MODELS OF
THE SELF

ALSO OF INTEREST FROM IMPRINT ACADEMIC
Full details on: http://www.imprint.co.uk

Series Editor: Professor J.A. Goguen
Department of Computer Science and Engineering
University of California, San Diego

Thomas Metzinger, ed.
Conscious Experience

Francisco Varela and Jonathan Shear, ed.
The View from Within:
First-person approaches to the study of consciousness

Benjamin Libet, Anthony Freeman and J.K.B. Sutherland, ed.
The Volitional Brain: Towards a neuroscience of free will

Rafael Núñez and Walter J. Freeman, ed.
Reclaiming Cognition: The primacy of action, intention and emotion

Joseph A. Goguen, ed.
Art and the Brain

Published in the UK and USA by Imprint Academic
PO Box 1, Thorverton EX5 5YX, UK
World Copyright © Imprint Academic, 1999

ISBN 0 907845 40 1 (cloth)

British Library Cataloguing in Publication Data
A catalogue record for this book is available from the British Library

Cover illustration: Claire Harper
Cover design: J.K.B. Sutherland

Printed in Exeter, UK by Short Run Press Ltd.

MODELS
OF
THE SELF

edited by
Shaun Gallagher
and
Jonathan Shear

IMPRINT ACADEMIC

Contents

Contributors

José Luis Bermúdez
Philosophy, University of Stirling, Stirling FK9 4LA, Scotland

James Blachowicz
Philosophy, Loyola University, 6525 North Sheridan Road, Chicago IL 60626, USA

Andrew Brook
Cognitive Science, Carleton University, Ottawa, Ontario K1S 5B6, Canada

George Butterworth
Psychology, University of Sussex, Brighton BN1 9QU, UK

Jonathan Cole
Clinical Neurophysiology, Poole Hospital, Poole BH15 2JB, UK

Arthur J. Deikman
Psychiatry, UCSF, 401 Parnassus Avenue, San Francisco CA 94143, USA

Mait Edey
PO Box 2681, Vineyard Haven, MA 02568, USA.

Robert K.C. Forman
Religion, Hunter College, CUNY, 695 Park Avenue, New York NY 10021, USA

Shaun Gallagher
Philosophy and Cognitive Science, Canisius College, Buffalo NY 14208, USA

Tamar Szabó Gendler
Philosophy, Syracuse University, Syracuse NY 13244-1170, USA

Jeremy Hayward
Shambhala Training Institute, Halifax, Nova Scotia, Canada

William Hirstein
Philosophy, William Patterson University, Wayne, NJ 07470, USA

Stephen W. Laycock
Philosophy, University of Toledo, Toledo OH 43606, USA

Maria Legerstee
Psychology, York University, Toronto, Canada

Anthony J. Marcel
MRC, Cognition and Brain Sciences Unit, 15 Chaucer Road, Cambridge CB2 2EF, UK

Mary Midgley
 1a Collingwood Terrace, Newcastle-upon-Tyne NE2 2JP, UK

Eric T. Olson
 Churchill College, Cambridge CB3 0DS, UK

Jaak Panksepp
 Psychology, Bowling Green State University, Bowling Green, OH 43403, USA

Josef Parnas
 University Dept. of Psychiatry, Hvidovre Hospital, Copenhagen, Denmark

Donald Perlis
 Computer Science, University of Maryland, College Park MD 20742, USA

John Pickering
 Psychology, Warwick University, Coventry, CV4 7AL, UK

Jennifer Radden
 Philosophy, University of Massachusetts, Boston MA 02125, USA.

V.S. Ramachandran
 Brain & Perception Laboratory, 1019, UCSD, La Jolla CA 92093, USA

Louis A. Sass
 Clinical Psychology, GSAPP, Rutgers University, Piscataway, NJ 08854-8085, USA

Jonathan Shear
 Philosophy, Virginia Commonwealth University, Richmond, VA 23284-2025, USA

Maxine Sheets-Johnstone
 Philosophy, University of Oregon, Eugene, OR 97403, USA

Galen Strawson
 Jesus College, Oxford OX1 3DW, UK

Jun Tani
 Sony Computer Science Laborator, 3-14-13 Higashi-gotanda, Tokyo, 141 Japan

Kathleen Wilkes
 St. Hilda's College, Oxford OX4 1DY, UK

Dan Zahavi
 Philosophy, University of Copenhagen, Denmark

Shaun Gallagher and Jonathan Shear

Editors' Introduction

There is a long history of theoretical inquiry about human nature and the nature of the self. It stretches from the ancient tradition of Socratic self-knowledge in the context of ethical life to contemporary discussions of brain function in cognitive science. It includes a variety of theories developed in either first-person (from the point of view of the experiencing subject) or third-person (from the point of view of an external observer) approaches. On one reading of this history, the Western notion of the self continually narrows. The history of this issue begins with a conflict among the ancients. On one view, which comes to be represented most clearly by Aristotle, the issue is settled in terms of a composite and very complex human nature. Who I am is closely tied to my embodied existence and yet transcends it. The soul or *psyche*, as the form of the body, involves a multitude of life functions, including nutrition, repro- duction, locomotion and sensation, but also action and philosophical contemplation. The rational (and for Aristotle this means social and linguistic) part of the soul lifts all of these functions to a higher, human and close to divine level. The other view, found as early as the Pythagoreans, clearly expressed in the texts of Plato, and later devel- oped in Neoplatonic authors such as Augustine, held that genuine humanness is not the result of an integration of 'lower' functions, but a purification of those functions in favour of a liberating spirituality. The animal elements are excluded from the human essence.

Along this same Platonic line, Augustine prefigures Descartes. For Descartes, and many modern thinkers, however, medieval spirituality was reducible to an important but narrow conception of rationality. The self is nothing other than the cogito, that is, one's own conscious mental events, a *res cogitans,* which is a mind composed of a unique, non-physical substance. At the beginning of the modern era, Descartes was led to the conclusion that self-knowledge provided the single Archimedean point for all knowledge. His thesis that the self is a single, simple, continuing and unproblem- atically accessible mental substance resonated with common sense, and quickly came to dominate European thought. Against this background, the specifically modern philosophical problem (or group of problems) pertaining to the nature of self identity arises and continues to define much of the contemporary discussion. Notably, it arises in the context of the first sustained discussion of consciousness in the philosophical literature, and at a precisely definable point in space and time, in an important few pages in John Locke's *Essay Concerning Human Understanding* (1690). Locke defines it as the problem of personal identity. Briefly stated, the problem involves finding criteria that can account for the unity of the self in conscious experience over time. In consciousness itself we find 'a thinking intelligent Being, that has reason and reflection, and can consider itself as a self, the same thinking thing in different times and places' (1690, # 9). To find the essence of the self, for someone like Locke, one needs to look within the central flux of the mind, the successive passage of consciousness. If we are anything, we must be able to find ourselves within the continuous becoming of experience which is constantly blooming forth from and continuously receding into what, without memory, would be nothingness.

Locke's solution was that consciousness maintains its identity over time only so far as memory extends to encompass past experience. This view almost immediately produced philosophical controversy. In the opinion of some, Locke was teetering on the edge of a dark precipice, the abyss of irrationality. Thus Bishop Butler (1736) and Thomas Reid (1785), expressing the anxiety that was common to both theologians and scientists of their age, helped to define the centrality of the problem of the self. If we cannot trust our own perceptions about ourselves, how can we know anything else? The very foundations of reason would be made unsure if we could not have certitude about the nature of the self. They had cause to worry. In particular, David Hume, in a very short time, was arguing that introspection does not display anything corresponding to what philosophers call the self, either Cartesian substance or Lockean identity.

> For my part, when I enter most intimately into what I call *myself*, I always stumble on some particular perception or other, of heat or cold, light or shade, love or hatred, pain or pleasure. I never can catch *myself* at any time without a perception, and never can observe any thing but the perception. . . . [We] are nothing but a bundle or collection of different perceptions, which succeed each other with an inconceivable rapidity, and are in a perpetual flux and movement. . . . The mind is a kind of theatre, where several perceptions successively make their appearance; pass, re-pass, glide away, and mingle in an infinite variety of postures and situations. There is properly no *simplicity* in it at one time, nor *identity* in different; whatever natural propension we may have to imagine that simplicity and identity (Hume, 1739, pp. 252–3).

Thus, Hume, contemplating these problems and challenging the foundational principles of science, was unable to find any introspective evidence of the self, and he attributed the concept to a misinterpretation, a fantasy, a fiction of the imagination. As a result, the self, which once flourished as the Aristotelian fullness of human life, and which had been stabilized in a Cartesian substance, became subsequently distilled to a flowing consciousness in which it dissipated and finally disappeared.

In part, contemporary responses have been attempts to explain how it is possible that we still experience a sense of self, notwithstanding Hume's analysis. If the self is not a soul, not a Cartesian substance, if its psychological continuity is tenuous, then why do we still believe that we have a certain identity over time? Thus, the variety of responses to the problem of self include assertions that there is no self; that the idea is a logical, psychological, or grammatical fiction; that the sense of self is properly understood and defined in terms of brain processes; that it is merely a constructed sociological locus, or the center of personal and public narratives, or that it belongs in an ineffable category all its own. Among these responses there is no consensus about how to approach the problems of self, much less what the appropriate resolution might be. In short, modern philosophers have rendered both our commonsensical and our philosophical notions of self utterly problematic.

The current lack of consensus suggests that the problem of the self is a complex and multi-dimensional phenomenon like consciousness itself, and that no one discipline on its own will be able to capture it in an adequate way. The aim of this volume is to explore various dimensions of the self by drawing on a diverse set of disciplines and approaches. The essays collected here develop divergent models of the self, representative of approaches that involve philosophy, psychology, neuroscience, theories of development and embodiment, as well as meditation-based approaches and artificial intelligence. They address many questions, including the following: What is the meaning of the self, and how does it arise? What are the minimal conditions for possession of a sense of self? Does the self consist of an enduring thing or function, or is it constituted from moment to moment in the flow of consciousness? Can the self be reduced to neuronal activity, and, if so, what is the precise neuronal mechanism that accounts for self and self-consciousness? Is it possible to model the self in computational terms? To what extent does a sense of self depend upon linguistic activity? Are there aspects of the self that are simply not reducible to such things as brain functions, linguistic and social phenomena, or consciousness, or all of them collectively?

This volume opens with an intriguing essay by **Galen Strawson**, and most of the other authors make reference to it. Strawson then responds to their comments and criticisms in the final chapter. He begins by asserting that the problem of the self is a real problem, one that arises not from improper use of language but from a phenomenologically prior and independent sense that there is such a thing as the self. Answering the question of whether a self really exists requires a metaphysical approach — but metaphysics in this case has to start with phenomenology. The question of a human sense of self is distinguishable from questions about the possibilities of self in general, and Strawson holds that these more general questions have to be answered in order to answer the factual question for human beings about whether there is — or could be — such a thing as a self.

Strawson starts with the phenomenological fact that people generally have a sense of themselves as being some kind of mental presence or 'thing' that is single, both at one time and over time, and a conscious subject of experience distinct from all its particular experiences. Thinking that we are such mental 'things' is not to deny that we also think of ourselves as complex embodied mental-and-non-mental human beings considered as wholes. Nor is it incompatible with a sophisticated materialism which recognizes mental and non-mental phenomena as distinguishable aspects of physical things and holds that all mental phenomena have a non-mental mode of being as well. Strawson argues that the mental self is properly thought of as a strong unity having internal connectedness. This unity is recognizably mental inasmuch as it is independent of any singleness or multiplicity the self might have as a non-mental being (body, brain, etc.). He also argues that personality is not essential to one's sense of being a unitary mental self; for it is possible to experience oneself as a bare locus of consciousness. This apparently necessary unity of self, however, is only synchronic, (existing momentarily at single, phenomenologically defined, generally quite short units of time) and not diachronic (existing across time), despite the common conviction to the contrary. Furthermore the fundamental sense of the synchronically unitary mental self is quite distinguishable from the so-called 'stream of consciousness' which is in fact full of hiatuses, continually stopping and restarting out of phenomenological 'nothingness'.

Thus, for Strawson, the 'core conditions' for a thing to be a mental self are that it be a single, mental thing which is distinct from all other things, and a subject of experience. Strawson concludes that each of us is in fact properly understandable as a sequence of many mental selves, existing and following each other one at a time, like a string of pearls. This conclusion prompts him to suggest that each of these short-lived 'pearls' or mental selves is an individual physical thing, namely a set of neurons in a certain state of activation.

The initial section of this volume is devoted to philosophical disputations sparked, at least in part, by Strawson's essay. Several questions are raised by **Kathleen Wilkes**. On the one hand, is it possible that what we call the self can have, as Strawson maintains, so little to do with temporally extended experiences such as psychological dispositions, time-related emotions like guilt or remorse, or practices such as planning for a future? On the other hand, although it is very useful to talk about the self, is the self anything more than an abstraction — an abstraction which does not refer to anything real? That might prompt us to ask precisely what we mean by the term 'self'. Indeed if there is no one thing that we call 'the self' there may not exist any problem that pertains to it. It may be impossible to find consensus on what counts as characteristic features or paradigm examples of the self. In this case, as **Eric Olson** suggests, we should give up the superfluous concept of self, at least in philosophical and scientific analyses. Some theorists resist this idea, however. Indeed, is there not some consensus about the self reflected in language and in social practices? **John Pickering** suggests that this social sense of self has an ontological status that is best modelled on a process view of reality. The self can be legitimately regarded as a semiotic and social process and its importance as a concept, and indeed as a reality, can be found in the ethical implications that follow from this. Still, some agreement is required on precisely how we might access and understand the self if we are to properly use the concept. **Andrew Brook** thinks that Strawson is largely right about the importance of phenomenology. Indeed, he thinks that how the self *appears* is essential to what the self actually *is*. But what the self is, according to the materialist metaphysics that Brook and Strawson agree on, is both mental and non-mental.

The essays in the section entitled 'Cognitive and Neuroscientific Models' are devoted to exploring the non-mental aspects of self. Two of the essays take up this question in terms of computational theory. **Donald Perlis** seeks to elucidate the notion of self in functional and computational terms. He offers a concept of self-modelling which he calls 'strong self-referential computation'. Self-modelling depends on working out an algorithm that allows a system to discriminate between self and non-self, and to do so in a double way, specifically in a way that allows a first-person perspective to cope with itself from a third-person perspective, that is, to cope with itself as an element in its own world. Is it possible to translate this idea of self-referential computation into a dynamical systems language that employs a neural-net model? This is precisely what **Jun Tani** does in his revolutionary essay on building a robot with a structure analogous to a phenomenological self. Traditional robotics design employs either a top-down predictive or a bottom-up perceptual control scheme. Tani has designed robots that work according to an interactive dynamics between top-down and bottom-up systems. In cases of coherence between internal and environmental dynamics, no conflict develops between top-down prediction and bottom-up information and the robot performs automatically without problem (steady phase state). In cases that involve incoherence and conflict, however, an open dynamic structure characterized by the co-existence of stability of goal-directedness but instability with respect to robotic movement develops. During such states, Tani suggests, the system undergoes a transition to an unsteady phase state which for resolution requires the ability to discriminate self from non-self. As he points out, these practical insights from robot construction are quite consistent with various phenomenological insights and with Strawson's pearl view of the self.

Strawson, as well as Brook, Perlis, and many of our other authors, are keen to understand the self in terms of brain function. This is precisely the aim of **Ramachandran and Hirstein** in their essay on qualia and the biological functions of consciousness. Like several other authors, they explore neuropathologies to discover what can be learned about qualia and one's sense of self. They conclude that, like qualia, the experience of self arises from a specific kind of brain activity (mapped anatomically to limbic and associated structures, and linked functionally to frontal executive processes). For Ramachandran and Hirstein, however, this means that the self as a unitary, enduring thing is an illusion. At best, the self is a certain function that mediates between motivational-emotional processes and control of action. **Jaak Panksepp** takes this idea further: the self and the contours of its affective awareness are generated in neural mechanisms responsible for emotions (in the subcortical, brainstem PAG area) and in their reiterated role in more rational forms of consciousness. Panksepp's discussion of neural reiterations of the self-structure provides a valuable insight into why the self is a multifaceted and multiply-represented phenomenon, and why, therefore, the problem of the self is such a complex one.

The final chapter in this section takes as its theme what may be the very cognitive core of rationality, the mental dialogue that constitutes thinking. **James Blachowicz** focuses on the performance dimension of interior conversation as an essential component in the development of self. The central question is whether interior dialogue is simply the internalization of external conversation, in effect, a product of socialization, or whether it is motivated by more strictly cognitive factors. Blachowicz argues that inner speech is a logical rather than a social or phenomenological demand. He pictures it as a dialogue between established meaning and logical articulation which is central to the constitution of the self. On this view, in contrast to Panksepp, Ramachandran and Hirstein, the self is not something that is formed deep inside the physical brain, but is something that develops as a virtual extension of the brain in linguistic behaviour. This does not rule out the idea that the self is generated in certain executive functions, but in verbal ones rather than the purely cognitive ones described by Ramachandran and Hirstein. This idea is not incompatible with Wilkes' suggestion that the work done by Strawson's experiential self is more economically done by the first-person pronoun.

As the chapters in the next section make clear, developmental issues are important for any discussion of how the self is generated. The contributions by **George Butterworth** and **Maria Legerstee** are consistent in their criticisms of Strawson's model, criticisms that would equally apply to Blachowicz's idea that the self is generated in linguistic behaviour. Butterworth's starting point actually goes back to a previous question: what do we mean by 'the self'? He points out that prior to finding a self in introspective consciousness, there is already an implicit ecological self involved from the very beginning of perceptual experience; and prior to filling out the self in linguistic narrative, there is an interpersonal self evidenced by the imitation of facial gestures in early infancy. The cognitive or conceptual aspects of self are built upon more fundamental, preconceptual beginnings. The details of such beginnings in the self-awareness of infants are explored by Legerstee in her own empirical studies. Her experiments show that social and bodily factors play an important role in the development of early self-awareness, and these factors are reiterated in the mature sense of self.

Maxine Sheets-Johnstone puts similar studies of development to work in her phenomenological critique of Strawson. What Strawson fails to take into consideration in his analysis of the self is agency, one of the characteristics he names but disqualifies as unessential. Agency, however, as an aspect of the activity of the tactile-kinaesthetic body is evident from the very first year of life, and as various psychologists have shown, is indispensable for the development of a sense of self. Furthermore, as Legerstee, Daniel Stern, and others have shown, certain aspects of the early experience of agency are reiterated in later domains of self-formation. Sheets-Johnstone argues that what these developmental studies show is in precise accord with the results of a phenomenology that is more methodical than the one proposed by Strawson. Specifically, if one pursues methods outlined by Husserl, one finds that a sense of agency is an essential component of a phenomenology of the self. Like Sheets-Johnstone, **Zahavi and Parnas** take issue with Strawson's understanding of phenomenology. They argue that only a phenomenology guided in a methodological fashion, of the sort initiated by Husserl, would be adequate to discover a genuine sense of self. Strawson's phenomenology, like Hume's phenomenology, amounts to pre-scientific introspection and as such is not trustworthy. The advantages of more controlled phenomenological methods are demonstrated in a discussion of their importance for an understanding of disorders of the self in schizophrenia.

The discussion of schizophrenia leads directly to the issues explored in the fourth section of this volume on 'Pathologies of the Self'. We normally feel some guarantee that we have direct phenomenological access to ourselves and that in this regard we are immune to error. Yet this immunity is clearly disrupted in psychopathologies that involve dissociation (Dissociative Identity Disorder and schizophrenia). **Jennifer Radden** explores ways in which the synchronic unity of the self is fractured in such dissociations. She makes it clear that the study of dissociative pathologies can help to clarify the normal and seemingly guaranteed ability to self-ascribe, that is, to say that 'This is my experience'. Dissociative states, Radden argues, even in causing trouble for self-ascription, nonetheless fall within the framework of a synchronic mental unity.

In a broad-ranging chapter that moves easily from a Foucauldian cultural critique to a discussion of neurobiology, **Louis Sass** presents his influential interpretation of schizophrenia as characterized by a form of hyperreflexive self-consciousness. This is one part of a larger experiential paradox which makes schizophrenia so difficult to understand, namely, a contradiction between two opposite experiences of self: a loss or fragmentation of self, and an inflationary solipsistic self-aggrandizement. On the neurobiological level, Sass's suggestions are quite consistent with Ramachandran and Hirstein's focus on limbic executive functions. On the phenomenological level they are consistent with proposals made by **Gallagher and Marcel** who consider neurological disorders, and disorders of intention, as guides to clarifying the notion of self, not as an object of awareness, but as a point of origin for action. They explore various modes of self-awareness that are embedded in action and are 'on-line' rather than detached in reflective or retrospective self-consciousness. Like Wilkes and Pickering, they suggest that certain dimensions of self-experience pertaining to character and action were left undeveloped by Strawson, but have significant ethical implications. This idea, especially in its embodied and social dimension is nicely captured in **Jonathan Cole**'s chapter on the importance of facial embodiment. Citing Wittgenstein's dictum, that 'the human body is the best picture of the human soul', Cole focuses on the face and, we might say, attempts to look the self squarely in the eye. The face, which is the most personal of body parts, is the locus that reveals, in certain indefinite and subjective ways, important objective facts about who we are. It is a medium upon which our emotions and our character are written. The face allows the sharing of those emotions and refines our communication with other persons. Pathologies that involve the face, from stroke to blindness, from Möbius Syndrome to autism, reveal what we otherwise take so much for granted. Cole suggests that the face represents something that goes beyond both neurological and cognitive accounts of what it means to be a person. His essay is a mirror which reflects the significance of one's own face in the constitution of one's personal and interpersonal life.

The next section, 'Meditation-Based Approaches', also examines how experiences that lie outside the everyday range can shed light on questions concerning the nature of the self. The section includes **Steven Laycock**'s Buddhist-based examination of Sartre's notion of the transparency of consciousness. As Sartre pointed out, each of us naturally *feels* that we are a self, a subject who is having one's own experience. But whenever we attempt to focus on this subject, it seems to recede from view, always somehow just behind, beyond or otherwise outside the focus of one's awareness. This, Laycock argues, is because consciousness itself is always utterly transparent, and has no thematizable mark or feature to identify it or distinguish it from the objective contents of one's awareness. Thus, since, as the Buddhist view holds, it would have to look like nothing at all, the 'I' necessarily remains hopelessly anonymous. Any self that we can grasp can only be a dead image. As a result, none of Strawson's 'pearls' can succeed in representing the self, even the self of a moment.

Robert Forman also examines the notion of consciousness with no distinguishing empirical marks. His focus is on 'pure consciousness events', defined as consciousness itself entirely devoid of empirical content, reported in many (Hindu, Buddhist, Christian, etc.) mystical traditions, and produced by specific meditation procedures. Forman then describes more advanced states, where pure awareness is experienced (dualistically) along with other experiences, and finally (non-dually) as permeating all other experiences. These experiences are widely held to display the underlying nature of the self, already there (although ordinarily not clearly recognized) in one's everyday awareness. As Forman points out, when we formulate our theories of consciousness and self it appears at least as reasonable to take account of these experiences, associated with exceptional degrees of self-actualization, as it is to take account of pathological conditions.

Arthur Deikman, like Laycock, emphasizes the essential featurelessness of consciousness itself. However, unlike Laycock, but like Forman, he identifies this featureless pure consciousness with the 'I' or self within. On Deikman's account, the core of subjectivity, the 'I', is independent of all objective content because it is precisely that which observes — not that which is observed. The 'I' is consciousness itself, the *ground* in which the mind's contents manifest themselves. It is prior to and more fundamental than all such content, and necessarily featureless, lacking all form, texture, colour, spatial dimensions, etc. We know the internal observer, consciousness itself, not by observing it, but by *being* it. Like Forman, Deikman holds that first-hand experience of pure consciousness as produced by Eastern meditation disciplines should prove clarifying for Western investigators.

Jeremy Hayward also holds that practice of Eastern meditation techniques can provide a much-needed platform for investigating consciousness and self. Writing from the Tibetan Buddhist *rDzogs-Chen* perspective of Insight-Awareness (*shamatha-vipashyana*) meditation, he reports how long practice can allow one to recognize how our ordinary experience is in fact composed of collections of minute components rapidly flashing in and out of existence from a boundless background (*rigpa*). This background is experienceable as a Void or nothingness — a nothingness which is (at the same time) something, an unbounded, non-localized openness. Here one's self comes to be perceived as constituted by flashings of a sense of self that, moment by moment, come into and go out of existence from that non-dual background. Hayward's account thus agrees with Strawson's 'pearl' view with regard to the discontinuity of self. But it rejects the notion that the self is a momentary physical thing, or even a string of such things.

Jonathan Shear reexamines some traditional Western problems of self in the context of common meditation experiences. Since Hume it has seemed clear that nothing corresponding to Descartes' commonsensical notion of self is discoverable introspectively. And Kant, supporting both Descartes and Hume, famously argued that all experience presupposes the existence of a self which, as a 'pure consciousness' with no distinguishing features of its own, cannot possibly be experienced. Shear points out, however, that the experience of pure consciousness discussed in other chapters of this section appears to provide the relevant experience, and he argues that this allows us to resolve important tensions between Descartes', Hume's and Kant's analyses. He also argues (consonant with Forman and Deikman, but in contrast with Laycock and Hayward) that these analyses serve in turn to identify the pure consciousness experience as experience of self. Finally, he suggests that the experience clarifies our ordinary sense of self by raising to clear awareness what is usually merely subliminal.

In the penultimate section we take note of further questions to be explored, questions that are broadly methodological and that pertain to the various strategies that philosophers and scientists take when addressing the problem of the self. **José Bermúdez** examines the legitimatacy of a reductionist approach to the notion of the self. Resistance to reductive strategies reflects claims that the concept of a self has a central and irreducible role to play in our understanding of mental events, and that personal-level phenomena cannot be reduced to subpersonal processes. Bermúdez suggests that the eliminativist side of reductionist strategy is complemented by a legitimizing side. A successful reduction of one theory to another can actually legitimize aspects of the reduced theory. Thus Bermúdez defends the idea of a reductionist strategy that would eliminate at least a substantialist conception of the self as something over and above a collection of mental events within one psychological space.

Mait Edey sets aside the assumption, operative in a number of the previous essays, that the self is a discrete part of the universe with a boundary (physical, functional or conceptual), marking the distinction between me and the rest of the universe. He focuses on the more basic distinction between subject and object which informs our thoughts about these matters prior to any theory about what the self is. I already realize the fact of my being as subject before I can even raise questions about what I am. Consistent with much of what Butterworth and Legerstee say in the section on development, Edey maintains that whenever I am conscious of some object (taken in the most general sense) I automatically distinguish it from myself as subject. He cautions that working out a proper concept of the self requires, not some external measure or objective criterion, but an unmediated realization. We begin to move away from this immediacy, in the wrong way, when we pose questions about the self using categories that are not present in that original realization. Thus any quest to identify the self with the mind, or the body, or the brain, is already misdirected.

Tamar Szabó Gendler takes up precisely this question of how theorists go about identifying the self with mind, body, or brain. Gendler works out her answer in the framework of traditional approaches to the problem of personal identity in which philosophers since the time of Locke have employed imaginary thought experiments. She suggests that this methodology may be less reliable than its proponents take it to be. Gendler argues that the use of thought experiments is productive only when the concept at stake is structured around a set of necessary and sufficient conditions that play a role in identifying a particular thing as falling under that concept. The concept of personal identity, however, is not this kind of concept. This means that the use of imaginary thought experiments will be inconclusive. In making her case Gendler takes us on a tour of several of the more fascinating thought-experiments in the Lockean tradition. Her analysis of these imaginary cases suggests that there is no easy way to separate self from the physical, psychological, or social factors that constrain experience.

Is it, then, possible to have a science of the self? **Mary Midgley** does not ask this question directly, but indirectly, and she makes it a question about science as much as about the self. It is a question that draws together two notions that seem very different: scientific knowledge and self-knowledge. Midgley's question may be put in this way: to what extent is self-knowledge, which is a moral or practical form of knowledge, necessary for an adequate scientific knowledge of the self? She argues that the kind of moral judgments that come with self-knowledge are necessarily preliminary to framing the scientific project. That is, a scientist will select to study what matters about the self, but what matters is a function of value-judgment without which we would be unable to formulate even a general view of human existence. A self, as Midgley points out, is not an egg: it is difficult to know where precisely it begins and how far it extends. Science rests on pre-scientific judgments about such matters and scientific criteria do not help us to make such judgements. But this does not make a science of the self impossible, it should rather make us rethink and expand the notion of science to meet the real practice of science.

In the final essay, **Strawson** acts as his own attorney, and as counsel for the self. He mounts a convincing defence of his position from the many criticisms advanced in the previous chapters. His brief covers the range from phenomenological testimony about self-experience, to very basic ontological considerations about the nature of matter. As Strawson suggests, the many different approaches that can be pursued in addressing the question of the self appear to yield a multitude of conceptions of the self: the cognitive self, the conceptual self, the dialogical self, the ecological self, the embodied self, the emergent self, the empirical self, the existential self, the extended self, the fictional self, the interpersonal self, the material self, the narrative self, the physical self, and so on. The cross-examinations will necessarily be extensive, and we leave that to Strawson himself.

This situation, however, suggests the following question, with methodological implications. Does the sense of the self that we can discover depend upon the variety of modes of access that we have to it? Posed at the level of theoretical model-building, insofar as our various authors approach the topic of the self in different ways, through phenomenological analyses of consciousness, or by empirical research into brain function, or from perspectives that involve normal, exceptional, and/or pathological behaviour, language, or embodiment, do they target the same ontological subject-matter or do they end up with different models because, on their chosen approaches, they discover different conceptions of the self? We leave this as a question that readers might explore as they work their way through a controversial collection of essays.[1]

References

Butler, Joseph (1736), *The analogy of religion, natural and revealed, to the constitution and course of nature: to which are added two brief dissertations, On personal identity and On the nature of virtue, and fifteen sermons* (London: G. Bell, 1902).
Hume, David (1739), *A Treatise of Human Nature*. ed. L.A. Selby-Bigge (Oxford: Clarendon Press, 1888, 1975).
Locke, John (1690), *An Essay Concerning Human Understanding* (London).
Reid, Thomas (1785), *Essays on the Intellectual Powers of Man* (Edinburgh; ed. A.D. Woozley, London: Macmillan, 1941).

---

[1]   All the essays in this book were selected from a series of special issues of the *Journal of Consciousness Studies*.

Part 1

Philosophical controversies

I know that I exist; the question is, what is this 'I' that I know?

Descartes 1641

The soul, so far as we can conceive it, is nothing but a system or train of different perceptions. *Hume 1739*

What was I before I came to self-consciousness? . . . *I* did not exist at all, for I was not an I. The I exists only insofar as it is conscious of itself. . . . *The self posits itself*, and by virtue of this mere self-assertion it exists. *Fichte 1794–5*

The 'Self' . . . , when carefully examined, is found to consist mainly of . . . peculiar motions in the head or between the head and throat.

James 1890

The ego continuously constitutes itself as existing. *Husserl 1929*

Any fixed categorization of the Self is a big goof. *Ginsberg 1963*

The self which is reflexively referred to is synthesized in that very act of reflexive self-reference. *Nozick 1981*

The self . . . is a mythical entity. . . . It is a philosophical muddle to allow the space which differentiates 'my self' from 'myself' to generate the illusion of a mysterious entity distinct from . . . the human being.

Kenny 1988

A self . . . is . . . an abstraction . . . , [a] Center of Narrative Gravity.

Dennett 1991

My body is an object all right, but my self jolly well is not!

Farrell 1996

Galen Strawson

The Self

I: Introduction[1]

The substantival phrase 'the self' is very unnatural in most speech contexts in most languages, and some conclude from this that it's an illusion to think that there is such a thing as the self, an illusion that arises from nothing more than an improper use of language. This, however, is implausible. People are not that stupid. The problem of the self doesn't arise from an unnatural use of language which arises from nowhere. On the contrary: use of a phrase like 'the self' arises from a prior and independent sense that there is such a thing as the self. The phrase may be unusual in ordinary speech; it may have no obvious direct translation in many languages. Nevertheless all languages have words which lend themselves naturally to playing the role that 'the self' plays in English, however murky that role may be. The phrase certainly means something to most people. It has a natural use in religious, philosophical, and psychological contexts, which are very natural contexts of discussion for human beings. I think there is a real philosophical problem about the existence and nature of the self, not just a relatively uninteresting problem about why we think there's a problem. It is too quick to say that a 'grammatical error . . . is the essence of the theory of the self', or that ' "the self" is a piece of philosopher's nonsense consisting in a misunderstanding of the reflexive pronoun' (Kenny, 1988, p. 4).

The first task is to get the problem into focus. I will recommend one approach, first in outline, then in slightly more detail. (I will model the problem of the self, rather than attempting to model the self.) I think the problem requires a straightforwardly metaphysical approach; but I also think that metaphysics must wait on phenomenology, in a sense I will explain. Most recent discussion of the problem by analytic philosophers has started from work in philosophical logic (in the large sense of the term).[2] This work may have a contribution to make, but a more phenomenological starting point is needed.

I will use the expression 'the self' freely — I am already doing so — but I don't want to exclude in advance the view that there is no such thing as the self, and the

[1] I am grateful to Derek Parfit, Shaun Gallagher, Jonathan Shear, Keith Sutherland, and P.F. Strawson for their comments. This essay was originally published in *JCS*, **4**, No.5/6, 1997, pp. 405–28. Sources of quotations on the facing page: Descartes (1985, vol.2, p. 18); Hume (1978, p. 657); Fichte (1982, pp. 97–8); James (1950, vol. 1, p. 301); Husserl (1973, p. 66); Ginsberg (1963); Nozick (1981, p. 91); Kenny (1988, pp. 3–4); Dennett (1991, pp. 426–7); Farrell (1996, p. 519).

[2] See, for example, the essays collected in Cassam (1994).

expression will often function as a loose name for what one might equally well call 'the self-phenomenon', i.e. all those undoubtedly real phenomena that lead us to think and talk in terms of something called the self, whether or not there is such a thing.

II: The Problem of the Self

Many people believe in the self, conceived of as a distinct thing, although they are not clear what it is. Why do they believe in it? Because they have a distinct sense of, or experience as of, the self, and they take it that it is not delusory. This sense of the self is the source in experience of the philosophical problem of the self. So the first thing to do is to track the problem to this source in order to get a better idea of what it is. The first question to ask is the *phenomenological question*:

What is the nature of the sense of the self?

But this, in the first instance, is best taken as a question explicitly about human beings: as the *local phenomenological question*

   (1) What is the nature of the human sense of the self?

Whatever the answer to **(1)** is, it raises the *general phenomenological question*

   (2) Are there other possibilities, when it comes to a sense of the self? (Can we describe the minimal case of genuine possession of a sense of the self?)

The answers to **(1)** and **(2)** raise the *conditions question*

   (3) What are the grounds or preconditions of possession of a sense of the self?

and this question raises a battery of subsidiary questions. But progress is being made, at least potentially. For, if one can produce satisfactory answers to **(1)**, **(2)** and **(3)**, one will be in a good position to raise and answer the *factual question*, the fundamental and straightforwardly metaphysical question

   (4) Is there (could there be) such a thing as the self?

I think one has to answer **(1)** and **(2)**, and probably **(3)**, in order to answer **(4)** properly.

III: The Local Question; Cognitive Phenomenology

I will now go through the plan in more detail, and sketch how I think some of the answers should go. The first question is the local phenomenological question: What is the nature of the ordinary human sense of the self? This raises a prior question: Can one generalize about the human sense of the self? I think the answer is Yes: the aspects of the sense of the self that are of principal concern, when it comes to the philosophical problem of the self, are very basic. They are situated below any level of plausible cultural variation.[3] They are conceptual rather than affective: it is the *cognitive phenomenology* of the sense of the self that is fundamentally in question, i.e. the conceptual structure of the sense of the self, the structure of the sense of the self considered (as far as possible) independently of any emotional aspects that it may have.

---

[3] Work in evolutionary psychology suggests that doubts about the possibility of generalization that derive from considerations of cultural difference can be easily dealt with. See e.g. Barkow *et al.* (1992).

The cognitive phenomenology of the self is bound up with the affective phenomenology of the self in complicated ways, but emotional or affective aspects of the sense of the self will be of concern (e.g. in section VIII) only in so far as emotions shape or weight conceptions.

What, then, is the ordinary, human sense of the self, in so far as we can generalize about it? I propose that it is (at least) the sense that people have of themselves as being, specifically, a mental presence; a mental someone; a single mental thing that is a conscious subject of experience, that has a certain character or personality, and that is in some sense distinct from all its particular experiences, thoughts, and so on, and indeed from all other things. It is crucial that it is thought of as a distinctively mental phenomenon, and I will usually speak of the 'mental self' from now on (the qualifier 'mental' may be understood wherever omitted).

Is the sense of the mental self, as so far described, really something ordinary? I believe so. It comes to every normal human being, in some form, in childhood.[4] The early realization of the fact that one's thoughts are unobservable by others, the experience of the profound sense in which one is alone in one's head — these are among the very deepest facts about the character of human life, and found the sense of the mental self. It is perhaps most often vivid when one is alone and thinking, but it can be equally vivid in a room full of people. It connects with a feeling that nearly everyone has had intensely at some time — the feeling that one's body is just a vehicle or vessel for the mental thing that is what one really or most essentially is. I believe that the primary or fundamental way in which we conceive of ourselves is as a distinct mental thing — sex addicts, athletes, and supermodels included. Analytic philosophers may find it hard to see — or remember — this, given their training, and they risk losing sight of the point in derision.

This is not to deny that we also naturally conceive of ourselves as mental-and-non-mental things, human beings considered as a whole. We do. Nor is it to claim that the sense of the mental self always incorporates some sort of belief in an immaterial soul, or in life after bodily death. It doesn't. Philosophical materialists who believe, as I do, that we are wholly physical beings, and that the theory of evolution by natural selection is true, and that animal consciousness of the sort with which we are familiar evolved by purely physical natural processes on a planet where no such consciousness previously existed, have this sense of the mental self as strongly as anyone else.

In more detail: I propose that the mental self is ordinarily conceived or experienced as:

(1) a *thing*, in some robust sense

(2) a *mental* thing, in some sense

(3 ,4) a *single* thing that is single both *synchronically* considered and *diachronically* considered

(5) *ontically distinct* from all other things

(6) a *subject of experience*, a conscious feeler and thinker

(7) an *agent*

(8) a thing that has a certain character or *personality*

---

[4] It certainly does not require the special kind of experience recorded by Nagel (1986, pp. 54–7) or Richard Hughes (1929, ch. 6), for this is by no means universal.

This is an intentionally strong proposal, and it may be thought to be too strong in various ways. Most of (1)–(8) can be contested, and the list may well contain redundancy, but it provides a framework for discussion. There are various entailment relations between the eight elements that need to be exposed; (1) – (6) are closely linked. (1) also raises the general question 'What is a thing?' — a question that will be important when the fundamental factual question ('Is there such a thing as the self?') is considered.

I don't think the list omits anything essential to a genuine sense of the mental self, even if it includes some things that are not essential. I will assume that this is true for the purposes of this chapter: a primitive framework can show the structure of a problem even if it is not complete. It can be the best way to proceed even if the problem resists regimentation in terms of necessary and sufficient conditions. If an omission were identified, it could simply be added in to the existing framework.

(2) is the only one of the eight properties that is not attributed as naturally to the embodied human being as to the putative mental self, and it may be suggested that the sense of the mental self is just a delusory projection from the experience of embodiment. Perhaps the so-called self is just the human being incompletely grasped and illegitimately spiritualized. This is a popular view, but I am not yet in a position to assess it.[5] Some argue from the fact that use of the word 'I' to refer to the supposed mental self does not ordinarily stand out as distinct from use of the word 'I' to refer to the human being considered as a whole to the conclusion that we have no good reason to distinguish them. To this it may be replied that appeal to facts about public language use is often irrelevant when considering facts about meaning and reference, and is spectacularly inappropriate in the case of the problem of the self.[6]

IV: Phenomenology and Metaphysics

Equipped with an answer to the local question, one can go on to raise the general question: 'Are there other possibilities, so far as a sense of the mental self (or SMS) is concerned?' Given the assumption that the list of eight properties doesn't omit anything essential to a genuine sense of the self, this amounts to the question whether one can dispense with any of (1)–(8) while still having something that qualifies as a genuine SMS. It enquires, among other things, after the minimal case of a SMS. The answer is partly a matter of terminological decision, but for the most part not.

How might the answer go? I don't yet know, but if I had to commit myself it would be as follows: (4) and (8) are not necessary to a sense of the mental self, even in the human case (see sections VIII and IX). (6) is secure, but a serious doubt can be raised about (7). (2) and (5) need careful qualification if they are to survive. (1) and (3) can be challenged but effectively defended.

Objection: 'Surely the phenomenological investigation loses something crucial at this point? It is no longer rooted in the human case, so it is no longer independent of specifically philosophical theories about what selves actually are or can be: such theories are bound to be part of what governs our judgements about whether some thinned down SMS can count as a genuine SMS, once we go beyond the human case.'

[5] For older versions of the view, see e.g. James (1950, ch 10). See also Bermúdez et al. (1995).

[6] This point is developed in Strawson (forthcoming).

I believe that a detailed attempt to answer the general phenomenological question will show that this is not so: our basic judgements about whether anything less than (1)–(8) can count as a genuine SMS can remain comfortably independent, in any respect that matters, of metaphysical philosophical theorizing about the nature of the self. In fact I think they can be sufficiently supported by reference to unusual human cases.

So much for the claim that phenomenology is substantially independent of metaphysics. What about the other way round? Here I think there is a fundamental dependence: metaphysical investigation of the nature of the self is subordinate to phenomenological investigation of the sense of the self. There is a strong phenomenological constraint on any acceptable answer to the metaphysical question which can be expressed by saying that the factual question 'Is there such a thing as the mental self?' is equivalent to the question 'Is any (genuine) sense of the self an accurate representation of anything that exists?'[7]

This equivalence claim can be split in two:

(E1) If there is such a thing as the self, then some SMS is an accurate representation of something that exists,

(E2) If some SMS is an accurate representation of something that exists, then there is such a thing as the self.

(E1) and (E2) may seem trivial, but both may be challenged. The first as follows:

(C1) There is really no very good reason to think that if the self exists, then there is some SMS that is an accurate (if partial) representation of its nature. Perhaps the mental self, as it is in itself, is ineffable, quite unlike any experience of it.

(C1) is Kantian in spirit. The second rejection is a response made when some particular SMS has been presented:

(C2) This SMS you have outlined is indeed an accurate representation of something that exists, but the thing of which it is an accurate representation does not qualify for the title 'the mental self' because it does not have feature F (e.g. it is not an immaterial, ± immortal, ± whatever, substance).

The force of (E1) and (E2) consists precisely in the fact that they reject proposals like (C1) and (C2). In this way they impose a substantial constraint on metaphysical theorizing about the self. According to (E1), nothing can count as a mental self unless it possesses all the properties attributed to the self by some genuine SMS, whatever other properties it may possess. It rules out metaphysical claims about the self that fail to respect limits on the concept of the self revealed by the phenomenological investigation. It states a necessary condition on qualifying for the title of self. (E2), by contrast, states that nothing can fail to count as a mental self if it possesses all the properties that feature in some SMS, whatever other properties it may possess or lack. It states a sufficient condition on qualifying for the title of self — it lays it down that there is no further test to pass.

To make the equivalence claim, then, is to say that one must have well-developed answers to phenomenological questions about the experience of the self before one can begin to answer metaphysical questions about the self. The equivalence claim excludes two forms of metaphysical excess — extravagance and miserliness.

---

[7] I take it that a representation R of a thing X is accurate if (and only if) X really has the properties R represents it as having. R need not be complete to be accurate.

Extravagance is blocked by showing that we cannot answer the question 'Is there such a thing as the self?' by saying 'Yes there is (or may be), but we have (or may have) no understanding of its ultimate nature'. Miserliness is blocked by showing that we cannot answer by saying 'Well, there is *something* of which the sense of the self is an accurate representation, but it does not follow that there is any such thing as the self.'

If the answers to the phenomenological questions go well, we should be left with a pretty good idea of what we are asking when we ask the factual, metaphysical question 'Is there such a thing as the self?' Any metaphysical speculations that are not properly subordinate to phenomenology can be cheerfully 'commit[ted]. . . to the flames' (Hume, 1975, p. 165).[8]

V: Materialism

In sections VI–IX I will give examples of more detailed work within this scheme. Before that I must give a brief account of the sense in which I am a materialist.

Materialists believe that every thing and event in the universe is a wholly physical phenomenon. If they are even remotely realistic in their materialism they admit that conscious experience is part of reality. It follows that they must grant that conscious experience is a wholly physical phenomenon. They must grant that it is wholly physical specifically in its mental, experiential properties. (They must grant that the qualitative character of the taste of bread, considered just as such and independently of anything else that exists, is as much a physical phenomenon as the phenomenon of an electric current flowing in a wire.)

It follows that materialists express themselves very badly when they talk about the mental and the physical as if they were opposed categories. For on their own view, this is exactly like saying that cows and animals are opposed categories — for all mental phenomena, including conscious-experience phenomena *considered specifically as such*, just are physical phenomena, according to them; just as all cows are animals.

So what are materialists doing when they talk as if the mental and the physical were different things? What they presumably mean to do is to distinguish, within the realm of the physical, which is the only realm there is, according to them, between the mental and the non-mental, and, more specifically, between the experiential and the non-experiential; to distinguish, that is, between (A) mental (or experiential) aspects of the physical, and (B) non-mental (or non-experiential) aspects of the physical.[9] This is the difference that is really in question when it comes to the 'mind–body' problem, and materialists who persist in talking in terms of the difference between the mental and the physical perpetuate the terms of the dualism they reject in a way that is inconsistent with their own view.[10]

---

[8] I should say that I'm rejecting, and not claiming to refute, more unbridled approaches to the metaphysics of the self.

[9] I need to make the distinction between mental and experiential phenomena, because although all experiential phenomena are mental phenomena, not all mental phenomena are experiential phenomena: according to ordinary usage, beliefs, likes and dislikes, and so on are mental phenomena, though they have no experiential character.

[10] There is tremendous resistance to abandoning the old mental/physical terminology in favour of the mental/non-mental, experiential/non-experiential terminology, even though the alternative is very clear and is exactly what is required. Cf. Searle (1992, p. 54); also A. Campbell (1994).

Let me rephrase this. When I say that the mental and the experiential are wholly physical, I mean something completely different from what some materialists have apparently meant by saying things like 'experience is really just neurons firing'. I don't mean that all that is really going on, in the case of conscious experience, is something that can be discerned and described by current physics, or by any non-revolutionary extension of current physics. Such a view amounts to some kind of radical eliminativism, and is certainly false. My claim is quite different. It is that the experiential considered specifically as such — the portion of reality we have to do with when we consider experiences specifically and solely in respect of the experiential character they have for those who have them as they have them — that 'just is' physical. No one who disagrees with this claim is a serious and realistic materialist.[11]

A further comment is needed. As remarked, thoroughgoing materialists hold that all mental phenomena, including all experiential phenomena, are entirely physical phenomena. But triviality threatens when things are put this way. For now even absolute idealism (in one version, the view that only experiential phenomena exist) can claim to be a materialist position.

The trivializing possibility can be excluded by ruling that anything deserving the name 'materialism' must hold that there are non-mental and non-experiential phenomena as well as mental or experiential phenomena. But one can plausibly go further, and take materialism to incorporate what one might call 'the principle of the necessary involvement of the mental with the non-mental'. Most realistic materialists take it that the existence of each particular mental or experiential phenomenon involves the existence of some particular non-mental, non-experiential phenomenon. More strongly expressed: each particular mental or experiential phenomenon has, essentially, in addition to its mental or experiential character or mode of being, a non-mental character or mode of being. One might call this 'mental-and-non-mental' materialism. When I talk of materialism in what follows, I will take it to involve this view.

According to materialism, then, every thing or event has non-mental, non-experiential being, whether or not it also has mental or experiential being. More needs to be said (given that we have knowledge of central aspects of the fundamental reality of the mental just in having experience in the way we do, we need to ask whether it is possible to give some basic positive characterization of the non-mental, perhaps in terms of properties like time, length, position, mass, electric charge, spin, 'colour' and 'flavour' in the quantum theory sense). But this is enough to make it clear that the present question about whether the self exists in the human case is not a question about whether we might possibly be 'Cartesian egos' or immaterial substances. It is the question whether the mental self exists given that we are ordinarily embodied, entirely physical living human beings.

VI: Singularity

I have sketched how I think answers to the phenomenological questions should go, described the constraint that phenomenology places on metaphysics, and characterized the sense in which I am a materialist. I will now give samples of more detailed work on the phenomenological questions.

---

[11] Hurlburt *et al.* discuss a superficially 'zombie'-like subject who has 'no reportable inner experience' (1994, pp. 391–2), but it becomes clear he does have experience in the current sense.

The proposal for consideration is that the mental self is conceived or experienced as (1) a *thing*, (2) a *mental* thing, a *single* thing that is single both (3) *synchronically* considered and (4) *diachronically* considered, (5) a thing that is *ontically distinct* from all other things, (6) a *subject of experience* and (7) an *agent* that has (8) a certain personality. In this section I will discuss (3) and (4) in the framework of the *local* phenomenological question, after very brief comments on (1) and (2). In sections VII–IX I will discuss of (4) and (8) in the framework of the *general* phenomenological question. In section IX I will say something about (5).

Thinghood and mentality
What about the claim (1) that the self is conceived of as a thing? In a way, this is the least clear of the eight claims, but the general idea is this: the self isn't thought of as merely a state or property of something else, or as an event, or process, or series of events. So, in a sense, there is nothing else for it to seem to be, other than a thing. It's not thought of as being a thing in the way that a stone or a cat is — it's not thought of as a sort of ethereal concrete object. But it is thought of as a thing of some kind. In particular, it is thought of as something that has the causal character of a thing; something that can undergo things and do things. Bishop Berkeley's characterization of the self as a 'thinking ... principle' seems as good as any (1975, p. 185). A principle, in this old use, manages to sound like a thing of some sort without sounding anything like a table or a chair.

The second claim, (2), that the self is thought of as something mental, is also unclear. Very briefly, the idea is something like this: when the self is thought of as a thing, its claim to thinghood is taken to be sufficiently grounded in its mental nature alone. It may also have a non-mental nature, as materialists suppose, but its counting as a thing is not thought to depend on its counting as a thing considered in its non-mental nature: the self is the *mental* self. (It's true and important that many people naturally think of themselves as possessing both mental and non-mental properties, but this doesn't affect the truth of (2).)

Singularity
Clearly, to think of the self as a thing is already to think of it as single in some way — as a thing. But in what way? I have three main claims in mind.

First: in so far as the mental self is thought of as single, it is not thought of as having singularity only in the sense in which a group of things can be said to be a single group. Rather it is thought of as single in the way in which a single marble (e.g.) is single when compared with a single pile of marbles. Developing the Lockean point just made about the fundamental causal component in our idea of a thing, one might say that the mental self is conceived of as something that has the kind of strong unity of internal causal connectedness that a single marble has, as compared with the much weaker unity of internal causal connectedness found in a pile of marbles.[12]

Second: the mental self's property of singleness is thought of as sufficiently and essentially grounded in its mental nature alone. This closely parallels the idea that the

---

[12] Cf. Campbell (1995). A marble, of course, is made of atoms, and is a collection of things from the point of view of an atom. An atom is a collection of things from the point of view of an electron, and perhaps the series continues. This is the point of the comparative formula 'single in the way in which a marble (e.g.) is single when compared with a pile of marbles'.

self's claim to thinghood is thought of as sufficiently grounded in its mental nature alone, and the same moves are appropriate. We may suppose that the mental self has non-mental being (the brain-as-revealed-to-physics, say) as well as mental being, and it may be *believed* to have non-mental being. The fact remains that it is thought of as having singleness in a way that is independent of its having singleness when considered in its non-mental nature.

One may express this by saying that its *principle of unity* is taken to be mental. What does 'principle of unity' mean? Well, it is arguable that everything that is conceived of as a single thing or object — electron, atom, neuron, sofa, nation-state — is conceived of as a single thing relative to some principle of unity according to which it counts as a single thing. An atom counts as a single thing relative to one principle of unity, and it *counts* as many things relative to other principles of unity — those which discern subatomic particles. Many associate this point with the view that there are no ultimate facts of the matter about which phenomena are things or objects and which are not; they hold that all principles of objectual unity, as one might call them, are ultimately subjective in character. But this is a further claim. In itself, the claim that everything that is taken to be a single object is so taken relative to some principle of objectual unity is compatible with the view that there are objective principles of objectual unity given which there are right answers to questions about which things are genuinely single objects.

Let me try to put the point about the self in another way: we may suppose that the mental self (the self-phenomenon) has non-mental being as well as mental being, and it may even be widely believed that this is so (few give the matter much thought). The fact remains that it is thought of as having singleness in its mental being in a way that is independent of any singleness that it may have in its non-mental being. In this sense it is taken to be single just as something mental.[13] I will illustrate this idea after introducing the third main point about singleness.

This is that the mental self is standardly thought to be single in the two ways just characterized both when it is considered (3) synchronically, or as a thing existing at a given time, and when it is considered (4) diachronically, i.e. as a thing that persists through time.

In what follows, I will stretch the meaning of 'synchronic' slightly, and take it to apply to any consideration of the mental self (or self-phenomenon) that is a consideration of it during an experientially unitary or unbroken or hiatus-free period of thought or experience. The notion of a hiatus-free period of thought or experience is important for my purposes, and needs further description (see section IX). For the moment let me simply assert that in the normal course of events truly hiatus-free periods of thought or experience are invariably brief in human beings: a few seconds at the most, a fraction of a second at the least. Our eyes are constantly engaged in saccadic jumps, and reflection reveals the respect in which our minds function in an analogous — if more perceptible — way. (Research by Pöppel and others provides 'clear evidence that . . . the experienced Now is not a point, but is extended, . . . that the [human] conscious Now is — language and culture independent — of the duration

---

[13] Compare 'X is taken to be single just qua something physical (i.e. non-mental)'. The thought that this expresses is not problematic for ordinary thought, and the thought expressed by 'X is taken to be single just qua something mental' is no more problematic.

of approximately 3 seconds', and although this proves nothing about the existence of hiatuses, or about the nature of the self, it is undeniably suggestive.)[14]

'Diachronic' complements 'synchronic' and applies to consideration of the mental self (or self-phenomenon) during any period of conscious thought or experience that includes a break or hiatus. Such periods may range from a fraction of a second to a lifetime.

Now reconsider the second claim — that the mental self is taken to be single just as something mental. This has a synchronic and and diachronic aspect. I will begin with the former. Suppose that someone fully convinces you (perhaps by hypnosis) that your current mental life with all its familiar characteristics, which incorporates your current sense of the single mental self, depends on the activity of three spatially separated brains in three different bodies. Will this immediately annihilate your natural sense of your mental singleness? Surely not. Your thought is likely to be 'Wow, I have got three brains — I, the single thing or person that I am' (Kant (1996, A353–4) makes a related point). Your sense of the mental self is overwhelmingly likely to continue unchanged. It doesn't depend on your believing that you have a single brain or body. Suppose that you find out that there are three separate brains in your single body, collaborating to produce your experience. Again this will not override the experience of mental singleness.

It may be objected that in the case imagined you still have experience as of inhabiting a single body. This is true, given that you are an ordinary human being. But one can equally well imagine a three-bodied creature that naturally experiences itself as three-bodied, and as receiving information (perhaps via different sense modalities) from all three bodies, while still having a strong sense of the single mental self, and thinking of itself as 'I'. Here the experience of three-bodiedness is likely to make the sense of the singleness of the mental self particularly vivid. It is true that ordinary human experience of oneself as mentally single is deeply shaped by experience of having a single body, but it hardly follows that any possible experience of oneself as mentally single depends essentially on such experience.[15]

That is the sense of synchronic singleness I have in mind. Now for the diachronic case. Suppose one experiences one's mental life as something that has strong diachronic singleness or unity (some do more than others). And suppose that one is then convinced — that it depends for its existence on the successive existence of a series of numerically distinct brains or neuronal entities. Will this annihilate one's sense of the mental self as a single thing persisting through time? It would be extraordinary if it did: for, by hypothesis, everything else is the same, experientially, as it was before one made this discovery. This suggests that confrontation with the fact of one's non-mental multiplicity will have no more force to undermine one's sense of the singleness of the mental self in the diachronic case than in the synchronic case.

There is a famous footnote in Kant's discussion of the Third Paralogism (Kant, 1996, A363–4):

---

[14] Ruhnau (1995, p. 168); Pöppel (1978). Citing this research in his essay *The Dimension of the Present Moment*, the Czech immunologist and poet Miroslav Holub writes that 'in this sense our ego lasts three seconds' (1990, p. 6).

[15] This is the kind of issue that arises when one asks (3), the 'conditions' question.

An elastic ball which strikes another similar ball in a straight line communicates to the latter its entire motion, and therefore its entire state (if we take account only of positions in space). If, in analogy with such bodies, we postulate substances such that the one communicates representations to the other together with consciousness of them, we can conceive a whole series of substances of which the first transmits its state to the second, the second its own state with that of the preceding substance to the third, and [so on]. The last substance would then be conscious of all the states of the previously changed substances as being its own states, because they would have been transferred to it together with consciousness of them.

Kant's aim is to argue that no experience of the diachronic singleness of the mental self can possibly establish that the mental self or 'I' is in fact a diachronically single substance. My different, compatible claim is that even if one came to believe that the existence of the mental self did *not* involve the existence of a diachronically single substance, there is no reason to suppose that this would undermine one's experience of the mental self as so single.

To summarize: even if one takes it for granted that the mental self (or self-phenomenon) has a non-mental nature or being, one's experience of the mental self as single is independent of any belief that it is single — either synchronically or diachronically — in its non-mental nature or being. This, then, illustrates the respect in which the singularity of the mental self is conceived of as being essentially grounded in its mental nature alone.

It's also true — to diverge from merely phenomenological concerns — that thoughts that occur in a single body or brain (or substance of some other sort) may fail to seem anything like the series of thoughts of a single self or thinker, both when considered 'from the inside' (i.e. from the point of view of the thinker of any given one of the thoughts in question) and when considered from the outside (i.e. by someone who is not the thinker of any of the thoughts, but who has access to the contents of the thoughts, as in a novel). Consider the diachronic case first: imagine that a series of self-conscious thoughts or 'I-thoughts' occurs in the same brain, one at a time, while none of them ever involves any awareness of any thought earlier (or indeed later) than itself, and while no two of them ever stand in any of the relations (of content, temperamental coherence, etc.) in which temporally close pairs of thoughts so often stand when they are the thoughts of a being that we naturally think of as a single thinker.

In this case, it may be said that we lack any mentally grounded reason for saying that there is a single thinker. Some may want to say that there is nevertheless a single thinker, simply because a single brain is the locus of all the thoughts. But why should the fact of non-mental diachronic singleness decisively overrule the natural judgement that there is no plausible candidate for a diachronically single mental self in this case? The fact of non-mental multiplicity in the three-bodies case had no power to defeat the natural judgement of mental singleness. Why should the fact of non-mental singleness in this case defeat the natural judgement of mental multiplicity (lack of mental singularity)?[16]

Now consider the synchronic case: imagine that a single brain is the site of experiential phenomena that are just like the experiential phenomena taking place simultaneously in the brains of three different people (the first thinking exclusively about

---

[16] The phenomena of dissociative identity disorder may also support the idea that non-mental singleness is compatible with a multiplicity of mental selves, but the present example is much more extreme.

Vienna, the second exclusively about menhirs, the third exclusively about DNA).
Here it is natural to judge that there are three subjects of experience. If one counts the
whole brain non-mentally considered as the non-mental being of each of the three
apparently distinct thought-thinking selves, then one has multiplicity of selves in
spite of non-mental singleness.

The judgement that there are three subjects of experience may seem natural in this
case, but it can be cogently challenged. It is very difficult to draw firm conclusions
about the number of subjects of experience associated with a single brain from facts
about the contents of the experiences associated with that brain. As far as the synchronic case is concerned: it may be a fact about human beings that they can only
genuinely entertain one conscious thought at a time, but it does not seem to be an *a
priori* truth about conscious thinking in general. As far as the diachronic case is concerned: it is not clear that there is any lower bound on the connectedness of the successive thoughts and experiences of a single subject of experience, any point at which
we can confidently say, 'These experiences are too unconnected and disordered to
count as the experiences of a single subject of experience.'[17]

Multiplicity?

So far I have taken it for granted that human beings standardly have some sense of the
singleness of the mental self. But some may claim to experience the mental self as
fragmentary or multiple, and most of us have had experiences that give us — so we
feel — some understanding of what they mean.

It seems, however, that the experience of multiplicity can at most affect (4), the
sense of the mental self as diachronically single (recall that a sense of the mental self
as diachronically single may well be concerned with short periods of time; when I
want to consider longer periods of time — weeks, months, years, lifetimes — I will
talk about 'long-term' continuity). It cannot affect (3), the sense of the mental self as
synchronically single (single during any one 'hiatus-free' period of thought or experience). Why not? Because any candidate for being an experience of the mental self as
synchronically multiple at the present moment will have to be an episode of explicitly
self-conscious thought, and there is a crucial (trivial) respect in which no such episode could be experience of the mental self as synchronically multiple. Explicitly
self-conscious thought need not always involve some explicit sense of the mental self
as something present and involved, even when it has the form 'I f ', or 'I am F' ('I forgot the key', 'I'm late for my exam'). But whenever it does — and it must if there is to
be anything that is a candidate for being an *experience* of the mental self as synchronically multiple at the present moment — there is a fundamental respect in which the
mental self must be experienced as single, for the space of that thought at least.

This may seem obvious, but it can be disputed. It may be said that even experience
of the mental self synchronically considered can seem to be experience of something
shattered and multiple ('My name is legion', *Mark* 5.9). There seem to be forms of
human experience that invite such a description. One may be under stress and subject
to rapidly changing moods. One may feel oneself pulled in different directions by
opposed desires. Human thought-processes can become extraordinarily rapid and
tumultuous. But what exactly is being claimed, when it is said that the self may be
experienced as synchronically multiple? There seem to be two main possibilities:

---

[17] See Snowdon (forthcoming); also Van Inwagen (1990, section 16, pp. 196–202).

either the experience is that there are many selves present, or it is (just) that the self is complex in a certain radical way. But in the second case, the experience of radical complexity that is claimed to justify the description 'synchronically multiple' clearly depends on a prior sense of the mental self as synchronically single: in this case 'mult-iple' is a characterization that is applied to something that must have already pre-sented as single in order for the characterization to be applied at all. What about the first case, in which the experience is that there are many selves present? Well, we may ask who has the experience that there are many selves present. To face the question is to realize that any explicitly self-conscious experience has to present as experience from one single mental point of view. (The word 'mental' is not redundant here, for the three-bodied person that has sensory experience of being three-bodied may have three sensory points of view while still having only one mental 'point of view'.) If so, the experience that there are many selves present is necessarily experience from some single point of view. Even if a single brain is the site of many experiences that there are many selves present, each such experience is necessarily experience from a single point of view. This is the trivial aspect of the claim that experience of the mental self as synchronically multiple is not really possible.[18]

It may be added that when one's mind races and tumbles, it is natural to experience oneself as a largely helpless spectator of the pandemonium. To this extent, experience of chaotic disparateness of contents reinforces a sense of singleness rather than diminishing it. Nor can one experience conflict of desire unless one experiences both desires as one's own.

VII: Personality

So much for a consideration of (3) and (4) — synchronic and diachronic singleness — in the framework of the local phenomenological question (What is the human sense of the self?) I will now consider (4) and (8) — diachronic singularity and personality — in the framework of the general phenomenological question (What senses of the self are possible?) I will begin with personality, and, like William James, I will sometimes talk 'in the first person, leaving my description to be accepted by those to whose introspection it may commend itself as true, and confessing my inability to meet the demands of others, if others there be' (1950, vol. 1, p. 299).

It seems plain that (8) is not a necessary component of any possible sense of the mental self — that experience of the self does not necessarily involve experience of it as something that has a personality. Most people have at some time, and however temporarily, experienced themselves as a kind of bare locus of consciousness — not just as detached, but as void of personality, stripped of particularity of character, a mere (cognitive) point of view. Some have experienced it for long periods of time. It may be the result of exhaustion or solitude, abstract thought or a hot bath. It is also a common feature of severe depression, in which one may experience 'depersonaliz-

---

[18] I take it that this conclusion is compatible with the possibility of Husserlian *splitting of the I* in transcendental–phenomenological reflection (Husserl, 1973, p. 35), and also with a thought-experiment of Parfit's in which he imagines being able to 'divide his mind' in order to do two separate calculations in two separate streams of consciousness, and then reunite it. He considers his attitude to the process after several divisions and reunions: 'in each of my two streams of consciousness I would believe that I was now, in my other stream, having thoughts and sensations of which, in this stream, I was unaware' (Parfit, 1984, pp. 246–8).

ation'. This is a very accurate term, in my experience and in that of others I have talked to.

Sustained experience of depersonalization is classified as psychotic relative to the normal human condition, but it is of course experientially real, and one can imagine human beings getting stuck in this condition; some do. Equally, one can imagine aliens for whom it is the normal condition. Such an alien may still have a clear sense of the self as a specifically mental thing. It may still have an unimpaired sense of itself as a locus of consciousness, just as we ordinarily do—not only when we suffer depersonalization, but also in everyday life.[19]

A very strong form of what may be lost in depersonalization is recorded by Gerard Manley Hopkins, who talks of considering

> my self-being, my consciousness and feeling of myself, that taste of myself, of *I* and *me* above and in all things, which is more distinctive than the taste of ale or alum, more distinctive than the smell of walnutleaf or camphor, and is incommunicable by any means to another man . . . . Nothing else in nature comes near this unspeakable stress of pitch, distinctiveness, and selving, this selfbeing of my own.[20]

My enquiries suggest that while some people feel they know exactly what Hopkins means, most find this deeply bewildering: for them, their personality is something that is unnoticed, and in effect undetectable, in the present moment. It's what they look through, or where they look from; not something they look at; a global and invisible condition of their life, like air, not an object of experience. Dramatic differences like these back up the view that we need a phenomenology of the sense of the self before we try to answer the factual question about whether or not there is such a thing.

VIII: The Self In Time; Effects of Character

So much, briefly, for (8). Must any sense of the mental self involve experience of the self as (4) something that has long-term diachronic continuity as a single thing? I think not. The sense of the single mental self may be vivid and complete, at any given time, even if it has to do only with the present, brief, hiatus-free stretch of consciousness, at any given time. Nor do I think that this is just some alien or logical possibility, though it is also that. It lies within the range of human experience. One can be fully aware of the fact that one has long-term continuity as a *living human being* without *ipso facto* having any significant sense of the *mental self* or *subject of experience* as something that has long-term continuity. One can have a vivid sense of oneself as a mental self, and a strong natural tendency to think that that is what one most fundamentally is, while having little or no interest in or commitment to the idea that the I who is now thinking has any past or future.

Human beings differ deeply in a number of ways that affect their experience of the mental self as diachronically continuous. Some people have an excellent 'personal'

---

[19] A friend who recently experienced depersonalization found that the thought 'I don't exist' kept occurring to him. It seemed to him that this exactly expressed his experience of himself, although he was aware of the force of Descartes' 'I think, therefore I am', and knew, of course, that there had to be a locus of consciousness where the thought 'I don't exist' occurred. (The case of Meursault is also worth considering, in Camus' book *The Outsider*. So too is his remarkable description of his mother in *The First Man*. See Camus, 1982; 1995.)

[20] Hopkins (1959, p. 123); quoted in Glover (1988, p. 59).

memory (i.e. memory of their own past life) and an unusual capacity for vivid recollection. Others have a very poor personal memory. And it may not be simply poor. It may also be highly quiescent, and almost never intrude spontaneously into their current thought. These deep differences of memory are matched by equal differences in the force with which people imagine, anticipate, or form intentions about the future.

These differences interact with others. Some people live deeply in narrative mode: they experience their lives in terms of something that has shape and story, narrative trajectory. Some of them are self-narrators in a stronger sense: they regularly rehearse and revise their interpretations of their lives. Some people, again, are great planners, and knit up their lives with long-term projects.

Others are quite different. They have no early ambition, no later sense of vocation, no interest in climbing a career ladder, no tendency to see their life in narrative terms or as constituting a story or a development. Some merely go from one thing to another. They live life in a picaresque or episodic fashion. Some people make few plans and are little concerned with the future. Some live intensely in the present, some are simply aimless.

Many things can encourage or obstruct a sense of the mental self as something that has long-term diachronic continuity. Some people are very consistent in personality or character, whether or not they know it. And this form of steadiness may in some cases strongly underwrite experience of the mental self's continuity. Others are consistent only in their inconsistency, and may for that reason feel themselves to be continually puzzling, and piecemeal. Some go through life as if stunned.

Neither inconsistency nor poor memory is necessary for the episodic experience of life. John Updike writes 'I have the persistent sensation, in my life and art, that I am just beginning' (1989, p. 239). These are the words of a man who has an extremely powerful personal memory and a highly consistent character. I have the same persistent sensation, and learn from Updike that it is nothing essentially to do with my extremely poor personal memory. I believe that it is an accurate description of how things are for many people, when it comes to that sense of oneself as a mental self that is — whether or not it is acknowledged — central to most people's self-conception.

I'm somewhere down the episodic end of the spectrum. I have no sense of my life as a narrative with form, or indeed as a narrative without form. I have little interest in my own past and little concern for the future. My poor personal memory rarely impinges on my present consciousness. Even when I am interested in my past, I'm not interested in it specifically in so far as it is mine. I'm perfectly well aware that it is mine, in so far as I am a human being considered as a whole, but I do not really think of it as mine at all, in so far as 'mine' picks out me as I am now. For me as I am now, the interest (emotional or otherwise) of my personal memories lies in their experiential content considered independently of the fact that what is remembered happened *to me* — i.e. to the me that is now remembering.[21] They're certainly distinctive in their 'from-the-inside' character, but this in itself doesn't mark them as mine in any

---

[21] Here I am strikingly different from J. Campbell, who argues that 'fission' (in which one person is imagined to split into two separate people) 'would mean loss of the right to one's autobiographical memories, my memories of what I have seen and done' in some way that mattered (1994, p. 189).

emotionally significant sense. The one striking exception to this, in my case, used to be — but no longer is — memory of recent embarrassment.

I make plans for the future. To that extent I think of myself perfectly adequately as something that has long-term continuity. But I experience this way of thinking of myself as utterly remote and theoretical, given the most central or fundamental way in which I think of myself, which is as a mental self or someone. Using 'Me*' to express this fundamental way in which I think of myself — or to denote me thinking of myself in this way, looking out on things from this perspective — I can accurately express my experience by saying that I do not think of Me* as being something in the future. It is also accurate to shift the 'not', and say, more strongly, that what I think of as being in the future is not Me*.

As I write these words, the thought that I have to give a lecture before a large audience in two months' time causes me some worry, which has familiar physiological manifestations. I feel the anxiety naturally and directly as pertaining to me even though I have no sense that it will be Me* that will be giving the lecture. Indeed it seems completely false to say that it will be Me*. And this is how it feels, not something I believe for theoretical reasons. So why do I feel any anxiety now? I believe that susceptibility to this sort of anticipatory anxiety is innate and 'hard-wired', a manifestation of the instinct for self-preservation: my practical concern for my future, which I believe to be within the normal human range, is biologically grounded and autonomous in such a way that it persists as something immediately felt even though it is not supported by any emotionally backed sense on the part of Me* now that Me* will be there in the future. (Not even half an hour away—and certainly not tomorrow.) In so far as I have any sense of Me* (rather than the living human being that I am) as something with a history and future, it seems that this sense is a wispy, short-range product of, and in no way a ground of, my innate predisposition to physiological impulses that develop into experience of anxiety or regret. It dislimns when scrutinized, and it is more accurate to say that it does not exist.

Now for an exception. You might expect me to say that when I think of my death at some unspecified future time, I think that it is not Me* who is going to die, or at least that I do not think that it is Me*. But I do think that it is Me* that is going to die, and I feel fear of death. It's only when I consider future events *in life* that I do not think it's Me*. This seems odd, given that my death necessarily comes after any future events in my life, and ought therefore to seem to have even less to do with Me* than any future events in life. But it can be explained. This feature of my attitude to death is principally grounded in susceptibility to the following line of thought: When eternity — eternal nonexistence — is in question, the gap between Me* and death that is created by the fact that I still have an indefinite amount of life to live approximates to nothing (like any finite number compared with infinity). So death — nonexistence for ever — presents itself as having direct relevance for Me* now even if Me* has no clear future in life — not even tomorrow. On the vast scale of things that one naturally thinks in terms of when thinking of death, death is no significant distance away from Me*, and looms as something that will happen to Me*. This is not to say that I feel or fear that I am going to die now. The thought of eternity doesn't override common sense. But it has an emotional force that makes it seem plain that death faces Me*. If this is Heideggerian authenticity, then Heideggerian authenticity is compatible with lack of any belief in the persisting self.

Note that this line of thought will have equal force for someone who *does* think of their Me* as having a future in life: for if eternity of nonexistence is what you fear, a few years is not a protection. This idea was vivid for me every night as a young child combining an atheist upbringing with great difficulty in going to sleep.

One indirect lesson of this case is important. It is that one's sense of one's temporal nature may vary considerably depending on what one is thinking about. But the general conclusion I draw is that a sense of the self need not necessarily involve (4) a sense of it as something that has long-term continuity.[22]

IX: The Self In Time; The 'Stream' of Consciousness

How does the moment-to-moment experience of consciousness relate to the sense of the self? Does it underwrite (4)? I will now consider this question.

I think William James's famous metaphor of the stream of consciousness is inept.[23] Human thought has very little natural phenomenological continuity or experiential flow — if mine is anything to go by. 'Our thought is fluctuating, uncertain, fleeting', as Hume said (1947, p. 194). It keeps slipping from mere consciousness into self-consciousness and out again (one can sit through a whole film without emerging into I-thinking self-consciousness). It is always shooting off, fuzzing, shorting out, spurting and stalling. William James described it as 'like a bird's life, . . . an alternation of flights and perchings' (1950, vol. 1 p. 243), but even this recognition that thought is not a matter of even flow retains a strong notion of continuity, in so far as a bird traces a spatio-temporally continuous path. It fails to take adequate account of the fact that trains of thought are constantly broken by detours — byblows — fissures — white noise. This is especially so when one is just sitting and thinking. Things are different if one's attention is engaged by some ordered and continuous process in the world, like a fast and exciting game, or music, or a talk. In this case thought or experience may be felt to inherit much of the ordered continuity of the phenomenon which occupies it. But it may still seize up, fly off, or flash with perfectly extraneous matter from time to time, and reflection reveals gaps and fadings, disappearances and recommencements even when there is stable succession of content.[24] It is arguable that the case of solitary speculative thought — in which the mind is left to its own resources and devices — merely reveals in a relatively dramatic way something that is true to a greater or lesser extent of all thought. There is an important respect in which James Joyce's use of punctuation in his 'stream of consciousness' novel *Ulysses* makes his depiction of the character of the process of consciousness more accurate in the case of the heavily punctuated Stephen Daedalus than in the case of the unpunctuated Molly Bloom. Dorothy Richardson, acknowledged as the inventor of the 'stream of con-

---

[22] Narrative personalities may feel there is something chilling and empty in the Episodic life. They may fear it, and judge that it shows lack of wisdom, conduces to lack of moral responsibility, and is 'deficient and empty' (Plutarch, 1939, p. 217). This, however, is ignorance: even in its extreme form this life is no less intense or full, no less emotional and moral.

[23] James (1984, p. 145). Husserl is also heavily committed to the image of the stream, the '*flowing cogito*', the 'flowing conscious life in which the . . . ego lives' (1973, pp. 66, 31). For an excellent discussion of Buddhist uses of the metaphor of the stream see Collins (1982, ch. 8.4).

[24] This is just a phenomenological report; compare Dennett's discussion (1991, pp. 189, 237–42) of the 'pandemonium' in the mind–brain as different words, ideas, thoughts, impulses vie for emergence into consciousness.

sciousness' novel in English, remarked on the 'perfect imbecility' of the phrase to describe what she did.[25]

My claim is not just that there can be radical disjunction at the level of subject matter. Switches of subject matter could be absolute, and still be seamless in the sense that they involved no sensed temporal gap or felt interruption of consciousness. It seems to me, however, that such experience of temporal seamlessness is relatively rare.[26] When I am alone and thinking I find that my fundamental experience of consciousness is one of *repeated returns into consciousness from a state of complete, if momentary, unconsciousness.* The (invariably brief) periods of true experiential continuity are usually radically disjunct from one another in this way even when they are not radically disjunct in respect of content. (It is in fact often the same thought — or nearly the same thought — that one returns to after a momentary absence.) The situation is best described, it seems to me, by saying that consciousness is continually *restarting.* There isn't a basic substrate (as it were) of continuous consciousness interrupted by various lapses and doglegs. Rather, conscious thought has the character of a (nearly continuous) series of radically disjunct irruptions into consciousness from a basic substrate of non-consciousness. It keeps banging out of nothingness; it is a series of comings to. It's true that belief in the reality of flow may itself contribute to an experience of flow. But I think that the appearance of flow is undercut by even a modest amount of reflection.[27]

'But perhaps the experience of disjunction is an artefact of introspection. Perhaps unexamined consciousness has true flow, and the facts get distorted by the act of trying to observe what they are.'

---

[25] This is Richardson's Miriam Henderson in church:

> Certainly it was wrong to listen to sermons . . . stultifying . . . unless they were intellectual . . . lectures like Mr Brough's . . . that was as bad, because they were not sermons . . . . Either kind was bad and ought not to be allowed . . . a homily . . . sermons . . . homilies . . . a quiet homily might be something rather nice . . . and have not Charity — sounding brass and tinkling cymbal . . . .*Caritas* . . . I have *none* I am sure . . . (Richardson, 1979, p 73).]

Compare Molly Bloom in bed:

> I want to do the place up someway the dust grows in it I think while Im asleep then we can have music and cigarettes I can accompany him first I must clean the keys of the piano with milk whatll I wear a white rose or those fairy cakes in Liptons at $7^1/_2$d a lb or the other ones with the cherries in them and the pinky sugar 11d a couple of lbs of those a nice plant for the middle of the table Id get that cheaper in wait wheres this I saw them not long ago I love flowers . . . (Joyce, 1986, p. 642).]

And Stephen Daedalus walking on the beach:

> Who watches me here? Who ever anywhere will read these written words? Signs on a white field. Somewhere to someone in your flutiest voice. The good bishop of Cloyne took the veil of the temple out of his shovel hat: veil of space with coloured emblems hatched on its field. Hold hard. Coloured on a flat: yes, that's right (Joyce, 1986, p. 40).

[26] Molly Bloom might seem to be an example of seamlessness across radical change of content, but Shaun Gallagher argues that 'such radical disjunctions of content actually do disrupt the flow structure — content and form are not independent of one another' (private correspondence).

[27] This experience seems to be in affinity with the Buddhist theory of the way in which consciousness is an interruption of ongoing, unconscious *bhavanga* mind, although the Buddhist theory has many special further features. See Collins (1982, pp. 238–47).

This seems highly implausible. Awareness of radical disjunction sometimes surfaces spontaneously and unlooked for. We can become aware that this is what has been happening, we do not see it only when we look. This is my experience, and the claim seems strongly supported by work described by Dennett (1991, e.g. ch. 11). Even if the appearance of disjunction were partly an artefact of intentional introspection, this would be a striking fact about how consciousness appears to itself, something one needed to take account of when considering the underpinnings of the sense of the self. There's a sense in which this issue is undecidable, for in order to settle it one would need to be able to observe something while it was unobserved. Nevertheless, the view that there is radical disjunction might receive independent support from experimental psychology, and also, more indirectly, from current work on the non-mental neural correlates of consciousness.

I have been arguing — if that's the word — that the sense of the mental self as something that has long-term continuity lacks a certain sort of direct phenomenological warrant in the moment-to-moment nature of our thought processes. It is not supported at the level of detail by any phenomenon of steady flow. If there is any support for belief in the long-term continuity of the self in the nature of moment-to-moment consciousness, it is derived indirectly from other sources — the massive constancies and developmental coherencies of *content* that often link up experiences through time, and by courtesy of short-term memory, across all the jumps and breaks of flow. One (the human being, the mental-and-nonmental whole) walks from A to B, looking around, thinking of this and that. One works in a room for an hour. Examined in detail, the processes of one's thought are bitty, scatty, and saccadic in the way described; consciousness is 'in a perpetual flux', and different thoughts and experiences 'succeed each other with an inconceivable rapidity' (Hume, 1978, p. 252). And yet one is experientially in touch with a great pool of constancies and steady processes of change in one's environment including, notably, one's body (of which one is almost constantly aware, however thoughtlessly, both by external sense and by proprioception). If one does not reflect very hard, these constancies and steadinesses of development in the *contents* of one's consciousness may seem like fundamental characteristics of the *operation* of one's consciousness, although they are not. This in turn may support the sense of the *mental self* as something uninterrupted and continuous throughout the waking day.

I am not claiming that belief in the flow of consciousness is *necessary* to a sense of the self as something that has long-term continuity. One could think and feel that consciousness was gappy and chaotic and still believe in a mental self that had long-term continuity. This is probably the most common position among those who believe in the self, and the present, weak suggestion is only that belief in the flow of consciousness may be one interesting and suspect source of support for a sense of long-term continuity.

There is more to say, but not here. My central claim remains unchanged: one can have a full sense of the single mental self at any given time without thinking of the self as something that has long-term continuity. According to Reed 'our sense of self is intimately related to the subjective awareness of the continuity of life. Any break in personal time [or 'time-gap experience'] is alarming, because it suggests some disintegration of psychic synthesis' (Reed, 1987, p. 777). I believe that this is not generally true.

X: The Conditions Question

I have given examples of how one might set about answering phenomenological questions **(1)** and **(2)** in preparation for **(4)**, the factual question 'Does the self exist?' I have no space to consider **(3)**, the conditions question 'What are the grounds or pre-conditions of possession of a sense of the mental self?', but I think it is best approached by asking the more familiar question 'What are the grounds or necessary conditions of self-consciousness?', which has been widely discussed—e.g. by Kant, Fichte, Wundt, James and their followers, and, more recently, by P.F. Strawson (1966, pp. 97–112), Evans (1982, ch. 7), and others (see e.g. the contributors to Bermúdez et al., 1995, and Cassam, 1997). I believe that all discussions in the analytic tradition overestimate the strength of the conditions that can be established as necessary for self-consciousness, but this is a question for another time, and I will now conclude with a wild sketch of how I think the factual question is to be answered.

XI: The Factual Question

Suppose — for the sake of argument — that the answer to the general phenomenological question is as follows: any genuine sense of the self must involve a conception of the self as $[(1) + (2) + (3) + (5) + (6)]$ — as a single, mental thing that is distinct from all other things and a subject of experience — but need not involve a conception of it as (7) an agent, or as having (8) character or personality or (4) longer-term diachronic continuity. If we couple this answer with the equivalence claim (p. 5 above) we get the result that if there is such a thing as a mental self, it must at least fulfil conditions (1), (2), (3), (5) and (6) — one might call these the 'core conditions'. It must be a distinct, mental thing that is correctly said to be a subject of experience and a single thing within any hiatus-free period of experience; whatever else it may be.[28]

Is there such a thing? If there is, is it right to call it a self? I can't legislate on how anyone should use the words 'self' and 'thing' (cf. note 8 above). It seems to me that the best answer is Yes, but many will think my Yes is close to No, because I don't think a mental self exists in any sense that will satisfy most of those who want there to be a self. I believe the Buddhists have the truth when they deny the existence of a *persisting* mental self, in the human case, and nearly all of those who want there to be a self want there to be a persisting self.

I will call my view the Pearl view, because it suggests that many mental selves exist, one at a time and one after another, like pearls on a string, in the case of something like a human being.[29] According to the Pearl view, each is a distinct existence, an individual physical thing or object, though they may exist for considerably different lengths of time. The Pearl view is not the view that mental selves are necessarily of relatively short duration—there may be beings whose conscious experience is uninterrupted for hours at a time, or even for the whole of their existence (if I believed in God, this is how I'd expect God to be). But we are not like this: the basic form of

---

[28] Obviously the view that mental selves can have personality and can be agents and have longer-term continuity is not excluded by this proposal. Very few would agree with me that agenthood is dispensable with.

[29] It is unlike the 'bundle' theory of the self, described but not endorsed by Hume, according to which the self, in so far as it exists at all, is a diachronically extended — perhaps non-continuous — thing constituted of a series of experiences (Hume, 1978, pp. 251–3, 259–63, 633–6, 657–8).

our consciousness is that of a gappy series of eruptions of consciousness from a sub-strate of apparent non-consciousness.

I don't suppose the Pearl view will be much liked. It sounds linguistically odd and counterintuitive. It offends against the everyday use of expressions like 'myself' to refer to enduring human beings, and nearly all theoretical speculation about the self incorporates a deep presumption that if one is arguing for the existence of the mental self one is arguing for something that exists for a substantial period of time. The Pearl view sounds even more implausible as an account of the subject of experience.[30]

Sometimes we need to speak oddly to see clearly. I think it is important to defend the Pearl view, giving its linguistic counterintuitiveness a chance to diminish through familiarity so that one can judge it on its merits rather than on linguistic gut feeling. Perhaps the most that can be said for it is that it is the best we can do if we commit our-selves in advance to answering Yes to the question 'Is there any straightforward and metaphysically robust sense in which it is legitimate to talk of the mental self as a thing, something that really exists, like a chair or a cat, rather than merely as a Humean or Dennettian fiction?' In my view, that means that there is a lot to be said for it.

The proposal, in any case, is that the mental self — *a* mental self — exists at any given moment of consciousness or during any uninterrupted or hiatus-free period of consciousness.[31] But it exists only for some short period of time. But it is none the less real, as real as any rabbit or Z-particle. And it is as much a *thing* or *object* as any G-type star or grain of salt. And it is as much a *physical* thing as any blood vessel or jackhammer or cow.

I can think of three overlapping tasks one has to undertake in order to develop the proposal. One has to say more about what it is to be a materialist, address the question 'What is a thing (or object)?', and explain further what is meant by 'ontic distinct-ness'. I will make one comment about each.

(i) In saying that a self is an 'ontically distinct' thing, I mean — at least — that it is not the same thing as anything else ordinarily or naturally identified as a thing. But I don't mean that it is an 'independent or separately existing entity' (Parfit, 1995, p. 18) relative to all other things naturally identified as things — such as atoms, neu-rons, and brains. Parfit takes a Cartesian immaterial ego to be a paradigm instance of such a separately existing entity, but I take it that a mental self's existence from t_1 to t_2 (I'll suppose this to be a two-second interval) is part of the existence from t_1 to t_2 of a set of neuron-and-neurotransmitter-(etc)-constituting atoms or fundamental particles in a certain state of activation.[32]

Note that this is not any sort of reductionist remark, for the phrase 'a set of . . . parti-cles in a certain state of activation', as used by a consistent and realistic materialist, does not refer only or even especially to non-mental phenomena that can be ade-

---

[30] Dennett's account of the self as an 'abstraction', a 'Center of Narrative Gravity' (1991, pp. 426–7) may be the best one can do if one is determined to conceive the self as something that has long-term continuity.

[31] The notion of uninterruptedness remains vague. Note that many will think that the period of consciousness must be one of explicit self-consciousness (cf. the opening quotation from Nozick), or must at least occur in a being capable of such self-consciousness. But I am not sure that this is the best thing to say.

[32] Compare Van Inwagen's account (1990, pp. 94–5) of how an atom may be 'caught up in the life of an organism' while existing both before and after it. One may equally well say that each member of the set of fundamental particles is 'caught up in' the life of a mental self.

quately described by current physics or something like it. It refers just as it says, to a set of neuron-and-neurotransmitter-(etc)-constituting particles in a certain state of activation; and this existence and activity, as all genuine and realistic materialists agree, is as much revealed by and constituted by experiential phenomena as by any non-experiential phenomena discernible by physics.

The plausibility of the claim that a mental self is a *thing*, given the way it is characterized in the penultimate paragraph, depends on the success of arguments sketched in (iii) below. But it is at least clear that ontic distinctness is not separate existence. Nor, it seems, is it what Parfit has in mind when he himself distinguishes distinctness from separate existence.

Consider a human being X. I will call the portion of physical reality that consists of X the 'X-reality'. This is a rough notion — as a physical being X is enmeshed in wide-reaching physical interactions, and is not neatly separable out as a single portion of reality — but it is serviceable none the less. Parfit offers two examples of things that stand in the relation of distinctness without separate existence: a statue and the lump of bronze of which it is made, and a nation and 'a group of people, on some territory, living together in certain ways'.[33] By contrast, I propose that there is an analogy between the following two relations: (1) the relation between one of X's little fingers and X, where X is considered statically at a particular moment in time; (2) the relation between a mental self that exists in the X-reality and the X-reality, where the X-reality is considered dynamically as something essentially persisting in time. In other words, I propose that there is some sort of part-whole relation to be discerned, although there is more to be said in description of the whole of which the self is a part. It seems to me that selves are as real, and as much things, as little fingers (actually it is arguable that they have a better claim to count as things than fingers do).

(ii) Genuine, realistic materialism requires acknowledgement that the phenomena of conscious experience are, considered specifically as such, wholly physical, as physical as the phenomena of extension and electricity as studied by physics (section V). This in turn requires the acknowledgement that current physics, considered as a general account of the nature of the physical, is like *Hamlet* without the prince; or at least like *Othello* without Desdemona. No one who doubts this is a serious materialist, as far as I can see. Anyone who has had a standard modern (Western) education is likely to experience a feeling of deep bewilderment — category-blasting amazement — when entering into serious materialism, and considering the question 'What is the nature of the physical?' in the context of the thought that the mental (and in particular the experiential) is physical; followed, perhaps, by a deep, pragmatic agnosticism.[34]

(iii) The discussion of materialism has many mansions, and provides a setting for considering the question 'What is a thing or object?' It is a long question, but the answer suggests that there is no less reason to call the self a thing than there is to call a cat or a rock a thing. It is arguable that disagreement with this last claim is diagnostic of failure to understand what genuine, realistic materialism involves.

---

[33] The statue just consists in the lump of bronze, and is therefore not a separately existing entity, but it is not the same as a lump of bronze: for example, we can melt down the statue and so destroy it without destroying the lump of bronze. The existence of the nation 'just consists in the existence of a group of people, on some territory, living together in certain ways': it is not a separately existing entity. But it is also 'not the same as that group of people, or that territory'.

[34] Cf. Chomsky (1995, pp. 1–10); Russell (1954, ch. 37).

'Come off it. Even if we grant that there is a phenomenon that is reasonably picked out by the phrase "mental self", why should we accept that the right thing to say about some two-second-long mental-self phenomenon is (a) that it is a *thing* or *object* like a rock or a tiger? Why can't we insist that the right thing to say is simply (b) that an enduring ('physical') object — Louis — has a certain *property*, or (c) that a two-second mental-self phenomenon is just a matter of a certain *process* occurring in an object — so that it is not itself a distinct object existing for two seconds?'

I think that a proper understanding of materialism strips (b) and (c) of any appearance of superiority to (a). As for (c): any claim to the effect that a mental self is best thought of as a process rather than an object can be countered by saying that there is no sense in which a mental self is a process in which a rock is not also and equally a process. So if a rock is a paradigm case of a thing in spite of being equally well thought of as a process, we have no good reason to say that a self is not a thing.[35]

'But if there is a process, there must be something — an object or substance — in which it goes on. If something happens, there must be something to which it happens, something which is not just the happening itself.' This expresses our ordinary understanding of things, but physicists are increasingly content with the view that physical reality is itself a kind of pure process — even if it remains hard to know exactly what this idea amounts to. The view that there is some ultimate stuff to which things happen has increasingly ceded to the idea that the existence of anything worthy of the name 'ultimate stuff' consists in the existence of fields of energy — consists, in other words, in the existence of a kind of pure process which is not usefully thought of as something which is happening to a thing distinct from it.

As for (b): the object/property distinction is, as Russell says of the standard distinction between mental and physical, 'superficial and unreal' (1954, p. 402). Chronic philosophical difficulties with the question of how to express the relation between substance and property provide strong negative support for this view. However ineluctable it is for us, it seems that the distinction must be as superficial as we must take the distinction between the wavelike nature and particlelike nature of fundamental particles to be. Obviously a great deal more needs to be said. But Kant seems to have got it exactly right in a single sentence: 'in their relation to substance, [properties] are not in fact subordinated to it, but are the manner of existence of the substance itself' (1996, A414/B441).

XII: Conclusion

So much for the sketch of my answer to the factual question. I think it expresses a difficult truth, but it is exiguous and probably looks very implausible. It is not designed to persuade, however; it simply marks a possible path. One can think it monstrously implausible without rejecting the approach to the problem of the self proposed in this chapter: one can agree about the importance of answering **(1)** and **(2)**, the two phenomenological questions and **(3)**, the conditions question, even if one wants to give a very different answer to **(4)**, the factual question.

---

[35] In saying this, I don't mean to show any partiality to the 'four-dimensionalist' conception of objects.

References

Barkow, J.H., Cosmides, L. and Tooby, J. (1992), *The Adapted Mind: Evolutionary Psychology and the Generation of Culture* (New York: Oxford University Press).
Berkeley, G. (1975), *Philosophical Works*, edited by M. R. Ayers (London: Dent).
Bermúdez, J. L., Marcel, A. and Eilan, N. (ed. 1995), *The Body and the Self* (Cambridge, MA: MIT Press).
Campbell, A. (1994), 'Cartesian dualism and the concept of medical placebos', *Journal of Consciousness Studies*, **1** (2), pp. 230–3.
Campbell, J. (1994), *Past, Space, and Self* (Cambridge, MA: MIT Press).
Campbell, J. (1995), 'The body image and self-consciousness', in Bermúdez *et al.* (1995).
Camus, A. (1982), *The Outsider*, translated by Joseph Laredo (London: Hamish Hamilton).
Camus, A. (1995), *The First Man*, translated by David Hapgood (London: Hamish Hamilton).
Cassam, A-Q.A. (ed. 1994), *Self-knowledge* (Oxford: Oxford University Press).
Cassam, A-Q.A. (1997), *Self and World* (Oxford: Clarendon Press).
Chomsky, N. (1995), 'Language and nature', *Mind*, **104**, pp.1–61.
Collins, S. (1982), *Selfless Persons* (Cambridge: Cambridge University Press).
Crabbe, J. (ed. forthcoming) *From Soul to Self* (London: Routledge).
Dennett, D. (1991), *Consciousness Explained* (Boston, MA: Little, Brown).
Descartes, R. (1985), *The Philosophical Writings of Descartes*, Volumes 1 and 2, translated by J. Cottingham *et al.* (Cambridge: Cambridge University Press).
Evans, G. (1982), *The Varieties of Reference* (Oxford: Oxford University Press).
Farrell, B. (1996), Review of Bermúdez *et al.* (1995), *Journal of Consciousness Studies*, **3** (5–6), pp. 517–19.
Fichte, J.G. (1982), *The Science of Knowledge*, trans. Peter Heath and John Lachs (Cambridge: CUP).
Ginsberg, A. (1963), 'Statement to the Burning Bush', *Burning Bush II*.
Glover, J. (1988), *I: The Philosophy and Psychology of Personal Identity* (Harmondsworth: Penguin).
Holub, M. (1990), *The Dimension of the Present Moment* (London: Faber).
Hopkins, G.M. (1959), *Sermons and Devotional Writings*, ed. C. J. Devlin (London: Oxford University Press).
Hughes, R. (1929), *A High Wind in Jamaica* (London: Chatto & Windus).
Hume, D. (1947), *Dialogues Concerning Natural Religion*, ed. N. Kemp Smith (Edinburgh: Nelson).
Hume, D. (1975), *Enquiries Concerning Human Understanding*, ed. L.A. Selby-Bigge (Oxford: OUP).
Hume, D. (1978), *A Treatise of Human Nature*, ed. L.A. Selby-Bigge and P. H. Nidditch (Oxford: OUP).
Hurlburt, R., Happ, F. and Frith, U. (1994), 'Sampling the form of inner experience in three adults with Asperger syndrome', *Psychological Medicine*, **24**, pp. 385–95.
Husserl, E. (1973), *Cartesian Meditations*, translated by D. Cairns (The Hague: Nijhoff).
James, W. (1950), *The Principles of Psychology* (New York: Dover).
James, W. (1984), *Psychology: Briefer Course* (Cambridge, MA: Harvard University Press).
Joyce, J. (1986), *Ulysses* (Harmondsworth: Penguin).
Kant, I. (1996), *Critique of Pure Reason*, translated by W. S. Pluhar (Indianopolis: Hackett).
Kenny, A. (1988), *The Self* (Marquette: Marquette University Press).
Lowe, E. J. (1996), *Subjects of Experience* (Cambridge: Cambridge University Press).
Nagel, T. (1986), *The View From Nowhere* (New York: Oxford University Press).
Nozick, R. (1981), *Philosophical Explanations* (Oxford: Clarendon Press).
Parfit, D. (1984), *Reasons and Persons* (Oxford: Clarendon Press).
Parfit, D. (1995), 'The unimportance of identity', in *Identity*, ed. H. Harris (Oxford: Clarendon Press).
Plutarch (1939), 'On tranquillity of mind' in Plutarch, *Moralia*, volume VI, translated by W. C. Helmbold (Cambridge, MA: Harvard University Press).
Pöppel, E. (1978), 'Time perception', in *Handbook of Sensory Physiology*, Vol. VIII, ed. R. Held, H.W. Leibovitz and H.L. Teuber (New York: Springer).
Reed, G. (1987), 'Time-gap experience', in *The Oxford Companion to the Mind* (Oxford: OUP).
Richardson, D. (1979) *Pointed Roofs, Pilgrimage*, Vol 1 (London: Virago Press).
Ruhnau, E. (1995), 'Time gestalt and the observer', in *Conscious Experience*, ed. T. Metzinger (Paderborn: Schöningh / Thorverton, UK: Imprint Academic).
Russell, B. (1954), *The Analysis of Matter* (London: Allen and Unwin).
Searle, J. (1992), *The Rediscovery of the Mind* (Cambridge, MA: MIT Press).
Snowdon, P. (forthcoming), 'Personal identity and the unity of consciousness', in *Persons, Animals and Ourselves*.
Strawson, G. (forthcoming), 'The sense of the self', in Crabbe (forthcoming).
Strawson, P.F. (1966), *The Bounds of Sense* (London: Methuen).
Updike, J. (1989), *Self-Consciousness* (London: Deutsch).
Van Inwagen, P. (1990), *Material Beings* (Ithaca, NY: Cornell University Press).

Kathleen V. Wilkes

ΓΝΩΘΙ ΣΕΑΥΤΟΝ
(KNOW THYSELF)

The burden of this chapter is that although the idea of 'the self' which Galen Strawson describes in his target chapter is initially very attractive, it eventually doesn't work. There is a lot of competition for a 'pole position' notion — 'human', 'person', 'psuche', 'soul', even 'sake' — and the idea of 'self' does not seem to deserve the prize. What Strawson wants to do with the notion of a 'self' can be done equally well, and more economically, by the first-person pronoun. Perhaps the greatest area of disagreement with Strawson's chapter is with his idea that 'the self' needs to have little or nothing to do with time-related plans and emotions: guilt and remorse; pride; hope and expectation; career choices . . . even such apparently mundane things as pension-plans — in fact, any long-term forward- or backward-looking psychological phenomena. The question of realism (about 'the self') is pressed.

Introduction

'Know thyself', or 'know thy *self*'? In his subtle and intriguing chapter, Galen Strawson[1] has a variety of things to say about 'the self', or 'the sense of the self', well-supported by examples and analogies. I have some difficulty in reconciling the several strands of the chapter; but he begins, at least, in a way that is clear and beguilingly acceptable: with an appeal to common sense and everyday usage. We all know what we want of the notion of 'a self', or what we are trying to do with it; in English at least it has a role to play; as Strawson says, it 'means something to most people' (p. 1). The *sense* of the self, too, can be an 'ordinary, human' sort of phenomenon, a feeling for a mental thing that 'is what one really or most essentially is' (p. 3).

There are questions to do with 'I', 'myself', 'my sense of myself'; changes in me (or 'Me*'),[2] identified by Strawson, which can puzzle and bewilder. I want in this

---

[1] Unless otherwise stated, all references to 'Strawson' in the current chapter are to Galen Strawson's opening chapter in this volume (pp. 1–24).

[2] Strawson describes this 'Me*' as

> the most central or fundamental way in which I think of myself, which is as a mental self or someone. Using 'Me*' to express this fundamental way in which I think of myself — or to denote me thinking of myself in this way, looking out on things from this perspective — , I can accurately express my experience by saying that I do not think of Me* as being something in the future. (p. 16.)

As will become clearer later, I am not quite happy with this notion.

chapter to work towards a different sort of view of, way of thinking about, these questions; but will develop the picture in large part by setting out and explaining some of my difficulties with some of Strawson's arguments.[3]

A word of warning, though. Over the years, increasingly, I have been coming to think that the terms that might be described as the 'keywords' of Strawson's chapter cannot sustain the weight demanded of them. I mean, especially, 'self', 'mind', and 'consciousness'.[4] It seems to me that whatever is said by these terms can be said as well or better without them; so arguing in these terms has become somewhat analogous, for me, to using a foreign language. However, I cannot use this as an excuse, since Strawson says that 'all languages have words which lend themselves naturally to playing the role that "the self" plays in English' (p. 1). (I find myself doubting that this is true of, say, Aristotle; but that would have to be an argument for another paper.) In any case, I shall try as much as possible to stick with the terminology of selves, consciousness, etc.

One more preliminary. Unless I have badly misunderstood, it seems that the 'sense of the self' stands to 'the self' as scanner to scanned; the self is the object sensed. Thus, the list of elements (1)–(8) in Strawson's section III[5] describe the *self*, not the sense of it. The sense of the self is the sense *of* something, a something with some or all of the features given in (1)–(8). This is a point worth making, because from time to time Strawson writes as if some or all of the eight features are features of the *sense* of the mental self, rather than of (just) the self; for example, when talking about our judgements, he puts a question this way: 'whether anything less than (1)–(8) can count as a genuine SMS [sense of the mental self]' (p. 5). I think he cannot mean this. Put another way, there could be a self with (some or all of (1)–(8)) without any SMS. The notion of the 'Me*', introduced in his section VIII, and introduced in this chapter above, also seems sometimes to wander between the self, and the sense of it; I shall need to return to the 'Me*'.

I shall attempt to spell out what I would expect from a notion of 'the self' that is worth wanting, something which we may have a sense of, 'conceive', and 'experience; and where 'consciousness' , and 'self-consciousness' play their parts. *En route* my unhappiness with these terms (as with 'sensation' and 'experience') will show itself, as will some of my disagreements with Strawson's overall thesis.

I: *My* 'Self'

I want to insist that a self worth wanting is a self that must meet at least part of element (4) in Strawson's list (see my own footnote 5 on this page; the relevant bit is that 'the mental self is . . . a *single* thing . . . [when] *diachronically* considered'). In other words, I shall be disagreeing almost *in toto* with his arguments in section VIII, 'The

---

[3] By no means all of them. With his section V in particular ('Materialism') I am in almost complete agreement.

[4] I admit that these concepts have been bothering me for some time. I have tried to describe my unhappiness with 'mind' and 'consciousness' in Wilkes (1988).

[5] It might be worth rehearsing these briefly: according to Strawson, 'the mental self is ordinarily conceived or experienced as (1) a *thing*, in some robust sense (2) a *mental* thing, in some sense (3,4) a *single* thing that is both *synchronically* considered and *diachronically* considered (5) *ontically distinct* from all other things (6) a *subject of experience*, a conscious feeler and thinker (7) an *agent* '(8) a thing that has a certain character or *personality* (p. 3; italics in original).

Self in Time'. (I shall be returning to the general point about 'singleness', whether considered synchronically or diachronically, later.)

Remember that we are starting from a notion of the self that 'means something to most people'; it is meant to be an everyday notion. There are many reasons for requiring duration over time for one's self (which Strawson acknowledges), but one of them must be simple and incontrovertible: however brief the existence of the self here, now (and even if it is for but 3 seconds: see Strawson' footnote 14, p. 10, where — *inter alia* — he cites Moroslav Holub arguing that our ego might perhaps last three seconds) my conscious mind might be filled with intense remorse, contrition, grief. Now: remorse and contrition are among the (self-referring; experiential) mental phenomena that make no sense apart from the idea that I (or the 'Me*') had on some occasion in the past behaved badly or dishonourably; mourning is a form of sorrow that, like remorse and contrition, reaches into the present from the past. (Note that emotions such as pride, or shame, could not be used to make this point securely; it is possible to experience these emotions vicariously, on behalf of another, and hence presumably could do so for a former self which I no longer identify with any 'Me*'. They may not, that is, presuppose self-consciousness.)

Just as for the past, so also for the future. Consider a feeling/experience of bated-breath anticipation, or a terror of what might happen to me within the next few hours. These two seem to me to be indisputably *current* phenomena; but are impossible to understand unless we acknowledge that they are forward-looking. There are indeed experiences of being *just* a 'bare locus of consciousness'; but fortunately (because such experiences can be terrifying or disorientating) not often with most people, and no doubt with some people perhaps never.

Strawson wants the fleeting, 'episodic', life to be 'no less intense or full, emotional or moral' than the lives of the 'narrative personalities' (footnote 22, p. 17).[6] However, this cannot be; consider what it would mean. Morality is a matter of planning future actions, calculating consequences, experiencing remorse and contrition, accepting responsibility, accepting praise and blame; such mental phenomena are both forward- and backward-looking. Essentially. We require also the capacity to have thoughts *about* our own mental states; and about the needs, desires, thoughts of others. The inability to do or to experience such things would make one a-moral, a 'wanton' (see Frankfurt, 1971). Some people with extreme autism are perhaps a bit like that. Even more tragically, such an inability would mark one off as someone with a condition such as Alzheimer's disease. Similarly, emotions such as love or hate, envy or resentment, would not deserve the name — except in some occasional rare cases — if they lasted for but three seconds, and were thereafter claimed, not by any Me*, but by some former self. Our life would be 'a sort of Humean froth, a meaningless fluttering on the surface' (Sacks, 1970, p. 37). We make contracts, promise this or that. In sum, the 'Episodic' life could not be richly moral and emotional; we must have a life, or self, with duration. We are, and must consider ourselves as, relatively stable intentional systems. Essentially. To support this, Stevenson (1886) could never have given

---

[6] To remind the reader, Strawson describes people who 'live deeply in narrative mode: they experience their lives in terms of something that has shape and story, narrative trajectory. Some of them are self-narrators in a stronger sense: they regularly rehearse and revise their interpretations of their lives.' These are contrasted with those who live an 'episodic' life — 'some live intensely in the present, some are simply aimless' (p. 15).

us a convincing story if Jekyll's and Hyde's selves had had very fleeting and transient existences: we simply would not *call* such entities 'selves'.

None of this prevents me from agreeing with Strawson that people fall on a spectrum between those who 'live deeply in narrative mode', who 'experience their lives in terms of something that has shape and story', at one extreme; and, at the other, those who are 'simply aimless', living life in a 'picaresque or episodic fashion' (p. 15). Or, as William James described them, there are those 'whose existence is little more than a series of zig-zags' (1890, p. 145). Manic depressives, for example, 'zig-zag' a lot. Most of us, I suppose, are somewhere in the middle. Indeed, given that we have the statute of limitations for *most* (not all) crimes, and given that a declaration of bankruptcy 'clears the board' for the debtor, there is no doubt but that we treat responsibility on a sliding scale, and regard the sinner as being less culpable, at least for some of his past actions, as time goes by. Nevertheless, the point remains that the more short-lived the 'Me*'s — the more I treat past selves as *others* — the less moral and emotional can the 'episodic' person be. Indeed, *pace* Strawson, the less *complete* can he be. (Strawson, the reader may recall, said, 'The sense of the single mental self may be vivid and complete, at any given time, even if it has to do only with the present, brief, hiatus-free stretch of consciousness, at any given time' [p. 14].) Many would prefer a thought expressed by many, but here, for example, concisely put by Korsgaard (1989, p.114): 'When the person is viewed as an agent, no clear content can be given to the idea of a merely present self'.

For there is one important fact, which Strawson acknowledges in section IX. The most common position with respect to the self is that it *is* something with long-term continuity. This is surely due in large part to the social relations in which we engage: loving, hating, promising, trusting and being trusted; and to our admiration for values such as integrity or constancy. Such social relations, in a manner of speaking, 'go out', and 'come in': 'go out', in the sense that we see ourselves as agents, free to act and plan, responsible for the consequences of what we do; and 'come in', inasmuch as others have 'reactive attitudes' to us (P.F. Strawson, 1962/1974); attitudes of resentment, gratitude, respect, devotion, or — perhaps most commonly — simply, vaguely, liking or disliking. They do, and I have to, regard me (or 'Me*') as a self with continuity over time, if I am to be in the moral domain at all. What (P.F.) Strawson (*ibid.*) calls 'moral solipsism' would be the only way to describe the state of a fugitive, transient 'Me*'; which does not make for a self worth wanting. Nobody would want Sacks' (1970) 'Humean froth', later characterized by him as 'de-pithed, de-soiled and scooped-out'. We cannot, and should not, ignore the role of what others say about me; or about 'Me*'.

All this helps to explain why virtually all psychotherapists,[7] when confronted with a patient suffering from some kind of disorder of identity, spell out their aims as trying to (re-)discover an 'authentic', 'true', 'real', or 'unified' self, and to integrate the patient, even in the most bizarre cases of synchronous or diachronic dissociation; seeing it as their goal to reintroduce integrity and self-determination. Rightly or wrongly? Rightly, given that whether we like it or not we are complex *social* animals, and needs must cope with the short-term and long-term obligations and responsibilities that that entails. Charles Taylor expressed this attitude at its most extreme: '. . . as

---

[7] Not all of them. See, among others, Coons (1984); Chase (1987, p. 411f.); and Schemen (1993, p. 103).

a being who grows and becomes I can only know myself through the history of my maturations and regressions, overcomings and defeats' (1989, p. 50). We have obligations; we are culpable; we need to keep our promises; we have rights.

It is unclear (and unclear in more writers than Strawson; unclear whenever people take seriously successive or synchronous selves) how they should be counted, individuated, distinguished. And, when counting, do we *discover*, or *decide*?[8] The fact that 'trains of thought are constantly broken by detours — byblows — fissures — white noise' (p. 17); or that 'truly hiatus-free periods of thought or experience are invariably brief in human beings' (p. 9); neither of these as yet entails or even suggests that each break or hiatus heralds a new self. Put another way, single selves can be the sorts of things that can be in a state of 'pandemonium' (see Strawson's footnote 24, p. 17); why not? We are, most of us, beings of exactly this kind: beings in whose heads thoughts, memories, emotions come and go, 'pass, re-pass, glide away, and mingle in an infinite variety of postures and situations' (Hume, 1739, I, iv, vi). The brute fact of saccadic eye-jumps, to which Strawson (to my mind ill-advisedly) appeals on p. 9, is or may be a useful tool for some theoretical purposes, to distinguish something from something (but usually only saccadic eye-fixations!) for some scientists; (Strawson, footnote 14, p. 10, cites Holub, 1990; Ruhnau, 1995; Pöppel, 1978). Nevertheless, it would be entirely *arbitrary* to call the stages before and after a saccadic jump a *self*. Moreover, even if it were to be defensible to choose some clear physiological change to distinguish one kind of state from another, why stick to the eyes? Why not go deeper into the brain, to successive patterns of neural-net activation? That would be no *less* unmotivated. Indeed, many people nowadays swear by it. The claim that there is radical disjunction in a (highly philosophical-theoretical) notion of a 'self' can only be supported very weakly, at best, by empirical conjectures in experimental psychology or 'current work on the non-mental neural correlates of consciousness' (p. 19). More to the point, though: psychologists, neuropsychologists, and neurophysiologists rather *rarely* talk about 'the self'.

A self worth wanting — a 'complete', 'emotional', 'moral' sort of thing, to which adjectives such as 'true', or 'authentic' tend to be attached — is something with a character; where emotions, decisions, actions, and reactions spring from a reasonably coherent cluster of beliefs and values. A complex sort of thing; an 'oddly bright sundriness' (Nietzsche, 1966, pp. 287 f.). Different sorts of things have different identity conditions, and criteria for continuity (this is not a new point!). An antique Greek vase; the Niagara Falls; a shaft of sunlight; a government policy . . . we would need *arguments*, and strong arguments at that, to propound and defend any single criterion, or set of criteria, for counting or for individuating selves. I shall need next to consider 'consciousness', 'non-consciousness', and 'self-consciousness' to support this point. For the moment, though, the fact that I *can*, and sometimes do, see myself just as a 'bare locus of consciousness . . . a mere (cognitive) point of view' (p. 13), does not establish that *this* is the important thing about being me, or a Me*. A bare locus of consciousness, minus the dualism, is Descartes' stripped-down *res cogitans*, no more.

---

[8]   For these questions see Hacking (1995), especially chapters 11 and 12.

II: Consciousness and Its Cognates

Consciousness (and here, just and only for the purposes of this argument, I shall consider only those kinds of consciousness that fall under the heading of 'reportable thinking')[9] jumps all over the place, as Strawson's quotations (footnote 25, p. 18) from Richardson (1979) and Joyce (1986) show beautifully. Whether or not this militates against 'seamlessness' (p. 18) though, is *highly* unclear. In any case, we cannot possibly talk about a smooth flow of consciousness unless we know where the seams are; how we can identify 'periods of true experiential continuity' (*ibid.*). Whatever our decision, it will be contestable; maybe fuelled by a bundle of theoretical intuitions. Consider: many psychoanalysts have for a long time used, and still do sometimes use, the method of free association to inform them about the nature of the patient's mind, which suggests that they are hypothesizing some intricate stitching between *prima facie* unrelated thoughts. Hume, after all, had his three principles of association to stand-in for the stitches; and subsequent associationist philosopher-psychologists (e.g. both Mills; Hamilton; Brown; Hartley; etc.) found from one to twelve 'principles of association' between mental elements. Alternatively, the decision may be fuelled by introspective intuition, as it seems to be with Strawson; his 'fundamental experience is one of *repeated returns into consciousness from a state of complete, if momentary, unconsciousness*' (*ibid.*, italics in original). I cannot make sense of this until I get clearer about the 'unconsciousness' bit. There seems to me to be a great deal that isn't sharply 'conscious' or 'unconscious'.

For the mental is not, *pace* Strawson's footnote 9,[10] simply either 'the experiential', or 'beliefs, likes and dislikes, and so on'. By the sound of it (and perhaps I am over-interpreting) it looks as if his 'mental' is either experiential, or potentially conscious; if asked 'do you believe that *p*, do you like *x*?' the subject could answer 'yes' or 'no' — but before he was asked, his belief or desire was 'mental', and only *potentially* 'experiential'. Yet there is *far* more to the mental than this tip of the iceberg. We do not need Freud to tell us that there is much in the mind of which we are not conscious; which we don't know about; which we can get to know about, if at all, only with difficulty; and which is deeper than 'beliefs, likes and dislikes'.

There is a mass of evidence for this. Shakespeare is, as usual, the best:

> . . . my affection hath an unknown bottom, like the bay of Portugal.
>
> (*As You Like It*, IV, i, 212.)

> My mind is troubled, like a fountain stirr'd;
> And I myself see not the bottom of it. (*Troilus and Cressida*, III, iii, 311.)

> *Prince.* I never thought to hear you speak again.
> *King.* Thy wish was father, Harry, to that thought. (*King Henry IV, Part II*, IV, v. 92.)

> In sooth, I know not why I am so sad:
> It wearies me; you say it wearies you;
> But how I caught it, found it, or came by it,

---

[9] I do not believe that conscious phenomena should be thus restricted, but will restrict them for the sake of the debate. (I think there are indeed conscious phenomena which are *not* reportable; those of non-human animals, for example.)

[10] This footnote says: '. . . because although all experiential phenomena are mental phenomena, not all mental phenomena are experiential phenomena: according to ordinary usage, beliefs, likes and dislikes and so on are mental phenomena, though they have no experiential character'(p. 6).

What stuff 'tis made of, whereof it is born,
I am to learn;
And such a want-wit sadness makes of me,
That I have much ado to know myself. (*Merchant of Venice*, I, i, 1.)

Thousands and thousands of examples could be thrown in here. Let me offer just one more, from Wordsworth:

I held unconscious intercourse with beauty.
Caverns there were in my mind which sun could
Never penetrate. (*Prelude*.)

Whyte (1962) lists examples starting from 50 BC; and claims that even earlier examples could be found in the Indian *Upanishads* and the literature of ancient Egypt and Greece. He quote Margetts (1953, p. 115): 'Almost since the dawn of civilization man has had an inkling of understanding that mind activity outside of our waking consciousness does exist'.

I find this strongly and intuitively self-evident, compelling, obvious. To stoop to the mundane from the sublime, the mere *fact* of self-deception puts the fact of not-conscious parts of the mind beyond doubt. For various — perhaps theoretical — purposes, we can if we choose divide up the not-conscious mind, and label parts of it with quasi-technical terms such as 'preconscious', 'subliminal', 'subconscious', 'unconscious'; or we could swallow the Freudian 'System Ucs'; or we could rest content with, simply, 'not- (or non-) conscious'. Some mental phenomena are indeed best known through introspection (e.g. pain); others are publicly observable (e.g. generosity), and might be self-ascribed *either* by using the same evidence that is available to others, *or* introspected; with other ascriptions, another may have far better grounds for ascribing them than does the subject himself (e.g. racism, anti-Semitism, any other kind of prejudice or self-deception). Furthermore: consciousness, whatever else it may be, is not a simple or an all-or-nothing phenomenon. We can be more or less conscious, intensely conscious, barely conscious; activities can be 'on automatic control', as we tend to think it to be with the (hackneyed example of the) skilled driver, negotiating bends and gear-changes while arguing heatedly with his passengers. A different sort of example, a trivial one: we can be said to hold beliefs that we never have or never will entertain consciously. Although, evidently, I cannot give an example without instant self-refutation, I am thinking of beliefs *such as* 'Rome is not in Sri Lanka', 'elephants are larger than dachshunds'.

Now unless (as I said before) I have misunderstood badly, it seems to me that the *sense* of the self is essentially — indeed, almost by definition — a matter of self-consciousness, while the self itself primarily requires consciousness. This, I think, matters. I find, paradoxical as it may seem, the concept of self-consciousness to be much easier to understand than simple (sic!) consciousness. Self-consciousness is a matter of my thoughts having as their content either me *qua* subject or agent; or thoughts, desires, fears, expectations (etc.) of mine. Second-order thoughts. The capacity for second-order thoughts generally (whether they be self-conscious ones, or thoughts about the thoughts of another) seem to be necessary, although far from sufficient, for responsibility, freedom of action; necessary, again, for 'what matters' in 'what is worth wanting', if we are to talk about selves (as I have argued above);[11] nec-

---

[11] Useful here is an influential article by Frankfurt (1971).

essary, finally, in order to make sense of the idea of 'true', or 'authentic', selves. Now, such thoughts as these (second-order thoughts) are indeed interrupted — indeed, they may be very infrequent. I can spend hours engrossed in a book, or a film, or an argument; conscious, but with scarcely any thoughts that are self-conscious in the sense sketched above; but the capacity to think second-order thoughts I must have. By contrast, when we turn to the *sense* of the self . . . this must, clearly, be a matter essentially of *self*-consciousness, because it is in that mode that I am said to be having an *experience* of the (conscious) self: *it* is the object before me. Selfconsciousness is, indeed, one of the things that can *interrupt* a stream of consciousness. ('I'm thinking this!' — a clear distraction.)

So to have a *sense* of the self is and must be an exercise of self-consciousness; which can, interestingly, disrupt the continuity of the self.

Where 'the self' is at issue, rather than the (meta) 'sense of the self', then we need no more than the conscious-experiential (plus, as noted above, the *capacity* for self-consciousness). For only so would it be at all relevant for Strawson to bring into play the arguments he deploys against James' 'stream of consciousness' in his section IX. Only so would it be at all plausible to say that a 'fundamental experience of consciousness is one of repeated returns into consciousness from a state of complete, if momentary, unconsciousness', a matter of 'banging out of nothingness'; or, not quite equivalently, 'a gappy series of eruptions of consciousness from a substrate of apparent non-consciousness' (p. 21). The alternatives cannot be self-consciousness and unconsciousness. It must be consciousness *versus* unconsciousness; or, as I would prefer to put it (and must, since I have undertaken *pro tem.* to use the terminology of consciousness), *versus* not-consciousness.

On the other hand, though, Strawson is not clear on this point; and indeed admits some ambivalence. Consider his footnote 31 (p. 21), in which he refers to his opening footnote from Nozick: 'the self which is reflexively referred to is synthesized in that very act of self-reference' (Nozick, 1981). That, insofar as I understand it,[12] would be *self*-consciousness, and Strawson goes on to say in the same footnote that 'many will think that the period of consciousness must be one of explicit selfconsciousness'. This would be bizarre, and Strawson should surely reject it; he would not need any *arguments* for hiatuses, gaps, discontinuities, if explicit self-consciousness were at issue: nobody, surely, would dispute that. Explicit self-consciousness is surely the exception rather than the rule with most of the experiences of most lives. Even if this point is granted, though, there are further puzzles. His introduction of the 'Me*' (p. 16, and see my footnote 2) is 'to express this fundamental way in which I think of myself — or to denote me thinking of myself in this way'. I cannot understand this unless it is self-reflective, i.e., self-conscious, thinking. But then the 'Me*' is not the self; it is what thinks of the self. Yet it should be the self! Because it is that, surely, not the *sense* of it, which he says he will not be in the future. He seems to want this 'Me*' to be both a self, and a sense of the self.

There are hiatuses, breaks, discontinuities, disruptions in the sequence (let us, neutrally, call it 'sequence' — Strawson argues against the term 'stream') of experience, of consciousness. There are often long gaps between episodes of *self*-conscious occasions of thought. Since it is, to put it mildly, *difficult* to consider one's own flow of

---

[12] I am not quite sure that I do.

consciousness, or to give a running report, Molly Bloom style, without 'going meta' into *self*-consciousness, it is easy to confuse the two. However, if the 'Me*' is *self*-conscious, then disruptions and disorderliness in the sequence of (merely) conscious thoughts, or saccadic eye-jumps, are just irrelevant and unnecessary.

We can indulge in 'me-here-now' thoughts, self-conscious thoughts, thoughts stripped down to a 'bare locus of consciousness'. But I chose the verb 'indulge' with some reason. Most of life isn't like that. The day-to-day boring routines are finding means to ends (which airport bus should I catch, if I'm to get the plane? What can I buy X, for a Christmas present? Should I send this chapter to the editor by fax, by regular mail, by express mail? The ceiling in my bathroom is leaking: what to do?). It seems to me that consciousness (conscious thoughts), and not-fully conscious, and not-conscious thoughts, traits, dispositions, memories, styles, etc., constitute a self, or any self worth wanting. It is impossible to accept this point, though, if the 'conscious/unconscious' dichotomy is taken to be exclusive and exhaustive.

III: Synchronous Selves

Strawson begins with phenomenology, and defends the strategy in his section II. So it would not be unfair to use phenomenology to quibble with his arguments that the self must be *single* when synchronically considered. (See his sections III and VI, too; and my footnote 5.)

There are consistent reports, from those suffering from the bunch of disorders that generally go by the name of 'dissociative-identity' disorders, of *synchronous* multiplicity. Medieval talk of 'possession' would probably pick out conditions that would be labelled as 'dissociative' today; so does multiple personality. Literature has fun with the idea — consider only Stevenson: 'I hazard the guess', he writes at the end of *Dr. Jekyll and Mr. Hyde*, that man 'will ultimately be known for a mere polity of multifarious, incongruous, and independent denizens' (Stevenson, 1886, p. 49). Granted, Jekyll and Hyde swapped in sequence; but Stevenson's remark suggests that he might have had more in mind than *successively* existing 'denizens'. However that may be, though, we need to examine some of the reported experiences of 'co-presence', or 'co-consciousness'.

Strawson could easily accommodate multiple personality, supposing that he believed that there were such a condition,[13] if the selves succeeded each other; that is, if there were only one 'aware' self, one 'locus of consciousness', at any given moment. Yet there is a substantial degree of consistency in the reports about different patients, treated by different doctors, to the effect that one (or more) of their 'selves' is (or are) aware of the experiences of other selves (or 'selves').

Braude (1991), when talking about 'coconsciousness', distinguishes between the states of being 'intraconscious', and of being 'cosensory'. 'Cosensoriness' is when two selves are simultaneously aware of the same thing, at the same time; 'intraconsciousness' is when one self is, or claims to be, not only cosensory but also aware of another self's thoughts and feelings (and dreams) although not *as* his or her own. However, with multiple personalities, we must gloss 'cosensory' a bit. Sometimes, or

---

[13] Which he need not do. The existence (or not) of any condition such as multiple personality — which it is now more politically-correct to call 'dissociative-identity disorder' — is much challenged. I would refer the reader to the Hacking (1995) book, mentioned in the bibliography.

so we are told, one of the alternate personalities is aware of *what another individual self is seeing and that the other is seeing it too*. They both 'see', in a way; but one of them is said to be — or is described as — 'seeing' *by* being aware of the other's seeing. The best example, and also one of the earliest, is the personality called 'Sally' in Morton Prince's extraordinary book, *The Dissociation of a Personality* (1905). Sally was, or claimed to be, intraconscious with the BI personality; to be cosensory with BIV; and to be intraconscious with BII, the personality whom Prince thought to be 'the real' Miss Beauchamp, and whom he eventually established in charge of the physical reality of Miss Beauchamp.

I use this example at such length, because none of the trio: BI, BIV, and the final BII, had any direct knowledge of Sally. The point is that when Sally was, so to speak, 'latent' , she knew what BI was doing and thinking (and dreaming); and what BIV was doing. But she did not regard their thoughts and actions as *her* thoughts and actions; if we are to believe Prince, she was an amused — and often malicious — observer.

Well: apart from the florid (but fascinating) cases — or alleged cases — of multiple personality, there is also abundant testimony, from patients with some other form of dissociative disorder, of experiences that they disown. They have a strong sense that various feelings and impulses belong to someone else, but are forced upon the patient; she (it is usually, but by no means always, 'she') describes herself as being used, the passive screen upon which another's thoughts are projected, a passive tool for someone else's impulses. These, and many more instances of apparently non-singular selves (which, for reasons too complicated to explain in the space available here, should *not* be thought of as schizophrenia), selves that are somehow simultaneously present, can be found in Davidson and Neale (1986). I am not clear how Strawson would cope with these.

IV: Thing-hood: Realism

Realism in psychology, whether it be examined with respect to everyday, common-sense psychology[14] or to the scientific psychology conducted in laboratories and white coats, is a deeply vexed and vexing business. A sudden agonising pain, and a memory from childhood that is currently not being accessed, are very different 'things'. (The pain has relatively clear temporal parameters, for a start.) All the same, there is nothing too disturbing here: we find analogous sorts of questions that could be raised in physics: magnetic fields are very different sorts of 'things' from lumps of gold, or quarks. Strawson's materialism (see his section V; with which, as I have said, I *almost* unreservedly agree) gives every mental or experiential phenomenon a non-mental, non-experiential being. That form of being, I assume, we can be realists about. 'Me*' thoughts would — really! — have a non-mental existence. Presumably as hyper-complex neural events.[15] I suppose that one can call events 'things'; any-

---

[14] Most people call this 'folk psychology'. This is a mistake. Calling our incredibly sophisticated apparatus of common-sense psychology 'folk psychology' makes it sound too simple and naive, too 'folksy'. It is in fact one of the richest and densest parts of our conceptual apparatus. And, besides, Wilhelm Wundt got the label first, with his *Volkerpsychologie*.

[15] As will probably be obvious, I am thinking here about connectionism, or 'parallel distributive processing' ('PDP').

thing can be a 'thing', after all. Moreover, we could be realists about dispositional states too, and about not-conscious mental states; they might have not-mental existence inasmuch as they might be, for example, 'things' that exist as some readiness-potential of neural nets. One could perhaps say, in a token–token way,[16] that *since* they have a non-experiential or non-mental character too, mental or experiential phenomena exist — being as real as are the sets of neural happenings, neurotransmitter flows, or potentials-for-activation. Further, if we had a secure neurophysiological principle of individuation for the non-mental happenings that (also) have a mental or experiential character, we might (again token–token) have an hypothesis to secure Strawson's 'Pearl' idea (p. 20): mental selves existing, one after another, like beads on a string. Or, if we are unconvinced by the arguments for the temporal brevity of *selves*, at least distinct *thoughts* so succeeding each other. (The 'Pearl' view, of course, can work only for clockable mental phenomena. Otherwise it is totally implausible.)[17] Dispositional mental states won't come along one by one; in fact they do not 'come along' at all. But I find it hard to believe that they don't make me, me. (Even if not 'Me*'.)

This seems to me to be a 'straightforward and metaphysically robust' sense in which it might indeed be legitimate to talk of mental or experiential phenomena as being real; reality tends not to come in degrees. But real in their own several ways ('a real X'; 'a real Y'); atomic lattices, magnetic fields, 'medium-sized samples of dry goods', beliefs, prejudices, fences, positrons. I think that Strawson's comparisons with chairs, cats, rabbits, jackhammers, and cows tend to mislead; why not introduce dispositions, thoughts, hallucinations, photons, light waves, shafts of sunlight, shadows, sunsets: these are surely all *real*, but not at all for the same reasons, and not in the same way. (Or ways.)

Moreover, since these non-mental, non-experiential 'things', be they events, states, or whatever, will have (by hypothesis) a mental and/or experiential character, they can — and probably most conveniently will — be picked out by the description under which they are thoughts. Consider: it is often far easier to pick something out by the expression 'that program' rather than by the hugely-complex description of the machine code and the strings of 0s and 1s that in fact drive the computer. At any given time a complex sequence of strings of 0s and 1s is 'enmeshed', and 'revealed by' the currently-running state of the program. Without the program, the hardware description would indeed be like *Othello* without Desdemona. (I think that this is a better analogy than that of X's little finger to X's body — see Strawson, p. 22 — one can always amputate fingers.)

I find it easier to accept most of section XI ('the factual question') in terms of the *reality* of experiential phenomena rather than of their thing-hood. Inevitably 'thing'

---

[16] Example of token–token (said at a party): 'The man drinking the martini is my brother'. I am not committing myself to the idea that every martini-drinker is a brother of mine; nor that all my brothers drink martinis. Contrast with type–type; 'that dolphin is a mammal' (explaining something to a child who thought that dolphins were fish, and was watching one).

[17] Even in cases of extreme amnesia or fugue states, the victims know a language, how to use the currency, how to drive (or, in one of the earliest reported examples, how to harness a horse and cart). The more general point, though, is that even if 'Me*' thoughts come along irregularly, and even if I were suffering from extreme amnesia; even then, my dislike of broccoli, my preference for Bach over Oasis, my small ability at speaking Croatian, or solving the Rubik cube, or playing chess, or knowing that Rome was not in Sri Lanka — such things would remain.

makes one think of spatiotemporally bounded *objects*, made of *stuff*. Granted that contemporary physics is retreating from a 'substance/properties' ontology towards one of fields of energy and pure processes, this is still not the way that the layman understands 'thing'. A phenomenon of any kind is a 'thing' to the layman, roughly to the extent that it comes close enough to a prototype; where the prototype is probably like Austin's 'medium-sized samples of dry goods'. We should not forget that with talk of 'selves' we are engaging with the vernacular, not with the vocabulary or the theoretical terminology of subatomic physics.

V: And Yet . . .

I still do not want to be a realist about *selves*, although I am happy to agree that some thoughts (occasions of thinking) are real. Occurrent conscious (and self-conscious) thoughts have temporal location. But *selves*? There is indeed utility in talk about selves; but it has utility if (and only if) selves are given the flexibility that would come if we ascribed to them duration (even if not lifetime-long); the warp and weft of character traits, foibles, quirks, memories, ambitions — in short, a sort of three-dimensionality. We create and construct our 'selves'. Consciousness will be intrinsic to any notion of a self; but so will the rest of the iceberg of not-conscious mentality; 'conscious or not?' is often (and I would say usually) not the most interesting question to ask about 'what matters' to my being me. Or, perhaps better: the issue that such a question is meant to address is more often than not better posed and examined in terms of thinking, feeling, wanting, anticipating, grieving, and so on (and on). However that may be, though — and I do not expect many to share my deep unease about the serviceability of the term 'conscious' and its cognates — so long as we treat selves as 'abstracta',[18] to talk in terms of them might prove useful; especially when we have puzzling cases of mental dissociation or breakdown, extreme manic depression, and their ilk. No: more than 'might prove useful'; we know that talk in such terms *is* useful. We need, and badly need, terminology with which to describe (say) manic depressives. All the same, the fact that a mode of expression may be useful does not mean that it has to be used to say something true; nor that all the terms deployed in it must really refer. Consider: 'I believe it with all my heart', 'it's weighing on my mind', 'I am in two minds', 'my heart went out to her', 'I had this gut feeling'. But note that this is not only true about mental terms: even the Astronomer Royal might say impatiently to his wife that she should get up, because the sun had risen long ago.

Conclusion

Although I agree with Strawson that the fact that other civilizations and cultures do, or do not, share terms with our 1990s' western culture is in no way decisive . . . still, it ought to give us pause. 'Bigger' terms than 'self' — in particular, perhaps, 'person', 'mind', 'belief', and 'consciousness' — are virtually impossible to translate into some other languages.[19] So are 'smaller' terms, such as 'sake'. My overall thought is

[18] This is a term picked up by Dennett (1981) from Reichenbach (1938). Reichenbach thought of *abstracta* as calculation-bound entities, logical constructs. Dennett suggests as examples centres of gravity, and the Equator — and (possibly) beliefs, desires.

[19] Take, for example, Chinese — the oldest civilization of all. 'Consciousness' was not anything that featured in their literature until it became necessary to translate Marx. Then there was a problem about

that 'self' is a rather *small* term, particularly if it can last for just three seconds; and that being a *person*, particularly if seen in the Aristotelian way as a human animal with all sorts of diverse capacities (including capacities to change) is substantially *more* important. What emerges very clearly, though, is that a person can change dramatically over time. But we already know that: the water over the Niagara Falls changes dramatically over time too.

Thus I think that Strawson is, to some extent, giving to 'airy nothings' a 'local habitation and a name'.

References

(*Asterisked items are those also cited by Strawson in his opening keynote chapter)

Braude, S.E. (1981), *First Person Plural: Multiple personality and the philosophy of mind* (London: Routledge).

Chase, T. (1987), *When Rabbit Howls* (New York: E.P. Dutton).

Coons, P. (1984), 'The differential diagnosis of multiple personality: a comprehensive review', *Psychiatric Clinics of North America*, **7**, pp. 51–67.

Davidson, G. and Neale, J. (1986), *Abnormal Psychology: An experimental clinical approach*, 4th edition (New York: John Wiley & Sons).

Dennett, D. (1981), 'Three kinds of intentional psychology', in *Reduction, Time and Reality*, ed. R. Healy (Cambridge, Cambridge University Press). Reprinted in Dennett [1987], *The Intentional Stance* (Cambridge, MA: MIT/Bradford).

Frankfurt, H. (1971), Freedom of the will and the concept of a person', *Journal of Philosophy*, **68**, pp. 5–20.

Hacking, I. (1995), *Rewriting the Soul: Multiple personality and the sciences of memory* (Princeton: Princeton University Press).

*Holub, M. (1990), *The Dimension of the Present Moment* (London: Faber).

Hume, D. (1739/1978), *A Treatise on Human Nature*, 1978 edn., ed. L.A. Selby-Bigge (Oxford: Oxford University Press).

*James, W. (1890), The Principles of Psychology (New York: H. Holt and Co.). Edition cited by Strawson is [1950] (New York: Dover).

*Joyce, J. (1986), *Ulysses* (Harmondsworth: Penguin).

Korsgaard, C. (1989), 'Personal identity and the unity of agency: a Kantian response to Parfit', *Philosophy and Public Affairs*, **18**, pp. 101–32.

Margetts, E.L. (1953), 'Concept of the unconscious in the history of medical psychology', *Psychiatric Quarterly*, **27**, p. 115.

Nietzsche, F. (1966 edn.), *Werke in drei Banden*, ed. K. Schlechta (Munich: Hanser).

*Nozick, R. (1981), *Philosophical Explanations* (Oxford: Clarendon Press).

*Pöppel, E. (1978), 'Time perception', in *Handbook of Sensory Physiology*, vol. VIII, ed. R. Held, H.W. Leibovitz and H.L. Teuber (New York: Springer).

Prince, M. (1905), *The Dissociation of a Personality* (London: Longmans, Green). Reprinted [1968] (New York: Johnson Reprint Company).

Reichenbach, H. (1928), *Experience and Prediction* (Chicago: University of Chicago Press).

*Richardson, D. (1979), *Pointed Roofs, Pilgrimage*, vol. I (London: Virago Press).

*Ruhnau, E. (1995), 'Time gestalt and the observer', in *Conscious Experience*, ed. T. Metzinger (Paderborn: Schöningh / Exeter: Imprint Academic).

Sacks, O. (1970), *The Man Who Mistook His Wife For a Hat and Other Clinical Tales* (New York: Summit Books).

Schemen, N. (1993), *Engenderings: Constructions of knowledge, authority and privilege* (London: Routledge).

how to translate 'the consciousness of the proletariat'. The Chinese solved this by putting 'yi' (which means 'know') together with 'shi' (which means 'know'): Yishi. This is, certainly, an uninformed remark — I know very few words of Chinese — but I have been interrogating Chinese friends for a long time about this.

Stevenson, R.L. (1886), *Dr Jekyll and Mr Hyde and Other Stories* (London).

Strawson, G. (1997), '"The self"', *Journal of Consciousness Studies*, **4** (5–6), pp. 405–28. Reprinted in this volume, pp. 1–24.

Strawson, P.F. (1962), 'Freedom and resentment', *Proceedings of the British Academy*, **48**. Reprinted in Strawson [1974], *Freedom and Resentment and Other Essays* (London: Methuen).

Taylor, C. (1989), *Sources of the Self: The making of the modern identity* (Cambridge, MA: Harvard University Press).

Whyte, L.L. (1962), *The Unconscious Before Freud* (London: Tavistock Publications).

Wilkes, K.V. (1988), '— , yishi, duh, um, and consciousness', in *Consciousness in Contemporary Science*, ed. A.J. Marcel and E. Bisiach (Oxford: Clarendon Press).

Andrew Brook

Unified Consciousness and the Self

I am in complete sympathy with Galen Strawson's conclusions in 'The Self'.[1] He takes a careful, measured approach to a topic that lends itself all too easily to speculation and intellectual extravaganzas. The results are for the most part balanced and plausible. I am even in sympathy with his claim that a memory-produced sense of continuity over time is less central to selfhood than many researchers think, though he may go too far in the opposite direction. Thus my purpose in these comments is not to criticise his conclusions. Instead, I want to look at certain aspects of the framework of argument and observation that he uses to reach them.

In particular, I want to look at elements (3) and (4) in his list of features that we conceive a self to possess. (3) concerns synchronic singularity, i.e. being one mental being at a time, and (4) concerns diachronic singularity, i.e. being one mental being over time. I will argue that the spirit of Strawson's claims about (3) and (4) is supportable but that the letter of them is flawed, due mainly to a failure to distinguish *singleness* of self from a self being *unified*. The feature relevant to Strawson's overall analysis is being unified, not being single. Before we take up the relationship between unity and singularity, I must do some stage-setting.

I: Phenomenology and What the Self is Like

Strawson puts phenomenology, that is, how the self appears to itself, at the centre of his picture of what the self is like. It is unusual to let how things appear to us influence our view of how things are in this way. It is not done in science and if it had been, we would never have discovered all those laws where how things appear is quite different from how they are. ('Feathers and cannonballs fall at the same rate in a vacuum? Nonsense!' — that is what appearances would suggest. Yet for all that, they do.) Nonetheless, I think that Strawson is right to put phenomenology at the centre of what the self is like. Here is why.

What is 'the self'? In my view, my 'self' is simply me, specifically, me as I am aware of myself. The '. . . self' locution ('myself', 'yourself', 'itself') is a grammatical device for marking the turning, we might say, of a thing onto that very thing — onto (how else can we say it?) itself. In my view, what we have in mind when we

[1] All references to 'Strawson' in the current article are to Galen Strawson's keynote paper in this volume (pp. 1–24).

speak of 'the Self' is simply the person; specifically, the person from the standpoint of that person — the person from the standpoint that she has on herself. There is a huge literature on the Self, capital 'S', in which it is viewed as an entity. Statements of this view should always be checked to make sure that they are not simply pumping a grammatical device up into a metaphysical postulate.

We need to be a bit more specific. What gets pumped up into a supposed entity, the Self, is the result of *one special way* in which persons can turn back on themselves. What gets mistaken for a Self, a special kind of entity, is the person *as she appears to herself in those representations of herself in which she is aware of herself 'from the inside'*, to use an old but still suggestive metaphor of Sydney Shoemaker's. Note that I have used the term 'herself' three times in this 'definition'. That was deliberate. The 'self' is simply the human person — as she appears to herself. And whatever thus appears, that is the self. Pictures of the self as an entity notwithstanding, that is what we are actually talking about when we talk about the self.

What is the difference between awareness of myself 'from the inside' (merely a useful metaphor, of course) and awareness of myself by using an external sense? This is a complicated matter and we can only sketch the story here. To be aware of the colour of my hair, I have to use my eyes (or, in extreme cases, hear or read what someone else's eyes have seen). But to know what I want for this sentence — and also what it feels like in my arm muscles to be typing this sentence, what attitude my body is in, whether I am happy or unhappy with how this chapter is going, and so on and so forth — I do not need to use any external senses. These are things that I could be aware of in myself even if I were in a sensory deprivation chamber.

Take my desires for the sentence that I'm typing, that it come out clear, that it say what I want it to say, etc. There are two ways in which I could become aware of these desires:

(1) by having the desires, and

(2) by encountering evidence of various kinds indicating that I have them.

The kind of evidence envisaged in (2) might include: how I am behaving, others' judgments about what is motivating my behaviour, (perhaps someday) readouts from brain scanning devices, and so on and so forth. However, it is (1) that is relevant to the self. It is when I am aware of myself in this special way that I am aware of what we call 'the self'. And that is all that 'the self' consists in: a person aware of him- or herself in this special way.

More specifically, it is when I am experiencing my thoughts by thinking them, my desires by feeling them, my perceptions by having them, my actions by doing them, etc., that I am aware of myself as a self. I could and others do infer that I have a self by observing what I say and do, but no one can be directly (i.e. non-inferentially) aware of me as a self via such observations, not anyone else and not me either. To be directly aware of myself as a self, I must have the kind of awareness of myself that I get when feeling desires, thinking thoughts, having perceptions, etc. The self in me is what I am aware of when I am aware of myself and my mental states and activities by having those states and doing those activities.

If so, we see just the major difference between what defines a self and what defines virtually everything else that we mentioned earlier: unlike the situation with virtually everything else, phenomenology is central to what it is to be a self. If the self is what I am aware of when I am aware of myself from the inside, then how the self *appears* is central to what the self *is*: a self simply *is* what one is aware of when one is aware of oneself from the inside. For this reason, Strawson is right to put phenomenology at the centre of his picture of what the self is. And he is also right to make the self's mental properties central to determining what it is like. The self has to be brain states of some kind on the materialist metaphysics that he and I both accept, but it is the brain states that are one's introspectible properties that will define what the self is like. And introspectible properties are mental properties. Properties described in or requiring description in the language of the brain will be peripheral to what selves are.

II: The Self — Just Results Or Also Activities?

If the self is simply what one is aware of when one is aware of oneself from the inside, this will hold implications for a number of features of selves. First, what the self is will be largely an empirical question. The reason is this: the self in any given person is simply whatever that person happens to be aware of when aware of him- or herself from the inside, and what anyone actually is aware of in this way is an empirical question. Indeed, how much and what kinds of thing a given person is aware of in him- or herself is likely to vary and even vary enormously from person to person. A completely task-oriented athlete is likely to be aware of very different things in herself, for example, from what a psychologically-minded novelist who has had years of psychoanalysis is aware of. Equally, what one is aware of in him- or herself varies widely from occasion to occasion within a single person: compare the extent and intensity of self-awareness when you are trying to describe how you are reacting to something and when you are completely absorbed in some task. On my account, these variations are all variations in what the self *is* — in different people or in a single person at different times.

If the nature and contents of the self is an empirical matter in this way, that would hold implications for any attempt such as Strawson's to lay down a list of essential features of selfhood (p. 3). There are apt to be severe limitations on such a project, limitations arising from the large element of sheer variability in what the self is from person to person and time to time. Strawson makes *some* allowance for this feature of selfhood in (8), selves are things that have a certain character or personality. Character or personality vary from person to person and, within a person, from time to time. There is a risk, however, that this variability is virtually the whole story, that there is little or nothing that is constant across persons and times, certainly much less than Strawson's or any other essentialist analysis requires.

We may be able to rescue Strawson's kind of analysis if we add a further element to the picture. What we have so far is the idea that the self is what I am aware of when I am aware of myself from the inside. What we need to add is this: the self is also made up of *acts of awareness,* including perhaps the acts in which we become aware of ourselves. On this new proposal, the self would include *both* what one is aware of as oneself *and* activities that yield awareness. This suggested addition has some plausibility. In our conception of the self, we view it as not just an inert residue of psychological properties. We also view it as active — the self can be forceful, inauthentic, kind, mean, warm, connected to other people, alienated, and so on and so forth. To be such things, it has to be active. If so, the activities of the self are part of the self, including perhaps the activity of being aware of ourselves.[2]

Now, if the self is activities as well as psychological states (by 'psychological states', I mean something like Strawson's (8), having a personality — i.e. things like traits, capacities, dispositions to behave, etc.), then we can resuscitate a good portion of Strawson's essentialist analysis. For even if the *contents* of the self can vary widely from person to person, it is likely that the *activities* characteristic of selves will have much the same general form from person to person, a form, moreover, that these activities have to have to be the activities that they are. In particular, and this brings us to the details of Strawson's analysis, such a self will have to be:

- mental; the activities in question would (mostly) be conscious and consciousness is a form of mentality (Strawson's (2)),
- ontically distinct from other things, in particular all those things whose states one is not aware of by having or doing them (5), and
- a subject of experience (6).

This supports Strawson in three of his eight claims about what characterizes selves.

III: The Self: Unity versus Singularity

In addition to these three features of selves (we also took a side glance at a fourth, namely, (8), personality), the activities characteristic of selves and the contents that these activities generate have a certain kind of *unity* — or perhaps a number of different kinds of unity. Kant argued just this point 200 years ago and it brings us to claims (3) and (4) in Strawson's analysis:
A self is,

- a single thing synchronically (3), and
- a single thing diachronically (4).

Strawson accepts that (3) is an essential feature of selves but has doubts about (4). He recognizes that (4) is very commonly found in selves as we know them, of course, but doubts whether singularity over time is strictly *essential* to being a self (p. 4).

In my view, Strawson is right to accept (3), though my reasons for accepting it are a bit different from his (as we will see shortly). He is also right to reject (4) *as he words it*. There is a different version of (4), however, that we should not reject.

Let us return to the distinction mentioned earlier between singularity and unity. Strawson spends a lot of time on principles of unity and I agree with everything he says about them. However, he may not have noticed that the unity distinctive to conscious cognition is a very particular kind of unity (we may find this particular kind of unity in some nonconscious cognition, too, though I cannot go into that here). Following Kant, let us call it *unity of consciousness*:

The unity of consciousness = *df.* an act of representing in which a number of objects and/or representations of them are combined in such a way that to be aware of any of these items is to be aware of others of these items as connected to it.

---

[2] And when we are not aware of those activities? That is a difficult and tricky question that for reasons of length I will not attempt to resolve.

I am using the broadest possible notion of representation here, one in which a representation is:

(1) any state or activity of a person[3] that gives that person epistemic access to an object, where:

(2) 'object' is also used in the broadest possible sense to mean physical things, ideas, non-existent entities (e.g. Santa Claus), abstract objects (e.g. numbers) and so on; and,

(3) the access may or may not be conscious.

Put more simply but less accurately, unity of consciousness consists in being aware of a number of objects and/or the representations of them at the same time: I am aware, not just of A, and, separately, of B, and, separately, of C, but of A-and-B-and-C, as we say, 'all together'. That is to say, to be aware of any of them is to be aware of others of them. This is what we mean, or one of the things that we mean, when we talk about being aware of a number of items as the contents or object of *a single representation*.

Note that the unity being delineated here may be more than just unified 'phenomenology' — i.e. more than the unified items *appearing* as one of some sort in experience. That was certainly Kant's view. As Kant saw it, to *appear* as one in this way, the items thus appearing *must actually be related to one another* in certain ways. We cannot pursue this interesting byway here. I mention it merely to indicate that while the unity of consciousness is at least a matter of unified 'phenomenology', of how things appear, it may be more than that. This unity, delineated as I have delineated it, is, and so far as I can see must be, a feature of the activities of awareness that are part of what we take a self to be (according to the account of the self given in Section II).[4]

Two points may help clarify the claims I am making about unity. First, even if unity of consciousness is more than things appearing as unified, it would be another question whether unity at the level of consciousness requires singularity or anything else for that matter at the level of the cognitive system itself. In fact, this question will be central to the next Section.

Second, it has been objected that it is not clear that we can be aware of more than one item at a time, something that my account of the unity of consciousness requires. In fact, this seems very clear: right now I am consciously looking at a screen, monitoring my fingers on the keyboard, thinking about what I want to say, feeling the heat and humidity of the current heat wave, wishing that these comments were finished, and a number of other things — all simultaneously. So there is no objection to my account of the unity of consciousness here.

---

[3] I define 'representation' in terms of states of *people* but elements in the environment of a person may play a role in representation, too. I am taking no stand on this, the issue of externalism about representations, or many other things to do with representations.

[4] Unity of consciousness as I have defined it here is only one of the relevant kinds of mental unity. Others include: cognitive unity (ability to bring a vast range of cognitive resources to bear on a single problem), unity of focus (ability to focus resources, including attention, on an objective), and unity of behaviour (ability to keep all our vast repertoire of bodily motions and dispositions coordinated). Even within unity of consciousness a distinction needs to be made between unity of simple consciousness and unity of consciousness of self (Brook, 1997).

Strawson makes use of a similar notion of unity, though not so precisely articulated (p. 12). As he also sees, such unified awareness is closely related to our sense of what a *single* self or mind consists in. There is actually evidence for such a link. When we suspect a duality or plurality of selves (as in brain bisection and dissociative identity disorder cases), it is precisely the absence of such unity that gives rise to the suspicion. In these cases, it appears that the representations in such persons can be divided into two groups such that there is a subject of experience for whom it is true that: the items in one group are unified in a single representation, but the items of the other group are not part of that unified consciousness. Yet the items in the second group often make up a substantial group and there is often evidence for a second subject, 'secondness' here being based on the notion that items in the second group are unified in a single representation but items in the first group are not included in it. No unity, no single self; duality of unified groups, duality of selves.

Strawson himself claims that 'explicitly self-conscious thought' *must* experience the self as synchronically single (p. 12) and I think that he is right. I have examined this issue (and the others under discussion) elsewhere but let me note just one argument (Brook, 1994, esp. ch. 7 and 8). Suppose I am told that I am to undergo fission into two persons (two minds, two selves, two souls — the terminology does not matter). I am given a detailed account of how the fissioning machine works and I set out to imagine myself going through the process. I have no difficulty with imagining myself lying down on the table, the table moving into the fissioning machine, the machine starting to work to divide me into two, . . . and then what? I cannot go any further. I cannot imagine myself, i.e. me as I am aware of myself from the inside, becoming two selves (Brook, 1994, p. 172). To think of anything happening to myself, as Bennett noted many years ago, 'pre-requires an undivided *me*' (Bennett, 1974, p. 83). If so, Strawson is right that a self is synchronically a single thing. The reason is that, synchronically, a self must have unified consciousness and *unity* of consciousness at a given time requires a *single* conscious being at that time.

Put in terms more familiar to some, synchronic unity at the level of phenomenology, i.e. in how things appear, requires synchronic singularity at the level of ontology, i.e. in the cognitive system 'housing' these unified appearances. Let us now turn to the parallel question concerning diachronic unity and diachronic singularity.

IV: Diachronic Unity and Singularity

Strawson urges that *diachronic* singularity is *not* needed for selfhood and I agree with him here, too. However, diachronic *unity* is another matter. This distinction gives rise to two questions:

(1) Does diachronic unity of self require diachronic singularity of self?

(2) Whatever the story may be with diachronic singularity, is diachronic *unity* an essential feature of selfhood?

Strawson is inclined to answer 'no' to both questions. I agree with him about (1) but am not so sure about (2).

Diachronic singularity (what philosophers call personal identity) is persisting as one and the same person over time. It is a central notion of our legal system (you can only be found guilty for what *you* did or caused to have done), concept of property (you own what *you* legally acquired earlier), and interpersonal relationships (if I love you, we are separated and you are killed, I will not be consoled by being told that you had an identical twin who is ready to step in).

Diachronic unity is achieved by remembering past experiences, etc., and anticipating future experiences, etc., from the inside, in such a way that I can combine the representation of the remembered earlier or anticipated future states and events with current experienced states and events. This process of combination (or as Kant called it, synthesis) produces a form of synchronic unity, i.e. the unity that results when I combine a number of current states with one with another. If so, diachronic unity is simply synchronically unified consciousness where the representations being unified represent past and future states and events, the past ones in memories, the future ones in anticipations, etc.

I agree with Strawson that diachronic unity does not require diachronic singularity. All that is required for diachronic unity backward is that something of earlier experiences, actions, etc., be carried forward in such a way that the earlier experiences, actions, etc., are represented to me now from the inside (i.e. as if *I* had had or done them originally). As Kant showed, such memories (or q-memories, to use the philosopher's fastidious term)[5] and the unity over time that they make possible could well survive transfer of the memory 'trace' (i.e. whatever it is that carries the memory) from one person to another over time. (Strawson quotes a relevant passage from Kant and offers a related analysis on p. 11.) Strawson calls this picture the Pearl (string of pearls) view of diachronic unity (p. 20) and I agree with him entirely that it is a possibility. If so, unity of self backwards over time does not require that the self persists over time, paradoxical as that may sound.

The same is true and even more true of unity of self forward into the future. Since the self does not yet exist in the future, all that unity forward in time *could* consist in is some present state. And all this present state consists in is the anticipation of certain future states as states of myself, i.e. 'projecting' myself into the future. If the unity achieved by projection into the future does not require that the self already exists in the future, then it would seem likely, by parity of reasoning, that unity backward over time does not require that the self actually existed earlier (though perhaps *someone* had to exist earlier, the self that actually had and did the q-remembered experiences and actions, whoever that was). Anticipations of the future are one kind of experience in the present and memories are merely another. If so, Strawson is right to hold that what counts for determining the nature of the self is how we appear to ourselves in the present moment, including what (q-)memories we have right now and what anticipations of the future we are engaged in right now, not how we were or how we will be.[6]

It is time to turn to (2): If diachronic *singularity* is not essential for selfhood, what about diachronic *unity?* Do we need to have memories of having and doing *some* past

---

[5] Starting with Shoemaker (1970), philosophers have used the term 'q-memory' in contexts like the current one because of an objection that, by the very definition of 'remember', we can *remember* having and doing only our own earlier experiences and actions. Response: switch to talk of q-memories, where q-memories are exactly like memories except that this definitional link is absent. It then becomes an open question whether I can q-remember having and doing experiences and actions that, when they were done, were in fact done by someone else (Parfit, 1984).

[6] The term 'present moment' needs clarification. The experienced present is not the infinitesimal point of modern physics. What we experience as 'now' is in fact a stretch of time — a very small stretch, but a stretch nonetheless. Philosophers call this phenomenon the 'specious present'.

experiences and activities? Do we need in at least *some* degree to be able to imagine a future conceived of as our own? Here, I am inclined to think, Strawson's story needs to be qualified. On the one hand, I am inclined to agree with him that one would not lose one's selfhood by losing *most* of one's sense of having existed, of having experienced things and done things in the past. (On my analysis, this sense consists in unifying *current* awareness of having had and done the earlier things with awareness of one's *current* life and world.) Likewise if one lost or perhaps even never had most of the normal ability to anticipate a future as one's own.

However, I am not so sure about a complete loss of all diachronic unity, a complete lack of any sense of personal continuity from the past to the present and into the future. I think Strawson may be inclined to understate how very, very different creatures who lost all sense of personal continuity would be from us. Oliver Sacks has explored cases in which virtually all sense of continuity over time has been lost (for example, cases in which the patient has to introduced to the medical staff anew on every meeting). While these patients continue to be aware of themselves as they are in the present moment (ask if they are happy and they can answer yes or no), something is profoundly different. It would hardly be an exaggeration to say that, in the sense that matters for forming interpersonal relationships, there is no person there in these patients. At least some sense of the history and the possible future(s) of a relationship is just that important to the very existence of an interpersonal relationships.

Now consider a hypothetical patient with no ability to anticipate a future as his or her own. (I have no idea if such patients exist. I certainly hope not.) A person who could not think of him- or herself as existing in the future, who could not, for example, plan what to have for dinner, wonder what tomorrow will hold, think about who might visit next week, would be even more uncanny than the patients with no ability to form memories. Strawson may tend to understate the importance of a sense of continuity from past to present to future to the question of having a self. As he tells us, his own sense of personal continuity with any past or future being is quite limited. I have no reason to doubt what he says. However, I suspect that there is a huge difference between a limited sense of personal continuity and no sense at all.

For one thing, beings with *no* sense of personal continuity would also *and for that very reason* be cognitively impaired in a certain way. The ability to retain the contents of earlier experiences and, via remembering (or q-remembering) them from the inside, synthesize them with current experiences is an unsubstitutable feature of virtually all forms of cognition of any complexity. But when I (q-)remember an earlier experience from the inside, I also remember that experience as though *I* had it. (If our earlier analysis is right, I can (q-)remember earlier experiences this way even if it were not in fact me who had had them. We are talking about *sense* of personal continuity here, not actual continuity.) If so, a *measure* of diachronic unity is essential for virtually all cognitive activity of any complexity.

This argument for diachronic continuity is not enough to undermine Strawson's most radical doubts completely. All it shows, strictly speaking, is that selves *of any cognitive complexity* must be unified over time. It is still possible that cognitively very simple selves do not have to be. Because of what I just said about Sacks' cases, I am inclined to resist even this weaker claim but I am also inclined to think that it is not very important. As Strawson articulates in his (8), selves have a certain personality — when we think of selves, we think of beings fairly richly endowed with personal characteristics. Indeed, we think of beings rather like us. If my argument shows only that selves *like us* must have significant diachronic unity, I would be quite content.

V: Remaining Issues

I have not said anything about two of the features that Strawson identifies in his account of selves, namely, (1), that a self is a thing of a certain kind, and, (7), that a self is an agent. (1) is easy: if the self is simply me as I am aware of myself from the inside, then, since I am a thing of a certain kind, the self is a thing of a certain kind. (7) is trickier. I find it hard to imagine a subject of experience, a thing able to be aware of itself, that had no volitional, action-initiating abilities of any kind whatsoever. Surely such a being must have at least the ability to initiate certain *mental* actions, e.g. directing and changing the focus of attention. However, I do not know how to *prove,* against Strawson's suspicions, that selves must have such volitional abilities. For now, that is where I will leave the matter.[7]

To sum up: if we push the notions of the unity of consciousness and singularity of person a bit further than Strawson pushes them, his conclusions appear in an even more convincing light. However, one of them needs to be qualified, namely, the suggestion that unity over time may not be required for something to be a self. For a self like us at any rate, some measure of unity over time is needed.[8]

References

Bennett, J. (1974), *Kant's Dialectic* (Cambridge and New York: Cambridge University Press).
Brook, A. (1994), *Kant and the Mind* (New York and Cambridge: Cambridge University Press).
Brook, A. (1997), 'Unity of consciousness and other mental unities', *Proceedings of the 19th Annual Conference of the Cognitive Science Society, 1997* (New York: Ablex Press), p. 875.
Parfit, D. (1984), *Reasons and Persons* (Oxford and New York: Oxford University Press).
Shoemaker, S. (1970), 'Persons and their pasts', *American Philosophical Quarterly*, 7, pp. 269–85.
Strawson, G. (1997), 'The self', *Journal of Consciousness Studies*, 4 (5–6), pp. 405–28. Reprinted in this volume, pp. 1–24.

---

[7] I have also said relatively little about (8), that selves have personalities. That may not matter very much. Strawson is probably right when he suggests that having a personality is a less important feature of selves than any of (1) – (7).

[8] An anonymous referee for the *Journal of Consciousness Studies* raised some interesting and provocative questions in an effort to help me make my analysis clearer and more accessible. I am not sure how successful I have been in meeting these challenges but I am certainly grateful for them.

Eric T. Olson

There Is No Problem of the Self

Because there is no agreed use of the term 'self', or characteristic features or even paradigm cases of selves, there is no idea of 'the self' to figure in philosophical problems. The term leads to troubles otherwise avoidable; and because legitimate discussions under the heading of 'self' are really about other things, it is gratuitous. I propose that we stop speaking of selves.

I

People often speak as if there were a serious philosophical problem about *selves*. Is there a self? Is the self knowable? How does the self relate to the body? These and other questions are thought to make up something called the *problem of the self.*

I doubt seriously that there is any such problem. Not because the self is unproblematic, or because there are unproblematically no such things as selves. My trouble is that a problem must be a problem *about* something: even if there are no selves, there must at least be some problematic idea or concept of a self, if there is to be a problem of the self. As far as I can see there is no such idea. What is a self? For every answer to this question, there is another answer not only incompatible with it, but wholly unrelated. There is virtually no agreement about the characteristic features of selves: depending on whom you believe, selves may be concrete or abstract, material or immaterial, permanent or ephemeral, naturally occuring or human constructions, essentially subjective or publicly observable, the same or not the same things as people. There are not even any agreed paradigm cases of selves, things we could point to or describe and say, 'A self is one of *those*.' But no concept could be so problematic that no one could agree about *anything* to do with it. For lack of a subject matter, then, there is no problem of the self.

So I shall argue, anyway. I am not just quibbling about a word. Real philosophy is at stake. Many philosophers assume that there is something properly called the problem or problems of the self, and write as if everyone knew what they meant by 'self'. This often leads to obscurity and muddle. If I am right, the muddle arises because those philosophers believe in a concept that doesn't exist.

I claim also that if we look at those books and articles with titles like 'The Self' or 'Problems of the Self', we will find that they are most typically not about 'selves' at all, but about other things — different things in different cases. In fact the matters discussed under the heading of 'self' are *so* various that no one can seriously say that they are all about some one thing, the self. Because legitimate inquiries that go under the heading of 'self' are really about something else, and can be (and typically are) put in other terms, we can easily do without the word 'self'.

For these reasons, I believe that philosophers would do well to avoid the word 'self' in their theorizing.[1]

II

What would the problem of the self be about, if there were such a problem? What is this 'self' whose existence and properties appear to be the subject of so much debate? What distinguishes problems about the self from problems about other topics — causation or intrinsic value, say? If there is any genuine problem of the self, there must be *some* nontrivial answer, however vague or incomplete, to these questions.

There are several ways of trying to meet this demand. The most satisfactory would be to give a definition of the term or an analysis of the concept. A definition of 'self' would say, 'x is y's self if and only if . . .', with the dots filled in by some synonymous or at least logically equivalent phrase. I say that the phrase to be explained is 'x is y's self' rather than 'x is a self' (less formally, 'one's self' rather than simply 'a self') because it is part of the meaning of the word 'self', in its typical philosophical uses, that a self be *someone's* self. (That much, anyway, seems clear.) Or if there could be 'unowned' selves, it is part of the idea of a self that it at least be the sort of thing that *could* be the self of a particular person or thing. If someone could explain 'x is a self' but not 'x is y's self', or if someone could distinguish selves from non-selves but had no idea what made a given self the self of a particular person, I think most 'self'-users would doubt that he knew what the word meant. The word 'self' is like the word 'body', as in the phrase 'human body': anyone who knows what the words 'human body' mean must have at least some idea of what it is for something to be the body, or at least a body, of a particular person (van Inwagen, 1980). We can easily define 'x is a self' in terms of 'x is y's self': x is a self just in case there is (or could be) some y such that x is y's self. But there is no obvious way of deriving an account of the meaning of 'x is y's self' from a definition of 'x is a self'. Thus, even if we succeeded in defining 'x is a self' we should still face the task of accounting for 'x is y's self'.

If we use a word that we can't define, or that we can't define in a way that others who use it will accept, we must be on our guard — the more so if the word is a piece of philosophical jargon that has no place in ordinary language. (Part of the trouble with 'self' is that it is jargon masquerading as ordinary language.) It will be a real question whether those who use the word are in any sense talking about the same thing. Anyone who uses a word whose definition is disputed is obliged to say what she means by it. If we cannot do so, we have to wonder whether we understand what we are saying.

---

[1] This idea is not new. F.H. Bradley once wrote, 'Self has turned out to mean so many things, to mean them so ambiguously, and to be so wavering in its applications, that we do not feel encouraged' (1893, p. 101). Alston (1977), Flew (1949; 1993), and Toulmin (1977) have said similar things. Since many seem to have paid no heed, however, it seems worthwhile making the point again in a different way.

I hope it will be obvious that I have no quarrel with the word 'self' as it appears within reflexive pronouns or as a prefix (or even as it appears in idioms such as 'self and other', which, I take it, means nothing more than 'oneself and other beings'). I understand well enough what it means to say that Jane burned or contradicted herself, or that Fred lacks self-control or is self-taught. But I don't understand what it could mean to say that you and I might exchange selves, or that a human being may have more than one self, or that the self is unobservable or doesn't exist — or at least not without some special explanation of what the word 'self' means here. Likewise, I understand what it means to say that I am thinking, but not what it means to say that *the I* (or *the 'I'*, as it often appears) is thinking.

But a word isn't necessarily in serious trouble just because it has no agreed definition. There are other ways of saying what a self is than by explicitly defining it. We could mention some characteristic features of selves — features that may not necessarily be shared by all and only selves, but which selves at least typically have and non-selves typically lack. A longish list of such features would give us a fair idea of what a self is.

Failing both a definition and a list of characteristic features, we could at least begin to answer the question, What is a self? by referring to some paradigm cases of selves — particular things that everyone agrees are selves, or that would be selves if there were any selves — and some paradigm cases of non-selves. Of course, this strategy faces well-known difficulties: even if you can figure out which particular things I am referring to, you might not be able to guess what it is about those things that makes them all selves, and so have no idea what other things count as selves or why. (If I point to a shoe, a lampshade, a book, and a carrot, and say, '*Melves* are things like those,' obviously that won't suffice to tell you what I mean by 'melf'; nor will it help much if I go on to tell you that stones and forks are not melves.) Still, I should have given you at least *some* information about what a self is.

Let me illustrate these rather abstract points with a concrete example. There is no agreed account of the meaning of the term 'mind' or 'mental', of what makes a phenomenon mental rather than non-mental. Intentionality ('aboutness'), subjectivity ('what it is like'), immediate accessibility to consciousness, and many other features have been proposed as 'marks of the mental'; but none of these accounts is widely accepted. This is a problem. In a sense, we don't know what the mind is. At the same time, we know rather a lot about the mind. Nearly everyone agrees that mental phenomena, if there are any, often *have* intentionality and subjectivity, and are often accessible to consciousness, even if these features don't suffice to define the mental. We agree on a wide range of typical and characteristic features of mental phenomena: everyone agrees, for instance, that the desire for rain is satisfied by rain and frustrated by persistent dry weather, and that being in the presence of rain usually causes one to believe that it's raining. And we agree on paradigm cases: no one doubts that beliefs, wants, memories, intentions, sensations, emotions, and dreams, if there are such things, are mental phenomena, and that earthquakes and temperatures are not. Even those who deny that there are any mental phenomena can reasonably claim to understand what it is whose existence they are denying. Thus, although there is some dispute about just what the subject matter of psychology or the philosophy of mind may be, there seems to be enough agreement that many of our questions can be said to be questions *about the mind*.

On the other hand, if a large minority of philosophers and psychologists thought that beliefs, though they exist, were not mental phenomena at all, but took something completely different — photosynthesis, say — as paradigmatic of the mental, it would be clear that there was serious confusion afoot. Matters would be even worse if there were respected participants in the debate who thought that many non-mental but few mental phenomena had properties like intentionality or subjectivity. Although there would certainly be a problem about the *word* 'mind' in that case, it would be a good deal less clear that there was a philosophical problem *of the mind*. For what, beyond the word, could it be a problem about? The case of the self is rather like that.

III

Let us consider some attempts to say what a self might be. It doesn't matter whether we take these proposals to be definitions of 'self' or only as giving essential or paradigmatic or at any rate salient features of selves. Take them as proposed answers to the ordinary question, What is a self?

Account 1. One's self is that unchanging, simple substance to which one's impressions and ideas have reference.

This is apparently what Hume sought in vain within himself (1978, p. 251). We may wonder what Hume meant by ideas 'having reference to' one's self. But the main thing to be said about this account is that most present-day philosophers see no reason to believe that any unchanging, simple substance has anything to do with anyone's ideas or impressions. If this is what selves are, there are simply no selves, and the problem of the self is of little more than historical interest. For an account of 'self' that reflects today's concerns we must look elsewhere.

Here is an updated version of something like Hume's account:

Account 2. One's self is the inner subject of one's conscious experiences.

(Campbell, 1957, p. 74; Harré, 1987, p. 99.) Variants include 'One's self is the bearer of one's personal identity over time' (Berofsky, 1995, p. 234); '. . . that which views the world through one's eyes' (Nagel, 1986, p. 55); '. . . the tautological subject of one's actions' (Rée, 1974, p. 188n.); 'the cause of everything one does' (Minsky, 1985, p. 232); etc.

Now I take it that *I* am the subject of my conscious experiences, the bearer of my identity over time, and the cause of everything I do. Otherwise they wouldn't be *my* experiences, *my* identity, or things that *I* do. On this account, then, I am my self, and you are yours. Everyone is identical with his self. If there should turn out to be no selves, there would be no such beings as you and I. And although some philosophers accept this inference, others reject it: they think that the existence of selves is problematic in a way that the existence of midwives and plumbers, or of you and me, is not (e.g. Harré, 1987, p. 103). In fact those who argue that 'there is no self' rarely go on to conclude from this that they themselves do not exist. *Their* problem of the self must be about something else.

Although the above account seems to imply that selves are people, it doesn't say that the two terms are synonymous. But many philosophers use the terms interchangeably (e.g. Mellor, 1991; Bermúdez, 1997). So we might say:

Account 3. One's self is just that person, himself.

Selves are just people, human beings. To say that the self is so-and-so is to say that people, you and I, are so-and-so. This makes it rather awkward to say that one *has* a self. What could it be for me to *have* a person, or to *have* myself? The truth, rather, is that we *are* selves. But we could presumably explain away talk of having a self as a hangover from the eighteenth-century use of the word 'self'.

If this account were widely accepted, I shouldn't be writing this essay. To be sure, the word 'person' is problematic enough that anyone who relies on it in philosophical discussion had better say what she means by it. There is a good deal of dispute about its definition, and about whether it can be defined at all. Compared with 'self', though, 'person' is a model of clarity and accord. Everyone agrees that people (persons) characteristically have certain mental capacities such as rationality and self-consciousness, and certain moral attributes such as accountability for their actions (or at any rate that they are capable of acquiring such features). There is a fair consensus about what things count as people: no one doubts that you and I and Boris Yeltsin are people, and that houses and bronze statues of people aren't. Although there are disputed cases (foetuses, infants, adults suffering from severe senile dementia), their number is small compared with the number of items we can confidently classify as people or non-people. In this respect 'person' is no worse off than most other nouns. We know how many people there are (a few hard cases aside, once more) and how to count them. The word 'person' is well enough understood for there to be philosophical problems about people.

But many philosophers explicitly deny that 'self' and 'person' are interchangeable. For example, some say that dogs and dolphins are, or have, selves, even though they aren't people (Lowe, 1996, p. 49n.). More seriously, it is often said that 'person' has to do with a publicly observable, social being whereas a self is essentially something inner or private (e.g. Harré, 1984, p. 26; McCall, 1990, pp. 12–15; see also Campbell, 1957, p. 93; Hamlyn, 1984, p. 188). Others say that people but not selves can be described, identified, and counted (Abelson, 1977, p. 87). This suggests that you and I are not selves, but rather have them — assuming, at least, that *we* are people, or that we are publicly observable or countable or identifiable. What, then, are selves? We might say:

Account 4. One's self is that indescribable and unidentifiable private, inner being within one.

('By "self" I mean the personal unity I take myself to be, my singular inner being, so to speak' [Harré, 1984, p. 26].)

Now this is completely unhelpful. We might as well say that the self is 'the elusive "I" that shows an alarming tendency to disappear when we try to introspect it', a definition (tongue in cheek, I assume) found in a popular philosophical dictionary (Blackburn, 1994, p. 344). You can't explain what a self is by saying that it is something inner and ineffable, any more than you can do so by saying that it is a certain kind of 'I'. Of course, if the self really is something ineffable, this is no criticism. You can't describe the indescribable. The challenge for those who think they understand this account is to persuade the rest of us to take them seriously.

'One's self is what one identifies oneself with, what a person cares most about, the loss of which amounts, for him, to self-destruction, either partial or total' (Abelson, 1977, p. 91; see also James, 1905, p. 291; Berofsky, 1995). Thus we might write,

Account 5. One's self is what one values above all else.

Of course, there may be a number of things that someone values above all else, and whose destruction would be as bad for her as her own destruction. So it would not be uncommon for someone to have several different selves at once, on this account ('The piano is my second self,' said Chopin), as well as having different selves at different times; and different people would often share the very same self. The phrase 'Mary's self' wouldn't necessarily have unique reference. It would be more like 'Mary's brother'. In fact, Mary's self might *be* her brother. There would be people whose selves were houses, political causes, children, or pets. Many of those who use the word 'self' would reject this consequence as absurd.

Let us continue our catalogue:

Account 6. One's self is the unconscious mechanism responsible for the unity of one's consciousness.

(Brooks, 1994, pp. 36, 51.) On this account, there is nothing subjective or ineffable or immaterial about the self; nor are selves people. My self may be literally an organ, a part of my brain, a matter for physiologists to investigate.

Others suggest that the self is not a material part of one but rather an attribute, typically an aspect of one's personality or character or behaviour:

Account 7. One's self is a psychological or behavioural attribute of one.

But which psychological or behavioural attribute? No one would count my fear of close spaces as a serious candidate for being my self. One view is that one's self is the way one sees oneself, or a certain set of one's beliefs about oneself: one's self is roughly one's self-image (Rogers, 1951, pp. 498; Harré, 1984, p. 26; Marx and Hillix, 1973, p. 605). I suppose Dennett's account of the self as a 'center of narrative gravity' might be something like this, though it is far from clear just what he means by that phrase (1991, pp. 416, 427). On this view a person's self is typically unique, and one may have different selves at different times, perhaps even more than one self at once. Others say that one's self is by definition unique: it is (for example) what is expressed by one's uniquely characteristic actions (Kenny, 1988, p. 33). In that case, for all I know I may not have a self at all, as I cannot rule out the possibility that somewhere in the universe there is someone exactly like me in the relevant respects. For that matter, it is consistent with everything we know that no one has a self. Even those who consider it an open question whether there are any selves are unlikely to accept that there could fail to be selves for *that* reason. By contrast, others take the self to be 'man as he really is, not as he appears to himself' (Jung, 1968, p. 186), or that collection of features shared by all and only human beings in all times and places (Solomon, 1988, p. 4). One's self is something like universal human nature. The very idea of the self, on this account, ensures that we all have the same self, and that there could not be more than one.

Naturally none of these variants will be acceptable to those who think that *we* are selves, or that selves are things that think or experience. No one seriously supposes that *he* is a psychological attribute. No psychological attribute could think about Vienna, or sleep badly, or drink coffee.

Let us consider one more popular account:

Account 8. One's self is an aggregate of or a construction out of one's sense-experiences.

(Ayer, 1946, p. 125; see also Broad, 1925, p. 282; Marx and Hillix, 1973, p. 605.) Let us set aside the serious question of just what an 'aggregate' or 'construction' might be. We might put the view more loosely by saying that one's self is one's mental life, the sum-total of all of one's thoughts and experiences, or perhaps some selected portion thereof. This, I suppose, is the 'bundle theory of the self' often attributed to Hume. Are you and I selves on this account? That depends on whether we are literally made out of thoughts and experiences — whether an aggregate of thoughts and experiences is the sort of thing that can do and be all of the things that you and I can do and be. (Can a bundle of thoughts ride a bicycle? Could a bundle of thoughts have consisted of completely different thoughts?) This is a familiar problem about personal identity.

IV

What, then, of the problem of the self? What is it a problem about? There is clearly nothing that satisfies all of these accounts. There aren't even two or three similar kinds of things that each satisfy most of them. It should be equally clear that there is no one thing — no single idea — that all of these accounts could reasonably be seen as trying to capture. There is no one sort of thing that some believe is a construction out of sense-impressions and others take to be a mental attribute, a simple substance, an organ, a human being, or in some cases even a house or a hamster. It should also be clear that there are no agreed characteristic attributes of selves, or even any generally accepted cases. (We can't even pick out a self in a purely relational way, for example as 'Bertrand Russell's self', without controversy, for on some accounts of 'self' there are no selves to pick out, while on others Russell might have had any number of different selves.) I conclude that those who use the word 'self', if they are saying anything coherent at all, must be talking about completely different things. Thus, there is no such idea as the idea of the self, and therefore nothing for the 'problem of the self' to be a problem about.

There are several replies that someone might make to this argument. First, our catalogue of answers to the question, What is a self? is incomplete. We may have neglected one that would solve the problem. Of course, the mere fact that there are other accounts different from those mentioned is no help to those who believe in the problem of the self. Simply extending the list will only make matters worse. What we need is not just an account of the self that would command wider assent than any of these, but one that would synthesize them and show them all to reflect a part of some larger, common idea. But we can say no more about this possibility until someone produces a candidate for that role.

Second, one might argue that this lack of agreement about selves is part of the very problem I claim not to exist. Doesn't this just show that the problem of the self is more serious than we thought? That it is not only about the nature and existence of selves and their relation to more familiar entities such as people and human beings, but about the very meaning of the term? I can imagine someone comparing the problem of the self with the problem of *race*. There is no accepted account of what the term 'race' or any of its determinates such as 'black', 'white', 'coloured', 'slavic', 'oriental', etc. mean. For this and other reasons, there is no end to the rubbish that has been said and written about race. But aren't those confused writings and sayings *about race*? If there were no problem of the self for the reasons I have given, wouldn't it follow, absurdly, that there was no race problem?

The analogy is strained. Even if no one knows what race or individual races are, there is wide agreement about a great deal of 'race lore'. Whatever 'black' or 'white' might mean, everyone agrees that 'black' people *typically* (though not always) have dark, curly hair and dark skin compared with 'white' people. Everyone agrees that race, if there is such a thing, is an inherited trait, even if there is dispute about how the race of one's parents determines one's own race. Most of us are disposed to class most people into 'black', 'white', etc. in the same way, however arbitrary or unfair those classifications may be. Everyone accepts certain paradigm cases: Nelson Mandela is clearly 'black', Margaret Thatcher is 'white', Mao Tse-Tung is 'oriental', and so on. So even the problematic term 'race' fares far better than 'self' in terms of characteristic features, consistency of application, and paradigm cases.

At any rate, the comparison with 'race' can hardly be cheering for theorists of the self. Of course there is a *social* 'race problem'. But that problem is not so much about race itself, whatever that may be, as about people's attitudes. It arises not because different people belong to different races, but because people think they do, or rather because they treat others differently on the basis of their outward appearance or that of their ancestors. If everyone stopped doing that, the problem would go away. In this sense there is indeed a 'problem of the self'. The problem is that people use the word 'self' as if everyone knew what it meant when in fact there is no agreement about what it means, and that this leads them into needless troubles. *That* 'problem of the self' would be solved if people simply stopped using the word and others like it. But that is not the problem of the self that my opponents believe in. There is a social problem about the *word* 'self'. There is no philosophical problem about selves.

A third reply would be to concede that there is no single concept of the self, but to insist that there are, nonetheless, many different concepts properly so called. There are different kinds of selves. Since the term is ambiguous, it may be a mistake to speak of *the* self without specifying which 'self' we mean. But we do have 'the Humean self', 'the inner-subject self', 'the personal self', 'the ineffable self', 'the evaluative self', and so on, each with its own set of problems. Don't these ideas give us a set of problems of the self?

Only in the most trivial sense. Once we concede that the various uses of the term 'self' have nothing more in common than the word, we can see that it could be a pun to say that they are all nevertheless problems of the self. We might as well say that the 'problem of property' includes both debates about the legal institution of ownership and the metaphysical problem of universals. On the other hand, if the various accounts of the self do have some interesting content in common, we ought to be able to say what it is, and thus give an account of the meaning of the word, however vague or incomplete, that everyone can accept.

V

I said I was going to argue not only that there is no problem of the self, properly so called, but also that careless use of the term 'self' creates trouble we could otherwise avoid. I will mention a few examples of that trouble.

Some philosophers seem to be aware that the term 'self' is wildly ambiguous. Owen Flanagan, for example, writes,

> The word 'self' has many meanings — personality, character, an individual's central character traits, the way(s) one carries oneself in the world, the way one represents oneself to oneself and to others, the dynamic integrated system of thoughts, emotions, lived events, and so on, that make up who one is from the God's eye point of view. All these senses are useful (1996, p. vii).

We should expect someone of this view to take care always to explain what he meant when he used the word 'self'. But Flanagan goes on to say that Augustine's *Confessions* is 'the story of a single self', and to ask whether every individual has 'one and only one self', without giving any indication of whether he means central character traits, the way one represents oneself to others, or any of the other items on his list, leaving the reader to guess what claim is intended (pp. 95 f.).[2]

This can lead to more serious trouble. Consider this quotation:

> If A's brain is put into B's body, would A's Self move into B's body? Clearly, if the bodies were different (A might be a man, and B a woman) then the Self could hardly be the same — for our notion of Self is surely bound up with our potentialities and our behaviour. At most there could be but a kind of inner core of Self (which might be memories?) remaining after a radical change of body. Suppose, though, that A and B are identical twins and equally fit. Would they swap selves with a brain transplant?' (Gregory, 1981, p. 491)

Well, *would* the result of putting your brain into the head of your identical twin and his brain into yours be that you got what was previously his self and he got the self that was once yours? There are many questions we might ask about this imaginary case. We can ask what would happen to *you*: which, if any, of the two resulting people, if they would be people at all, would be you. We can ask whether the being got by putting your brain into your twin's cranium would have memories, personality, self-image, and other psychological features that were more like yours or more like those of your twin, or which person — you or your twin or someone else — he would think he was. And so on. But what could it mean to ask whether you and he would exchange *selves*? Suppose someone insisted that you would indeed exchange selves. Would you agree or disagree? What sort of argument would support or undermine this claim? What consequences, if any, would it have for the way the other questions are answered? Until the author tells us what he means by 'self', we can have no idea. Yet he apparently sees no need to do so.

The same trouble arises when people ask whether someone with a split personality has more than one self, or whether we create two different selves by cutting the cerebral commissures, or whether one can become a different self through religious conversion, psychic trauma, education, or some other experience. Anyone familiar with philosophical writing that purports to be about the self will recognize claims like these:

> The self exists (does not exist).
> The self is identical (is not identical) with the body.
> The self is not an object.
> A human being can have (cannot have) more than one self at once.
> Human beings have selves but lobsters don't.
> The first-person pronoun purports to pick out a self *qua* self.

Without further elucidation, I don't understand any of these claims well enough to know even whether I agree or disagree. And for anyone who thinks he understands them perfectly well, there will be another who feels equally confident, but who understands them in a completely different way. The reason is that unless the word 'self' as it figures in these sentences is explicitly given some special meaning, they simply don't say anything at all.

---

[2] Elsewhere he writes, 'One useful way of conceiving of the self is as a kind of structured life . . .' (p. 67), and then says on the next page that the various twists and turns in one's life 'have to be part of the life of a single self'. Unless something can both be and have a life, the point would have been more clearly put in different words.

Let us consider one more example. Galen Strawson[3] writes,

> I will call my view the Pearl view, because it suggests that many mental selves exist, one
> at a time and one after another, like pearls on a string, in the case of something like a
> human being (p. 20).

Each self, apparently, exists for as long as one's attention is focused on some one
thing, typically two or three seconds, then perishes. But what is it that a human being
gets a new one of every few seconds? That is not so clear, despite Strawson's attempts
to explain what he means by 'self'. The idea seems to be something like this:

> One's self is that distinct, mental thing within one that is a subject of experience and a
> single thing within any hiatus-free period of experience.

(The bit about one's self being 'within' one is a guess; Strawson doesn't say what
makes a self the self of a particular person.) I take it that something is a 'subject of
experience' just in case it *has* experiences — just in case it sees, feels, hears, and so
on. But *I* see, feel and hear. The question, then, is whether I am 'distinct', 'mental', or
'a single thing' (it doesn't matter for present purposes what those terms of art mean).
If I am, it appears to follow from Strawson's view that I am my self, and that Strawson
is Strawson's self. Otherwise, if I have a self at all, it must be a subject of experience
other than me — something *else* that sees, feels, and hears everything that I see, feel,
and hear. I hope we may assume that there aren't *two* sentient beings living within my
skin, I and my self. And Strawson seems inclined to think that there are such things as
selves. Thus, although he never says so explicitly, his view seems to be that each person is ordinarily identical with his self.

If this is right, then Strawson is telling us that he himself exists (or existed) for only
two or three seconds. Or rather, he, Galen Strawson, does not exist at all — for what
could make it the case that one rather than any other of those billion or so two-second
beings that are the successive 'selves' of a certain tall, blond-haired human being was
Strawson? The chapter attributed to him was in fact written by a vast committee of
authors, none of whom contributed so much as an entire sentence. And the same goes
for you and me, unless your attention span is considerably longer: you are not the
being who read the previous sentence a moment ago. You didn't exist then. The
slightest lapse of attention is literally fatal: it destroys you and replaces you with
someone else — someone rather like you, but numerically different.

That, surely, is incredible. Anyone who reaches the conclusion that none of us
exist, or at least none for longer than a few seconds, must have gone wrong somewhere, just as certainly as someone who concludes that motion is impossible. At any
rate, we can accept Strawson's conclusion (or try to accept it) only if it is clear that it
follows inexorably from premises whose truth is even more obvious than that you and
I exist, and that we existed ten seconds ago. Strawson apparently thinks that it follows
inexorably from the fact that our thoughts don't flow in a single, unified stream, but
are disjointed and gappy. The premise is probably true. But I can't begin to see how
this entails Strawson's conclusion. Even if there *are* things that last only as long as
one's attention remains focussed on something — 'sets of neuron-constituting atoms
in a certain state of activation' (p. 21), if you like — why suppose that you and I are

---

[3] All references to 'Strawson' in the current chapter are to Galen Strawson's opening chapter in this
     volume (pp. 1–24).

such things? Why couldn't we be human beings? Why couldn't human beings be the subjects of disjointed thoughts and experiences? What is it about lapses of attention that makes it impossible for *anything* to survive them?

My point is not to criticize Strawson's view as implausible or unsupported, but rather to illustrate the perils of relying on terms like 'self' in doing philosophy. I doubt that Strawson would have reached this absurd conclusion had he put his questions in other terms. If he had simply asked, What sort of thing am I? (Am I a mental thing, a substance, unified synchronically and diachronically, etc.? Am I the sort of thing I ordinarily believe myself to be?) instead of asking about the nature of 'the mental self', I doubt that he would have answered, 'I am a thing that lasts only as long as its attention remains fixed and then perishes and is replaced by something else.' The claim that a human being acquires a new 'mental self' every few seconds may sound surprising. The claim that *you and I* did not exist five seconds ago turns the world upside down. I suspect that Strawson didn't mean to endorse this view at all, and that he was lured into saying something that implies it by the seductions of the word 'self'. (If he did mean it, why not make it plain? As if the nonexistence of people were a corollary too trivial to mention!) But if that is not what he meant, I have no idea what 'the Pearl view' is meant to be a theory about.

VI

If there is nothing properly called the problem of the self, what of those books and articles that appear to be about the self? Must we commit them to the flames? Not at all. Despite their titles, they are typically not about 'the self' at all. They are about issues like these:

Personal identity. What does it take for you and me to persist through time? What determines how many people there are at any given time? (Is the number of human people always the same as the number of human animals, for example?) What sort of things are you and I? Are we immaterial substances? Mere 'bundles' of thoughts? Living organisms? Material objects different from but 'constituted by' organisms?

Semantics. What are the semantic properties of first-person pronouns such as 'I'? How and to what do they refer, if they refer at all? What distinguishes first-person beliefs such as my belief that I have brown eyes from third-person beliefs such as the belief that Eric Olson has brown eyes? Does this difference involve irreducibly subjective facts?

Philosophy of mind. What is it for one's mental contents to be unified, and to what degree is this ordinarily the case? What, if anything, causes this unity? To what extent are we aware of what goes on in our minds? What is self-consciousness, and how does it relate to consciousness in general?

Moral psychology. What is it that one cares about most, that one identifies with in the sense of regarding its flourishing as a large part of one's own well-being? What makes a project, belief, value, pattern of behaviour, or personality trait autonomous or authentic, fully one's own, and not merely the result of our upbringing or peer pressure? How do these issues connect with moral responsibility?

Cognitive psychology. What is involved in forms of reflexive conduct such as knowing one's own mind, in the sense of having settled, consistent and realistic intentions? Or knowing one's own capacities and propensities, in the sense of being able to judge realistically what one can do and is likely to do? Or recognizing one's standing as one agent among others and seeing one's desires in relation to those of others? Or being in command of oneself, in the sense of being able to match one's conduct to one's intentions? How do these reflexive abilities relate to one another? How are they acquired? What happens when they are absent? How does one's mental picture of oneself relate to the way one really is? How does one acquire that distinctiveness that makes one different from others?

Epistemology. What are the varieties of first-person knowledge? How do we get knowledge of our own psychological states? Is it something like sense perception? What kinds of first-person knowledge are immune to error through misidentification? What is the nature and extent of proprioception and other forms of first-person knowledge of one's physical properties?

And so on.

You might think that these, and others like them, are the very 'problems of the self' whose existence I have denied. I grant that they are not completely unrelated. When you pick up a book whose title includes the free-standing noun 'self', you have at least some idea of what it will be about. (It won't be about cookery or geology.) But we shouldn't make too much of this. These problems have even less in common than the various accounts of what a self is discussed earlier. If they did have some idea in common, then once again we ought to be able to use that idea to explain what everyone means by 'self'. Yet no one has been able to do this.

Moreover, all of these problems can be put without using the word 'self', as the way I put them shows. *All* of the intelligible content of what are called problems of the self can be captured in this way. If we had answers to all of these questions, there would be no further 'problem of the self' remaining to be solved. There is nothing left over that can be expressed only in terms of words like 'self'. One of the unfortunate consequences of using the word 'self' in doing philosophy is that it encourages us to look for entities that we have no other reason to believe in. Once we have accounted for people, their mental features, their relation to those human animals we call their bodies, and so on, we think we need to say something about 'the self' as well. There is no good reason to think so.

Or so I claim. Of course, merely putting a number of so-called problems of the self in other terms doesn't show that the term 'self' is superfluous. I may have overlooked legitimate problems or questions that can be put only in terms of the free-standing noun 'self' or some equivalent term. In that case I should have to retract my claim that there is no legitimate problem of the self — though the problem so revealed is unlikely to be the problem commonly thought to bear that name.

But if the word 'self' really has no agreed meaning, and leads us into troubles we could otherwise avoid, and if we can easily get on with our legimate philosophical inquiries without it, there can be no reason, other than tradition, to continue to speak of the self.[4]

References

Abelson, Raziel (1977), *Persons: A study in philosophical psychology* (London: Macmillan).
Alston, William P. (1977), 'Self-intervention and the structure of motivation', in *The Self: Psychological and philosophical perspectives*, ed. Theodore Mischel (Oxford: Blackwell).
Ayer, A.J. (1946), *Language, Truth and Logic*, 2nd. ed. (New York: Dover).

[4]   For helpful comments on earlier versions of this chapter I thank Shaun Gallagher, Hugh Mellor and two referees for the *Journal of Consciousness Studies.*

Bermúdez, José (1997). 'Reduction and the self', *Journal of Consciousness Studies*, **4** (5–6), pp. 459–66.
Berofsky, Bernard (1995), *Liberation From Self: A theory of personal autonomy* (Cambridge: Cambridge University Press).
Blackburn, Simon (1994), *Dictionary of Philosophy* (Oxford: Oxford University Press).
Bradley, F.H. (1893), *Appearance and Reality* (London: Allen and Unwin).
Broad, C.D. (1925), *The Mind and its Place in Nature* (London: Routledge and Kegan Paul).
Brooks, D.H.M. (1994), *The Unity of the Mind* (London: St. Martins).
Campbell, C.A. (1957), *On Selfhood and Godhood* (London: Allen and Unwin).
Dennett, Daniel C. (1991), *Consciousness Explained* (Boston, MA: Little, Brown).
Flanagan, Owen (1996), *Self Expressions: Mind, morals, and the meaning of life* (New York: Oxford University Press).
Flew, Antony (1949), 'Selves', *Mind*, **63**, pp. 355–8.
Flew, Antony (1993), 'People themselves, and/or their selves?', *Philosophy*, **68**, pp. 546–8.
Gregory, Richard (1981), *Mind in Science* (Harmondsworth: Penguin).
Hamlyn, D.W. (1984), *Metaphysics* (Cambridge: Cambridge University Press).
Harré, Rom (1984), *Personal Being: A theory for personal psychology* (Cambridge, MA: Harvard University Press).
Harré, Rom (1987), 'Persons and selves', in *Persons and Personality: A contemporary inquiry*, ed. A. Peacocke and G. Gillet (Oxford: Blackwell).
Hume, David (1978), *A Treatise on Human Nature* (Oxford: Clarendon Press; original work published in 1739).
James, William (1905), *The Principles of Psychology*, Vol. 1. (London: Macmillan; original work published in 1890).
Jung, C.G. (1968), *The Archetypes and the Collective Unconscious*, 2nd. ed. (London: Routledge).
Kenny, Anthony (1988). *The Self* (Milwaukee, WI: Marquette University Press).
Lowe, E.J. (1996), *Subjects of Experience* (Cambridge: Cambridge University Press).
McCall, Catherine (1990), *Concepts of Person: An analysis of concepts of person, self and human being* (Aldershot, UK: Avebury).
Marx, Melvin and Hillix, W. (1973), *Systems Theories in Psychology* (New York: McGraw Hill).
Mellor, D.H. (1991), *Matters of Metaphysics* (Cambridge: Cambridge University Press).
Minsky, Marvin (1985), *The Society of Mind* (New York: Simon and Schuster).
Nagel, Thomas (1986), *The View from Nowhere* (New York: Oxford University Press).
Rée, Jonathan (1974), *Descartes* (London: Allen Lane).
Rogers, Carl R. (1951), *Client-centered Therapy* (Boston, MA: Houghton).
Solomon, Robert (1988), *Continental Philosophy Since 1750: The rise and fall of the self* (Oxford: Oxford University Press).
Strawson, Galen (1997), '"The self"', *Journal of Consciousness Studies* 4 (5–6), pp. 405–28. Reprinted in this volume, pp. 1–24.
Toulmin, Stephen E. (1977), 'Self-knowledge and knowledge of the "self"', in *The Self: Psychological and philosophical perspectives*, ed. Theodore Mischel (Oxford: Blackwell).
van Inwagen, Peter (1980), 'Philosophers and the words "human body"', in *Time and Cause*, ed. van Inwagen (Dordrecht: Reidel).

John Pickering

The Self Is a Semiotic Process

Introduction

Galen Strawson[1] accepts that the common experience of being a social self is of
something that continues through time. However, he excludes this from what 'the
self' means in a stricter ontological sense. Here I will argue that this experience of self
as enduring can be taken to be ontologically real as well. I will suggest that selfhood
arises from the assimilation of cultural signs by a semiotic process that is a fundamental aspect of nature. I will also consider how the phenomenological encounter with
'the self' is conditioned by prior beliefs and their ethical entailments.

Phenomenology and Its Limitations

A welcome feature of Strawson's chapter is that he takes phenomenology as a necessary starting point for his inquiry. He distances himself from philosophers who have
concluded that 'the self' is merely some sort of error of language (e.g. Kenny, 1998).
To inquire into 'the self', they might say, is mere metaphysical speculation since
careful analysis of how the phrase is used would show that nothing really corresponds
to it. But the actual experience of selfhood is nonetheless convincing despite linguistic analysis, however careful it might be. Therefore, the danger of falling into metaphysics notwithstanding, it seems reasonable to start with the experience rather than
the analysis.

Strawson identifies eight aspects of 'the self' which, in condensed form, are: a
single mental thing that is distinguished, both momentarily and over longer periods of
time, from all other things by virtue of being the subject of experience and the bearer
of agency and personality. These, he claims, would be common to all adults irrespec-
tive of their cultural background. However, not all of the elements of this description
are, in Strawson's view, essential as preconditions for what 'the self' might mean,
ontologically speaking. These more essential preconditions are: a single mental thing
that is momentarily the distinct subject of experience. Of particular interest here is the
distinction between a momentary awareness of the self as a single thing (synchronic
awareness, item 3 in Strawson's list of 8) and a temporally extended awareness of the
same thing (diachronic awareness, item 4). The synchronic sense is what James
called the 'specious present' — the span of awareness in which experiences are uni-

---

[1] All references to 'Strawson' in the current chapter are to Galen Strawson's opening chapter in this
volume (pp. 1–24).

fied. Here James uses 'specious' in the sense of 'appearing to be directly known or experienced'.

Pathological conditions aside, our experience of being a single unified centre of awareness in this sense is compelling. However, the diachronic sense is just as powerful. This is the common experience of passing from one moment of time to the next and from one situation to another whilst maintaining continuous unified identity. This is a precondition of being a social self, that is, a centre of awareness that carries identity and intentionality from one situation to another and which enables persons to participate in the give and take of social life. To be social in the manner of human beings or some of the more advanced apes requires that individuals are recognized as having a consistent identity and that their actions are predictable.

Strawson feels that while the synchronic sense is primordially part of the experience of selfhood, the diachronic sense is not (p. 20). The basis for this is a careful consideration of the singleness and multiplicity of experience. He concludes, more on analytic than on phenomenological grounds it might be noted, that there is no *thing* underlying the experience of mental continuity. To this he adds the phenomenological finding (p. 18) that, when he is alone and thinking, his 'fundamental experience of consciousness is one of repeated returns into consciousness from a state of complete, if momentary, unconsciousness'.

Now under similar conditions my experience is not like this at all. There are jumps and breaks in the *contents* of consciousness certainly, but I find no break in the flow of consciousness itself. This is particularly the case when practising *Vipassana* meditation, which is, in effect, an inquiry into selfhood through the investigation of the contents of consciousness. One tries to pay continual bare attention to what mentally arises but without evaluating it or becoming involved with it. This is difficult, and what usually occurs is that one engages with one's own thoughts or with the sensory impressions that constantly arise and thereby create moments of specious awareness.

However, after much practice, it is occasionally possible to maintain a somewhat greater distance from one's own mental processes than usual, from where its nature becomes a little clearer. For example the passage from one thought to the next, which might have been taken to be the free mental action of 'the self', is recognized as far more habitual than might have been supposed. However, it also appears to me that the process itself is continuous.

My encounter with consciousness then leads me to conclude, in the terms of Strawson's chapter, that item 4, diachronic self-awareness, as well as, or perhaps even in preference to, item 3, synchronic self-awareness, should also be in the list of 'core conditions' to be fulfilled by that to which 'the self' refers.

Things or Processes?

A difficulty with phenomenological inquiry is what to do when the experiences of the same phenomenon are different. The differences in the present case probably arise because the underlying assumptions of the investigators are different. What we experience the self to be will depend in a quite fundamental way on what we believe anything to be. Now, I take processes to be as real as things. I approach the self from the framework of organic process created by Bergson, Bohm and, most fundamentally, Whitehead. Whitehead considered that 'inherent in the very character of what is real is the transition of things' (Whitehead, 1933, p. 116) and that nature consists of 'structures of activity, and the structures are evolved' (p. 135). These structures endure, actively and collectively, creating what Whitehead called the 'continual creative advance' of nature. What we think of as 'things', like material particles, are abstractions from what are actually processes.

Approaching the self from this basis, then, predisposes one to experience it as something that *goes on*, is continuous and is actively self-perpetuating. Strawson is predisposed to a thing-like view of the self because: 'any claim to the effect that a mental self is best thought of as a process rather than an object can be countered by saying that there is no sense in which a mental self is a process in which a rock is not also and equally a process' (p. 23). For the thoroughgoing Whiteheadian a rock is indeed a process, but we treat it as a thing, since it is unproductive to do otherwise. But it seems unproductive to treat selfhood as if it were a thing like a rock since selves and rocks are at such different levels of order. Rocks are not active in their own construction nor do they make the effort to persist; selves do both.

It appears that to take the self as a thing or a process is an option. I prefer the latter since it matches my worldview and my phenomenological encounter with selfhood. Strawson prefers the former because it matches his. But since our worldviews condition our encounters, there is something of an *impasse* here. Going beyond the phenomenological encounter, Strawson also claims that to treat the self as thing-like demonstrates a 'proper understanding of materialism' (p. 23). He distinguishes his materialism from simple reductionism or eliminativism by claiming that the experiential realm, while real, 'just is' physical (pp. 6–7).

This hints at an old project, that of denying the existence of non-material entities such as souls. But, as Strawson notes, contemporary physics, biology and psychology are rich in process-like ideas that show how matter, organic organization and psychological life can all be approached in properly material non-dualistic terms (e.g. Kauffman, 1995; Scott, 1999). On this basis, selves need not to be identified with anything soul-like and Strawson also notes with approval the Buddhist doctrine of *anatta* which takes just this position (p. 20). But care is needed in adopting Buddhist thinking, which in any case offers a number of different notions of selfhood. Perhaps just as significant here would be the Buddhist doctrine of *pattica samupada*, usually translated as 'dependent origination' or 'dependent co-arising', which bears some remarkable similarities to dynamic systems theory (Rosch, 1994; Macy, 1991). It is notable how dynamic systems theory is increasingly used to describe the process which actively balances stability and change during growth and evolution, whether growth is of organisms in general, of human individuals or even of organizations (Van Geert, 1994; Thelen & Smith, 1994; Mingers, 1995).

Pattica samupada describes mental life as bound up with a self-perpetuating cycle of psycho-physical causality, which is one meaning of the symbol of the wheel in Buddhist iconography. Selfhood is bound to this cycle, and the point of the doctrine is to help individuals to see past the merely contingent contents of their personal consciousness to the process underlying it. Buddhism indeed rejects soul-like, notions of selfhood, but what is proposed in its place is a process (Pickering, 1997). Awareness of this process may be intermittent, but the process itself is not.

If treating the self as a thing or a process is an option then a way forward is to ask what is gained by treating it in one way or the other. The answer here will be that the process view corresponds more naturally with what selves do and how they change. Processes develop, allowing new capacities, new identities and new levels of meaning to emerge (Fogel *et al.*, 1997, p. 4). But while the content of the process may change, the process persists. The self is just such a process and we can understand it, in semiotic terms, as something that has emerged, or evolved.

Semiotics and Selfhood

To ask what 'the self' *is*, ontologically speaking, is a metaphysical question, and Strawson's view is that: 'metaphysics must wait on phenomenology' (p. 1). But phenomenological inquiry is into what consciousness *is*, or what the contents of consciousness *are*. Perhaps then, phenomenology and metaphysics cannot be so easily separated, and we will have to take them forward together to ask how selfhood has come into existence, which is after all what makes phenomenological inquiry possible.

Both animals and humans are conscious, but only humans become selves. This is the more remarkable since animals are self-aware to a degree (Savage-Rumbaugh & Lewin, 1994; Parker *et al.*, 1994), primates are highly socially aware (de Waal, 1996) and some types of self knowledge are as available to animals as they are to people — at least two of the five types distinguished by Neisser (1988), which will be discussed below.

The key to human selfhood is the capacity to symbolize. Symbols condition experience and turn processes into things. Including selfhood — as Mead pointed out, once the actions of others and of the self are internalized in symbolic form, the basis for self-awareness is created. Human selfhood depends on the human form of consciousness being conditioned by the symbols that are assimilated from the cultural milieu. However, consciousness *qua* awareness existed prior to the appearance of this milieu and arose along with the evolution of all living beings. The phrase 'along with' could mean a range of things. At the dismissive end would be Thomas Huxley's famously trenchant view that consciousness is no more necessary to the workings of organisms than the whistle is to a steam engine (Huxley, 1893, ch. 5). At the other extreme might be Teilhard de Chardin's vision of consciousness as participating in a transcendental unfolding of the universe towards a pre-ordained point (Chardin, 1959).

As a middle way between these extremes I will take it that consciousness is not merely contingently associated with organisms but that it is functional in the sense that many psychologists have proposed (e.g. Mandler, 1985; Humphrey, 1983). Moreover, it is bound up with the exploratory action that, in Piaget's phrase, is 'the motor of evolution' (Piaget, 1979) and is therefore present in organisms to the extent that they are able to make discriminative choices between actions (Greenfield, 1995; Reber, 1997). This is akin to Bergson's sense of consciousness as a link between memory and choice: 'the hyphen that joins what has been to what will be' (e.g. Bergson, 1921). In the broadest Whiteheadian sense, consciousness is a fundamental aspect of reality, at all levels. It participates in the continual creative advance that, in bringing the past into the present, opens up a space of possibilities from which choice makes a bridge to the future. But what is this space of possibilities? What is the process itself? And what has all this got to do with selfhood?

Since the key to human selfhood is the capacity to use symbols, answers here can be framed in the language of semiotics. The space of possibilities is not, not immediately at least, that of material structures or even of physically realized actions, although these are eventually the result. The space is one of signs, of internal dialogue, interpretation and evaluation of both what has happened and what might happen. The process, in Mead's terms, is one of symbolic interaction, both within the self and between the self and the sign-world it inhabits. It is this process, and in particular its inner structure, that is unique to human mental life and which provides the basis for human self-awareness. In brief, 'the self' is a semiotic process.

Here 'semiotic' is used in Peirce's three-valued sense of the relationship between sign–interpretant–signified rather than in Sassure's two valued sense of the relationship between signifier–signified. The latter usage is perhaps more common to European semioticians, like Eco or Barthes, who primarily deal with cultural signifiers. The former is more characteristic of pragmatists such as Peirce, James, Cooley, Mead and Dewey, who pay more attention to the internal process of signification. It is this process on which human selfhood depends. Indeed, Wiley has recently brought together Peirce and Mead to produce an account of what he calls 'The Semiotic Self' (Wiley, 1994). This account captures very well the Bergsonian notion of consciousness above, but adds to it what is required in order to cover the human experience of being a mental self that persists over time.

Wiley begins from Peirce's fundamental triad of the sign, interpretant and object. The sign is something that can stand for something else. The object is what it stands for: the signified. The interpretant is a process that derives the object from the sign. So, to illustrate, take a pattern of marks on paper which is encountered on a particular occasion of reading. The pattern itself is the sign. The interpretant is the process that begins with activity on the retina, continues with the retrieval of information from the internal lexicon and ends with the integration of this information with the flow of the reading process. The object is the meaning, for a reader on a particular occasion, of this information.

Signification looked at in this way is a process. The interpretant encounters the sign and the object is produced. This process, in the human case, involves components both inside and outside the individual. Mead suggested that the internalization of this process creates the human sense of self. What is internalized initially derives from the actions and gestures of human social interaction. At later stages in the development of the individual cultural symbols such as speech and writing also become important.

Wiley brings together Peirce's and Mead's ideas into a semiotic account of the self as a process of internal dialogue between components of the self which he terms 'me', 'I' and 'you'. The 'me' is the past. It is that which a person knows of their history: names, relationships, memories, habits, tastes, possessions and so on. The 'you' is the future. It is the person referred to when one thinks to oneself: 'you need to get going or you'll miss the bus', whether or not it is in these actual words, or even whether it is in words at all. The 'I' is the present. It is the experiential centre of choice and of reflexive awareness, the point at which experiences are added to the episodic history.

Selfhood is a process of interchange:

> The self on this view is a constant process of self-interpretation, as the present self interprets the past self to the future self . . . the I and the you interpret the me in order to give direction to the you. Semiotically the I-present functions as a sign, the me-past as an object and the you future as the interpretant. As the self moves down the time-line its

semiotic process is constantly transformed, with a past interpretant becoming a present sign and then a future object (Wiley, 1994, p. 14).

As these components of the self interact and exchange identities, the process moves from situation to situation. This internal cycle is continuous circulation of signifiers. For adults they will be words for the most part, though not exclusively. Prior to the development of speech the signifiers will be the actions and gestures which precede language (Lock *et al.*, 1989). As the human being develops the signifiers increasingly reflect linguistic and cultural patterns. It is in this more familiar linguistic sense that infants become selves by acquiring the means to reflect on themselves.

Selfhood involves self-interpretation and self-direction. As the individual develops, the basis on which these processes occur will change but the process itself remains fundamentally the same. This is the continuity of selfhood. Research on the interaction between infants and caregivers shows rich patterns of social interchange which require an active centre of agency on both sides (e.g. Fogel & Branco, 1997; Trevarthen, 1993; Tomasello, 1993). In this case one side of the interaction, the self-aware adult, might be able to reflect on themselves and their participation in the interaction while the other side, the infant, cannot. However, the process in the infant, in its semiotic essentials, prefigures that of the adult. It is a process of transaction within the network of social relations in which people participate. Through being enriched and made reflexive by language it is internalized and gradually transforms into the adult process by the assimilation of cultural signifiers. This, as Mead pointed out, makes 'the self' an object of thought, transforming the aware infant into the self-aware adult. Something like this transformation remains at the heart of contemporary views of how selfhood emerges within infant–adult interaction (e.g. Butterworth, 1998; Stern, 1993; Hobson, 1993; Bowlby, 1969).

Selfhood is thus a process that emerges from social interaction and is sustained by cultural signifiers and practices. But the process itself exists prior to culture. Semiosis is a fundamental aspect of the way the living world works.

Signs of Life

The process that supports human selfhood is, in its adult form, a cultural-semiotic one (Smolka *et al.*, 1997). However, its origins are biological (e.g. Sebeok & Umiker-Sebeok, 1992; Uexküll, 1982). This semiotic interpretation of biology is set out by Hoffmeyer who suggests that organic relations are based on meaning (Hoffmeyer, 1996). He combines Peirce and the *Umwelt* theory of Jacob von Uexküll to show how the interaction, exchange and development that underlie biological order are fundamentally semiotic processes.

Hoffmeyer's interpretation extends from the more obvious cases, such as communication between animals, to cases where things as fundamental as the actual organization of matter are involved. For example, in considering embryogenesis, he suggests that we should not regard genetic material as an explicit code but rather as a sign which, if made available to an appropriate interpretant (the egg and other relevant structures) produces the object, in this case the embryo. DNA is not a blueprint, since the same DNA can be interpreted in different ways, as happens in organisms like the locusts and alligators where the same genetic material produces different adult forms depending on circumstances.

Hoffmeyer develops Peirce's view of semiosis as a universal medium of causality and a way of moving beyond a picture of the world as governed by physical necessity (e.g. Hoopes, 1991, page 9). Peirce claimed that:

> Thought is not necessarily connected with a brain. It appears in the work of bees, crystals and throughout the purely physical world. . . . Not only is thought in the organic world, but it develops there. . . . But as there cannot be a General without Instances embodying it, so there cannot be thought without signs (Peirce, 1906, p. 497).

Peirce treats the tendency of nature to follow patterns, even though they may seem deterministic, as more like interpretative habits. These habits are so highly prescribed at the physical level, that we refer to them as 'laws'. But as we pass from physical through biological towards psychological levels of organization, habits move away from ineluctable physical laws and towards organic flexibility, eventually arriving at human self-awareness and freedom to choose. In this sense, evolution from physical through biological to cultural levels of organization can be seen as a process of semiotic enrichment, the concentration of a primordial sentience in proportion to the degree of evolved order.

This enrichment enhances the transactions between organisms and their surroundings. When animals perceive patterns in their surrounding and use them to guide what they do, they are not only responding to stimuli but also interpreting signs. This semiotic coupling of perception and action is the product of both phylogenetic and ontogenetic learning. Both species and individual animals learn to notice what their surroundings offer and to use what they learn in the service of action. This is what James Gibson called 'affordance' in his theory of direct perception (Gibson, 1979), a term for which he proposed an interesting ontological status:

> I mean by it something that refers to both the environment and the animal in a way that no other term does. It implies the complementarity of animal and environment (p. 173).

> An affordance is neither an objective nor a subjective property; or it is both if you like. An affordance cuts across the dichotomy of subjective–objective and helps us understand its inadequacy. It is both physical and psychical, yet neither. An affordance points both ways, to the environment and to the observer (p. 129).

Affordance, the directly perceivable meaning of the environment, is in these terms inherently attached to action. It implies a mutualist ontology in which stable relations between co-evolved things is taken as being as real as the things themselves (Still and Good, 1998). In Peirce's terms, affordance is a sign for which the organism acts as interpretant to produce action in a given situation as the object. Thus organisms do not merely respond to stimuli, but act on the basis of meaning. This identification of affordance with meaning echoes David Bohm's (1985; 1988; 1990) claim that meaning is the fundamental nature of organic action. The reason is the co-evolution of physical, biological and psycho-social levels of organization:

> Most of the material environment . . . can be described as the somatic result of the meanings that material objects have had for human beings over the ages. These meanings fundamentally affect our actions towards nature and the action of nature back on us . . . some of the simpler kinds . . . are just reflexes that are built into the nervous system, or instincts that reflect the accumulated experience of a species . . . With higher animals this operation of meaning becomes more evident and in man it is possible to develop conscious awareness, and meaning is then most central and vital (Bohm, 1985, p. 79).

Bohm's usage of 'meaning', like Gibson's observation that 'affordance points both ways' above, brackets human selfhood (Bohm, 1985, p. 79). On the one hand, when humans perceive objects and events, we describe it as discovering what they 'mean' to the perceiver. On the other hand, when human beings voluntarily act on the world, we also describe that as carrying out what we 'mean' to do. In the human case this bi-directionality of 'meaning' has been hugely amplified by culture, the accumulated products of human action. Affordance has thereby become primarily social (Costall, 1995) and the social is fundamentally a semiotic system (Lotman, 1990; Elias, 1991).

But, as Hoffmeyer shows, human meaning is not thereby isolated or *sui generis*. Quite the reverse in fact, it is a recent manifestation of a semiotic process that has been part of evolution at all stages. For example Manfred Eigen, in discussing the origins of life, remarks that: 'The transition from inanimate to living structures took place with the increasing ability to wield information in a quasi-intelligent way. . . . The genotype, the information contained in the nucleic acids, develops phenotypic semantics' (Eigen, 1992, p. 125). If this acquisition by matter of the capacity to mean something marks the start of evolution, self-awareness is what marks the stage to which it has come. This, along with language is what has made the semiotic processes available to itself.

As Hoffmeyer puts it: 'This world has always meant something. It just did not know it' (p. 146). Now, with the evolution of self-awareness, it knows it, or rather, we know it. In Wiley's sense, human self-awareness is an aspect of a semiotic processes which continually produces itself. In much the same sense as Maturana and Varela represent an organism as a self-producing material process (Maturana & Varela, 1987) so I am proposing here that human selfhood is a self-producing semiotic process. Moreover, the process has developed an almost unique capacity for reflexivity. The next section discusses how this capacity both permits inquiry into the nature of the self but obscures it at the same time.

Ecological Psychology

Human beings are so immersed in cultural signification that it is almost impossible to experience the world apart from it. People live amid signs somewhat as fish live in water, although the relationship is more active and reciprocal. As the Soviet semiotician Yuri Lotman puts it: 'Thought is within us but we are within thought; just as language is something engendered by our minds and directly dependent on the mechanisms of the brain, and we are within language. And unless we were immersed in language, our brain could not engender it (and vice versa: if our brain were not capable of generating language, we would not be immersed in it)' (Lotman, 1990, p. 273). Accordingly how we experience selfhood will be conditioned by our social identities and, more impersonally, by our implicit assumptions about the physical nature of the world and the place of mental life in it.

The assumption being made here is that the self is a semiotic process that emerges within a web of relationships. The process has biological origins but in the human case is strongly influenced by the world of cultural meaning and this influence grows as selfhood takes shape. Just how soon this influence starts is an open question, but recent research indicates that experience may have its effects earlier in development than previously thought. Edelman suggests that environmental influences may play an early role in the development of the brain (Edelman, 1992). Connectionist models of brain development have fundamentally altered our notion of 'innateness' in ways that mean that the very functional anatomy of the brain may reflect sensory interaction with the environment (Elman *et al.*, 1996). Consequently, the distinction between innate and learned factors is now approached in a far more dynamic and interactive manner (Johnston *et al.*, 1991; Johnston and Morton, 1991). Studies of transnatal sensory capacities suggest that this may effect the developmental process from its very beginnings (DeCasper & Spence, 1986; Gallagher, 1996; Gallagher & Meltzoff, 1996; Van der Meer et al., 1995; van Geert, 1994; Thelen & Smith, 1994).

Thus, the neurological basis of selfhood also emerges from a process of interaction with the environment and is incorporated into the various levels of organization, physical, biological and psychological that eventually comprise the semiotic basis of selfhood. Selfhood is bound to a body, although it is not merely physical and is bound to a flow of organic action although it is not merely psychic. This shifts the emphasis from internal components of the self process towards the relationships between the individual and the environment, that is, to what we can call the ecology of selfhood.

Starting from an ecological position, Neisser has proposed that selfhood has five components, or, as he puts it, that there are five varieties of self-knowledge (Neisser, 1988). These five varieties of knowledge are: ecological, interpersonal, remembered, private and conceptual. Little more will be said here about the last three varieties, which primarily depend on adult use of memory, reasoning and language. Ecological and interpersonal knowledge, by contrast, depend on perception and action that are present in the earliest stages of development and persist throughout life. Ecological knowledge, following James Gibson, is based on the directly perceivable dynamic structure of the sensory array. This specifies a point of view, a trajectory of a centre of awareness and reveals the immediate sensory consequences of actions. Taken together, this comprises an unambiguous structured body of experience which directly discloses the existence of an individual human or animal perceiver at a particular point in space and time. As James Gibson put it: 'To perceive the world is to co-perceive oneself' (Gibson, 1993, p. 25).

External physical conditions and the active perceptual exploration of them provide what Neisser calls the ecological self and what Eleanor Gibson calls 'the rock bottom essential self that collects information about the world and interacts with it.' (Gibson, 1993, p. 41). It is the experiential entailment of embodiment and enaction. Any organism that is able to act, that has a body substantial enough to maintain a particular position in space and which has sensory organs of sufficient power to give a spatially organized response to the ambient array of energy surrounding it has, thereby, the sensory basis for recognizing that it is an individual distinct from the world around it.

Interpersonal knowledge is closely related to ecological knowledge but in addition reflects what are, especially for the infant, probably the most important components of human perceptual ecology, namely, other human beings. Converging lines of research show how the initiation of the self process intimately depends on early social give and take. In the subtle patterns of interaction with caregivers the human infant engages in highly structured social interchange (Fogel, 1993; Murray & Trevarthen, 1985). From this interchange there emerges the awareness of the self as perceivable by others (Hobson, 1993). Human beings seem both cognitively (Johnston *et al.*,

1991) and emotionally (Bowlby, 1969; Stern, 1993) predisposed to achieve self awareness through discovering how their actions are reflected in the actions of others.

Considered together, the ecological and the interpersonal types of self-knowledge emphasize once again that the sense of mental self emerges from a history of interaction. This interaction occurs, dialectically, between a growing centre of psychological resources and an environment to which those resources are adapted. The process of growth is initiated by innate tendencies towards active exploration of physical and social affordances. What grows is not a static or finalized structure but a dynamic set of relationships which persist through being enacted. In short, what develops in human development is a process.

In this genetic account, the origins of selfhood are in ecological relations and cannot in any realistic sense be considered apart from them. Although internal symbolic conditions are the most salient aspect of the adult experience of selfhood, external conditions must, in a very fundamental sense, also be present in what is experienced internally. On a short time-scale external conditions give content and direction to internal processes as the human being encounters and responds to the environment. But in the longer developmental perspective, external conditions have a more enduring and formative role. They bring the internal process into existence and give it structure and historical identity. Although the semiotic self described by Wiley rests on an internal symbolic interchange, the contents of the interchange reflect a history of external circumstances. The participants in the interchange themselves derive from the internalization of external conditions.

Thus, although the process of selfhood involves internal events, these cannot be isolated from the larger external system which they reflect. Internal symbols may come to dominate in the human case, but they derive from and reflect a larger pattern of organic action. This pattern, as Hoffmeyer shows, is not originally symbolic in the cultural sense. Rather, it consists of mutually evolved processes of signification carried in the constant circulation of matter, energy and meaning in biological systems. Within this circulation, smaller dynamic sub-processes of meaning arise. Here 'meaning' is used in Bohm's sense of the input–output boundaries of the self.

As an analogy, consider how smaller dynamic processes are produced and then maintain themselves for a while within the flow of a larger fluid body. These may be distinguished from it by being called 'eddies', 'tornadoes' or 'vortices'. In a like manner, what we call 'selves' are self-producing semiotics that are produced by the larger flow of meaning, like a 'whirlwind in a turbulent nature' as Prigogine and Stengers put it (1984, p. 301).

Now, eddies appear and disappear depending on the larger fluid flow and on the emergent properties of the eddies themselves. But, clearly, selves are more active in promoting their own existence than fluid swirls. Human selfhood depends to a far greater extent on emergent properties, the most obvious of these being the capacity to use symbols. But this too, as Lotman points out, is closely bound up with the symbolic systems of human culture, which in turn has come into being within the broader field of semiotic processes. This emphasizes once again the need for an ecological and genetic understanding of selfhood as process-like.

The symbolic resources of culture may make the self process available for reflection, but much of it is initiated prior to any cultural system for describing it. In the very act of encountering the world, which in the human case means encountering a culturally structured and highly social world, the fundamental vehicle for the self process is created. This encounter is developmentally and phylogenetically primary, as Neisser points out (1993, p. vii). In the human case, culture influences this encounter from very early stages and provides an experiential variety of self-knowledge on which later cultural structures can rest.

If, in Strawson's terms, the experiential 'just is' physical, then this process of encountering the world, which begins in experiential self-knowledge and continues into the realms of cultural signification, has a strong claim to ontological significance. The self is something that arises and persists through action. Its basic components are in the directly perceivable self-specification that that action produces in the sensory field. From this it develops via the world of social exchange towards the reflexive worlds of language and cultural symbols. It is a self-organizing process comprising a perceiver, an environment to be perceived and a process that connects the two in a cycle of perception and action.

Thoughts about the self — that is, symbolically mediated descriptions of the self — eventually participate in this process. They are not, however, an especially privileged or distinctive part of it, although their privacy may make them appear to be so. It is perhaps significant that Strawson identifies the origin of the sense of mental self in childhood with 'the early realization of the fact that one's thoughts are unobservable by others, the experience of the profound sense in which one is alone in one's head . . .' These insights, he suggests, are 'among the deepest facts about the character of human life, and found the sense of the mental self' (Strawson, p. 3).

Now I proposed that there is an aspect of selfhood that is deeper yet, although it may be more difficult to become aware of it. Thoughts are very real to be sure, but they arise and are born along within a process that precedes thought. This process is quite different from being alone in one's head. In it, inner and outer meaning arise together in a process of mutually evolved interchange. This means that selfhood and its environmental support are primordially interdependent.

The self is a process that persists by virtue of interaction within the world. The world created by language and other cultural artefacts influences this interaction from the earliest stages. It is very difficult to resist the lure of the symbolic, and we are so apt to think in cultural categories that it can easily obscure the precultural origins of human selfhood. However, selfhood is not to be exclusively identified with reflexive thought, although it is a unique characteristic of the human case. The foundations of selfhood, both ontogenetically and phylogenetically speaking, precede reflexive awareness.

This suggests that the sense of mental self has two elements that are marginalized in Strawson's account. These are process and interdependence. That the self is a process follows from the fact that selfhood arises from consciousness which, in Bergson's sense, is the process of continual choosing. Choice is the one-way bridge between past and future, between memory and action, it is a sign of participation in what Whitehead called the continual creative advance of nature. This is the primordial process-like ground from which thing-like abstractions may be made. Consciousness participates in this process in various ways depending on the form of life of which it is part. The uniquely reflexive human form of consciousness, created by cultural signifiers, gives rise to the sense of mental self. It also makes it possible to abstract sections from the process and hence make them appear thing-like. These have particularly compelling phenomenological presence, but compelling or not, selfhood remains essentially a process.

This process, in line with Sperry's view of consciousness, is an emergent aspect of the activity of the system comprising the body, nervous system of an organism and that portion of the environment with which the organism interacts (e.g. Sperry, 1985; 1994). Consciousness, and hence the capacity for selfhood, is present to different degrees depending on complexity of that interaction which in turn depends on the level of biological and psychological organization (e.g. Reber, 1997; Greenfield, 1995). The unity and continuity of consciousness depends upon fields of active information that link one state or configuration of the world to the next, emphasizing its process nature (Bohm & Hiley, 1993, pp. 381–90; Goodwin, 1989; Beckermann, 1995; Pickering, 1995).

The process standpoint presented here will, like any presuppositions about the nature of the mind and world, condition the phenomenological encounter with selfhood. But scientific practices and findings need to be interpreted hermeneutically (Griffin, 1988; Rorty, 1979). This is as true for phenomenological investigation as for any other type. Looked at in this light, the process-like and thing-like views of selfhood are not just options in an ontological debate. What we assume to be the value, that is the ethical entailments of one or the other view, are also likely subtly to condition what we experience 'the self' to be.

Selfhood, Actions and Consequences

That people have enduring identity to which legal and moral responsibility can be attached is a fundamental assumption in social science, law and theology. If philosophical inquiry suggests that this enduring notion of 'the self' is an error, where does that leave us? One option might be to set philosophy aside and to treat people as subject to the ethical entailments, rights, duties etc., that are commonly ascribed to them.

But philosophical inquiry, happily, resists being set aside as much as it resists ethical neutrality. Moreover, the deeper the inquiry, the more significant it eventually appears to be. Spinoza's inquiry into the effort of all things to persist in their own being has come to have a central place in contemporary environmental debates (e.g. Naess, 1995). Heidegger's effort to go past the lure of language and recover a presocratic encounter with a world of intrinsic value now figures centrally in discussions of the consequences of industrialisation (e.g. Zimmerman, 1981). Philosophical inquiry is intrinsically ethical and inquiry into the nature of the self will be no exception.

What then might be at stake, ethically speaking, when deciding whether to consider the self as a thing or as a process? My judgement is that it is an engagement with environmental issues. This connection is well brought out by Macy (1991), who, from the premise:

> To be interdependent and reciprocally affecting is to be a process. In this fluid state of affairs, the self is no exception (p. 107),

draws the conclusion:

> If the self is a pattern . . . or transformations of energy and information arising in interaction with the surrounding world, its nature is profoundly participatory in that of other

beings ... then this involves an extension of constructs of self-interest, in which the needs of other beings begin to emerge as covalent with one's own (p. 194).

This touches directly on environmental issues. There is presently deep concern at the loss of diversity of habitats and species. Since human action is often a major cause of the loss itself, people may also feel that it is a human responsibility to do something about it. But such feelings depend on the degree to which people feel threatened and on how strongly they feel they belong to the natural order and have a duty of care towards it. Now to treat selfhood as a thing helps us to see it apart from rather than a part of the natural world. It emphasizes the isolation of the human from the natural by diminishing the sense of experiential continuity, on which empathetic connection with the world depends. This is the internalized culmination of the 'disenchantment of the world' that Max Weber saw as an experiential consequence of the shift from medieval to modern world views. Not only is the world divested of intrinsic meaning but the self which encounters that world is also diminished.

However, shifts in the opposite direction, towards re-enchantment as it were, have been clear for decades now (e.g. Griffin, 1988). These seek to repair a fundamental dislocation of our sense of belonging to the natural order (Matthews, 1991). Similar moves towards ecological contextualization in other areas of science have, as Michel Serres puts it, 'to do with the recent passage from local to global and with our renewed relationship to the world, which was long ago our master and of late our slave, always and in all cases our host, and now our symbiont' (Serres, 1995, p. 38).

It is in the spirit of this move against alienation that I offer a view of human self-hood as a process intimately connected to the environment. The process involves the circulation of meaning, both within Wiley's 'semiotic self' and within the larger bio-semiotic arena described by Hoffmeyer. In the human case this circulation is amplified by cultural practices transmitted in language and in other symbolic systems. The emergence of selfhood depends on interaction with the human environment which, even as encountered by infants, is fundamentally shaped by human action. The artefacts of human culture and the practices that go with them, are assimilated as the human individual develops. The psychological (Sinha, 1988) and even the physical (Ingold, 1996a) characteristics of the individuals that emerge as this assimilation develops are thus significantly shaped by culture. Indeed, Ingold shows how the technological practices of cultures comprise a transmission system that runs in parallel with and indeed cannot be properly distinguished from the genetic transmission system (Ingold, 1996b). As human beings develop within an environment shaped by human action, so the cultural scaffolding for selfhood is encountered anew and new individuals, new self-processes, appear within it.

A loop is closed here, which is the basis of human self-awareness. The human environment being a cultural product, it requires the human brain for its development and preservation. But much of the structure, and hence the operation, of the human brain likewise requires the cultural environment for its development and preservation. In which case human beings are 'self-made', produced by a looped system of semiotic circulation (Kingdon, 1993). This is the looped semiotic relationship noted by Lotman in which language and thought are both part of the brain and the brain is a part of language and thought.

If important aspects of selfhood, especially those aspects of which human being are reflexively aware, emerge from looped cultural semiotic processes, then they are to that extent fictions. As Becker set out so clearly in *The Birth and Death of Meaning*:

> The world of human aspiration is largely fictitious, and if we do not understand this we understand nothing about man. It is a largely symbolic creation by an ego-controlled animal that permits action in a psychological world, a symbolic-behavioural world removed from the boundness of the present moment . . . (Becker, 1971, p. 139).

Here Becker's position has been amplified by treating selfhood as a process of semiotic interaction between individuals and their surroundings. Note, however, that what is fictional is the content of the process; the process is real. It is the ground for the diachronic sense of selfhood. This ground persists over time since the effects of action persist over time. For example, the flow of consciousness will be accompanied by neurochemical events in the brain. These, neurochemical dynamics being what they are, will create patterns of activity that persist from one moment to the next. States of strong emotion, for example, will persist by virtue of the hormonal changes to the body and brain that they cause. Action itself preserves and extends the intentional structure of psychological states. An act of attention results in orientation movements of the body and sense organs which necessarily extend over time. Indeed, any movement once initiated will tend to persist because of the mass-spring nature of the human body.

Beyond the body, objects acted on will draw out further and related action, as when a car, once set in motion, then requires steering, or a wall that is being painted indicates, by the extent of the painted area, how far a goal has been achieved. Other people are special objects in this sense, as Neisser and Gibson both point out. They are uniquely responsive to human acts and this response draws out, modulates and makes of those acts a continuous flowing process. Not only people, but the physical structure of the world, especially the world of cultural artefacts, is also apt to create selfhood. This would be to say that organisms and the environment itself, being co-evolved, anticipate each other, as Maturana and Varela proposed with their notion of structural coupling (Maturana & Varela, 1987, p. 75).

In short, the self is a process with components both inside the individual and in the environment around the individual. This underlines the difficulty of ascribing consciousness to events within the head alone (e.g. Velmans, 1990). The persistent identity of the social self reflects its coupling to a culturally structured milieu. Becker shows the symbols we use to name the self process are fictions, but the process itself is real.

The process view advanced is a response to James Hillman's claim that 'There is only one core issue for all psychology. Where is the "me"? Where does the "me" begin? Where does the "me" stop? Where does the "other" begin?' (Hillman, 1995, p. xvii). Hillman wants a radical revision of how we view the self within the natural order. Like Serres, he shows that we are moving into a time of re-connection, where the human phenomenon is being re-positioned with respect to a world seen as process. The rapid socio-cultural evolution of human beings has produced layers of symbolic order that obscure the place of the human phenomenon in the natural order. Growing concern about the effects of human action on that order has prompted the effort to discern that place anew.

A process view of selfhood answers Hillman's questions by stressing the inter-relatedness of selfhood and the world around it, thus opposing strong self–other boundaries. A thing-like view by contrast draws attention to the internal world, leaving people 'alone in their heads'. Such isolation might lessen concern for the effects of human action on the environment. It is worth noting that Buddhism, in which can be found something like the process view of the self that has been sketched here, comes to a very strong ethical position on the responsibility each person has for their actions. In recommending that we 'tread lightly' upon the earth, many environmental writers start from a Buddhist consideration of the self (Aitken, 1985, page 232):

> That the self advances and confirms the myriad things is called delusion.
> That the myriad things advance and confirm the self is enlightenment.

The point here is that selves are causally continuous with the processes occurring around them. Boundaries between self and other are socially real enough, but these are reified within human symbolic culture. Exploring these boundaries and trying to go beyond them is to change the encounter between self and world. We move away from an encounter between an isolated centre of awareness, a separate thing in a world of separate objects. Instead, self and world are participants in a flow of meaning, making it easier to integrate selfhood into a wider framework of political action and responsibility, as Wiley points out (1994, p. 223). A change, in Martin Buber's terms, from the encounter between 'I' and 'It' to that between 'I' and 'Thou' (Neisser 1993, p. 13; Gustafson, 1993).

The view of selfhood that I have set out here is bound to have been conditioned by what I *wish* the self to be. I advance it because it helps me to maintain certain political and ethical positions that I favour. This is likely to condition my observations of the mind and, hence, the self. But such conditioning is intrinsic to the condition of knowing anything. Perhaps the best that may be expected, then, is to become as aware as possible of this conditioning, thus to see past it.

A great *Vipassana* teacher said that the essence of the practice is 'being the knowing' (Sumedho, 1992, p. 54). He might well agree, in the spirit of *anatta*, that there is no self. There is, however, in the spirit of *pattica samupada*, a persistent process which is the bearer of selfhood. Perhaps the feeling of being thing-like is an illusion caused by naming. Attending to the process itself discloses a very different reality.

References

Aitken, R. (1985), 'Gandhi, Dogen & deep ecology', in *Deep Ecology*, ed. W. Devall & G. Sessions (Salt Lake City, UT: Peregrine Books).

Becker, E. (1971), *The Birth & Death of Meaning: An Interdisciplinary Perspective on the Problem of Man*, second edition (New York: Free Press).

Beckermann, A. (1995), 'Visual information processing and phenomenal consciousness', in *Conscious Experience*, ed. T. Metzinger (Thorverton, UK: Imprint Academic / Paderborn: Schöningh).

Bergson, H. (1921), 'Life and consciousness', Huxley Lecture delivered at Birmingham University on May 24th. 1911, in *Mind-Energy*, H. Bergson, trans. H. Wildon Carr (New York: Holt Publishing Co., 1921) and in *From Sentience to Symbols*, ed. J. Pickering & M. Skinner (Brighton: Harvester, 1990).

Bohm, D. (1987), *Unfolding Meaning* (London: Routledge).

Bohm, D. (1988) , 'Postmodern science and a postmodern world', in *The Reenchantment of Science: Postmodern Proposals*, ed. D.R. Griffin (Albany, NY: State University of New York Press).

Bohm, D. (1990), 'A new theory of the relationship between mind and matter', *Philosophical Psychology*, **3** (2), pp. 271–86.

Bohm, D. & Hiley, B. (1993), *The Undivided Universe* (London: Routledge).

Bowlby, J. (1969), *Attachment & Loss* (London: Hogarth Press).

Butterworth, G. (1998), 'A developmental-ecological perspective on Strawson's "The self"', *Journal of Consciousness Studies*, **5** (2), pp. 132–40.

Costall, A. (1995), 'Socializing affordances', *Theory & Psychology*, **5** (4), pp. 467–81.

de Chardin, P.T. (1959), *The Phenomenon of Man* (London: Collins).

de Waal, F. (1996), *Good Natured: The Origins of Right and Wrong in Humans and Other Animals* (Cambridge, MA: Harvard University Press).

DeCasper, A. & Spence, M. (1986), 'Prenatal maternal speech influences newborns' perception of speech sounds', *Infant Behavior and Development*, **9**, pp. 137–50.

Edelman, G. (1992), *Bright Air, Brilliant Fire* (New York: Basic Books).

Eigen, M. (1992), *Steps Towards Life: a Perspective on Evolution*, trans. P. Wooley (London: Oxford University Press).

Elias, N. (1991), *The Symbol Theory*, ed. with an introduction by Richard Kilminster (London: Sage).

Elman, J. *et al.* (1996), *Rethinkng Innateness: A Connectionist Perspective On Development* (London: MIT Press).

Fogel, A. (1993), *Developing Through Relationships : Origins of Communication, Self, and Culture* (London: Harvester Wheatsheaf).

Fogel, A. & Branco, A. (1997), 'Metacommunication as a source of indeterminism in relationship development', in Fogel *et al.* (1997).

Fogel, A., Lyra, M. & Valsiner, J. (ed. 1997), *Dynamics and Indeterminism in Developmental and Social Processes* (Hillsdale, NJ: Erlbaum).

Gallagher, S. (1996), 'The moral significance of primitive self-consciousness', *Ethics*, **107** (1), pp. 129–40.

Gallagher, S. & Meltzoff. A. (1996), 'The earliest sense of self and others: Merleau-Ponty and recent developmental studies', *Philosophical Psychology*, **9** (2), pp. 213–36.

Gibson, E. (1993), 'Ontogenesis of the perceived self', in Neisser (1993).

Gibson, J. (1979), *The Ecological Approach to Visual Percepetion* (Boston, MA: Houghton Mifflin).

Goodwin, B. (1989) , 'Organisms and minds as dynamic forms', *Leonardo*, **22** (1), pp. 27–31.

Greenfield, S. (1995), *Journey To the Centers of the Mind: Toward a Science of Consciousness* (London: Freeman).

Griffin, D.R. (1988), 'Introduction', in *The Reenchantment of Science: Postmodern Proposals*, ed. D.R. Griffin (Albany, NY: State University of New York Press).

Gustafson, J. (1993), 'G.H. Mead and Martin Buber on the interpersonal self', in Neisser (1993).

Hillman, J. (1995), 'A psyche the size of the earth', in *Ecopsychology: Restoring the Earth, Healing the Mind*, ed. T. Roszak, M. Gomes & A. Kanner (San Francisco, CA: Sierra Club Books).

Hobson, R. (1993), 'Through feeling and sight to self and symbol', in Neisser (1993).

Hoffmeyer, J. (1996), *Signs of Meaning in the Universe*, trans. B. Haveland (Bloomington, IN: University of Indiana Press).

Hoopes, J. (1991), *Peirce on Signs* (London: University of North Carolina Press).

Humphrey, N. (1983), 'Nature's psychologists', in *Consciousness Regained*, ed. N. Humphrey (Oxford: Oxford University Press).

Huxley, T. (1893), *Methods and Results* (London: Macmillan).

Ingold, T. (1996a), 'The history and evolution of bodily skills', *Ecological Psychology*, **8** (2), pp. 171–82.

Ingold, T. (1996b), 'A comment on the distinction between the material and the social', *Ecological Psychology*, **8** (2), pp. 183–7.

Johnston, M. *et al.* (1991), 'Newborn's preferential tracking of face-like stimuli and it's subsequent decline', *Cognition*, **40** (1), pp. 1–19.

Johnston, M. & Morton, J. (1991), *Biology and Cognitive Development : The Case of Face Recognition* (Oxford: Blackwell).

Kauffman,S. (1995), *At Home in the Universe: The search for laws of self-organization and complexity* (London: Viking).

Kenny, A. (1998), *The Self* (Marquette: Marquette University Press).

Kingdon, J. (1993), *Self-made Man and His Undoing* (London: Simon & Schuster).

Lock, A., Service, V., Brito, A. and Chandler, P. (1989), 'The social structuring of infant cognition', in *Infant Development*, ed. A. Slater & G. Bremner (London: Erlbaum).

Lotman, Y. (1990), *Universe of the Mind: A Semiotic Theory of Culture* (London: I.B. Taurus).

Macy, J. (1991), *Mutual Causality in Buddhism and General Systems Theory* (Albany, NY: SUNY Press).

Mandler, G. (1985), *Cognitive Psychology* (Hillsdale, NJ: Erlbaum).

Matthews, F. (1991), *The Ecological Self* (London: Routledge).

Maturana, H. & Varela, F. (1987), *The Tree of Knowledge: The Biological Roots of Human Understanding* (Boston, MA: Shambala).

Mingers, J. (1995), *Self-Producing Systems:Implications and Applications of Autopoiesis* (London: Plenum).

Murray, L. & Trevarthen, C. (1985), 'The infant in mother-infant communication', *Journal of Child Language*, **13**, pp. 15–29.

Naess, A. (1995), 'The apron diagram and self-realisation: An ecological approach to being in the world', in *The Deep Ecology Movement: An Introductory Anthology*, ed. A. Drengson and Y. Inoue (Berkeley, CA: North Atlantic Books).

Neisser, U. (1988), 'Five kinds of self knowledge', *Philosophical Psychology*, 1 (1), pp. 35–59.

Neisser, U. (ed. 1993), *The Perceived Self* (London: Cambridge University Press).

Parker, A. *et al.* (1994), *Self-Awareness in Animals & Humans* (Cambridge: Cambridge University Press).

Peirce, C. (1906), 'Prolegomena to an apology for pragmatism', *The Monist*, 16, pp. 492–7.

Piaget, J. (1979), *Behaviour and Evolution*, trans. Donald Nicholson-Smith (London: Routledge and Kegan Paul).

Pickering, J. (1995), 'Active information in physics and in ecological psychology', in *New Directions in Cognitive Science*, ed. P. Pykkänen and Pylkkö (Helsinki: Hakapaino).

Pickering, J. (1997), 'Selfhood is a process', in *The Authority of Experience*, ed. J. Pickering (London: Curzon Press).

Prigogine, I. & Stengers, I. (1984), *Order Out of Chaos* (London: Flamingo).

Reber, A. (1997), 'Caterpillars and consciousness', *Philosophical Psychology*, 10 (4), pp. 437–49.

Rorty, R. (1979), *Philosophy and the Mirror of Nature* (Princeton: Princeton University Press).

Rosch, E. (1994), 'Is causality circular? Event structure in folk psychology, cognitive science and Buddhist logic', *Journal of Consciousness Studies*, 1 (1), pp. 50–61.

Savage-Rumbaugh, E. & Lewin, R. (1994), *Kanzi: The ape at the brink of the human mind* (London: Doubleday).

Scott, A. (1999), *Nonlinear Science: Emergence and the dynamics of coherent structures* (Oxford: Oxford University Press).

Sebeok, T. & Umiker-Sebeok, J. (1992), *Biosemiotics: The Semiotic Web* (Berlin: Mouton de Gruyter).

Serres, M. (1995), *The Natural Contract* (Ann Arbour: University of Michigan Press).

Sinha, C. (1988), *Language & Representation* (Brighton: Harvester).

Smolka, A, Góes, M. & Pino, A. (1997), '(In)determinacy and the semiotic constitution of subjectivity', in Fogel *et al.* (1997).

Sperry, R. (1985) , *Science and Moral Priority: Merging Mind, Brain and Human Values* (New York: Praeger).

Sperry, R. (1994), 'Consciousness and the cognitive revolution: A true worldview paradigm shift', *Anthropology of Consciousness*, 5 (3), pp. 3–7.

Stern, D. (1993), 'The role of feeling for an interpersonal self', in Neisser (1993).

Still, A. & Good, J. (1998), 'The ontology of mutualism', *Ecological Psychology*, 10 (1), pp. 39–63.

Strawson, G. (1997), ' "The self" ', *Journal of Consciousness Studies*, 4 (5–6), pp. 405–28. Reprinted in this volume, pp. 1–24.

Sumedho, A. (1992), *Cittaviveka: Teachings From the Silent Mind* (Hemel Hempstead: Amaravati Publications).

Thelen, E. & Smith, E. (1994), *A Dynamic Systems Approach to the Development of Cognition and Action* (London : MIT Press).

Tomasello, M. (1993), 'On the interpersonal origins of self-concept', in Neisser (1993).

Trevarthen, C. (1993), 'The self born in intersubjectivity: The psychology of an infant communicating', in Neisser (1993).

Uexküll, T. von (1982), 'Jacob von Uexküll's theory of meaning', *Semiotica*, 42, pp. 1–88.

Van der Meer, A. *et al.* (1995), 'The functional significance of arm movements in neonates', *Science*, 267, pp. 693–5.

Van Geert, P. (1994), *Dynamic Systems of Development: Change Between Complexity & Chaos* (London: Harvester).

Varela, F., Thompson, E. and Rosch, E. (1991), *The Embodied Mind* (Boston, MA: MIT Press).

Velmans, M. (1990), 'Consciousness, the brain and the physical world', *Philosophical Psychology*, 3 (1), pp. 77–99.

Whitehead, A. (1933), *Science and the Modern World* (Cambridge: Cambridge University Press).

Wiley, N. (1994), *The Semiotic Self* (Cambridge: Polity Press).

Zimmerman, M. (1981), 'Beyond "Humanism": Heidegger's understanding of technology', in *Heidegger: The man and the thinker*, ed. Thomas Sheehan (Chicago, IL: Precedent Publishing).

Part 2

Cognitive and neuroscientific models

V. S. Ramachandran and William Hirstein

Three Laws of Qualia

What Neurology Tells Us about the Biological Functions of Consciousness, Qualia and the Self

Neurological syndromes in which consciousness seems to malfunction, such as temporal lobe epilepsy, visual scotomas, Charles Bonnet syndrome, and synesthesia offer valuable clues about the normal functions of consciousness and 'qualia'. An investigation into these syndromes reveals, we argue, that qualia are different from other brain states in that they possess three functional characteristics, which we state in the form of 'three laws of qualia' based on a loose analogy with Newton's three laws of classical mechanics. First, they are irrevocable: I cannot simply decide to start seeing the sunset as green, or feel pain as if it were an itch; second, qualia do not always produce the same behaviour: given a set of qualia, we can choose from a potentially infinite set of possible behaviours to execute; and third, qualia endure in short-term memory, as opposed to non-conscious brain states involved in the on-line guidance of behaviour in real time. We suggest that qualia have evolved these and other attributes (e.g. they are 'filled in') because of their role in facilitating non-automatic, decision-based action. We also suggest that the apparent epistemic barrier to knowing what qualia another person is experiencing can be overcome simply by using a 'bridge' of neurons; and we offer a hypothesis about the relation between qualia and one's sense of self.

Introduction

Nothing is more chastening to human vanity than the realization that the richness of our mental life — all our thoughts, feelings, emotions, even what we regard as our intimate self — arises exclusively from the activity of little wisps of protoplasm in the brain. The distinction between mind and body, illusion and reality, substance and spirit has been a major preoccupation of both eastern and western thought for millenia (Aristotle, 1961; Descartes, 1986; Fodor, 1975; Dennett, 1978; Searle, 1980). And although these distinctions have generated an endless number of debates among philosophers, little of lasting value seems to have emerged. As Sutherland (1989) has said, 'Consciousness is a subject on which much has been written but little is known.' Our primary goal in this paper is to forge a fresh approach to the problem, by treating it not as a philosophical, logical, or conceptual issue, but rather as an empirical problem. Our focus is on showing the *form* a scientific theory of consciousness might take, something which is independent of the truth of all of the more detailed claims and suggestions we will make. Our essay will consist of two sections. In part one, which philosophers can profitably skip, we describe some thought experiments to illustrate the problem of qualia, since in our experience, most neuroscientists and even most psychologists dispute the very existence of the problem. In part two, we offer numerous examples from neurology and perceptual psychology that, together with a new theoretical framework we offer, will help eventually solve the problem of consciousness. Our theory should be seen as complementing rather than replacing a host of other recent biological approaches to the problem such as those of Crick and Koch (1992), Pat Churchland (1986), Baars (1988), Edelman (1989), Llinás (Llinás & Paré, 1991), Plum (Plum & Posner, 1980), Bogen (1995a,b), Gazzaniga (1993), Humphrey (1993), Damasio (1994) and Kinsbourne (1995).

Much of our discussion will focus on the notion of qualia. It is our contention, however, that the problem of the self and the problem of qualia are really just two sides of the same coin. In part, our argument is that the self is indeed something that arises from brain activity of a certain kind and in certain brain areas, and that this activity is also closely tied to functions related to qualia. In contrast to the idea that qualia are private, subjective, and unsharable properties belonging exclusively to a private self, we suggest two thought experiments to show that there is no insurmountable barrier to sharing them. We then explore various issues involved in how qualia are generated and managed by neural systems, and by examining pathological and experimental cases that clarify these functions, we propose at the same time to clarify the nature of the self. We conclude that the self, or the thing that leads to the illusion of a unitary, enduring self, is neither a separable subject of consciousness nor a homunculus, but it can be mapped anatomically to limbic and other associated structures which 'drive' frontal executive processes. This view contrasts sharply with the widely held view that consciousness is based on the frontal processes themselves.

Part I: Epistemological Prolegomena

The qualia problem

We will illustrate the problem of giving an account of conscious experience, referred to by philosophers as the problem of *qualia*,[1] with two simple thought experiments.

First, imagine that you are a future superscientist with a complete[2] knowledge of the workings of the brain. Unfortunately however, you are a rod monochromat: you don't have any cone receptors in your eyes to delineate the different colours; you are colour blind. For the sake of argument, however, let's also assume that the central processing mechanisms for colour in your brain are intact, they haven't withered away. This is not an illogical assumption; it's fanciful perhaps, but not illogical.

You, the superscientist, study the brain of X, a normal colour perceiver, as he verbally identifies colours he is shown. You've become very interested in this curious

---

[1] Qualia are the 'raw feels' of conscious experience: the painfulness of pain, the redness of red. Qualia give human conscious experience the particular character that it has. For instance, imagine a red square; that conscious experience has (at least) two qualia: a colour quale, responsible for your sensation of redness, and a shape quale, responsible for the square appearance of the imagined object.

[2] The assumption that anyone could ever have a complete knowledge of the brain is questionable, depending of course on what one means by 'complete'. All we mean by this is that the super-scientist's theory has no obvious explanatory gaps in it, and that it allows him to predict behaviour with an extremely high level of accuracy. This example borrows liberally from Jackson's ingenious 'Mary' scenario (Jackson, 1986).

phenomenon people call colour; they look at objects and describe them as red or green or blue, but the objects often all look like shades of grey to you. You point a spectrometer at the surface of one of the objects and it says that light with a wavelength of 600nm is emanating from the object, but you have no idea what *colour* this might correspond to, or indeed what people mean when they say 'colour'. Intrigued, you study the pigments of the eye and so on and eventually you come up with a complete description of the laws of wavelength processing. Your theory allows you to trace out the entire sequence of neural events starting from the receptors all the way into the brain until you monitor the neural activity that generates the word 'red'. Now, once you have completely understood the laws of colour vision (or more strictly, the laws of wavelength processing), and you are able to predict correctly which colour word X will utter when you present him with a certain light stimulus, *you have no reason to doubt the completeness of your account.*

One day you come up with a complete diagram. You show it to X and say, 'This is what's going on in your brain.' To which he replies, 'Sure that's what's going on, but I see red, where is the red in this diagram?' 'What *is* that?' you ask. 'That's part of the actual experience of the colour which it seems I can never convey to you,' he says. This is the alleged epistemological barrier which you confront in trying to understand X's experience. Our thought experiment is also useful in that it allows us to put forward a clear *definition* of qualia: they are that aspect of X's brain state that seems to make your scientific description incomplete *from X's point of view.*

Second, imagine there is a species of electric fish in the Amazon which is very intelligent, in fact as intelligent and sophisticated as us. But it has something we lack: the ability to sense electrical fields, using special organs in its skin. You can study the neurophysiology of this fish and figure out how the electrical organs on the sides of its body transduce electrical current, how this is conveyed to the brain, what part of the brain analyses this information, how it uses this information to dodge predators, find prey, and so on. If the electric fish could talk, however, it would say, 'Fine, but you'll never know what it *feels* like to sense electricity.' These two thought experiments exemplify the problem of qualia. They are vaguely similar to Nagel's 'what is it like to be a bat' problem ('You'll never know what it's like to *be* a bat', Nagel, 1974), except that our examples are better, for the following reason. In the Nagel version, it's the whole bat experience, the qualia produced by the bat's radar system *along with everything else* in its conscious mental life, which Nagel claims we cannot know. But this misses the point. Most people would agree that you couldn't know what it is like to *be* a bat unless you are a bat — after all, the bat's mental life is so completely, utterly different. In our electric fish example, however, we are deliberately introducing a creature which is similar to us in every respect, except that it has *one* type of qualia that we lack. And the point is, even though your description of the fish is complete scientifically, it will always be missing something, namely the actual experience of electrical qualia. This seems to suggest that there is an epistemological barrier between us and the fish. What we have said so far isn't new, except that we have come up with a thought experiment which very clearly states the problem of why qualia are thought to be essentially private. It also makes it clear that the problem of qualia is not necessarily a scientific problem, because your *scientific* description is complete. It's just that the description is incomplete epistemologically because the experience of electric current is something you never will know.

This is what philosophers have assumed for centuries, that there is a barrier which you simply cannot get across. But is this really true? We think not; it's not as though there is this great vertical divide in nature between mind and matter, substance and spirit. We will argue that this barrier is only apparent,[3] and that it arises due to *language*. In fact, this barrier is the same barrier that emerges when there is *any translation*. The language of nerve impulses (which neurons use to communicate among themselves) is one language; a spoken natural language such as English is a different language. The problem is that X can tell you about his qualia only by using an intermediate, spoken language (when he says, 'Yes but there's still the experience of red which you are missing'), and the experience itself is lost in the translation. You are just looking at a bunch of neurons and how they're firing and how they're responding when X says 'red', but what X is calling the subjective sensation of qualia is supposed to be private forever and ever. We would argue, however, that it's only private *so long as he uses spoken language* as an intermediary. If you, the colour blind superscientist, avoid that and take a cable made of neurons from X's area V4 (Zeki, 1993) and connect it directly to the same area in your brain, then perhaps you'll see colour after all (recall that the higher-level visual processing structures are intact in your brain). The connection has to bypass your eyes, since you don't have the right cone cells, and go straight to the neurons in your brain *without an intermediate translation*. When X says 'red', it doesn't make any sense to you, because 'red' is a translation, and you don't understand colour language, because you never had the relevant physiology and training which would allow you to understand it. But if you skip the translation and use a cable of neurons, so that the nerve impulses themselves go directly to the area, then perhaps you'll say, 'Oh my God, I see what you mean.' The possibility of this demolishes the philosophers' argument (Kripke, 1980; Searle, 1980; 1992) that there is a barrier which is insurmountable. Notice that the same point applies to any instruments I might use to detect activity in your brain — the instrument's output is a sort of translation of the events it is actually detecting.

In principle, then, you *can* experience another creature's qualia, for example even the electric fish's. It's not inconceivable that you could find out what that part of the brain is doing in the fish and that you could somehow graft it onto the relevant parts of your brain with all the associated connections, and that you would then start experiencing the fish's electrical qualia.[4] Now we could get into the philosophical debate over whether you need to be a *fish* to experience it, or whether as a human being you could experience it, but we've already made the distinction between the entire experience of being a fish, and the qualia themselves, which are just part of that experience. Thus qualia are not the private property of a particular self; other selves can experience a creature's qualia.

---

[3] This idea emerged in discussions with F.H.C. Crick. See the acknowledgements at the end of this paper.

[4] The same thought experiment can be performed within a single subject. Anaesthetize the corpus callosum of a human at birth, expose the right brain alone to colours, then at age twenty-one de-anaesthetize the callosum, in order to see if the left brain then begins to experience the right brain's qualia.

What are qualia for?

So far we've talked about the epistemology of qualia and we've suggested that there is no barrier, and that you can in principle experience someone else's qualia by using a bridge of neurons — this problem may simply be a translation problem. We now want to address the question of why qualia evolved. Many others have raised this question before and come up with a wide range of different answers. One could also put on the sceptic's hat and say, 'Since you have already shown that the scientific description is complete without qualia, it is meaningless to ask why it evolved or what its function is. Doing so would entail converting a closed system — the physical universe — into an open one, and that would be a logical fallacy.' We could, however, temporarily set aside scepticism[5] and instead search for a reply to the questions 'Why did qualia emerge in evolution; or, why did some brain events come to have qualia?' Is it a particular *style* of information processing that produces qualia, or is it a particular neural locus, or perhaps only some types of neurons are associated with qualia? Crick (1996; Crick & Koch, 1992) has made the ingenious suggestion that the neural locus of qualia is a set of neurons in the lower layers of the primary sensory areas, because these are the ones that project to the frontal lobes. His approach has galvanized the entire scientific community (cf. Horgan, 1994) and has served as a catalyst for those seeking biological explanations for qualia. Similarly, people have suggested that it's the synchronization of oscillations that leads to conscious awareness (Paré & Llinás, 1995; Purpura & Schiff, 1997). This seems somewhat *ad hoc*, however — why this rather than something else? These approaches are attractive, if only for one reason — that reductionism has been the single most successful strategy in science.

---

[5] Epiphenomenalism cannot be rejected on strictly logical grounds and can be defended on grounds of parsimony; we may not *need* qualia for a complete description of the way the brain works. Since when, however, has Occam's razor been useful for scientific *discovery*? In fact, all of science begins with a bold conjecture of what *might* be true. The discovery of relativity, for example, was not the product of applying Occam's razor to our knowledge of the universe at that time. The discovery came from rejecting Occam's razor and asking what if some deeper generalization were true, which is not required by the available data, but which makes unexpected predictions (which later turn out to be parsimonious after all). It is ironic that most scientific discoveries come not from brandishing (or sharpening) Occam's razor — despite the view to the contrary held by the great majority of scientists and philosophers — but from generating seemingly *ad hoc* and ontologically promiscuous conjectures which are *not* called for by the current data.

For the same reason, we are sympathetic to Penrose's (1994) view that some hitherto undiscovered physical principles may be required for explaining conscious experience. Although his particular theory may turn out to be wrong (see, e.g., Grush and Churchland, 1995), we would argue that his idea should not be rejected on the grounds of parsimony alone. The fact that nothing we know about consciousness demands the postulation of new physical principles is not a sound argument against seeking such principles.

In general then, although philosophical scepticism may be logically justified (just as we cannot prove with complete logical certainty that we are not dreaming, or that your 'red' is not my 'green'), it is misplaced in the scientific realm, where one is concerned most often with what is likely to be true 'beyond reasonable doubt' — rather than with absolute certainty. Unless we set aside such misgivings one is trapped in an intellectual stalemate. In this respect we are in complete agreement with Crick and Koch (1992).

Another famous sceptic's challenge (also known as Molyneux's question) is 'Can a person blind from birth ever experience visual qualia?' Although this is often posed as a conceptual dilemma, we believe that it can be solved empirically by simply delivering localized transcranial magnetic stimulation to visuotopic V1 in blind human volunteers, to see whether it evokes completely novel, yet visuotopically organized visual qualia. (There is a paper by Ramachandran, Cobb & Hirstein, on this topic in preparation.)

Unfortunately however, it is not always easy to know *a priori* what the appropriate *level* of reductionism is for a given scientific problem (Churchland, 1996). Elucidation of the role of the double helix in heredity turned out to be the most important scientific discovery in this century (Medawar, 1969), because Crick and Watson had the foresight and genius to realize that the *molecular* level was the appropriate one. Had they chosen the quantum level, they would have failed! In a similar vein, we wouldn't expect an exhaustive description of the molecular structure of a mousetrap to reveal its function. Nor would a parthenogenetic (asexual) Martian scientist understand how the testicles worked by simply studying their structure, *unless* he knew about sex! And yet this is precisely the strategy adopted by the vast majority of neuroscientists trying to understand the functions of the brain.

Part II: The Biological Functions and Neural Basis of Qualia

In this essay we would like to try something different. We will deliberately begin at a 'higher' level of analysis, and use simple introspection as a strategy for elucidating the biological functions of consciousness. Toward this end we will first present some simple demonstrations of the 'filling in' of the natural blind spot of the eye (Ramachandran, 1992) and argue that this can provide some strong hints about the functions of qualia. Following these demonstrations we will examine a number of neurological syndromes in which qualia seem to *malfunction*, which raises the possibility that far from being a holistic property of the entire brain, qualia are indeed associated with the activity of a small subset of neural structures, as suggested by Crick (1994; 1996). We do not claim to have solved the problem of qualia, but at the very least the examples and thought experiments should provide food for thought.

First, consider the well-known example of the blind spot corresponding to the optic disc — the place where the optic nerve exits the back of the eyeball. To demonstrate the blind spot to yourself, shut your right eye and hold Figure 1 about 10 inches away from your face while looking at the small fixation star on the right. Now move the page toward or away from your eye very slowly, and you will find that there is a critical distance at which the spot on the left completely disappears. Notice, however, that when the spot disappears, it does not leave a gap or a dark hole behind in the visual field. Indeed, the entire field looks homogeneous, and the region corresponding to the blind spot is 'filled in' with the same texture as the background. Sir David Brewster, who discovered filling in, believed it was evidence for a benevolent deity (1832): 'The Divine Artificer has not thus left his works imperfect . . . the spot, in place of being black has always the same colour as the ground.' Curiously, Sir David was not troubled by the question of why the Divine Artificer should have created an imperfect eye to begin with!

Now close your right eye and aim the blindspot of your left eye at the middle of your extended finger. The middle of the finger *should* disappear, and yet the finger looks continuous. In other words, the qualia are such that you do not merely *deduce* intellectually that the finger is continuous — 'after all, my blind spot is there' — you literally *see* the missing piece of your finger. A dramatic demonstration of this phenomenon is the following: if you show someone a donut shape so that the donut is 'around' the blind spot, say a yellow donut, and if the inner diameter of the donut is slightly smaller than the blind spot, the donut will look like a complete, homogeneous

Figure 1. The eye's natural blind spot
Close your right eye and fixate the star with your left eye. Slowly move the page back and forth about ten inches from your eye until the dark circle on the left disappears.

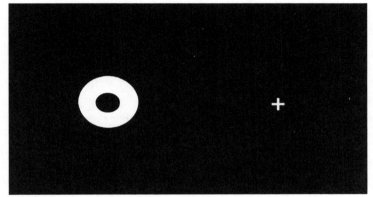

Figure 2a. Filling in
Cover your right eye and fixate your left eye on the small white cross. Move the figure back and forth until your blind spot encompasses the centre of the ring on the left. Visual processes fill in the centre of the ring so that it looks like a solid disc.

Figure 2b. Salience of filled-in objects
Cover you right eye and fixate your left eye on the small white square. Move the figure back and forth until your blind spot encompasses the centre of the ring on the left of the square. The solid filled-in disc will perceptually 'pop out' from the other rings.

disk. In fact, the size of the donut can be such that you're actually seeing three times as much yellow now as you did before (see Figure 2a), which in turn means that your brain actually 'filled in' your blind spot with qualia. The reason we emphasize this is that there are some who have argued you simply ignore the blind spot and don't notice what's going on (Dennett, 1991), so that there really is no filling in. But this can't be right, because if you show someone several rings, one of which alone is concentric with the blind spot, that single one will look like a disc and will actually 'pop out' perceptually (see Figure 2b). How can something you are ignoring pop out at you? This means that not only does the blindspot have qualia associated with it, but that the qualia can provide 'sensory support'and therefore are being filled in preattentively, so to speak.

As we have emphasized in previous papers (Ramachandran, 1993; 1995a,b; Churchland and Ramachandran, 1993) we use the phrase 'filling in' in a somewhat metaphorical sense. We certainly do not wish to imply that there is a pixel-by-pixel rendering of the visual image on some internal neural screen, which would defeat the whole purpose of vision (and would imply a 'Cartesian theatre', an idea which Dennett has brilliantly demolished). We disagree, however, with Dennett's specific claim that there is no 'neural machinery' corresponding to the blind spot. (There is, in fact, a patch of cortex corresponding to each eye's blind spot that receives input from the other eye as well as the region surrounding the blind spot in the same eye; Fiorini *et al.*, 1992; see below.) What we mean by 'filling in' is simply this: that one quite literally sees visual stimuli (e.g. patterns and colours) as arising from a region of the visual field where there is actually no visual input. This is a purely descriptive, theory-neutral definition of filling in and one does not have to invoke — or debunk — homunculi watching screens to accept it. We would argue that the visual system fills in not for the benefit of a homunculus but in order to make some aspects of the information explicit for the next level of processing (Ramachandran, 1993). In the last section we will argue that filling in is just one example of a general coherencing of consciousness, which perceptual systems undertake in order to prepare representations to interact with limbic executive structures, an interaction from which both the experience of qualia and intentionality emerge.

Now consider a related example. Suppose I put one finger in front of another finger and look at the two fingers. Of course I see the occluded finger as continuous. I *know* it's continuous. I *sort of* see it as continuous. But if you ask me, do you *literally see* the missing piece of finger, I would say 'no' — for all I know, someone could have actually sliced two pieces of finger and put them on either side of the finger in front to fool me. I don't literally *see* that missing part.

Compare these two cases, the blind spot and the occluded finger, which are in fact quite similar in that they are both cases where there is missing information which the brain supplies. What is the difference, however? What difference does it make to you, the conscious person, that the representation of the yellow donut now has qualia in the middle and that the representation of the occluded finger part does not? The difference, we suggest, is that *you cannot change your mind* about the yellow in the middle of the donut. In other words, you can't think '*Maybe* it's yellow, oh well, maybe it's pink, maybe it's blue. You can't think 'Well, it's *probably* yellow, but who knows, it may be pink.' No, it's shouting at you 'I am yellow', with an explicit representation of yellowness in its centre. In other words, the filled-in yellow is not revocable, not

Figure 3
The irrevocability of shape qualia

Once you see the dalmation dog in the picture on the left, it is impossible to go back to the state of not seeing it.

changeable by you. In the case of the occluded finger, however, you can think 'there's a high probability that there is a finger there, but some malicious scientist could have pasted two half-fingers on either side of it', or, 'there could be a little Martian sitting there for all I know'. These scenarios are highly improbable, but not inconceivable. Another way, then, to capture the difference between the two types of cases is that I could choose to assume that there is something else behind the occluding finger, but that I cannot do that with the filled-in region of the blind spot.

Thus the crucial difference between a qualia-laden percept and one that doesn't have qualia is that the qualia-laden percept is irrevocable, whereas the one which lacks qualia is flexible; you can choose any one of a number of different 'pretend' inputs using top-down imagery. Once a qualia-laden percept has been created, you're stuck with it. A good example of this is that high-contrast photo of the dalmatian dog (Figure 3). Initially, as you look it, it's all fragments, then suddenly everything clicks and you see the dog, you've got the dog qualia. The next time you see it, there's no way you can avoid it, and *not* see the dog. Indeed, we have recently shown that neurons in the brain have permanently altered their connections once you have seen the dog (Tovee *et al.*, 1996).

Three laws of qualia

We now describe three laws of qualia (with apologies to Sir Isaac Newton) which we hope will serve as guideposts for future inquiry. The examples we have just described demonstrate an important feature of qualia: if something is revocable, it isn't a quale (or has only weak qualia associated with it). To put it less strongly, there is a link between the strength or vividness of a quale and the degree of its irrevocability, i.e., this may be quantitative, rather than a qualitative distinction. However, although something's being irrevocable may be necessary, it is certainly not *sufficient* for the presence of qualia. Why? Well, imagine that I shine a light into the eye of someone who is in a coma. If the coma is not too deep, the patient's pupil will constrict, even though she will have no subjective awareness of any qualia caused by the light. The entire reflex arc is irrevocable, and yet there are no qualia associated with it. You can't change your mind about it, you can't do anything about it, just like you couldn't do anything about the yellow filling in your blind spot in the donut example. So why is it that only the latter has qualia? The key difference, we submit, is that there are no qualia in the case of the pupil's constriction because *there is only one output available*. But in the case of the yellow, even though the representation which was created is irrevocable, *what you can do with the representation is open-ended*; you have the luxury of choice. This is the second important feature of qualia: sensations which are qualia-laden afford the luxury of choice. So now we have identified *two* functional features of qualia: irrevocability on the input side, and flexibility on the output side.

There is a third important feature of qualia. In order to make decisions on the basis of a qualia-laden representation, the representation needs to exist long enough for executive processes to work with it. Your brain needs to hold the representation in an intermediate buffer, in other words, in 'working memory'. Again this condition is not enough in itself, because there could be other reasons why a neural system needs to hold some information in a buffer where qualia are not involved (e.g. spinal cord 'memory'). Typically in these cases, however, there is only one output possible, in which case the second important feature of qualia would be missing, on our scheme. There is some physiological evidence for such a connection between qualia and memory. Goodale has reported a certain type of 'blindsight' patient who can correctly rotate an envelope to post it in a horizontal or a vertical slot, even though he does not consciously perceive the slot's orientation and cannot tell you whether the slot is vertical or horizontal (Milner & Goodale, 1995). But if the room lights are switched off just before he puts the letter in, 'he' forgets the orientation of the slot almost immediately and is unable to get the letter in. This suggests that the unconscious 'dorsal stream' visual system which discerns orientation and affects arm movements accordingly is not only devoid of qualia but also does not have memory; it is the 'ventral stream' visual system that is conscious and has memory. We would maintain that *the reason the qualia-laden ventral system has memory is because it is involved in making choices* based on perceptual representations. In contrast, the system without qualia engages in continuous real-time processing running in a tightly closed loop and consequently doesn't need memory — it is not involved in the making of choices.

This suggests a testable prediction: in patients with blindsight, and in Goodale's visual zombie, if you give the patient a *choice*, the system should go haywire. Not only should it not have short-term memory as Goodale showed, but also it should be incapable of making choices. For example if the person is asked to mail a letter and shown *two* orthogonal slots simultaneously, he should fail, being unable to *choose* between the two (or alternatively, the system might always go for the first one it detects). This is consistent with the Crick-Koch view that the neurons which project to the frontal lobes are the qualia neurons because, obviously, the frontal lobes are important for the *execution* of choices. We would argue, however, that what we think of as the choice itself is really the work of a *limbic executive* system consisting of the amygdala, anterior cingulate cortex, and other areas, and that the frontal lobes are needed only for fully working out the long-range implications and possible alternatives which the decision entails, and for dealing with complications arising as the decision is executed (more on this in the final section).

Let's extend the account to the qualia associated with pain. Say you prick somebody with a pin. It's well known that there are two components: there is an immediate withdrawal, involving no qualia, followed a couple of seconds later by the experience of pain qualia. This dissociation is itself striking evidence for our view because the non-qualia-laden pathway is irrevocable, but has a fixed output (withdrawal) and therefore doesn't have qualia in our scheme. The pain you experience, on the other hand, is irrevocable, and what you do about it is flexible. You can put some medication on it, or you can run away from whatever caused it. This is a nice example because it's a case of the same stimulus producing two different streams of processing, one involving qualia and the other not.

Bistable percepts

Let's take bistable figures; how would our account apply to them? Here, the sensory stimulus can specify two qualia with equal certainty, so the output system can only choose between those two in creating an intermediate-level representation (Figure 4). Once you settle on an interpretation, however, it clicks and if it's revocable it's only in favour of a *single* other percept. You can only see that famous ambiguous figure as a duck or a rabbit, for instance. But when you finally do see it, the *implications* are infinite — this fulfills our criterion about output flexibility. In the spinal cord on the other hand there are neural circuits that display a type of bistability, but the implications are finite. So for qualia to exist you need potentially infinite implications, but a stable, finite, irrevocable representation as a starting point. But if the starting point is revocable, then the representation will not have strong, vivid qualia. Good examples of this are something seen behind an occluder, or imagining that there is a monkey sitting on that chair. These do not have strong qualia, for good reason, because if they did you wouldn't be able to survive long, given the way your cognitive system is structured. As Shakespeare said: 'You cannot cloy the hungry edge of appetite by bare imagination of a feast.' Very fortunate, for otherwise you wouldn't go eat, you would just generate the qualia associated with satiety in your head. In a similar vein, one could argue that a mutant creature that could imagine having orgasms is unlikely to pass on its genes to the next generation. *Therefore (real perceptual) qualia are protected; they are partially insulated from top-down influences.*

Figure 4
Bistable drawings

'Ambiguous figures' such as this one are designed to allow two possible interpretations. Such figures offer a sort of limited revocability: one set of shape qualia is revocable only in favour of the other.

At the same time, however, you occasionally need to run a virtual reality simulation using less vivid qualia generated from memory representations in order to make appropriate decisions in the absence of the objects which normally provoke those qualia. The memories one normally evokes in this case are not fully laden with qualia; they have qualia which are just vivid enough to allow you to run the simulation. If they possessed full-strength qualia, again, that would be dangerous; indeed that's called a hallucination. Presumably that's what happens in temporal lobe seizures; some mechanism has gone awry, and the virtual reality simulation has now become like real sensory input. The simulation loses its revocability and generates pathological qualia.

Why don't these internally generated images, or beliefs for that matter, have strong qualia? We can explain that. Percepts need to have qualia because they are driving ongoing, decision-laden behaviour. You can't afford the luxury of hesitating over the percept itself, however. The stimulus ensemble determines it, and you don't have time to say, 'Maybe it determines something else.' You need to 'plant a flag' and say 'This is it.' Beliefs and internal images on the other hand should not be qualia-laden, because they should not be confused with real perception; you need to be constantly aware of their tentative nature. And by virtue of their tentative status beliefs lack strong qualia — they are indefinitely revocable. So you believe — and you can imagine — that under the table there is a cat because you see a tail sticking out, but there *could* be a pig under the table with a transplanted cat's tail. You must be willing to entertain that hypothesis, however implausible, because every now and then you might be surprised.

What is the computational advantage to making qualia irrevocable? One answer is stability. If you constantly change your mind about qualia, then the number of potential outputs will literally be infinite; there will be nothing constraining your behaviour. At some point you need to say 'this is it' and plant a flag on it, and *it's that planting of the flag that we call qualia*. The perceptual system follows a rationale something like this: given the available information, it is 90% certain that the object perceived is red. Therefore for the sake of argument, I'll assume that it is red and act accordingly, because if I keep saying 'maybe it's not red', I won't be able to take the next step. In other words, if I treated percepts like beliefs, I would be blind. *Qualia are irrevocable in order to eliminate hesitation and to confer certainty to decisions.*

Charles Bonnet syndrome

This system can break down, however. For example, consider the curious neurological disorder known as Charles Bonnet syndrome. Patients with this disorder typically have damage to the retina, to the optic nerve, optic radiations, or sometimes even to area 17, producing blindness in either a large portion or in the entire visual field. But remarkably, instead of seeing nothing, they experience vivid visual hallucinations. Typically these are 'formed' hallucinations rather than abstract patterns; i.e., the patients claim to see little circus animals, or Lilliputian beings walking around. No adequate explanation of the syndrome has been proposed to date, although the hallucinations are sometimes referred to as 'release hallucinations' in the older clinical literature.

We recently had the opportunity to examine two patients with this syndrome, both of whom present certain novel features, which may help to elucidate the neural mechanisms underlying this disorder. These patients had a sharply circumscribed region in the visual field where they were completely blind; i.e., they had a blind spot, or scotoma. The remarkable thing is that their hallucinations are confined entirely to the blind region. For example, patient MB had a left paracentral scotoma, about the size of her palm (held out at arm's length), caused probably by damage to area 17 and the optic radiations, as a result of laser surgery to destroy an arteriovenous malformation. She was of course completely blind in this region, and yet as often as twenty or thirty times a day she would experience the most vivid hallucinations *confined entirely to the blind spot*. Surprisingly, these were static, outline drawings, like cartoon drawings, filled in with colour, but having no depth or motion.

We suggest that the hallucinations associated with Charles Bonnet syndrome arise because of the massive feedback projections (Ramachandran, 1993) that are known to exist from higher cortical areas to visual areas that precede them in the hierarchy; for example from area 17 to the LGN, or from IT and MT to areas 17 and 18 (Zeki, 1978; van Essen, 1979; Churchland *et al.*, 1994). When a normal person imagines something, such as a rose, we usually assume that some sort of activity is evoked in the higher centres such as the temporal lobes, where the memory of this rose is stored in the form of altered synaptic weights (and perhaps new synaptic connections). So when you imagine a rose, one expects activity in the temporal lobes. But there is a great deal of evidence now to suggest that in addition to the expected activity in IT, there is also activity in area 17, as though somehow this information was being projected back onto your 'neural screen' corresponding to area 17 (Cohen *et al.*, 1996; Farah, 1989). It's as though, to enable you to make certain fine spatial discriminations, your brain needs to run a sort of virtual reality simulation, and for some reason this requires the participation of area 17. (In particular, discrimination of topological features of the image, for example, may require that it be represented again in area 17).

However, when a normal person imagines a rose, she does not literally hallucinate a rose; what she experiences is typically a faint, ghostlike impression of one. Why? One possibility is that the normal person, unlike the Charles Bonnet patient, has real visual input coming in from the retina and optic nerve. This is true, by the way, even when the eyes are closed, because there is always spontaneous activity in the retina, which may function to provide a null signal informing the higher centers that there is no rose here, and this prevents her from literally hallucinating the rose. (Indeed, this may be one reason why spontaneous activity in the peripheral receptors and nerves evolved in the first place.) Again, all this is very fortunate, otherwise your mind would be constantly flooded with internally generated hallucinations, and if you begin confusing internal images with reality, you will be quickly led astray.

In the Charles Bonnet patient the visual input is completely missing, therefore the internally generated images which are sent back to V1, or perhaps V2 (areas 17 and 18), assume a degree of vividness and clarity not seen in normal people. This explains why the images are confined entirely to the scotoma, why they are so extremely vivid (one patient told us that the colours 'look more real than real colours'), and why they have the irrevocable quality of genuine, stimulus-evoked qualia. In other words, ordinarily your top-down imagery will produce only weak images because there is competing real visual input (or spontaneous activity), but when the input goes away, then you start confusing your internal images with external reality.

It is not clear why in the case of MB the images lacked depth and motion. One possibility is that for some reason the feedback information arises only from the ventral stream (the IT-V4 pathway), which is concerned primarily with colour and form, and there was no feedback from the dorsal stream and MT which would have conferred the appropriate spatial attributes, such a depth and motion, to the image.

Perhaps a more important general implication of this syndrome which has been overlooked in the past is that it is strong evidence for the idea that vision is not the one-way cascade or flow of information which it is often thought to be. For example, one simple-minded view of vision (Marr, 1982) holds that visual processing is sequential, modular, and hierarchical: each box computes something and sends it to the subsequent box, a model proposed frequently by AI researchers. This is clearly not how human vision works (Edelman, 1989); instead, there seems to be a constant echo-like back-and-forth reverberation between different sensory areas within the visual hierarchy and indeed (as we shall see) even across modalities. To deliberately overstate the case, it's as though when you look at even the simplest visual scene, you generate an endless number of hallucinations and pick the one hallucination which most accurately matches the current input — i.e., the input seems to *select* from an endless number of hallucinations.[6] There may even be several iterations of this going on, involving the massive back-projections — a sort of constant *questioning*, as in a game of twenty questions, until you eventually home in on the closest approximation to reality (a *partially* constrained hallucination of this sort is, of course, the basis of the well-known Rorschach ink blot test). Thus what you finally see is the result of a compromise between top-down processes and bottom-up processes, a very different view from the conventional one in which vision is seen as involving a hierarchical upward march of information; a bucket brigade.

Synesthesia

A second illustration of breakdown in the functions of qualia is provided by the extraordinary phenomenon of synesthesia, where sensations evoked through one modality produce vivid qualia normally associated with another modality. Many of these cases tend to be a bit dubious — the claims of 'seeing' a sound or 'tasting' a colour turn out to be mere metaphors. However, we recently examined a patient who had relatively normal vision up until the age of seven, then suffered progressive deterioration in his sight due to *retinitis pigmentosa*, until finally at the age of forty he became completely blind. After about two or three years, he began experiencing visual hallucinations similar to those experienced by Charles Bonnet patients. For example, he

---

[6] This is analogous to the way in which the immune system works. When I inject you with killed or denatured smallpox virus (antigens), they generate antibodies and lymphocytes that are *specific* to smallpox. It was once believed by medical scientists (and is still believed by many laypeople and philosophers) that upon entering your blood, the smallpox antigens — a protein molecule — *instruct* the formation of specific antibodies by acting as a template. We know now that this view, while intuitively plausible or obvious, is wrong. In fact, your body has antibody-producing cells for *every conceivable antigen*; even 'martian' antigens, so to speak. What the antigenic challenge (smallpox, for example) does is simply to select the appropriate clone of cells causing them to multiply and produce the specific anti-smallpox antibody. This is a useful analogy, but there is of course a difference: the random gene shuffling that leads to a multiplicity of antibodies has already been accomplished in the fetus, and no longer goes on in the adult. In the case of perception, on the other hand, the random combinations are tried out online even as you watch the stimulus.

would see little spots of red light which initially lacked depth, but which coalesced over time to form the clear visual impression of a face, including depth and shading. More interestingly however, this patient began to notice that whenever he palpated objects while negotiating the visual environment, or held an object in his hand, or even just read braille, this would conjure up the most vivid visual images, sometimes in the form of unformed flashes, sometimes a movement or 'pulsation' of pre-existing hallucinations, or sometimes the actual shape of the object he was palpating (e.g. a corner). These images were highly intrusive, and actually interfered with his braille reading and object palpation. We suggest that in this patient, as indeed in normal people, palpating an object evokes visual memories of that object, as a result of a previously established Hebbian association.[7] Of course, when a normal person closes his eyes and palpates a ruler, he doesn't hallucinate a ruler, even though he will typically visualize it. The reason, again, is because of the presence of normal, countermanding visual input in the form of spontaneous activity from the retina and visual pathways. But when this information is removed, as with the Charles Bonnet patient, our patient begins hallucinating. This can be verified by directly recording evoked potentials from his visual cortex while he is palpating objects (Cobb *et al.*, in preparation).

Finally, this line of speculation is also consistent with what we have observed in amputees with phantom limbs. After amputation, many of these patients experience a vivid phantom arm, and while most of them are able to 'move' their phantom, a subset of them find that the phantom is in a fixed position, i.e., their phantom is paralysed. But what would happen if one were to somehow create the visual illusion that the phantom had come back, and could move? To do this, we placed a vertical mirror on the table in front of the patient in the sagittal plane. The patient then puts his normal (say) right hand on the right side of the mirror and 'puts' his phantom left hand on the left side of the mirror. He then looks at the mirror reflection of his right hand, and moves his right hand around until its reflection is exactly superimposed on the felt position of the phantom limb. If he now starts making movements with his right hand, he gets the distinct *visual* illusion that his phantom hand is moving. Remarkably, this also seems to produce vivid sensations seeming to come from joints and muscles in the phantom limb, i.e., the patient experiences a curious form of synesthesia.

Such effects do not occur in normal individuals, supporting our conjecture that the presence of real (somatosensory) input somehow prevents such synesthesia. In a normal person, even though there is a visual impression that their left hand is moving (when they are actually looking at the mirror image of their right hand) this is contradicted by somatic sensations which inform the brain that the left hand is not in fact moving. The fact that this does not happen in the phantom limb patient may imply that the visual signals are causing activation to travel back all the way to the primary

---

[7] A second possibility is 'remapping'. We have previously shown that upon amputation of an arm in a human patient the brain area corresponding to the missing hand gets 'invaded' by sensory input from the face. Consequently, touching the face evokes sensations in the missing phantom hand (Ramachandran *et al.*, 1995).

In a similar vein, when the visual areas — either cortical or subcortical — are deprived of input it is not inconceivable that input from the somatosensory area 'invades' the vacated territory so that touching stimuli begins to evoke visual sensations. The two hypotheses, haptically-induced visual imagery vs 'remapping' can be distinguished by measuring the latency of evoked MEG responses (Cobb *et al.*, in preparation).

somatosensory areas concerned with proprioception. Again, this can be tested using imaging techniques.

Filling in the blind spot

Is there an absolute, qualitative distinction between qualia-laden percepts and those which are not; between perception and conception? Let us illustrate this point with three thought experiments. Consider the obvious phenomenological distinction between the region corresponding to my blind spot, where I can't see anything, and another sort of 'blind spot': the region behind my head, where I also can't see anything. In other words, each of us actually has three blind spots, one in the field of view of each eye, and a third behind our heads, which is much larger. Now, ordinarily you don't walk around experiencing an enormous gap behind your head, and therefore you might be tempted to jump to the conclusion that you are in some sense filling in the gap. But obviously, you don't: there simply is no visual neural representation in the brain corresponding to this area behind your head. You fill it in only in the trite sense that, for example if you are standing in a bathroom with wallpaper in front of you, you assume that the wallpaper continues behind your head. But the important point to emphasize here is, even though you assume (imagine, believe) that there is wallpaper behind your head, you don't literally see it. In other words, any 'filling in' is purely metaphorical and does not fulfill our criterion of being irrevocable. In this fundamental sense there is an important distinction between filling in of the blind spot, and our failure to notice the presence of a big gap behind your head (even though it is the conceptual similarity between these two cases that has misled many psychologists and philosophers to conclude that the eye's blind spot is not filled in). Put very simply, this means that in the case of the blind spot, as we said earlier, you can't change your mind about areas which have been filled in, whereas in the region behind your head, you are free to think, 'In all likelihood there is wallpaper there, but who knows, maybe there is an elephant there.'

It would appear then, that filling in of the blind spot is fundamentally different, both phenomenologically and in terms of what the neurons are doing, from your failure to notice the gap behind your head.[8] But the question remains, is the distinction between what is going on behind your head and the blind spot qualitative or quantitative, and is the dividing line completely arbitrary (cf. 'Is a man bald if he has only three hairs on his head?')? To answer this, let us consider the following thought experiment. Imagine we continue evolving in such a way that our eyes migrate toward the sides of our heads, while at the same time preserving the binocular visual field. The fields of view of the two eyes encroach further and further behind our heads until they are almost touching. At that point let's assume you have a blind spot behind your head (between your eyes) which is identical in size to the blind spot which is in front of you. The question then arises: Would the completion of objects across the

---

[8] Gattass *et al.* (1992) showed that there is a patch of neurons in area 17 corresponding to the blind spot. The neurons in this patch fire when there are two bars on either side of the blind spot, creating an irrevocable representation in area 17. That is about as close as you can get to arguing that there is a neural mechanism for filling in. To argue otherwise is pedantic.

The converse of qualia-laden filling in would be qualia-less 'repression' or inhibition of irrelevant, confusing, or destabilizing information that would otherwise clutter up consciousness and 'distract' executive structures (Ramachandran, 1995b). Analogously, one might leave non-urgent mail sitting in one's mailbox lest it clutter up one's desktop and distract one from more pressing matters.

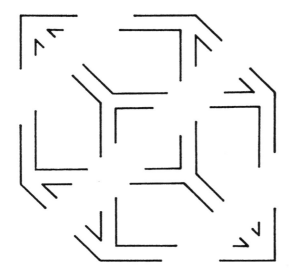

Figure 5
Intermediate case

There is a strong impression that there is a complete cube underneath the three slates, but is this due to genuine filling-in, or to conceptual 'amodal completion'?

(After Kanizsa, 1979, and Bregman, 1981.)

blind spot behind your head be true filling in of qualia, as with the real blind spot, or would it still be conceptual, revocable imagery or guesswork of the kind that you and I experience for the region behind the head? The answer to this question, we suggest, is that there will be a definite point when the images become irrevocable, and when representations are created, or at least recreated and fed back to the early visual areas, and at that point it becomes functionally equivalent to the blind spot. If this account is true, there is indeed a fundamental qualitative change, both in the phenomenology and in the corresponding information-processing strategies in the nervous system that are used to create the representations.

Thus, even though blind-spot completion and completion behind the head can be regarded as two ends of a continuum, evolution has seen fit to partition this continuum in order to adequately 'prepare' the completed data for subsequent processing in the case of blind spot completion. We suspect that the motive behind the partition has to do with balancing the need to reduce the workload of higher-level processes by passing them definite, perspicuous, gap-free representations on the one hand, with the need to avoid error on the other. In the case of the eye's blind spot, the chance that something significant is lurking there is small enough that it pays simply to treat the chance as zero. In the case of the blind area behind my head, however, the odds of something important being there are high enough that it would be dangerous to fill in this area with wallpaper or whatever pattern is in front of the eyes.

The second experiment might again be used to undermine the case for a strong qualitative distinction between qualia-laden percepts and conceptual representations, however. Let us go back to the example of the finger occluded by another finger. We argued there that the region behind the occluder is at least partially revocable. However, consider the following intermediate case: a cat behind a picket fence. Or even better, a cube hidden by three slats (Figure 5). It is very hard not to see a cube in this figure. Here you have an intermediate case where the representation seems to be filled in and yet not filled in. However, the existence of such intermediate cases should not forbid us from arguing that there may be separate neural mechanisms at the two ends of the spectrum.

It is very unlikely that the visual system has evolved dedicated neural machinery for the specific purpose of filling in the blind spot. What we are seeing here, instead, may be a manifestation of a very general visual process — one that we may call surface interpolation (Ramachandran, 1992; 1993; 1995b). It is very likely that the process may have much in common with — and may involve some of the same neural machinery as — the sort of filling in one sees in the example of the occluded finger (which Kanizsa (1979) termed 'amodal completion'). There are nevertheless important differences between completion across the blind spot and amodal completion (e.g. the occluded finger example), which implies that, although the two processes are similar, they are not identical (contrary to the views of Durgin *et al.*, 1995). The most important difference, of course, is that filling in across the blind spot is modal, whereas filling in behind occluders is amodal. What this means is simply that in one case you literally see the filled-in sections, in the other case you don't. (This distinction will not appeal to behaviourists but should be obvious to anyone who has carefully observed such stimuli and is not wholly devoid of common sense.)

A second difference between genuine filling in and conceptual or amodal completion is that the corner of a square or the arc of a circle will get completed amodally behind an occluder but will not get completed modally across the blind spot (Ramachandran, 1992; 1993). In fact, subjects sometimes report the corner or arc being completed amodally behind an 'imaginary' occluder corresponding to the blind spot; the occluder is usually reported to resemble an opaque smudged 'cloud'.

In spite of the differences, it is very likely that the two completion processes share some neural activity *up to a certain stage* in visual processing. Evidence for this comes from the work of Gattass *et al.* (1992). They found that neurons in the patch of area 17 corresponding to (say) the left eye's blind spot respond not only to the right eye (as expected) but also to two collinear line segments lying on either side of the left eye's blind spot — as though they were filling in this segment. Intriguingly, they also noted that similar effects could sometimes be seen in the rest of the normal visual field if a small occluder was used instead of the blind spot. The implication is that, at least in the early stages of processing, both modal completion across the blind spot (i.e. the filling in of qualia) and amodal completion behind occluders may be based on similar neural mechanisms. But if so, why is there such a compelling phenomenological difference between the two? One possibility is that the presence of the occluder itself might be signalled by a different set of neurons which vetoes the modal completion process. This makes good functional sense, for if you were to hallucinate something in front of the occluder you might be tempted to grab it!

Consider a third example: the peculiar mental diplopia or 'multilayer' qualia associated with locating objects in a mirror. Assume you're looking into the rearview mirror of your car, when suddenly you see the reflection of a red car zooming towards you from behind. You accelerate rather than brake, even though, optically, the image is in front of you and expanding. It is as if, when you look at the rearview mirror, you are dealing with bilayered qualia. There is a sense in which you continue to localize the image in front of you, and there is a sense in which you localize it behind you. This raises an interesting question, namely, does the 'location quale' represent the object as being in front of you or behind you? (Qualia represent an object as being red or square, but they also represent it as being in a certain location, egocentrically specified.)

Now imagine that, instead of a rearview mirror, there is a small window in front of you, and through that window you see a missile being hurled at you. Now of course, you duck backwards. Even though the two situations are exactly equivalent optically — there is an expanding retinal image — in the former case you accelerate forward because somehow, at some level, your visual system performs the appropriate transformation.

Another possibility is that when you look into the mirror you accelerate forward, not because the location qualia are now actually behind you, but because you've learned a reflex avoidance manoeuver, using the dorsal stream system alone. (So, in this situation, the input is irrevocable, and the output is also not open-ended, i.e. it's a single behaviour.) On the other hand, the high-level revocable aspect of the experience — where you think, 'Hey this is a mirror, so the object must be behind me,' doesn't have qualia either — it is more conceptual in nature. But at the critical *intermediate* level, which is still qualia-laden, the object is still represented as being in front of you. You look at the red object, and it's clearly in front of you, and if a fly appears on the mirror, it is right next to the red object. You certainly don't experience it behind your head. So what initially seems to be a disturbing borderline case, in fact can be readily explained in terms of our overall conceptual scheme. But even so, the example is thought-provoking and it leads to experimental questions,[9] such as: If someone were to hurl a missile at you from behind, as you watched in a mirror, would you duck forward or backward?

A fourth example of 'bilayered' (or bistable, really) qualia is shown in Figure 6 (below). What you see initially is a grey rectangle occluded partially by an opaque white square with Swiss-cheese like holes in it. Obviously the grey of the rectangle is not seen where it is occluded, but with a bit of practice you can get yourself to see this as a *transparent* grey film stuck *in front* of the white square with holes. When you see it this way, the film does have qualia because you 'choose' to see it in front and to flag it with the appropriate qualia — preparing it for further processing, as it were.

Anosognosia, schizophrenia, and other delusional states

Notice that in the 'cognitive' realm this sort of completion or filling in is not unlike the confabulations that right hemisphere stroke patients generate to 'deny' that they are paralysed — an anomaly is simply explained away (Ramachandran, 1995c). Some process located in the left hemisphere fills in gaps and smooths over contradictions in the patient's belief system (e.g., the contradiction between 'I can use both arms' and 'I can't see my left arm moving'). We have suggested elsewhere that such psychological defences evolved mainly to stabilize behaviour (they prevent your having to orient to every kind of anomaly that threatened the *status quo*) and should be seen as part of a general strategy for the 'coherencing' of consciousness: they help avoid indecisive vacillation and serve to optimize resource allocation, and to facilitate rapid, effective action. Similarly, perceptual filling in occurs to keep conscious qualia coherent, perspicuous, and distraction-free — it is another example of a general strategy of coherencing consciousness.

---

[9] Intriguingly, we have recently described a new neurological sign of right hemisphere disease, which we call the looking glass syndrome, in which patients, while looking at a mirror, will reach for objects 'inside' the mirror, and assert that the object is inside or behind the mirror, even though they realize they are looking into a mirror (Ramachandran *et al.*, 1997).

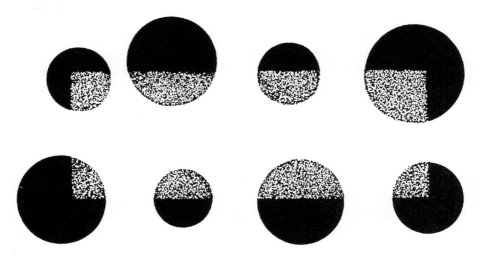

Figure 6. Bilayered qualia
Look at the figure and try to see the grey areas as part of a single translucent rectangle. This represents a higher level of filling in located somewhere between the filling in of the blind spot and amodal filling in. (After Kanizsa, 1979)

The cognitive styles of the two hemispheres might be fundamentally different; when faced with an 'anomaly' or discrepancy in sensory input, the left hemisphere tries to 'smooth over' the discrepancy (employing denial, repression, or confabulation) in the interest of preserving stability, whereas an 'anomaly detector' in the right hemisphere tends to orient to the discrepancy and generate a paradigm shift in the brain's representation of the situation (Ramachandran, 1995c).

The dialectic between the opposing tendencies of the two hemispheres that we are proposing also bears a tantalizing resemblance to what physicists refer to as the 'edge of chaos' in dynamical systems: the emergence of 'complexity' at the boundary between stability and chaos. Chaos arises in deterministic systems that show a highly sensitive dependence on initial conditions. This is not unlike the sensitivity to perturbation (or 'anomalies') that we have postulated for the cognitive style of the right hemisphere. In marked contrast, the left hemisphere is relatively *insensitive* to change and tries to preserve stability. Interesting or complex types of behaviour, on the other hand, seem to emerge spontaneously at the boundary between the two — a place where there is just enough novelty to keep things interesting and predictable but also just enough stability to avoid complete anarchy and instability. And it is precisely these little eddies of complexity at the border zone that may correspond roughly to what we call human caprice, innovation and creativity.

There is a similarity between anosognosics and schizophrenics who have 'positive' symptoms. In the former, we have argued, there is a failure to register a mismatch between expectation and current sensory input — leading to hallucinations (e.g. 'I can see my arm moving') as well as delusions ('My left arm is fine') and memory distortions ('I know that I am paralysed now; therefore I never denied that I was paralysed'). We suggest that such a failure results from damage to an anomaly or mismatch detector in the right frontoparietal cortex of anosognosics but it is entirely possible that some similar pathology may also underlie schizophrenia. Indeed, Frith

& Dolan (1997) have recently performed an ingenious experiment using the same mirror box we use on our phantom limb patients (Ramachandran & Rogers-Ramachandran, 1996) to demonstrate that a mismatch between vision and proprioception results in right frontal activation (during a PET scan), independently of whether the mismatch occurred on the right or left side of the body!

Surprisingly, there is no neurological syndrome in which one sees exactly the same types of 'positive symptoms' — i.e. combinations of hallucinations and delusions — that occur in schizophrenia (Frith & Dolan, 1997). We would venture to predict, however, that if someone developed Charles Bonnet syndrome (from ocular pathology) *combined with* a right frontoparietal lesion (causing a failure to register a mismatch between fantasy and reality) then you would come pretty close to a neurological equivalent of schizophrenia, for such a patient would take his hallucinations quite literally — not recognizing them to be illusory. Surprisingly, we have recently seen a phantom limb patient who precisely fits this general description. He lost his left arm in a car accident in which he also suffered bilateral frontal damage. While most people who lose an arm experience the illusion of a persisting arm, i.e., a phantom limb, they obviously do not literally see the arm or believe that the arm still exists. Our patient (DS), on the other hand, insisted that his arm was still there and had not been lost, even though he was quite lucid mentally in other domains (Hirstein and Ramachandran, 1997).

Qualia of percepts vs. qualia of beliefs

Beliefs are also associated with 'partial qualia' and conscious awareness, once they are made explicit in 'working memory'. In the absence of sensory support, however, the qualia associated with beliefs are fleeting and less robust than the real qualia-laden percepts associated with sensory stimuli. Therefore the distinction between qualia associated with *percepts* and those associated with explicit (or occurrent) *beliefs* may be quantitative rather than qualitative. Tacit beliefs, on the other hand, are completely qualia-free.

As an analogy, consider the distinction between 'knowing' and 'remembering' or between 'procedural' and 'episodic' memory in humans. We know that episodic memories are partially qualia-laden, whereas skills are not (Tulving, 1983). However, when a bee does a waggle dance, it is communicating an episodic memory. Why does this not qualify as an episodic memory analogous to human episodic memory? To argue that the bee is not conscious, and true episodic memories are conscious, would be circular, and does not answer the question. The problem is readily solved in our scheme, however, since in the bee, the alleged episodic memory is available for the production of only one (or two) outputs, and hence the bee lacks the second of our defining features of consciousness: flexibility of output.[10]

This is one advantage that our scheme has over other theories of consciousness: it allows us to unambiguously answer such questions as, Is a sleepwalker conscious? Is the spinal cord of a paraplegic conscious? Is a bee conscious? Is an ant conscious when it detects pheromones? In each of these cases, instead of the vague assertion that one is dealing with various degrees of consciousness, which is the standard answer,

---

[10] One prediction here is that a non-conscious zombie, such as Milner's visual zombie, or perhaps certain sleepwalkers should not have episodic memories.

one should simply apply the three criteria we have specified. For example, Can a sleepwalker make choices? Does he have short-term memory? Does a patient with akinetic mutism have short-term memory? Can the bee use its waggle dance for more than one output?, etc., thereby avoiding endless semantic quibbles over the exact meaning of the word 'consciousness'.

The importance of the temporal lobes for consciousness and qualia

'Does any of this yield clues as to where in the brain might qualia might be?', you ask. It is ironic that people have often thought that the seat of consciousness is the frontal lobes, because nothing dramatic happens to consciousness if you damage the frontal lobes. We suggest instead that most of the action is in the temporal lobes. Admittedly this allows us only a fourfold reduction in the problem space, since the brain has only four lobes; but at the very least it may help us narrow down the problem by allowing us to focus on specific neural structures and their functions. In particular, we suggest, one needs the amygdala and other parts of the temporal lobes for seeing the *significance* of things to the organism. Without this structure you are like Searle's Chinese room (Searle, 1980): capable of giving a single correct output in response to a demand, but with no ability to sense *the meaning* of what you are doing or saying.[11]

Our claim that qualia are based primarily in the temporal lobes is consistent with the idea put forward by Jackendoff (1987) and Crick (1996) that qualia and consciousness are associated not with the *early* stages of perceptual processing (at the level of the retina, for instance), where (in our scheme) obviously multiple choices are not possible. Nor are they associated with the *final* stages of perceptual processing and behaviour planning, where behavioural programs are executed. Rather, they are associated with the *intermediate* stages of processing. The temporal lobes are in fact the interface between perception and action.

Another piece of evidence for the idea that the temporal lobes are the neural locus of consciousness and qualia is that the brain lesions which produce the most profound disturbances in consciousness are those which generate temporal lobe seizures. Researchers who electrically stimulate the temporal lobes of epileptics prior to performing lobectomies have found the temporal lobes to be the best place for producing conscious experiences in their subjects (Penfield & Perot, 1963; Gloor *et al.*, 1982; Gloor, 1992; Bancaud *et al.*, 1976). Stimulating primary sensory areas, such as the visual cortex, can produce strange, unformed qualia, such as phosphene flashes, but only, we suspect because the events set in place by the stimulation eventually follow the natural course of processing into the temporal lobes, and produce (weak) effects there. Stimulating the amygdala is the surest way to 'replay' a full, vivid experience, such as an autobiographical memory complete with intense emotions, or a vivid hallucination (Gloor, 1992). The seizures which temporal lobe epilepsy (TLE) sufferers endure are associated not only with alterations in consciousness in the sense of personal identity, personal destiny, and personality, but also with vivid, qualia-laden hallucinations such as smells and sounds (MacLean, 1990; Bear, 1979; Waxman & Geschwind, 1975; Gloor, 1992; Bancaud *et al.*, 1994). If these are mere memories as they are sometimes claimed to be, why would the person say 'I literally feel like I'm

---

[11] This reminds one of the old quip in which one behaviourist zombie turns to his mate after passionate lovemaking and says, 'I know it was good for you, but was it good for me?', a question which encapsulates the entire Searle/Dennett debate.

reliving it'? What characterizes these seizures is the *vividness* of the qualia they produce. So the smells, the pains, the tastes and the emotional feelings, all of which are generated in the temporal lobes, suggest that they are in fact the seat of consciousness.

Another reason for choosing the temporal lobes — especially the left temporal lobe — as the main player in generating conscious experience is that this is where much of language — especially semantics — is represented. If I see an apple, it is the activity in the temporal lobes that allows me to *apprehend all its implications* almost simultaneously. Recognition of it as a fruit of a certain type occurs in IT (infero- temporal cortex), the amygdala gauges its significance for my well-being, and Wernicke's and other areas alert me to all the nuances of meaning that the mental image — including the word 'apple' — evokes; I can eat the apple, I can smell it, I can bake a pie, remove its pith, plant its seeds, use it to 'keep the Doctor away', tempt Eve, and on and on.

If one enumerates all of the attributes that we usually associate with the words 'consciousness' or 'awareness', each of them, you will notice, has a correlate in temporal lobe seizures:

(1) *Sensory Qualia — the raw feel of sensations, such as colour or pain.* TLE: Vivid visual and auditory hallucinations; the patient always notices that these look and feel like the real thing — they do not merely have the fleeting qualia of memories (Penfield & Jasper, 1954).

(2) *The attachment of emotional significance and value labels to objects and events.* TLE (especially seizures involving the amygdala): The patient may see cosmic significance in everything around him (Waxman and Geschwind, 1975), or feel intense fear (Strauss *et al.*, 1982). Conversely, bilateral damage to the amygdala may lead to a loss of emotion and empathy, or to the 'psychic blindness' and unthinking, automatic behaviour characteristic of the Kluver-Bucy syndrome (Lilly *et al.*, 1983). It is a moot point whether such a person would have any visual qualia. (One could regard the zombie-like behaviour of Goodale's patient as an extreme example of this.)

(3) *Body image — the sense of being corporeal and of occupying a specific location in space.* TLE: Autoscopic hallucinations (Devinsky *et al.*, 1989), 'out of body' experiences. Also, the temporal lobes and the limbic system receive a more massive projection form the viscera than any other part of the brain. The construction of a body image is one of the foundations of our sense of self but, as we will show in the next section, the body image is a merely a temporary construct, and in the next section we will describe experiments that clearly demonstrate its transitory nature.

(4) *Convictions of truth or falsehood.* TLE: An absolute sense of omnipotence or omniscience (Bear, 1979; Trimble, 1992). It seems ironic that our convictions about the absolute truth or falsity of a thought should depend not so much on the propositional *language* system but on much more primitive limbic structures which add a form of emotional qualia to thoughts, giving them a 'ring of truth'. This would explain why the more dogmatic assertions of priests as well as scientists are so notoriously resistant to correction through intellectual reasoning!

(5) *Unity — the sense of being a single person despite experiencing a lifetime of diverse sensory impressions.* TLE: Synesthesia; doubling of consciousness; multiplication of personal identity, e.g. in Capgras syndrome (which we have argued is due primarily to a temporal lobe lesion, see Hirstein & Ramachandran, 1997) and other reduplicative paramnesias, the patient may come to regard himself as more than one person. Similarly, multiple personality disorder (MPD) is often seen in association with TLE (Schenk & Bear, 1981; Ahern *et al.*, 1993).

(6) *Free will — the sense of being able to make a decision or control one's movements.* TLE: Even though the ability to engage in long range-planning is lost mainly in frontal disease, it is damage to the cingulate (which is part of the limbic system) that often results in something like 'disorders of *the will*' (e.g. the alien hand syndrome (Goldberg *et al.*, 1981), akinetic mutism: 'loss of will' (Nielson and Jacobs, 1951). Zombie-like automatisms are a frequent concomitant of TLE seizures, and also result from stimulation of the anterior cingulate gyrus (Bancaud *et al.*, 1976). It would be interesting to find out whether the patient can make actual *choices* during such states (we would argue that they cannot).

Furthermore, one frequently sees profound alterations in conscious experience — such as loss of contact with reality (de-realizations) and dream-like trance states during TLE seizures. While each of the disorders listed above can also be seen when other brain areas are damaged (e.g. body image distortions in parietal lobe syndromes), almost all of them can be seen in various combinations when the temporal lobes are damaged. Thus if there is a single brain region that can be regarded as critical for generating conscious experience, it would be the temporal lobes and various interconnected parts of the amygdala, the inferotemporal cortex, Wernicke's area and other associated structures (e.g. the cingulate gyrus). Remove these and you have the prototypical zombie of philosophers' thought experiments.

A new illusion of decapitation

We will now describe an illusion which demonstrates how the body image — despite its apparent durability and permanence — is an entirely transitory internal construct that can be profoundly altered by the stimulus contingencies and correlations that one encounters. Consider the following two illusions, the 'phantom nose' and the 'phantom head' that we recently discovered in our laboratory. In the first experiment, the subject sits in a chair blindfolded, with an accomplice sitting at his right side, or in front of him, facing the same direction. The experimenter then stands near the subject, and with his left hand takes hold of the *subject's* left index finger and uses it to repeatedly and randomly tap and stroke the nose of the accomplice, while at the same time, using his right hand, he taps and strokes the subject's nose in precisely the same manner, and in perfect synchrony. After a few seconds of this procedure, the subject develops the uncanny illusion that his nose has either been dislocated, or has been stretched out several feet forwards or off to the side, demonstrating the striking plasticity or malleability of our body image. The more random and unpredictable the tapping sequence the more striking the illusion. We suggest that the subject's brain regards it as highly improbable that the tapping sequence on his finger and the one on his nose are identical simply by chance and therefore 'assumes' that the nose has been displaced — applying a universal Bayesian logic that is common to all sensory systems. Interestingly, once the illusion is in place, if a drop of ice-cold water is now applied to the subject's nose, the cold is sometimes felt in the new location of the nose. The phantom nose illusion is a very striking one, and we were able to replicate it on twelve out of eighteen naive subjects.[12] Rather surprisingly, the illusion sometimes works even if the accomplice sits *facing* the subject; the logical absurdity of the situation seems not to veto the effect. This simple experiment demonstrates the single most important principle underlying the mechanisms of perception and conscious experience: that they may have evolved exclusively for *extracting statistical* regularities from the natural world.

In the second experiment we had a naive subject looking at his own reflection in a half-silvered mirror, and placed a dummy's head on the other side of the mirror, optically superimposed in exact registration on the subject's own reflection. The lights are switched off and the upper half of the dummy's face, including the nose, is illuminated with one spotlight and the lips alone of the subject are illuminated separately with a different light source. When the subject looks at the mask, he sees a combination of the top of the mask and, reflected in the glass, the bottom of his face. If the subject is asked to make large lip and tongue movements (and baring of the teeth), he develops the uncanny experience of being in direct control of the dummy's facial movements, as though his 'will' was manifesting itself through the dummy's mouth. It is as though the brain regards it highly improbable that the lips of the dummy should be so perfectly synchronized with his own motor speech commands, and therefore assumes that the subject's own free will has taken over the dummy.[13]

To test this objectively, we pinched the dummy's face and found that this evoked a striking increase in the subject's skin conductance response, whereas simply pinching the dummy without the initial lip movements evoked a much smaller response (Ramachandran *et al.*, in preparation). The extraordinary implication is that, using this relatively simple procedure, we had successfully 'decapitated' the subject, inducing the self to temporarily cast off its mortal coil to inhabit the dummy. The subject comes to experience the dummy's head as being his own to such an extent that it is now hooked up to his own limbic system and autonomic output. Even intermittent, unpredictable tactile stimulation (touch, cold, pain) delivered to the subject's face were occasionally referred to the dummy in a modality-specific manner (in a manner analogous to the referral of tactile stimulation to visually resurrected phantom limbs; Ramachandran and Rogers-Ramachandran, 1996). The observation also lends credibility to the reports of the self temporarily deserting the body: out of the body experiences and 'autoscopic hallucinations' in parietal lobe syndrome and ketamine anesthesia.

---

[12] It has not escaped our notice that if a willing accomplice were available, the effect could also be produced using other body parts.

[13] The sceptic could ask, How is this situation fundamentally different from ordering another human being — such as a valet — to perform an elaborate series of actions, or controlling a marionette on strings with one's fingers? The answer is that in the former case there is no perfect *temporal synchrony* between the orders issued and the actions performed by your subordinate; and in the latter case, even though there is some degree of synchrony, the movement trajectories and the body parts involved in the marionette are different from those of the puppeteer. This explains why the transfer of free will requires an experimental setup similar to the one we describe.

Qualia and 'the self'

We have discussed qualia and the body image,[14] but what about the self? Even though the notion of a unitary, enduring self may turn out to be a form of adaptive self- deception or delusion (Ramachandran, 1995b) we must consider why the illusion arises. We also need to consider the question of who the so-called observer is in the two thought experiments we began with. Since qualia-laden percepts are generated *for* someone or something — presumably 'the self' — the problem of the self and the problem of qualia are really just two sides of the same coin.

One way to approach the question of how our account of qualia relates to the question of the self is to ask from a scientific point of view why something like filling in of the blind spot with qualia-laden representations occurs. The original motive many had for arguing that the blind spot is *not* filled in was that there is no one there to fill them in for — that no homunculus is there looking at them (Dennett, 1991). This is an argument against the following line of reasoning: 'If qualia are filled in, they must be filled in for some *viewer*, i.e., a homunculus.'

There is reason to think that the conclusion is false (i.e., there is no homunculus), it was argued, and hence reason to think that the antecedent is also false: qualia are not in fact filled in, and that the appearance that they are is an illusion (Dennett, 1991). Now, since we have argued that qualia are in fact filled in (Ramachandran, 1992; 1993; 1995a; Ramachandran & Gregory, 1991), does this mean that we believe they are filled in for a homunculus? Of course not, but the fallacy may not be in the *form* of the reasoning, just in the illegitimate specificity with which the conclusion is stated. The above argument is really a 'straw man'; the line of reasoning should run: 'If qualia are filled in, they are filled in for *something*.'

Now, what is the 'something' here? There exists in certain branches of psychology the notion of an executive, or a control process (McKay, 1969). These processes are generally taken to be frontal, or prefrontal, but we would like to suggest that the something which qualia are filled in for is a sort of executive process, but a limbic[15]

---

[14] Our 'phantom nose' effect is quite similar to one reported by Lackner (1988) except that the underlying principle is different. In Lackner's experiment, the subject sits blindfolded at a table, with his arm flexed at the elbow, holding the tip of his own nose. If the experimenter now applies a vibrator to the tendon of the biceps, the subject not only feels that his arm is extended — because of spurious signals from muscle stretch receptors — but also that his nose has actually lengthened. Lackner invokes Helmholtzian 'unconscious inference' as an explanation for this effect (I am holding my nose; my arm is extended; therefore my nose must be long). The illustration we have described, on the other hand, does not require a vibrator and seems to depend entirely on a Bayesian principle — the sheer statistical improbability of two tactile sequences being identical. (Indeed, our illusion cannot be produced if the subject simply holds the accomplice's nose.) Not all subjects experience this effect, but that it happens at all is astonishing: that a lifetime's evidence concerning your nose can be negated by just a few seconds of intermittent tactile imput.

[15] The limbic system includes the hypothalamic nucleii, amygdala insula, interstitial nuclei of the striae terminalis, fornix and fimbria, septum, mamillary bodies and cingulate gyrus, but the exact definition is not critical to our argument. The cholinergic lateral dorsal tegmental and pedunculopontine nuclei and the intralaminar thalamic nucleii that project to limbic structures may be an integral part of the qualia-linked circuitry, but it remains to be seen whether they merely play a 'supportive' role for qualia (as indeed the liver and heart do!) or whether they are a part of the actual circuitry that embodies qualia; i.e. are they analogous to the power supply of a VCR or television set, or to the actual magnetic recording head and cathode ray tube? Hyperactivity of this system may contribute to peduncular hallucinosis. Also the doubling of dorsal tegmental and pedeuneulopontine cell numbers which is known to occur in schizophrenia may help explain hallucinations. (This idea emerged in conversation with John Smythies.)

one, rather than a frontal one. This would be a process involved in connecting motivation and emotion with the choice of actions to perform, based on a certain definite incoming set of qualia — very much the sort of thing which the self was traditionally supposed to do. A control process is not something which has all the properties of a full human being, of course — it is not at all a homunculus. All the notion of a control process entails, as we are employing it, is that control processes are guided by some brain areas (i.e. perceptual areas and motivational areas) as they control the activities of other brain areas (i.e. motor and planning areas).

Seen this way, filling in is a kind of treating and preparing of qualia in order for them to interact properly with limbic executive structures. Qualia may need to be filled in before they causally interact with these structures because gaps interfere with the proper working of these executive structures. To speak metaphorically, perhaps the control structures are prone to be distracted by gaps in a way which greatly reduces their efficiency and their ability to select appropriate output. The processes involved in generating qualia smooth over anomalies in their product in the same way in which the president's advisers might remove any little confusions or fill in any gaps in the data they give him, inconsequential confusions and gaps which might unnecessarily distract his attention from the main message of the data, causing him to take longer to make a decision, or worse, to make the wrong decision.

Where in the limbic system are these control processes? Perhaps a system involving the amygdala and the anterior cingulate, given the amygdala's central role in emotion (LeDoux, 1992; Halgren, 1992), and the anterior cingulate's apparent executive role (Posner & Raichle, 1994; Devinsky *et al.*, 1995), and the connection between its damage and disorders of the will, such as akinetic mutism and alien hand syndrome. It is not difficult to see how such processes could give rise to the mythology of a self as an active presence in the brain — a 'ghost in the machine'.

Acknowledgments: We thank P.S. Churchland, F.H.C. Crick, R.L. Gregory, D.C. Dennett, M. Kinsbourne and J. Smythies for stimulating discussions, and the NIMH for support. The idea that the Charles Bonnet syndrome might arise from the activity of feedback pathways projecting back to areas 17 and 18 was first suggested by one of us (VSR) in two interviews (Grady, 1993; Nash, 1995). The notion that the epistemic barrier to sensing another person's qualia results entirely from a translation problem emerged from conversations (and correspondence) with F.H.C. Crick in 1984. Our ideas about bees emerged from discussions with M. Hauser.

References

Ahern, G.L., Herring, A.M., Tackenberg, J. *et al.* (1993), 'The association of multiple personality and temporolimbic epilepsy', *Archives of Neurology*, **50**, pp. 1020–5.

Aristotle (1961), *DeAnima* (Oxford: Clarendon Press).

Baars, B. (1988), *A Cognitive Theory of Consciousness* (New York: Cambridge University Press).

Bancaud, J. *et al.* (1976), 'Manifestations comportmentales induites par la stimulation electrique du gyrus cingulaire anterieur chez l'homme', *Revue Neurologique*, **132**, pp. 705–24.

Bancaud, J., Brunet-Bourgin, F., Chauvel, P. & Halgren, E. (1994), 'Anatomical origin of *deja vu* and vivid ''memories'' in human temporal lobe epilepsy', *Brain*, **117**, pp. 71–90.

Bear, D.M. (1979), 'Personality changes associated with neurologic lesions', in *Textbook of Outpatient Psychiatry*, ed. A. Lazare (Baltimore, MD: Williams and Wilkins Co.).

Bogen, J.E. (1995a), 'On the neurophysiology of consciousness: Part I. An overview', *Consciousness and Cognition*, **4**, pp. 52–62.

Bogen, J.E. (1995b), 'On the neurophysiology of consciousness: Part II. Constraining the semantic problem', *Consciousness and Cognition*, **4**, pp. 137–58.

Bregman, A. (1981), 'Asking the ''what for'' question', in *Perceptual Organization*, ed. M. Kubovy & J. Pomerantz (Hillsdale, NJ: Lawrence Erlbaum Associates).

Brewster, D. (1832), *Letters In Natural Magic* (London: John Murray).

Churchland, P.S. (1986), *Neurophilosophy* (Cambridge, MA: The MIT Press).

Churchland, P.S. (1996), 'The hornswoggle problem', *Journal of Consciousness Studies*, **3** (5–6), pp. 402–8.

Churchland, P.S. & Ramachandran, V.S. (1993), 'Filling in: Why Dennett is wrong', in *Dennett and His Critics: Demystifying Mind*, ed. B. Dahlbom (Oxford: Blackwell Scientific Press).

Churchland, P.S., Ramachandran, V.S. & Sejnowski, T.J. (1994), 'A critique of pure vision', in *Large-scale Neuronal Theories of the Brain*, ed. C. Koch & J.L. Davis (Cambridge, MA: The MIT Press).

Cobb S., Ramachandran, V.S. & Hirstein, W. (in preparation), 'Evoked potentials during synesthesia'.

Cohen, M.S., Kosslyn, S.M., Breiter, H.C. *et al.* (1996), 'Changes in cortical activity during mental rotation. A mapping study using functional MRI', *Brain*, **119**, pp. 89–100.

Crick, F. (1994), *The Astonishing Hypothesis: The Scientific Search for the Soul* (New York: Simon and Schuster).

Crick, F. (1996), 'Visual perception: rivalry and consciousness', *Nature*, **379**, pp. 485–6.

Crick, F. & Koch, C. (1992), 'The problem of consciousness', *Scientific American*, **267**, pp. 152–9.

Damasio, A.C. (1994), *Descartes' Error* (New York: Putnam).

Dennett, D.C. (1978), *Brainstorms* (Cambridge, MA: The MIT Press).

Dennett, D.C. (1991), *Consciousness Explained* (Boston, MA: Little, Brown and Co.).

Descartes, R. (1986), *Meditations on First Philosophy*, trans. J. Cottingham (Cambridge: Cambridge University Press).

Devinsky, O., Feldmann, E., Burrowes, K. & Broomfield, E. (1989), 'Autoscopic phenomena with seizures', *Archives of Neurology*, **46**, pp. 1080–8.

Devinsky, O., Morrell, MJ, Vogt, BA. (1995) 'Contribution of anterior cingulate cortex to behavior', *Brain*, **118**, pp. 279–306.

Durgin, F.H., Tripathy, S.P. & Levi, D.M. (1995), 'On the filling in of the visual blind spot: some rules of thumb', *Perception*, **24**, pp. 827–40.

Edelman, G. (1989), *The Remembered Present* (New York: Basic Books).

Farah, M.J. (1989), 'The neural basis of mental imagery', *Trends in Neurosciences*, **10**, pp. 395–9.

Fiorini, M., Rosa, M.G.P., Gattass, R. & Rocha-Miranda, C.E. (1992), 'Dynamic surrounds of receptive fields in primate striate cortex: A physiological basis', *Proceedings of the National Academy of Science* **89**, pp. 8547–51.

Fodor, J.A. (1975), *The Language of Thought* (Cambridge, MA: Harvard University Press).

Frith, C.D. & Dolan, R.J. (1997), 'Abnormal beliefs: Delusions and memory', Paper presented at the May, 1997, *Harvard Conference on Memory and Belief.*

Gattass, R., Fiorini, M., Rosa, M.P.G, Pinon, M.C.F., Sousa, A.P.B., Soares, J.G.M. (1992), 'Visual responses outside the classical receptive field RF in primate striate cortex: a possible correlate of perceptual completion', in *The Visual System from Genesis to Maturity*, ed. R. Lent (Boston, MA: Birkhauser).

Gazzaniga, M.S. (1993), 'Brain mechanisms and conscious experience', *Ciba Foundation Symposium*, **174**, pp. 247–57.

Gloor, P., Olivier, A., Quesney, L.F., Andermann, F., Horowitz, S. (1982), 'The role of the limbic system in experiential phenomena of temporal lobe epilepsy', *Annals of Neurology*, **12**, pp. 129–43.

Gloor, P. (1992), 'Amygdala and temporal lobe epilepsy', in *The Amygdala: Neurobiological Aspects of Emotion, Memory and Mental Dysfunction*, ed J.P. Aggleton (New York: Wiley-Liss).

Goldberg, G., Mayer, N. & Toglis, J.U. (1981), 'Medial frontal cortex and the alien hand sign', *Archives of Neurology*, **38**, pp. 683–6.

Grady, D. (1993), 'The vision thing: Mainly in the brain', *Discover*, June, pp. 57–66.

Grush, R. & Churchland, P.S. (1995), 'Gaps in Penrose's toilings', *Journal of Consciousness Studies*, **2** (1), pp. 10–29.

Halgren, E. (1992), 'Emotional neurophysiology of the amygdala within the context of human cognition', in *The Amygdala: Neurobiological Aspects of Emotion, Memory and Mental Dysfunction*, ed J.P. Aggleton (New York: Wiley-Liss).

Hirstein, W. & Ramachandran, V.S. (1997), 'Capgras syndrome: A novel probe for understanding the neural representation of the identity and familiarity of persons', *Proceedings of the Royal Society of London*, **264**, pp. 437–44.

Horgan, J. (1994), 'Can science explain consciousness?', *Scientific American*, **271**, pp. 88–94.

Humphrey, N. (1993), *A History of the Mind* (London: Vintage).

Jackendoff, R. (1987), *Consciousness and the Computational Mind* (Cambridge, MA: The MIT Press).

Jackson, F. (1986), 'What Mary did not know', *Journal of Philosophy*, **83**, pp. 291–5.

Kanizsa, G. (1979), *Organization In Vision* (New York: Praeger).

Kinsbourne, M. (1995), 'The intralaminar thalamic nucleii', *Consciousness and Cognition*, **4**, pp. 167–71.

Kripke, S.A. (1980), *Naming and Necessity* (Cambridge, MA: Harvard University Press).

Lackner, J.R. (1988), 'Some proprioceptive influences on perceptual representations', *Brain*, **111**, pp. 281–97.

LeDoux, J.E. (1992), 'Emotion and the amygdala', in *The Amygdala: Neurobiological Aspects of Emotion, Memory and Mental Dysfunction*, ed J.P. Aggleton (New York: Wiley-Liss).
Lilly, R., Cummings, J.L., Benson, D.F. & Frankel, M. (1983), 'The human Kluver-Bucy syndrome', *Neurology*, **33**, pp. 1141–5.
Llinás, R.R. & Paré, D. (1991), 'Of dreaming and wakefulness', *Neuroscience*, **44**, pp. 521–35.
MacLean, P.D. (1990), *The Triune Brain in Evolution* (New York: Plenum Press).
MacKay, D.M. (1969), *Information, Mechanism and Meaning* (Cambridge, MA: The MIT Press).
Marr, D. (1982), *Vision* (San Francisco: Freeman).
Medawar, P. (1969), *Induction and Intuition in Scientific Thought* (London: Methuen).
Milner, A.D. & Goodale, M.A. (1995), *The Visual Brain In Action* (Oxford: Oxford University Press).
Nagel, T. (1974), 'What is it like to be a bat?', *Philosophical Review*, **83**, pp. 435–50.
Nash, M. (1995), 'Glimpses of the mind', *Time*, pp. 44–52.
Nielson, J.M. & Jacobs, L.L. (1951), 'Bilateral lesions of the anterior cingulate gyri', *Bulletin of the Los Angeles Neurological Society*, **16**, pp. 231–4.
Paré, D. & Llinás, R. (1995), 'Conscious and preconscious processes as seen from the standpoint of sleep-waking cycle neurophysiology', *Neuropsychologia*, **33**, pp. 1155–68.
Penfield, W.P. & Jasper, H. (1954), *Epilepsy and the Functional Anatomy of the Human Brain* (Boston, MA: Little, Brown & Co.).
Penfield, W.P. & Perot, P. (1963), 'The brain's record of auditory and visual experience: a final summary and discussion', *Brain*, **86**, pp. 595–696.
Penrose, R. (1994), *Shadows of the Mind* (Oxford: Oxford University Press).
Plum, F. & Posner, J.B. (1980), *The Diagnosis of Stupor and Coma* (Philadelphia: F.A. Davis and Co.).
Posner, M.I. & Raichle, M.E. (1994), *Frames of Mind* (New York: Scientific American Library).
Purpura K.P. & Schiff, N.D. (1997), 'The thalamic intralaminar nuclei: a role in visual awareness', *The Neuroscientist*, **3**, pp. 8–15.
Ramachandran, V.S. (1992), 'Blind spots', *Scientific American*, **266**, pp. 85–91.
Ramachandran, V.S. (1993), 'Filling in gaps in logic: Some comments on Dennett', *Consciousness and Cognition*, **2**, pp. 165–8.
Ramachandran, V.S. (1995a), 'Filling in gaps in logic: Reply to Durgin *et al.*', *Perception*, **24**, pp. 41-845.
Ramachandran, V.S. (1995b), 'Perceptual correlates of neural plasticity', in *Early Vision and Beyond*, ed. T.V. Papathomas, C. Chubb, A. Gorea and E. Kowler (Cambridge, MA: The MIT Press).
Ramachandran, V.S. (1995c), 'Anosognosia in parietal lobe syndrome', *Consciousness and Cognition*, **4**, pp. 22–51.
Ramachandran, V.S. & Gregory, R.L. (1991), 'Perceptual filling in of artificially induced scotomas in human vision', *Nature*, **350**, pp. 699–702.
Ramachandran, V.S., Rogers-Ramachandran, D. & Cobb, S. (1995), 'Touching the phantom limb', *Nature*, **377**, pp. 489–90.
Ramachandran, V.S. & Rogers-Ramachandran, D. (1996), 'Synaesthesia in phantom limbs induced with mirrors', *Proceedings of the Royal Society of London*, **263**, pp. 377–86.
Ramachandran, V.S, Altschuler, E.L. & Hillyer, S. (1997), 'Mirror agnosia', *Proceedings of the Royal Society of London*, **264**, pp. 645–7.
Ramachandran, V.S., Hirstein, W. & Stoddard, R. (in preparation), 'The phantom head: An illusion of decapitation'.
Schenk, L. & Bear, D. (1981), 'Multiple personality and related dissociative phenomena in patients with temporal lobe epilepsy', *American Journal of Psychiatry*, **138**, pp. 1311–16.
Searle, John R. (1980), 'Minds, brains, and programs', *Behavioral and Brain Sciences*, **3**, pp. 417–58.
Searle, John R. (1992), *The Rediscovery of the Mind* (Cambridge, MA: The MIT Press).
Strauss, E., Risser, A. & Jones, M.W. (1982), 'Fear responses in patients with epilepsy', *Archives of Neurology*, **39**, pp. 626–30.
Sutherland, N.S. (1989), *The International Dictionary of Psychology* (New York: Continuum).
Tovee, M.J., Rolls, E.T. & Ramachandran, V.S. (1996), 'Rapid visual learning in neurones of the primate temporal visual cortex', *Neuroreport*, **7**, pp. 2757–60.
Tulving, E. (1983), *Elements of Episodic Memory* (Oxford: Clarendon Press).
Trimble, M.R. (1992), 'The Gastaut-Geschwind syndrome', in *The Temporal Lobes and the Limbic System*, ed. M.R. Trimble and T.G. Bolwig (Petersfield: Wrightson Biomedical Publishing Ltd.).
van Essen, D.C. (1979), 'Visual areas of the mammalian cerebral cortex', *Annual Reviews of Neuroscience*, **2**, pp. 227–63.
Waxman, S.G. & Geschwind, N. (1975), 'The interictal behavior syndrome of temporal lobe epilepsy', *Archives of General Psychiatry*, **32**, pp. 1580-6.
Zeki, S.M. (1978), 'Functional specialisation in the visual cortex of the rhesus monkey', *Nature*, **274**, pp. 423–8.
Zeki, S.M. (1993), *A Vision of the Brain* (Oxford: Oxford University Press).

Jaak Panksepp

The Periconscious Substrates of Consciousness

Affective States and the Evolutionary Origins of the Self

An adequate understanding of 'the self' and/or 'primary-process consciousness' should allow us to explain how affective experiences are created within the brain. Primitive emotional feelings appear to lie at the core of our beings, and the neural mechanisms that generate such states may constitute an essential foundation process for the evolution of higher, more rational, forms of consciousness. At present, abundant evidence indicates that affective states arise from the intrinsic neurodynamics of primitive self-centred emotional and motivational systems situated in subcortical regions of the brain. Accordingly, a neural understanding of 'the self' may arise from a study of how various biological value-coding systems (emotional circuits) converge and interact with coherent brainstem representations of the body and nearby attentional/waking systems of the brain. Affective feelings may be caused by the neurodynamics of basic emotional circuits interacting with the neural schema of bodily action plans. One key brain area where such interactions occur is found within centromedial diencephalic midbrain areas such as the periventricular and periaqueductal gray (PAG) and nearby tectal and tegmental zones. Here I will envision that a Simple Ego-type Life Form (a primitive SELF structure) is instantiated in those circuits The ability of this 'primal SELF' to resonate with primitive emotional values may help yield the raw subjectively experienced feelings of pleasure, lust, anger, hunger, desire, fear, loneliness and so forth. A study of such systems is a reasonable starting point for the neurological analysis of affective feelings, which may lie at the periconscious core of all other forms of animal consciousness. If such a neurodynamic process was an essential neural preadaptation for the emergence of higher levels of consciousness, it may help us close the explanatory gap between brain circuit states and the psychological nature of affective feelings. Thereby, it may also help us conceptualize the nature of psychological binding within higher forms of consciousness in new ways.

Toward a Neurobiological Conception of the Self

It is generally agreed that the self is experienced as a stable mental presence that provides a sense of felt affective unity and continuity to humans, commonly with strong cognitive overtones (Strawson, 1997). Indeed, some believe 'the self' is a natural conceptual category not much different than that of *fish* or *fowl*, created out of higher brain matters, while others believe it is largely a 'narrative fiction' (Dennett, 1991).

Yet others, like myself, believe the matter goes much deeper, to a time in neural evolution when organisms first started to experience existence through the affective qualities of consciousness. I will here explore the proposition that those evolutionary passages yielded the essential brain system dynamics that need to be recognized and understood in order to clarify the emergence of a pre-propositional form of consciousness on the face of the earth.

Of course, the fundamental nature of the self remains a matter of controversy, as highlighted by the contributions to this volume devoted to the topic. However, two critical aspects of the self continue to receive comparatively little attention, namely its neural and affective underpinnings. Here, I advocate the position that the roots of the self go back to specific mesencephalic and diencephalic sensory-motor action circuits within the mammalian brain which can generate a primitive sort of intentionality (an automatized action readiness) and primitive forms of psychic coherence (global affective states of the brain) by interacting with various emotional and attentional circuits that encode basic biological values (for summary of systems, see Panksepp, 1998). These interacting circuits have specific neurochemical codes that may generate distinct types of neurodynamics within primitive core systems of self-representation that first symbolized organisms as coherently active creatures in the world. This view of the self is based on the following five assumptions:

(1) I ascribe to the evolutionary view which assumes that the primordial self arises from certain body-linked neurosymbolic brain processes that we share homologously with all other mammals and perhaps a diversity of other creatures as well. Since clarification of such issues in mammalian species is hard enough, I will not dwell on the others, even though I am admittedly fond of the possibility that all vertebrates and perhaps even some other creatures have a smidgen of the neural architecture that permits a primitive (affective) consciousness that still lies at the root of our own immediately felt sense of existence.

(2) Being a materialist, I believe that consciousness evolved from unconscious neural processes, and an essential key to all higher levels of analysis may lie in our ability to recognize and specify the primordial interface between the two. I ascribe to the proposition that every moment of our conscious lives is undergirded by feelings, and that if the biological infrastructure of those intrinsic value-signalling systems were destroyed, one's sense of self would degrade.

(3) Considering the evident fact that deeply valenced feelings reside at the core of our being, most especially when we are young, I favour the view that the fundamental nature of the self and affective experience is closely related to the hard problems of consciousness (Chalmers, 1995; Gray, 1995), the hardest of which, in my estimation, is understanding the nature of the most ancient *evolutionary qualia* (I shall here refer to them as *equalia*). Equalia directly reflect the neuronal encoding within mammalian brains of the animals' most important bodily concerns. They reflect how basic emotional and motivational feelings (i.e. internal value indicators) inform animals of major survival issues. In other words, equalia tell organisms where they stand with respect to environments and actions that will enhance or detract from the likelihood of their own survival as well as of their kind.

(4) Considering the importance of such values for all subsequent levels of brain organization, I would anticipate that selfness is a neural process that is re-represented hierarchically at many levels of neural and mental development. Hence, while the

roots and trunk lines may be similar across all mammalian species, the activities within the cerebral canopies and resulting psychological consequences are bound to vary considerably. The essential neural roots of consciousness may, by necessity, be embedded in fundamentally unconscious dynamics of the brain. The level that most critically needs to be explained is the interface between the unconscious properties of neural tissues and those that permitted the emergence of consciousness. I refer to the latter as the 'periconscious substrates of consciousness'.

(5) Since the self should be established on very stable neural coordinates, I believe the sources of primary process core-consciousness are intertwined more intimately with intrinsic motor than with exteroceptively driven sensory processes within the brain. This is not to deny the importance of afferent and reafferent processes converging at the core of the self (e.g. Sheets-Johnstone, 1998), but to bring to the forefront of discussion the potentially essential role of central motor processes in anchoring the periconscious substrates of consciousness.

In essence, the proposal is that within the very core of the self, we must find a neural 'stage manager' who does not observe, but rather, has the ability to generate various coherent acts in response to archetypal survival challenges. The resulting neural resonances that can inundate this central stage manager (henceforth, the SELF), and which can radiate widely in the brain, may constitute the foundation of our basic feelings — the affective equalia we experience as we navigate the major challenges of the world. Among the prototypic equalia, we find the feelings of eagerness, fear, anger, lust, loneliness, nurturant warmth and playful joy, as well as the pleasures and displeasures of various consummatory acts (Panksepp, 1998). Although highly valenced feelings can certainly be triggered by external events and higher appraisals, they are not created from those transient sensations (qualia) and thoughts, but from the stable evolutionary equalia that are neurosymbolically coded, as cladistic birthrights, by the efferent/integrative subcortical emotional circuits of the mammalian brain.

To restate the above view, I assume that the most fundamental forms of affective consciousness within the mammalian brain arise from a neurodynamic scaffolding that provided a stable self-referential set of internal motor coordinates upon which various sensory and higher perceptual/learning mechanisms could operate. This self-referential scaffolding is essential for ever more sophisticated forms of psycho-behavioural coherence as encephalization proceeded in each species' quest for fitness (i.e. as monitored by internal affective homeostasis). Indeed, the neural substrates for our rich exteroceptive qualia, apparently more recently evolved (Deacon, 1990),[1] may be integrally dependent, in some presently unfathomed way, on primitive integrative functions that give rise to affective equalia — the global internal feeling states that reflect the various intrinsic emotional and motivational values that all mammals share in remarkably homologous ways. It may be that the evolution of a coherent self, that could participate in the generation of global internal states, suffices to bind many other psychic activities of the brain.

---

[1] Throughout this manuscript, I will assume that neural tissues which reflect more rostral and lateral expansions of the neuroaxis generally reflect more recent evolutionary developments than those that are situated more caudally and medially. Although we obviously do not have fossilized brains that can affirm such evolutionary assertions, this principle is generally accepted by neuroembryologists since it confirms how neural systems are typically laid out in development.

If this perspective is on the right track, the way to search for the neural foundations of the self would be to identify the areas of the brain where there is a massive convergence of a diversity of basic emotional systems (fundamental value schema),[2] various simple sensory abilities (perceptual schema), and primitive but coherent response systems (action schema). I believe such essential convergence zones may be quite ancient in brain evolution, existing perhaps among the evolutionarily conservative neural bridgeworks of mesencephalic and diencephalic circuits residing in primitive midline regions of the brain. I assume we may be able to gain considerable insight into the nature of the core SELF within human brains by studying the dynamics of such homologous structures in animal brains (Panksepp, 1982; 1998).

To help guide the search for specific brain systems that subserve basic SELF functions, a focus on three neuro-empirical attributes may help us: (1) At key brain areas, global psychobehavioural abilities should be compromised to the greatest extent with the smallest amounts of brain damage across a diversity of species. (2) The most intense and coherent affective/emotional behavioural states should be capable of being provoked with the lowest levels of exogenously applied brain stimulation, whether it be electrical or chemical. (3) Anatomically, such information-rich convergence zones should receive the greatest concentrations of inputs from other brain areas, and they should also have, neuron for neuron, the most prolific outputs.

In my estimation, the brain area that would win in any such competition is the periaqueductal gray (PAG). Accordingly, the PAG and closely related brain areas will be postulated to be the epicenter of the primordial self.

Although no one has pursued a systematic programme of empirical investigations with these empirical goals in mind, a great deal of evidence suggests that midbrain areas such as the PAG as well as the adjacent colliculi do have all the needed characteristics (Strehler, 1991). There is much indirect evidence for the existence of foundational self-referential types of neuronal functions within the centromedial midbrain and diencephalon which may be essential for purely affective types of consciousness — global states commonly referred to by terms such as fear, anger, desire, joy and the other basic emotional and motivational feelings. All of these feelings appear to be embodied in specific types of neural circuits, and presumably distinct types of neurodynamics (Panksepp, 1998). If this idea is on the right track, then future neurophysiological recordings from well-positioned electrodes within such core brain systems may provide objective dynamic signatures reflecting the various archetypal, global states of the self, and hence the various dynamic forms of primary processes 'affective consciousness' (Panksepp, 1999a).

Let me highlight some reservations at the outset. If such a basic system for 'the self' and 'primary affective consciousness' exists, it will certainly not directly help explain higher forms of human consciousness, including the various qualia created by our more recently evolved neocortex and exteroceptive apparatus. However, it might begin to explain the fundamental nature of equalia, the distinct affective states that

---

[2] Here, it is assumed that certain basic affective feelings reflect the types of psychobiological issues that constitute evolutionary memories as opposed to matters learned during the individual life span of an organism. The affective feeling states are envisioned as evolutionary memories (i.e. equalia) that help to efficiently sustain behavioral plans into the future, and to provide a general purpose mechanisms for allowing organisms to efficiently learn about the potential values that appear to be embodied in environmental events (see Panksepp, 1998).

arise from the arousal of the basic emotional systems of the brain. It may also provide insights into how higher and lower processes become interdependent in the brain during development — with emotional faculties emerging earlier and more cognitive-rational faculties later in life. In early development, cognitive abilities may be strongly linked to and limited by affective correlates, and only later in development may they emerge as seemingly self-sufficient entities. There are many conceptual and empirical opportunities to be pursued when we consider the possibility that coherences within the lower substrates of the emotional self may be essential for creating the binding that is subjectively evident in the more recently evolved processes, either through the 'glue' of specific neuro-rhythms (Jefferys *et al.*, 1996) or neurochemicals (Panksepp, 1986; 1993). Although perceptual binding may require neural coherences of much higher frequencies than can be sustained by slowly firing (i.e. visceral) neuronal systems such as the PAG, the integrity of those higher functions may be critically dependent on the types of lower functions we will consider here. In short, my aim is to try to elucidate the necessary rather than the sufficient neural substrates for the sense of self within the brain.

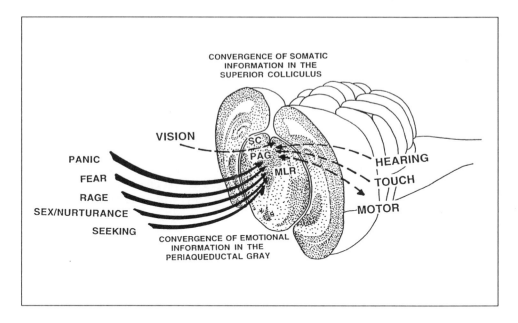

Figure 1

An overview of emotional circuitry converging on the mesencephalic periaqueductal gray (PAG) which is the lowest region of the brain to orchestrate various coordinated emotional responses via a variety of motor outputs. Motor representations for bodily orientation are found in the deep layers of the SC and for forward locomotor activity in the mesencephalic locomotor region (MLR), upon which there is a massive convergence of somatic information dorsally from the superior colliculus (SC), and visceral information from the PAG. Diverse ascending and descending connections of the PAG can integrate coherent emotional reactions throughout the neuroaxis.

The figure is copyright by Oxford University Press and is reprinted from Panksepp (1998) with the publisher's permission.

The Roots of the SELF within the Midbrain
and the Neural Nature of Emotional Feelings

I will henceforth consistently refer to this postulated fundamental neural substrate for primary process affective integration as the SELF (a Simple Ego-Type Life Form). The use of capitalization here for this ancient brain system serves as a convention to highlight that a distinct brain system is the referent as opposed to all the associated psychological states that coalesce during development. This precedent was originally used to designate the basic emotional systems of the brain by Panksepp and Miller (1996). Because of many converging facts, some already alluded to, I will situate this system's epicenter in the PAG and the immediately surrounding tectal and tegmental layers, with substantial spread into midline diencephalic areas that are most intimately connected to the PAG (Cameron et al., 1995a,b).

The converging anatomy of emotional circuits upon the SELF can be schematized effectively within the midbrain (see Figure 1). Around the aqueduct of Sylvius, we have the PAG (also historically known as the 'central gray') whose more rostral extensions in the diencephalon are typically called the periventricular gray. The PAG receives input from all of the major emotional systems of the brain. Just dorsal and lateral to the PAG, there are several simple motor maps of the body which are used for orienting reflexes (the deepest layers of the superior colliculus) as well as for generating stereotyped forward locomotor patterns (i.e., via the more laterally situated mesencephalic locomotor region (MLR)). Surrounding these simple motor orientation and coordination maps, there are multi-modal layerings of major sensory systems, starting with somatosensory and vestibular (deep tectal), as well as auditory (inferior colliculi) and visual (superior colliculi) processing areas. Each of these layers of control has neuronal interconnections with the others, affording various types of coherent interactions that may constitute a coherent SELF-representation comprised of a generalized body map that can be buffeted from the ventral side by distinct affective processes and from dorsal inputs by a variety of simple perceptual states. The rostral, caudal and lateral relations to many brain areas (Cameron et al., 1995a,b), provide many avenues for the interaction of these value systems with attentional and exteroceptive consciousness mediating systems of the brain, as recently discussed in Panksepp (1998) and Watt (1998).

As Bandler (Bandler & Keay, 1996) and others have shown, the PAG has a columnar structure for many emotions such as fear and anger, as well as for sexuality at the lateral edges of the PAG (Shipley et al., 1996). The PAG is also integrally involved in pain modulation and may well contain the primordial 'ouch' generators in response to painful stimuli. An evolutionary outgrowth of the pain regulatory circuits, the separation response system, is also well represented in the PAG (Panksepp, 1998). Although most physiologists have preferred to focus on this structure as the 'efferent motor system' (for a comprehensive recent review, see Holstege et al., 1996), it surely elaborates brain processes more subtle than the mere motor outflow of coordinated emotional responses. There are good reasons to believe that the PAG lies at the very root of many integrated affective feelings of the brain.

This core system of the SELF interacts closely with other nearby components for exteroceptive consciousness such as the Extended Reticular and Thalamic Activating System (ERTAS) introduced by Newman & Baars (1993), and most recently elaborated in Newman (1997) and Baars (1998). However, this SELF system is conceived to be anatomically distinct, albeit functionally interactive, with the ERTAS. According to the present view, the ERTAS is a slightly more recently evolved neural mechanism whereby endogenous commotion within the extended SELF system (reflecting bodily homoestatic imbalances) as well as primitive sign-stimuli from the environment are able to tune the various perceptual systems of the brain (i.e. the various higher tools of consciousness). Thus, the PAG-centred emotional SELF system may be seen as the very core of the visceral-hypothalamic-limbic axis (which is essential for affective, interoceptive consciousness), while the ERTAS is the core of the adjacent somatic-thalamic-neocortical axis (which is essential for exteroceptive consciousness). As Watt (1998) has recently elaborated, the interaction between these systems is one way that biological values may persistently penetrate into higher cognitive activities. The most obvious linkages would be through modulation of the massive ascending acetylcholine, histamine, norepinephrine, and serotonin systems, which convey a variety of very generalized biases to all higher brain regions (Panksepp, 1986; 1993).

Although investigators continue to debate whether internally experienced feeling states are elaborated within the lower or higher reaches of the brain (Damasio, 1994; LeDoux, 1996; Panksepp, 1998; Watt, 1998), it is next to impossible to evoke affective responses via localized electrical stimulation of the neocortex, and quite difficult from most areas of the thalamus. Fragments of emotional feelings can be more easily evoked from higher limbic areas — of cingulate, frontal and temporal cortices — but one needs quite high current levels, often establishing epileptiform activities that invade lower brain systems (Gloor, 1997). By contrast, coherent and powerful emotional responses along with affective states are much easier to obtain by stimulating subcortical brainstem sites (for review, see Panksepp, 1985; 1998).

Some of the most compelling evidence for mesencephalic epicenters for affect comes from attempts to localize the areas of the brain that are essential for opioid and psychostimulant reward processes. It is becoming evident that affective states are more integrally related to the lower than the higher reaches of emotional systems, since opioid reward is easier to establish there (Olmstead & Franklin, 1997; David & Cazal, 1996), while psychostimulant reward has been related to higher aspects of certain emotional systems such as the shell of the nucleus accumbens (Olmstead & Franklin, 1997; Schildein et al., 1998). As even this small sampling of available studies indicates, it would be extreme to believe that affective consciousness is simply elaborated by the PAG (since there are so many other hot spots for drug reward in the diencephalon and midbrain), but the main point of the present argument is that the PAG provides an essential multi-modal module where empirical enquiries into core features of many distinct affective states can be conducted. In my estimation, the PAG is the major epicenter for the generation of emotional feelings which is presently most susceptible to broad-scale empirical enquiry in animal models but not in human beings. In contrast, the amygdala is one convergence zone for various forms of emotional learning (LeDoux, 1996), that can now be readily studied in humans (Lane et al., 1997). Although the effects of extreme pain have been visualized in the PAG of humans (Hsieh et al., 1996), special techniques may need to be developed in order to adequately image milder forms of emotional arousal in such small, functionally diverse, slowly firing visceral areas of the brain.

Although affective consciousness, like every other brain function, is surely organized hierarchically, there is presently little evidence that the elaboration of affective valence requires the participation of higher brain areas such as the neocortex. Indeed, if decortication is done at a very young age in altricial animals such as rats, their affective apparatus appears to be largely spared, indeed intensified, perhaps because of diminished inhibition of lower processes by higher ones (Panksepp *et al.*, 1994). Cortical areas appear only to modulate and to regulate the basic emotional tendencies — to increase the duration, intensity and subtlety of affective expressions in real-life interactions. Cortical modules do not appear to create emotional feelings locally.

In sum, there are many reasons, only some of which can be reviewed here, to believe that the evolutionary roots of a coherent, albeit primitive, self-centred affective awareness first emerged subcortically. A great deal of evidence implicates the PAG as the most essential component of the many relevant neural systems.

On the Potential Neural Reiterations of the SELF

Throughout ontogenetic development, primordial affective capacities may be reiterated within higher brain areas to help organisms extend their basic feelings in space and time to more complex situations so as to allow basic psychobiological values to anchor and to interpenetrate long-term behavioural choices and strategies. From this point of view, the normal moral and cognitive development of a human child could be envisioned to be dependent as much on the various regulatory processes for affect as on the ability to elaborate propositional knowledge. Indeed, many cognitive abilities could be seen to be adaptive skills for maintaining desired levels of emotional stimulation and mood homeostasis (Panksepp *et al.*, 1998; Panksepp & Miller, 1996). I am especially fond of Nietzsche's (1885/1996) insightful assertion that 'moralities are also merely a *sign language of the affects*' (p. 100).

In its basic form, the SELF is presumably reflexive and intentional[3] only to the extent that a certain type of baseline neural activity in the system acts like a 'settling-point' or 'attractor' to which various behaviours are referenced in a feedback manner (Panksepp, 1999a). Behaviours that reduce affective disturbances (i.e. represented perhaps as shifts in the resting neurodynamics of the reverberatory networks of the SELF) will be increased, and those that increase deviations from equilibrium will generate withdrawal behaviours. In simple terms, what has been added to a primordial form of affectively modulated SELF-representation during subsequent brain evolution is, (1) the ability of this SELF-process to migrate (or perhaps more precisely, be reiterated) and thereby to develop extensively throughout neuroanatomically related areas of the brain, yielding widely distributed fractal representations of itself in many areas of the brain, and (2) the addition of various specialized cognitive tools, such as sophisticated forms of working memory to facilitate SELF-regulation. As the reverberatory patterns of the SELF come to be developmentally re-represented in many brain areas, perhaps a neural mirroring is established that can lead not only to increasing degrees of self-reflection and greater mind-reading abilities (Baron-Cohen, 1997; Rizzolatti & Arbib, 1998; Snodgrass & Thompson, 1997) but also po-

[3] In the present context, primary process intentionality is envisioned to be the natural action readiness that is instrinsically coded within the interaction of emotional processes with the neural representation of the SELF.

tentials for multiple personalities in a single individual, with different persona being under the control of different global emotional state variables.

Central Motor Processes and the Neural Architecture of the SELF

Let me now discuss in a bit more detail why the primal neural scaffolding for the SELF could be concentrated in the PAG and overlying tectum. Briefly, the deeper layers of the colliculi constitute a basic motor mapping system of the body which interacts not only with visual, auditory, vestibular and somatosensory sytems (Strehler, 1991), but also with nearby emotional circuits of the PAG (Figure 1). The extended PAG elaborates a visceral type map of the body along with basic neural representations of pain, fear, anger, separation-distress, sexual and maternal behaviour systems (Depaulis & Bandler, 1991; Holstege et al., 1996; Panksepp, 1998).

The primacy of motor functions within the neural representation of the SELF is suggested by the fact that functional eye-movement maps bordering the PAG remain geographically more stable than do the overlying sensory maps. In other words, the local sensory maps shift markedly in reference to stable motor coordinates when the motor map initiates specific actions (Sparks, 1988). Embedded within these primitive body orientation maps, we also find many neurons that can respond to pain, facilitating arousal of whole body attentional responses (Redgrave et al., 1996). In addition, there is a powerful executive motor system just adjacent to the PAG, namely the MLR, which is able to coordinate forward locomotion to achieve a variety of goal-directed activities (Brudzynski et al., 1993).

Contrary to traditional thinking on the matter, the above analysis affirms that affective consciousness may be more (or at least as) integrally linked in evolution to endogenous motor-related processes than to incoming sensory ones. It would be surprising if it were the other way, for ancient organisms needed broad and coherent motor plans before distal sensory guidance could produce anything useful. This pattern is also evident in the higher reaches of the brain. Emotional systems appear to be much more concentrated in frontal motor/planning areas than posterior sensory/perceptual regions. As a consequence, much greater personality disturbances result from frontal cortex damage than injuries of comparable size occuring to posterior sensory cortices (Damasio, 1994; MacLean, 1990). The critical role of motor processes in the elaboration of consciousness may also help solve the paradox of the infinite regress of observers within sensory sytems. To put it in Dennettian (1991) terms, the stable feature of the 'Cartesian Theater' may not be any ultimate observer but a virtual actor,[4] the SELF, which resonates with bodily needs as well as external inputs signifying values that may alleviate those needs. In other words, the stable features of our experience may not be due to an internal self-observing function, but an agent, made capable of instinctual action by the neural structures of the SELF.

It is admittedly hard to envision how subjective feelings might be critically linked to the motor apparatus. After all, our most vivid and common perceptual qualia

---

[4] 'Virtual actor' is used here in the sense that this neural circuit represents the prioridal body which emerged in a distant evolutionary past, and hence may be quite homologous in all mammalian species. When the term 'neurosymbolic' is used in this essay, there is a similar evolutionary referent: namely, functional circuits that have been evolutionarily constructed to represent ancestral memories, as opposed to memories derived during the lifespan of an organism. For a discussion of issues concerning such virtual realities in consciousness, see Revonsuo (1995).

(vision and hearing) are quite obviously tightly linked to our sensory processors. However, we should not be too easily tempted to assume that our equalia must be similarly controlled. Our tendency to relate primary consciousness more to sensory than to motor processes, may be largely an illusion created by the captivating complexity of our exteroceptive sensory inputs (Ramachandran & Hirstein, 1997). There is certainly no intrinsic reason to believe that the internally experienced qualities of central affective states are more critically linked to sensory processing than motor control and planning functions within the brain. For this reason, psychobiologists call many of the intervening abilities 'sensory-motor functions'.

Although it would be foolish to neglect the various sensory components, the probability is high that the stability of primary-process consciousness is created as much by the intrinsic stability of motor coordinates as by any power inherent in sensory processing. As is being increasingly recognized, proprioceptive feedback from motor actions is critical in allowing our brains to actively create conscious perceptions in many realms (Sheets-Johnstone, 1998). In affective experience, a direct motor preparatory linkage appears to be especially evident, although the induction of feelings is surely strongly facilitated by reafferents aroused by the ensuing motor acts. Of course, the higher cortical 'tool-boxes' of consciousness are more intimately linked to sensory processes.

In line with the above, I would suggest that emotional feelings depend critically on the convergence of evolutionarily derived information (from various emotional sensory-motor command circuits — Panksepp, 1998) onto a primordial integrative map of the body that finds its evolutionary origin within the central zones of the midbrain. Ontogenetically, this brain function may migrate or reiterate through the medial zones of the diencephalon and telencephalon to more rostral limbic cortical areas that have long been recognized as higher repositories of emotion regulation (MacLean, 1990). Indeed, considering how closely human language appears to be related to feelings of selfhood, it is noteworthy that the medial limbic cortex of the anterior cingulate is essential for motivating the use of language; when anterior cingulate is damaged, a syndrome of akinetic mutism emerges, where people can speak but they do not desire to do so (Devinsky et al., 1995). Although such higher areas, including distinct specializations of the cerebral hemispheres (Ross et al., 1994) are clearly important for regulating affective processes, the massive convergence of information onto a primitive representation of the body makes the centromedial areas of the midbrain an excellent candidate for the essential integrative framework that first permitted a primitive form of emotional awareness. For instance, the endogenous oscillatory activity of the SELF may establish a resting tone throughout the brain and body which serves as a ground state for deviations from equilibrium that are experienced as affectively valenced forms of bodily arousal.

The intrinsic neurodynamics of such affective, motor tone-setting circuits, along with various converging somatic and visceral inputs, may create a pervasive and fractally propagated feeling of self-ness within the organism. When the shift in this feeling tone is precipitous, we call the response an emotional one; when the changes are more gradual and sustained, we may call them moods. If the system becomes chronically imbalanced, the changes may be deemed of psychiatric significance. If this view is on the right track, we may anticipate that the neurodynamics of emotions may eventually be reliably measured via EEG recordings from electrodes placed in the neural trajectories of these systems as well as from the concurrent quantification of the dynamics of spontaneous bodily movements (Freeman, 1995; Panksepp, 1999a). Although it should be possible to monitor the activities of the SELF using modern neurophysiological tools, whether they can be captured clearly on the neocortical surface remains uncertain. By the time the neurodynamic ripples reach such distant shores, the signals may be so degraded that only a modest amount of emotion-specific information remains evident (Panksepp & Bekkedal, 1997). Only the effects of general positive and negative arousal may be measureable from the cortex.

It should again be noted that since neural firing tends to be quite slow in the ancient visceral areas of the brain such as the PAG, and many functionally opposing emotional systems are concentrated in very small absolute areas of brain tissue, the slower imaging procedures which rely on blood flow and metabolic changes (fMRI and PET) may not be very effective in studying these regions. Watt (1998) has also emphasized that many forms of subcortical arousal may be washed out during brain imaging because of the overwhelming signals generated by cortical activites.

A Naturalistic Proposal of How Feelings Emerge from the Neurodynamics of the SELF

How might such a system of SELF-representation actually generate intrinsic affective value structures within the organism? If various distinct emotional and motivational inputs (i.e. the specific emotional circuits described in Panksepp, 1998) modulate the SELF-schema in distinct ways, each with characteristic neurodynamic and neurochemical signatures (Panksepp, 1993; 1999a), the result may be a variety of fundamental subjectively experienced feeling states. For instance, feelings of anger may reflect the generation of an energized bodily stance — a forceful pounding-type of sensory-motor dynamic that inundates the SELF schema when RAGE circuits of the brain are aroused. FEAR circuits may generate a qualitatively different, up-tight, trembly type of neural dynamic within the SELF. PLAY and LUST circuits may establish more flexible, rounded and flowing types of neurodynamics, while separation distress circuit may lead to repeated spikes (pangs), followed by shallow waves of distress characteristic of sadness. In other words, the neurodynamics of the various basic emotional states may eventually be visualized as topographically unique chaotic attractors within the extended neural representation of the SELF (Panksepp, 1999a). Even though this type of neuronal isomorphism is not a mandatory prediction of the present view, I share these analogical images in the hope that they may help us fathom, in neuro-theoretical terms, how the conceptual gap between our verbal concepts and our subjective experiences can be narrowed.

According to such a view of affective experience, the various neurodynamics of emotions will be characterized as hedonically desirable or distressing (i.e. the various positive and negative affects), not only by higher neural monitors but also via reafferents within the instinctual motor apparatus. In other words, the natural types of emotion-specific neurodynamic may have evolved not only to regulate motor outputs through various relatively stereotyped action tendencies in both somatic and visceral output systems, but also to continually gauge the physical consequences of actions in a feedback manner. Those types of arousal that are not resonant with the resting rhythms of the SELF, may generate withdrawal behaviours and be experienced as undesirable. Those that are resonant with the resting rhythms or facilitate certain harmonics of those rhythms may be deemed desirable. At this level of analysis, the 'explanatory gap' between neural, bodily and affective activities appears narrowed considerably. In any event, whether such understandable neural dynamics actually mediate affective experience becomes an empirically testable proposition (Freeman, 1995; Panksepp, 1999a). Only with additional encephalization, and the emergence of sophisticated learning abilities, including facility with languages that can re-symbolize such basic neuronal firing patterns, might a 'conceptual gap' have emerged. In other words, I think the explanatory gap is constructed by the ways we think about these matters linguistically rather than by the underlying primary-process brain matters themselves.

Predictions of This Model of the SELF

The credibility of any evolutionary view of consciousness or 'the self' must be based on the empirical neurobehavioural predictions that can be generated from the hypotheses. A prediction based on the views articulated above would be that extensive damage to the PAG should have profound and generalized effects on all forms of affect and conscious activities. Indeed, the initial brain-damage studies of Bailey & Davies (1942; 1943), in which remarkably precisely placed lesions of the PAG were created with electrodes threaded from the fourth ventricle up the aqueduct to the caudal edge of the diencephalon, revealed strikingly compromised consciousness in cats and monkeys as operationalized by their failures to exhibit any apparent intentional behaviours and global unresponsiveness to powerful emotional stimuli. While damage to many other brain areas can compromise the modular 'tools of consciousness', they typically do not eliminate the core of affective responsivity and intentionality in such broad ways. To my knowledge, full PAG lesions compromise consciousness with the smallest absolute destruction of brain tissue, even though a formal comparison with damage to the ERTAS remains to be conducted. However, to be highly effective, damage must run from the caudal to the rostral limits of the PAG — in other words, from the fourth to third ventricles. Simply lesioning a cross-section at one anterior-posterior extent of the PAG does not compromise consciousness to the same extent, suggesting that psychobehavioural competence may be sustained by a limited amount of PAG, which may be able to maintain affective functions via many radial connectivities to surrounding brain stem tissues.

It is also noteworthy that lower intensities of electrical stimulation in the PAG arouse animals to a larger variety of coordinated emotional actions than stimulation of any other brain area (Panksepp, 1998 and Unpublished data). The PAG is also one of the most highly interconnected areas of the brain (Cameron, et al., 1995a, b). If one accepts the criteria enunciated earlier, these compelling facts point toward the existence of a very powerful primordial foundation for various primary forms of affective consciousness within these lower reaches of the brain. Clearly, primary-process consciousness circuits are not simply restricted to the classical ascending reticular activating systems, coursing upward just ventrolateral to the PAG, as is commonly assumed (Petty, 1998), but must be seen as integrally interactive with the more medial strata of the brainstem (Panksepp, 1998; Watt, 1998).

In sum, to the best of our current knowledge, the PAG is an initial source of the anguish and suffering that suffuses self-awareness during stressful circumstances when the SELF is significantly out of homeostatic balance. The PAG is the brain area where pain and all the other basic emotions, including sexuality, leave strong neuronal footprints as measured by cFos immunocytochemistry (Bandler & Shipley, 1994; Shipley et al., 1996).[5] It is here where pain apparently begins to arouse the unconditional state of fearfulness (Depaulis & Bandler, 1991; Panksepp, 1990) and where neural circuits induce creatures to first cry out in distress and pleasure (Jürgens, 1976; Panksepp et al., 1988), where the anguish of separation and the joys of social contact first begin to be manifested (Herman & Panksepp, 1981; Panksepp, 1998). Emotional vocalizations are most easily evoked from this brain zone (Yajima et al., 1980), and it seems reasonable to assume that the neural sources of affective calls are closely intermingled with the basic mechanisms of the SELF. All of these observations lead to a cornucopia of objective empirical predictions.

Such emotional responses are not affectively vacuous motor outputs, but appear to reflect emotionally relevant central states of organisms, as can be monitored with affect-sensitive measures such as place-preference and avoidance. Often vocalizations and other emotional behavioural responses outlast the stimulation, and affective responses from higher sites are often directly dependent on the integrity of the PAG sites. The fact that compromising consciousness with diverse anaesthetics leads to some of the most powerful and consistent effects in such neural tissues (Takayama et al., 1994), further highlights the cardinal importance of the PAG for consciousness. Midline thalamic and hypothalamic circuits that are intimately related to the PAG (e.g. Cameron et al., 1995a,b) are next in the line of importance, and a close study of the higher brain areas that regulate these tissues is bound to be of importance in generating a lasting understanding how affective consciousness is generated within the brain. Surely the cortex serves to regulate — to sustain, deepen and dampen — emotions, but to my knowledge there is little substantive evidence that such higher processes create affective feelings from 'working memory', as hypothesized by LeDoux (1996). Of course, such an updated form of the James-Lange theory of emotions, where the subcortical circuits simply provide the raw materials for the creation of feelings, is certainly one way to logically deal with the empirical problems encountered by peripheralists' theories of emotions, but there is a great deal of evidence such views tend to overlook (Panksepp, 1998).

Although a high level of awareness is certainly not a local property of the PAG itself, such functions may emerge from the higher brain areas that are recursively linked to the PAG, especially in cingulate, frontal and temporal lobes (Damasio, 1994; Mantyh, 1982; Panksepp, 1991; Sesack et al., 1989). In a very similar way, it is to be expected that the SELF mechanisms of the extended PAG will be tightly interlinked with the ERTAS control of sensory-perceptual systems of the thalamic-neocortical axis as well as the REM mechanisms that appear to have antedated those systems (Panksepp, 1993). Obviously, affective feelings, as all other forms of con-

[5] This and related techniques allow neuroscientists to visualize neurons in brain circuits that have recently been aroused. In other words, the new synthesis of cFos protein as can be visualized with immunocytochemistry can provide a map of potentially critical neural systems for those behavioural and psychological process that we can bring under experimental control. For a most interesting example, see Beckett et al., 1997.

sciousness, are hierarchically organized in the brain, with the higher functions being decisively dependent on the integrity of the lower functions, but not vice versa. In other words, the convergence of visceral, somatosensory, and kinesthetic information on this primal body map, may have first generated affective feeling states that reflect the intrinsic biological values of an organism.

If so, I am willing to make one especially telling prediction. If the neuronal tissue of the SELF is essential for so many brain functions, then it should also be the most vital of neural tissues in a biophysical sense. Accordingly, if one were to take the living brain from the cranium, this tissue should be the last to die (i.e. its intrinsic neurodynamics would fade most slowly). Likewise, in tissue culture, where slabs of brain disconnected from all peripheral connections can be kept alive for days, the PAG and closely associated midline diencephalic zones should sustain endogenous activity more intensely than other tissues. Such results, not yet collected to my knowledge, could highlight the importance of these zones for all other brain activities.

Conclusions and Implications

The recognition of an embodied affective SELF, and its many moods, as a key actor rather than an observer, within the 'Cartesian Theater', may help us cultivate a more satisfactory understanding of both emotional feelings and the primal nature of the self. The SELF is fundamentally a primal sensory-motor mechanism with intrinsic resting rhythms and many emotional and integrative reafferent interlinkages that can intrinsically inundate the brain with differential psychobiological values. It has abundant somatic-perceptual and visceral-affective inputs, and working in conjunction with ERTAS architectures, it can establish certain transient as well as sustained states of being within the many neuronal workspaces of the mind. I would suggest that these states of being constitute the basic feelings (the various emotions and motivations), and we could even fantasize how the nature of the higher qualia (e.g. colours and the qualities of sound) might be closely linked to certain types of affective resonances: Harmonious or disharmonious neuro-emotional states of being might be established in the ontogenetically extended neural trajectories of the SELF. I would suggest that the emotional power of music may arise from the ability of sound to establish various resonances with the extended neural infrastructure of the SELF, yielding such magnificent bodily effects as chills (Panksepp, 1995). These possibilities can be constructed into concrete empirical predictions. The recognition that such processes may be central components of human development (Panksepp, 1999a) may also encourage us to consider undertaking positive forms of social engineering (e.g. emotional and motor education) that have so far been left to chance within our educational system (Goleman, 1995; Panksepp, 1999b).

The present view also highlights a potential dilemma for modern neuroscience, which has largely eschewed the existence of internal affective states that might control behaviour: If such processes actually exist in the brain, the neuroscientific enterprise will be critically flawed unless it takes them into consideration in its studies of various integrative brain functions.

Also, if affects are at the core of neural organization, they would obviously have to be strongly linked to genetic mechanisms. Affect, as a genetically coded property of the brain, is not widely discussed, but in evolutionary terms, one could argue that it is a special language of the genes (an idea developed by Buck & Ginsburg, 1997). Such processes could allow animals to communicate effectively in rather subtle ways, and could help explain the likelihood that genes are not simply selfish, but also capable of generating intrinsic psychological dynamics that can promote various pro-social activities enhancing genetic selection at the group, as opposed to individual, level (Sober & Wilson, 1998). Again, I would here resurrect the voice of Nietzsche (see previous quote, p. 573) that affects constitute the core of being for many of our higher faculties.

Finally I note that the neuropsychic properties that distinguish us from zombies, as the term is used in current philosophical parlance, may be these deeply felt emotional and motivational values that are closely related to our bodily survival as well as the survival of our kin (a concept that could be extended, in our rich imaginations, to many other species). For those interested in simulating mind and feelings through computational approaches, the lesson may be that at the heart of such a futuristic beast we should find a virtual body that can intrinsically reverberate, in certain presently unknown ways, with a host of deeply experienced emotional values (Picard, 1997).

Another aspect of this view is the fundamental similarly of the SELF across mammalian species, and no doubt, some other animals. This may help explain why we can resonate emotionally so well with many other creatures — we share a host of basic affective values, from rage to affection, through evolutionarily shared equalia. However, since the instantiation of equalia may require the existence of a virtual body image within the brain, constructed of living neurodynamics, the continuity of individual SELVES through space and time, after death, seems improbable. However, if there is a core similarity (i.e., a cladistic homology) of the SELF across all mammals, the shared emotional attributes offer us a variety of special resonances that can be tapped and cultivated across individuals, species and societies through affectively rich artistic, intellectual and other cultural practices. The rest of the activity of such a SELF system, broadcast gently through the resting brain, may constitute the still point of consciousness — the inner light of the soul — that is so widely recognized in many meditative and religious traditions as the central aspect of our lives.

References

Baars, B.J. (1998), *In the Theater of Consciousness. The Workspace of the Mind* (Cambridge, MA: MIT Press).

Bandler, R. & Shipley, M.T. (1994), 'Columnar organization in the midbrain periaqueductal gray: modules for emotional expression', *Trends in Neurosciences* 17, pp. 379–89.

Bandler, R. & Keay, K.A. (1996), 'Columnar organization in the midbrain periaqueductal gray and the integration of emotional expression', in Holstege *et al.* (1996).

Bailey, P. & Davis, E.W. (1942), 'Effects of lesions of the periaqueductal gray matter in the cat', *Proceedings of the Society for Experimental Biology and Medicine*, **351**, pp. 305–6.

Bailey, P. & Davis, E.W. (1943), 'Effects of lesions of the periaqueductal gray matter on the Macaca Mulatta', *Journal of Neuropathology and Experimental Neurology*, **3**, pp. pp. 69–72.

Baron-Cohen, S. (1997) *Mindblindness* (Cambridge, MA: MIT Press).

Beckett, S.R., Duxon, M.S., Aspley, S. & Marsden, C.A. (1997) 'Central c-Fos expression following 20kHz/ultrasound induced defence behaviour in the rat', *Brain Research Bulletin*, **42**, pp. 421–6.

Buck, R. & Ginsburg, B. (1997), 'Communicative genes and the evolution of empathy', in *Empathic Accuracy*, ed. W. Ickes (New York: Guilford Pubs.).

Brudzynski, S.M., Wu, M. & Mogenson, G.J. (1993), 'Decreases in rat locomotor activity as a result of changes in synaptic transmission to neurons within the mesencephalic locomotor region', *Canadian Jouranl of Physiology and Pharmacology*, **71**, pp. 394–406.

Cameron, A.A., Khan, I.A., Westlund, K.N., Cliffer, K.D. & Willis, W.D. (1995a), 'The efferent projections of the periaqueductal gray in the rat: a Phaseolus vulgaris-leucoagglutinin study. I. Ascending projections', *Journal of Comparative Neurology*, **351**, pp. 568–84.

Cameron, A.A., Khan, I.A., Westlund, K.N. & Willis, W.D. (1995b), 'The efferent projections of the periaqueductal gray in the rat: a Phaseolus vulgaris-leucoagglutinin study. I. Descending projections', *Journal of Comparative Neurology*, **351**, pp. pp. 585–601.

Chalmers, D.J. (1995), 'Facing up to the the problem of consciousness', *Journal of Consciousness Studies*, **2** (3), pp. 200–19.

Damasio, A.R. (1994), *Descartes' Error* (New York: G.P. Putnam's Sons).

David, V. & Cazal, P. (1996), 'Preference for self-administration of a low dose of morphine into the ventral tegmental area rather than into the amygdala of mice', *Psychobiology*, **24**, pp. 211–18.

Deacon, T.W. (1990), 'Rethinking mammalian brain evolution', *American Zoologist*, **30**, pp. 629–705.

Devinsky, O., Morrell, M.J., & Vogt, B.A. (1995), 'Contributions of anterior cingulate cortex to behaviour', *Brain*, **118**, pp. 279–306.

Depaulis, A. and Bandler, R. (ed. 1991) *The Midbrain Periaqueductal Gray Matter: Functional Anatomical and Neurochemical Organization* (New York: Plenum Press).

Dennett, D.C. (1991), *Consciousness Explained* (Boston: Little, Brown & Co.).

Freeman, W.J. (1995), *Societies of Brains: A Study in the Neuroscience of Love and Hate* (Hillsdale, NJ: Lawrence Erlbaum).

Gloor, P. (1997), *The Temporal Lobes and Limbic System* (New York: Oxford University Press).

Goleman, D. (1995), *Emotional Intelligence* (New York: Bantam Books).

Gray, J.A. (1995), 'The contents of consciousness: A neuropsychological conjecture', *Behavioral and Brain Sciences*, **18**, pp. 659–722.

Herman, B.H. & Panksepp, J. (1981), 'Ascending endorphin inhibition of distress vocalization', *Science*, **211**, pp. 1060-62.

Holstege, G., Bandler, R. & Saper, C.B. (ed. 1996), *The Emotional Motor System: Progress in Brain Research,* Vol. 107 (Amsterdam: Elsevier).

Hsieh, J.C., Stahle-Backdahl, M., Hagermark, O., Stone-Elander, S., Rosenquist, G. & Ingvar, M. (1996), 'Traumatic nociceptive pain activates the hypothalamus and the periaqueductal gray: A positron emission tomography study', *Pain*, **64**, pp. 303–14.

Jefferys, J.G.R., Traub, R.D. & Whittington, M.A. (1996), 'Neuronal networks for induced '40 Hz' rhythms', *Trends in Neurosciences*, **19**, pp. 202–8.

Jürgens, U. (1976), 'Reinforcing concomitants of electrically elicited vocalizations', *Experimental Brain Research*, **26**, pp. 203–14.

Lane, R.D., Reiman, E.M., Bradley, M.M., Lang, P.J., Ahern, G.L., Davidson, R.J. & Schwartz, G.E. (1997), 'Neuroanatomical correlates of pleasant and unpleasant emotion', *Neuropsychologia*, **35**, pp. 1437–44.

LeDoux, J. (1996), *The Emotional Brain: The Mysterious Underpinnings of Emotional Life* (New York: Simon and Schuster).

MacLean, P.D. (1990), *The Triune Brain in Evolution* (New York: Plenum Press).

Mantyh, P.W. (1982), 'Forebrain projections to the periaqueductal gray in the monkey, with observations in the cat and rat', *The Journal of Comparative Neurology*, **206**, pp. 146–58.

Newman J. (1997), 'Putting the puzzle together: Towards a general theory of the neural correlates of consciousness', *Journal of Consciousness Studies*, **4** (1&2), pp. 47–66, 101–21.

Newman, J. & Baars, B.J. (1993), 'A neural attentional model for access to consciousness: A Global Workspace perspective', *Concepts in Neurosciences*, **4**, pp. 255–90.

Nietzsche, F. (1996) *Beyond Good and Evil* (New York: Vintage).

Olmstead, M.C. & Franklin, K.B. (1997), 'The development of a conditioned place preference to morphine: effects of microinjections into various CNS sites', *Behavioral Neuroscience*, **111**, pp. 1324–34.

Panksepp, J. (1982), 'Toward a general psychobiology of emotions', *Behavioral and Brain Sciences,* **6**, pp. 407–67.

Panksepp, J. (1985), 'Mood changes', in *Handbook of Clinical Neurology,* Vol. 1. (45): *Clinical neuropsychology*, ed. P.J. Vinken, G.W. Bruyn & H.L. Klawans (Amsterdam: Elsevier).

Panksepp, J. (1986), 'The neurochemistry of behavior', *Annual Review of Psychology*, **37**, pp. 77–107.

Panksepp, J. (1990), 'The psychoneurology of fear: evolutionary perspectives and the role of animal models in understanding anxiety', in *Handbook of anxiety*, Vol. 3: *The Neurobiology of Anxiety*, ed. G.D. Burrows, M. Roth & R. Noyes Jr. (Amsterdam: Elsevier).

Panksepp, J. (1991), 'Affective neuroscience: A conceptual framework of the neurobiological study of emotions', in *International Review of Studies on Emotion*, ed. K.T. Strongman, (Chichester: John Wiley & Sons Ltd.).

Panksepp, J. (1993), 'Neurochemical control of moods and emotions: Amino acids to neuropeptides', in *Handbook of Emotions*, ed. M. Lewis & J.M. Haviland (New York: Guilford Press).

Panksepp, J. (1995), 'The emotional sources of 'chills' induced by music', *Music Perception*, **15**, pp. 171–207.

Panksepp, J. (1998), *Affective Neuroscience: The foundations of human and animal emotions* (New York: Oxford University Press).

Panksepp, J. (1999a), 'The neurodynamics of emotions: An evolutionary-neurodevelopmental view', in *Emotion, Self-Organization, and Development*, ed. M.D. Lewis & I. Granic (New York: Cambridge University Press) in press.

Panksepp, J. (1999b), 'A critical analysis of ADHD, psychostimulants, and intolerance of childhood playfulness: A tragedy in the making?', *Current Directions in Psychological Science*, **8** (in press).

Panksepp, J. & Bekkedal, M.Y.V. (1997), 'The affective cerebral consequences of music: Happy vs sad effects on the EEG and clinical implications', *International Journal of Arts Medicine*, **5**, pp. 18–27.

Panksepp, J., Knutson, B. & Pruitt, D.L. (1998), 'Toward a neuroscience of emotion: The epigenetic foundations of emotional development', in *What Develops in Emotional Development*, ed. M.F. Mascolo & S. Griffin (New York: Plenum Press).

Panksepp, J. & Miller, A. (1996), 'Emotions and the aging brain. Regrets and remedies', in *Handbook of Emotion, Adult Development and Aging*, ed. C. Magai & S.H. McFadden, (San Diego: Academic Press).

Panksepp, J., Normansell, L.A., Herman, B., Bishop, P. & Crepeau, L. (1988), 'Neural and neurochemical control of the separation distress call', in *The Physiological Control of Mammalian Vocalizations*, ed. J.D. Newman (New York: Plenum).

Panksepp, J., Normansell, L., Cox, J.F. & Siviy, S.M. (1994), 'Effects of neonatal decortication on the social play of juvenile rats', *Physiology & Behavior*, **56**, pp. 429–43.

Petty, P.G. (1998), 'Consciousness: A neurological perspective', *Journal of Consciousness Studies*, **5** (1), pp. 86–96.

Picard, R.W. (1997), *Affective Computing* (Cambridge, MA: MIT Press).

Ramachandran, V.S. & Hirstein, W. (1997), 'Three laws of qualia: What neurology tells us about the biological functions of consciousness', *Journal of Consciousness Studies*, **4** (5–6), pp. 429–57.

Redgrave, P., Telford, S., Wang, S., McHaffie, J.G. & Stein, B.E. (1996), 'Functional anatomy of nociceptive neurones in rat superior colliculus', In eds. G. Holstege, R. Bandler & C.B. Saper *The emotional motor system. Progress in Brain Research,* Vol. 107 (Elsevier, Amsterdam), pp. 401-415.

Revonsuo, A. (1995), 'Consciousness, dreams, and virtual realities', *Philosophical Psychology*, **8**, pp. 35–58.

Rizzolatti, G. & Arbib, A. (1998), 'Language within our grasp', *Trends in Neurosciences*, **21**, pp. 188–94.

Ross, E.D., Homan, R.W. & Buck, R. (1994), 'Differential hemispheric lateralization of primary and social emotions', *Neuropsychiatry, Neuropsychology and Behavioral Neurology*, **7**, pp. 1–19.

Schildein, S., Agmo, A., Huston, J.P. & Schwarting, R.K.W. (1998), 'Intraaccumens injections of substane P, morphine and amphetamine: Effects on conditioned place preference and behavioral activity', *Brain Research*, **790**, pp. 185–94.

Sesack, S.R., Deutsch, A.Y., Roth, R.H. & Bunney, B. (1989), 'Topographic organization of the efferent projections of the medial prefrontal cortex in the rat: An anterograde tract-tracing study with Phaeolus vulgaris leucoagglutinin', *The Journal of Comparative Neurology*, **190**, pp. 213–42.

Sheets-Johnstone, M. (1998), 'Consciousness: A natural history', *Journal of Consciousness Studies*, **5** (3), pp. 260–94.

Shipley, M.T., Murphy, A.Z., Risvi, T.A., Ennis, M. & Behbehani, M.M. (1996), 'Olfaction and brainstem circuits of reproductive behavior in the rat', in Holstege *et al.* (1996).

Snodgrass, J.G. & Thompson, R.L. (ed. 1997), *The Self Across Psychology: Self-recognition, Self-awareness, and the Self Concept. Annals of the New York Academy of Sciences,* vol. 818 (New York: New York Academy of Sciences).

Sober, E. & Wilson, D.S. (1998), *Unto Others: TheEvolution and Psychology of Unselfish Behavior* (Cambridge, MA: Harvard University Press).

Sparks, D.L. (1988), 'Neural cartography: sensory and motor maps in the superior colliculus', *Brain Behavior and Evolution*, **31**, pp. 49–56.

Strawson, G. (1997), 'The self', *Journal of Consciousness Studies,* **4** (5–6), pp. 405–28. Reprinted in this volume, pp. 1–24.

Strehler, B.L. (1991), 'Where is the self? A neuroanatomical theory of consciousness', *Synapse*, **7**, pp. 44–91.

Takayama, K., Suzuki, T. & Miura, M. (1994), 'The comparison of effects of various anesthetics on expression of Fos protein in the rat brain', *Neuroscience Letters*, **176**, pp. 59–62.

Watt, D. (1998), The Association for the Scientific Study of Consciousness Electronic Seminar on Emotion and Consciousness, Sept. 21– Oct. 9, 1998, http://www.phil.vt.edu/assc/esem.html

Yajima, Y., Hayashi, T. & Yoshii, N. (1980), 'The midbrain central gray substance as a highly sensitive neural structure for the production of ultrasonic vocalization in the rat', *Brain Research*, **298**, pp. 446–52.

Donald Perlis

Consciousness as Self-Function

I argue that (subjective) consciousness is an aspect of an agent's intelligence, hence of its ability to deal adaptively with the world. In particular, it allows for the possibility of noting and correcting the agent's errors, as actions performed by itself. This in turn requires a robust self-concept as part of the agent's world model; the appropriate notion of self here is a special one, allowing for a very strong kind of self-reference. It also requires the capability to come to see that world model as residing in its belief base (part of itself), while then representing the actual world as possibly different, in other words, forming a new world-model. This suggests particular computational mechanisms by which consciousness occurs, ones that conceivably could be discovered by neuroscientists, as well as built into artificial systems that may need such capabilities.

Consciousness, then, is not an epiphenomenon at all, but rather a key part of the functional architecture of suitably intelligent agents, hence amenable to study as much as any other architectural feature. I also argue that ignorance of how subjective states (experiential awareness) could be essentially functional does not itself lend credibility to the view that such states are not essentially functional; the strong self-reference proposal here is one possible functional explanation of consciousness.

Introduction

This chapter outlines the beginnings of a theory of mind based in large part on the notion of self. However, I do not take self as a fundamental irreducible notion, rather I seek to elucidate self in computational terms. The picture I wish to present has the following outline: Mind, consciousness/awareness, and qualia, are notions coherent only in relation to the concept of self, which in turn can be given functional and computational characterization. On that basis can be built the beginnings of a general theory that at least is not obviously incapable of explaining the former notions, and that holds suggestions for how to go about finding such explanations.

My theses in this chapter are, roughly, (i) that consciousness is synonymous with self, and self with a special sort of self-modelling I call strong self-referential computation; (ii) that there is an indivisible 'something it is like to be' a strongly-self-modelling (or referring) entity, constituting a sort of ur-quale,[1] and without which no experience, no subjectivity, is possible; and (iii) out of the ur-quale can arise fancier sorts of ineffable qualia: colours, emotions, and so on.

Since there is so much disagreement on basic terminology, it will be helpful to set out at the beginning how I understand certain terms.

---

[1] 'Ur' is used here in the sense of *prototypical* or *fundamental* or *primitive*.

Paradigms and Definitional Gestures

Concepts mature as we learn more. We cannot expect to grasp the nature of the mind at the outset, nor to have adequate definitions. As we study conscious systems, e.g. brains, we may find out about new structures and processes that will utterly amaze us because they are so different from anything we had imagined before. Who in 1900 had thought of self-replicating molecules? — yet in principle it would have been possible to do so. Who in Flatland thinks of 3-dimensional space? — yet it is possible in Flatland to do so, indeed to give a mathematical description of its properties, once someone has the idea.

I conjecture that we may find in the brain special amazing structures that facilitate true self-referential processes, and that constitute a primitive, bare or ur-awareness, an 'I'. I will call this the *amazing-structures-and-processes paradigm*. I take it that it is shared by many working in the allied computational cognitive neurosciences, e.g. Baars, Crick, Damasio, Edelman, Harth; but not Block, Chalmers, Deikman, Dennett,[2] Penrose. Such entities once understood may indeed 'stand up and grab us' as obviously self-experiencing and hence possessed of experiential awareness. Such an outcome would then close the explanatory gap.

In order to relate the above to other pieces of the consciousness debate, I provide some definitional guides. Block (1995) notes that the term 'consciousness' is used in many distinct ways; it is Block's *P-consciousness* — i.e., phenomenal consciousness, or subjective experiential awareness — that is the subject of our concern. It is worth noting that Block, along with Crick and others, seems to regard it as almost obvious that P-consciousness is not the same thing as self-consciousness, in apparent strong contrast with the position I shall argue. One small part of my argument is a rather trivial one that I shall reveal here: subjectivity involves a subject, a self, a 'me', simply on the terminological face of things.

We can provide another characterization of P-consciousness in a paraphrase of Nagel (1974): An entity is conscious if it is in a state such that it is 'like something' for it to be in that state. This seems to help us separate examples of consciousness from examples of non-consciousness. Rephrased again, consciousness is experiential awareness, and experience is like something for the experiencer; what it is like, how it feels, is the experience. This may seem a bit circular, but it is usefully suggestive. We will see something analogous (strong-self-reference) come up in an important role in what follows.

Qualia are the individuating aspects of experiences that allow us to distinguish experiences from one another; e.g. we distinguish red from blue by its redness. We distinguish a square from a triangle by its four-sidedness as an aspect of the experience of seeing a square. These examples illustrate that some qualia are partially effable (e.g. square-percepts) and some are not (e.g. redness). Qualia are not restricted to visual experiences: they are found also in emotions, touches, smells, sounds, and so on. They may also occur in thoughts, since a thought has a particular aspect that distinguishes it from, say, a touch: to use Nagel's terminology, it is like something to be

---

[2] Dennett (1991) however is hard to pin down. He undoubtedly agrees that the brain achieves an amazing feat of information-processing, and that this is all there is to consciousness. But he also argues that consciousness is an illusion, leaving the impression that once all detail is worked out nothing so very novel will have been discovered.

thinking, it feels different from not-thinking.[3] A quale is an aspect of an experience such that it is recognizably different (i.e. like something different) for it to be absent.

So defined, qualia occur only as aspects of consciousness; but consciousness might not, at least prima facie, be accompanied by qualia. We will explore this further below.

Functional explanations

Let us recall the challenge by Chalmers (1995, loosely paraphrased): where's the beef (qualia) in many of the proposed 'scientific' accounts of consciousness? He in particular argues that consciousness, unlike the usual objects of study in science, is not itself a behaviour (function or process), and that attempts at scientific explanation simply replace consciousness by some function or process that may result from or contribute to — but is itself not — consciousness. It is the subjective sense of awareness, the qualitative 'feels' of consciousness, pains and pleasures, vivid experiences, that seem to be lacking in the processes or functions.

But why is consciousness not a process, simply an amazing one well beyond the poor pale processes we are currently able to envision, much as a living cell is an amazing but physical structure-and-process far beyond what any chemist could have envisioned in 1900? To be sure, consciousness is something special, beyond cellular chemistry. It's amazingness will be different, perhaps far more astounding, than that of the cell. But we should not assume we currently see the ultimate limits of what processes or functions can entail.

Chalmers argues that past perplexities as to the nature of living things, for instance, were ones of behaviours and thus did not present the same kind of fundamental challenge as does conscious experience: to be a living thing is to perform certain kinds of function, such as reproduction, adaptation, metabolism.

But it was not always thus: the apparent purposiveness of (many) living things did not once seem to be a function. It is only now with the enormous success of the evolutionary, biochemical and computational paradigms that we can at last see biological purposiveness as a kind of evolved electro-chemical computational process: the wasp builds a nest 'purposively' but not in ways that call for explanations beyond ordinary causal mechanisms. Similarly, conscious experience might turn out to be a function, such as an appropriate form of self-modelling, which we might come to understand when we are further along in the quest. How could 'mere' self-modelling have a feel? That remains to be seen, and I will make some tentative suggestions here.

Looking ahead to the thesis — defended below — that there is an ur-quale necessary and sufficient for consciousness, and that it is a special but effable sort of strongly-self-modelling computational process, we can ask: How are fancier qualia to be recaptured, how are the ineffable to be added-on to the effable ur-consciousness? How is it that a presumably mechanical process of distinguishing self from other, itself based ultimately on geometric (spatio-temporal) distinctions in the nervous system, can be green-perceiving rather than red-perceiving? How can geometric distinctions amount to the differing feels of red and green?[4]

---

[3] Thinking feels different from, say, drinking, or from listening to music, or from writhing in pain, or from lying awake but unfocused. And thinking about a calculus problem in a general way feels different from trying to solve it, and in turn different from comparing two solutions.

[4] Not to be confused with mere wavelength differences.

But perhaps such feels can be found in a deeper analysis of colour experiences, as based on the self, and on emotional factors such as fear, envy, rage, despondency (yellow, green, red, blue). Emotions[5] in turn might prove to be bodily conditions that are also self-based (fear might involve a condition of unwanted reduction in self-governance). Wants might involve recognition of physiological needs and what might satisfy them. Needs may be perceptions of built-in drives as well as of the organism's inability to act so as to disobey those drives.

Another challenge to the amazing-structures-and-processes paradigm (see McGinn, 1995; Shear, 1996) is that whereas physical (process) phenomena occur in spatial arrangements, subjective phenomena do not. A full discussion would take us far from the main theme of this chapter, but the following suggestions may serve to indicate that there is more spatiality to subjectivity, and less to physicality, than meets the eye. Our percepts very often have spatial arrangement: my tooth-ache does seem higher than my stomach ache. And while my thought that Nixon was a scoundrel may not be above or below my thought that he was a Quaker, there is a sort of metric tying them together: I turn attention from one to the other, then back again, as if moving through a mental space. Moreover, a thought is not indivisible, it is a complex built out of parts arranged among themselves, e.g. subject and predicate, with a specific linkage that may be metrical in significant ways. Finally, the physical world is not all spatio-temporal: gravity is weaker than the electromagnetic force; but gravity is not above or below electromagnetism. Physically real entities of suitable abstraction need not be spatially arranged.

The amazing-structures-and-processes paradigm then is directly in opposition to Chalmers' view. We proceed to explore the paradigm by reconsidering the role of qualia in consciousness.

Getting by without qualia?

It may be that qualia are not essential for consciousness after all. This can be argued by direct appeal to our experience. We can certainly be conscious with our eyes closed, or indeed with no eyes at all. We can lack a visual cortex, auditory cortex, and certain other portions of our brains, and still be conscious. And even without missing brain parts, we can simply be in a state of not having any of the qualitative experiences so common in discussion of consciousness: touch, sight, sound, smell, taste, pain, pleasure, and so on. For any particular experiential quality we may mention, it seems that we can quite clearly be without it and yet be conscious. If so, then why cannot we also be without any qualia at all and yet be conscious? Is there perhaps a special sacrosanct quale that must remain, an ur-quale? If so, the ur-quale would be the only quale necessary and sufficient for consciousness, all others being contingent.

To be more specific, suppose an experience with quale Q to be modified so that Q is missing from the experience. For instance, suppose the redness of an apple-perception disappears and the apple is seen as a shade of grey. There are still qualia present in the modified experience, namely brightness and shape qualia among others. Now suppose the brightness and shape qualia absent as well; in fact suppose the experience is 'reduced' simply to that of knowing there is an apple ahead. Still qualia remain in the experience, for it is like something to experience knowing an apple is ahead, even without seeing it; and we can distinguish knowing about an apple from

---

[5] See O'Rorke and Ortony (1994) for a distinct suggestion.

other experiences. What if now we remove that knowing as well, and are left with bare experience with no distinguishing features to single out: no apple, no thoughts, just bare experiential awareness, pure consciousness.[6]

Let us pursue this a little further. Suppose such a state of experience is possible. Then can it too be distinguished from other experiences? Can one imagine it removed? Is it imaginably absentable? Since all experience would be gone then, it would seem that it is not like anything at all for such a pure consciousness to be gone. But if we cannot even imagine it absent, i.e. what it is like for that experience to be absent, this seems to fly in the face of the property of distinguishability stated as our definition of qualia. This might mean that pure consciousness, if it exists at all, is not a quale. But how can an an experience be like something and yet not be distinguishable from other experiences (i.e. possessed of qualia)?

We are at a seeming impasse. Yet there is a way out: it may be that an experience can be distinguished in and of itself, by its own intrinsic character, rather than by comparison to something else. While everyday qualia such as redness and square-ness, perhaps even thinkingness, are distinguishable from one another and also by their presence or absence, perhaps bare consciousness is in and of itself a self-distinguishing process, a process that takes note of itself. If so, it could still be considered a quale, the ur-quale, what it's like to be a bare subject, and distinguishable from other fancier experiences simply in virtue of the additional qualia attending the latter but not the former.

What might this be? That is unclear, and yet it has a certain familiarity to it, in the sense that our experiences are, after all, known to us to be ours, private, personal. If we strip away incidental properties due to our situated histories, do we end up simply with a 'me', a bare awareness, not in touch with objects or environment, but simply having a self-presence *simpliciter*? What is it for a process to distinguish itself, and from what is it distinguished? We will return to this below. The potential beauty of this is that it is not totally implausible that such a kind of self-perceiving process may be computational. Much of the rest of this paper is a tentative exploration of that possibility.

Robots, perceptual awareness, perceptual management, mantises
Some (e.g. Crick) hope to find keys to the nature of conscious experiential awareness by studying particular behaviours such as visual perception. While such work is valuable and important, I think there is serious question whether it alone will get us very far in this issue. One reason is that consciousness can go on quite nicely in the complete absence of vision. Another is that visual processing can go on without consciousness. I think that expressions such as 'perceptual awareness' are risky ones that mislead us into thinking, for example, that visual processing in and of itself is a kind of consciousness. When we are conscious, there can be visual qualia present as part of that experience, but that is not to say that visual processing constitutes visual qualia, the 'what it's like' to be seeing.

Indeed, robot vision systems today routinely perform complex tasks of visual perception, even visuo-motor coordination, binocular focusing of cameras, motion-tracking, and so on. It is startling to observe such systems in operation, hard to avoid

---

[6] See Deikman (1996) and Shear (1996) for evidence of such a state coming from various cultural traditions. Below I offer some contrasts of detail in our respective views.

the uncanny sense of being watched, their paired robot eyes swivelling suddenly as you walk across the room. Yet no one seriously regards these as in any way conscious or aware of anything at all. I suspect that the impressive physiological work being done on the vision systems of mammals is going to show us structures and processes much like those of today's robots, and little at all about awareness.[7] This is not to say, of course, that consciousness is not a physiological phenomenon: it is, but one that is at quite a different level from processing of perceptual data. I prefer to call the latter 'perceptual management' rather than perceptual awareness.

Another interesting perception management system is that of the praying mantis. The mantis has in the order of 100,000 neurons,[8] roughly half of which are grouped in two large clumps, one behind each eye. The mantis has excellent visual abilities, and can utilize these as well as auditory processing in navigating a powerdive to avoid bats which feed on them. The mantis can launch an attack of its own as well, for instance cannibalistically on its own species. Thus if mantises are not conscious — and I am not taking sides on this — then a high degree of sensori-motor facility need not endow consciousness even in biological systems.

Such systems nevertheless can have a high degree of self-modelling; e.g. the mantis does not mistakenly attack itself instead of another mantis. But when self-modelling is present in *sufficient* degree, it may confer, or may simply be, what consciousness is. Just what that degree might be is considered below.

Self: A Hypothesis

I will set out a (possible) function of consciousness that I think might in fact *constitute* consciousness. I state this baldly as a hypothesis; later we will have to refine it a bit: *Consciousness is the function or process that allows a system to distinguish itself from the rest of the world*, conferring a point of view on the system, hence providing Perry's essential indexical 'I' (Perry, 1979); this plays an important role in error-correction, and bears on the problem of intentionality. Consciousness is then, first and foremost, a special kind of self-reference.[9]

Moreover, I think that this particular function is one that may be able to bear the weight of qualitative demands; at least the notion of self seems like a hopeful start: to feel pain or have a vivid experience requires a self. There is no such thing as pain *simpliciter*, or experience *simpliciter*, in the absence of an agent that is (has) a self, an 'I' to be the feeler (as in 'I am feeling pain').[10] Thus I think that recognition of self (personal identity) is an essential ingredient in conscious experience; I think it may even be *what it is* to be consciously experiencing. Note that recognition of self can go on in many particular contexts, some of which would be pain experiences, some colour-perceptions, some ruminatory excursions, and so on.

---

[7] That is, one needs to go to much deeper and higher levels of processing to get to consciousness.

[8] Compare to the 100 *billion* or so in the human brain.

[9] Refinements to come below include the idea that non-self can be one's own past remembered self, so that no *external* perception is needed.

[10] Try to imagine a system noting 'there is pain' but not that it is *its* pain. If not its, then whose? No-one's pain? Or consider visual experience: a scene appears as seen from a direction and at a particular distance, namely from the position and at the distance of the observing agent.

It is fair to ask, however, what good self-modelling is. This brings us to the general issue of error-recognition and repair, which means we must talk about meaning and reference.

Intentionality and self

No one mistakes a symbol for what it stands for; we easily distinguish the two.[11] The symbol is something we use in our thinking, hence instances of it occur in us, in our belief base, in our self model. By contrast the *symbolled* is in the world, and merely represented by the internal symbol in our self-model. We have direct control over the one (the internal symbol) and not the other (the symbolled world). Thus we can alter our images or ideas or words: we alter the expression 'this is a dog' to 'this is a wolf' at will (whether for whim or speculation or to correct a false belief), but we do not so easily change a dog into a wolf. This symbol–symbolled distinction suggests several things, which I will detail in what follows. But I will note first that this rather obvious distinction is not currently put to much use in artificial intelligence systems, nor in psychology, linguistics, and neuroscience; it has been largely ignored, except in developmental psychology, where it surfaces in the appearance–reality distinction. I suggest that it may in fact play a very key role in intelligence and consciousness. Its proper handling requires the self-*vs*-world models as stated above, and can be seen in computational terms in part as a kind of quotation mechanism, i.e., 'Ralph' is a word in my thoughts and stands for Ralph in the world. Here we see the beginning outlines of our computational theory of consciousness.

When an agent's reasoning behaviour is reflected into its self-model, then it has become recorded as part of its narrative self-history, a term suggestive of Dennett's interno-phenomenological report.[12] I suggest that this is a key component of that behaviour's being conscious: it takes its place in episodic memory, as something that occurred in or to the agent. Without this double-layer of representation (as being outside the agent and also symbolled inside the agent), there is no 'I' and no awareness.[13]

Thus for a brain structure to provide consciousness, it must be complex enough to be able to provide a self-in-the-world, a symbol-to-symbolled tie that links a self model to a world model and can adjust the latter if errors are encountered. Various neural maps come to mind here, that may be part of a larger system of self–world representations: tectal maps, efference copies, thalamic maps, sensori-motor homunculi.

The above ideas with respect to language are further developed in several papers (Perlis, 1987; 1990; 1991; 1994; 1995). Newton (1988; 1992) develops a similar line of argument. We look more closely at this now, since it further illustrates some of the computational/quotational thesis.

Double representation and error

Even though double, the distinction between symbol and symbolled is useful, perhaps crucial, for it allows us tremendous flexibility to reconsider our beliefs, to see our

---

[11] Voodoo dolls and cave-paintings notwithstanding. The belief in a deep causal connection between two objects, or even that they are two aspects of the same thing, is entirely consistent with — and even built on — the ability to distinguish the one from the other.

[12] A special self-reporting case of his hetero-phenomenological report (Dennett, 1991).

[13] The self/non-self or inside/outside distinction will be refined below, however, bringing it in line with the idea of the ur-quale.

beliefs as mere beliefs rather than brute truths: it allows us the wisdom that we are after all holders of imperfect views of reality, and the further wisdom that we can try to improve our views by finding our errors and correcting them. It allows what at one moment is a pure symbol undistinguished from what it stands for, to become at a later moment quoted or otherwise seen as an object of thought, something inside and not the outer reality.[14]

To relate this to a familiar subjective sense: We find ourselves engaged in a nearly constant back-and-forth between naive belief and circumspect self-querying, as we go through the day thinking about things. We are aware of thinking, aware of time passing, of ourselves with goals and being part-way through an ever-evolving effort. This can be the profound wisdom of a philosopher; or the profane wisdom of a raccoon rubbing water out of its eyes, not long mistaking its still-watery view with the dry world it has struggled to from the lake.[15]

We are constantly bombarded by such clashes in our perceptions, and we iron them out by noting, first of all, that we are possessed of views and that not all of them are correct (if they are in mutual conflict). This I think is a very basic phenomenon, not requiring explicit human-style language, but more like a very primitive (perhaps mostly bodily-and-visual) language of thought.

I suggest that an agent G cannot be conscious of event Y unless G represents an intentionality relation between G and Y: G must record the *fact* of its representing Y by means of a symbol (or image) 'Y' that is inside G. G not only represents Y with 'Y', G also represents the relationship between Y, 'Y' and G itself, along with means to adjust it. Thus G's situatedness in the world that includes Y is central to this notion of consciousness. There can be no box of pure unsituated consciousness, no box of 'perceiving redness', without an observer that is itself part of what is observed.[16] Again then we come to the idea of self as central to consciousness, and self-referral as ur-consciousness: Y and 'Y' are absentable, but not G's self-representation.

In Perlis (1994) I offer suggestions as to how an account based on self might be given for bodily reference and beyond, based on internal geometry and bodily situatedness and recalibration during motion. This yet again fits into my claim above that self is crucial: meaning is measured by reference to the agent's own body, e.g., via homuncular and other cortical and tectal maps, and involving that body's situatedness in the environment: this pain is in my leg; that red ball is in front of me. When we are conscious of Y, we are also conscious of Y in relation to ourselves: it is here, or there, or seen from a certain angle, or thought about this way and then that. Indeed, without a self model, it is not clear to me intuitively what it means to see or feel something: it seems to me that a point of view is needed, a place from which the scene is viewed or felt, defining the place occupied by the viewer. Thus I question (e.g. Crick, 1994, p. 21) that self-consciousness is a special case of consciousness: I suspect it is the most basic form of all.

[14] For a similar view see Humphrey (1992).

[15] The reader wary of my presumptive claims about raccoons, may simply substitute humans.

[16] Thus quotation or some similar device for internal referring may be a key ingredient in the processes by which an entity may be a self, i.e. a self-distinguishing self-presence. More will be said on this below. Note the double-representation implicit in representing an intentionality relation: this is precisely a matter of representing a representation. But it need not require a third level, let alone an infinite regress; we return to this below as well.

Appearance–reality distinction and self

Error-recognition has ties to nonmonotonic reasoning (Perlis, 1990; Alchourron *et al.*, 1985) in which reasoners may change their minds based on finding conflicts in their beliefs. I think that this too can be seen as an appearance– (or belief–) reality distinction (ARD, see Flavell *et al.*, 1986 and Gopnik, 1993). The ARD provides an interesting handle for studying much of what passes as 'mind' and it is amenable to technical study (in psychology, AI, linguistics, and — hopefully — neuroscience). (So far it has mainly been studied only in developmental psychology; but see Miller, 1993.) The ARD is the capacity to distinguish conceptually between how something appears and how it is. This usually is applied to perceptual judgments (that ball looks blue in this light but it is really white); however, the concept makes sense in far broader settings.

Consider the example of having the belief that John is old (you see that he has grey hair). Later you discover that he is 25 years old and prematurely grey. Then 'John is old' comes to be seen by you as a belief or appearance, out of line with reality. As a result your beliefs change as they form a new current view of reality. So, there is a loop of belief-to-reality updates. The ARD then is in effect simply the self-*vs*-world modelling discussed earlier.

Note that ARD can involve temporal information: *that* is how it appeared to me (how I thought it was a moment ago) but *this* is how it is. Such reasoned change in belief involves recognition of passage of time and with it a passage of belief-state. Note also that the ARD applies equally both to perceptual judgments and to perceptual experiences. One can judge a past judgment to be in error, and so may one judge a past perceptual experience to be in error. Just as one's judgment or belief that a blue object is directly ahead may later be rejected, so may the experiencing of blueness be rejected as an error: did I really experience that, or is my memory fooling me?

Gopnik (1993) discusses an interesting study of 3-year-olds that bears on our claims. When questioned as to what they think is inside a closed candybox, they state it has candy; when shown that inside are pencils and asked again, they state it has pencils; and when then asked what they had thought it contained before it was opened, they state (falsely) 'pencils'. On the other hand, 4-year-olds do not make such mistakes. There are many subtleties to the design and interpretation of this and related studies. However, on the face of it, my theory might be taken to suggest that 3-year-olds are not conscious of seeing the pencils; or do not consciously see pencils: or perhaps are not conscious of meaning pencils by 'pencils'; or of having seen anything ten seconds ago as opposed to now. That is, they do not seem to distinguish the (former) appearance (a box with candy) from the reality (a box with pencils). The simplest explanation, perhaps, is that they do not remember what they had thought at first; this of course does not entail that 3-year-olds are not conscious. Thus the theory of consciousness I am proposing is not contradicted by ARD data. It is noteworthy that the inside of the closed box is not available in appearance, yet it is believed to be there by the three-year-old. It is unavailable 'perceptions' that seem to present the difficulty. To what extent then must cognitive self-modelling occur, to count as conscious? I have been urging at least some form of this, but it need not extend to time periods long enough to be captured in language.

Consider an individual unable to distinguish a seen object from how it looks. Such a person may be puzzled, for instance, at things becoming blurred in rainy weather, (compare the raccoon example above), or in their disappearing as night falls. This would, to say the least, be a very severe disorder of thought. If I am right, it would amount to the loss of thought altogether — at least if it extended to all modes of representation rather than visual alone — leaving only a mindless and slavish recording of inputs with possible reactive responses (no weighing of alternatives). According to the theory being advanced here, such a person would not be conscious at all.[17]

We have been discussing self-*vs*-world modelling at some length, but now we must ask what constitutes a self, and how it can be distinguished from non-self. This will add a further dimension to the quotation–computation mechanism.

Strong Self-reference

If it is like something to be conscious, then that something, that experiential feel, is not imaginably absentable, i.e. it is not like anything at all to be without that feel. How then can it be noted, be a part of awareness? How can we note something without thereby noting a difference from an absence of that something?

Ordinarily we may distinguish experiences by differences, but perhaps this is not essential. Perhaps certain notings can be done in such a way that they can only occur positively, never as an absence. In particular, an inherently self-noting process may be exactly that: not imaginably absentable. Whether such occurs in the conscious brain, and whether we can discover such computational processes, is an empirical matter.

Why would such a not-imaginably-absentable feature be important? What is its functional role? Here we come to the crux of the debate, and the crux of this paper. The forms of self-reference most widely cited and studied, from antiquity to the present are weak forms. They tend to come in two types: delegated self-reference[18] and meta-self-reference. Delegated self-reference has been made famous in the sentence 'This sentence is false' as well as others such as 'This sentence has five words' and 'This sentence no verb', not to mention 'This proof-system is consistent'. On their own, such sentences express nothing; it takes a linguistic community to interpret them and close the loop, so that 'this' comes to mean that very expression itself.

Meta-self-reference is another kind of weak self-referring, most easily described with the help of a robot, Ralph. Suppose in Ralph's knowledge base (KB) are various sentences, including 'Sue is Canadian' and 'Ralph is American'. The latter does not in itself amount to Ralph's referring to himself, i.e. it does not form a closed loop back to Ralph (without delegated help from us), unless Ralph also has further sentences or processes that do just that: link the name 'Ralph' to Ralph. Replacing 'Ralph' with 'I' will not in itself achieve this; a special treatment of 'I' is needed (Perry, 1979). Links

---

[17] This hinges crucially on the phrase *all modes of representation*, including self-representation. Such a person would not have a self in the sense argued here. We discuss this at greater length below.

[18] Self-reference has an illustrious role in intellectual history, from antiquity (the Liar paradox) to modern times (Cantor's, Gödel's, and Turing's theorems). However, the form of self-reference in these cases is a delegated one: the actual action of referring is done by an interpreter outside the supposedly self-referential objects (sentences). Moreover, such delegated-self-reference is, when treated with technical care, quite well-understood, not quite tail-chasing after all despite how it may seem to beginning logic students. This alas is not enough for our purposes; no one proposes that, for example, a formal system of arithmetic prone to Gödelian incompleteness is in any sense conscious, or is even an active entity that can perform or partake in processes.

that tie 'I' to Ralph's own body are a beginning, permitting Ralph to order replacement parts for his broken arm. But he could do the same for robot Sue's broken arm, from knowing Sue was built at a certain Canadian factory. The fact that in the former case Ralph is replacing his own arm, as opposed simply to the arm of a robot named 'Ralph', is irrelevant. We can keep adding to Ralph's KB: 'I am Ralph', ' "I" means the robot with serial number xyz', etc, in a hierarchy of referrings, but none seeming to get to a final self-contained self. What is of interest for us is not such meta or delegated self-reference, but rather entities that self-refer all on their own.

Why do we need a self-contained self, where referring stops? Negotiating one's way in a complex world is a tough business, for a robot or for a biological system, and complex behaviours have come about as a result. Dealing with the inevitable errors that crop up is one big part of the problem, necessitating commonsense reasoning, as above in the case of Ralph noting the need to order a new arm. But now something interesting happens. Suppose the new arm is needed within 24 hours. He cannot allow his decision-making about the best and quickest way to order the arm get in his way, i.e. he must not allow it to run on and on. He can use meta-reasoning to watch his reasoning so it does not use too much time, but then what is to watch the meta-reasoning? Since he is a finite system, his resources are limited and he cannot do all kinds of reasoning simultaneously. He must budget his time. Yet the budgeting is another time-drain, so he must pay attention to that too, and so on in an infinite regress. Treating his planning as one thing and his time-tracking of his planning as another, and so on, by separate modules responsible for each level of reasoning, clearly will not work. Somehow he must regard it all as himself, one (complex) system reasoning about itself, *including that very observation*. He must *strongly self-refer*: he must refer to that very referring so that it's own time-passage can be taken into account.

Do we ever find ourselves having such a 'conscious' state? I think we do so all the time, it is the essence of barebones consciousness: 'here I am'. Not 'here is Joe' and 'Joe is me' and 'me is the person who just thought his name is Joe' and so on. We catch ourselves in the present, in a strongly self-referring (SSR) loop. It is the recognition that 'this is now', where 'this' is my present experience that this is now. Circular, yes, but not quite paradoxical.

Now we can look back and say that even a sentence such as 'I am Ralph' can strongly self-refer in the appropriate system in which the pronoun 'I' is treated in a special way. So, what is *strong self-reference*, what is that special way? I do not have a technically precise answer, but I do claim that this problem is a technical one, not a philosophical one. Robots, like humans and many other biological entities, need this ability, and it is one that is functionally defined. Moreover, it is not so apparent that it does not have, in and of itself, an attendant quality, a something-it-is-like-to-be. It might be a nearly qualeless-consciousness, but with a bare 'I am here' aspect to it that is distinguishable even though it is never noticeably absent: the ur-quale.

In light of the above, let us now again ask, what is a self?

I suggest that a self is best thought of as an entity G that can refer to G as that entity doing that very referring. This might for instance be associated with the gloss 'here I am now thinking about myself'. There is a peculiar kind of tail-chasing mind-bogglingness to such a description. It is this that I suggest is at the heart of self and therefore of consciousness.

I will now advance a tentative semi-technical definition of strong-self-reference. An entity G strongly-self-refers by an action A if:

1. G models the performance of A;
2. that same modelling is part of that very performance of A;
3. this reflexive aspect of the modelling is itself part of the modelling.[19]

These three 'axioms' are admittedly not as clear as one would like. I present them as very rough guides to further study. However, one thing seems clear: time and memory must play very special roles in this, for it is a self-modelling *process* we are dealing with, not a frozen formula. Perhaps these models run on a very fast basic time cycle, perhaps a few milliseconds long, in which there is a blurred notion of the present, i.e. in which there can be several things occuring that manage to refer to one another.

I will now offer several observations that appear to be in line with the idea of a self-referring final-self.

First, our earlier comments that qualia must be *someone's* qualia, that to be in pain one must take the pain to be one's own, does not sit well unless there is a final self. A hierarchy of selves, each referring to the one below, does not self-refer, and so does not take anything to be its own. To say 'the system' as a whole feels the pain, or is aware, simply backs away from the problem. Maybe a system as a whole can be aware, but we need an account of how that might be.

Second, the only kind of reference that does not pass the buck is reference to itself, i.e. a referring that refers to that very referring. This sounds very odd, but we have seen examples: 'this current action of expressing' or 'I am now referring to my referring'. While strained (unfelicitous) these are still intelligible. I am proposing that something akin to this goes on literally all the time when we are conscious, and that this *is* our consciousness. It is of course not usually spoken, and probably is on a much faster time-frame, and would not normally be under our control. On the contrary, it is the very matrix of awareness that gives us control over slower behaviours.

Third, it seems to me that we *explicitly* do something very much like this at times when we think about ourselves. For example, in making the utterance 'I am now speaking English', we refer to our very referring. This I think satisfies the three axioms above; in particular, the reflexive character ('I . . . now') is what makes it be us and not Joe Blow that we refer to. Note that this example exploits a time cycle well beyond a few milliseconds; but it is not a blur, since we easily pick out earlier and later parts of it. But there may be an elementary 'I'-cognition that has no observed subparts: it is observation at its most primitive.

Fourth, we need to do this, at least in deadline-coupled situations. Here is a more difficult example, but one that makes the point.[20] I decide 'I'll get on with things', implicitly meaning not only to stop whatever I had been doing, but also to pass beyond that very decision and on into some other action. Here the decision seems in part to refer to that very process of decision, i.e. to get on past even it. There may appear to be an infinite regress of meta-levels, but I believe this is incorrect and that we do in fact refer to our own very act of referring. Otherwise there is nothing in the

---

[19] Here 'modelling' is an ambiguous term perhaps nearly synonymous with 'referring' or 'representing'. Presumably the utility of modelling is that it allows the individual the ability to draw inferences and make plans, especially in deadline-coupled situations.

[20] A bit along the lines of the earlier one of Ralph seeking a new robot arm.

represented pattern of thought that ties it back to the thinker's ongoing actions. That is, we might actually either (i) get into an infinite regress and never come to a full stop to get on with other tasks, or (ii) we might simply stay at a particular meta-level and never note that it too is keeping 'us' from those tasks. Somehow we must (and do) tie our ongoing sense of time passing to our ongoing planning and acting, and get the right things done at the right time (sometimes!).

A question then is how can an active system G genuinely self-refer? Does it take something more than information processing? And does it confer consciousness? On the latter, since we do not currently have an independent definition, we are left with intuition. I think that only by careful examination of human behaviour and the design of smarter robots will we be able to position ourselves to have more than merely prejudicial intuitions. At present I simply offer this as a tentative characterization of consciousness, namely: a process of self-referring that satisfies the three axioms above.

No one, to my knowledge, has built, or even tried to build, strongly-self-referring machines. This in large part is due simply to the fact that no one has tried to build robots that can do very much reasoning, or even that can do very much common-sensical self-protection in a complex world. But strong self-reference is what an intelligent robot needs, to avoid the infinite meta-regress, as well as to appropriately take action to protect itself, say, when it infers that 'it' is in danger.

One may retort that although *at times* one is aware mostly of oneself and no more, this is more often not the case. One may think about the Moon, and not oneself. But this is a misunderstanding of my point. The strongly-self-referring ur-quale (which we might give as the gloss 'here I am') is always there, whether or not the 'here' includes the Moon or anything else as part of it. There can be many types of contents to consciousness; the ur-quale is always among them even if it is not in central focus, and indeed it might never be so.[21] It is perhaps better put 'here I am as this noting of things including this noting'[22] or more simply 'this is itself a noting of XYZ going on'. One's activity keeps bordering on focusing on itself and then (necessarily) getting pushed aside by its own activity; and yet this very fact is somehow recorded or observed as part of that activity. Very puzzling stuff, but we should not assume a physical device cannot do just this.

Discussion

The above presents a number of complicated notions that require further comment to appreciate their interconnections. I specially wish to consider some particular areas of possible misunderstanding of my intent. In this I avail myself of some very helpful comments and questions by the editors, Jonathan Shear and Shaun Gallagher.

I have argued that consciousness involves a self/non-self distinction, and then I assert that the ur-quale, the essential ingredient of consciousness, is devoid of the usual cognitive modalities (vision, touch, and even thought with external content) by which we know non-self. This seeming inconsistency touches on a key refinement of my initial definition: the self is also non-self when it is remembered as one's past self:

---

[21] This is one way of reading of Searle's claim that 'I cannot *observe* my own subjectivity' (1992, p. 99).

[22] Grice's views on speech acts (Grice, 1975) are similar to this, as well as more recent work on mutual knowledge (Barwise, 1989). Both involve self-reference not unlike the strong sort here.

it no longer is the self of the moment — subject becomes object — and this 'sliding along' in self-observation is another way to describe strong self-reference. This need not be a rich memory of years gone by; it is enough that it be a memory of one's immediate past activity, even if that activity is simply internal self-observation, an ongoing 'here I am'.

What is the computational mechanism I have promised, as a possible basis for the ur-quale? It is strongly self-referring computation, probably facilitated by some sort of quotational syntax. However, it is a computational research paradigm, not a precisely defined notion at present. I have presented examples intended to show the need of such a thing in intelligent behaviour, especially deadline-coupled planning in complex environments. This in turn suggests two places to look in evolutionary terms for the appearance of consciousness: (i) where behaviour of that sort does or does not arise[23] and (ii) where there are brains with suitable processing power to allow such strong self-reference.

Note, however, that very likely in evolution, the processing of external perceptual data became important early on, and so the first appearance of the ur-quale may well have coincided with the arrival of 'fancier' qualia. That is, the devices for processing perceptual data likely were well in place long before the ur-quale appeared and made possible the 'translation' of that perceptual processing into fancy qualia. It seems unlikely that evolution would have wasted the energy to build self-meditating worms that could not utilize that ability to better survive. But when deadline-coupled planning becomes essential to survival, when planning and acting need to be subtly dovetailed and what has just been done needs to be factored into what is to be done next, yet without letting that deliberation take too long, we may be nearing a strong self-loop of now-into-then processing tantamount to the ur-quale.

Thus the ur-quale probably evolved in conjunction with very complex external perceptual processing. Still, it need not be tied to the latter once it is present. This is not to say, however, that the ur-quale is something simple. It will be a complex process, one requiring memory (of itself) and temporal processing. Quite possibly the ability to access the ur-quale in isolation, as in a meditative state, is an accidental by-product of evolution; at least I see no survival value in being able to strip away fancy qualia altogether, despite possible philosophical, psychological and aesthetic value.

With the refinement above, we can now reinterpret my argument for a double-layer of representation (both outside the agent and also symbolled inside) as being outside the present activity of the agent and yet also symbolled in that present activity, namely as one refers to one's immediate past. Thus my theory does not require, for consciousness, sophisticated views of external reality found in, say, adult humans but not in three-year-olds. It is enough that a now–then distinction be made, even on a short time-cycle, enough for self-representation as an ongoing-ness of the self from present into future.

Moving from appearance to reality with regard to conscious experience makes sense precisely in terms of time-passage. We access the process of a moment ago, taking it as the present (i.e. as reality) until we reject it and take the next moment as the

---

[23] The Sphex wasp, for instance, seems not to be able to distinguish very well what it has done from what it must still do: if its multi-step routine of stocking its nest with supplies is even slightly disrupted, it begins all over again, repeating many unnecessary steps. This suggests that it has little if any internal model of its own behaviour.

present, and so on. We are caught permanently in a now-to-then loop. How such a loop can also refer to itself, i.e. to its own self-referring processing, is an open question. But we have seen reasons to believe something of that sort may well be requisite for survival in complex entities such as ourselves.

Comparisons

Deikman (1996) argues a related position: content is not enough, there must be a self (which he calls the 'I', reserving 'self' for more incidental aspects of the aware agent, such as personality). This deep inner 'pure' self is bare awareness in itself, as suggested by the answer 'yes' that one is likely to give to the question, 'Are you conscious?'

He further says we *are* awareness and do not need to observe awareness; being awareness is a different kind of knowing awareness, from the inside. But what does this mean, and why is it not also a kind of self-observing, perhaps different from but related to other-observing? He seems to suggest self-knowing occurs in a largely different sphere from that of space and time, but this is a large leap that may not be needed.

Contrary to Deikman, I suggest the observer can be and is observed by itself, and so can be content as well as observer. Awareness does always have an object, but that object can be pure awareness of itself.

The SSR theory being advanced here has some common ties with the higher-order theory, HOT, of Rosenthal (1986). However, the latter (actually more meta-theory than higher-order theory) is not genuinely self-referential, and thus cannot avail itself of the suggestive hints we have urged here, toward closing the explanatory gap on awareness and qualia. Rather, HOT postulates distinct levels or layers of representation directed from one to another. By contrast, SSR postulates a single reflexive level.

Rosenthal distinguishes creature-consciousness from higher-order consciousness; the former may come close to what I above called perceptual management, while the latter, a form of self-consciousness, is proposed as the consciousness of interest, Block's P-consciousness. However, it is not defined that way by Rosenthal; it is defined as a kind of meta-propositional information, about creature consciousness for instance. Thus the information that 'one is hungry' — itself distinct from the gastrointestinal facts of the matter — is a higher-order piece of information a system may have about itself. This in turn may be further modelled at a yet higher level as 'I have the belief that I am hungry'.

Harth (1993) espouses a recursive notion of awareness as a process in which successive passes of processing provide a deepening of representational 'bias'. However, the self-reference described in his account does not appear to be that of representation of the process to itself; there is only content, no subject. What we need, according to the SSR theory, is a genuinely self-reflecting loop, one that takes its own activity into account, that sees itself as a self-seeingness.

There is a frequently-heard view (e.g. Crick, Block) that self-consciousness is a special and unusual form of consciousness. We suggest a distinction between strong-self-reference on the one hand, and introspective consciousness on the other. The former is always present in a conscious system, on my theory: it is consciousness. But the latter is an additional feature, in which the noting includes, say, historical information about oneself, such as 'I tend to be shy'. Here the 'I' reveals SSR at work, and the rest is introspection or meta-knowledge. As such the latter adds much to the cognitive repertoire of the system, but little at all to our understanding of the nature of consciousness. It is not so much a special kind of consciousness as simply a special kind of information. Indeed, many introspective mechanical systems have been built, but none that are conscious.

To sum up: consciousness is the function of strongly-self-noting that allows a system cognitively to get out of its own way, to avoid an infinite regress.

So, does this 'stand up and grab us' as being obviously right, obviously a fount of an inner life of the mind? I cannot claim so. But I do think that it is at least not obviously wrong, that there is something to the idea of a bare, stripped consciousness that only knows its own knowingness, and that such would not be vividly populated with colours and smells and urges. And I think it also is at least not obviously wrong that it is like something to be in such a state.

Conclusions and Neural Connections

Much of the consciousness debate hinges on qualia — the felt qualities of experiential awareness: colours, pains, moods, what it feels like to do or be or undergo this or that. Yet one can be colourblind and assuredly conscious. While not denying the philosophical challenge that qualia present, we might still consider whether consciousness itself is something more basic than qualia. If we strip away colour experience, pain experience, emotional experience, and so on, is anything left? Is it like something simply to be conscious, and if so, what is it like? Intuition suggests it is like something, but perhaps a very primitive something. Might this not be simply strong self-reference? Note that complex time-situated and memory-bound processing must occur as part of strong-self-reference. It might not be like very *much* to be a pure ur-consciousness/self/strongly-self-referrer: no personal feelings, no goals, no cares. But it is not so evident that it is like nothing, surely not so evident as that it is like nothing at all to be a rock or a Macintosh computer.

Where are we to look in the brain for such amazing structures and processes? A camera can take a picture of itself (via a mirror, and can even take a picture of itself that includes the mirror); this is an elementary example of self-reference. But there may be far more subtle ones in the brain. Known neural loops are a start, from efference copy in VOR to the reentrant loops emphasized by Harth and Edelman. But that's only a beginning. We'll need far better models of strong self-reference, self-modelling temporal loops that take now into then on and on, while also being able to get out of their own way. Perhaps the diagonal method of Cantor, used so well by him and Gödel and Turing in explicating self-referential mysteries of mathematics and computation, has yet more in store for us in the brain.

This paper has sketched one possible 'scientific' (function or process) theory of consciousness. To be sure, I have not given a detailed account of exactly how subjectivity might arise in systems with the functional capacities I describe; but this I think is not to be expected in advance. It is far too early to give up on traditional 'function or process' modes of scientific inquiry regarding consciousness. My hope is that the amazing-structures paradigm will little by little lead to just that, in computational, cognitive, and neuroscientific terms.

References

Alchourron, C., Gardenfors, P. and Makinson, D. (1985), 'On the logic of theory change', *Journal of Symbolic Logic*, **50**, pp. 510–30.

Barwise, Jon (1989), *The Situation in Logic*, chapter 9: On the Model Theory of Common Knowledge. CSLI Lecture Notes: Number 17. Center for The Study of Language and Information.

Block, N. (1995), 'On a confusion about a function of consciousness', *Behavioral and Brain Sciences*, **18** (2), pp. 227–87.

Chalmers, David J. (1995), 'Facing up to the problem of consciousness', *Journal of Consciousness Studies*, **2** (4), pp. 200–19.

Crick, F. (1994), *The Astonishing Hypothesis* (New York: Scribners).

Deikman, Arthur (1996), ' "I" = awareness', *Journal of Consciousness Studies*, **3** (4), pp. 350–6.

Dennett, D. (1991), *Consciousness Explained* (New York: Little, Brown).

Flavell, J., Green, F. and Flavell, E. (1986), 'Development of knowledge about the appearance–reality distinction', *Society for Research in Child Development Monographs*, **51**, No. 1, Series No. 212.

Gopnik, A. (1993), 'How we know our minds: the illusion of first-person intentionality', *Behavioral and Brain Sciences*, **16** (1), pp. 1–14.

Grice, H.P. (1975), 'Logic and conversation', in *Syntax and Semantics 3: Speech Acts* (New York: Academic Press).

Harth, Eric (1993), *The Creative Loop* (New York: Addison-Wesley).

Humphrey, N. (1992), *A History of the Mind* (New York: Simon and Schuster).

McGinn, Colin (1995), 'Consciousness and space', *Journal of Consciousness Studies*, **2** (4), pp. 220–30.

Miller, M. (1993), 'A view of one's past and other aspects of reasoned change in belief', PhD thesis, Department of Computer Science, University of Maryland, College Park, Maryland.

Nagel, T. (1974), 'What is it like to be a bat?', *Philosophical Review*, **83**, pp. 435–50.

Newton, Natika (1988), 'Machine understanding and the Chinese Room', *Philosophical Psychology*, **1**, pp.207–15.

Newton, Natika (1992), 'Dennett on intrinsic intentionality', *Analysis*, **52**, pp. 18–23.

O'Rorke, P. and Ortony, A. (1994), 'Explaining emotions', *Cognitive Science*, **18**, pp. 283–323.

Perlis, D. (1987), 'How can a program mean?', in *Proceedings, International Joint Conference on Artificial Intelligence*, Milan, Italy, 1987.

Perlis, D. (1990), 'Intentionality and defaults', *International J. of Expert Systems*, **3**, pp. 345–54 [Special issue on the Frame Problem, ed. K. Ford and P. Hayes].

Perlis, D. (1991), 'Putting one's foot in one's head — part I: Why', *Nous*, **25**, pp. 435–55 [Special issue on Artificial Intelligence and Cognitive Science].

Perlis, D. (1994), 'Putting one's foot in one's head — part II: How', in *From Thinking Machines to Virtual Persons: Essays on the intentionality of computers*, ed. Eric Dietrich (New York: Academic Press).

Perlis, D. (1995), 'Consciousness and complexity: the cognitive quest', *Annals of Mathematics and Artificial Intelligence*, **15**, pp. 309–21 [Special issue in honor of Jack Minker].

Perry, J. (1979), 'The problem of the essential indexical', *Nous*, **13**, pp. 3–21.

Rosenthal, David (1986), 'Two concepts of consciousness', *Philosophical Studies*, **49**, pp. 329–59.

Searle, John (1992), *The Rediscovery of the Mind* (Cambridge, MA: MIT Press).

Shear, Jonathan (1996), 'The hard problem: Closing the empirical gap', *Journal of Consciousness Studies*, **3** (1), pp. 54–68.

Jun Tani

An Interpretation of the 'Self' from the Dynamical Systems Perspective
A Constructivist Approach

This study attempts to describe the notion of the 'self' using dynamical systems language based on the results of our robot learning experiments. A neural network model consisting of multiple modules is proposed, in which the interactive dynamics between the bottom-up perception and the top-down prediction are investigated. Our experiments with a real mobile robot showed that the incremental learning of the robot switches spontaneously between steady and unsteady phases. In the steady phase, the top-down prediction for the bottom-up perception works well when coherence is achieved between the internal and the environmental dynamics. In the unsteady phase, conflicts arise between the bottom-up perception and the top-down prediction; the coherence is lost, and a chaotic attractor is observed in the internal neural dynamics. By investigating possible analogies between this result and the phenomenological literature on the 'self', we draw the conclusions that (1) the structure of the 'self' corresponds to the 'open dynamic structure' which is characterized by co-existence of stability in terms of goal-directedness and instability caused by embodiment; (2) the open dynamic structure causes the system's spontaneous transition to the unsteady phase where the 'self' becomes aware.

I: Introduction[1]

One of the crucial problems in consciousness studies is that terms such as 'consciousness' and 'self', which ought to describe subjective human experiences, are rarely defined in an objective and scientific manner. Dennett (1991) made this point when he wrote 'every author who has written about consciousness has made what we might call the first-person-plural presumption'. In considering this problem, this chapter explores the possibility that the constructivist approach using the power of system analysis reinforces some theories about the 'self' obtained from phenomenological observations.

By the constructivist approach, what we mean here is an approach to understanding various cognitive and behavioural functions of humans and animals by modelling them with artificial systems — i.e. building computer simulators, robot systems, etc.

[1] I would like to thank Joseph Goguen for discussion and encouragement with this study from its inception. I would also like to thank the journal's referees who suggested various ideas to improve the contents and J. Yamamoto and H. Nishi for their assistance in building the robot platform.

Although the constructivist approach in the field of artificial intelligence, artificial neural networks and machine learning has made a contribution towards the understanding of general cognitive mechanisms such as recognition, learning or planning, it has not made a great contribution towards understanding the problems of consciousness. Although some might be able to build their own models of consciousness by embodying them with some 'conscious robots', such attempts would just end up with Dennett's problem of 'the first-person-plural presumption' again. Once Thomas Metzinger (1998) argued that the problems of consciousness cannot be solved if people focus on only those problems, but they can be naturally resolved when mutual relations among other elements of human cognition are well understood. This argument can be extended further to say that consciousness or self might be seen in *a hermeneutic process* which appears in the iterative interaction among elemental cognitive processes, as Tsuda discussed (Tsuda, 1984.) This interpretation is supported also by Varela (Varela *et al.*, 1991) who claims that consciousness is not self-existential but appears as a co-dependent structure among others. In this sense, the constructivists may not be able to design or model functions of consciousness or self directly but some analogies for them may appear in terms of structures and regularities in the interactions among cognitive and behavioural processes that are properly configured.

Varela argued in the book *The Embodied Mind* (Varela *et al.*, 1991) that the essence of the embodied mind resides in the structural coupling which is established in the interaction between the bottom-up process originated from the objective world and the top-down process originated from the subjective mind. In our study, we attempt to reconstruct this sort of interactive process between the subjective mind and the objective world in a robot platform by which we examine what sort of structures can emerge from such interactions. (Here the word 'the subjective mind' is used only metaphorically in our robot studies to indicate a process that attempts to interpret the 'objective world' by means of its accumulated sensory-motor experience.) If certain structures are observed in our experimental results, we investigate whether the structure corresponds with any phenomenological observations that have been obtained in other disciplines. Although it might be true that the descriptions of the 'self' or 'consciousness' from the constructivist side can never be more than metaphorical, we expect that such comparison with the phenomenological observations can serve to strengthen the metaphors for connecting aspects of robot and human behaviours more closely. The following subsections will discuss our framework in detail.

1. Puzzles involving 'bottom-up' and 'top-down' in robotics

For more than four decades, robots have been good experimental platforms for constructivist research investigating human mechanisms of intelligence and cognition. The first biologically inspired robot was developed by Grey Walter as shown in his book *The Living Brain* (Walter, 1953) in the 1950's. Walter describes robots built on cybernetic control principles which demonstrated goal-seeking behaviour, learning capability, and Ashby's (1952) idea of homeostasis. His 'turtle' robot, which was equipped with a simple cybernetic controller using optical sensors, exhibited quite complex navigation trajectories by avoiding obstacles and approaching light sources in the environment. This illustrated well that even simple control functions can generate quite complex behaviours when interacting with the environment.

From the 1970s to the 1980s, robots were often used as platforms for artificial intelligence (AI) research. Typical research objectives in those days were to study how to represent abstract models of the world and how to build action plans efficiently using the acquired representation of the world. In these studies, researchers believed that the most essential feature of intelligence was the logical manipulation of symbols. The studies of Shakey (Nilsson, 1984) at SRI and CART (Moravec, 1982) in Stanford represent well such research attitudes. Although this type of research produced rich results for the theories and methodologies of AI, the understanding obtained usually exhibited poor performance when implemented in physical robots and tested in the real world. More specifically, the robot could not tolerate the discrepancies between the given model and its actual experiences in the real world; the robot could not plan its actions in real time.

So-called behaviour-based robotics were initiated by Rodney Brooks (1991) at the end of the 1980s in reaction to conventional AI research. The new research put less emphasis on the performance of higher-order cognition such as abstraction, representation or planning. Instead, the focus was on the interactions between the robot and its environment at the sensory-motor level. A robot perceives the sensory input from the environment, and the motor actions are directly determined by means of reflex responses to the sensory input. As the result of the iterative sensory-motor interactions, certain structures and regularities emerge in the coupled dynamics between the robot and its environment (Beer, 1995). The goal of the adaptive behaviour is to adapt the internal controller such that the emergent structure and regularity sustain the robots inside their zones of viability (Meyer & Wilson, 1991). This claim is actually a reintroduction of the one by Ashby (1952), Walter (1953) and Braitenberg (1984) in the cybernetic era. The main difference between the behaviour-based robotics in the 1980s and the turtle robot of Grey Walter in the 1950s is the use of digital computers instead of vacuum tubes for the internal controllers. The microprocessor technology allowed researchers to build small self-contained robots, while implementing various sophisticated control and adaptation algorithms on them. Regardless of such sophistication, the old and new robotics share the same principle — the internal processes are naturally situated in their environment by means of their structural coupling via sensory-motor loops.

It can be said that robotics has fluctuated between the two extremes — putting strong emphasis either on the top-down process of the subjective mind or the bottom-up process from the objective world. The strong negation of 'representation' in the behaviour-based robotics left no room for 'subjective mind' by which the realities perceived from the 'objective world' can be anticipated and interpreted in the top-down manner. On the other hand, it can be said that AI researchers have been underestimating the significance of realities that arise in a bottom-up fashion from the objective world. This underestimation of the difference between the abstract model in the subjective mind and the reality of the objective world causes the so-called symbol grounding problems which have been discussed by Harnad (1990). We consider that constructivists need to focus seriously on the relation between the bottom-up process from the objective world and the top-down process from the subjective mind, since the problems of consciousness are very likely to be found in the middle of these two pathways (Varela et al., 1991.).

2. *Symbol grounding problems*

A common approach for combining the bottom-up and top-down pathways is to use hybrid-type models which consist of a lower level processing the real world signals with analogue pattern-matching (often by using the connectionism technique) and a higher mental level which deals with symbolic manipulations of the abstract world models. These two levels are interfaced by a device, called a categorizer, by which patterns can be categorized into clusters represented by particular symbols. The patterns can then be projected back by indexing the symbols. Harnad considered that the categorizer device is a strong candidate for solving the symbol grounding problems (Harnad, 1990). He further argued that hybrid symbolic/analogue models employing the categorizers can be scaled up to human capacity levels more readily than pure symbolic models or purely neurodynamics models (Harnad, 1993). This argument might be overly optimistic. In reality, such architectures could still suffer from symbol grounding problems. Let us describe such an example in autonomous robot research.

The example that we introduce is about the landmark-based navigation of mobile robots that has been studied by many robot researchers (Kuipers, 1987; Mataric, 1992). A typical mobile robot, which is equipped with simple range sensors, travels around a certain office environment while sensing the range reading of its surrounding environment. The continuous flow of the sensory image is categorized into one of several predefined landmark types such as a straight corridor, a corner, a branch or a room entrance. The upper level constructs a chain representation of landmark types by observing sequential outputs of the categorizer while the robot explores the environment. Such an internal map consists of nodes representing landmark types and arcs representing transitions between them. This representation takes exactly the same form as a symbolic representation known as finite state machine (FSM).

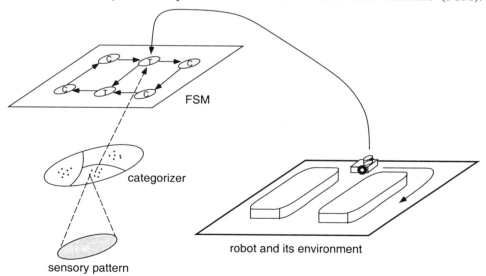

Figure 1.

Landmark-based navigation of a robot using hybrid-type architecture consisting of FSM and categorizer.

(A FSM consists of a finite number of discrete states and their state transition rules.) Once the robot acquires the internal map of the environment, it becomes able to predict the next sensation of landmarks during its travel by looking at the next state transition in the FSM. When the actual perception of the landmark types matches the prediction, the robot proceeds to the prediction of the next landmark to be encountered. An illustrative description is shown in Figure 1.

The problems take place when this matching process fails. The robot will become lost since the operation of the FSM halts upon receiving an illegal symbol/landmark type. This is the symbol grounding problem. Some may argue that the addition of certain exception handling procedures to the FSM operations will remedy the situation. For example, one could write a program such that when unexpected landmarks occur, the current state transition rules of the FSM could be modified suitably. However, we argue that such exception handling procedures could face another symbol grounding problem since there is no logical way of knowing whether unexpected landmarks appear by means of temporal noise or due to permanent changes in the environment.

When systems involve the bottom-up and the top-down pathways, the systems inevitably encounter inconsistencies between the two pathways. The problem is how such inconsistencies can be treated internally without causing a fatal catastrophe in the system's operations. In hybrid systems, the higher symbolic levels, which are designed to resolve such inconsistencies, simply halt their operations upon facing a contradiction between the expectation of the FSM and the observation. We consider that both levels are jointly responsible for any inconsistency and that the conflicts should be resolved through cooperative processes between the two levels. The cooperation entails iterative interactions between both sides through which optimal matching between the two sides is sought dynamically. The iterations in time are necessary not for the complete resolution of the conflict but for the postponement of the current inconsistency to a future time via which the systems can at least continue their consisting current operations. The major drawback of hybrid systems is that two pathways of the bottom-up analogue processes and the top-down symbolic processes cannot interact with each other intimately since the two pathways are defined in different metric spaces. In this chapter, we propose an alternative — the dynamical systems approach (Beer, 1995; Freeman, 1995; Kawato *et al.*, 1990; Smith & Thelen, 1994; Tani, 1996; van Gelder, 1998) — in which all systems including the mind, body and environment are defined as dynamical systems to enable their interaction to take place in the shared metric space.

3. Dynamical systems approach

The computational metaphors of dynamical systems have been discussed by many others (Crutchfield, 1989; Blum *et al.*, 1989). It is, however, important to say that in dynamical systems we cannot recognize the separable entities 'representation' and 'manipulation' as one does in conventional computation. Esther Thelen and Linda Smith wrote in their recent book (Smith & Thelen, 1994), 'Although behaviour appears rule-driven, there are no rules. There is a multiple, parallel and continuously dynamic interplay of perception and action, and a system that, by its thermodynamic nature, seeks a certain stable nature.' In the dynamical systems view, all that exists is the dynamical structures of the system and the resulting system's behaviour. The dynamical structure corresponds to the configuration of the vector flows in the phase space of the system. For example, if all vectors in the phase space of a system converge onto a point, the system behaves as characterized by equilibrium fixed point dynamics. If all the vectors converge onto a closed cycling orbit, the system behaviour is characterized by periodic oscillations known as 'limit cycling dynamics'. If the configuration of the vector flows becomes more complex and satisfies certain conditions, the system's behaviour is characterized by randomness and nondeterminism which is known as 'chaotic dynamics'. The new question is from where all the dynamical structures originate. We consider that the dynamical structures of the system are not something to be given or to be designed, but they emerge as self-organized through the iterations of the system itself. The dynamical structures generate the iterations of the system that, in turn, modify the original dynamical structure. The dynamical structure for cognition is established through such self-referential processes.

A difficulty exists in the embodiment of the higher cognitive levels by means of the dynamical systems approach. The question is how the dynamical systems approach can embody the complex subjective processes without employing the AI scheme of symbolic representation and manipulation. The key to solving the problem can be found in a recent scheme developed in the field of artificial neural networks, called recurrent neural network (RNN) learning (Elman, 1990; Pollack, 1991). The RNNs are considered to be adaptive dynamical systems from which dynamical structures can be tuned by means of neural connective weight modification using certain self-learning schemes. Elman (1990) and Pollack (1991) showed that the RNNs can learn certain language syntactic structures from example sentences. The particular finding in their research is that grammatical rules cannot be seen explicitly in the neural internal representation, but the rules are actually embedded in complex attractor dynamics. Using the RNNs is suitable for our objective since we can exclude the 'homunculus' from the systems which attempts to look down at the representation from the top and to manipulate the elements of the representation. The symbol grounding problem may not exist for RNNs since there exist no explicit forms for the symbols in the RNNs which need to be grounded.

Our cognitive architecture, which will be described in this chapter, employs the RNN scheme for embodying the top-down subjective processes of the robot. We expect that intimate interactions will take place between the top-down processes of the RNN and the bottom-up pattern matching processes of the other conventional neural nets, since the processes share the same metric space comprising the real number system. In the experiments, we investigate how the total dynamical system evolves through the iterative interactions between the internal neural systems and the environment, focusing especially on the bottom-up and the top-down issues. We will show our finding of specific dynamical phenomena from the results of iterated experiments and discuss its analogy to the notion of 'self' found in the literature of phenomenology. Finally we shall describe our model of the 'structure of the self', which is obtained by extending Strawson's (1997) and Hayward's (1998) studies about discontinuous occurrences of 'selves'.

II: The Robot and Its Cognitive Tasks

Our experimental investigations concern the navigation learning of a mobile robot. For the experiment, we built a small mobile robot which is equipped with vision and tactile sensors as shown in Figure 2. The robot controls camera-targeting, both hori-

zontally and vertically, in addition to the manoeuvering of its wheels. We will now describe
the task setting more specifically.

1. The task

The robot travels clockwise around a closed
workspace following its outside wall as shown
in Figure 3. The robot has to switch its attention
between two visual tasks: wall edge following
(for detecting the configuration of the wall on
the left-hand side) and object recognition (for
coloured objects appearing on the right-hand
side of the robot). These two tasks are alternated
while the robot travels smoothly along the detected wall at a constant speed. The robot encounters two types of landmarks in the
workspace: objects with coloured patterns on
their surface, and corners in the wall. As the robot sequentially encounters these landmarks
while travelling around the same workspace,
the landmark sequences are learned via consolidation into a long-term episodic memory. The
robot then becomes able to anticipate which
landmark will be encountered and when it will
do so from the episodic memory. The recognition of a landmark proceeds as a cooperative
process between the anticipation in the higher
level and the perception in the lower level. The
anticipation also activates the robot's attention
towards a visual target. The visual attention is
switched to searching for coloured objects on the
right hand side of the robot when a coloured object is expected to be encountered in the near future. Otherwise, the vision is engaged in the wall
edge following task. It is considered that the robot becomes situated to the environment when

Figure 2.

The vision-based mobile robot used in the experiments.

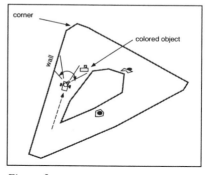

Figure 3.

Robot navigation with landmark objects and corners.

the anticipation and the perception match well for the event sequences. This navigation learning experiment was conducted in both a constant and an inconstant environment.

2. Cognitive problems in the task

The tasks described here are not trivial since the robot must perform them utilizing
only the finite cognitive resources available. What neural networks can do are always
constrained in time and space. For example, the recognition of a visual object requires
a certain convergence time for the network since a neuron's activation evolves according to its inherent time constant. The learning capacity is limited since the
number of synaptic connections is finite. Moreover, the physical embodiment con-

strains the robot's cognitive processes significantly. The robot's vision can only see within a finite range in the workspace at one moment. The visual attention switch takes a nonzero time in order to rotate the motors of the camera head. The difficulty is that the robot has to interact with the world in a real time manner under various cognitive and physical constraints. This difficulty is explained more specifically in the following.

- The time delays in the visual recognition and the attention switch make the visual processes of the robot difficult. Problems take place when the robot travels in the workspace while alternating its visual attention between wall-following and object recognition. If attention is engaged in the recognition of a coloured object for too long, the robot might overlook the wall and collide with it. On the other hand, if object recognition is engaged for only a shorter period, the recognition process could result in mis-identification of the object since the process might be terminated before complete convergence.

- The cooperation scheme between the top-down anticipation and the bottom-up perception is a non-trivial problem. The correct top-down anticipation could stabilize the lower perception processes. However, if the learning of the event sequences is insufficient, the resulting incorrect anticipation may interfere badly with the perception of the next event in the lower level. Strong top-down anticipation could override the bottom-up perception, which might cause 'illusions'. The problem is that it is hard to determine in what ratio the top-down and the bottom-up processes should contribute to the recognition processes.

- The incremental learning scheme in the inconstant environment faces a dilemma between stability and plasticity since learning new experiences often interferes with what was learned in the past. When the new experience and the former memory conflict with each other, the conflict cannot be resolved easily since the robot itself cannot judge on this occasion whether it should acquire the new experiences as being the correct one and forget the former memory as being obsolete, or to ignore the new experience as being a misleading result and to preserve the former memory.

III: Models

This section introduces the cognitive architecture employed in our robot. The architecture consists of several neural network modules in which some aspects of the modelling are based on physiological findings shown in the literature, but only in quite an abstract manner. The architecture is, rather, built to reflect our interpretation of how the bottom-up and the top-down interactions might take place in the cognitive processes of animals or humans. In the following, we first describe our modelling procedure, including the neural architecture, the learning scheme and the arbitration mechanism between the top-down and the bottom-up pathways, in a very abstract manner in order that non-technical readers can understand the content. The later subsections will describe the details which non-technical readers may like to skip.

Figure 4 shows a schematic diagram of our proposed neural net (NN) architecture consisting of multiple modules. The architecture consists of three parts, namely the perception part, the association part and the prediction part. The perception part consists of the PE module and the TE module which recognize the current object of visual

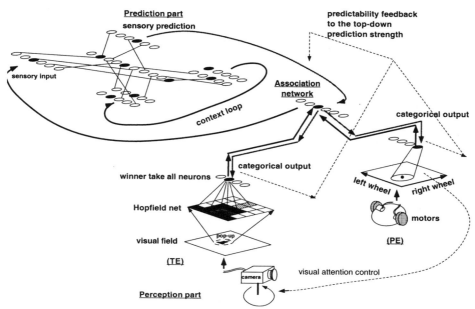

Figure 4. Proposed architecture consisting of multiple neural networks.

focus (a landmark) in terms of a 'where and what' manner (Ungerleider & Mishkin, 1982). (PE and TE are actually the names of specific regions in the parietal lobe and the inferior temporal lobe in the human neo-cortex.) Two streams of neural activities of 'where and what' are sent to the association part where they are represented as integrated neural activities.

The associated neural activities corresponding to the current visual object are also sent to the top-down prediction part where a prediction of the next landmark to be encountered is generated. This prediction in terms of 'where and what' is sent back to the perception part through the association part so that recognition can be carried out by taking account of the top-down prediction. The neurodynamics, with two input forces from the top-down prediction of 'what' and the bottom-up perception, determine the actual recognition outcomes. The prediction in terms of 'where' is used to direct the visual attention of the robot to the direction expected for the next landmark encountering.

The learning in both the perception part and the association part is conducted each time the stimulus comes. The learning in the prediction part is conducted incrementally, which models the consolidation processes of memory transfer from short-term to long-term that Squire (Squire *et al.*, 1984) observed in some animals and humans.

The architecture employs another adaptation mechanism that arbitrates the interaction between the top-down prediction and the bottom-up perception. In this mechanism, the top-down prediction is more biased when the predictability becomes better. On the other hand, the bottom-up perception is more biased with allocating longer time for the visual perception when the predictability gets worse.

1. Neural net architecture

In this subsection each module in the proposed neural architecture is described in detail.

(a) The perception part: In the perception part, the TE module receives the visual image from a video camera and the PE module receives the dead-reckoning vector from the rotation encoder of the wheels.

When a coloured object is detected in the visual field during the object search, the object is foveated by targeting the camera head towards it. The region of colour 'pops-up' and pixels in the region are sent to an associative memory implemented using a Hopfield network (Hopfield & Tank, 1985) in the TE module. The Hopfield network consists of 10x10x3 neurons corresponding to the 10x10 pixel size with three-colour information for each pixel. The Hopfield network can memorize the pixel patterns by associative learning using the pixels through iterative exposures to the patterns. It is well known that each memory pattern is stored in a corresponding fixed point in the hypothetical potential field defined in the network (Hopfield, 1986). The Hopfield network is bi-directionally connected to an array of winner-takes-all neurons (Amari & Arbib, 1977; Waugh & Westervelt, 1993). Each neuron in the winner-take-all array is inhibitively connected. Each neuron also receives the top-down prediction inputs from the integration part. In the recognition process, the neural activation of the Hopfield net and the winner-takes-all neurons are dynamically computed simultaneously upon receiving the continuous video image from the bottom and the landmark prediction from the top. The neural state of the Hopfield net converges onto a fixed point attractor in the potential field and at the same time each neuron in the winner-take-all neuron array competes to be a winner. The winning neuron represents the categorical output of 'what' in this module. Convergence takes up to several seconds in the real implementation using the robot. After convergence, associative learning is conducted for the internal connective weights in the Hopfield network as well as for the cross-connective weights between the Hopfield network and the winner-takes-all network so that all the connections among the activated neurons can be reinforced.

In the PE module, the winner-takes-all neurons dynamically compute the categorical output representing 'where' by receiving the dead-reckoning data from the wheels and the top-down prediction from the integral part. The dead-reckoning data represents the rotation sum of the left and right wheels starting from the previous encounter with a landmark to the current encounter. Therefore, the categorical outputs of 'where' represent the movement of the robot relative to the position of the previous landmark encountered.

(b) The association part: The association part receives categorical outputs from both the TE and PE modules. When the association network receives a new combination of categorical outputs from the TE and PE modules, a neuron is allocated and positive connections are made to this neuron from each winning neuron in the TE and PE modules. In this manner, a single neuron activated in the association network represents the association of two categorical outputs of 'what' and 'where'. The activity of top-down prediction from the higher level propagates through these established connections to both the TE and PE modules.

(c) The prediction part: The prediction part in our architecture may correspond to the prefrontal cortex in a primate. Higher order cognitive functions such as working memory, prediction and planning have been widely studied in primates (Fuster, 1989). Some researchers consider that such episodic memory of event sequences are stored in the so-called place-cells (O'Keefe & Nadel, 1978) in the hippocampus

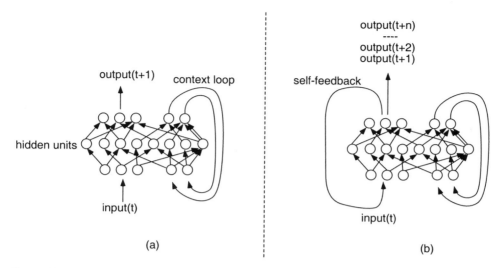

Figure 5.

The RNNs operated in (a) the open loop for the one-step prediction and in
(b) the closed loop for the look-ahead prediction.

rather than the prefrontal cortex, as a large body of lesion studies shows evidence of
hippocampal involvement in spatial cognition and episodic memory in rodents
(O'Keefe & Nadel, 1978; Wilson, 1994.) It is, however, still unclear whether this hippocampus theory can be applied to monkey or human cases and if the theory accounts
not only for the short-term memory but also for the long-term memory. Therefore,
what we assume in the current model is that the hippocampus stores the episodic
memory of event sequences only for temporary memory, and these sequences are
incrementally transferred to the prefrontal cortex in order to form the long-term memory through the so-called consolidation process (Squire *et al.*, 1984). Then we assume
that the actual prediction of the next coming event sequence is conducted by using
this long-term memory which is embodied by a RNN in the current model. A later
section will describe more details about the implemented consolidation mechanism.

In the proposed architecture, a conventional RNN, receiving its current activation
state, (Elman, 1990; Jordan & Rumelhart, 1992; Pollack, 1991) learns to predict the
activation in the association part due to the next landmark encounter. Figure 5 shows
details of the RNNs operating in open-loop mode and in closed-loop mode. Upon
receiving the inputs, the activation of the output units is calculated by means of nonlinear mapping using the synaptic weights shown in Fig. 5 (a), where the outputs represent the prediction. This operation mode of the RNN is called the open-loop mode.
We employ Jordan's idea of context re-entry that enables the network to represent the
internal memory (Jordan & Rumelhart, 1992). The current context input is a copy of
the previous context output: by this means the context units remember the previous
internal state. The navigation problem is an example of a so-called 'hidden state problem': a given sensory input does not always represent a unique situation/position of
the robot. (For example, quite similar shapes of corners or objects can be observed
from different locations.) Therefore the current situation/position is uniquely identifiable not by the current sensory input, but by the memory of the sensory-motor

sequence stored during travel. Such memory structure using the context re-entry is self-organized through the learning process.

The RNN can function as an autonomous dynamical system by installing a closed loop from the outputs to the inputs as shown in Fig. 5 (b). The prediction for the next step obtained from the current output units is re-entered into the input units for the next step of computation. By iterating the dynamical map with the closed loop, the RNN can conduct lookahead prediction for input sequences of arbitrary length, which resembles the performance of memory rehearsal. This iteration of the RNN with the closed loop can exhibit various dynamical structures depending on the connective weights developed though learning (Tani & Fukumura, 1995). This is similar to the logistic map (Devaney, 1989) which can exhibit bifurcations from a fixed point, limit cycling, or chaotic dynamics depending on its initial parameters. In the later sections, it will become apparent that the understanding of such dynamical structures within the RNN is essential to the current study.

The RNN used in our experiment has 9 input units, 9 output units, 25 context units and 25 hidden units. The input units adopt a discrete local representation (only one unit is set to 1.0; the others are set to 0.0 which corresponds to the winner in the association part), while the context units and the hidden units are activated to take a grey distribution of values. The output units are also activated to take on grey values, where a high activation state of an output unit denotes a high confidence that the corresponding neuron in the integration part is to be activated in the next event step. The grey valued top-down prediction by the output units is sent to both the TE and the PE module through the association part. The expectation of landmarks in the form of 'what' and 'where' is utilized for the visual attention switch.

2. Visual targeting

The two visual tasks of wall following and object recognition are alternated according to the top-down prediction obtained in the neural net architecture described in the previous section. In the following, details of the visual targeting mechanism for these two task modes are described.

The basic mechanism for camera targeting is realized by a hand-coded program using the assumption that the walls and the coloured objects appear on the left-hand side and on the right-hand side of the image space respectively. In the wall following task, the camera head turns maximally to the left and focuses on the edge between the wall and the floor. The camera head then turns gradually to the forward direction, following the perceived edge line as foveated in the centre of the visual field. The measured trajectories of the head's rotation in the horizontal and vertical directions represent the shape of the wall edge. This single movement of the camera head from the extreme left to the forward direction takes about 2 seconds. The current motor commands for the wheels are determined by a hand-coded function to enable the robot to travel smoothly, thus avoiding collisions with the wall.

In the object search and recognition, the camera head sweeps from the frontal side to the right-hand side in searching for a coloured object. Once a coloured object is targeted, the vision recognition process is initiated. One important note is that the robot cannot manoeuvre its wheels while it engages in the object search and recognition task. The robot risks colliding with the walls during this engagement. The next section will describe how attention is switched between these two visual tasks using the top-down prediction.

3. Arbitration between the top-down and the bottom-up

As we have described in the previous section, the visual recognition processes face two essential problems concerning (1) the conflicts between the top-down and the bottom-up processes and (2) the time delay. While the robot is new to the workspace with a small amount of learning experience, the predictions of the RNN are vague and erroneous. Therefore, an erroneous prediction can lead to fluctuations in the timing of the attention switch; erroneous prediction might also interfere with the bottom-up perception in the Hopfield net. Moreover, under these circumstances convergence of the visual recognition takes a longer time, since the pressure from the top-down prediction is weak and the attractors organized in the Hopfield network are shallow. On the other hand, when the robot becomes familiar with the workspace, more accurate prediction enables correct timing of the attention switch for the upcoming landmarks; accurate prediction also enables the bottom-up perception processes in the Hopfield net to be stabilized more rapidly.

In this situation, what is lacking in this cognitive architecture is a type of 'awareness' property, one which means that the robot can be aware of its own state of familiarity or 'situatedness' in the environment in which it is currently engaged. Such a self-measured state can be utilized internally to arbitrate between the top-down and the bottom-up processes. For this purpose, the predictability measure in the network is introduced, which represents the degree of agreement between the top-down expectation and the bottom-up perception. (The measure is the sum of the dot products between the two vectors corresponding to the prediction and the outcome for each TE and PE module.) The following arbitration scheme is considered using this predictability measure.

(1) When the predictability measure is more than a certain threshold value, the visual attention is switched to the right-hand side in preparation for object recognition by following the top-down prediction. On the other hand, when the predictability measure is less than a certain threshold value, attention is switched alternately between the wall following on the left-hand side and searching for the objects on the right-hand side, ignoring the top-down prediction.

(2) The strength of the top-down prediction with respect to the winner-takes-all neurons in the TE module and in the PE module is modulated in proportion to the predictability measure. Therefore, the actual top-down input given to the winner-takes-all neurons is obtained from the prediction value from the RNN multiplied by this strength.

(3) The maximum iteration time allocated for the convergence dynamics in the Hopfield net is modulated in inverse proportion to the predictability measure.

These schemes mean that the robot tends to rely on the bottom-up process, ignoring the top-down process if the robot becomes suspicious about its own prediction reliability; otherwise the robot tends to be relatively unreliant on the bottom-up process, being dependent primarily on the top-down process.

4. Incremental learning and consolidation process

It is difficult for RNNs to learn the information received incrementally. It is generally observed that the contents of the current memory are severely damaged if the RNN attempts to learn a new teaching sequence. One way to avoid this problem is to save all the past teaching data in a database. When new data is received, it is added to the former data in the database, and all the data is then used to re-train the network. Although this procedure may work well, it is not biologically plausible.

Observations in biology show that some animals and humans may use the hippocampus for temporary storage of episodic memories (Squire *et al.*, 1984). Some theories of memory consolidation postulate that the episodic memories stored in the hippocampus are transferred into some regions of the neocortical systems during sleep. Recent experiments (Wilson, 1994) on the hippocampal place-cells of rats show evidence that these cells reinstate the information acquired during daytime active behaviour. McClelland (McClelland *et al.*, 1994) further assumes that the hippocampus is involved in the reinstatement of the neocortical patterns in long term memory and that the hippocampus plays a teaching role in training the neocortical systems.

We apply these hypotheses to our model of RNN learning. In our system, the sequence of events experienced, which may correspond to a temporary episodic memory, is stored in the 'hippocampal' database. In the consolidation process, the RNN that corresponds to the prefrontal cortex rehearses the stored memory patterns. This rehearsal can be performed in the closed-loop mode, as described in the previous section. The sequential patterns generated by the rehearsal are sent to the hippocampal database. The RNN can be trained using both the rehearsed sequential patterns which correspond to the former memory and the current sequence of new experience, by using the back-propagation through time learning algorithm (Rumelhart *et al.*, 1986). The re-training of the RNN is conducted by updating the connective weights obtained in the previous training.

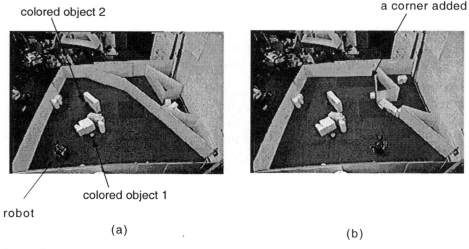

Figure 6.

(a) The original workspace and (b) the modified workspace used for the learning experiment.

IV: Experiment

The learning experiments were conducted in the 'original workspace' and in the 'modified workspace' shown in Figure 6 (a) and (b), respectively. Five landmarks consisting of two visual objects and three wall corners exist in the original workspace. The robot navigates until it encounters 15 landmark steps during each travel.

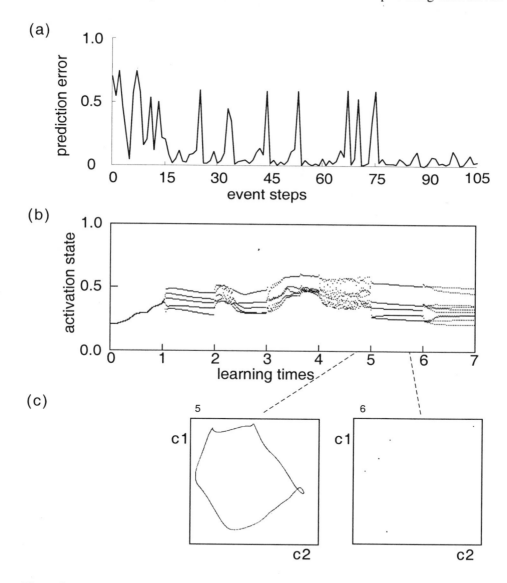

Figure 7.

Trial-1: (a) the prediction error,
(b) the bifurcation diagram of the RNN dynamics and
(c) the phase plots at particular times.

The times are indicated by the dashed lines.

After each travel, the robot 'sleeps' to produce the memory consolidation process as has been described in the previous section, in which the RNN is trained for 6000 learning steps. After sleeping, the robot starts to travel again; the training process is terminated. This cycle involving travel and learning is repeated.

In this experiment we focus on how the internal dynamical structure of the system evolves in the course of incremental learning and also on how the interactions evolve between the internal and the environmental dynamics. For this purpose we observed the evolutionary paths of the RNN dynamics and of the prediction error. The evolutionary path of the RNN dynamics is observed by means of plotting the bifurcation

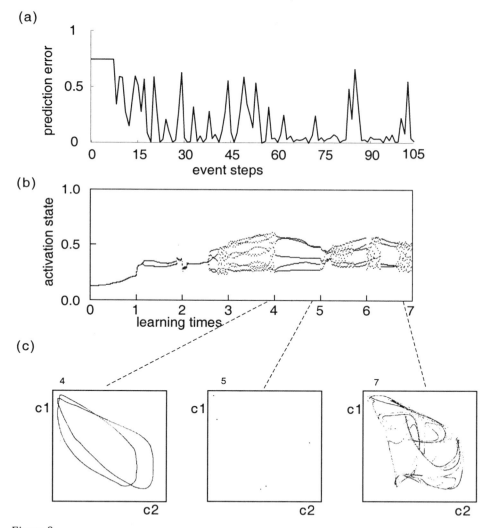

Figure 8.

Trial-2: (a) the prediction error,
(b) the bifurcation diagram of the RNN dynamics and
(c) the phase plots at particular times.

The times are indicated by the dashed lines.

diagram of the RNN dynamics during the learning process as well as by making phase plots of the RNN dynamics at particular instants in time. The prediction error is given by 1 less the normalized predictability as defined in the previous section. In the following subsections, we describe two experiments: the adaptation to the original workspace and the re-adaptation to the modified workspace. We devote the last sub-section to the brief summary of the experimental results. Non-technical readers may skip the following two sub-sections and need read only this summary in order to understand the basic results.

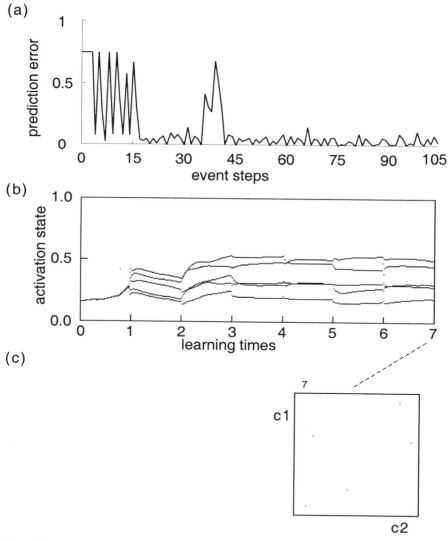

Figure 9.

Trial-3: (a) the prediction error,
(b) the bifurcation diagram of the RNN dynamics and
(c) the phase plots at particular times.

The times are indicated by the dashed lines.

1. Adaptation to the original environment

Three independent trials of adaptation to the original environment were conducted. In each trial, the cycle involving travel and learning was repeated seven times. Figures 7, 8 and 9 show the prediction error at each landmark encounter, the bifurcation diagram of the RNN dynamics and the phase plot at a particular time for each trial.

The bifurcation diagram of the RNN shows the evolutionary path of the closed loop RNN dynamics for each learning period during 'sleep'. For example, the plotted values from the 0th learning period to the 1st learning period in the diagram show how the activation state of the RNN evolves due to the learning of the landmark sequence experienced during the first 15 steps. We plotted the average of the context neuron's activation state generated by each iteration of the closed-loop dynamics of the RNN. We observed how this activation state changed while the connective weights gradually changed due to the learning process.[2] The phase plot was drawn using the connective weights sampled in the particular learning period in order to show snap-shots of the evolving attractor. We plotted the c_1 and c_2 values that are average activation over one half of the context neurons and over the other half of the context neurons, respectively. The (c_1, c_2) points were plotted from the results of 6000 iterations of the closed loop RNN dynamics using the sampled connective weights.

In all three trials, the prediction error is quite high in the beginning because of the initially random connective weights. After the first learning period, the predictability is improved to a certain extent in all three trials but the errors are not minimized completely except in trial-3. Prediction failures take place intermittently during the course of the trials. From the bifurcation diagram, we can also see that the dynamical structure of the RNN varies from time to time in trial-1 and trial-2. In the first learning period, fixed point dynamics — i.e. converging onto one activation state — appear in all three trials. Thereafter, phase transitions take place during the second learning period for all trials; limit cycling dynamics with a periodicity of five appear in trial-1 and in trial-3, while dynamics with a periodicity of two appear in trial-2. We observe that limit cycling dynamics with a periodicity of five appear frequently in the course of the trials. The periodicity of five is significant since it corresponds to the five landmarks which the robot encounters in a circuit of the workspace. It should be noted that the observed limit cycling dynamics with a periodicity of five do not remain stationary. The periodicity of five disappears intermittently and other dynamical structures emerge. The phase plots show such emergent dynamical structures more clearly. We observe a non-periodic attractor in the 5th learning period in trial-1 in the phase plot. The attractor was identified as being weakly chaotic since its Lyapunov exponent[3] (Devaney, 1989) was computed to be slightly positive at 0.0011. These weakly chaotic dynamics disappear soon after and the periodicity of five, which corresponds to the five points in the phase plots, appears in the 6th learning period. In trial-2, we observed quasi-periodic dynamics, limit cycling dynamics with a periodicity of 5 and a strange chaotic attractor with a Lyapunov exponent of 0.14 in the 4th, 5th and 7th learning periods, respectively.

---

[2] The bifurcation diagram is usually obtained by gradually changing a parameter in the target dynamical system. In the current case, the connective weights correspond to the system's parameters being changed.

[3] In dynamical systems theory, it is well-known that a positive, zero or negative Lyapunov exponent denotes chaos, quasi-periodic, and limit cycling and fixed point dynamics, respectively.

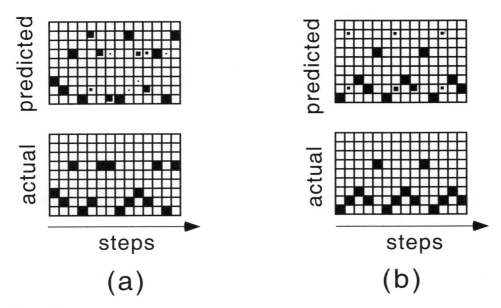

Figure 10.

Comparison between the actual perception and its corresponding RNN prediction sequence
   (a) in the unsteady phase (60th step to 74th step) and
   (b) in the steady phase (75th step to 89th step), both in trial-1.

Based on the results, we see that there exist two distinct phases which are the steady phase represented by the limit cycling dynamics with a periodicity of five and the unsteady phase characterized by non-periodic dynamics. It is also seen that the shifts between two phases take place arbitrarily in the course of the time development. In order to clarify the differences between these two phases, we selected two sequences, namely from the 60th step to the 74th step and from the 75th step to the 89th step, both in trial-1, which represent the unsteady phase and the steady phase, respectively. We compared the actual perception sequence and its prediction made by the RNN for the

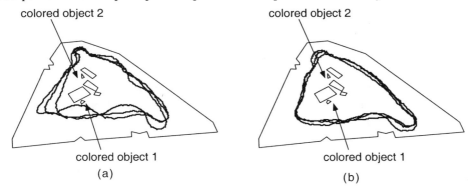

Figure 11.

The robot trajectories measured (a) in the unsteady phase (60th step to 74th step) and
                      (b) in the steady phase (75th step to 89th step).

two sequences. Figure 10 shows such a comparison. In Fig. 10 (a), we see that the prediction is inaccurate with the actual perception in some parts of the sequence while the prediction is highly accurate for the sequences in Fig. 10 (b). A more important observation is that the actual perception sequence in these two sequences differs in some parts even though the robot travelled through the same workspace in both periods. We can see the periodicity of five in the actual perception sequence in Fig. 10 (b) while such a periodicity cannot be seen in the sequence in Fig. 10 (a). In order to elucidate this observation, we compare the actual robot trajectories observed in these two periods.

Figure 11 shows the robot trajectories measured in these two periods by a camera mounted above the workspace. It is seen that the trajectory winds more in (a) than in (b) especially in the way objects or corners are approached. We infer that the manoeuvering of the robot is more unstable in (a) because the robot spent a longer period on the visual recognition of objects due to the higher value of the prediction error. (Recall that the maximum iteration time allocated to visual recognition is inversely proportional to the predictability measure.) Therefore the robot took a higher risk of mis-detection of landmarks when its trajectory meandered during this period. In fact, the robot mis-detected corners and objects when its trajectory meandered severely during this period. On the other hand, in the period from the 75th step to the 89th step, the detection sequence of landmarks became more deterministic and the robot travelled smoothly with greater prediction success.

An important comment on the above is that the observation of the steady and unsteady dynamics is attributed not only to the internal cognitive processes arising in the neural networks but also to the physical movements of the robot's body as it interacted with the external environment. It was observed that the change in the visual attention dynamics due to the change in predictability caused drifts in the robot's manoeuvring. These drifts resulted in mis-recognition of the upcoming landmarks, which led to the re-adaptation of the internal memory and a consequent change in the predictability. The dynamical interactions took place between all processes including attention, prediction, perception, learning and behaviour that led to a non-trivial time development of the total system.

2. Re-adaptation to the modified environment

When the robot learning experiment in trial-3 reached to the 105th step, the original workspace was modified by adding one sharp corner as shown in Fig 6 (b). Thereafter, the re-adaptation experiment was conducted until the 225th step was reached, which included fifteen learning periods. Figure 12 shows the normalized prediction error at each landmark encounter, the bifurcation diagram of the RNN dynamics and the phase plot at particular times. In this figure, it can be seen that the prediction error becomes larger soon after the workspace is modified and this tendency continues until around the 165th step. The bifurcation diagram shows the appearance of nonperiodic dynamics in the RNN during this period; the emergence of strange chaotic attractors is seen in the corresponding phase plots. We found that the strange attractors have positive Lyapunov exponents. The prediction error decreased after eleven learning periods and a periodicity of six was observed in the RNN closed-loop dynamics after fourteen learning periods.

It was observed that the re-adaptation process is a non-trivial task for the robot, since the former memory based on limit cycling dynamics with a periodicity of five and the new experience with a periodicity of six conflict with each other in the learning processes. Immediately after the modification of the workspace, relatively strong top-down prediction based on the former memory tends to override the actual perception because the averaged predictability is still high. This destabilized the pre-learned associations between the actual sensory patterns received in the lower level modules and the corresponding structures in the RNN. In fact, the structures corresponding to

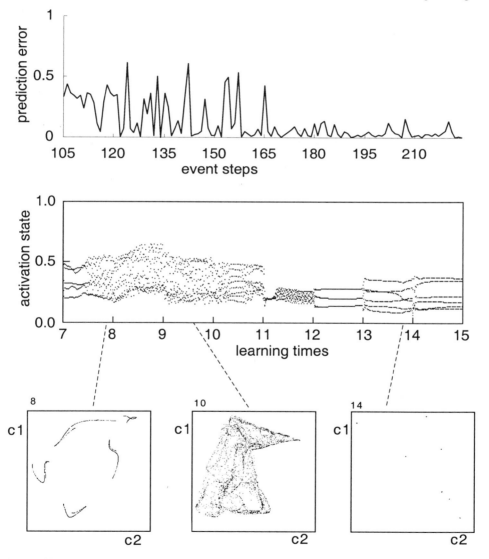

Figure 12.

Trial-3 continued in the modified workspace:
   (a) the prediction error,
   (b) the bifurcation diagram of the RNN dynamics and
   (c) the phase plots at particular times. The times are indicated by the dashed lines.

the landmarks changed after the modification of the workspace — i.e. the RNN outputs corresponded differently to the images, in comparison with the period prior to the modification. Such reorganization of the association between the higher and the lower level representation increased the confusion of the system during the re-adaptation.

3. Summary of the experimental results

This subsection gives a summary of our experimental results. In the experiments with the original environment, the time-development of the system dynamics in the course of the incremental learning of the environment exhibits spontaneous switching between the steady phase and the unsteady phase. In the steady phase, the robot travels smoothly, showing good prediction of the coming landmark sequences where a simple periodicity is observed in the internal neural dynamics. This periodicity corresponds to the number of landmarks allocated in the workspace. On the other hand, the prediction goes wrong in the unsteady phase where non-periodic chaotic attractors are observed in the internal dynamics. The actual trajectory of the robot manoeuvring becomes much more unstable in the unsteady phase since more visual attention is directed to the landmark objects than to the walls to be followed. The experiment in the modified environment shows that the unsteady phase lasts for a while before the re-adaptation of the internal neural dynamics is achieved.

V: Analysis and Discussion

1. The open dynamic structure

Our experiment demonstrated that the internal dynamics of the RNN evolved by switching intermittently between limit cycle, quasi-periodic and chaotic dynamics. These fluctuations in the RNN learning are caused mainly because (a) the sequences to be learned contain a certain nondeterminism and (b) the learning process of the

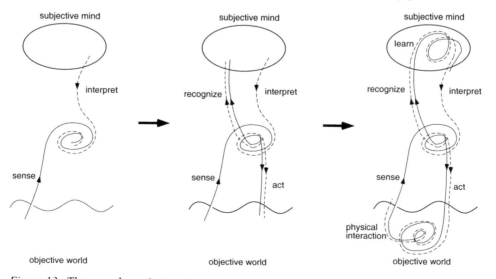

Figure 13. The open dynamic structure.

RNN behaves arbitrarily in determining its connective weights as has been shown by Ikegami and Taiji (1998). As described above, the RNN obtains nondeterministic sequences of landmark recognition events. This RNN learning involving finite sequences can result in various interpretations of the data obtained. Let us consider an example. Suppose that the RNN receives in one instance a sequence such as 'a b c a d c a b c'. The RNN learning process could interpret the rules underlying the sequence as being a simple periodic pattern of 'a b c', ignoring the appearance of 'd' in the second period. Other possibilities include a long periodic pattern of all the nine letters in the sequence, or a periodic sequence of three containing nondeterminism, in that 'a' can be followed by 'b' or 'd' in a nondeterministic fashion. The third case is especially interesting as it implies that the observed nondeterminism in the sequence is embedded in the deterministic chaos of the RNN dynamics. Mathematical and numerical analysis of this case is given in Tani & Fukumura (1995). It is important to note that the learning is somewhat arbitrary since all three of the above interpretations of the given sequence are possible. By this means, it can be said that our robot reinterprets the world as being deterministic or nondeterministic in an arbitrary manner after every learning process.

The dynamical structure observed in the system can be characterized as shown in Figure 13. The sensory flow enters the system from the environment, and encounters the top-down interpretation process of what metaphorically we can refer to as the subjective mind. These two flows interact with each other intimately in between from which a new set of recognitions and actions is generated. The actions lead to changes in the environment, which result in new sensations coming from the objective world. The recognition, on the other hand, causes the re-adaptation of the currently organized memory obtained through previous learning, which produces a new interpretation for the next sensation. What we see here is the open dynamic structure in which the relationship between the subjective mind and the objective world changes continuously through their mutual interaction.

Figure 13 is analogous to Varela's (Varela et al., 1991) views of the sense of the groundlessness of embodied cognition as well as to Matsuno's (1989) view of the internal observer. Varela wrote that nothing can be found as responding to the ultimate existence of the subjective mind or the objective world since all one can find is their co-dependent structures. He argued that such structures can be grounded in neither side, but reside in between. Matsuno (1989) and Gunji (Gunji & Konno, 1991) used the term 'observation' as mostly equivalent to the term 'interaction'. They considered that the original relationship between the observer and the observed changes because of the interactions between them. This observer is called the 'internal observer' since it is included in the internal loop of the interactions. The observation consists of a set of embodied processes that are physically constrained in various ways — e.g. delays in neural activation and body movement, limitation in learning capacity and so on. Such physical constraints in time and space do not allow the system to be uniquely optimized and give rise to incompleteness, nondeterminism and inconsistency. In fact in our robot experiment, such inconsistency arises in every aspect of system performances including recognition, learning and behaviour. However, at the moment of facing such an inconsistency, the processes cannot be terminated; instead, each process attempts to change its current relations to others as if it were expected that the inconsistency would be resolved. It is interesting to note that the open dynamic structure maintains both stabilizing and unstabilizing mechanisms. The goal-directedness is an attempt to achieve the stability of the system by resolving the currently observed inconsistencies of the system. All processes of learning, perception, interpretation, behaviour and so on are regarded as goal-directed activities. However, such goal-directed attempts always entail instability because of their embodiment, as we have mentioned above. The co-existence of the stable and the unstable nature does not allow the system state to simply converge or diverge in its time-development. The trajectory of the system state is likely to show chaotic itinerary wandering among marginally stable attractors in a diverse manner as shown by Tsuda's memory dynamics simulation using a chaotic neural network (Tsuda *et al.*, 1987). The essential difference of Tsuda's model from ours is that in Tsuda's formulation the instability originates from the non-equilibrium term explicitly represented in the neuro-dynamics model.

To the end of the discussion of the open dynamic structure, we would like to describe briefly its analogy to the Freeman analysis (Skarda & Freeman, 1987; Freeman, 1995) which is based on the electrophysiological studies of the olfactory systems of animals in the following two respects. First, in experiments on the conditioned behaviour of an animal, a chaotic attractor appears in the neural activities in the olfactory systems when the animal experiences a new scent. This means that the internal chaotic dynamics imply the novelty of the subjective experience. The second respect is that the correspondence between the spatio–temporal neural activation patterns and the scents vary if the animal continues to learn new experiences day by day. This corresponds to our observation that the relation between the subjective mind and the objective world is always changing through incremental learning.

2. A model of the 'structure of the self'

In this section, we first show our interpretation of the 'self-consciousness' of the robot which has been obtained especially by observing the system dynamics characteristics of spontaneous phase transitions between the steady and the unsteady phases. Then we discuss and evaluate this interpretation by considering possible correspondences in the literature on the discipline of phenomenology. Finally, we propose a possible model that represents the 'structure of self'.

In the steady phase in our experiment, good coherence is achieved between the internal dynamics and the environmental dynamics when the subjective anticipation agrees well with observation. All the cognitive and behavioural processes proceed smoothly and automatically; no distinction can be made between the subjective mind and the objective world. In the unsteady phase, this distinction becomes rather explicit as the conflicts are generated between what the subjective mind expects and its outcome from the objective world. Consequently, we say that the 'self-consciousness' of the robot arises in this moment of incoherence since the system's attention is now directed to the conflicts to be resolved. On the other hand, in the steady phase, the 'self-consciousness' is diminished substantially since there are no conflicts to which the system's attention needs to be directed.

This interpretation of 'self-consciousness' might be supported by Heidegger's (1962) example of the hammer. For the carpenter, when everything is going smoothly, the carpenter himself and the hammer function as a unity. But, when something goes wrong with the carpenter's hammering or with the hammer, then the independent existences of the subject (the carpenter) and the object (the hammer) are noticed. Here, the carpenter becomes self-conscious just as he or she becomes conscious of the world as problematic. Another traditional phenomenologist, Merleau-Ponty (1962), describes illness in the similar way. The healthy organism and environment function as a closely coupled unity in which we usually do not pay much attention to the organism. But when the organism becomes sick and goes wrong with the interaction with environment, then our attention goes to the organism. The essential claim shown in these two examples is quite analogous to our claim that 'self-consciousness' emerges when the relation between the subject (top-down process) and the object (bottom-up process) becomes incoherent.

If we take it that 'self-consciousness' and 'non-self-consciousness' correspond to the unsteady and steady phases, respectively, then this leads to the further interesting idea that the 'self-conscious' situation takes place not as continuous in time but as discontinuous in time accompanied by the spontaneous phase transitions. This observation would correspond to Strawson's (1997) view in which he suggests the image of a string of pearls, as an image of a self. He claims that each self should be considered as a distinct existence, an individual thing or object, yet discontinuous as a function of time, as he inherited the idea from William James (1984). Hayward (1998) commented on Strawson's model by raising further questions: 'do the continuous moments of experience themselves have structure; how are they held together so that we have the sense that they all belong to the same string'. For these questions he investigates the structure of the self from the point of view of the Buddhist analysis of experience which is based on the disciplined examination of first-person experience through the method of shamatha-vipashyana meditation (Varela *et al.*, 1991). From this study, he concludes that a particle-field analogy for the self is more apt than the string-of-pearls analogy. He claims that conscious experience is particle-like in that our sense of self appears to be ontologically distinct and relatively localized, but it also has a field-like and a non-local aspect.

Regarding this remark of Hayward, we further speculate that the field-like aspect is actually the dynamical systems aspect and also that the structure of the self corresponds to the dynamical structure of the system and not simply to what is captured by self-conscious operations. It is important to remember that all the characteristics of the time-development of the system are determined by this dynamical structure. Therefore, it is assumed that the particle-like aspect of self-consciousness accompanied by the phase transitions could be naturally explained when the structure of the self in terms of the dynamical structure of the system is well understood.

In order to clarify this idea, we first discuss the essential differences between machines and cognitive systems in general. A machine is basically operated in a way that its designer intended. Machines are designed to perform in a deterministic way such that their trajectory exactly repeats for the same sequences of inputs from the outside. In this sense, the performance of machines is completely controllable and observable from the outside. On the other hand, the behaviour of cognitive systems does not always follow this principle. For cognitive systems, it looks as if they maintained certain extents of autonomy to self-determine their own activities independent of the outside environmental interactions. Generally speaking, such systems encourage us to refer to their 'selves'. On the other hand, we cannot imagine any 'selves' for machines, which are not allowed to maintain such autonomy. Then the question is how the autonomy of self-generating activities is enabled. Our answer is that such autonomy originates with the open dynamic structure that is characterized by the co-existence of the stable and the unstable mechanisms in terms of goal-directedness and embodiment respectively. As we have discussed previously, the open dynamic structure enables the system to continue to develop by changing the relation between the subjective mind and the objective world, accompanied by the spontaneous transitions between the unsteady and the steady phases. When the system exhibits a non-repeatable and diverse trajectory, then the 'self' of the system is seen in the uniqueness of the trajectory. (On the other hand, if the trajectory converges into a stable one for good, no 'self' would be seen.) Consequently, such a 'self' becomes explicit internally (by observing the gaps between the subjective mind and the objective world), especially when the system comes across the unsteady phases in an unexpected manner. To the end of this section, our essential claims are summarized as:

(1) There is an essential structure of the 'self' in the system and occurrences of 'self-consciousness' are explained in terms of unfolding of this structure in time.

(2) The structure of the 'self' corresponds to the open dynamic structure which is characterized by stability in terms of goal-directed activities and instability caused by the embodiment.

(3) When the system develops an ever-changing relation between the subjective mind and the objective world in its non-repeatable trajectory, the uniqueness of the trajectory represents the 'self' of the system.

(4) The 'self' becomes aware discontinuously when incoherence arises between the subjective mind and the objective world in a non-deterministic manner in the course of the time-development of the system.

VI: Conclusion

We have attempted to explain our model of the 'self' from our constructivist approach. Our experiments on robot learning showed that the incremental learning process evolves while the steady and unsteady phases appear intermittently. Our dynamical systems analysis showed that these fluctuations arise because of the intimate interaction between the bottom-up and the top-down processes. The comparison of this finding with phenomenological observation leads to a conclusion that the structure of the 'self' corresponds to the dynamical structure of the system and that the 'self' is made aware when the unsteady phase appears in the course of the time-development of the system.

What the current chapter has shown is just one of many possible interpretations of the 'self'. It is expected that future collaborative studies between constructivists, phenomenologists and various empirical researchers would dramatically improve the current model of the 'self'.

References

Amari, S. and Arbib, N. (1977), 'Competition and cooperation in neural nets', in *Systems Neuroscience*, ed. J. Metzler, (San Diego, CA: Academic Press).
Ashby, W.R. (1952), *Design for a Brain* (London: Chapman and Hall).
Beer, R.D. (1995) 'A dynamical systems perspective on agent-environment interaction', *Artificial Intelligence*, **72** (1), pp. 173–215.

Blum, L., Shub, M. and Smale, S. (1989), 'On the theory of computational complexity over the real number', *Bulletin of the American Mathematical Society*, **21** (1), pp. 1–47.

Braitenberg, V. (1984), *Vehicles: Experiments in Synthetic Psychology* (Cambridge, MA: MIT Press).

Brooks, R. (1991), 'Intelligence without representation', *Artif. Intell.*, **47**, pp. 139–59.

Crutchfield, J.P. (1989), 'Inferring statistical complexity', *Phys Rev Lett*, **63**, pp. 105–8.

Dennett, D. (1991), *Consciousness Explained* (Boston, MA: Little Brown).

Devaney, R.L. (1989), *An Introduction to Chaotic Dynamical Systems*, Second edition (Reading, MA: Addison-Wesley).

Elman, J.L. (1990), 'Finding structure in time', *Cognitive Science*, **14**, pp. 179–211.

Freeman, W. (1995), *Societies of Brains: A Study in the Neuroscience of Love and Hate* (Hillsdale, N.J: Erlbaum).

Fuster, J.M. (1989), *The Prefrontal Cortex* (New York: Raven Press).

Gunji, Y.P. and Konno, N. (1991), 'Artificial life with autonomously emerging boundaries', *App. Math. Computation*, **43**, pp. 271–98.

Harnad, S. (1990), 'The symbol grounding problem', *Physica D*, **42**, pp. 335–46.

Hayward, J. (1998), 'A rDzogs-chen Buddhist interpretation of the sense of self', *Journal of Consciousness Studies*, **5** (5–6), pp. 611–26.

Heidegger, M. (1962), *Being and Time* (New York: Harper and Row).

Hopfield, J.J. (1986), 'Computing with neural circuits', *Science*, **233**, pp. 625–33.

Hopfield J.J. and Tank, D.W. (1985), 'Neural computation of decision in optimization problems', *Biological Cybernetics*, **52**, pp. 141–52.

Ikegami, T. and Taiji, M. (1998), 'Structure of possible worlds in a game of players with internal models', in *Proc. of the Third Int'l Conf. on Emergence*, pp. 601–4 (Helsinki).

James, W. (1984), *Psychology: Briefer Course* (Cambridge, MA: Harvard University Press).

Jordan, M.I. and Rumelhart, D.E. (1992), 'Forward models: supervised learning with a distal teacher', *Cognitive Science*, **16**, pp. 307–54.

Kawato, M., Maeda, Y., Uno, Y. and Suzuki, R. (1990), 'Trajectory formation of arm movement by cascade neural network model based on minimal torque-change criterion', *Biological Cybernetics*, **62**, pp. 275–88.

Kuipers, B. (1987), 'A qualitative approach to robot exploration and map learning', In *AAAI Workshop Spatial Reasoning and Multi-Sensor Fusion*, pp. 774–9 (Chicago).

Mataric, M. (1992), 'Integration of representation into goal-driven behavior-based robot', *IEEE Trans. Robotics and Automation*, **8** (3), pp. 304–12.

Matsuno, K. (1989), *Physical Basis of Biology* (Boca Raton, FL: CRC Press).

McClelland, J.L., McNaughton, B.L. and O'Reilly, R. (1994), 'Why there are complementary learning systems in the Hippocampus and Neocortex', Technical Report PDO.CNS.94.1 (Carnegie Mellon Univ.).

Merleau-Ponty, M. (1962), *Phenomenology of Perception*, trans. Colin Smith (London: Routledge and Kegan Paul).

Meyer, J.A. and Wilson, S.W. (ed. 1991), *From Animals to Animats: Proc. of the First International Conference on Simulation of Adaptive Behavior* (Cambridge, MA: MIT Press).

Moravec, H.P. (1982), 'The Stanford Cart and the CMU Rover', in *Proceeding of the IEEE*, **71** (7), pp. 872–84.

Nilsson, Nils J. (1984), 'Shakey the Robot' *SRI A.I. Center Technical Note 323*.

O'Keefe J. and Nadel L. (1978), *The Hippocampus as a Cognitive Map,.* (Oxford: Clarendon Press).

Pollack, J.B. (1991), 'The induction of dynamical recognizers', *Machine Learning*, 7, pp. 227–52.

Rumelhart, D.E., Hinton, G.E. and Williams, R.J. (1986), 'Learning internal representations by error propagation', in *Parallel Distributed Processing*, ed. D.E. Rumelhart and J.L. Mclelland (Cambridge, MA: MIT Press).

Skarda C.A. and Freeman W.J. (1987), 'Does the brain make chaos in order to make sense of the world?', *Behavioral and Brain Sciences*, **10**, pp. 161–5.

Smith L.B. and Thelen E. (1994) *A Dynamic Systems Approach to the Development of Cognition and Action* (Cambridge, MA: MIT Press).

Squire, L.R., Cohen, N.J. and Nadel. L. (1984), 'The medial temporal region and memory consolidation: A new hypothesis', in *Memory consolidation*, ed. H. Weingartner & E. Parker (Hillsdale, N.J: Erlbaum).

Strawson, G. (1997), '"The self"', *Journal of Consciousness Studies*, **4** (5–6), pp. 405–28. Reprinted in this volume, pp. 1–24.

Tani, J. (1996), 'Model-based learning for mobile robot navigation from the dynamical systems perspective', *IEEE Trans. System, Man and Cybernetics Part B, Special issue on learning autonomous robots*, **26** (3), pp. 421–36.

Tani, J. and Fukumura, N. (1995), 'Embedding a grammatical description in deterministic chaos: an experiment in recurrent neural learning', *Biological Cybernetics*, **72**, pp. 365–70.

Tsuda, I. (1984), 'A hermeneutic process of the brain', *Progress of Theoretical Physics*, **79**, pp. 241–59.

Tsuda, I., Koerner, E. and Shimizu, H. (1987), 'Memory dynamics in asynchronous neural networks', *Progress of Theoretical Physics*, **78**, pp. 51–71.

Ungerleider L.G. and Mishkin. M. (1982), 'Two cortical visual systems', in *Analysis of Visual Behavior*, ed. D.G. Ingle, M.A. Goodale, and R.J. Mansfield (Cambridge, MA: MIT Press).

van Gelder .T.J. (1998), 'The dynamical hypothesis in cognitive science', *Behavioral and Brain Sciences*, (in press).

Varela, F.J., Thompson, E. and Rosch, E. (1991), *The Embodied Mind* (Cambridge, MA: MIT Press).

Walter, W.G. (1953), *The Living Brain* (Harmondsworth: Penguin).

Waugh, F. and Westervelt, R. (1993), 'Analog neural nets with local competition, dynamics and stability', *Phys. Rev. E*, **47**, pp. 4524–36.

Wilson, M. (1994), 'Reactivation of hippocampal ensemble memories during sleep', *Science*, **265**, pp. 676–9.

James Blachowicz

The Dialogue of the Soul with Itself

What is the cognitive significance of talking to ourselves? I criticize two interpretations of this function (the reflection model and the social model), and offer a third: I argue that inner speech is a genuine dialogue, not a monologue; that the partners in this dialogue represent the independent interests of experienced meaning and logical articulation; that the former is either silent or capable only of abbreviated speech; that articulation is a logical, not a social demand; and that neither partner is a full-time subordinate of the other. I examine the views of Plato, Arendt, Gadamer, Ryle, Piaget and Vygotsky on the nature of inner speech, and the views of Gazzaniga and Dennett on the role of inner speech in the constitution of human consciousness.

Given the fact that talking to ourselves so dominates our private experience, it is surprising that classical and contemporary philosophers and psychologists have not appreciated more fully its significance for a theory of human cognition and human consciousness. We find Plato fond of this idea, but it is neglected by Aristotle and most other early philosophers. Kant has a sentence on it. Hegel, for whom it might have proved a useful idea, says nothing about it. Perhaps most surprisingly, continental philosophy has shown little interest in this phenomenon. The philosophers who have had something substantial to say about it — Plato, Hannah Arendt, Gilbert Ryle, George Herbert Mead — still did not penetrate very far into the inner logic beneath the surface of its conversational appearance.

Among early psychologists, Piaget and Vygotsky found 'inner speech' an important developmental phenomenon and parts of their analysis may at least help clarify its nature if not directly contribute to a logical theory. More recently, psychologists have also begun to relate the duality implicit in the internal dialogue with inter-communication among brain systems and with lateralization phenomena. Daniel Dennett's (1991) theory of brain function and consciousness has perhaps come closest to appreciating the importance of this phenomenon, but it fails, I shall argue, to grasp the whole picture.

This chapter has three purposes: to show the relevance of this distinctive phenomenon for our understanding of human cognition — in part through an acquaintance with the views of those who have had something substantial to say about it; to distinguish and criticize two principal interpretations (the reflection model and the social model) which run through these various accounts; and to propose instead a third interpretation of its function.

Two Models of Inner Speech

For someone who hasn't considered the question seriously before, talking to oneself may seem a relatively trivial practice related to short term memory. I look up a telephone number and, if there is some delay either in writing it down or dialing it, I may repeat it to myself aloud so that I don't forget it. I have to write down my ideas (whether a philosophical conception or a sketch of a piece of furniture I'm designing) because my imagination is unable to present all of their various details at once before my mind. It seems that I represent my thoughts to myself, therefore, because by expressing them in some perceptual medium (an inner voice, written speech, drawings, etc.), I am able to hold on to them more completely and securely. Inner speech is thus explained as a way of artificially expanding the size of the 'working table' of my cognition — that is, as augmenting the quantity and/or sharpness of the content of what is present to me. Many who have examined the structure of inner speech more carefully, however, have suggested another, more fundamental role for it. It is not simply that 'representation-to-myself' serves the purely quantitative aim of aiding my memory;[1] these representations may also possess a *cognitive* form which the represented material lacks. This is the possibility I will explore in the interpretations which follow.

1. The reflection model

One such interpretation takes inner speech to be the manifestation of *reflection*, that is, of the act by which I am able to think *about* some content within my consciousness. I may, for example, possess a moral intuition of the virtue of *justice*, and live according to its principles; but in reflecting on it (when challenged to define it, for example), I examine this content from some higher or more abstract perspective. That is, where the original level is merely 'lived' and relatively unexamined, the higher level is evaluative and critical. Since this evaluation requires conceptual analysis, I talk to myself when I reflect on things. I may consider alternatives as my evaluation proceeds, perhaps even taking different sides in arguing for or against candidate definitions.

For those who adopt this model of inner speech, 'conversational' duality is more apparent than real. It is only the reflecting 'self' that does the talking; inner speech is monologue, not dialogue. My taking of different sides of an issue is merely a device for organizing what may be a variety of positions, rather than any indication of cognitively different parties in communication. The reflection model of inner speech is *foundationalist* — preserving an asymmetrical relation between a foundation of basic lived experience and a higher dependent level of conceptual judgment and reflection.

The reflection model fails to account for a specific type of inner speech which, even if it does not monopolize our consciousness, may still play a more vital cognitive role than any of the other types. We need first to consider that type of inner speech in which we *propose* something to ourselves; then that subtype in which our proposals must meet *multiple requirements* of some kind; and finally that subsubtype in which these requirements themselves represent *different cognitive interests*.

---

[1] We should also not underestimate the role of memory in thinking. Memories are perhaps the first form in which cognition breaks away from the pure immediacy of experience; and recalling from memory can provide a useful model for both perception and thinking, as Plato and Augustine realized. (For Augustine on memory and thinking, see O'Daly, 1987, pp. 138–45).

(a) Proposals. What exactly is the point of proposing something to myself? I may, for example, sketch out a rough version of a piece of furniture I'm trying to design; on subsequent inspection, I may reject it or at least edit it in some way. But if this particular design thus turns out to be unacceptable, why did I bother to propose it in the first place? One plausible answer is that the party doing the proposing has informatiom that is different from the party doing the 'disposing' or criticizing. The reflection model would identify the critic with the higher-level reflecting self, but would probably take the criticized material to be 'available' to reflection without having to bring in any secondary agent who proposes this material to the critic. Even if this were true, it would still be the case that the critic must possess some capacity for discrimination beyond that whereby we grasp the proposed material itself — otherwise the whole procedure of proposing something to oneself would be gratuitous. Of course, this superior power of discrimination may (so far) be merely quantitative: the critic may simply have a sharper eye for detail.

(b) Multiple requirements. My problem may require than I juggle and simultaneously satisfy multiple requirements. For example, I might require the piece of furniture I am designing to be both stylish and yet inexpensive to make. I may find it easy enough to satisfy one of these requirements, but not both; stylishness can be expensive, while economy can be ugly. When I make proposals to myself in this circumstance, I may be torn, one side arguing for style and the other for economy. What is significant about this type of talking-to-myself is that, because there are two distinct kinds of requirement to be met, the two sides can exchange places as critic and criticized. One side can propose a stylish design; the other side may criticize this proposal on the grounds that it's too expensive and offer a counter-proposal; the first side may then criticize this amended design, etc. The unidirectionality of the reflection model is replaced by a more reciprocal (more 'conversational') relation between the two sides.

The defender of the reflection model might grant this point and try for a compromise — admitting the reciprocity of multiple interests, while still denying the existence of two distinct 'speakers' on their behalf. Rather, this is just reflection 'doubled' — like having a single person arbitrate a dispute between two other parties. The arbitrator (or the designer) may well engage in a self-dialogue in this negotiation but, while there are two interests, there is ultimately one voice and one agent. Despite the fact that we often speak of ourselves being 'torn' or 'of two minds' on some matter, still, in coming to a decision after a dialogue with myself, I have the consciousness that it is *my* decision, and not the result of one of two 'selves' getting the upper hand.

(c) Different cognitive interests. A different situation may obtain, however, when the two 'interests' are themselves cognitive in nature. Consider the relation between such distinct cognitive interests in the articulation of meaning: In writing a poem, for example, I may first offer a rudimentary formulation of the first two lines. I know the meaning I want to articulate, and this first rough attempt does in fact bear this meaning; but in reading these lines to myself, I may judge that they fail on other grounds: that is, I may find that they need to be re-formulated in order to improve their poetic effect or their logical coherence. The critic in this phase of my thought invokes standards of (poetic) articulate speech: 'This may well capture the intended meaning,' this critic may say, 'but it fails as a clearly formulated articulation.' This critic then reformulates the proposal, improving its form. But in doing so, some of the material

content (the intended meaning) may have been lost. The critic now becomes the criticized, for the original proposer is now in a position to say: 'You may well have improved the form of my speech, but you have lost something of my intended meaning.' Here a re-editing occurs, changing the expression once again — not with a view to improving its form but for the sake of retrieving some lost content.

If this case is to be treated like the previous one — a single arbitrator in a dispute — we should expect the speech on both sides to be on a par in syntax and semantic content. What we often have in inner speech, however, is a qualitative difference between the two — even to the point of having one party speaking little if at all, but nevertheless communicating by other means. That is, while one side seems more adept at articulation (this *is* its cognitive interest), the other is richer in experience and meaning (the other cognitive interest). While I do not deny that there exists *some* important sense of the unity of the self, the reflection model does not appreciate sufficiently the composition of cognitive interests comprising this unity, where it is more difficult to separate the represented interest from the speaker. It is this form of more genuinely dialogical inner speech — serving the articulation of meaning — that may lie at the heart of cognition and distinctively human consciousness.

2. The social model

Other accounts of inner speech invoke a more overtly dialogical structure. Among these is the idea that my inner conversation takes place among different *personae*; I might adopt the role of 'parent', 'child', 'teacher' or 'victim', etc., in relation to another such role within my self. My self might in fact be taken largely as a set of such roles, determined to a significant extent by my social relationships. While communication among such various 'players' may indeed occur, as well as among the multiple personalities that may exist in more pathological cases, these role performances do not in themselves, I shall argue below, reveal the basic cognitive function of our internal dialogue.

There is, of course, a danger in even using the terms 'dialogue' and 'conversation', for we usually take such an interaction to be precisely between cognitively equivalent parties. Even among those philosophers and psychologists who have taken talking-to-oneself most seriously, there is a tendency to model the internal dialogue on *social* conversation. In place of the foundationalist asymmetry of the reflection model, they propose a kind of *coherence* among quantitatively different but qualitatively equivalent internal speakers.

In order to criticize each of these interpretations in more detail, I must develop my own proposal. What I offer here, however, is no more than an outline of a third model.[2]

Meaning, Articulation and Reciprocal Correction

The two conversational partners of our internal dialogue each correct the proposals of the other. Since it's easier to appreciate the logic of this reciprocal correction if it's

---

[2] More complete discussions of various aspects of this model are to be found elsewhere: my approach to meaning and articulation is developed in 'Unarticulated meaning' (1994); the theory of correction which is at the heart of the logic of the dialogue may be found in 'Discovery as Correction' (1987); and my analysis of Plato's original understanding of inner speech is included in 'Platonic "True Belief" and the Paradox of Inquiry' (1995b). All of this material (together with a more comprehensive treatment of the present topic) is integrated into a complete statement in *Of Two Minds: The Nature of Inquiry* (1998).

'writ large', let me first point to its main features in the large-scale projection of this dialogue found in scientific inquiry.[3]

Philosophers of science have in general rejected the possibility of a distinctive 'logic of discovery'. This rejection arises from grounds similar to those explored in Plato's *Meno*: if discovery is a reasoned procedure, it must proceed deductively and therefore cannot generate anything truly new; but if discovery does generate novelties, it cannot have arrived at that result through a reasoned procedure (cf. Plato, 1961). This is the exclusive choice offered by 'evolutionary epistemologists' like Donald Campbell, who defends the establishment view with the disarmingly simple formula: 'When we venture beyond that which we already know, we have no choice but to explore without benefit of wisdom: blindly, stupidly, haphazardly' (1974, p. 142).

My own theory (1987; 1989; 1998) attempts to reopen the question, showing how reasoning may reach novel conclusions even through deductive inference. It responds to the *Meno* paradox by arguing that we can generate something new only if we first have something to 'edit'. That is, the discovery of a new hypothesis is really the variation or intelligent *correction* of an antecedent hypothesis. A scientist may employ an initial hypothesis with the full knowledge that it is erroneous as it stands: the point is to see where we want to be as a variant of where we are. To determine more precisely the nature of this variation (the heart of the problem), sets of hypotheses are mapped onto sets of predictions and we establish how the actual data fall in the series of predictions. Any intelligent correction, I have argued, requires such mapping and interpolation.

A new hypothesis, like a portrait sketched by a police artist and guided by a witness's memory, is the result of a collaborative effort. The artist makes proposals which are each aesthetically correct but factually deficient; these are corrected by the witness. But if the witness tries personally to re-draw an eye sketched by the artist, a second type of corrective procedure is evident: now a factually correct but aesthetically inadequate proposal is made by the witness, which the artist can correct. The rhythm of proposal and disposal in scientific discovery is analogous. An initial hypothesis may meet all the requirements of a good explanation but be factually deficient. However, in fitting the hypothesis to the facts (through the use of ad hoc hypotheses, for example), it may cease to be fully explanatory. There is therefore a double procedure, each part of which involves a sequence of proposals and corrective disposals — and also, therefore, two distinct mapping operations.

The procedures by which we generate an explanation of an observed phenomenon have the same form as those by which we articulate an initially grasped meaning for ourselves. In crafting a poem, I will try various formulations, observe how the resultant meaning of these formulations falls short of the meaning intended, and alter the expression to bring its resultant meaning closer to the intended one. Like a scientist, a poet may begin with an expression fully aware that it will have to be changed. The point is to see the original intended meaning as a *variant* of the meaning of this initially inadequate expression. That is, the articulation of a new expression is the intelligent correction of an antecedent expression in response to the divergence between the meaning of that antecedent expression and the desired meaning. Further, the prod-

---

[3] This is the strategy I adopt in *Of Two Minds* (1998): the first third of the book outlines the structure of inquiry in science; the remainder explores the analogous structure we find in the articulation of meaning.

uct of such a correction, now adequate to the desired meaning, is subject to a second type of correction, for its articulating form may not be satisfactory.

I propose viewing the 'dialogue of the soul with itself' as a series of proposals and disposals similar in function to the exchange between the police artist and the witness in their collaboration. The two parties represent the independent interests of meaning and articulation. At one moment we may possess a meaning but fail to articulate it; at another moment we may possess just such an articulation, but find that its meaning fails to correspond with our intended one. We talk to ourselves when we think because only a dialogue where each side provides proposals and corrective disposals for the other can achieve a simultaneous satisfaction of these twin requirements. The 'method' writ so large in science may initially be inscribed in this deceptively simple universal cognitive act.

A Conversation Between Cognitively Different Partners

The social model of inner speech fails to appreciate the fact that the partners in the internal dialogue represent cognitively different interests. I want to reject this model and yet not dismiss the very palpable intuition that some kind of conversation is indeed taking place. What sort of conversation is possible where the less articulate partner is either silent or at best capable only of abbreviated speech?

Consider trying to communicate with a person either incapable of speech or deliberately withholding it (as in a game of charades): we might ask our own highly articulated questions; the mute person would then indicate a response through gestures (which are certainly less articulate — I here exclude the possibility that the person knows a hand-sign language). Then *we* might say what it is that we think the other person is trying to communicate, thus speaking for the other person. Our verbal representation might at first be quite sketchy; if the other person confirms this verbal formula through non-verbal means, we might then rephrase it (while trying to preserve its meaning) to explore more precisely and logically what is being said. In this exchange, there is indeed a conversation occurring between independent parties, but one party is doing all the talking. While it is a conversation between equals, it is not a conversation between cognitively equivalent partners.

It is also possible that the more laconic partner is capable of some limited speech — some rudimentary, sketchy articulation, but still lacking specification and logical clarity. I would maintain even in this case, however, that there is more than a quantitative difference between these two forms of speech; that is, that there still exists a significant cognitive difference between the partners. I will consider this point more closely below.

Communicating in a game of charades more closely approximates the dynamics of inner speech than does ordinary social conversation. Another suggestive model is the classic representation of a petitioner's consultation with the Delphic oracle. Julian Jaynes (1977) has proposed that the oracle was less a projection of wishful thinking than an actually functioning (really heard) voice (pp. 321–6). The interchange between supplicant and oracle, he hypothesized, was really a (rather one-sided) dialogue between our left (petitioning) cerebral hemisphere and our right (commanding) hemisphere. Even in classical times, he suggests, we had not attained the unity of consciousness we experience today. The abbreviated speech of the right hemisphere was experienced rather as the command of the gods or the inspiration of the descending muse; in any case as someone else's voice.

Whatever the merits of Jaynes' speculations, the Delphic oracle provides an instructive model for talking to ourselves. I ask myself a question. This question is completely articulated, and I (the petitioner) listen for an answer. The answer I (the oracle) supply may be sketchy or abbreviated, but I (the petitioner) then amplify this response, exploring its logical consequences in a detailed articulation. According to many commentators, the actual delivery of the Delphic answer was provided by a woman (the Pythia) who would sit on a tripod suspended over a chasm within the temple of Apollo, inhaling the fumes emanating therefrom and chewing laurel leaves.[4] The Pythia's mumblings would then be interpreted and summarized by attending priests. Here we have one party, capable of privileged intuitions, but lacking the power of articulation, communicating with a second party (priests or petitioner), devoid of such intuitions, but capable of articulate speech. This hardly resembles social conversation with a friend (a cognitive equivalent).

But this provides only half the picture. To complete the story, we would need a second mirror-oracle. Here the petitioner would possess rich personal experience and intuition (as did the Pythia), but would be either unable to communicate beyond a mumble or at most be capable of abbreviated speech. The oracle in this case would be a person gifted with analytical skill and articulational power, but would be more shielded from the world of experience — far from the influences of fumes and intoxicating substances. On hearing the crude mumblings of the petitioner, this type of oracle might respond: 'What you may mean is . . .', providing some precise spelling-out of the implications of the petitioner's blunt declaration. Such wisdom resembles that available from a teacher in a classroom. The conversation may not be between cognitive equivalents, but it is not one-sided.

A more mundane, but perhaps more accurate analogy for the internal dialogue takes us back to the police artist, but with a minor modification. The witness to the crime possesses the experience lacked by the artist, but the witness's ability to draw is meagre and crude (the witness is therefore comparable to someone filled with actual meaning, but capable only of abbreviated speech). The artist, of course, possesses this skill (is capable of articulation), but does not have the witness's experience. In order to match more closely the relation of the two partners in the internal dialogue, we need to alter this last feature somewhat. It might well be true that, just as the partner possessing rich experience might nevertheless still have *some* degree of articulational ability (abbreviated speech, a crude ability to draw), so too the other partner will possess not only a high degree of this same ability but also *some* measure of experience (yet to sustain the symmetry, nothing to match the richness of the first partner's). That is, both the artist and the witness can draw and both got a look at the suspect, but the artist isn't as observant as the witness. The fact that each shares the capacity of the other to some degree, of course, will make their collaboration more productive. This

---

[4] See Guthrie (1970) for this traditional description. Fontenrose (1978) however, challenges almost all of this characterization, insisting that there is no evidence for fumes, laurel-leaf consumption, or semi-intelligible mumblings, basing his conclusions only on what he considers to be reliable historical accounts, rather than on the legends that accumulated in pre-classical times. Yet even if the traditional view of the oracle's function is erroneous, it still proves a useful metaphor.

may be an important feature of communicating brain systems as well. I will return to this idea below.

This conversation also occurs in stages. One party doesn't provide the other with all of the desired information all at once. While the aim of the conversation is agreement, one side lags behind the other until that agreement is reached. This leap-frogging — in which satisfying the two cognitive requirements is 'out of phase' — is one of the most prominent phenomenological features of inquiry: it's what makes our internal conversation a conversation.

Talking to Ourselves: Other Views

Let me now turn to what others have said about this phenomenon,[5] attending to which of the three models is supported by their accounts.

(a) Plato   In his description of the connection between judgment and the internal dialogue, Plato observed:

> . . . I have a notion that, when the mind is thinking, it is simply talking to itself, asking questions and answering them, and saying yes or no. When it reaches a decision — which may come slowly or in a sudden rush — when doubt is over and the two voices affirm the same thing, then we call that 'its judgment' (*Theaetetus* 189e–190a).

Let us consider more closely the dynamic interplay of these 'two voices'.

There is an obvious connection between Plato's understanding of the nature of the internal dialogue and his understanding of dialectic, that is, of conversational argument with another person.[6] While the two partners in such a conversation may not at first appear to have equal standing in the Platonic dialogues — for Socrates obviously introduces most if not all of the new points and surely directs the 'dialogue', with his partners hardly playing equivalent roles — still, at least ideally, this equivalence is something on which Plato and Socrates insisted. Socrates tells us that he 'would be no less happy to be refuted myself than to refute' (*Gorgias* 458a).

Plato thus seems to have adopted the social model of the internal dialogue.[7] That is, he often treats the two internal parties as 'two voices' in simple agreement — modelled on the agreement you and I might come to after a fruitful exchange. He also tends to see the dialogue as achieving a kind of *logical consistency*, so that I am freed from 'self-contradiction'. Beliefs which simply 'contradict' each other, even if materially different, may still be cognitively equivalent (have the same cognitive status). A different situation would arise if one of my conflicting beliefs was taken as reliable

---

[5]   Space does not permit considering the views of George Herbert Mead (1934), Mikhail Bakhtin (see Wertsch, 1991), or Sokolov (1972). I provide some discussion of these three contributions in *Of Two Minds* (1998), chapter 19.

[6]   Conversation (but not the monologue of writing?) provides two voices, and is necessary for inquiry. See Robinson (1953), pp. 77, 79–80.

[7]   In this respect, Augustine has a more sophisticated conception of inner speech. O'Daly (1987) argues that, for Augustine,

> it is not . . . because we *communicate* memories [to others] that we utilize inner-words; we need the inner word to realize private memories as well. Inner words are thus not so much the necessary preludes or 'cues' . . . to the generations of outer words, as the mental recovery and articulation of memories that need never be expressed in language. The inner word serves initially as the means whereby we communicate our memory-image to our consciously thinking selves, in a purely introspective manner (p. 141).

because it was derived from some experiential or otherwise intuitive source, while the other was taken as reliable because it depended on a more discursive or logical principle: such would be the conflict between facts based on experience and an explanation based on antecedent theoretical knowledge. In such a case, the 'voices' (if we could call them voices at all) would *not* be cognitively equivalent, and it would therefore be misleading to characterize their agreement or disagreement in language that suggests mere logical consistency or logical contradiction.

Yet despite what Plato often *says* with regard to the agreement between the two voices, he himself provides some evidence for a kind of talking-to-oneself that involves non-equivalent partners. In the *Philebus*, Socrates asks Protarchus:

> If a man sees objects that come into his view from a distance and indistinctly, would you agree that he commonly wants to decide about what he sees? [Protarchus agrees.] Then the next step will be that he puts a question to himself. . . . 'What is that object which catches my eye there beside the rock under the tree?' Don't you think that is what he would say to himself, if he had caught sight of some appearance of the sort? [Protarchus agrees.] And then he would answer his own question and say, if he got it right, 'It is a man' (38cd).

Here the questioning voice represents the interests of conceptual clarity, while the voice which responds is obviously the voice of experience. This does not fit the social model.

Plato's inaccurate parallel between internal and external dialogues cuts both ways: not only did he usually describe the internal dialogue as a conversation between equivalent partners (which might be true for an external, social dialogue); he may also have erroneously portrayed the true dynamic of the social dialogue by reproducing, not such real conversations with others, but his own internal conversation. That is, his 'dialogues', ostensibly between equivalent partners (a point on which he insisted), hardly provide anything like an actual argument with another human being, even allowing for editing out the messy contingency of such experiences. The one-sidedness of these arguments reflects at least one aspect of the *internal* dialogue, namely, that one side does most of the talking. Consider the striking example he provides at *Gorgias* (506c–507c), where he carries an argument through quite a number of stages, but where he is talking solely to himself (although Callicles is listening). The form of this discourse appears quite the same as that of his other social dialogues. Thus, despite both the appearance that the internal dialogue is modelled on the external, social variety and Plato's failure to make clear the cognitive difference between the two partners, it is the form of the internal variety that seems to predominate.[8]

(b) Arendt   Hannah Arendt (1978) positioned the internal dialogue close to the centre of her theory of cognition. She refers to the reflecting self as the 'two-in-one' (pp.179–93). She retrieves the Platonic conception in order to insist that moral sensibility depends utterly on the capacity for reflective thought — the capacity to think about and criticize myself and my thought; this in turn presupposes the duality of the self-in-dialogue: 'It is this *duality* of myself with myself that makes thinking a true activity in which I am both the one who asks and the one who answers' (p. 185).

Arendt does not want a foundationalist version of this duality (as the reflection model by itself might require) — where, for example, one part would only formulate

---

[8]   I provide a more developed account of Platonic inquiry in 'Platonic "true belief" and the paradox of inquiry' (1995b), which reappears (in a longer version) as chapter 16 of *Of Two Minds* (1998).

hypotheses while the other would only provide the evidence by means of which the hypotheses would be tested (that is, where one party only proposes while the other only disposes):

> The criterion of the mental dialogue is no longer truth, which would compel answers to the questions I raise with myself, either in the mode of Intuition, which compels with the force of sense evidence, or as necessary conclusions of reckoning with consequences in mathematical or logical reasoning, which rely on the structure of our brain and compel with its natural power (pp. 185–6).

Intuitive evidence and logical necessity could each function as foundations, as relatively guaranteed suppliers of truths. What Arendt wants to avoid is a trivialization of the process of criticism and inquiry, as would occur if it were simply a matter of evaluating proposals in the light of foundational 'answers' already provided. In all this she correctly perceives the need to sustain the *equality* of the two sides of the partnership, so that neither becomes a permanent subordinate.

But in thus rejecting the foundationalism of the reflection model, Arendt seems to move toward the kind of coherence on which the social model relies: 'The only criterion of Socratic thinking is agreement, to be consistent with oneself' (p. 186); the 'supreme law' of dialogue, she argues, is 'Do not contradict yourself' (p. 189). A dialogue might be carried on with a friend 'just as well as with yourself' (*ibid.*). While my 'self' is thus taken to be extended in some fashion — to have 'parts' in dialogue — these parts apparently are not very differentiated in function, but somehow collectively 'know'. I might talk to myself simply because one part doesn't happen to have some information in possession of another part. But on this reading, there would be no principled explanation of why the self should be *dual*, rather than multiple, with three, ten or a hundred different parts, rather like a committee. She does not consider the possibility that we may reject foundationalism while preserving a cognitive difference between the dialoguing partners.[9]

Arendt herself seems to recognize that such a simple quantitative conception of the extension of the self would not account for the sharpness of our experience of duality (as distinct from simple multiplicity). She appeals, therefore, to a Hegelian conception, in which a 'self' has no meaning apart from an 'otherness' which contributes to its constitution:

> . . . the specifically human actualization of consciousness in the thinking dialogue between me and myself suggests that difference and otherness, which are such outstanding characteristics of the world of appearances as it is given to man for his habitat among a plurality of things, are the very conditions for the existence of man's mental ego as well, for this ego actually exists only in duality. And this ego — the I-am-I — experiences difference in identity precisely when it is not related to the things that appear but only related to itself (p. 187).

While Arendt fails to explain the cognitive differences entailed by the two sides of this duality, her concrete examples reveal more (this was true of Plato as well). The voice of conscience is essentially a critic, disposing but not proposing: 'This conscience, unlike the voice of God within us or the *lumen naturale*, gives no positive prescriptions (even the Socratic *daimôn*, his divine voice, only tells him what *not* to do) . . .' (p. 190). The Socratic question we usually ask ourselves, Arendt observes, is 'What do you mean when you say . . . ?' (p. 185). This is a question that asks for the

---

[9]   I argue for this compromise between foundationalism and the coherence theory elsewhere (1997; 1998).

articulation of a meaning. It is asked *by* the party demanding articulation and logical clarity; it is asked *of* the party possessing the relatively unarticulated meaning (or moral intuition). But because Arendt does not also see how these two parties may reverse positions as critic and criticized, we are back once again at the reflection model. She does not sort any of this out.

(c) Gadamer   Hans-Georg Gadamer has a brief treatment of inner speech in *Truth and Method* (1989). He insists that talking-to-oneself does not involve two stages, where we first conceive the thought and then, relying on 'reflection', proceed to express it. Rather, we think immediately in language. This is consistent with the basic principle of his hermeneutics — that interpretation is not the 'means' for understanding, but is understanding itself. But this intimate relation which he believes to hold between thought and word tends to make the expression of a thought more immediate and less problematic than I believe it is. The direct relation he has in mind is perhaps more applicable to the process of expressing (in language) an articulation, than to the process of articulating a meaning. The relation between meaning and articulation is not straightforward: we do not simply and directly articulate what we mean.

While Gadamer takes the expression of a thought in language to be direct, he does recognize that it is discursive; and it is the discursiveness of human thought, he believes, that accounts for inner speech: 'Because our understanding does not comprehend what it knows in one single inclusive glance, it must always draw what it thinks out of itself, and present it to itself as if in an inner dialogue with itself. In this sense, all thought is speaking to oneself' (1989, p. 422). That is, the 'inner word, by expressing thought, images the finiteness of our discursive understanding' (*ibid.*). And again: 'the imperfection of the human mind consists in its never being completely present to itself but in being dispersed into thinking this or that' (p. 425). Thus, whereas the human word is many, the divine word is one.

While the discursiveness of inner speech certainly derives in part from the task of the articulating partner, its conversational character cannot be explained on these grounds alone, without considering its finer details — the 'taking turns' of the two partners and the twin cognitive requirements they represent. Indeed, in rejecting reflection as an essential component of inner speech, Gadamer himself glosses over this duality.

Gadamer tends to see the need for articulation itself as a mark of thought's finitude (God's word is 'one'); Hegel, in contrast, would probably have taken God's word to be 'one' only in the sense of an articulated system; that is, articulation contributes to the *constitution* of thought, whether human or divine. Hegel's project in his Logic — his account of divine thought ('truth without veil') — is not 'meaning without articulation'.[10] And so, elaborating on Gadamer's speculations on the nature of divine thought, we might say that whereas in both human and divine thought, meaning needs to be articulated (and so both are discursive in this sense), this task in human thought is 'out of phase' with the parallel task of investing our articulations with actual meanings — and it is this duality, rather than the discursiveness of articulation *per se*, which more directly accounts for the phenomenon of the internal dialogue.

(d) Ryle   Ryle (1979) has an unsurprisingly less romantic view of talking to ourselves. He wants to remove some of the 'barnacles' that have attached to this

---

[10] I develop this point in both 'Discovery and dialectic' (1991) and ch. 18 of *Of Two Minds* (1998).

otherwise interesting idea, and consequently rejects the notion (to which he admittedly once subscribed) 'that a person who is non-absentmindedly and non-gramophonically saying things to himself is conversing with himself, that is, [the notion] that soliloquy is colloquy with one's Alter Ego, or that internal monologue is dialogue with a cryptic Siamese Twin' (p. 34). He doesn't mention who held or holds this idea, although he may be referring to some interpreters of Plato. Further, he rejects both the view that, in talking to ourselves, we *think* 'in' the particular language, such as English, being used (*ibid.*), as well as the more general view that speech is necessary for thought (a musical composer, after all, is thinking without speech) (p. 33).

While there are a number of ways of saying things to others that have parasitically attached themselves to the idea of saying things to oneself, Ryle still wants to defend the importance of the latter for an adequate conception of creative thinking. He takes the sorts of thoughts that occur in this talking as *means* or intermediate thoughts, stepping stones that take us from one thought to another, whether we are engaging in something as simple as counting the number of hockey-players on a field or constructing complex inferences. There is, he says, 'no conversational or didactic point [to such talking], but only an heuristic point' (p. 45). Of course, he continues, it is also true that much talking to oneself, while employing sentences, has no real propositional intent; that is, while we may be remarking to ourselves about something, we do not necessarily do so with the purpose of 'trying to decide what to think' (p. 46). While not all talking to oneself is heuristic or creative, he observes, the kind which is is as instrumental for thinking as Plato once supposed.

All of this suggests that Ryle would reject the idea that the internal dialogue functions in the way that conversation with a cognitive equivalent does. But then he surprises us. He asks: 'How is Pythagoras *employing* the things that he is saying in his head or muttering *sotto voce*?' (p. 89). After considering a number of possibilities (holding in memory, rehearsing, re-savouring, involuntary muttering), he settles on an activity modelled on discussion with a friend: 'Though neither of us participants can pilot the other or himself, yet between us we may (though also we may not), make steady or erratic, great or slight progress towards our hidden goal' (p. 90). That is, Ryle invokes the social model after all.

Ryle recognizes that the goal is achievable only through an interaction between the two parties, with neither dictating to (or acting as the foundation for) the other. But how is progress actually made? By means of the fact that what two discussants say to each other is said 'experimentally'. This, he claims, is plausible in discussing with oneself as well as with another: Pythagoras' mutterings or notes to himself

> too can be heuristic experiments, moves made in the dark, in the faint but not foolish hope that they may prove to be self-proddings forward. Our question 'With what heuristic intention?' can have for its answer, 'In order to try out whether or not it has eye-opening, memory flogging, or cramp-easing potencies' (p. 91).

But this doesn't get us much further than the observation that, when we talk to ourselves, we *propose* things to ourselves. Much remains to be explained.

Ryle does not look favourably on the stiff characterization of dialogue found in Plato's *Meno*. A true discussion between friends would be two-sided, where neither Socrates nor the slave boy would at first know how to proceed or even what questions to ask. Ryle observes that it is this sort of genuine discussion that more closely resembles what had to have occurred in Pythagoras' own mind in discovering his theorem. Ryle is fond of calling such an exploration 'pathfinding' (in contrast to path-following): *somehow* (and the problem is that Ryle fails to explain how) a path is marked out where none existed before:

> How does he achieve this? Not by following tracks, since there are none to follow. Not by sitting down and wringing his hands. But by walking over ground where tracks certainly do not exist, but where, with luck, assiduity, and judgment, tracks might and so perhaps *will* exist. All his walkings are experimental walkings on hypothetical tracks or candidate-tracks or could-be tracks, or tracks on appro; and it is by so walking that, in the end, while of course he finds lots and lots of impasses, he also finds (if he *does* find) a viable track (p. 74).

Ryle's 'track' here does not lead anywhere very interesting, for he fails to offer even a hint of the processes whereby some proposals are fruitfully edited — assuming, that is, that he sees this blind exploration as anything more than a process of elimination. Nor does he seem to realize that two parallel editing procedures occur simultaneously, each guided by its own distinctive cognitive interest. Further, despite his own warnings not to allow conversations with others to become the overriding model for conversations with ourselves, his notion of two parties in experimental discussion threatens to do just that.

(e) Vygotsky   Vygotsky's (1962) contribution to our understanding of 'inner speech' (as he calls it) is to be found in his sensitivity to its peculiar syntax and his judgment that important qualitative differences exist between inner (private) and outer (social) speech.

He reviews Piaget's distinction between autistic thought (imagistic, emotive, unrealistic and linguistically incommunicable) and 'directed' thought (realistic and linguistically communicable) and considers Piaget's view that, as children develop, their thought moves from the former to the latter. He rejects much of this claim and holds that egocentric speaking-to-oneself, far from atrophying with age, remains an important tool for problem-solving in adult cognition (p. 16).

Such speech is highly attenuated. Its syntax is markedly abbreviated; not only are subjects of sentences often omitted, but entire complex thoughts may be compressed into compact short phrases, even single words (pp. 100, 139, 147–8). In this respect, it is the very opposite of the syntax found in formal writing (p. 99). Inner speech is speech with maximum meaning, but with the bare minimum of articulational structure. 'The change from maximally compact inner speech to maximally detailed written speech,' Vygotsky observes, 'requires what might be called deliberate semantics — deliberate structuring of the web of meaning' (p. 100). He rejects the idea of thoughts without words (or of meanings with no articulation). Inner speech

> ... still remains speech, i.e., thought connected with words. But while in external speech thought is embodied in words, in inner speech words die as they bring forth thought. Inner speech is to a large extent thinking in pure meanings. It is a dynamic, shifting, unstable thing, fluttering between word and thought, the two more or less stable, more or less firmly delineated components of verbal thought (p. 149).

Vygotsky contrasts inner speech with outer, social speech. I would rather strike the contrast between a proto-speech anchoring a wealth of actual meaning and a highly precise form of speech representing the interests of clarity and articulation. *Both* forms, I maintain, can be 'inner'. Highly articulated speech may have to be written down, for it may be impossible to sustain the totality of its detail and structure in our limited memories, but this does not automatically constitute a transformation from private to social. As I write these words, I am endeavouring to articulate ideas which were once captured in my very sketchy note pads; but my first expanded articulation of these notes is written *for myself*, so that I might be satisfied with the extent to which I have clarified and articulated my original ideas. It is true, of course, that in successive drafts, these articulations will be changed, owing to the necessity of communicating them to others; but this social constraint is not the principal stimulus for articulation. The demand for articulated thought is one I am quite capable of imposing on myself for myself. *It is a logical, not a social, demand.*[11]

Vygotsky seems to conceive of abbreviated inner speech as resulting from the fact that I know what I mean, and that I would need to provide more complete articulations only for someone else who does not know my meaning. That this is his view can be seen from the fact that he admits the possibility that a close psychological and intellectual acquaintance with another person's thoughts 'may establish a mutual perception leading to the understanding of abbreviated speech' (p. 145). That is, if you and I understand each other very well, 'practically wordless ''communication'' of even the most complicated thoughts is the rule' (*ibid.*). In saying this, he seems to see articulation as a vehicle for the *communication* of thought — a kind of necessary evil derivative from the fact that you can't know what I mean without my telling you. I would insist, on the contrary, that because this articulation in fact occurs *within* myself and not just (or even principally) for others, its function is partly constitutive of fully realized thought. My conversation with the person I know best — myself — does not and cannot remain at the level of abbreviated speech, for I must, even at mundane levels of experience, explain and articulate my experience for myself.[12] In holding that the abbreviated nature of inner speech derives simply from our *familiarity* with what that speech is to convey and not from the fact that it lacks *logical articulation*, Vygotsky failed to grasp the fundamental logic of the interior dialogue.

(f) Piaget   Piaget (1959) also attributed the need to articulate a meaning to the social demands for clarity and facile communication. We initially have a satisfying sense of full understanding when some solution to a problem has been grasped, 'but as soon as we try to explain to others what it is we have understood, difficulties come thick and fast' (p. 65). He attributes these difficulties to the fact that our initial insight was largely imagistic and perhaps expressed in abbreviated language with many lacunae: to communicate this insight, we have to fill in the gaps with intermediate links left out before. Such is the difference, he claims, between 'personal understanding and spoken explanation' (*ibid.*).

---

[11] None of this denies, of course, that linguistic development must also be social; but, as I have argued elsewhere (Blachowicz, 1994; 1998, ch. 13), the capacity for logical articulation is itself to be distinguished from the capacity for linguistic expression. Space does not permit reconstructing that argument here.

[12] Sokolov (1972), who developed a number of Vygotsky's ideas, was perhaps closer to the mark in his observation that 'at times . . . especially in solving difficult problems, we enter into a kind of discussion with ourselves: we formulate mentally a number of propositions, criticize them from various points of view, and finally select one of them, rejecting the rest' (p. 34). Although Sokolov did not distinguish the two different cognitive functions represented by the two parties in the internal dialogue, he at least noticed more clearly than Vygotsky that *criticism* of an internally advanced proposal by oneself within oneself is a significant feature of inner speech.

It is noteworthy, however, that this 'filling in' is more than the supplying of words once omitted; it does indeed require the inferences and logical clarifications which constitute articulation. This is an indication that Piaget may have conceived of the distinction between the functions of the two partners of the dialogue along the lines I have proposed; but he neither clarifies the nature of these functions nor sufficiently distinguishes the logical demand we impose on ourselves in self-articulation from the demands of communication with others.

Conclusion   I have suggested that the 'conversation' in our internal dialogue is between cognitively different partners; that one of these partners is either silent or capable of only abbreviated speech; that it is not the interests of social communication *per se* that guide the articulate partner; and that, although the partners are cognitively different, their function is not divided as subordinate and primary, for two distinct channels of communication exist between them: where one party must conform to the constraints of the other in one channel, the reverse is true for the other channel.

Let us now consider what implications this model may have for those who have linked inner speech with human consciousness.

Self-Consciousness

It is not surprising that various recent theories of the nature of 'consciousness' have not used the term uniformly. Humphrey (1992) restricts the term to *sensation* (p. 115), so that no non-sensory process (abstract thinking without a sensory component, for example) would be conscious. Jackendoff (1987) holds a similarly negative view with respect to the possibility of conscious thought without a sensory medium. He also takes to task those (Jaynes, R. Dawkins, Hofstadter) who seem to have restricted 'consciousness' solely to human awareness (p. 6). Gazzaniga and LeDoux (1978) should probably be included with this latter group since they associate true consciousness with the linguistic capabilities of the left cerebral hemisphere of most right-handed people and thus question whether consciousness should be ascribed without qualification to non-humans (p. 145).

These differences may be more semantic than substantive. My own preference is for using 'consciousness' to apply to waking mental states of human beings and higher animals; I thus side with Jackendoff and Humphrey. Yet there may be a problem in denying that mental states which lack a sensory (visual, auditory or tactile) medium can be conscious (as both Jackendoff and Humphrey do). I will refer to peculiarly human consciousness as *self-consciousness*. Talking with oneself is probably sufficient evidence for self-consciousness; might it be constitutive of it as well?

(a) Brain lateralization

The difference in cognitive interest between the two parties in the internal dialogue may be related in some way to brain lateralization. Lateralization studies have provided much material for highly speculative extrapolations into whole psychologies of 'left brain/right brain' personalities. Many of these theoretical musings lack a scientific footing and have been deservedly criticized.[13] However, it is also true that such

---

[13] Gazzaniga and LeDoux (1978) and Gazzaniga (1985) obviously take some care in their reflections on lateralization to discourage simple-minded divisions of consciousness into left and right; Gazzaniga (1985) suggests that the operation of human intelligence, for example, is more evident in inter-modal

studies have attracted this attention (leading to abuse) because brain laterality is one of the most fundamental and fascinating of psycho-physiological facts. There may be some tendency on the part of the scientific community to avoid more soundly based speculation on this matter (more than it would have in normal circumstances), for fear of confusing its own perspective with that of these other popular views. I hope my own suggestions here, therefore, succumb to neither of these temptations.

There can be little doubt that some early views of brain laterality were based on overly-simplified dichotomies. Consider the view that the left 'dominant' cerebral hemisphere is the locus for human language, while in the right is found the abilities for spatial perception, drawing and art. In time, more careful distinctions were introduced which recognized the fact that *both* hemispheres were involved in important ways in both types of function.[14]

Gardner (1974), among many others, observed that the left hemisphere favours sequential while the right favours parallel processing (p. 376). A more careful judgment, offered in the wake of the growing appreciation of the role of parallel processing in brain physiology, suggests rather that both hemispheres are basically parallel processors, but that a serial processing may have arisen on a parallel substructure in the left hemisphere.[15] Gazzaniga and LeDoux (1978) speculate that, while manipulational skills may have arisen in both hemispheres in the higher animals, these skills were crowded out of the left hemisphere of human beings by the development of language (p. 59). They question the plausibility of positing a unique serial (hard-wired) structure for the left hemisphere, for, if that were the case, how is it that the right hemisphere can assume linguistic function when the left becomes damaged? (p. 48).

It is the fact that the serial processing of the left hemisphere may not have evolved with full physiological integration with the more basic parallel processors that has led Gazzaniga and LeDoux (1978), Gazzaniga (1985) and Dennett (1991) to suggest that communication between these two systems may have had to resort to an expediency to circumvent this limitation. In lieu of hard-wiring, the parallel and serial systems had to communicate through *overt behaviour* and *speech* 'outside the brain' (a form of talking to oneself). Gazzaniga and LeDoux appreciate how behaviour may provide the channel by which the affective experience of the right hemisphere is communicated to the linguistic system of the left; indeed, this phenomenon is the focus of their writing. They hypothesize a variety of separate 'memory banks' which do not communicate in the brain: 'If this is true, then the only way for the organism — which is to say the cognitive sub-system in the forefront of consciousness at any one point in time, which is the verbal system in humans — to discover its total resources is to watch itself as it behaves' (Gazzaniga and LeDoux, 1978, p. 134).

They provide a number of striking examples of this phenomenon. In some cases, they tested patients with split or partially-split hemispheres who also possessed the unique ability to read or even speak to some extent with both hemispheres: this enabled them to design experiments in which verbal cues were provided to the right hemisphere (which normally wouldn't be able to decipher them) with subsequent

---

sensory processing within a hemisphere, than in inter-hemispheric processing (p. 176). Even Ornstein (1976), whose earlier work on consciousness and laterality helped fuel much of these popular simplifications, has warned of the dangers implicit in such unconstrained exploration.

[14] See Gardner's (1974) descriptions; pp. 304, 372.

[15] See Dennett (1991, ch. 7), for example.

inquiries about the cues made to the left hemisphere, which could report verbally but which lacked any cerebral connection to the right. When the instruction was to assume the position of what was suggested in the word flashed to the right hemisphere, and the word was 'boxer,' for example, the patient assumed a stance with two fists raised; when she was then asked (to her left hemisphere) what word was flashed, she correctly guessed 'boxer.' It was a *guess*, however, for she was reading, not the original word, but her own behaviour (pp. 146–7).

In another experiment, a picture of a chicken claw was flashed to the left hemisphere while a picture of a house in a winter scene was flashed to the right; the patient was instructed to point to which of another set of pictures was relevant to the ones he saw. He correctly pointed with his right hand to a chicken and with his left hand to a shovel. However, when asked what he had seen (a question directly only to the left hemisphere), he responded: 'I saw a claw and I picked the chicken, and you have to clean out the chicken shed with a shovel' (p. 148). That is, he could see that he had also pointed with his left hand to a shovel, and therefore integrated this response into the framework established by the left hemisphere, but *without* awareness that he was 'rationalizing' this anomalous datum. Gazzaniga and LeDoux conclude: 'We feel that the conscious verbal self is not always privy to the origin of our actions, and when it observes the person behaving for unknown reasons, it attributes cause to the action as if it knows but in fact it does not' (pp. 149–50).

In these two cases, a *behaviour* initiated by the right hemisphere was interpreted by the disconnected left; there is also the important case of simple *emotional states* (not behaviour as such) being similarly interpreted. Here a male subject was given the cue/command 'kiss' to his right hemisphere by a male investigator, after which the left disconnected hemisphere responded: 'Hey, no way, no way, you've got to be kidding' (p. 151). This is a particularly interesting case, for two reasons: not only was this person's disconnected hemisphere able to interpret an internal emotional reaction (and not simply an overt act), but this interpretation was relatively precise. That is, if the person has just experienced general embarrassment, he would probably not have responded with a refusal — which suggested that he had understood that he was being asked to perform an act. The response was appropriate to the *word* communicated, despite the fact that this word was only communicated to the other hemisphere by means of an emotional reaction.

By analogy, this suggests that the articulating partner of the internal dialogue may be able to interpret even silent responses by the experiencing partner — that meanings, for example, might be experientially differentiated to the extent that our verbal systems can 'read them' in our affective responses. Of course, in this particular case, the meaning involved was itself closely tied to a specific emotion. It would be interesting to see how discriminating our verbal systems might be in 'reading' other, less emotional types of semantic content.

Yet such wordless communication is not a necessary component of the model I have proposed. The experiential partner in the internal dialogue may be capable of abbreviated speech and would not have to communicate with the other partner through a silent (for example, affective only) channel.

Gazzaniga also provides some interesting evidence for such communication. It has been known for some time that the right hemisphere even of individuals with normal lateralization retains some limited capacity for speech. Zaidel (1978) showed that the right hemisphere could do about as well as a ten-year old child in vocabulary tests. Gazzaniga and LeDoux (1978) point out that while it is *expression* rather than *comprehension* that is highly lateralized, the right hemisphere has its share of expressive capacities as well. Gazzaniga (1985) describes an experiment with a woman with split hemispheres, but who possesses some capacity for speech in her right hemisphere (p. 91). When her left cerebral hemisphere was flashed a picture of a hurdler, dressed appropriately and running in a certain direction, she responded verbally in accurate detail. However, when this picture was flashed to her right hemisphere, she responded (at first) accurately, but only with a generalized term such as 'athlete'. Her left hemisphere, on hearing this word, however, embellished this crude information with its own more analytical (but erroneous) account, describing a basketball player. Here, as we have seen before, the verbal report is integrated with the rationalizing context provided by the other hemisphere. This contrast between the sketchy yet perceptive right hemisphere and the more analytic, detail-supplying, yet experientially isolated left hemisphere resembles the distinction in function between the two partners of the internal dialogue.

Gazzaniga (1985) himself suggests a neighbouring hypothesis:

> The more interesting case is one that is rankly speculative but is more closely related to the subtle and usually opaque process of creative cognition. It has to do with the process of writing. I believe it is usually the case that a writer is not fully aware of what the import of a sentence, paragraph or page will be. . . .
> . . . As sentences are formed, the words begin to elicit mental images, each accessing related images carrying different emotional valences. This fluctuating state of emotional energy leads to description of all these images by the continually active verbal system. In this dynamic way, the initial action is modified. It is an idea worth considering because . . . language is a system that is not intrinsically powerful. Language reports the cognitive computations of other mental modules (pp. 91–3).

When the articulate partner in the internal dialogue either reads the affective response of the other partner or hears its abbreviated speech, it draws out in a logical and analytic way the implications of this information: but, of course, in so extending and amplifying this knowledge, it may have concluded to items either not warranted by or at least not present in this knowledge. Like Gazzaniga's 'rationalizing' patients, we may not even be aware of the fact that we have, in our articulations, projected ourselves beyond our original experience. Gazzaniga (1985) observes that it is not simply language (which the right hemisphere also possesses), therefore, that explains the contribution of the left hemisphere to our distinctively human consciousness, but more especially systems that work to construct beliefs (one might also say 'hypotheses') about ourselves and the world (pp. 97–9).

The partner in the internal dialogue representing the interests of experience, therefore, probably possesses some capacity for abbreviated speech, perhaps because communication between these two systems might not be possible unless each were capable of some minimum 'skill' in the other's medium (a matter, of course, to be decided empirically). The sketchy language of the first partner may serve to provide a minimum vehicle for its experience (language supersaturated with meaning), and also orient the articulations of the second partner in the right *general* direction — but would provide no more than this sketchy indication. The fact that some language would thus be shared would not mean, therefore, that the linguistic differences between the two would be only quantitative: it may be that this type of abbreviated speech lacks many of the syntactical and logical features of that provided by the more articulate partner. We should also leave open the possibility that the articulate partner also possesses some minimum capacity for experience, allowing it to endow its proposed articulations with at least some experiential content; that is, it too must be capable of projecting its proposals with at least some degree of the content or vocabulary of its partner's medium.

(b) Dennett on human consciousness and the internal dialogue

Of all of the philosophical and psychological commentary on the role of the internal dialogue in self-consciousness, Dennett's (1991) analysis goes furthest toward identifying some of the components I have discussed. Like Gazzaniga and LeDoux, Dennett recognizes overt behaviour and speech as new (non-hard-wired) channels for communication among different cognitive systems (pp. 195–6). Human consciousness arises with a new system superimposed, as it were, on the existing structure of the brain. This new system, he claims, is 'one of *serial chaining*, in which first one "thing" and then another "thing" takes place in (roughly) the same "place". This stream of events is entrained by a host of learned habits, of which talking-to-oneself is a prime example' (p. 221). Evidence for this assertion is in part derived from introspection. In encountering a problem of some sort, we approach a solution by typically saying to ourselves: '. . . "Well, first I'd do this, and then I'd have to do that, etc." But if you ask yourself "What would I do in this situation if I were a thousand-channel-wide parallel processor?" you draw a blank; you don't have any personal familiarity with — any "direct access to" — processes happening in a thousand channels at once, even though that is what is going on in your brain' (p. 215). Such experience, Dennett observes, is presented in a sequential format, quite like a von Neumann machine.[16]

Dennett's account of the internal dialogue relies on the social model I have criticized. He advocated this model as long ago as 1976: genuine self-consciousness, he said, 'is achieved only by adopting toward *oneself* the stance not simply of communicator but of Anscombian reason-asker and persuader. . . . One's stance toward oneself *and access to oneself* in these cases is essentially the same as one's stance toward and access to another' (1976, p. 193). Reflective self-evaluation, he continues, 'cannot be there unless it is there in episodes of conscious thought, in a dialogue with oneself' (p. 193). In a note, he invokes both Marx and Nietzsche as supporting the view that self-consciousness arises only from a need for social communication with others (p. 196).

In his more recent discussion, Dennett puts the issue in an evolutionary perspective. There may well have been an initial evolutionary advantage in social communication, he speculates, insofar as an individual's problem-solving ability would thereby be enhanced. That is, as an individual puzzled about something, he or she might ask some companions nearby for help; the information offered might be just what the problem-solver needed to 'break out of a rut' or see things from a new perspective (1991, p. 195). Then, Dennett continues, 'one of these hominids "mistakenly" asked for help when there was no helpful audience within earshot — except itself!' (*ibid.*) and this may well have spurred it to answer its own question.

Presumably, Dennett does not mean that another hominid possessed information of a cognitively different kind from that of the inquirer, but only (quantitatively) other

---

[16] Dennett says that putting it this way is 'historically backwards', however, because the von Neumann machine was designed as a mirror of our own serial thinking (Dennett, 1991, p. 215).

information of the same type. I have proposed an alternative model: it's not simply that I don't know something that someone else knows in a cognitively equivalent way; what I lack in asking my question is a form of cognition which I (the questioner) cannot in principle possess in the way that my respondent does. Dennett sees human consciousness as having arisen as a jury-rig; it is the imperfection of the mind that calls for talking to oneself. 'None of this makes any sense,' he claims, 'so long as we persist in thinking of the mind as ideally rational, and perfectly self-transparent or unified. What good could *talking to yourself* do, if you already know what you intended to say?' (1991, p. 301). That is, it is the apparently contingent fact of a 'problematic intercommunication of parts' in the brain that calls forth the inner dialogue as an equally contingent solution.

This is not an impossible picture of the role of the internal dialogue in the constitution of self-consciousness, but I don't see that it is either necessary or likely. If the two partners are only quantitatively different, that is, if one merely has more information of the same kind as the other, and then communicates this to the other, then indeed, the communication seems to depend on the fact that, for some reason, one partner wasn't in possession of all this information; and the communication would then seem to be attributable to this contingent limitation. But if each partner possesses information of a cognitively different kind, then the duality is less the result of a quantitative division of information and more the result of a natural cognitive distinction — a distinction between material experience and formal expression.[17] Dennett's account, like other versions of the social model, would allow a conversation among many parties, not just between two. Talking to ourselves may be an efficient way in which two systems with the independent interests of meaning and articulation collaborate. Evolution may also have generated nicely designed systems meeting basic logical and methodological requirements.

But Dennett has more interesting things to say about the role of language in the structure of our consciousness, many of which are compatible with my own theory (or nearly so): 'Full fledged and executed communicative intentions — Meanings — could emerge from a quasi-evolutionary process of speech act design that involves the collaboration, partly serial, partly in parallel, of various subsystems none of which is capable on its own of performing — or ordering — a speech act' (1991, p. 239). My own claim is similar: neither the interests of articulation (which rely on 'serial' representation) nor of meaning (which rely on the 'parallel' processes by which we experience the world) by themselves are sufficient to constitute whole thought. Further, Dennett explicitly acknowledges the role of talking to oneself as a means for such collaboration.

We sometimes think that reflecting or self-conscious 'minds' must be in place somehow before material may be processed by them. It is much of this illusion of a central Self descending from above, and then acquiring a language for its special use that Dennett has rightly criticized. Reflective consciousness may be more the effect and less the cause of the differentiation of the language system from the other (perceptual) systems. That is, rather than having the two internal conversational partners established *so that* they can conduct a conversation, a more realistic view would

---

[17] I argue elsewhere (1998, Part II) that this coincides with the distinction between analogue and digital forms of representation.

derive the duality of these two agents from the duality of the representational systems found in linguistic and pre-linguistic experience, respectively.

Where Dennett diverges from the model I propose is on the question of the 'quasi-evolutionary' process he talks about. He observes, for example, that a 'generate-and-test' theory of perception supports a simple and powerful account of hallucination: '. . . the hypothesis-generation side of the cycle (the expectation-driven side) . . . operate[s] normally, while the data-driven side of the cycle (the confirmation side) goes into a disordered or random or arbitrary round of confirmation and discon-firmation . . .' (1991, p. 12). There is no Freudian 'playwright' responsible for dreams; its content emerges as the random data-confirmations prune away at the expectation-supplied proposals. We have here the familiar elements of Donald Campbell's 'blind-variation and selective retention' Darwinian model of inquiry.

Dennett feels a Darwinian account is necessary to explain the articulation of mean-ing, for otherwise we would have to resort to 'miracles' or an 'infinite regress of Mean-ers' (1991, p. 239). The idea that there is an agent — a 'Meaner' — whose thoughts simply come to be articulated and who directs the entire operation is unacceptable; rather there are 'content-demons' in feedback with 'word-demons'. Our final expres-sions are not, he claims, simply what we originally 'meant': what we *mean* and what we *say* emerge together as they interact. Thus, he rejects this top-down view: 'When the first bit of preverbal message arrives at the Formulator [Articulator], it triggers the production of the beginning of an utterance, and as the words get chosen by the For-mulator, this constrains how the utterance can continue, but there is minimal *collabo-ration* on revision of the specs' (p. 240). At the other extreme, which Dennett favours (although he allows that this is to be decided empirically),

> . . . are the models in which words and phrases from the Lexicon, together with their sounds, meanings and associations jostle with the grammatical constructions in a pande-monium, all 'trying' to be part of the message, and some of them thereby make a substan-tial contribution to the very communicative intentions that still fewer of them end up executing. At this extreme, the communicative intentions that exist are as much an effect of the process as a cause (pp. 240–1).

On this model, Dennett observes, 'we have to *abandon* the idea that the thought-*thinker* begins with a determinate thought to be expressed' (*ibid.*). He acknowledges Levelt's 'excellent negative evidence' against this model, and while expressing surprise at these results, holds that they are not conclusive. He also adds: 'But perhaps Levelt is right: perhaps the only feedback from Formulator to Conceptu-alizer is *indirect*: the sort of feedback that a person can produce *only* by explicitly talking to himself and then framing an opinion about what he finds himself saying' (p. 241, fn.2).

Here are the amendments which I would introduce into Dennett's account that would bring it closer to my own:

I would first emphasize how correction mechanisms (found in any notion of 'feed back') effect a major change in purely eliminative (Darwinian) models of adapta-tion.[18]

I would also reconstrue his conception of the *standard* against which the adequacy of trials in a feedback process is judged. He once believed in a 'Central Meaner,' he explains, because he believed 'there had to be . . . a place where meaning came

[18] This is the focus of a number of my earlier discussions (1987; 1995a; 1998).

from . . . since *something* has to set the standard against which 'feedback' can register failure to execute' (p. 246). I would agree that having an unqualifiedly invariant meaning functioning as the sole standard in such an adaptive process is no more plausible than having theory-free observation functioning as the sole foundation for scientific inquiry. Dennett tries to keep the function of a 'standard' in feedback and yet avoid this unfortunate consequence by allowing the standard itself to vary more constitutionally than I think necessary.

My own model is secured from a 'meaning-foundationalism' by two factors. The first is that there is a third choice besides Dennett's radical meaning-shifting model and a fixed meaning-foundation; for we can allow the *way meanings are taken* to vary, without a shift in the actual meanings themselves. While it may be true that there are no uninterpreted meanings (any more than there are theory-free observations), and that a given meaning can only be taken as a variant of an antecedent meaning which we supply (from an antecedent articulation), this variation need not amount to a constitutional alteration of the given meaning itself.[19] This latter more radical variation of meaning may sometimes occur, so that there may indeed be change in what we are trying to articulate as we try to articulate it, but I deny that this is either necessary or typical.

Dennett's example of Lincoln's famous line about 'fooling all of the people all of the time' might not even count as a case of a shifting meaning in the sense he wants (pp. 244–5). His point is that we sometimes say what we say because we like the way it sounds (the Formulator affecting the Conceptualizer), not simply because we want to communicate a fixed meaning. But we need to observe, first of all, that logical *articulation* should not be confused with verbal *formulation*: it may well have been the *logical*, and not merely the *auditory* or *rhetorical* effect that Lincoln liked. The preference for this logical form may admittedly effect a shift in the original meaning-to-be-articulated (although it might not as well): if it does, our response to this might be *either* (a) to abandon the original meaning in favour of the newly generated one, for the sake of the logical effect in this case (this is Dennett's point); or (b) to edit our articulation so that its effective meaning once again coincides with the original intended meaning. That is, we can just as easily imagine a case in which Lincoln would have rejected his pretty formula because it failed to communicate what he wanted to communicate. It didn't have to be a case of 'making it up as you go'.

This points to another feature of the dialogue between meaning and articulation which precludes a meaning-foundationalism. While a stable meaning may appear foundational, the fact that it functions as a standard in only one-half of the full reciprocal correction procedure (with purely logical or articulational requirements functioning as the other independent standard) will ensure that the whole process never becomes one-sided, with meaning always dictating to articulation. Dennett's Formulator (Articulator) can be a true collaborator to his Conceptualizer (Meaner), and not its subordinate, only if they don't butt into each other's affairs; with two standards, there is the recognition that *both* sets of requirements must be met — that, in the ideal

---

[19] As I argue at length elsewhere. I here rely on a distinction between *actual meaning* and *contrasted actual meaning*, modelled on an equivalent distinction between two senses of 'observation' (1987; 1994; 1998). I also argue elsewhere that because the term 'foundation' tends to preclude a sharing of power, the dual justificatory principles I describe here are probably best not referred to as 'foundations' (two 'foundations' in this case): 'reciprocal justification' is preferable (1997; 1998).

case, actual meaning is never sacrificed for articulation or vice-versa (in unideal cases, we recognize always that we have more work to do).

And so, the domination of meaning over articulation in some older cognitive theories need not be broken by surrendering the requirement of a non-shifting meaning, as Dennett proposes: it can also be broken both by recognizing a less radical variation of meanings, as well as by establishing the *equal* rights of articulation, thereby recognizing the existence of genuine and irreducible duality within cognition.

Dennett's account portrays these functions as more competitive than collaborative. While granting that there is much human behaviour that is naturally messy and falls short of ideal rationality, so that 'we don't know what we mean until we see what we say', there is also human behaviour that succeeds in satisfying both sets of requirements. This is, I admit, behaviour that we extol as ideal and rational; it is well that we do.

Conclusion

While self-consciousness seems to be closely tied to the internal dialogue, and the partners of this dialogue are equal, if not equivalent, this balance is often enough ignored, and self-consciousness (as well as our sense of 'self' in general), comes to be associated with the articulating partner alone. Both Dennett and Gazzaniga have implied as much as well. By what right would the articulating partner claim a privileged status in its partnership? It might be claimed that senses of self and self-consciousness more naturally attach to *executive* processing systems in the brain, and that the verbal system, although by no means dictatorial in its function, bears the responsibility for some general coordination of the other systems. The more primitive experiential systems had evolved first, and the verbal system may have developed to handle problems not taken care of at these more basic levels.

Executive coordination need not entail executive power, however. Jaynes' speculative account of the development of these two systems suggests that, prior to their integration (integration of the two cerebral hemispheres), 'I' was associated with the verbal system, while I received 'commands' (as from another person) from the nonverbal system (perhaps in abbreviated speech).[20] This 'I' has little if any executive power; it may have had more the function of an adviser to the real executive, interpreting and articulating the nuances of organizational function, and perhaps outlining alternatives, but with no power to actually originate an action or make a decision. From this standpoint, the articulating partner was the 'junior' partner, executing the commands of the other. In time, with integration, collaboration became so close that 'I' was no longer experienced as an isolated (powerless) facilitator, but as the origin of my decisions as well; that is, 'I' denoted this partnership itself.

We can still, of course, take our 'selves' to be more closely identified with our relatively inarticulate 'experiential' sides. The brilliance of clarity, conceptual analysis and rational control can quickly turn into an annoying glare without the depth and security of experience. Our sense of being moved by powers beyond our rational control need not be interpreted as a reversion to some primitive state; even Freud would have recognized that it might be in the self-interest of reason to portray this experiential side as childish and untrustworthy, in order to secure its own unilateral power.

---

[20] A familiar model for Freudian (and later) psychotherapy has the rational, conscious, articulating *ego* confronting its powerlessness in the face of the emotional, unconscious and nonverbal *id*.

We may, therefore, experience a duality of consciousness — be more acutely 'of two minds' — insofar as we fail to integrate fully the interests of our two dialoguing partners. This should come as no surprise: our mental life is full of conflict — a fact which convinced Freud that any adequate theory of the personality must embrace duality. He also realized that this duality derives, not from the conflict between my mind and other minds, but from the fundamental division between my desiring self and an unyielding world which I must represent to myself. This is analogous to my claim that the articulating partner in the internal dialogue does not arise merely in response to the need for social communication and adaptation, but represents one of two distinct internal cognitive interests. We can be 'of two minds' quite independently of reference to the minds of others.

References

Arendt, H. (1978), *The Life of the Mind, Volume I: Thinking* (New York: Harcourt, Brace, Jovanovich).

Blachowicz, J. (1987), 'Discovery as correction', *Synthese*, 71, pp. 235–321.

Blachowicz, J. (1989), 'Discovery and ampliative inference', *Philosophy of Science*, 56, pp. 438–62.

Blachowicz, J. (1991), 'Discovery and dialectic', *Idealistic Studies*, 21, pp. 1–28.

Blachowicz, J. (1994), 'Unarticulated meaning', *Erkenntnis*, 40, pp. 43–70.

Blachowicz, J. (1995a), 'Elimination, correction and Popper's evolutionary epistemology', *International Studies in the Philosophy of Science*, 9, pp. 5–17.

Blachowicz, J. (1995b), 'Platonic "true belief" and the paradox of inquiry', *The Southern Journal of Philosophy*, 33, pp. 403–29.

Blachowicz, J. (1997), 'Reciprocal justification in science and moral theory', *Synthese*, 110, pp. 447–68.

Blachowicz, J. (1998), *Of Two Minds: The Nature of Inquiry* (Albany, NY: SUNY Press).

Campbell, Donald T. (1974), 'Unjustified variation and selective retention in scientific discovery', in *Studies in the Philosophy of Biology*, ed. F.S. Ayala and T. Dobzhansky (London: Macmillan).

Dennett, D. (1976), 'Conditions of personhood', in *The Identities of Persons*, ed. Amelie Rorty (Berkeley, CA: University of California Press).

Dennett, D. (1991), *Consciousness Explained* (Boston, MA: Little, Brown and Company).

Fontenrose, J. (1978), *The Delphic Oracle* (Berkeley, CA: University of California Press).

Gadamer, Hans-Georg (1989), *Truth and Method*, second, revised edition. Translation revised by J. Weinsheimer and D. G. Marshall (New York: Continuum).

Gardner, H. (1974), *The Shattered Mind* (New York: Vintage Books).

Gazzaniga, M. (1985), *The Social Brain* (New York: Basic Books).

Gazzaniga, M. and J. E. LeDoux (1978), *The Integrated Mind* (New York: Plenum).

Guthrie, W. (1970), 'Delphic oracle', in *The Oxford Classical Dictionary*, ed. N. Hammond & H. Scullard (Oxford: Oxford University Press).

Humphrey, N. (1992), *A History of the Mind* (New York: Simon and Schuster).

Jackendoff, R. (1987), *Consciousness and the Computational Mind* (Cambridge, MA: MIT Press).

Jaynes, Julian (1977), *The Origin of Consciousness in the Breakdown of the Bicameral Mind* (Boston, MA: Houghton Mifflin).

Mead, George H. (1934), *Mind, Self and Society* (Chicago: University of Chicago Press).

O'Daly, G. (1987), *Augustine's Philosophy of Mind* (London: Duckworth).

Ornstein, R. (1976), *The Mind Field* (London: Octagon).

Piaget, Jean (1959), *The Language and Thought of the Child*, translated by Marjorie and Ruth Gabain (New York: Humanities Press).

Plato (1961), *Collected Dialogues*, edited by E. Hamilton and H. Cairns, Bollingen Series LXXI (New York: Pantheon).

Robinson, R. (1953), *Plato's Earlier Dialectic*, second edition (Oxford: Oxford University Press).

Ryle, G. (1979), *On Thinking* (Totowa, NJ: Rowman & Littlefield).

Sokolov, A. (1972), *Inner Speech and Thought*, translated by G. T. Onischenko, edited by D. B. Lindsley (New York: Plenum).

Vygotsky, L. (1962), *Thought and Language,* edited and translated by Eugenia Hanfmann and Gertrude Vakar (Cambridge: Cambridge University Press).

Wertsch, J. (1991), *Voices of the Mind* (Cambridge, MA: Harvard University Press).

Zaidel, E. (1978), 'Auditory language comprehension in the right hemisphere following cerebral commissurotomy and hemispherectomy: A comparison with child language and aphasia', in *Language Acquisition and Language Breakdown*, ed. A. Caramazza & E. Zurif (Baltimore: Johns Hopkins University Press).

Part 3

Developmental and phenomenological constraints

George Butterworth

A Developmental–Ecological Perspective on Strawson's 'The Self'

Introduction

Galen Strawson[1] considers the self to be best described as a cognitive, 'distinctively mental' phenomenon. He asserts that the mental sense of self comes to every normal human being in childhood and comprises the sense of being a mental presence, of being alone in one's head, with the body 'just a vehicle or vessel for the mental thing that is what one really or most essentially is' (p. 3). His thesis is determinedly cognitivist (although not naively so) and it is with this that I take issue. As Reed (1994) puts the problem, 'cognitivism, with its allegiance to the representational theory of mind and its focus on mental states as internal to the mind, is particularly susceptible to the dualistic separation of self from the environment' (p. 278). One may add that cognitivism is also susceptible to separating the self from the body. Reed suggests that perception not only provides information for the distinction between self and environment from the outset, but also it provides a means of keeping in contact with the world. Memory provides a means of bridging earlier and later aspects of self and integrating diverse elements of experience. Both perceiving and remembering entail aspects of self but in rather different ways. Perceiving is a spatio-temporal process which provides a continuous flow of information about the embodied self in its encounters with the physical and social world. Autobiographical memory requires a duplication of the self so that 'me-experiencing-now' can be related with 'a prior me-experiencing-a-prior-environment'. The question of interest is how a perceived self may, through development, give rise to a remembered self.

Extensive reviews on the early origins of self knowledge, well before the age of four years, have already been published and it would be inappropriate to present all the evidence again here (Butterworth, 1990; 1992a,b; 1995a,b). However, it will be necessary to state some of the fundamental premises of an ecological perspective in order to offer a developmental alternative to Strawson's cognitive phenomenology. The argument is that there are ways in which perception provides information for self before there is a self concept. This means that the mental self is not the 'essential' heart of the self system in the go-it-alone fashion suggested by Strawson's analysis.

---

[1] All references to 'Strawson' in the current chapter are to Galen Strawson's opening chapter in this volume (pp. 1–24).

The mental reflective self is just one relatively late-developing component of self. Although adult introspection may (unreliably) suggest differently, introspection cannot reveal the inter-related, mutually-embedded levels of self awareness which have been shown by empirical enquiry. Knowledge of the self as a singular 'entity', as an individuated object of one's own experience, is founded on and remains dependent upon information for the self situated in social and physical reality.

Five Kinds of Self Knowledge

Neisser (1988) made a useful distinction between five types of self knowledge which, taken together, comprise aspects of a single, complex self system. Although Neisser's taxonomy was not intended to be a developmental description, the aspects of self he describes make their appearance at different times in development and help in explaining the origins of a distinctively mental sense of self. The five aspects of self are:

1. The ecological self, which is directly perceived with respect to the physical environment.
2. The interpersonal self, also directly perceived, which depends on emotional and other species-typical forms of communication.
3. The extended self, which is based on memory and anticipation and implies a representation of self.
4. The private self, which reflects knowledge that our conscious experiences are exclusively our own, and this is also dependent on representation.
5. The self concept, defined as a theory of self based on socio-cultural experience.

From a developmental perspective, the problem is to relate the first two levels of self specified by the ecological approach (which are innate) via the development of self representation, to levels four and five. Levels three, four, and five correspond roughly to self recognition, the sense of being alone in one's head, and autobiographical memory. These three later appearing levels, which seem to be those which Strawson emphasises, only partially define the full-grown self since they omit those aspects which situate the self in the world (i.e. the synchronic problem is incompletely specified). Furthermore, even isolating the five aspects of self does not explain how the self is inter-related over time (i.e. the diachronic problem is not solved either).

The Ecological Foundations of Self Knowledge

The ecological approach proposes that the self exists objectively from the outset by virtue of its embodiment. Many of the characteristics of the body in action are specified by objective information about the location of the perceiver's own body provided by the ongoing physical and perceptual interaction with the physical and social environment. These forms of information are simultaneously 'exterospecific' (Gibson, 1987), that is they specify the perceived environment, and self specific, that is they specify the perceiving body. Much of this information is kinetic, consisting of structures which both change and remain invariant over time and which are equivalent across several perceptual systems. A prime example is the so called 'optic flow' pattern, the stream of textured visual information moving across the retina as the observer moves in relation to the ground. Among the earliest functions of such information is maintenance of posture, firstly over eyes and head, eventually over the trunk and then the whole body, as the baby gradually gains mastery over the main body segments. Self control emerges over static postures, such as sitting and standing and then over dynamic postures like, crawling, walking or running. In each case, the infant functions as an organised totality in making use of available visual information (this evidence and its implications for the origins of self are more fully discussed in Butterworth, 1995a).

It is a telling observation that adults also control posture using visual proprioception. Adults will lose their balance when presented with visual flow fields that are discrepant with other indices of postural stability, as in moving room experiments (Lee and Lishman, 1975). In these studies adults stand facing the interior end wall of a 'room' comprising three walls and a ceiling, which is suspended just above the ground. The suspended room is moved so that the end wall recedes from or approaches the observer, hence generating a flow of visual information which specifies postural instability (body sway). The visual information is in conflict with information from the vestibular and kinaesthetic systems which are actually stable with respect to the ground. The approaching wall provides visual information which specifies that the perceiver is falling forward with the result that the visually specified instability is corrected, and the adult loses balance in the backward direction. When the wall moves away from the observer, the visual information is consistent with loss of postural stability in the backward direction and the adult falls forward when the visually specified loss of stability is corrected. Babies show a similar loss of postural stability in experiments such as these. Vision serves to maintain a stable posture long before they can crawl or walk, as they first gain control over the stability of the head, then over the head and trunk in sitting and finally when they stand unsupported (Butterworth and Cicchetti, 1978; Butterworth and Pope, 1983).

Such experiments show that the primary sense of the embodied self is directly, perceptually tied to the stability of the visual environment, especially to the background perceived in the periphery of vision. Normally, specification of self through visual proprioceptive feedback is congruent with other levels of organisation of the self system and hence it passes unnoticed. When the normal, stable conditions of the ecology are violated (as, for example, when standing beside a waterfall), we become aware of the bodily self as a proprioceptive object of consciousness. We are not usually aware of the intimate link between self and the stable external environment but under perceptually incongruous conditions, even very young infants reveal such awareness, by compensating for visually-specified loss of postural control when subjected to discrepant optical flow. There is continuous specification of self agency within the optic flow pattern, which is tied to awareness of the body, and normally generated by the dynamics between the observer and the stable background. The agent revealed in this relational order may equally be called the self in its proprioceptive aspect.

Other recent sources of information for self specification in early infancy come from studies using video feedback whereby the baby sees her own arm or leg movements, not directly, but over a TV monitor (Bahrick and Watson, 1985; Van der Meer et al., 1995). These studies show that very young babies perceive the correspondence in patterning between self-generated kinaesthetic information, for instance as they kick their legs, and the visual feedback of the limb seen on the television monitor. Van der Meer et al. (1995) showed that a newborn baby would keep a weighted arm aloft when the limb was visible on a TV monitor but the baby would allow the arm to drop when the camera showed the other, non-weighted arm. This achievement requires more than simple detection of a contingent relation between kinaesthetically specified limb motion and visual feedback. It requires perception of the correspondence between the kinaesthetic output of one's own limbs and the patterned visual feedback consistent with that motion. The embodied aspect of self is constituted in perceiving the identity of patterning between kinaesthetic and visual proprioceptive processes.

The examples suggest that self specification emerges from the dynamic information available to perceptual systems, which cohere about a unitary, individual experiencer from the outset. That is, primary self awareness is both a process and a product of perception to which Strawson's principle of unity already applies. Individuation is not especially or essentially cognitive in the sense of being generated by self-conscious reflection. The cognitive or reflective aspect of self acquires its principle of unity from the perceptual-ecological aspect of self which engages the world with a unitary sense of self-agency. Unity of self is not a 'delusory projection' (Strawson, p. 4) but it is not purely cognitive either; such unity can be observed before it is reasonable to postulate any ability to reflect on experience.

Foundations of the Interpersonal Self

Similar arguments can be made for the importance of inter-personal aspects of self and for the role of emotional experience in underpinning later, more cognitively-defined aspects of self. Social relations depend on inter-relating one's own movements and facial expressions to those of others. The early origins of the interpersonal aspects of self are revealed most clearly by recent research on newborn babies' imitation of facial gestures such as tongue protrusion, which demonstrate that infants from the outset perceive some fundamental facts of human embodiment (e.g. Meltzoff and Moore, 1977; 1995). Infants' ability to share experiences with others in simple tasks requiring joint attention to the same object also reveals that even babies have a point of view which they are willing to share with others (Butterworth and Jarrett, 1991). Having a point of view may be taken as a criterion for existence of a self. The existence of a point of view however, may go only part of the way, developmentally speaking, towards the sense of possession of a point of view (Bermúdez, 1995). Development is needed to reach the level of reflective self awareness which supports the sense of ownership and which can bridge experience of self over discontinuous intervals.

The emotions as founding factors should also be considered as constitutive of self, rather than being excluded. Stern (1985; 1993) describes how the emergence of a core sense of a human self may depend on emotional experience. The parent, by imitating the expressive contours of the infant's behaviour, reveals she understands not only the infant's actions but also her feelings. This aspect of interpersonal synchrony does not involve literal imitation. Rather, the mother, in analogical fashion, matches the baby's mood through the vitality of her own responses. She thus provides the baby with important information about specifically human emotions and conveys that she understands the child's feelings. Such vitality effects may provide the essential, human information for the self which a 'cold blooded' cognitive analysis overlooks.

As Stern (1993) suggests it may be relatively easy to fake cognitive aspects of inter-personal co-ordination, whereas affect, more than cognition, determines whether one is engaged with another human being. Feelings may therefore occupy an important position in defining what makes a human self, rather than merely a ghost in the bodily machine. In infancy such qualitative aspects of self are directly experienced in the context of social relations, whereas they may be evoked within the autobiographical self in a more fragmentary fashion, depending on which aspect of a prior self is being remembered.

Stern (1993) distinguishes further between objective and subjective aspects of the interpersonal self. For the objective aspect of the interpersonal self all the necessary information must be available to the subject, the partner and an observer. For the sub-jective aspect of the interpersonal self, all the requisite information must be perceived by the subject. Given sufficient experience of both types of interaction, representa-tions of their invariant, affective properties are said to develop. Such representations may not include a subjective experience of reliving the interactions, especially if based on experiences in infancy. Nevertheless, it is from social experience that feel-ings of being attached, loved, or being alone in one's head are very likely derived.

Primary and Secondary Self Consciousness

The argument for the pre-reflective origins of self is not readily countered by Straw-son's distinction between the experiential and non-experiential aspects of the physi-cal self (p. 7). The level of consciousness involved in the earliest forms of self can be characterized as primary self awareness, in which the self is part of the direct, un-reflective object of experience. This thesis follows from the work of Edelman (1989), who distinguishes primary self awareness from the higher-order (cognitive) self con-sciousness at the core of Strawson's definition. Primary consciousness is based on being mentally aware of things in the world (including one's own presence in the world) whereas reflective self awareness, 'includes recognition by a thinking subject of his or her own acts or affections. It embodies a model of the personal and of the past, future and present' (Edelman, 1989). In essence then, the distinction between primary and higher-order self consciousness is similar to that between consciousness of self as a (proprioceptive) product of perception and reflective self consciousness, as a product of representation, memory and thought.

From Self Perception to a Self Concept

It still remains to bridge the gap between primary and higher-order aspects of self. One approach is to consider the classical evidence on the development of mirror self awareness. Mirror self recognition has long been considered a diagnostic indicator for the emergence of a self concept. The technique is to show the child her own face, on which has been surreptitiously dabbed a spot of rouge. Infants as young as 15 months (typically by 24 months), notice the anomaly in the mirror image and remove the offending red dot from their own face. There are developmental antecedents to this achievement, for example babies from about ten months will use the mirror image in a self-directed way, to grasp a hat lowered just above their head, or they may touch their own body as if they detect an anomaly but they fail to remove the rouge mark (Bertenthal and Fisher, 1978). That there is a substantial cognitive component in mirror self recognition is revealed by the fact that mentally retarded Down's syndrome children are delayed on rouge removal tasks until three to four years (Mans *et al.*, 1978). Mirror self recognition seems to be restricted to humans, chimpanzees [at about 8 years] and orang-utans [age unknown], (Gallup, 1982). The task probably requires a combination of perceptual and cognitive abilities including detection of the contingent nature of the mirror image, monitoring proprioceptive output, self identification by means of distinctive features, comprehension of the identity of the reflected image and attribution of the image to the self.

Mirror self recognition occurs at about the same time as Piaget (1954) describes the child acquiring the concept of the permanent object. The object concept includes knowledge that objects continue to exist when unperceived and that they retain their unique identity over time. On Piaget's theory the infant acquires a concept of person permanence, including a concept of self, at the same time as discovering the invariant properties of physical objects. These cognitive developmental achievements may be sufficient to account for the origins of a mental sense of uniqueness, although this very likely requires socio-emotional experience, especially as concerns the development of personality (Hinde, 1997). The relation between object concept development and the prior perceptual abilities of babies is also a matter of controversy which, although relevant, cannot be entered into here (Butterworth, 1981).

Even with a concept of self as a permanent object, which we may postulate to be in place by the end of infancy, there is much development still to come in establishing an autobiographical self. Recent research by Povinelli and Simon (1998) extends our understanding of the spatio-temporal envelope within which the child comprehends the mirror image to be a reflection of the self. Children aged three, four and five years were seen on two successive occasions, separated by one week. On the first, preparatory visit, a sticker was placed surreptitiously on the child's head and a video-recording was made of the child playing an unusual game. The sticker was then removed so that its presence during the game was unknown to the child. One week later the children were filmed again, playing a different game at a conspicuously different place, and once more a sticker was surreptitiously placed on the child's head so that it was visible in the video-recording. Testing then began and half the children at each age were shown the recording made of them one week previously, while the remainder were shown the recording that had been made of them just three minutes before.

The children aged four and five years who were tested with the video-recording made just three minutes earlier reached to remove the sticker, thus demonstrating continuity of self over the three minute gap. They would refer to the video image using the first person pronoun 'me' or by their own name. In contrast, three-year-olds often used third-person descriptions to state that the sticker was on 'his' (or her) head, as if the brief delay was sufficient to disrupt the ability to attribute the video image to the self. The four- and five-year-old children tested with the video-recording made one week earlier generally made no attempt to remove the sticker, as if the transient anomaly in the appearance of the self of the distant past was understood to be irrelevant to the present self. Three-year-old children were as likely to attempt to remove the sticker when the film showed them one week before as when the film showed them three minutes earlier. That is, they identified the self but did not take into account the contextual information which showed them in the more distant past. Consequently they treated both old and more recent video-images as equivalent.

Thus, even though three-year-olds have no difficulty in identifying themselves in a mirror, they depend on spatio–temporal congruity between proprioceptive aspects of motor output and the video-image to attribute the image of the child with the sticker to the self. Povinelli (1995) suggests that they lack the 'duplicated' self which enables older children to connect 'me experiencing now' with 'me experiencing then', even across small gaps in time. Povinelli and Simon (1998) have suggested that such an autobiographical self emerges at the age of four years. The autobiographical self is capable of bridging the spatio-temporal gap in experience which the three-year-old cannot overcome.

A series of developmental changes underlie these differences in performance between two and five years (Povinelli, 1995; Povinelli and Simon, 1998). Children recognize themselves in mirrors by the age of two, perhaps by a combination of feature knowledge and proprioceptive information which links their own actions to the movements of the mirror image. Cognitive developmental changes related to object concept acquisition may also contribute. This aspect of self is specified within a continuous real-time spatio-temporal envelope since the three-year-old cannot relate the present self to the self in delayed visual feedback. This requires the child to consider simultaneously spatio-temporal information specifying the self as it is now with the incongruent dynamics which specified the self at a previous time. This requires more than simple perspective taking since it involves perspective duplication. However the capacity to link present to past aspects of self by internally duplicating perspectives is still incompletely developed. Fogel (1993) has discussed precursors of such 'dialogic' aspects of self which are revealed in real-time social interaction, as in turn taking during mother–infant play or in simple role switching in play at the age of three years. Such examples involve shifting of perspectives but they are less cognitively demanding than perspective duplication, which appears to be a relatively late-developing phenomenon at about four years.

Something has therefore changed by four years, when briefly-delayed video feedback can be related to currently transient aspects of self. This implies that the child can simultaneously consider the present and immediately past state of the self. The child is no longer so dependent on the congruence of the visual dynamics of the input with proprioceptive aspects of motor output to specify the self. Four- and five-year-old children also understand that currently transient aspects of self are not revealed in the long-delayed video images filmed one week before. They recognize that the context and game being played on the video-recording are out of date and they are unlikely to reach up for the sticker on their head, even though they will do so when contextual cues are constant and the delay is short.

It is not known whether four-year-old children will continue to respond to the transient anomaly displayed in visual feedback after longer delays than three minutes. Nevertheless, the evidence suggests that by four years previous states of the self can be linked to present states through a self system which binds successive instances in a temporal and causal sequence. This corresponds to the subjective, autobiographical aspect of self of Neisser's classification. It appears to be related to Strawson's description of a distinctively cognitive self but in fact, the autobiographical aspect of self depends on the duplication of perspectives; it comprises self as experienced now in relation to the remembered self. The extent to which such a duplication depends on language, or more precisely on symbolic representation, remains to be investigated. It is surely not coincidental that the autobiographical aspect of self emerges at about the same time as the child acquires a theory of mind, which may be defined as the ability to attribute a mental life to others (Perner, 1991). Consistent with my general position, I have suggested that the ability to mentalize may depend crucially on the capacity for symbolic processes which enable counterfactual states of affairs to be represented (Butterworth, 1994). From this perspective Strawson's 'distinctively mental' self is a symbolic aspect of self, whereas the ecological and interpersonal selves are better considered as non-symbolic aspects of experience. The autobiographical self requires a constant interplay between the ecological aspect of self (me as I am now) and the symbolic, remembered aspect of self. Perhaps it is only because such a self is symbolic that it can choose, counterfactually, to ignore its own embodiment.

Conclusion

A developmental analysis reveals many links between the conceptual self and its pre-conceptual underpinnings. It reveals the self as many faceted, as dependent on the proprioceptive functions of the body, on social and affective experiences and on cognitive developmental processes. Strawson's 'distinctively mental' self (p. 3) is just one facet of a complex interplay of self-specifying factors, only some of which are accessible to introspection. On a developmental model the notion of self changes as new layers are added around the fundamental core given by the ecological and interpersonal aspects. From an ecological perspective development is not best understood if the self is considered, in its essence, a purely cognitive phenomenon. On the contrary, those cognitive aspects of self are best understood to develop out of relations with persons and other aspects of embodiment. A symbolic form of self permits a conception of self as unique and supports reflective self awareness and a private perspective. Even these aspects of the cognitive self are best considered as extensions of the embodied, situated, ecological aspects of self. It is the primacy of the ecological aspect of self which makes the mental experience of self, to the introspective adult, so real.

References

Bahrick, L and Watson, J.S. (1985), 'Detection of inter-modal proprioceptive-visual contingency as a potential basis of visual self perception in infancy', *Developmental Psychology*, **21** (6), pp. 963–73.
Bermúdez, J.L. (1995), 'Ecological perception and the notion of a non-conceptual point of view', in Bermúdez *et al.* (1995).
Bermúdez, J., Eilan, N. and Marcel, A. (ed. 1995), *The Body and the Self* (Cambridge, MA: MIT Press).
Bertenthal, B.J. and Fisher, K.W. (1978), 'Development of self recognition in the infant', *Developmental Psychology*, **14**, pp. 44–50.
Butterworth, G.E. (1981), 'Object permanence and identity in Piaget's theory of infant cognition', in *Infancy and Epistemology, an evaluation of Piaget's theory*, ed. G.E. Butterworth (Brighton: Harvester).
Butterworth, G.E. (1990), 'Self perception in infancy' in *The Self in Transition*, ed. D. Cicchetti and M.Beeghly (Chicago: University of Chicago Press).
Butterworth, G.E. (1992a), 'Origins of self in human infancy', *Psychological Inquiry*, **2** (3), pp. 103–11 (with ten peer commentaries).
Butterworth, G.E. (1992b), 'Self perception as a foundation for self knowledge' *Psychological Inquiry*, **3** (2), pp. 134–6.
Butterworth, G.E. (1994), 'Theory of mind and the facts of embodiment', in *Origins of an Understanding of Mind*, ed. C. Lewis and P. Mitchell (Hove: Psychology Press).
Butterworth, G.E. (1995a), 'An ecological perspective on the origins of self', in Bermúdez *et al.* (1995).

Butterworth, G.E. (1995b), 'The self as an object of consciousness in infancy', in Rochat (1995).

Butterworth, G.E. and Cicchetti, D. (1978), 'Visual calibration of posture in normal and motor retarded human infants', *Perception*, 7, pp. 513–25.

Butterworth, G.E. and Jarrett, N.L.M. (1991), 'What minds have in common is space: Spatial mechanisms for perspective taking in infancy', *British Journal of Developmental Psychology*, 9, pp. 55–72.

Butterworth, G.E. and Pope, M. (1983), 'Les origines de la proprioception visuelle chez le nourisson', in *Le Developpement dans la Premiere Année*, ed. S. de Schonen (Paris: Presses Universitaires de France).

Edelman, G.M. (1989), *The Remembered Present* (New York: Basic Books).

Fogel, A. (1993), *Developing Through Relationships: Origins of communication, self and culture* (Hemel Hempstead: Harvester).

Gallup, G.G. (1982), 'Self awareness and the emergence of mind in primates', *American Journal of Primatology*, 2, pp. 237–48.

Gibson, J.J. (1987), 'The uses of proprioception and the detection of propriospecific information', in *Reasons for Realism : Selected essays of James J Gibson*, ed. E. Reed & R. Jones (Hillsdale, NJ: Erlbaum).

Hinde, R.A. (1997), *Relationships: A dialectical perspective* (Hove: Psychology Press).

Lee, D. and Lishman, J.R. (1975), 'Visual proprioceptive control of stance', *Journal of Human Movement Studies*, 1, pp. 87–95.

Mans, L., Cicchetti, D. and Sroufe, L.A. (1978), 'Mirror reactions of Down's syndrome infants and toddlers: Cognitive underpinnings of self recognition', *Child Development*, 49, pp. 1247–50.

Meltzoff, A.N. & Moore, M.K. (1977), 'Imitation of facial and manual gestures by human neonates', *Science*, 198, pp. 75–8.

Meltzoff, A.N. & Moore, M.K (1995), 'Infant's understanding of people and things: From bodily imitation to folk psychology', in Bermúdez *et al.* (1995).

Neisser, U. (1988), 'Five kinds of self knowledge', *Philosophical Psychology*, 1, pp. 35–59.

Perner, J. (1991), *Understanding the Representational Mind* (Cambridge, MA: The MIT Press).

Piaget, J. (1954), *The Construction of Reality in the Child* (New York: Basic Books).

Povinelli , D. (1995), 'The unduplicated self', in Rochat (1995).

Povinelli , D and Simon, B.B. (1998), 'Young children's understanding of briefly versus extremely delayed images of the self: Emergence of an autobiographical stance', *Developmental Psychology* (in press).

Reed, E.S. (1994), 'Perception is to self as remembering is to selves', *in The Remembering Self: Construction and accuracy in the self narrative*, ed. U. Neisser and R. Fivush (Cambridge: Cambridge University Press).

Rochat, P. (1995), *The Self in Early Infancy: Theory and research* (Amsterdam: Elsevier).

Stern, D. (1985), *The Interpersonal World of the Infant* (New York: Basic Books).

Stern, D. (1993), 'The role of feelings for an interpersonal self', in *The Perceived Self : Ecological and interpersonal sources of self knowledge*, ed. U. Neisser (Cambridge: Cambridge University Press).

Strawson, G. (1997), '"The self"', *Journal of Consciousness Studies*, 4 (5–6), pp. 405–28. Reprinted in this volume, pp. 1–24.

Van der Meer, A., Van der Weel, F.R. and Lee, D.N. (1995), 'Lifting weights in neonates : Body building in progress', *Science*, 267, pp. 693–5.

Maria Legerstee

Mental and Bodily Awareness in Infancy

Consciousness of Self-existence[1]

Introduction

I know that I exist, the question is, What is this 'I' that I know?

Descartes (1641/1985)

This question, posed by Descartes at the beginning of the modern era, has incited philosophers and psychologists to explain human existence. Descartes suggested that he knew that he existed because he thought. However, even if we have immediate evidence for our mental self, how can we be sure about the existence of our body, the external world, and even more challenging, how can we be sure about the thoughts and emotions of others? How do we know that the ideas we have about these things are not just aspects of our mind, such as our dreams or imaginations? If we do not want to introduce a superior being that gave us these ideas, then we have no choice but to rely on human reason or human experience. But how do we achieve self-awareness and what is its relation to the mind–body problem?

Many contemporary cognitive scientists emphasize the importance of mental states and thought when discussing self-awareness. They inherently adopt a particular stance on the nature of self-awareness by shifting to an exclusive concern with mental states and events, while neglecting the bodily dimensions. They believe that adults possess rich conceptions about internal cognitions and mental states of self and others, and that adults construe people's overt behaviour as the product of these states, such as the actors' intentions, beliefs and desires (Bennett, 1989; Searle, 1992). However, they do not discuss the developmental dimension that leads to the adult's competencies so fervently described in detail in these frameworks.

The problem of self-awareness is solved neither by adopting a position that eliminates the bodily dimension nor by a position that contests the notion of self-awareness or the mind. As is well known, many materialists and behavioural neuroscientists

[1] This work was supported by a grant from the Social Sciences and Humanities Research Council of Canada (410-98-1743). I would like to thank Thomas Teo, Shaun Gallagher and three anonymous reviewers of the *Journal of Consciousness Studies* for valuable comments on earlier drafts of this chapter.

propose that the mind is a wholly physical phenomenon. But how do the senses and experiences (e.g. Churchland, 1991; Hume,1739/1888; Locke, 1710/1975; Watson, 1928) lead to self-awareness? It seems that rationalist and empiricist epistemologies, monistic and dualistic mind–body positions, and contemporary neuroscientific frameworks are not really able to address the problem of self-awareness as long as they do not address the genetic (in the Piagetian sense of developmental) dimension of this problem. Developmental psychology in general and infancy research in particular have produced a vast literature to address these issues and are able to complement, falsify, or verify philosophical reflections (Teo, 1997).

The problem of how to define the nature of the self was recently addressed by Galen Strawson (1997). Strawson argues that the 'self' is a purely mental entity. It seems that Strawson takes a monistic view, but one where everything is cognitive. Strawson's account of the self not only differs from orthodox materialists and interactionists, but also from that of many genetic epistemologists, who propose that there are several levels of the self — such as the physical and social, as well as the mental — that are internal to the mind, and of which humans become conscious during their first years of life. These primitive levels of awareness of the self shape the individual's subsequent mature concept of self. Thus these scientists (primarily developmental psychologists) focus on how an awareness of the body and mind develops, and at what age humans become able to think about their actions and those of others. In fact, these questions have become hot topics in the past decades. Recent volumes have been edited describing children's discovery of their bodily and social selves (Neisser, 1993; Rochat, 1995a), as well as their mental selves (Astington *et al.*, 1988; Astington & Olson, 1995; Wellman,1993). For instance, Neisser's theoretical formulations predict that different kinds of self-knowledge become available through different forms of information processing. Through the innate mechanisms of amodal perception and imitation, the social or interpersonal selves are perceived when infants observe the expressive gestures of their caregivers who engage with them in social interaction. Thus, developmental psychologists investigate the origins of an awareness of mind and body and endeavour to determine what the self was before the human creature became conscious of it.

In this chapter, I will draw on my own work and related publications to present some intuitions and hypotheses about the nature of the self and the mechanisms that lead to the development of consciousness or self awareness in human infants during the first 6 months of life. My main purpose is to show that the origins of a concept of self include the physical and the mental selves. I believe that it is essential when trying to understand what a mental state is, that one identifies the social and physical aspects of the person to whom the mental state belongs. How can one identify a mental state or thought without making reference to a subject who experiences it (Hobson, 1990)? The other important feature of the self is that it is distinguished from other people and inanimate objects. 'One's concept of self is a concept of a person; one's concept of persons cannot be a concept applicable only to a single individual (oneself), for the reason that in this case it would no longer constitute a concept'(Hobson, 1990, p. 165). I would like to argue that infants must be able to represent their physical and social selves in order to recognize that they are similar and different from other people, and to develop expectations and predictions about the behaviour of others (theory of mind). Unlike Strawson, I do not believe that the social and physical aspects of the self are, or become redundant to the nature of the self. I posit that the mature conscious self is a unique mythical and constantly changing entity, the formation of which is *created* not by the individual alone, but through continuous dialectical inquiry with other people.

The view that this chapter puts forth about the origin of the concept of self — and will attempt to support with empirical data — is that infants, during their first six months of life, show a primitive concept of their physical/social and mental selves and impute mental states such as intentions and purpose to others. I will argue that a *structural constraint theory*, which proposes that the mind has innate knowledge, but that development is a process of constructing new knowledge from previous cognitive structures in interaction with the social and physical world, most adequately explains the empirical evidence we possess. For clarity, I will organize this review and evaluation according to two *methodological* approaches, perceptual or sensory awareness and conceptual awareness. This distinction however, does not mean to indicate that humans have perceptual experiences which they do not, or cannot represent, or that perceptual awareness precedes conceptual awareness; rather this distinction is related to different *experimental paradigms* researchers use to assess the infant's understanding of certain aspects of the self. Studies that provide information on *perceptual* (or sensory) self awareness in infants often rely on the products of the infant's perceptions of, or direct experience with *environmental stimuli* that identify the self. These studies, because of the type of method they use, cannot make claims about the infants' conceptual understanding of the self. Studies that aim to provide evidence for a *conceptual* or representational awareness of the self must show that infants are aware of aspects of the self that are *not* available to immediate sensory experience. In this case, infants' identifications of self are products of their *mental capacities* (e.g. memory, representation, etc.). Infants would be able to draw on this knowledge when perceptual stimulation is *not* available.

Perceptual or Conceptual Awareness?

What is the *relationship* between a perceptual and conceptual awareness of the self? According to Quassim Cassam (1994) a thorough theoretical account of self-awareness must include a discussion of the relationship between an awareness of our material or perceptual self, which includes such things as our voice and body, and our mental or conceptual self, which refers to the nature and the extent of the knowledge of our particular thoughts. In developmental psychology, just as in philosophy, the relationship between the two levels of self-knowledge is not straightforward. As Pascal-Leone and Johnson (1998) point out it was Plato who originated the idea that there are two distinct aspects of conscious awareness, 'the world of ideas and that of the senses, the world of being and that of becoming, the noetic, intelligible world and the world of appearance' (Jaspers, 1957, p. 30).

Some authors propose that perceptual self-awareness is a *precursor* to a conceptual awareness of the self in infants (e.g. Berkeley, 1975; James, 1890; Merleau-Ponty, 1942; Piaget, 1952). In this sense perceptual and conceptual awareness provide a continuum in the development of consciousness or self-awareness, but the two stages are *qualitatively* distinct in that perceptual awareness does not require mental awareness of self, and hence only when infants have a conceptual awareness can they be said to have self-awareness. Thus in the first stage, the self is an object of *perception*, and in the second stage of *thought*. Consequently, the infants' earliest understandings of self are limited to the earliest perceptual and sensorimotor experiences they have of their bodily self. With development, these earliest perceptions about the self are *overturned* and changed into a more appropriate (realistic), representational awareness of self. However, this position does not solve the problem of body and mind dualism. What does this representational self involve? Does it include knowledge of our bodily self or just of our thoughts? Another problem with the perception/conception distinction is how one can differentiate between these two cognitive processes (the conceptual or high functioning cognitive mode and the experiential or low-functioning cognitive mode), 'and at the same time explain the emergence of both modes of processing from the same origin: as resulting from interactions among innateness (maturation) and experience (learning)' (Pascual-Leone & Johnson, 1998).

Not all authors make the perceptual/conceptual distinction. Many propose that a primitive sort of self-awareness or consciousness exists at birth, and that with development a more complex consciousness develops (Butterworth, 1995; Gallagher, 1996; Gibson, 1995; Kant, 1781; Karmiloff-Smith, 1992; Legerstee, 1997b; Neisser, 1995; Pascual-Leone & Johnson, 1998; Spelke *et al.*, 1992). The developmental distinction is one of progressive differentiation rather than of qualitative changes in the way infants know themselves (Spelke,1988). Because infants experience the world in a veridical way, the initial conceptions of the self are appropriate (albeit limited), form the core for later mature self-consciousness, and become more refined as either their information systems (Gibson, 1995) or cognitive structures (Karmiloff-Smith, 1992; Legerstee, 1997b) develop. Thus according to this view, infants develop from a primary consciousness, which includes primitive representations of the physical/social as well as the mental aspects of self, to a higher-order consciousness, which entails a fully developed concept of self, rather than from an experiential/perceptual-motor to a qualitatively different mental/conceptual awareness of self. If this can be empirically supported, then it would mean that in addition to mental aspects, a mature concept of the self must include the components that comprise the primitive self; the mental, but also the social and physical aspects. Such a position would argue against Strawson's idea that the representational self only involves the mind and not the body.

Theoretical Speculations in Developmental Psychology

Because Piaget's theory with regard to the development of a representational or mental self remains influential in more recent theorizing about self-awareness and theory of mind, in particular his accounts of the relationship between perception (action) and conception (representation/operation) (see for instance Frye, 1981; Tomasello, 1995), current theories of representation must be contrasted with that of Piaget. Classical cognitive developmental theorists such as Piaget (1952), propose that at birth, infants are neither social nor cognitive creatures; they do not distinguish between self, other people and things. They come equipped with a set of reflexes, which become action schemes that for the first 10–12 months only allow infants to relate objects to their own actions rather than to other objects in space. Through repeatedly acting on objects (people and inanimates) during the first two years of life, these courses of action internalize; they become verbal or other types of symbolic schemes that permit infants to deal with the world in a conceptual manner. Consequently, the infants' first awareness of self is as a perceptual physical stimulus. During perceptual awareness infants are merely reacting to immediate sensory stimulation that distinguishes self from other people and inanimate objects. With conceptual knowledge, infants begin to change their subjective understanding of the world and self to an objective understanding, and to place themselves within a common space with other objects. Those theorists who propose that perceptual awareness precedes and is qualitatively distinct from conceptual awareness would argue that after an initial state of 'dualistic confusion'(Piaget, 1954) or of 'normal autism' (Freud, 1961; Mailer et al., 1975) at birth, during which infants are unable to differentiate between self and the environment, infants enter a state of dualism where a differentiation between self and other is made. According to Piaget, the reason that this process is protracted over the first 2 years of life is related to several aspects. First, being born without the ability to perceive depth, infants need considerable developmental experience with objects (reaching for them, bringing them to the mouth, etc.) in order to begin to understand that these objects occupy a permanent position in space, one that is different from their own. Second, Piaget proposes that at birth the senses are not connected. Until infants come to recognize correspondences between information perceived through different sense modalities, stable sensorimotor schemes of three-dimensional, solid, sound producing textured objects cannot be formed and hence cannot be thought about.

Contrary to Piaget, many neo-nativist (Karmiloff-Smith,1992; Legerstee, 1997b; in press; Mandler, 1992; Spelke, 1988) and neo-Piagetian (e.g. Pascual-Leone & Johnson, 1998) researchers view the young infant as more sophisticated than Piaget believed. They propose that simple representations can be found at earlier stages and that much of the so-called 'complicated cognition' (e.g. object permanence, imitation, categorization), can be found in the beginning rather than at the end of the infancy period. Some of these authors postulate that infants are born with domain specific knowledge that will be expressed when the appropriate sensorimotor skills have matured (Karmiloff-Smith, 1992; Legerstee, 1997b; Spelke, 1988). Thus, infants are biologically constrained to process certain classes of stimuli that are relevant to human existence, such as knowledge about the self and other people. Infants have innately specified structural information that enables them to recognize members of their own species and to differentiate them from physical objects right from the start. Infants treat faces and voices and bodily movements as special social parameters, and human behaviour as involving intentionality. It should be noted that knowledge in each domain is not complete, it is in an infancy state and provides minimal information about the environment for the organism to act upon. With development and because of plasticity of early brain development, domain specific structures not only become more specific but decentration occurs which allows for cross-connecting of the various domains. Thus, these structural constraint theorists part from the conventional epistemologists on two accounts. First, rather than viewing infants as having empty minds and various reflexes to act on the 'blooming, buzzing, confusion' out there (James, 1890), in the present state of developmental theorizing, the domain specific predispositions guide the infants' subsequent involvement with social and physical things in the environment. However, development is not determined by these domain-specific structures alone, rather this model views the environment as a co-determinant in the course of development. Thus, the present model uses the infant-environment system as the subject of study and ascribes change and variability to both the infants' cognitive structures and the physical and social environments.

Rather than proposing that infants *construct* a sense of self, either with the help of domain-specific abilities (Karmiloff-Smith, 1992) or through acting and moving about in the environment, thereby discovering planes of depth through their own activity (Piaget, 1954), Gibson (1969; 1995) puts forth an ecological theory which proposes that information about the self is veridically perceived from infancy. Thus, unlike the classical cognitive developmental view in which perception begins with a retinal image that needs to be interpreted, Gibson argues that perception is an activity. 'It is the obtaining of information from a dynamic array in the environment surrounding the perceiver. This activity begins immediately at birth (and to some extent before)' (1995, p. 5). Gibson claims that the first awareness of the infant's own body comes through proprioceptive experience, which includes both internal (muscle and joints) receptors and external (visual and auditory) senses. A conceptual aware-ness of self can be specified by simultaneously feeling the muscles and seeing the arms and legs move. The physical and social selves are the first levels to be perceived through bodily movements and social emotional forms of communication respec-tively (see also Neisser, 1995). Thus, the theory of *direct perception* proposes that proprioceptive specification of self (internal and external) is possible long before the infant can move around the environment. Consequently consciousness, which includes a sense or awareness of self as separate from environmental stimuli, appears at the onset of development for this developmental theory rather than at the end of the infancy period (2 years of age).

Evidence for a Physical Self

Consciousness of a physical self before independent locomotion would refute the notion that infants begin life unable to separate self from others and would counter Strawson's idea of the 'single mental thing' as 'grounded in its mental nature alone' (1997, p. 413). Evidence of a near-self-awareness, or at least of an awareness as a dif-ferentiated entity from the external environment, is provided by studies showing that within the first weeks of life, infants use either visual or proprioceptive information to control their posture (Berthental & Bai, 1989; Butterworth & Hicks, 1977). Such young infants also explore their own bodies, show coordinated hand–mouth move-ments, and accommodate their open mouth to their approaching hand (e.g. Butter-worth & Hopkins, 1988; Rochat *et al.*, 1988). They further engage in visually guided reaching (Hofsten, 1980). The fact that infants only reach for three-dimensional ob-jects rather than to two-dimensional representations of them (Rader & Stern, 1982) indicates that this behaviour is not unconscious or reflexive, but that infants perceive the distance of the object relative to their own. Similarly, when infants respond with avoidance reactions to looming objects and not to objects approaching on a 'miss' path (Ball & Tronick, 1971; Yonas *et al.*, 1979), they provide evidence that object knowledge and self-knowledge are inseparable. Further knowledge of the self is evi-denced when infants augment non-nutritive sucking to bring a picture into focus (Kalins & Bruner, 1973) and increase the movements of a leg, attached to a rotating mobile, in order to make it move (Rovee-Collier & Fagan , 1981). Thus, infants appear to act as individuals which suggests that they are conscious of their physical selves as separate from the external environment.

In addition to seeing and feeling themselves move, infants from birth experience contrasting auditory events that should inform them about their own sounds. When infants vocalize, the sounds they hear are paired with kinesthetic and proprioceptive feedback. Sounds produced by other people or objects do not provide infants with such intermodal information. There is evidence for an auditory specification of self in newborns. Martin & Clark (1982) compared the responses of day-old infants to pre-recorded sounds of their own cries as well as the cries of other newborns. Their results showed that infants discriminated their own cries from those of other infants; those that were calm at the commencement of the experiment vocalized considerably more when hearing the cries of other infants, but less when hearing their own cries.

Evidence for a Social Self

The above evidence seems to suggest that during the first 6-months of life, infants perceive, through various forms of proprioception, their own bodily movements and voice and through their responsiveness show an awareness of themselves as objects that have bodies and make sounds. Thus, situations that identify the physical self are continuously specified by acoustic, kinesthetic and vestibular information. Consciousness of the social self becomes evident when infants interact with the social environment (Legerstee, 1997b; in press; Neisser, 1995; Reed, 1995). From birth, infants demonstrate their abilities and motivation to interact with people. They express awareness of their social selves in interactions that are reciprocally controlled by human signals, such as imitative responses, smiles and vocalizations (Legerstee, 1990; 1997a; Legerstee & Bowman, 1989; Legerstee et al., 1987; Legerstee et al., 1990; Neisser, 1995; Stern, 1995; Trevarthen, 1979). By 5 weeks, infants imitate facial expressions modelled by people and not by inanimate objects simulating these movements. This suggests that imitation of facial expressions, actions which babies can only feel themselves perform, is the result of active intermodal mapping. That is, infants possess the ability to integrate information from two senses. They can observe the model (visual sense) and store the information in an abstract format so that the information can be compared to their own proprioceptive (tactile) information. Thus preverbal infants are able to translate, without language, information from one sense (in this case the visual — seeing a tongue protrusion) into non-modality specific or amodal information, so that it can be picked up and used by the tactile sense for action (protruding one's own tongue). Thus, infants are able to coordinate two sensory modalities many months before Piaget (1952) thought this possible. Although the ability to imitate proprioceptive movements may not need to rely on representation, imitation is not a reflexive or unconscious type of response elicited by particular stimuli moving toward the mouth (e.g. the protruding tongue of an actor). These 5-week old infants only imitated the mouth and tongue protrusions modelled by people and not those simulated by inanimate objects (a pen the size of a tongue, moving through a disk the size of a mouth). This indicates that imitation is a social mechanism intended to promote interpersonal communication through which the social self may be identified (Legerstee, 1991; Meltzoff, 1990).

That infants have an innate or instinctive motive for communication has long ago been suggested by Baldwin (1902), who proposed that from the beginning infants are sensitive to 'suggestions of personality' present in social objects, which allows for a differentiation between the social and non social. The social self, or 'socius' is created through such instinctive forms of communication with others. Trevarthen (1993) also claims that newborns have an inborn ability to communicate. In his view, during the first half of the year, infants display *subjectivity*, the ability 'to show by co-ordinated acts that purposes are being consciously regulated'. Evidence for this proposition comes from studies showing that infants expect people to communicate with them when in face-to-face interaction — if they don't infants become upset. For instance, when 2- to 3-month-olds are presented alternately with responsive and unresponsive people (mother and female stranger) and objects (dolls with schematic faces, partial faces, or no facial features) in naturally interactive paradigms, infants will smile and vocalize more to responsive people than to 'interactive' objects, whether the objects have facial features or not (Ellsworth *et al.*,1993; Legerstee *et al.*, 1987; Legerstee *et al.*, 1990). The results cannot be related to differences in movement pattern between the person and object stimuli because infants respond differentially also when the stimuli remain immobile. They show distress to unresponsive people, and vigorously attempt to regain their participation. They do not show this behaviour in front of immobile inanimate objects (dolls with facial features). This cannot be the result of the absence of familiar responses of the mother to which the infants have become accustomed, because they do not show these behaviours when mothers becomes engaged with adults (Murray & Trevarthen, 1985). Thus infants experience people differently than objects right from the start. They expect people (and not objects) to communicate reciprocally with them in face-to-face interactions, and to work actively with them to sustain and regulate the interactions (Stern, 1995; Trevarthen,1979; Tronick *et al.*, 1982). Gibson (1995) proposes that information about the self is obtained in the discovery of such social control; it is the expectation of intentional behaviour in other people that leads to the development of self as a social agent.

Evidence for a Representational Self

As is evident, young babies appear actively involved in investigating the intermodal, temporal contingencies and spatial congruencies that lead them to perceive their bodily selves during the first 6 months of life, and to respond in social ways to other people, but not to inanimate objects. Because the above studies investigated the infant's *perception of sensory stimulation* emanating from the self and from other stimuli, it could be argued that these studies do *not* provide evidence that infants *represent* this information. How can one reliably determine that infants are aware that the bodies they have been working with, and the visual and auditory stimulation that they are perceiving are aspects of the self? Young infants have limited communication skills and they do not begin to refer to themselves verbally until 18–24 months of age (Legerstee & Feider, 1986). In order to reveal that infants represent aspects of the self, researchers have focused on the infants' recognition of their own face in the mirror. Face recognition was taken as an important aspect of self-recognition. It was assumed that if infants recognized their own face, they would have an internal representation of their face to which they compared the face in the mirror. In a review of the self-system, Harter (1983) writes that throughout history the face seems to have been regarded as the primary representation of the self. She notes that the face, as an embodiment of the self, can be found in such metaphorical expressions as 'I won't be able to face myself in the mirror in the morning' (p. 218). Cole (1997) proposes that the face reveals important facts about ourselves, such as our age and gender, but also our psychological and mental healths. The face reveals our emotions and allows us to communicate nonverbally with others. Gallup (1982) demonstrated that the recognition of one's own physical features is crucial for the development of an awareness of self in higher primates. In a variety of studies, he found that after 3 days of experience with mirrors, chimps would change from making threatening gestures to self-directed behaviours such as picking food from their teeth. After 10 days of mirror experience, Gallup first anaesthetized the chimps and then painted red marks on their face. When the chimps recovered, they apparently recognized their facial features, because they touched the spots more than marked chimps who did not have mirrors. Studies using Gallup's procedure with infants reported that self-recognition as indexed by touching the rouge-spot on their faces did not occur until infants were at least between 18 and 24 months old. However, the rouge task should not be used with younger preverbal infants, since they (1) may not understand what the task demands, and (2) are confused by the reflective properties of the mirror (Loveland, 1986). In a recent study, Bahrick *et al.* (1996) showed that infants as young as 5-months recognized their facial features as *familiar* stimuli. They looked less long at their own previously filmed facial image (indicating familiarity) than at that of a same aged peer.

Although the Bahrick *et al.* (1996) study does not show whether infants recognize their face as belonging to self, the findings are of interest because the authors controlled for proprioceptive contingencies. Instead of having babies look in the mirror, in which case they could have distinguished between their peers' and their own faces because of differential contingencies between the visual stimulation of the mirror images and the proprioceptive feedback from their own body motion, the authors showed the infants previously recorded video images of self and a peer. They further controlled for other differences between the infants by dressing them in yellow robes. Because the infants only had featural differences to go by in their differentiation of the faces of peer and self, the authors provided evidence for *recognition* of the face in this study. This demonstrates that the activity cannot be regulated by sensory information alone, it must also involve information stored in memory (representation).

The finding that some of the bodily self is represented is interesting because it provides information about early *mental* abilities of infants during the first 6 months of life. However, do infants represent themselves as social creatures? It has already been established that by 2–3 months, infants respond differentially to people and inanimate objects, they treat people as social objects, smiling, vocalizing, and imitating their actions, but objects are treated as toys to be looked at and manipulated (see Legerstee, 1992, for a review of these studies). However, these studies have not revealed whether infants perceive *themselves as* similar to other social entities and different from nonsocial objects. Recent research suggests that such an awareness may exist in 5–8-month-olds (Legerstee *et al.*, 1998). The paradigm used was a modified version of the one used by Bahrick *et. al.* (1996). All infants received two visits. During the first visit, infants were filmed in interaction with their mothers in order to obtain visual and auditory material of a smiling and cooing baby. Of this 5-minute interaction

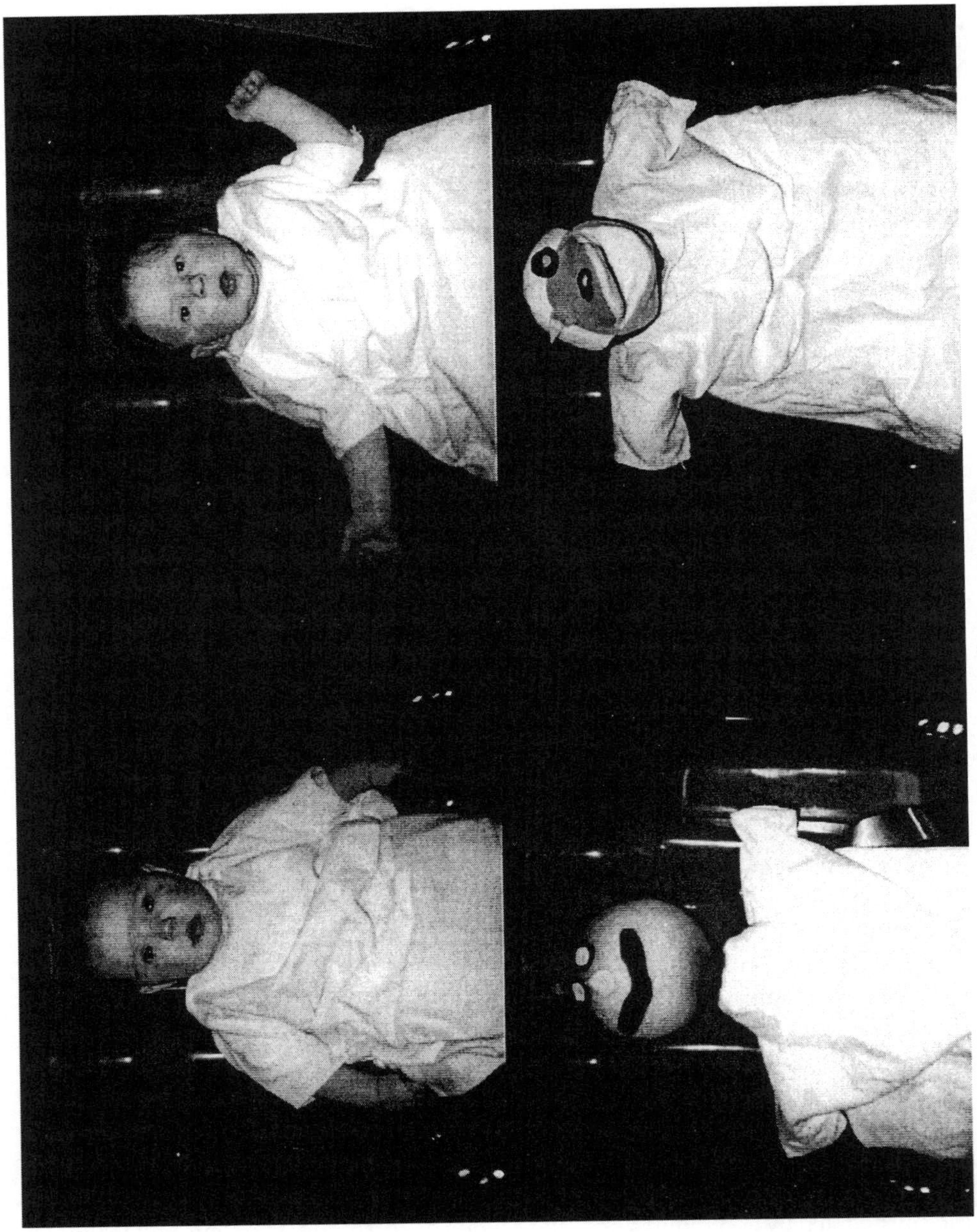

Figure 1.

Examples of faces of:

- self (top left),
- peer (top right),
- external moving object (bottom left), and
- internal moving object (bottom right)

Reprinted with permission of the Society for research in Child Development.

tape, a 60-second demonstration tape was cut for the second visit. These demonstration tapes showed babies that moved their faces, and vocalized in a burst-and-pause pattern (three successive bursts of vocalizations of a total of approximately 6 seconds and a 1-second pause during which the babies did not vocalize, repeated for a total of 60 seconds). Burst and pause pattern were used in order to simulate human interactional pattern. This pattern has been shown to motivate infants to action rather than to mere visual fixation (Legerstee, 1991). During the second visit, the infants were placed in front of a large television screen and were presented with the demonstration tapes of self, a peer and a doll. The stimuli were all matched on size and hair colour and were dressed in yellow robes (see Figure 1).

To examine the role of movement in the recognition of the faces, the images were presented in static and moving conditions. In the moving conditions, the doll would either move externally (the body swayed sideways and up and down) or internally (an experimenter would move the internal abstract facial features of a hand puppet), and the infants moved as they naturally do when interacting with adults. In the static condition the infants saw a frozen image of self, peer and doll. The moving and static visual conditions were presented *without sound*. The results showed that when 5- and 8-month-old infants were presented with *silent moving* video images of self, peer, and dolls they looked longer at the peer (novelty preference) and least long at self (familiarity) at both ages. However, whereas the 8-month-old infants also looked longer at the static image of the peer (novelty effect) the 5-month-olds looked longer at their own static facial image. The finding that the younger infants found their static facial image unusual but not their moving facial image supports the suggestion that recognition of one's own image develops through experience with dynamic facial stimulation during the first 5 months of life. Prior to the experiments, we had asked parents to fill out questionnaires about the amount of mirror exposure their babies experienced. These questionnaires revealed that all infants saw themselves at least once a day in the mirror during care-takers' activities. Parents reported that their infants would look first at their care-giver in the mirror, and would then notice themselves. It was when they observed their own face that they began to coo and smile. Our data reflected these natural observations of the mothers, because the infants also smiled and cooed more at their own facial image than at that of the peer and they smiled and cooed least at the doll. Thus infants learn through mirror exposure to identify their own face, because information about the face is specified both kinesthetically and visually. Infants become aware of themselves as social entities because infants do not view their faces in mirrors in isolation, but with caregivers while playing imitative and other socio/affective games with them (Fogel, 1993; Stern, 1995). As a result of the adults' responses to their infants' behaviours, infants learn to identify with people and to differentiate themselves from others. Thus, one may speculate that when infants recognize their distinctive features as familiar through exposure to mirror - images, they simultaneously recognize their faces and voices as socio/affective stimuli.

Aside from visual recognition of the face, infants also attend preferentially to human auditory input and recognize their own vocalizations as familiar sounds. In the auditory conditions, infants of both ages were presented with the social demonstration tapes, but now the visual image was obscured, so that only the vocalizations were heard. The nonsocial sounds were made either by bells or by a synthesizer and matched to the rhythm and frequency (burst-pause pattern) of the infant vocalizations. The results showed that the infants looked longer (novelty) when hearing the peer's vocalizations than when hearing their own (familiarity), and least long when hearing the inanimate sounds. Smiles and vocalizations occurred most frequently when infants heard human voices, with most of the vocalizations occurring when they listened to their own voices. Thus, the infants not only discriminated between their vocalizations and nonsocial sounds, but they recognized these vocalizations as familiar and similar to sounds they produce themselves. This indicates that the infants' responses were species-, peer- and self-specific.

Evidence for an Awareness of Intentionality

Thus during the first 6 months of life, infants distinguish between their own body and external stimulation, and they show that they *represent* parts of their bodily and social selves because they recognize these aspects of the self as familiar. The question that remains unanswered is whether infants have sufficiently elaborated concepts of causality to attribute these faces, voices and bodily parts to themselves. Various researchers have formulated theories for a domain specific predisposition in infants to detect animate causation (Gelman, 1990; Leslie, 1984; Michotte, 1963; Premack, 1990; Spelke *et al.*, 1995). A representational account of intentionality/causation has been proposed by philosophers such as Brentano (1874) who argued that intentionality is the main feature of self awareness. It has been shown that 9-month-old infants understand that people are purposive or intentional agents, who behave as independent actors. At that age, infants begin to use their vocalizations, gestures and gazes to direct others to an object external to the dyad (Bates *et al.*, 1979; Legerstee & Weintraub, 1997), and to read emotions of others when evaluating new events (Feinman, 1992). In a recent study with abstract objects, Rochat, Morgan and Carpenter (1997) investigated the precursors to the understanding of intentionality in infants in order to determine when infants first become sensitive to information specifying intentional action. Adults and infants aged 5–6 and 3–4 months, watched two computer screens simultaneously displaying two different dynamic events. In the chase display one disc approached another that then moved away and in the independent display, identical discs moved with the same velocity, but never in any systematic way. The adults and the 5- to 6-month olds looked longer at the independent display than at the chase display. The authors proposed that by 6 months, infants are sensitive to some properties of animate motions, such as independent motion and action at a distance.

If 6-month-old infants differentiate social causation from physical causation in the onset of motion (self-motion vs. caused) and two types of contingencies (at a distance vs. direct physical contact) in the chase events of two discs, then it becomes important to find out whether infants are able to associate animate motion with people. From birth, infants have had ample opportunities to participate in dyadic interactions with adults who respond from a distance to their actions. By 4 months, infants appreciate that people can reciprocate and that their actions can be caused at a distance. They react differently to people and objects in a game of hide and seek. Infants will reach toward the door behind which objects have disappeared, but they call for people in order to bring them back to view (Legerstee, 1994). Thus studies investigating infants' responses to abstract objects, and those investigating infants' abilities to differentiate between the properties of people and inanimate objects suggest that by 6 months infants must be able to relate motion identified as animate with people. If infants are able to infer from observing the actions of people what they intend to do, then infants impute mental states to others. Inferences of this kind are usually viewed as a theory of mind, because the predictions or inferences are not based on observable phenomena (Premack & Woodruff, 1978). A recent experiment suggests that 6-month-old infants are sensitive to social causality (Legerstee, 1998). The infants were randomly assigned to two conditions. In one condition, they saw an actor *talk* to something hidden behind a screen and in the other the actor *reached* for and *swiped* with something hidden behind the screen. After the infants were familiarized (habituated) the screen was removed to reveal that the actor had directed her actions to either a social or an inanimate object. The social objects were women, who wore blue or beige slacks, with white blouses and black shoes. The inanimate objects were matched on size and colour to the social objects. They consisted of a black broom with a blue handle, or a black shovel with a wooden handle and a Styrofoam ball attached to the top of the handles. The infants' looking time was coded in each condition. It was hypothesized that if infants are sensitive to social and physical causality, then they would expect the actors to talk to people, but act on inanimate objects. The

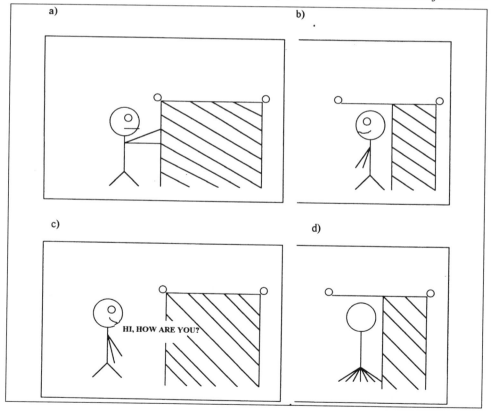

Figure 2.
(a) Actor reaching for occluded stimulus during habituation
(b) Test-event showing novel outcome
(c) Actor talking to occluded stimulus during habituation
(d) Test event showing novel outcome

results provided evidence that 6-month-old infants expect people to contact inanimate objects but not animates. They looked longer at the events where the actor had spoken to inanimate objects or reached for a person (see figure 2), (indicating that they found this event unusual or novel) than when the actor had spoken to another person or reached and swiped with the inanimate object. The finding that in this internally controlled experiment infants reacted differently to the person or the inanimate object depending on which condition (e.g. talking or reaching) the infants had been familiarized with, indicated that the infants had formed different predictions during habituation about the type of object (social or inanimate) the actors were acting on.

From these experiments one could infer that 6-month-old infants are able to adopt mentalist strategies to interpret and predict the behaviour of others and that 6-month-old infants have a primitive theory of mind (attributing purpose/intentions to others). One could argue that the results of these experiments can be interpreted with a version of classical associationism. That is, by 6 months, infants have learned through association that people talk to conspecifics and act on inanimate objects. Because infants have become familiar with this sequence, and exhibit these types of behaviours in their own repertoire, they should, when shown the incomplete version of this sequence of behaviours, choose the element that completes the sequence. However, this type of interpretation may seem plausible to adults, because they are capable of fitting in missing links. Infants and children younger than about four, cannot make sense out of picture stories when they are out of sequence (Poulsen *et al.*, 1979). Young infants would see for example 'a person talking, and a closed curtain'. The elements are joined together by imputing mental states to the actor e.g. 'the person is talking to someone. She wants something of someone'. According to Premack & Woodruff (1978, p. 525), only specifically trained adults and older children are able to give an account of human behaviour that does *not* impute states of mind to the participants. They may try to be objective and read the event and suppress the inference that whenever A precedes B, we believe that A causes B, and impose further tests: When does A occur and B not? When A does not occur and yet B does etc. 'Thus imputing mental states to someone is not an advanced behaviour, but a primitive one. All this is to say, that theory building is natural in man.'

Are Infants Social Creatures, Aware of their Minds and Bodies?

Various philosophers have suggested that self awareness originates in the mind. The problem to be solved is the discovery that we have bodies similar to the bodies of others and that the bodies of other people have minds. The present review of empirical evidence suggests that during the first 6 months of life, infants see themselves and other people as having minds and bodies, that together form one creature that both feels and acts. There is evidence that the perceptual abilities of infants play a seminal role in the development of the infant's awareness of the external environment and of a primary consciousness of the bodily self (Gibson, 1995). The special attention of infants to the faces, voices and movements of people contributes to the infant's sensitivity of humans as special entities. The role of the social environment appears important in the infants' awareness that the self is identical to other social objects, both in the primary stages of consciousness as well as in the higher forms of self-consciousness (Butterworth, 1995; Fogel, 1993; Legerstee, 1997b; Stern, 1995). This preferential attention to human behaviour plays an important role in infants' awareness of the mental states of others. Their primitive ability to assign mental states to other individuals allows them to 'organize scenes or events, holding together the disparate elements into which scenes otherwise threaten to dissolve' (Premack & Woodruff, 1978, p. 525). The finding that the foundations for a concept of self consist of mental, social and physical levels would argue against Strawson's notion that the self is made up of cognitive phenomena to the exclusion of physical and social influences (see also Butterworth, 1998)

What are the mechanisms that allow for such precocious awareness of body and mind? As the evidence indicates, infants from birth process information about the social environment in a special way and differently from nonsocial objects. This supports the idea that knowledge about the social and the physical environments may be driven by domain specific predispositions. In fact, it would be hard to explain the present data if the awareness of certain physical features of the self, the pattern of social interaction in which human infants engage, and of animate causation in such young infants, were not the result of domain specific structures that identify people. However, these attentional abilities may assist in the development of a theory of people by ensuring that the proper input gets into the system, it is through social interaction with conspecifics that infants acquire an understanding that the bodily and mental selves identify one person (Karmiloff-Smith, 1992).

The Self as a Unique Mythical Entity

The above account of the development of the self has detailed the universal awareness of infants physical, social and mental selves during their first six-months of life. However, the self represents something that goes beyond the neurological, physical/social and cognitive accounts. The self is in addition to a mental/social and physical self, a unique mythical creature (Kenny, 1988). What is the process by which such uniqueness is created? It appears from the data presented above that infants understanding of the self begins at birth and is guided by domain-specific 'cognitive' structures that identify the mental and physical/social selves. However, the existence of these structures does not imply that infants do not develop new structures, comprising more elaborate knowledge about the self. The evidence shows that many of the attributes that pertain to the self need to be constructed with age. The role of the predispositions is to give the epigenetic process a head start and to guide development in an orderly yet varied way. Although increasingly more complex interactions with the world will result in more sophisticated knowledge of self, it is through interactions with people that new structures are created. That is because during their joint activity, the two partners not only share the knowledge that each alone possesses, but there is a possibility that they construct knowledge that neither one of them possessed alone (Chapman, 1992). The generativity of one's own intelligence, which forms the foundation of a unique and mythical self, is not seen as resulting only from equilibrations in the self–environment relationship but also from intersubjective equilibrations. It is only during this dialectical inquiry that truly novel forms of knowledge, of unique and mythical selves can be created.

References

Astington, J.W., Harris, P.L. & Olson, D.R. (1988), *Developing Theories of Mind* (Cambridge: Cambridge University Press).

Astington, J.W. & Olson, D.R. (1995), 'The cognitive revolution in children's understanding of mind', *Human Development*, **38**, pp. 179–189.

Bahrick, L.E., Moss, L., & Fadil, C. (1996), 'Development of visual self-recognition in infancy', *Ecological Psychology*, **8** (3), pp. 189–208.

Baldwin, J.M. (1902), *Social and Ethical Interpretations in Mental Development* (New York: Macmillan).

Ball, W. & Tronick, E. (1971), 'Infant responses to impending collision: Optical and real', *Science*, **171**, pp. 818–20.

Bates, E., Camaioni, L. & Volterra, V. (1979), 'Determining intentionality prior to and at the onset of speech', in *Developmental pragmatics*, ed. E. Ochs & B.B. Schieffelin (London: Academic Press).

Bennett, J. (1989), *Linguistic Behaviour* (Indianapolis, IN: Hackett).

Berkeley, G. (1975), *PhilosophicalWorks*, edited by M.R. Ayers (London: Dent).

Bertenthal, B.I., & Bai, D.L. (1989), 'Infants' sensitivity to optical flow for controlling posture', *Developmental Psychology*, **25**, pp. 936–45.

Brentano, F. (1874/1973), *Psychology from an Empirical Standpoint*, trans. A.C. Rancurello, D.B. Terrell & L.L. McAlister (London: Routledge & Kegan Paul).

Butterworth, G.E. (1995), 'The self as an object of consciousness in infancy', in Rochat (1995a).

Butterworth, G.E. (1998), 'A developmental-ecological perspective on Strawson's 'The self' ', *Journal of Consciousness Studies*, **5** (2), pp. 132–40.

Butterworth, G.E. & Hicks, L. (1977), 'Visual proprioception and postural stability in infancy: A developmental study', *Perception*, **6**, pp. 255–62.

Butterworth, G. & Hopkins, B. (1988), 'Hand-mouth coordination in the newborn baby', *British Journal of Developmental Psychology*, **6**, pp. 303–14.

Cassam, A-Q. (ed. 1994), *Self-knowledge* (Oxford: Oxford University Press).

Chapman, M. (1992), 'Equilibration and the dialectics of organization', in *Piaget's Theory: Prospects and Possibilities*, ed. H. Beiling and P.Putfall (Hillsdale, NJ: Lawrence Erlbaum Associates).

Churchland, P.M. (1991), 'Folk psychology and the explanation of human behavior', in *The Future of Folk Psychology: Intentionality and Cognitive Science*, ed. J.D. Greenwood (Cambridge: Cambridge University Press).

Cole, J. (1997), 'On being faceless: Selfhood and facial embodiment', *Journal of Consciousness Studies*, **4** (5–6), pp. 467–84.

Descartes, R. (1641/1985), *The Philosophical Writings of Descartes*, Volumes 1 and 2, trans. J. Cottingham *et al.* (Cambridge: Cambridge University Press).

Ellsworth, C., Muir, D. & Hains, S. (1993), 'Social competence and person-object differentiation: An analysis of the still-face effect', *Developmental psychology*, **29**, pp. 67–73.

Feinman, S. (1992), *Social Referencing and the Social Construction of Reality in Infancy* (New York: Plenum).

Fogel, A. (1993), *Developing Through Relationships: Origins of Communication, Self and Culture* (Chicago: The University of Chicago Press).

Freud, S. (1961), 'The ego and the id', in *The Standard Edition of the Complete Psychological Works of Sigmund Freud (Vol. 19)*, trans. J. Strachey (London: Hogarth Press).

Frye, D. (1981), 'Developmental changes in strategies of social interaction', in *Infant Social Cognition*, ed. M. Lamb and L. Sherrod (Hillsdale, NJ: Erlbaum).

Gallagher, S. (1996), 'The moral significance of primitive self-consciousness: The response to Bermúdez', *Ethics*, **107**, pp. 129–40.

Gallup, G.G. (1982), 'Self-awareness and the emergence of mind in primates', *American Journal of Primatology*, **2**, pp. 237–48.

Gelman, R. (1990), 'First principles organize attention to and learning about relevant data: Number and the animate-inanimate distinction as examples', *Cognitive Science*, **14**, pp 79–106.

Gibson, E.J. (1969), *Principles of Perceptual Learning and Development* (New York: Appleton-Century-Crofts).

Gibson, E. (1995), 'Are we automata?', in Rochat (1995a).

Harter, S. (1983), 'Developmental perspectives on the self system', in *Handbook of Child Psychology, Vol. 4*, ed. M. Hetherington (New York: Wiley).

Hobson, P.R. (1990), 'On the origins of self and the case of autism', *Development and Psychopathology*, **2**, pp. 163–81.

Hofsten, C. von. (1980), 'Predictive reaching for moving objects by human infants', *Journal of Experimental Child Psychology*, **30**, pp. 369–82.

Hume, D. (1739/1888), *A Treatise of Human Nature*, ed. L.A. Selby-Bigge (Oxford: Clarendon).

James, W. (1890), *Principles of Psychology* (New York: Holt).

Jaspers, K. (1957/1962), *Plato and Augustine*, ed. H. Arendt, trans. R. Manheim (New York: Harcourt Brace Janovich).

Kalins, I.V. & Bruner, J.S. (1973), 'The coordination of visual observation and instrumental behavior in early infancy', *Perception*, **2**, pp. 307–14.

Kant, I. (1781/1996), *Critique of Pure Reason*, trans. W.S. Pluhar (Indianapolis: Hackett).

Karmiloff-Smith A. (1992), *Beyond Modularity: A Developmental Perspective on Cognitive Science* (Cambridge, MA: MIT Press).

Kenny, A. (1988), *The Self* (Marquette: Marquette University Press).

Legerstee, M. (1990), 'Infants use multimodal information to imitate speech sounds', *Infant Behavior and Development*, **13**, pp. 343–54.

Legerstee, M. (1991), 'The role of people and objects in early imitation', *Journal of Experimental Child Psychology*, **51**, pp. 423–33.

Legerstee, M. (1992), 'A review of the animate-inanimate distinction in infancy: Implications for models of social and cognitive knowing', *Early Development and Parenting*, **1**, pp. 57–67.

Legerstee, M. (1994), 'Patterns of 4-month-old infant responses to hidden silent and sounding people and objects', *Early Development and Parenting*, **2**, pp. 71–80.

Legerstee, M. (1997a), 'Contingency effects of people and objects on subsequent cognitive functioning in three-month-old infants', *Social Development*, **6**, pp. 307–21.

Legerstee, M. (1997b), 'Changes in social-conceptual development: domain-specific structures, self-organization, and indeterminism', in *Dynamics and Indeterminism in Developmental and Social Processes*, ed. A Fogel, M.C.D.P. Lyra, & J. Valsiner (Mahwah, NJ: Erlbaum).

Legerstee, M. (1998), 'Precursors to the development of intention: Understanding people and their actions', Paper presented at the *11th Biennial International Conference on Infant Studies*, Atlanta, GA, April 1998.

Legerstee, M. (in press), 'Domain specificity and the epistemic triangle in the development of animism in infancy', in *Transitions in Perception, Cognition and Action in Early Infancy*, ed. F. Lacerda, C. Von Hofsten & M. Heimann (Hillsdale, NJ: Erlbaum).

Legerstee, M., Anderson, D. & Shaffer, A. (1998), 'Five-and eight-month-old infants recognize their faces and voices as familiar and social stimuli', *Child Development*, **69**, pp. 37–50.

Legerstee, M. & Bowman, T. (1989), 'The development of responses to people and a toy in infants with Down Syndrome', *Infant Behavior and Development*, **12** (4), pp. 462–73.

Legerstee, M., Corter, C. & Kienapple, K. (1990), 'Hand, arm and facial actions of young infants to a social and nonsocial stimulus', *Child Development*, **61**, pp. 774–84.

Legerstee, M. & Feider, H. (1986), 'The acquisition of pronouns in French speaking children', *International Journal of Psychology*, **21**, pp. 629–39.

Legerstee, M., Pomerleau, A., Malcuit, G. & Feider, H. (1987), 'The development of infants' responses to people and a doll: Implications for research in communication', *Infant Behavior and Development*, **10**, pp. 81–95.

Legerstee, M. & Weintraub, J. (1997), 'The integration of person and object attention in infants with and without Down syndrome', *Infant Behavior and Development*, **20**, pp. 71–83.

Leslie, A.M. (1984), 'Infant perception of manual pick-up event', *British Journal of Developmental Psychology*, **2**, pp. 19–32.

Locke, John (1710/1975), *An Essay Concerning Human Understanding*, edited with a foreword by Peter H. Nidditch (Oxford: Clarendon Press).

Loveland, K.A. (1986), 'Discovering the affordances of a reflecting surface', *Developmental Review*, **6**, pp. 1–24.

Mahler, M.S., Pine, F. & Bergman, A. (1975), *The Psychological Birth of the Human Infant: The Symbiosis and Individuation* (New York: Basic Books).

Mandler, J. (1992), 'How to build a baby: Conceptual primitives', *Psychological Review*, **99** (4), pp. 587–604.

Martin, G.B. & Clark, R.D. (1982), 'Distress crying in neonates: Species and peers specificity', *Developmental Psychology*, **18**, pp. 3–9.

Merleau-Ponty, M. (1942/1963), *The Structure of Behavior*, trans. A.L. Fisher (USA: Beacon Press).

Meltzoff, M. (1990), 'Foundations for developing a concept of self: The role of imitation in relating self to other and the value of social mirroring, social modelling, and self practice in infancy', in *The Self in Transition: Infancy to Childhood*, ed. D. Cicchetti & M. Beeghly (Chicago: The University of Chicago Press).

Michotte, A. (1963), *The Perception of Causality*, trans. T. and E Miles (London: Methuen).

Murray, L. & Trevarthen, C. (1985), 'Emotion regulation of interactions between two-month-olds and their mothers', in *Social Perception in Infants*, ed. T.M. Field and N.A. Fox (Norwood, NJ: Ablex).

Neisser, U. (1993), 'The self perceived', in *The Perceived Self: Ecological and Interpersonal Sources of Self-knowledge*, ed. U. Neisser (Cambridge: Cambridge University Press).

Neisser, U. (1995), 'Criteria for an ecological self', in Rochat (1995a).

230   M. LEGERSTEE

Pascual-Leone, J. & Johnson, J. (1998), 'A dialectical constructivist view of representation: The role of mental attention, executives, and symbols', in *The Development of Representational Thought: Theoretical Perspectives*, ed. I.E. Sigel (forthcoming).

Piaget, J. (1952), *The Origins of Intelligence in the Child*, trans. M. Cook (New York: Basic Books; originally published in French 1936).

Piaget, J. (1954), *The Child's Conception of the World* (London: Routledge and Kegan Paul).

Poulson, K., Kintch, W., Kintch D. & Premack, D. (1979), 'Children's comprehension and memory stories, *Journal of Experimental Child Psychology*, **1**, pp. 515–26.

Premack, D. (1990), 'The infant's theory of self-propelled objects', *Cognition*, **36**, pp. 1–16.

Premack, D. & Woodruff, G. (1978), 'Does the chimpanzee have a theory of mind?', *Behavioral and Brain Sciences*.

Rader, N. & Stern, J. D. (1982), 'Visually elicited reaching in neonates', *Child Development*, **53**, pp. 1004–7.

Reed, E.S. (1995), 'Becoming a self', in Rochat (1995a).

Rochat, P. (ed. 1995a), *The Self in Infancy: Theory and Research, Advances in Psychology* (Amsterdam: North Holland-Elsevier).

Rochat, P. (1995b), 'Early objectification of the self', in P. Rochat (1995a).

Rochat, P., Blass, E.M. & Hoffmeyer, L.B. (1988), 'Oropharyngeal control of hand-mouth coordination in newborn infants', *Developmental Psychology*, **24**, pp. 459–63.

Rochat, P., Morgan, R. & Carpenter, M. (1997), 'Young infants' sensitivity to movement information specifying social causality', *Cognitive Development*, **12**, pp. 441–65.

Rovee-Collier, C.K. & Fagan, J.W. (1981), 'The retrieval of memory in early infancy', in *Advances in Infancy Research, 1*, ed. L.P. Lipsitt and C.K. Rovee-Collier (Norwood, NJ: Ablex).

Searle, J. (1992), *The Rediscovery of the Mind* (Cambridge, MA: MIT Press).

Spelke, E. (1988). 'The origins of physical knowledge', in *Thought Without Language*, ed. L. Weiskrantz (Oxford: Clarendon Press).

Spelke, E.S., Breinlinger, K., Macomber, J. & Jacobson, K. (1992), 'Origins of knowledge', *Psychological Review*, **9** (4), pp. 605–32.

Spelke, E.S., Phillips, A.T. & Woodward, A.L. (1995), 'Infants' knowledge of object motion and human action', in *Causal Cognition*, ed. D. Sperber, D. Premack and A. Premack (New York: Oxford University Press).

Stern, D. (1995), 'Self/other differentiation in the domain of intimate socio-affective interaction: Some considerations', in Rochat (1995a).

Strawson, G. (1997), 'The self', *Journal of Consciousness Studies*, **4** (5–6), pp. 405–28. Reprinted in this volume, pp. 1–24.

Teo, T. (1997), 'Developmental psychology and the relevance of a critical metatheoretical reflection', *Human Development*, **40**, pp. 195–210.

Tomasello, M. (1995), 'Understanding the self as social agent', in Rochat (1995a).

Tronick, E.A., Ricks, M. & Cohn J.F. (1982), 'Maternal and infant affective exchange. Patterns of adaptation', in *Emotions and Early Interaction*, ed. T. Field & A. Fogel (Hillsdale, NJ: Erlbaum).

Trevarthen, C. & Hubley, P. (1978), 'Secondary intersubjectivity: Confidence, confiding and acts of meaning in the first year', in *Action, Gesture and Symbol: The Emergence of Language*, ed. A. Lock (New York: Academic Press).

Trevarthen, C. (1979), 'Communication and cooperation in early infancy: A description of primary intersubjectivity', in *Before Speech: The Beginning of Interpersonal Communication*, ed. M. Bullowa (New York: Cambridge University Press).

Trevarthen, C. (1993), 'The self born in intersubjectivity: The psychology of an infant communicating', in *The Perceived Self: Ecological and Interpersonal Sources of Self-knowledge*, ed. U. Neisser (Cambridge: Cambridge University Press).

Watson, J.B. (1928), *Psychological Care of Infant and Child* (New York: Norton).

Wellman, H.M. (1993), 'Early understanding of mind: The normal case', in *Understanding Other Minds: Perspectives from Autism*, ed. S. Baron-Cohen, H. Tager-Flusberg & D.J. Cohen (Oxford: Oxford University Press).

Yonas, A., Pettersen, L. and Lockman, J.J. (1979), 'Young infants' sensitivity to optical information for collision', *Canadian Journal of Psychology*, **33**, pp. 268–76.

Maxine Sheets-Johnstone

Phenomenology and Agency

Methodological and Theoretical Issues in Strawson's 'The Self'

I: Specification of Methodological and Theoretical Issues

In his intriguing but methodologically puzzling and theoretically problematic chapter 'The Self', Galen Strawson[1] invites us to consider an innovative conception of the self, one that is compatible with — indeed centrally anchored in — 'the mental', but at the same time compatible with a thoroughgoing materialism. Summarily defined, his physicalist model of the self conjoins both mental (or experienced) and non-mental (or non-experienced) phenomena. In what follows, what is at issue is not his novel '"mental-and-non-mental" materialism' (Strawson, p. 7), which conceivably might profitably serve to legitimize that pervasively used but conceptually nettle-some lexical band-aid 'embodiment' (in all its variations — 'embodied', 'embodies', and so on),[2] but his so-called 'phenomenological' approach to 'the problem of the self' (p. 2) on the one hand, and his troubling inattention to an item on his own list of fundamental ways in which the self may be experienced or conceived on the other. Rather than treating each of these issues in a concentrated critical assessment of Strawson's essay, we will examine each issue constructively. After describing how Strawson's methodology is puzzling, we will proceed to a delineation of a properly phenomenological methodology with respect to the self, contrasting such a methodology with Strawson's putative phenomenological one. Similarly, after describing what is problematic about Strawson's theoretical structuring of the self, we will proceed to a delineation of a properly historical and dynamic conception of self, contrasting such a self with Strawson's 'mental self'. In conclusion, we will point out related liabilities and implications of Strawson's cognitive phenomenology, showing: (1) how his attempt to separate out 'the conceptual structure of the sense of the self' from 'any emotional aspects that it may have' (p. 2) constitutes a methodological misstep that compromises his putative phenomenology of the self from the start; (2) how, his claim to a '"mental and non-mental" materialism' notwithstanding, his conception of the self is wedded to a Cartesian dichotomization of mind and body; and (3)

---

[1] All references to 'Strawson' in the current chapter are to Galen Strawson's opening chapter in this volume (pp. 1–24).

[2] For a critical analysis and discussion of the term as a lexical band-aid, see Sheets-Johnstone (1998).

how his professed belief about 'the truth' of Buddhism with respect to the self (p. 20) is a belief at odds with the 'the mental thing' he specifies as the self.

II: A Properly Phenomenological Methodology
with Respect to the 'Problem of the Self'

To begin with, we should note that Strawson opens his chapter with eight epigraphs, one of which is a quotation from Edmund Husserl's *Cartesian Meditations: An Introduction to Phenomenology*, a book in which Husserl spells out phenomenological methodology and, in the context of the Fifth (and final) Meditation, gives an account of how one gets from a single existing self (or monad) to existing others (or intersubjectivity). The reader thus reasonably assumes that Strawson is not merely appropriating the term 'phenomenology' in a casual way or as a convenient lexical device, but is conversant with phenomenology both substantively and methodologically. Moreover, given his consistent methodological emphasis on phenomenology — he states, for example, that a metaphysics of the self 'must wait on phenomenology' (p. 1) and that 'one must have well-developed answers to phenomenological questions about the experience of the self before one can begin to answer metaphysical questions about the self' (p. 5) — the reader furthermore assumes that his phenomenological approach to the self will bear a basic resemblance to classical phenomenological methodology. Both assumptions are bolstered by the very manner in which Strawson opens his investigation.

Strawson begins by asking what he terms 'the *phenomenological question*: What is the nature of the sense of the self?' He immediately separates out 'the *local phenomenological question*' — 'What is the nature of the human sense of the self?' — from 'the *general phenomenological question*' — 'Are there other possibilities, when it comes to a sense of the self?' He says that answers to these questions raise 'the *conditions question*' — 'What are the grounds or preconditions of possession of a sense of the self?' He says further that answers to all of the foregoing questions are the basis for raising and answering 'the *factual [metaphysical] question* . . . Is there (could there be) such a thing as the self?' (p. 2).

The singular question of phenomenological concern is Strawson's first question, and this because, if the question is a *bona fide phenomenological question*, as Strawson claims, then a bifurcation of it into local and general questions is deflective if not out of place, and in turn, so also is his conditions question. In brief, *contra* Strawson, the local and general questions are deviant and inappropriate reductions of the original phenomenological question, and the conditions question is not a bona fide phenomenological offspring of the so-called local and general phenomenological questions. These procedural misconstruals of phenomenology are not the only methodological stumbling stones. Immediately after broaching a discussion of the local phenomenological question, Strawson states that this local phenomenological question 'raises a prior question: Can one generalize about the human sense of the self?' He answers with a simple 'Yes'. He gives no phenomenological or otherwise empirical justification whatsoever for his belief. Upon proceeding to ask, 'What, then, is the ordinary, human sense of the self, in so far as we can generalize about it?' he answers, 'I propose that it is . . .' (p. 3). Strawson's 'I propose' is a far cry from the practice of phenomenology, which deals not in propositions about, but in progressive elucidations of, phenomena.

Strawson's odd methodological way of doing phenomenological business warrants both finer commentary and rectification. In quite general terms, what is methodologically amiss about his phenomenology is the asking of a putatively phenomenological question and the giving of an answer that is far short of a phenomenological one. As we will see, what is needed in the way of an answer is not a Strawsonian *'cognitive phenomenology'* (p. 2), but a phenomenology anchored both in a descriptive account of the self and in a 'constructive phenomenology' in Eugene Fink's sense of the term (Fink, 1995), a phenomenology that ultimately reaches back to recover a past inaccessible to direct experience, a past in which the sense of self is originally formed. We are otherwise on both analytically speculative and adultist grounds, however 'phenomenological' we might think our account to be. Our first move toward rectification will be to delineate briefly just what is involved in a bona fide phenomenological methodology.

Bracketing is the first step in a phenomenological procedure. The natural attitude that frames one's everyday commerce with the world and that defines the character of one's many and diverse transactions in it is temporarily suspended. What is usually quite familiar thereby becomes strange; trees, cars, apples, geometric equations, hammers, symphonies — things in the world — no longer have their customary and comfortable knownness. By attending to something in this bracketed way, one comes first of all to know what is actually there, sensuously present in one's experience without its usual conceptual-affective-practical trappings. One perceives the thing as if for the first time. One thereby has the possibility, through progressive phenomenological work, of discovering how one's knowledge of the thing came to be what it is, how it was progressively built up, or, in phenomenological language, how the thing came to be epistemologically constituted. With the natural attitude suspended, a further phenomenological step is possible. One can freely vary the thing in question, imagine it in multiple guises and thereby determine its invariant features, that is, determine what remains unchanged throughout all its permutations. In this way, one arrives at a phenomenological account of the essential nature of the thing. In effect, one proceeds according to a certain method to answer questions about our experiential knowledge of something — hammers, geometric equations, or symphonies. In like fashion, one proceeds according to a certain method to answer questions about our experiential knowledge of the self.

Now to carry out a phenomenological investigation of the self and to give a phenomenological report on it — as Strawson explicitly professes to do[3] — one would have to proceed in a somewhat different fashion. Since it is not a question of something out there in the world but of something wholly personal, i.e., the self, one cannot bracket in the usual way. *One cannot make oneself strange.* One can, however, carry out a suspension — an *epoché* — very like the one Husserl initially carries out in his Fifth Cartesian Meditation, where his aim is to give an account of an intersubjective world, that is, an account of how we come to experience a world of other human beings. He proceeds first by marking off what he terms 'a sphere of ownness'

[3] See, e.g., Strawson, pp. 5 and 17 note 24; see also the, reference to 'phenomenological concerns' (p. 11). There is no doubt but that Strawson construes his modelling of the problem of the self to be phenomenological.

(Husserl, 1973, p. 93). He does this by performing '*a peculiar kind of epoché*' (*ibid.*). In the natural attitude, I and others exist; through the 'peculiar epoché', I abstract from others such that, as Husserl says, '*I "alone" remain*' (*ibid.*). The description that Husserl gives of this 'I alone' is clearly related to a phenomenological account of the sense of self, a phenomenon that exists apart from the world of others. If we limit our attention of his account to just those passages in the Fifth Cartesian Meditation where he is speaking of 'the sphere of ownness' and disregard his intermittent and subsequent descriptions of the constitution of the Other, we find some remarkable leads as to what a bona fide phenomenological answer would be to the phenomenological question, 'What is the nature of the sense of the self?'

To begin with, Husserl states that what is peculiarly his own is '*non-alien*' (p. 95). He describes his peculiar ownness in this way because, abstracting from any and all experiences connected with the natural attitude, the sphere of ownness is detached from any customary sense of other living beings; it is devoid of the customary meanings and values attaching to the surrounding world; it is not amenable to customary cultural predicates; and so on. Whatever phenomenon might present itself to me in the way of others and of the world in this phenomenological attitude, it is present solely within the sphere of my abstracted experience. It is in this sense that Husserl speaks of everything being 'reduced' (pp. 97–8). Others and the world generally do not have their customary meanings and values; they are not there for me as they are in the natural attitude. Most importantly, this means that Nature as it is understood by science and as it is objectified and known by others '*vanishes completely*' (p. 96). There is no longer for me such an objective natural world. Hence, as Husserl points out, when I reduce others to my sphere of ownness, there are bodies — what one might designate 'moving forms' — but only '*my animate organism*' (p. 97). Nature is thus not altogether omitted from my sphere of ownness. On the contrary, it is still there but in reduced, i.e., abstracted, form. What remains and remains centrally is that unique object of Nature '*my animate organism*', the sole such object left after severance from all that is alien.

Clearly, we can winnow clues toward a specification of the self from Husserl's initial delineation of a sphere of ownness in his phenomenological analysis of an intersubjective world, though to avoid misattributions we should emphasize that his aim is to show how an intersubjective world is built up, not to answer the question 'What is the nature of the self?' or 'What is the nature of the sense of self?' The clues are readily apparent in his description of what remains experientially following the procedure of abstracting from others. In particular, in his ensuing discussion, we can discern five distinct but intimately related experienced characteristics of the unique remaining object he designates 'my animate organism': I experience '*fields of sensation*' — e.g., 'a field of tactual sensations, a field of warmth and coldness, and so forth', with respect to my animate organism;[4] I and I alone hold sway with respect to the movement and activities of my animate organism; a particular and ready repertoire of 'I cans' is available to me with respect to my animate organism — I can push, pause, cling, test, verify, and run, for example; a reflexive relationship readily obtains between my animate organism as intentional subject and as object — I can, for exam-

---

[4] In the context of the 'non-alien' in which he speaks of them, 'fields of sensation' refer specifically to sensations of one's own animate organism and not to visual or auditory sensations of things in the world.

ple, perceive my leg by means of my hand and my lips by means of my tongue; I experience my animate organism as a psychophysical unity (Husserl, 1973, p. 97). Carrying out 'an abstractive *epoché*' (p. 95) — as Husserl also describes 'the peculiar procedure' — clearly discloses a corporeal subject of experience. In doing so, it discloses something strikingly akin to what one might regard as a self. Indeed, the five fundamental uniquenesses of 'my animate organism' appear straightaway amenable to being spelled out in ways consonant with a phenomenological answer to the question 'What is the nature of the self?' Closer phenomenological investigation will substantiate the consonance. So also, by comparison, will closer examination of the candidate Strawson proposes for 'the ordinary, human sense of the self' (p. 3).

Strawson writes, 'I propose that it ['the ordinary, human sense of the self'] is (at least) the sense that people have of themselves as being, specifically, a mental presence; a mental someone; a single mental thing that is a conscious subject of experience. . . . It is crucial that it [the self] is thought of as a distinctively mental phenomenon'. He specifies concretely what he means by a 'mental self' when he writes that 'The early realization of the fact that one's thoughts are unobservable by others, the experience of the profound sense in which one is alone in one's head — these are among the very deepest facts about the character of human life, and found the sense of the mental self'(p. 3). In contrast to this Strawsonian self, what an abstractive *epoché* brings to the fore and what the consequent sphere of ownness captures is not only a whole self over a fractured and disembodied one, but the possibility of a bona fide, richly-textured phenomenology of the self, precisely what Strawson intimates is needed when he writes that, 'one must have well-developed answers to phenomenological questions about the experience of the self before one can begin to answer metaphysical questions about the self' (p. 5). To link the sense of self to unobservable thoughts — most especially to link the sense *primarily* to unobservable thoughts — in advance of a proper phenomenological analysis is to do an injustice to any intended phenomenology of the self. From the methodological perspective of an abstractive *epoché*, unobservable thoughts obviously constitute a more sophisticated part of the phenomenological description of the self, since the very idea of 'unobservable thoughts' assumes full-fledged others; that is, while unobservable thoughts may certainly be characterized as 'non-alien', they also patently draw in a fundamental sense on what is alien. To put the same point in more elemental terms, we might note that findings from the methodological procedure Husserl follows coincide with what one would expect on intuitive grounds; namely, that the foundation of a sense of self lies in a sphere of ownness, a sphere that is not only distinguishable from, but that, to be known, *requires* distinction from, *all* that is alien. Clearly, from this perspective, I am alone not just 'in my head', but in much more. The sense of self, in turn, lies in much more than 'a thinking principle' (as Strawson, approvingly appropriating Bishop Berkeley's terminology, specifies the self; p. 8), with its unobservable processes of thought. It lies in 'my animate organism' with its fields of sensations, its power to govern, and with all those other distinct features Husserl identifies as aspects of his sphere of ownness. This sense of self is justly identified as a psychophysical unity. It is definitively not a self in the head, however much that 'mental self' might be said to include sensations, will, and so on, in the manner of Descartes.

To arrive at a bona fide phenomenological answer to the phenomenological question, 'What is the nature of the sense of the self?', and certainly to be able to propose

and list phenomenological aspects of that sense of self, one needs to proceed methodologically in such a way that one first of all arrives at a sense of the self. Only then can
one examine what is there. Only then can one consult one's actual experience, as is
proper to a phenomenological investigation, and in turn reap the benefits of that consultation, notably, in a delineation of essential aspects of the self. In this properly
phenomenological enterprise, one's point of departure is what Husserl terms 'a transcendental clue', a phenomenon in the everyday lifeworld which, when regarded
within the phenomenological attitude, i.e., regarded within the *epoché* rather than
within the natural attitude, is epistemologically transformed. It no longer resonates
with familiarity but appears strange; it is no longer the known but the unknown.
Regarded within a bracketed or equivalent attitude, the phenomenon taken as a clue
opens a phenomenological terrain. What may be taken as a clue in a phenomenological investigation of the sense of self is any experience of myself in the everyday lifeworld — walking to the store, for example, quenching my thirst, reading a book,
serving in tennis, jumping with joy, thinking about the contents of a letter I must
write, imagining something or deliberating about something, and so on. Placing
myself outside the natural attitude, I no longer take my-self for granted in any one of
these experiences. On the contrary, I intently regard the experience in order to find
what I have been taking for granted. I examine what is there in order to bring to light
what is wholly me and has no vestige of the other within it. Experiencing myself in
walking, drinking, reading, serving, feeling joyous, thinking, imagining, or deliberating, I discover — among other possible dimensions of self — myself as 'I-alone-
engaged-in-some-activity-or-other'. Even if I am merely standing still, or sitting still,
or lying quietly in bed in the dark before sleeping, I experience myself in this way:
'I-alone' standing, sitting, or lying. Everyday experience thus functions as a clue
leading to the experience of 'I-alone-doing'. In effect, everyday experience in the
natural attitude is epistemologically transformed, and of course can be transformed
much further, not only with respect to other dimensions of the self, but with respect to
the dimension just specified. Indeed, the phenomenological challenge is to fathom
exactly what 'I-alone-doing' portends in terms of a self, to elucidate exactly what
'I-alone' walking, reading, thinking, feeling, deliberating, standing, and so on, specifies and comprehends. As with any particular dimension discovered and examined,
the properly phenomenological task is to flesh out the abiding or invariant structures
of self inherent in the global experience.

     Methodologically speaking, the abstractive *epoché* is an essential step. To arrive at
the self, the initial move must be to separate out what is not-alien from everything
alien. The abstractive move is required even if one were bent on showing that the so-
called 'self' is an amalgam of self and other — 'other' in the sense of being the product of a particular familial and ethnic grooming, for example; one would necessarily
proceed in the same way — by abstracting — in order to be able to specify exactly not
only what is self and what is other, but how self and other intertwine. Abstracting
from all that is other, one then delineates what lies within the bounds of the non-alien.
As noted, what Husserl discovered was that fields of sensation lie within the bounds
of the non-alien; an 'I govern' lies within the bounds of the non-alien; a repertoire of
'I cans' lies within the bounds of the non-alien; a possible self-reflexive stance lies
within the bounds of the non-alien; intentionalities and habitualities play out in distinctive ways within the bounds of the non-alien. To flesh out these intimately-related

essential features of the non-alien in the direction of a full elucidation of the self would be to do painstaking phenomenological work, work that begins, as described above, with a clue from the everyday lifeworld and with 'a peculiar *epoché*', and that culminates in a thoroughgoing articulation of the invariant structures of the sense of self.

When we take the essential features of the non-alien that Husserl briefly describes as just such invariant structures of the sense of self, we immediately find them at sizeable odds not only with Strawson's 'mental self', but with the features Strawson proposes as defining the self to begin with. Most notable is the fact that, while clearly stated to be provisional, Strawson's proposed list of eight defining characteristics of the mental self emphatically specifies the mental self as a *thing*. As Strawson himself admits, a thing is rather vague; in fact, he states that characterization of the self as a thing is 'the least clear of the eight claims' (p. 8). But although he acknowledges that the characterization of the mental self as a thing can be challenged, and even that the particular characterization of the self as a *mental* thing must be qualified (p. 4), he nonetheless offers a defence of the characterization, stating ultimately that 'Bishop Berkeley's characterization of the self as a "thinking . . . principle" seems as good as any [characterization]', immediately remarking that 'A principle, in this old use, manages to sound like a thing of some sort without sounding anything like a table or a chair' (p. 8). What is remarkable is that there is no *thing* found in Husserl's phenomenological investigation of the sphere of ownness. Moreover although each of the five characteristics may be explicated in fuller and far richer ways, there is no vagueness whatsoever. On the contrary, the findings are concrete: fields of sensation, an 'I govern', a repertoire of 'I cans', and so on. What is furthermore remarkable in this respect is that Husserl's phenomenological findings can be verified by others who, adopting the procedure outlined, can examine the findings and validate them on the basis of their own experience. More than this, adopting the procedure outlined, others have the possibility of elaborating the findings on the basis of their own experience. Alternatively, adopting the procedure outlined, they have the possibility of questioning the findings on the basis of their own experience, or further still, the possibility of presenting findings at variance with the original. A bona fide phenomenological methodology inherently guarantees the possibility of verification, elaboration, questioning, and alternative findings by others. In this respect, phenomenology is very like science. It has a methodology that allows replication of results. Husserl in fact considered phenomenology a science.

Now in order to demonstrate the value and relevance of a bona fide phenomenological methodology to a study of the self — or sense of self — it is apposite to sketch out in further ways at least one of the dimensions that Husserl discovered remaining after the abstractive *epoché*, thereby illustrating how a dimension may be elaborated in the direction of a phenomenological account of the self. For quite specific reasons, it is most appropriate to choose the second of the essential features listed above — the 'I govern'. This dimension has a direct relationship to the one defining characteristic that Strawson lists but neglects discussing, and in this respect provides a direct link to what is problematic in his theoretical structuring of the self.

III: 'Governing Psychically':[5] A Question of Agency

When Husserl briefly specifies an 'I govern' in the Fifth Meditation, he amplifies the description minimally, on the one hand saying that 'organs' — hands, arms, torso, head, feet, legs — are immediately ruled by me, and on the other hand hinting that I am free to perceive with these, my organs, any time I wish (Husserl, 1973, p. 97). It is important to emphasize that this description is given in the context of the abstractive *epoché*, and in particular in the context of an abbreviated description of the reduced experience of the natural world — of 'Nature'. It is in turn important not to be misled by language and to think of the 'I govern my organs' as an indication, much less a vindication, of the Cartesian mind/body dichotomy. Within the *epoché*, my body alone has a special place as an *object of nature*; that is, unlike the bodies of others within the natural world, my body alone retains its sense as *animate organism* within the *epoché*. To specify what is there in the reduced experience of this animate organism is to specify what is sedimented or taken for granted in the everyday experience of my body in the natural attitude — precisely as with an 'I govern'. Hence, that arms, hands, torso, and so on, are *ruled by me* does not signify a mind on high directing a body down below what to do, but is a description of my animate organism as a natural object — what we can identify more specifically as a natural *tactile-kinesthetic-kinetic* object — within the *epoché*. Nature as it is constructed by science and Nature as it enters into the natural attitude with respect to an objective world do not enter into this reduced description. Only my own nature experienced as a privileged animate domain is of moment within this description. In other texts, Husserl describes the governing and freedom-to-perceive-with-my-organs more fully — e.g., 'The animate organism is not only sensing animate organism but also organ of motion. In it the psyche, or the psychic subject, senses; in it the subject moves and executes performances in the material world by such self-movement (I move — I move something)' (Husserl, 1980, pp. 106–7); 'I have the freedom to change at will my position in relation to [things in the world] and thereby at the same time vary at will the manifolds of appearance in which they come to givenness for me, . . . [but] I do not have the possibility of distancing myself from my Body, or my Body from me' (Husserl, 1989, p. 167). It is readily apparent from these citations just how intimately related the five essential characteristics of the non-alien are; how, for example, a psychophysical unity underlies the 'I govern'. Still, the 'I govern' may be fleshed out in ways that capture its peculiar character. As the citations indicate, the 'I govern' has to do with *self-movement*, movement issuing from *experienced motivations*, and from a *freedom to move*. In this respect it is an indispensable characteristic of the self. A self incapable of self-movement (or a backlog of experiences of self-movement) would be a self in name only,[6] what Aristotle would call a homonymous self. A self feeling no impe-

[5] See Husserl (1973), p. 91.

[6] Persons who become paralysed through injury or who become motorically disabled through disease have all had prior experiences of self-movement since infancy (and even in the womb). The richness and wealth of these experiences cannot be disregarded. This is as true of persons such as Stephen Hawking as of persons suffering motor paralysis. Studies of paraplegics (persons with spinal cord lesions) such as those carried out by Hohmann (1966) and by Bermond *et al.* (1991) in the related area of affective feelings make the present point rather than challenge it, in that in their basically comparative approach, they presume an unimpaired bodily life history, in these cases, a life history of bodily feelings which, whether determined now to be muted or not, were once untempered by bodily trauma.

tus propelling it to move — no experienced motivations toward or away from something in its surrounding world as in curiosity or fear, for example, no experienced motivations toward opening its mouth to receive food, no experienced motivations toward closing its eyes as a prelude to sleep — is a self hardly definable as such. What lacks experienced motivation verges on (or is an outright instance of) the mechanical or the inanimate. A self incapable of freely varied self-movement is similarly a homonymous self in that it is not a veritable corporeal subject; it cannot dynamically engage itself in self-chosen ways in the world — not only in acts such as reaching, speaking, smiling, or scratching one's leg, but in acts such as shifting one's eyes from left to right, or chewing, or blinking. In both cases — lacking experienced motivations and a freedom to move — the self cannot be said to be a proper self; it cannot be said in good faith to 'govern' — govern itself much less anything in its world. Being unmotivated to move, it is incapable of initiating movement to begin with, and if somehow it finds itself nonetheless moving, e.g., having been pushed into movement or otherwise passively manipulated, it cannot mediate its movement toward an end, e.g., toward avoiding an obstacle in its path or improving its view. Governing, ruling, or holding sway — all phrases Husserl uses in describing this aspect of ownness — encompass both the motivation to move such that one initiates movement — or, chooses *not* to initiate movement — and the capacity to move freely toward whatever end is desirable or desired. It is a self that, as Husserl points out, is not, and never can be, distant from its own Body. Albert Johnstone's Husserlian account of the self in 'Oneself as Oneself and Not as Another' (Johnstone, 1996) makes quite similar points, interestingly enough in showing how a central claim about the self by Peter Strawson in his well-known book *Individuals* (1959) — a claim that makes do with a self of passive movement — does not stand up to scrutiny. Of the motivation to move and the directedness of self-movement, Johnstone writes that 'An adequate account of a voluntary activity must include both constituents of the experiential flux'; he describes the two constituents in terms of 'experienced affective spring' — for example, 'a discomfort, an interest, an annoyance, a tenderness, the glow of an anticipation' — and 'anticipated result' or 'goal' (Johnstone, 1996, p. 5).

Explicated within the context of the abstractive *epoché*, the 'I govern' clearly shows itself to be an essential characteristic of the self. Just as clearly, it shows itself to be connected with 'agentivity', Jerome Bruner's term for a basic human concern that is evident in the very first year of human life: 'action directed toward goals controlled by agents' (Bruner, 1990, p. 77). Bruner has documented this concern in his lifelong studies of infancy and early childhood development and especially in the context of the learning of language. Given this fundamental concern, Strawson's treatment of agency — or rather non-treatment of agency — is near astounding. '[A]n agent' is actually the eighth and last defining characteristic of the mental self that Strawson proposes. It is the one characteristic that he omits from discussion, making merely three remarks in passing about 'an agent'. The first of these is to say simply and without elaboration that 'a serious doubt can be raised about (7)'; the second is to say, some fifteen pages later, after having discussed other features he has proposed, that these other defining features 'need not involve a conception of [the mental self or mental thing] as (7) an agent'; the third is to say (in a footnote on the same page) that 'the view that mental selves . . . can be agents . . . is not excluded by this proposal. *Very* few would agree that agenthood is dispensable with' (Strawson, pp. 4, 20). It is of course puzzling in the extreme to find that insofar as '*[v]ery* few would agree that agenthood is dispensable', that Strawson to all effects dispenses with it. One could easily and readily assume that his proposed *mental* self — or *mental* thing — and 'an agent' are incompatible, altogether discordant metaphysical bedfellows; all the more so if what defines the mental self is a *thinking principle*, rather than, say, a *thinker* on the order of Rodin's famous statue which, in a quite pointed way, well exemplifies the indispensability of a body to the act of thinking.[7] As described earlier, a self that is thinking — or doing anything — catches itself, or is capable of catching itself, in the act of doing something quite particular — reading, listening, waiting, wondering, and so on. Thinking is equally a form of doing.[8] If we claim to be selves, that is, if we claim, each of us, that we have a sense of self, then that self is engaged in some particular way at any and all particular moments of our lives any time we care to be aware of it, that is, any time we care to turn our attention to our *self*.

A developmental account of the self is bracingly instructive in this regard. In fact, if we trace out a particular domain within the ontogeny of self offered by Daniel Stern, we find ourselves on sound empirical grounds for affirming both the indispensability of agency and the indispensability of the tactile-kinesthetic body to a sense of self. Stern's developmental account is based on both clinical and developmental research findings, that is, on his own experience and research background as an infant psychiatrist and experimental psychologist. Although his concern is preeminently with the social relatedness of the self, thus similar in a way to Husserl's preeminent concern with an intersubjective world, his account, like Husserl's, is crucially concentrated, and in foundational ways, on 'I-alone'.

Stern delineates four successive domains in the formation of the self, all the while emphasizing that a previous domain never disappears even as a further one becomes dominant. 'Once formed', he says, 'the domains remain . . . as distinct forms of experiencing social life and self. None are lost to adult experience. Each simply gets more elaborated' (Stern, 1985, p. 32). He points out in fact that the term *domains* is used in preference to the term *stages* or the term *phases* precisely to call attention to abiding formative structures that, though superseded, are never effaced. He identifies the successive domains as those of an emergent self, a core self, a subjective self, and a verbal self. Our major concern here will be with the core self. After briefly describing aspects of the emergent self to mark the corporeal ground out of which the core self develops, we will turn full attention to the core self, showing how it centres on the tactile-kinesthetic body and on agentivity, and showing too how Stern's empirically-founded account of the core self accords with a bona fide phenomenological descriptive account of the self. We will then briefly consider the subsequent development of a subjective self, and finally, reconsider the sense of self in the broader philosophical context suggested by Strawson's essay.

An emergent self evolves on the basis of certain aspects of experience that stand out as 'primary organizers' in the life of an infant (Stern, 1985, p. 33). Stern identifies these organizers as 'amodal perception' — an infant's proclivity and capacity to

[7] For an interesting discussion of Descartes's notable omission of a corporeal subject in his account of thinking, a discussion that includes reference to Rodin's *The Thinker*, see Johnstone (1992), particularly pp. 39–43.

[8] For an extended analysis and discussion of the confluence of thinking and doing from an evolutionary perspective, see Sheets-Johnstone (1986); see also Sheets-Johnstone (1990).

grasp objects and their properties across presentation in different sense modalities; 'physiognomic perception' (or 'categorical affects') — an infant's proclivity and capacity to grasp the affective character of a face, a colour, a line drawing, a sequence of sounds, and so on, thus perceiving its happy, angry, or sad character, for example; and 'vitality affects' — an infant's proclivity and capacity to grasp the dynamic character of its experiences, their unfolding qualitative intensities and qualitative spatio-temporal features, including the unfolding qualitative intensities and qualitative spatio-temporal features of its experiences of its own felt body.[9] It is notable in this respect that Stern underscores the fact that *an infant experiences itself from the start*. The fact has sizeable consequences, especially for a theory about a sense of self, as we shall presently see in greater detail. It is of moment too that Stern calls attention to the fact that the idea that a sense of self is possible in the first two months of infancy 'is generally dismissed or not even broached, because the idea of a sense of self is usually reserved for some overarching and integrating schema, concept, or perspective about the self'. In partial accord with this general estimation, he says that '[C]learly, during this early period infants are not capable of such an overview. They have separate, unrelated experiences that have yet to be integrated into one embracing perspective' (p. 45). But this process of integration is precisely a process of emerging organization in Stern's view, and the *experience* of emerging organization is the foundation of 'the *emergent sense of self*. It is of interest that in answer to the question, '[C]an infants also experience non-organization?' Stern answers a definitive 'No!' (p. 46). Elaborating on the point with specific reference to the classical notion of infants' experiencing themselves as totally undifferentiated — fused with their mothers and all else in their environment — he remarks that 'The traditional notions of clinical theorists have taken the observer's knowledge of infants — that is, relative undifferentiation compared with the differentiated view of older children — reified it, and given it back, or attributed it, to infants as their own dominant subjective sense of things'. Traditional wisdom has in this way overlooked the discreteness of infants' experiences of themselves, the distinctive vividness and clarity of those experiences on the one hand, and their initial unrelatedness and progressive integration on the other. Specifying an infant's developing sense of self on the grounds both of its differentiated experiences of itself and of its experiences of emergent organization, Stern makes a highly compelling and significant observation. He states that 'In order for the infant to have any formed sense of self, there must ultimately be some organization that is sensed as a reference point. *The first such organization concerns the body*: its coherence, its actions, its inner feeling states, and the memory of all these' (Stern, 1985, p. 46; italics added). He goes on to discuss each of these dimensions *as*

---

[9] Stern does not explicitly single out movement or the tactile-kinesthetic body in his discussion of vitality affects; he is more specifically concerned with feelings in an affective rather than kinetic sense. Yet movement and the tactile-kinesthetic body are each unmistakably central aspects of vitality affects, as is evident when, likening vitality affects to a puppet show, Stern observes that 'It is from the way they move in general that we infer the different vitality affects' (Stern 1985, p. 56); or when, in describing experiences in the life of an infant, he writes of an infant's changing bodily dynamics during a '*hunger storm . . . that passes*' (Stern, 1990, pp. 31–43); or when, in specifying the nature of a feeling's 'vitality contours', he speaks of those contours as coming from movement, from 'sensations of accelerating, growing, fading, climaxing, etc.', and gives as example the fact that 'there are smiles that grow slowly and steadily, others explode, and some progress slowly and suddenly burst open, etc.' (Stern, forthcoming).

aspects of the core self under the headings of self-coherence, self-agency, self-affectivity, and self-history, respectively, showing in each case how 'islands of consistency'[10] are built up, that is, how an infant comes to identify and to integrate invariants in its experiences of itself (p. 45). He thus affirms — not explicitly, but without any doubt implicitly — a corporeal foundation of the self, an organizational matrix grounded in bodily life. As will become apparent, although Stern does not specify the tactile-kinesthetic body as being at the heart of this organizational matrix — or, in phenomenological terms, *at the heart of the psychophysical unity that is the self*— that body is everywhere apparent in his descriptive account of the core self. Indeed, although not singled out as such, proprioception figures consistently and centrally in his account of each dimension of the core self.

Now, in one sense, Stern's bodily 'reference point' seems so obvious it hardly warrants discussion. With respect to putting things together — organizing experience — what could be more basic than one's tactile-kinesthetic body, most particularly more basic than *making sense of one's body and learning to move oneself*? With respect to 'organization', the first task of an infant is to make just such sense and to serve just such an apprenticeship.[11] Stern's description of the 'coming-to-be' of bodily organization (Stern, 1985, pp. 45, 47) — what he identifies as the *processes* at the foundation of an infant's putting things together — is in fact edifying. Though connection is not expressly made to the tactile-kinesthetic body, descriptions of amodal perception, physiognomic perception, and vitality affects consistently validate, and in distinctive ways, the primacy of movement and kinesthesia; in particular, each facet of the emergent self resonates or can be shown to resonate not just in 'subjective experience' (pp. 47–61, 64–8),[12] but in *tactile-kinesthetic* subjective experience. For example, an infant's amodal ability to match a sound it hears with a moving mouth that it sees — a spoken sound with a seen facial dynamic — and to notice when the latter does not match the former, is testimony to a foundational attunement to movement, in this case, an attunement to *articulatory gestures*, an attunement grounded in the infant's own tactile-kinesthetic life in babbling, in smacking, pursing, and rounding its lips, in protruding its tongue, in gurgling, and in much more (Sheets-Johnstone, 1990, chapter 6).[13] I have shown elsewhere in detail how each dimension of Stern's emergent self is definitively tied to a tactile-kinesthetic body (Sheets-Johnstone, 1996; 1998, chapter 5). That *infants experience themselves* is clearly a fact not to be overlooked, especially in an account of the sense of self. Recognition of the fact entails recognition of the fact that tactility and kinesthesia are the bedrock of infant self-experience, the corporeal foundation on which a sense of self emerges and develops. That self-agency, self-coherence, self-affectivity, and self-history — features of the core self — are built up on this foundation and that they continue to be elaborated along the lines of the body is not surprising in the least.

---

[10] Stern borrows the phrase from Escalona (1953).

[11] For a detailed analysis and discussion of this sense-making and apprenticeship, see Sheets-Johnstone (1998), in particular, chapter 5.

[12] 'Subjective experience' is the global term Stern uses from the very beginning of his investigations of infant life. See in particular Stern (1985), chapter 1, pp. 3–12, and the summation section of chapter 3, pp. 64–8.

[13] For an empirical grounding of an infant's foundational attunement to movement, see Sheets-Johnstone (1998), chapter 5.

Stern's discussion of self-agency focuses on three invariants of experience: on 'the sense of volition that precedes a motor act'; on 'the proprioceptive feedback that does or does not occur during the act'; and on 'the predictability of consequences that follow the act' (Stern, 1985, p. 76). He conjectures that 'volition may be the most fundamental invariant of core self-experience' (pp. 76–7). Disregarding his reliance on 'motor programs' to explain volition — 'motor programs' (or 'motor plans') putatively issuing from a Central Program Generator having rightly given way in recent years to dynamically informed analyses of 'real-bodies' in the 'real-time' and 'real-circumstances' of self-movement[14] — we find a quite unique and impressive kind of empirical documentation for his estimation of volition. He reports on experimental research — research he and colleagues conducted — involving Siamese twins who, before their separation at four months, were joined between navel and sternum. The experiment consisted in determining any difference in the bodily movement of the twins when they were deterred from sucking their own fingers and when they were deterred from sucking the fingers of their twin. When the twin's own arm was pulled away from her mouth by a researcher — the pulling movement resulting in the twin's own fingers being pulled out of her mouth — the twin resisted the pull, i.e., *she attempted to pull her own arm back toward herself*; when her twin's arm was pulled away from her mouth by a researcher — the pulling movement resulting in her twin's fingers being pulled out of her mouth — the twin *strained forward with her head in pursuit of the retreating fingers*, i.e., in pursuit of something *alien* to her own body. In documenting two distinctively different bodily movements, the experiment documents a bodily sense of self in the form of both a tactile-kinesthetic body and volitional movement or self-agency. We can appreciate once more on the basis of this empirical documentation how fundamental Husserlian aspects of the sense of self are intimately connected. We can furthermore appreciate how empirical findings complement phenomenological ones. Stern's experimental evidence of volition makes a burgeoning 'I govern' plainly evident in the act of resisting and in the act of straining forward. There is, then, not only an epistemological dimension — each twin unmistakably knowing her own body, or in terms of the abstractive *epoché*, having a 'field of sensations' that is entirely *her own* — but a metaphysical dimension as well in that neither the movement of resisting nor the movement of straining forward is reflexive; each is, on the contrary, a voluntary movement, and one appropriate to the situation at hand. In effect, each twin is a free agent who rules in her own body: each is capable of initiating movement and of voluntarily moving in ways concordant with her own motivations in a given situation. In short, Stern's experimental evidence of volition clearly accords in fundamental ways with an 'I govern' as a basic dimension of the sense of self. It testifies empirically to a psychophysical unity in the form of a tactile-kinesthetic body, in the most basic metaphysical sense, to a kinetic tactile-kinesthetic being, a *Da-bewegung*. It clearly does not accord with the sense of self as a 'mental thing', an entity locked inside a head.

That a sense of self engenders an ontogenetic history and that that history must be taken into account if one is to solve the 'real philosophical problem about the existence and nature of the self' — as Strawson characterizes 'the problem of the self' (p. 1) — should by now be readily apparent. Indeed, when Strawson writes that 'the

[14] For in-depth studies of, and probing essays on, infants by a variety of dynamic systems researchers, see Smith and Thelen (1993); and Thelen and Smith (1994).

sense of the mental self . . . comes to every normal human being, in some form, in childhood' (p. 3), he actually leaves us to our own devices to imagine its provenence, which could be magical or genetic — or conceivably both, in a creationist sense. The realization that each one of us 'is alone in [his/her] head' is presented as a *deus ex machina* realization, but at the same time as a realization akin to the realization of a secondary sex characteristic. In such circumstances, the idea that the sense of self is an emergent, developmental phenomenon grounded through and through in experience, and the idea that its experiential character can be progressively charted, never surface. Yet clearly, both the origin (in the sense of a foundation) and history are crucially important. It is not enough merely to *propose* characteristics of the self in an attempt to solve the 'real philosophical problem about the existence and nature of the self'. It is essential to *uncover* defining characteristics in the first place, and to *trace* those characteristics to their experiential core — precisely through both a phenomenological and empirical methodology. On the one hand, a genetic phenomenology ('genetic' in Husserl's sense of the term; see Welton, 1977, and Sheets-Johnstone, 1990, chapter 14) is definitively required for a *phenomenology of the self* since phenomenology takes as its task a return to, and an elucidation of, origins; on the other hand, empirical evidence is required for that to which we, as adults, do not have direct phenomenological access. Genetic phenomenology and empirical evidence together comprise a domain that aptly falls within what Eugene Fink termed 'a constructive phenomenology'. Fink described this phenomenology in general terms, but also at one point with specific reference to *early childhood development*. He said that transcendental questions about genesis pertain to '*early childhood development* insofar as precisely this early period lies beyond the reach of our memory; these [transcendental questions] are all questions that are raised in psychology under the titles "the origin of the idea of space, of the idea of time", etc., and of course at the essentially inadequate level of the natural attitude. The *transcendental* [i.e., properly phenomenological] response to all these questions cannot proceed in intuitive fashion, i.e. it cannot bring the archaic building processes actually to a present or recollective self-givenness, it can only "construct" them' (Fink, 1995, p. 63). By its very nature, the phenomenology of the self — or the phenomenology of the sense of self — falls within Fink's framework of transcendental questions about genesis; it falls precisely within the framework of a constructive phenomenology. Husserl's remark concerning methodology, a remark to the effect that a question itself determines the method appropriate to its answer, is relevant in directing us to the same methodology. Husserl observed that 'A method, after all, is nothing which is, or which can be, brought in from the outside. [A] *determinate* method . . . is a norm which arises from the fundamental regional specificity and the universal structures of the province in question' (Husserl, 1983, p. 173). The 'fundamental regional specificity' of the self requires a phenomenological-empirical methodology, for only such a methodology can provide insights into both foundations and development, that is, into both the origin and history of the sense of self; 'universal structures of the province in question', i.e., the province of the self, require a phenomenological methodology for only such a methodology can provide ever-deepening elucidations of invariants of the sense of self, invariants Husserl delineated prelusively in his discovery of 'fields of sensations', an 'I govern', and so on.

Before discussing the broader implications of a constructive methodological approach to the self within the specific context of Strawson's essay — implications having to do in part with a constructive over a 'cognitive' phenomenology — it will be instructive to specify features of Stern's subsequent domain, 'the subjective self', that bear in a pointed way on what Strawson identifies as the 'alone-in-one's-head' basic character of the sense of self.

The subjective self, Stern says, evolves out of the core self and marks a dual recognition on the part of the infant: a recognition not only that it itself, but that others as well, have minds of their own. The 'subjective self' thus actually specifies an *intersubjective* domain and not simply what Strawson would term 'the sense of the self'. The distinction is important for it strongly suggests that what starts out in singular individual fashion on the basis of tactile-kinesthetic life, of agentivity, of 'I cans', and so on, evolves into a social conception of the self. The evidence Stern presents for the development of a subjective self and of an intersubjective domain comes from interactive experiences, in particular, from experiences of shared attention, shared intentions, and shared affective states, all *nonlinguistic* experiences that he documents by way of both experimental and clinical studies. Although he does not call attention to the fact, it is significant that, as with phenomena associated with the emergent self, phenomena associated with the development of a subjective self are fundamentally rooted in bodily life: shared attention, shared intentions, and shared affective states are played out in gestures, postures, movements such as pointing and reaching, eye contact, facial expressions, and so on. When Stern discusses shared affective states, he singles them out as 'the most pervasive and clinically germaine [sic] feature of intersubjective relatedness' (Stern, 1985, p. 138). He describes them in terms of attunement and delineates their dynamic features both broadly, considering their intensity, timing, and shape, and in greater detail by way of six categories, each of which has a highly particularized operational definition. The bodily nature of the dynamic features, particularly as they are operationally described, is unmistakable. They include reference, for example, to 'an abrupt arm movement performed by the infant', to a 'mother's vocal effort and [an] infant's physical effort [showing] an acceleration in intensity', to a temporal conformation between an infant's arm gesture and its mother's up-and-down (nodding) head movement, and so on (p. 146). Stern himself at one point calls attention to the fact that infants first learn about attunement features — 'vitality affects, or in Langer's term "forms of feeling"' — 'from their interactions with their own behavior and bodily processes and by watching, testing, and reacting to the social behaviors that impinge on and surround them' (p. 160; see also Langer, 1953; 1967). However unacknowledged or implicit its recognition, the centrality of the body to an infant's developing sense of a subjective self is nonetheless palpably evident throughout.

The quintessential nature of this bodily anchorage is equally evident throughout. That the tactile-kinesthetic body is the centre-pin of the developing 'subjective self' is already suggested both by Stern's thesis that successive domains of the self are not superseded but enfolded and by his explicit reference to the foundational relationship of the core self to the subjective self at the very beginning of his descriptive account of the latter: the core self, he says, 'is the existential bedrock of interpersonal relations' (p. 125). An infant's discovery of a 'subjective self' between the seventh and ninth month of its life is based upon months of prior life experiences, experiences that, at their core, are rooted in experiences of its own tactile-kinesthetic body. What Strawson speaks of as the realization 'in some form, in childhood . . . of the fact that one's thoughts are unobservable by others, the experience of the profound sense in which one is alone in one's head' is grounded in these bodily experiences, that is, in a prior experiential sense of self. Moreover as indicated, the realization of which Strawson speaks is not just of a fact about one's self, but of a fact about others. Thus the realization is not, *and cannot logically be*, the ground floor of a sense of self; realization of being 'alone in one's head', distinct from all others, is necessarily grounded in experiences of self — and in experiences of others — that have gone before, experiences that are substantively different in nature from the realization that Strawson pinpoints. The evidence Stern offers for a subjective self and an intersubjective relatedness is clearly contingent on these earlier experiences and makes the point at issue: *attention* can be shared only if an infant has itself first experienced attending and has thus experienced itself governing its 'organs' — as in focusing visually on a mobile, for example, or watching its hand intently as it opens it and closes it into a fist; *intentions* can be shared only if an infant has first experienced itself as intending certain meanings and has thus experienced itself as a psychophysical unity — as in reaching out its hand for something it wants to explore or examine; *affective states* can be shared only if an infant has first felt itself affectively engaged and has thus experienced itself as the locus of tactile-kinesthetic happenings — as in crying, smiling, feeling eager, curious, fearful, and so on. It is, then, no great leap to identify the tactile-kinesthetic body as the foundation of the development of the subjective self. Without this foundation, the sense of a subjective self — the sense Strawson defines in terms of having 'unobservable thoughts' and being 'alone in one's head' — could not possibly develop. What *is* observable — my own tactile-kinesthetic body and the visual bodies of others — is the foundation for realizing what is *not* observable: my visual body for others — which is precisely *not* observable to me in ways it is observable to others — and the tactile-kinesthetic body of another — which is precisely *not* observable to me as it is observable to the other. What *is* observable are experienced tactile-kinesthetic corporeal realities, realities we as infants live directly from the very beginning of our lives. From this perspective, one is easily and with sound reasons led to conclude that our first realizations of the unobservable are not realizations of unobservable *thoughts*, just as our first realizations of 'aloneness' are not of being 'alone in our heads'. They are, rather, realizations about bodies, the body we are and the bodies we are not,[15] thus realizations of tactile-kinesthetic lives commensurate with — or not commensurate with — our own tactile-kinesthetic life. By the very dynamic manner in which such experiences are lived, which is to say by their very nature, shared attentions, shared intentions, and shared affective states articulate this corporeal priority as the foundation of their possibility, the foundation of intersubjective attunement.

In sum, the primordial distinctive experience of aloneness — the distinctive mark of the sense of self — is not of being alone in one's head but of *being alone in one's body*, in particular, one's tactile-kinesthetic body. It is notable that in philosophical disquisitions on qualia, this body is consistently bypassed in favour of pain and the

---

[15] For an elucidation and discussion of how the question, 'What is it like to be an X', is, at its most elemental level, a question of what it is like to be a body we are not, see Sheets-Johnstone (1998); see also Sheets-Johnstone (1994).

colour red, philosophers' paradigmatic qualia.[16] Hence the qualia of movement —
suddenness, expansiveness, tenseness, smoothness, for example — never come to
light, and in consequence, *fields of sensation* that we as adults ascribe or could ascribe
to ourselves if we but noticed ourselves in movement and that we as adults could analyse phenomenologically if we but cared to delve into the origin of our spatio-
temporal concepts, do not come to light either but instead lie buried in our experience.

IV: Related Liabilities, Implications, and Conclusions

If we take Strawson's claim seriously that a phenomenology of the self must precede
a metaphysics of the self, then we have considerable phenomenological work to do,
work that is methodologically very different from the purported phenomenological
analysis Strawson offers, and certainly much more extensive and detailed than what
has been offered here. That further work aside, on the basis of what has been gleaned
from an examination of a bona fide phenomenological methodology and from a phenomenological examination of agency, we may point out certain related implications
and liabilities of Strawson's conception of the self as a mental thing, and in so doing
offer broader conclusions with respect to his *'cognitive phenomenology* of the sense
of the self' (Strawson, p. 2). Two of the implications are of pivotal metaphysical significance and are all but singled out as such in the examinations themselves. One concerns a conception of the self as a developmental phenomenon and a psychophysical
unity as against — in spite of Strawson's claims to a thoroughgoing materialism — a
thoroughly dichotomized subject;[17] the other moves us toward a process metaphysics
as against an entity-substance metaphysics. Before we spell out these implications, a
more immediate methodological liability warrants our attention.

When Strawson pointedly specifies a *'cognitive phenomenology'* of the sense of
self (p. 2), he does so with a view to separating out 'the conceptual structure of the
sense of the self' from 'any emotional aspects that it may have'. He certainly does not
deny affective aspects to a sense of self (in fact, he speaks of these aspects in terms of
a separate domain: 'the affective phenomenology of the self'), but he is interested in
such aspects only insofar as they 'shape or weight conceptions [of the self]'. His territorial narrowing of the phenomenological field before actually undertaking a phenomenological investigation of the self is, phenomenologically speaking, a
methodological misstep that is hazardous to, if not totally compromising of, his so-
called phenomenological results. The prior territorial narrowing assumes first of all
that the conceptual structure of the sense of self can be distilled — purified of any and
all contaminant structures — in advance of the phenomenological investigation
which is supposed to lay it bare; conversely, it assumes that one can delete — and
with surgical precision — all that lies outside the domain of the phenomenologically

---

[16] For a critical account of philosophers' paradigmatic treatment of qualia, see Sheets-Johnstone (1998),
chapter 3, Afterword; see also in the same text, chapter 2, Part II.

[17] With respect to dichotomization, it should be noted and emphasized that the mind/body problem is not
the mind/brain problem. One may on the basis of first-hand experience readily affirm that thoughts,
like dreams, are immaterial, hence that while thinking is tied to the body, thoughts themselves are
non-sensuous. The relationship of thoughts to brains — the mind/brain problem — is a different
question altogether from the mind/body problem, and one not broached in the present chapter. For a
discussion of the distinction, see Sheets-Johnstone (1998), particularly chapter 10, 'Why a Mind Is Not
a Brain and a Brain Is Not a Body'.

cognitive sense of self prior to a phenomenological determination of the sense of self. It assumes, in addition and most importantly, that the duly distilled cognitive — or conceptual — sense of the self is a phenomenological ready-made. As we have seen, Strawson indicates the ready-made nature of the cognitive sense of self when he says that 'the sense of the mental self . . . comes to every normal human being, in some form, in childhood' (p. 3). In denying straightaway a *developing* sense of the self, a sense tethered to experiences from birth (possibly even experiences before birth) onward — or if not straightaway denying, then straightaway espousing what might be called a 'mysterian' view of the sense of self,[18] the sense just 'comes' — Strawson can easily deny that the conceptual sense of self has any foundation in affectivity or, by extension, in agentivity (infants and very young children being not yet at that Rubicon point of awareness of 'the mental self' that Strawson says 'comes to every normal human being . . . in childhood'). What Strawson's cognitive phenomenology of the sense of the self in effect implies is an instant self fabricated on the spot — a pristine mental spot through and through. Indeed, as Strawson explicitly states — though oddly enough in terms of *feeling* (in fact *intense* feeling), hence in terms of *bodies* — 'nearly everyone has had intensely at some time . . . the feeling that one's body is just a vehicle or vessel for the mental thing that is what one really or most essentially is' (p. 3). His cognitive phenomenology thus appears to be an efficient twentieth-century Western method of securing in advance what Descartes arrived at three-and-a-half centuries earlier by meditating: a thoroughly mental self — or 'thinking principle'. Such methodological efficiency preempts completely the possibility that thinking is modelled on the body[19] or that thinking is a form of doing[20] or that a thinking self is a corporeal self.[21] All such phenomenologically-derived insights are blocked from view from the start. Anything more than *the mental*, or anything other than cognition, is adjudged beforehand to corrupt the terrain, not only because it purportedly introduces something other than concepts or thinking into the 'phenomenological investigation', but because anything other than *the mental* plainly opens the door to bodies. In the end, Strawson's cognitive phenomenology offers us two possible philosophical ways of construing 'the mental thing' that he identifies as the sense of self and that he says comes to all of us 'in some form, in childhood'. On the one (historical perspective on philosophy) hand, the realization that one has unobservable thoughts and is alone in one's head amounts to eating *nouvelle cuisine*-but-still-traditional Cartesian cake. On the other (wholly physicalist) hand, so long as one is eating wholly material cake, one can fearlessly have unobservable thoughts and be alone in one's head.

Like the methodological liability, the two implications of pivotal metaphysical significance both have a decidedly Cartesian cast. To begin with, however holistic the attempt to define the self in terms of a '"mental and non-mental" materialism' (Strawson, p. 7), the metaphysics ensuing from Strawson's cognitive phenomenology pres-

---

[18] For a discussion of Owen Flanagan's original coinage of the term 'mysterian' as a label for philosophers who, Flanagan says, 'think that consciousness will *never* be understood' (Flanagan, 1991, p. 313), see Sheets-Johnstone (1998), chapter 11.

[19] For a thoroughgoing analysis of this relationship, see Sheets-Johnstone (1990); see also Sheets-Johnstone (1994).

[20] For exemplifications and a discussion of this relationship, see Sheets-Johnstone (1986).

[21] For a descriptive analysis of this identity, see Johnstone (1992).

ents a problem in the form of a partial or fragmentary self. The idea that the self is 'really or most essentially' a mental thing strongly implies that one's sense of self is fundamentally unattached to anything bodily. The problem is not simply that of a dis-embodied self, of which more later, or a self of which psychotic case studies are made; the problem is more immediately whether we actually experience ourselves as the partial or fragmented self Strawson describes: Do we 'really or most essentially' find ourselves to be no more than a passing self-conscious thought in our heads? Tak-ing Strawson's sympathetic references to Buddhism seriously — he finds the Bud-dhist notion of consciousness and denial of a persisting self to be supportive of his own view (p. 18, note 27; p. 20) — we might think that, after all, there are or might be good reasons for agreeing with him and, in consequence, for answering the question affirmatively. But to follow Strawson along his putatively Buddhist-supported path, we would first of all have to take the actual experience of a passing self-conscious thought in an extremely broad sense, i.e., to include, *contra* Strawson, bodily sensa-tions and perceptions, bodily feelings and emotions, bodily-felt likings and dislik-ings, and so on, since the Buddhist notion of consciousness includes just such bodily phenomena. Moreover we would have to acknowledge that a Buddhist-based affirmative answer is actually a cultivated answer, that is, an answer that a practising Buddhist has laboured hard to achieve. It is an answer based on experience, in par-ticular, on what a Buddhist has discovered many times over in the crucible of his or her own experiences in meditating, namely, the arising and passing away of all phe-nomena and of all experiences of phenomena, including the phenomenon of that which is called 'the self'. In effect, the discovery on which a Buddhist's answer rests is precisely *not* a ready-made on the order of Strawson's 'mental self': it is precisely *not* the discovery of 'every normal human being'; and it is certainly *not* a discovery coincident with what Strawson describes as one's realization in childhood that one is 'alone in one's head' (or, for that matter, with what Stern describes as a 'quantum leap in the sense of self . . . when the infant discovers that he or she has a mind and that other people have minds as well' [Stern, 1985, p. 124]). In short, if we hew to a Bud-dhist perspective, what we discover is not 'a mental thing', but the transient nature of all that is. In turn, we discover no self in the form of a *thing*, even less in the form of a thing that, as Strawson assures us late in his essay, has the same '*physical*' status as 'any blood vessel or jackhammer or cow' (Strawson, p. 21) — though we should note that in assuring us unflinchingly in terms of blood vessels, jackhammers, and cows, Strawson contradicts himself.[22] What we discover from a Buddhist (Vipassana) per-spective is impermanence — 'the existential transiency of all experience' (Goldstein and Kornfield, 1987, p. 103). Every aspect of ourselves and of the world about us shows us 'that there is nothing solid, nothing static, nothing steady that goes from one year to the next, one month to the next, one moment to the next'. The point of moment here is that the 'we' that makes this discovery is not a partial or fragmentary self but a psychophysical unity, or, as the same Buddhist text terms it, a 'mind-body [that] is a

---

[22] Earlier in his essay (p. 8), Strawson tells us that the self is 'not thought of as being a thing in the way that a stone or a cat is'. It is here that, as indicated previously in the present text, he goes on to liken the thinghood of the self positively to Berkeley's 'thinking principle', which, he says, 'manages to sound like a thing of some sort without sounding anything like a table or a chair'. We are warranted in asking Strawson to address the contradiction, or to redress it by specifying for us the difference in thinghood between a stone, cat, table, and chair, on the one hand, and a blood vessel, jackhammer, and cow, on the other.

flux of constant creation and dissolution'. The basic Buddhist practice of mindfulness to breathing indicates as much, all by itself.

A further and intimately related aspect of the same metaphysical problem is rooted in Strawson's implicit attitude toward infancy, i.e., infancy is a period of life that may be ignored altogether, or a period in which we do not have thoughts (supposing Strawson would grant that we have thoughts at all) of the kind requisite to a sense of self. When we take infancy seriously, this aspect of the problem all but formulates itself. We rightfully wonder whether what starts out whole becomes severed from its original moorings by later adult theoretical musings and near-magical categorizations of language that lead us to believe that whatever we designate by a word has a totally independent existence, the end result being that the self that is originally and developmentally a psychophysical unity floats off into a mental vacuum — sometime in childhood. Has a self so conceived and so described been philosophically waylaid on its journey to adulthood? Its unobservable thoughts and aloneness in its head appear, as per Strawson's cognitive phenomenology, to drive it into an existential *angst* that runs away with itself. Its private thought experiences become philosophically magnified into a metaphysics of the self that is ahistorical as well as disembodied. Insofar as it lacks both a proper historical and psychophysical foundation, it is no surprise that its metaphysical moorings are tenuous in the extreme.

Strawson's cognitive phenomenology dictates not only an instant, body-less self fabricated of private adult mental ruminations, but a self tethered to a substance metaphysics. That self belongs to a classical physicist's worldview, a worldview that does not and cannot easily accommodate a process metaphysics. The classical physicist's fundamental concerns are not rooted in motion and change but in elementary particles or things, not in dynamic but in objective structures. Thus, although Strawson is at pains to show and emphasize that the sense of self is an intermittent yet 'hiatus-free' mental thing (Strawson, p. 9), in other words, a mental thing that, while fleetingly there, is nonetheless there for us any time we are 'I-thinking self-consciousness' (p. 17), he gives no indication of the mental thing being characterizable as a processual phenomenon. More precisely put, the mental thing that constitutes the sense of self is, according to Strawson, experienced synchronically rather than diachronically. It does not persist over time but is experienced in 'periods of thought . . . [that] are invariably brief . . . a few seconds at the most' (p. 9). Strawson calls his view 'the Pearl view' of the mental self and, as indicated above, likens it to the Buddhist denial of 'a *persisting* mental self' (p. 20). But the fundamentally dynamic notion of phenomena arising and passing away that informs a Buddhist's view of the self is not compatible with and does not inform Strawson's account. There is in fact a disjunction between the notion of a mental *thing* — 'a distinct existence, an individual physical thing or object' — and the kind of process metaphysics that underlies not merely a Buddhist's conception of the self — or non-self — but the actual meditative and mindful experiences on which that conception is based, experiences not only of passing thoughts, but of passing breaths, movements, inclinations to move, judgments, likings and dislikings, and with all of these, passing sensations and feelings. The recent text of a Buddhist (Vipassana) psychiatrist makes the point in unequivocal terms: '[T]he distinguishing characteristic of Buddhist meditation is that it seeks to eradicate, once and for all, the conception of self as an entity. In various critical ways, the three major meditative strategies — concentration, mindfulness, and insight — all work to this end' (Epstein, 1995, pp. 138–9). In sum, although 'the mental thing' that Strawson identifies as the self is something that comes and goes — we experience it 'gappily' (Strawson, pp. 17–19) — and is furthermore multiple — each distinctive experience of one's mental self is a different experience — its elemental thingness, as Strawson describes it, precludes its being considered dynamically, as something arising and passing away, and in turn as being concordant with a processual metaphysics. The mental materiality that firmly constitutes Strawson's sense of self is a *some-thing* — not a *non-thing* or a *no-thing*.

A non-entitative metaphysics of the self demands a radically altered materialism. In a very basic sense, it requires recognition of the metaphysical corollary of materialism: animism, animism in the simple sense of being imbued with life — animated.[23] In the most elemental metaphysical sense, it requires recognition of Aristotle's observation that 'Matter will surely not move itself' (*Metaphysics* 1071b30) and in this respect has both cosmological significance and phylogenetic implications. Examined from this perspective, the sense of self has a far more extensive history for which an account must be given: it has not just an ontogenetical history but a natural history. In turn, a constructive phenomenology of the self has a wider task than that indicated earlier. Subsumed in that task is consideration of those hominids who painted on the walls of caves in the palaeolithic; of those earlier hominids who buried their dead; of those still earlier hominids who made hafted tools; of those living pongids who, recognizing themselves in a mirror and seeing a paint spot on their face, wipe it off; and so on. From this vantage point, the domain of the *non-alien* opens onto a field of study that is neither relative nor arbitrary but that may be specified with the precision of phenomenologically-grounded invariants. That those invariants should ultimately be found to have their roots in animation — in movement — and the tactile-kinesthetic body should not be surprising to anyone taking animate organisms as well as phenomenology seriously. In this regard, a final concluding observation may be made. In the beginning of his chapter, Strawson makes the important point that, while the problem of the self 'requires a straightforwardly metaphysical approach . . . metaphysics must wait on phenomenology' (p. 1). A final and sanguine implication of his chapter is that, indeed, we can and do learn from doing phenomenology in advance of offering a metaphysics of the self.

References

Bermond, B., Fasotti, L., Nieuwenhuyse, B. and Schuerman, J. (1991), 'Spinal cord lesions, peripheral feedback and intensities of emotional feelings', *Cognition and Emotion*, **5**, pp. 201–20.

Bruner, Jerome (1990), *Acts of Meaning* (Cambridge, MA: Harvard University Press).

Epstein, Mark (1995), *Thoughts Without a Thinker* (New York: Basic Books).

Escalona, S.K. (1953), 'Emotional development in the first year of life', in *Problems of Infancy and Childhood*, ed. M. Senn (Packawack Lake, NJ: Foundation Press).

Fink, Eugene (1995), *Sixth Cartesian Meditation: The Idea of a Transcendental Theory of Method*, trans. Ronald Bruzina (Bloomington, IN: Indiana University Press).

Flanagan, Owen (1991), *The Science of the Mind*, 2nd ed. (Cambridge, MA: Bradford /MIT Press).

Goldstein, Joseph and Kornfield, Jack (1987), *Seeking the Heart of Wisdom* (Boston, MA: Shambala).

---

[23] For exemplifications and discussions of this metaphysical corollary, see Sheets-Johnstone (1992) and Sheets-Johnstone (1998), especially chapter 11.

Hohmann, G.W. (1966), 'Some effects of spinal cord lesions on experienced emotional feelings', *Psychophysiology*, **3**, pp. 143–56.

Husserl, Edmund (1973), *Cartesian Meditations*, trans. Dorion Cairns (The Hague: Martinus Nijhoff).

Husserl, Edmund (1980), *Ideas Pertaining to a Pure Phenomenology and to a Phenomenological Philosophy*, Third Book, *Phenomenology and the Foundations of the Sciences* (commonly known as *Ideas III*), trans. Ted E. Klein and William E. Pohl (The Hague: Martinus Nijhoff).

Husserl, Edmund (1983), *Ideas Pertaining to a Pure Phenomenology and to a Phenomenological Philosophy*, First Book, *General Introduction to a Pure Phenomenology* (commonly known as *Ideas I*), trans. Fred Kersten (The Hague: Martinus Nijhoff, 1983)

Husserl, Edmund (1989), *Ideas Pertaining to a Pure Phenomenology and to a Phenomenological Philosophy*, Second Book: *Studies in the Phenomenology of Constitution* (commonly known as *Ideas II*), trans. Richard Rojcewicz and André Schuwer (Dordrecht: Kluwer).

Johnstone, Albert A. (1992), 'The bodily nature of the self or What Descartes should have conceded Princess Elizabeth of Bohemia', in *Giving the Body Its Due*, ed. Maxine Sheets-Johnstone (New York: State University of New York Press).

Johnstone, Albert A. (1996), 'Oneself as oneself and not as another', *Husserl Studies*, **13**, pp. 1–17.

Langer, Susanne K. (1953), *Feeling and Form* (New York: Charles Scribner's Sons).

Langer, Susanne K. (1967), *Mind: An Essay on Human Feeling* (Baltimore, OH: Johns Hopkins Press).

Sheets-Johnstone, Maxine (1986), 'Hunting and the evolution of human intelligence: An alternative view', *The Midwest Quarterly*, **28** (1), pp. 9–35.

Sheets-Johnstone, Maxine (1990), *The Roots of Thinking* (Philadelphia, PA: Temple University Press).

Sheets-Johnstone, Maxine (1992), 'The materialization of the body: A history of western medicine, a history in process', in *Giving the Body Its Due*, ed. Maxine Sheets-Johnstone (New York: State University of New York Press).

Sheets-Johnstone, Maxine (1994), *The Roots of Power: Animate Form and Gendered Bodies* (Chicago, IL: Open Court Publishing).

Sheets-Johnstone, Maxine (1996), 'An empirical-phenomenological critique of the social construction of infancy', *Human Studies*, **19**, pp. 1–16.

Sheets-Johnstone, Maxine (1998), *The Primacy of Movement* (Amsterdam: John Benjamins).

Smith, Linda B. and Thelen, Esther (1993), *A Dynamic Systems Approach to Development: Applications* (Cambridge, MA: Bradford Books/MIT Press).

Stern, Daniel N. (1985), *The Interpersonal World of the Infant* (New York: Basic Books).

Stern, Daniel N. (1990), *Diary of a Baby* (New York: Basic Books).

Stern, Daniel N. (forthcoming), 'Vitality contours', in *Early Social Cognition*, ed. P. Rochat (Hillsdale, NJ: Lawrence Erlbaum Associates).

Strawson, Galen (1997), ' "The self" ', *Journal of Consciousness Studies*, **4** (5–6), pp. 405–28. Reprinted in this volume, pp. 1–24.

Strawson, Peter (1959), *Individuals* (London: Methuen & Co.).

Thelen, Esther and Smith, Linda B. (1994), *A Dynamic Systems Approach to the Development of Cognition and Action* (Cambridge, MA: Bradford Books/MIT Press).

Welton, Donn (1977), 'Structure and genesis in Husserl's phenomenology', in *Husserl: Expositions and Appraisals*, ed. Frederick A. Elliston and Peter McCormick (Notre Dame, IN: University of Notre Dame Press).

Dan Zahavi and Josef Parnas

Phenomenal Consciousness and Self-awareness

A Phenomenological Critique of Representational Theory

Given the recent interest in the subjective or phenomenal dimension of consciousness it is no wonder that many authors have once more started to speak of the need for phenomenological considerations. Often however the term 'phenomenology' is being used simply as a synonym for 'folk psychology', and in our chapter we argue that it would be far more fruitful to turn to the argumentation to be found within the continental tradition inaugurated by Husserl. In order to exemplify this claim, we criticize Rosenthal's higher-order thought theory as well as Strawson's contribution to this volume, and argue that a phenomenological analysis of the nature of self-awareness can provide us with a more sophisticated and accurate model for understanding both phenomenal consciousness and the notion of self.

Cette conscience (de) soi, nous ne devons pas la considérer comme une nouvelle conscience, mais comme *le seul mode d'existence qui soit possible pour une conscience de quelque chose.*

Sartre

I

'Phenomenal consciousness' has again become a respectable scientific and philosophical topic. After a long period of neo-behaviouristic confusion, it has become increasingly clear that an exhaustive and adequate account of consciousness cannot satisfy itself with a mere functional analysis of intentional behaviour, but must also take the first-personal or subjective dimension of experience seriously. As Nagel has pointed out, a necessary requirement for any coherent reductionism is that the entity to be reduced is properly understood (Nagel, 1974, p. 437). An attempt to naturalize consciousness must take its subjectivity seriously, that is, it must account for the fact that there is something it is like for the subject to be conscious, otherwise the procedure will be question-begging.

However, not only has the problem of phenomenal consciousness become a popular theme. Recently, a number of analytical philosophers have even started to emphasize the importance of *phenomenological* considerations. To take but two examples: In his book *Consciousness Reconsidered*, Owen Flanagan argues in favour of what he calls the natural method. If we wish to undertake a serious investigation of consciousness, we should not only make use of neuroscientific and psychological (functional) analyses, but also give phenomenology its due (Flanagan, 1992, p. 11). In the opening chapter of this volume Galen Strawson[1] has claimed that a phenomenology of the self must precede a metaphysics of the self, and that the former investigation into the *sense* of the self will put constraints upon the latter investigation into the *nature* of the self (Strawson, pp. 1–4). Thus, when studying consciousness, rather than, say, deep-sea ecology, we should take phenomenological considerations into account, since an important and non-negligible feature of consciousness is the way in which it is experienced by the subject.

But what exactly do Flanagan and Strawson refer to when they speak of 'phenomenology?' Neither makes the obvious move — namely a reference to the continental philosophical tradition bearing that name — nor, however, do they ever provide any particular clear definition, but appear to understand 'phenomenology' as a kind of a-theoretical and pre-scientific account of how things seem to be at a perceptual or introspective glance. That is, they tacitly identify phenomenology and the common-sense considerations of 'folk psychology'.

For anybody familiar with the continental tradition inaugurated by Husserl, and developed and transformed by, among many others, Scheler, Heidegger, Fink, Sartre, Merleau-Ponty, Lévinas and Henry, this notion of phenomenology will strike one as both vague and rather toothless.

The aim of this chapter will be to argue that phenomenology, understood in a far more strict and technical (continental) sense, can make significant contributions to a study of consciousness. In our view, it is counter-productive to continue to disregard the detailed analyses to be found in the phenomenological tradition in the context of the upsurge of theoretical and empirical interest in the subjective or phenomenal dimension of consciousness.[2] We will argue that the approach found in continental phenomenology provides us with a more sophisticated and accurate model of conscious experience than the models currently in vogue in cognitive sciences, namely the so-called higher-order representation theories. Our exposition will draw upon *arguments* found within the phenomenological tradition rather than on the corresponding phenomenological *analyses* which are behind these arguments. This limitation is deliberate, given the critical scope of the current chapter.

The main part of our chapter will be devoted to an analysis of the relation between phenomenal consciousness, the notion of self, and self-awareness. We will present a critique of higher-order representation theory of phenomenal awareness, which — in our view — is highly paradigmatic of the current cognitivist analyses of consciousness. This critique will be followed by an analysis of Strawson's approach to the nature of self. We will repeat our claim that continental phenomenology offers a better conceptual framework and is more faithful to the analysed subjective experience than his analytically inspired approach. Finally, we will present a brief case-study of a patient suffering from schizophrenia. Continental phenomenology, as a truly applied discipline, has long been influencing psychiatric research, especially in the domain of

[1] All undated references to 'Strawson' in the current chapter are to Galen Strawson's opening chapter in this volume (pp. 1–24).

[2] In a recent 'field guide' to the present status of philosophical issues in the study of consciousness, Güzeldere is cautious enough to point out that his guide is only an introduction to one particular perspective, namely the one to be found in the analytic tradition (Güzeldere, 1997a, pp.1, 46).

schizophrenia. This detour into psychopathology is intended to illustrate certain aspects of the phenomenological method as well as to shed some light upon the nature of self-awareness, because schizophrenia is a human affliction in which the conditions of normal self-experience are sharply illuminated.

II

Why introduce the question of self-awareness in connection with an examination of phenomenal consciousness? Often, self-awareness is taken to designate a higher-order representation, and surely no one is prepared to identify such a state with the mere occurrence of phenomenal consciousness? But although self-awareness can be used to describe the situation in which I reflectively recognize that *I* am perceiving a candle, or realize that *I* am the bearer of private mental states, or identify my own mirror image, or refer to myself using the first-person pronoun, it is also possible and legitimate to speak of self-awareness in a more basic but also more fundamental sense, namely whenever I am pre-reflectively aware of my feeling of sorrow, or my burning pain, or my perception of a candle, i.e., whenever I am acquainted with an experience in its *first-personal mode of givenness*. That is, it is possible to speak of self-awareness the moment I am no longer simply conscious of a foreign object, but of my *experience* of the object as well, for in this case my subjectivity reveals itself to me.

Thus, in much phenomenological literature, the discussion of self-awareness is not so much a discussion of how consciousness is aware of *a self* (understood as a distinct pole of identity, the one *having* or *possessing* the different experiences), as it is a discussion of how consciousness is aware of *itself*. In other words, the question of self-awareness is basically taken to be a question of how consciousness experiences itself, how it is given to itself, how it manifests itself. On this account, the only type of experience which would lack self-awareness, would be an experience I was not conscious of, that is, an 'unconscious experience'.

In the following we will speak of the *first-personal givenness* of phenomenal consciousness in terms of self-awareness. Whereas the object of my perceptual experience is intersubjectively accessible in the sense that it can in principle be given to others in the same way that it is given for me, my perceptual experience itself is given directly only to me. It is this first-personal givenness of the experience which makes it *subjective*. In contrast to physical objects which can exist regardless of whether or not they *de facto* appear for a subject, conscious experiences are essentially characterized by having a subjective 'feel' to them, i.e., a certain (phenomenal) quality of 'what it is like' or what it 'feels' like to have them (Nagel, 1986, pp. 15–16; Jackson, 1982; James, 1890, I, p. 478). Whereas we cannot ask what it feels like to be a piece of soap or a radiator, we can ask what it is like to be a chicken, an alligator or a human being, because we take them to be conscious, i.e., to have experiences. To undergo a conscious experience necessarily means that there is something it is like for the subject to have that experience (Nagel, 1974, p. 436; Searle, 1992, pp. 131–2). This is obviously true of bodily sensations like pain or nausea and moods such as depression or happiness. But it has also been taken to be the case with, for instance, perceptual experiences such as tasting an omelette, feeling an ice-cube, or seeing a bumblebee and for intentional feelings such as having a desire for chocolate. Ultimately it has been argued that it is a serious mistake to limit the phenomenal dimension of experience to *sensory* qualia (Smith, 1989, pp. 82, 95; Flanagan, 1992, pp. 61–8; Goldman, 1997,

p. 122; Van Gulick, 1997, p. 559; Strawson, 1994, pp. 12, 194). There is also something it is like for the subject to entertain abstract beliefs. Yes — there is even something it is like to contemplate the problem of self-awareness. But insofar as there is something it is like for the subject to have experiences, there must be some awareness of these experiences themselves; in short, there must be self-awareness. And obviously, this self-awareness is not of a very sophisticated, propositional type. There is something it is like to taste water or be scared even for creatures such as cows or chickens, which are (presumably) incapable of entertaining higher-order beliefs.[3]

One reason for being critical of this attempt to characterize mere phenomenal consciousness in terms of *self*-awareness, would be the holding of a so-called *no-ownership* view, according to which experiences are subject- or ego-less: They are not states or properties of anyone, but mental events which simply occur (Strawson, 1959, p. 95). A classical version of this position can be found in Hume, who is famous for the following statement:

> For my part, when I enter intimately into what I call *myself*, I always stumble on some particular perception or other, of heat or cold, light or shade, love or hatred, pain or pleasure. I never can catch *myself* at any time without a perception, and never can observe any thing but the perception (Hume, 1888, p. 252).

More recently, it has been claimed that it is possible to have strictly *impersonal* experiences, which do not include any (not even an implicit) reference to oneself as the subject of the experience.[4] Thus, even if one had to concede that two persons — who had two simultaneous and qualitatively identical experiences — would still have two

---

[3] As James writes (quoting Lotze): 'Even the trodden worm [. . .] contrasts his own suffering self with the whole remaining universe, though he have no clear conception either of himself or of what the universe may be' (James, 1890, I, p. 289). As should be clear, our view on the 'What is it like?' question is very much in line with Rudd's recent account (Rudd, 1998).

[4] One example given is the following:

> 'In a dream, I can seem to see myself from a point of view outside my own body. I might seem to see myself running towards this point of view. Since it is myself that I seem to see running in this direction, this direction cannot be towards myself. I might say that I seem to see myself running towards the seer's point of view.' In this case my dream-perception would not entail a reference to myself as the subject of experience, but merely as the object of experience (Parfit, 1987, p. 221).

As Klawonn has pointed out, however, this example is problematic, since Parfit is using the words 'I' and 'myself' to refer to two quite different things:

> Take for example the sentence, 'I might seem to see myself running towards this point of view', or the sentence, 'it is myself that I seem to see running in this direction'. Here the use of the word 'I' (in 'I seem to see . . .') is linked up with the first-person perspective of the seer, whereas 'myself' is used to refer to a body — or somebody — that is present in the visual field of the seer. And when Parfit talks about 'running towards the seer's point of view', it is certainly not any seer's point of view which is relevant in this context. What he is talking about is the point of view of the seer who is myself — seen from the point of view of the person who is having the dream. The uses of the word 'I' and 'myself' which are linked up with the first-person perspective are — as far as I can see — the fundamental ones, whereas the possibility of referring to my body as seen from the outside as 'myself' is a secondary one which is created by my tendency to identify with the body that I am normally associated with. If my body were to become 'an external object' more permanently, I would not continue using the word 'myself' about it; and if this body also had its own subjective field of experience — so that it was not just a body, but somebody — I would not consider this individual as being myself. It would be somebody else (Klawonn 1990, p. 47).

numerical distinct experiences, this would not be the case because each of the experiences had a different *subject*, but simply because 'one of these experiences is *this* experience, occurring in *this* particular mental life, and the other is *that* experience, occurring in *that* other particular mental life.' (Parfit, 1987, p. 517; cf. p. 252.)

An objection to this position comes to mind, however, the moment one adopts a first-person perspective. Is it really true that the primary difference between my perception and my friend's perception is that my perception is *this* one and his *that* one? Is this not, as Klawonn has argued, a parasitic and derived characterization? Is it not rather the case that my experience is *this* one exactly because it is *mine*, i.e., given in an irreducible *first-personal mode of presentation*, whereas the other's experience is not given in a first-personal mode for *me*, and therefore no part of *my* mental life? (Klawonn, 1991, pp. 28–9.) Let us assume that I encounter a crying child. In this case, we would say that I experience not my own sorrow, but the sorrow of somebody else. I am conscious of another subject. But what is it that permits me to distinguish between my own experience (of empathy) and the other's experience (of sorrow)? Why do I not occasionally confuse my own experience with the other's experience? Whereas my own experience is given to me directly in a first-personal mode of presentation, this is obviously not the case with the child's sorrow. On the contrary, the first-personal givenness of the other's experience is fundamentally inaccessible to me. It is exactly therefore that the other is given to me as an other.[5]

Thus, it has been suggested that it is exactly the *primary presence* or first-personal givenness of a group of experiences that constitutes their intrinsic *myness*. Whether a certain experience is experienced as mine or not, does not depend upon something apart from the experience but upon the givenness of the experience (Klawonn, 1991, pp. 5, 141–2; James, 1890, I, pp. 226–7; Smith, 1989, p. 93). In short, if the experience is given in a first-personal mode of presentation to me, it is (at least tacitly) given as *my* experience, and is therefore a case of self-awareness.

If this is the case, Hume did in fact overlook something in his analysis, namely, the specific givenness of his own experiences. He was looking for the self in the wrong place, so to speak. To be self-aware is not to apprehend a pure self apart from the experience, but to be acquainted with an experience in its first-personal mode of givenness, that is, from 'within'. The subject or self referred to in *self*-awareness is not something apart from or beyond the experience, but simply a feature of its givenness. As the French phenomenologist Michel Henry would say: It is the very first-personal mode of presentation of the experience, its very self-manifestation, which constitutes the self in its most basic form, as the dimension of subjecthood, *ipseity* (Henry, 1963, pp. 580–1; 1965, p. 53; 1989, p. 55). Thus, in our view, phenomenal consciousness is simply a primitive type of self-awareness, and we can therefore only agree with Flanagan when he writes: '. . . all subjective experience is self-conscious in the weak

---

[5] Husserl (1959), p. 175; (1962), p. 416; (1973a), p. 139; (1973b), pp. 28, 56; (1973c), p. 12. To quote James:

> No thought even comes into direct *sight* of a thought in another personal consciousness than its own. Absolute insulation, irreducible pluralism, is the law. It seems as if the elementary psychic fact were not *thought* or *this thought* or *that thought*, but *my thought*, every thought being *owned*. Neither contemporaneity, nor proximity in space, nor similarity of quality and content are able to fuse thoughts together which are sundered by this barrier of belonging to different personal minds. The breaches between such thoughts are the most absolute breaches in nature (James, 1890, I, p. 226).

sense that there is something it is like for the subject to have that experience. This involves a sense that the experience is the subject's experience, that it happens to her, occurs in her stream' (Flanagan, 1992, p. 194). This is perhaps also what Strawson is aiming at when he claims that one has to take the way in which *consciousness appears to itself* into account when considering the underpinnings of the sense of the self (Strawson, p. 19).

III

But what is the nature and structure of self-awareness? How is it brought about? Locke used the term *reflection* to designate our mind's ability to turn its view inward upon itself, making its own operations the object of its contemplation (Locke, 1975, pp. 107, 127). Thus we can describe a theory stating that self-awareness is the result of consciousness directing its 'gaze' at itself, taking itself as its object, and thus becoming aware of itself, as a *reflection theory of self-awareness*.

It is not difficult to find contemporary defenders of some version of this theory, although the discussion is often presented as being concerned with the nature of (phenomenal) consciousness, and not with the issue of self-awareness. (However, since we interpret the first-personal givenness of phenomenal consciousness as a primitive type of self-awareness, the discussion remains of immediate relevance for our topic).

In *A Materialist Theory of the Mind*, D.M. Armstrong advocates a higher-order representation theory, and claims that there is a close analogy between perception and introspection. A perception is a mental event whose intentional object is a situation in the physical world. Introspection is a mental event whose intentional object is other mental happenings occurring in the *same* mind. It is, he claims, only by becoming the *object* of an introspection that a mental state can be conscious, i.e., manifest itself subjectively. Thus, 'consciousness is simply a further mental state, a state "directed" towards the original inner states' (Armstrong, 1993, p. 94). Just as there are many features of our physical environment which we do not perceive, there are many mental states of which we are *unconscious*, namely all those which we do not currently introspect. Just as one must distinguish between the perception and that which is perceived, one must distinguish between the introspection and that which is introspected. A mental state cannot be aware of itself, any more than a man can eat himself up. But of course, the introspection may itself be the object of a further introspective awareness, and so on.[6]

Recently, David Rosenthal has argued in favour of refining Armstrong's higher-order perception (HOP) theory with a higher-order thought (HOT) theory. As Rosenthal points out, there is more to the fact of being a conscious mental state than being the thematic object of introspection. A state can be non-introspectively conscious, and in fact introspective conscious states presuppose non-introspective conscious states (Rosenthal, 1997, p. 730). On the face of it, the claim that a mental state can be conscious even when we do not pay explicit and thematic attention to it seems quite reasonable, and Rosenthal's distinction between introspective and non-introspective conscious states might at first be taken to mirror a traditional phenomenological distinction, namely the one between a thematic and reflective type of self-awareness on the one hand, and a tacit and unthematic kind of pre-reflective self-awareness on the other.

---

[6] Armstrong (1993), pp. 323–6. For further examples of the claim that conscious mental activity (in distinction from unconscious mental activity) is the result of an internal monitoring, cf. Lycan (1997).

The moment Rosenthal starts to analyse the nature of this non-introspective consciousness it becomes clear, however, that he has something quite different in mind. In fact, Rosenthal argues that if one wishes to come up with a non-trivial and informative account of consciousness one must at any price avoid the claim that consciousness is an intrinsic property of our mental states. To call something intrinsic is, for Rosenthal, to imply that it is something unanalysable and mysterious, and consequently beyond the reach of scientific and theoretical study: 'We would insist that being conscious is an intrinsic property of mental states only if we were convinced that it lacked articulated structure, and thus defied explanation' (Rosenthal, 1993, p. 157). Although Rosenthal acknowledges that there is something intuitively appealing about taking consciousness to be an intrinsic property, he still thinks that this approach must be avoided since it will impede a naturalistic (and reductionist) account, which seeks to explain consciousness by appeal to non-conscious mental states, and non-conscious mental states in non-mental terms (Rosenthal, 1993, p. 165; 1997, p. 735).

For Rosenthal, the property of being conscious is not an intrinsic property, but a *relational property*, that is, a mental state is only conscious if it stands in the appropriate relation to something else (Rosenthal, 1997, pp. 736–7). More precisely, for a state to be conscious is for it to be accompanied by a suitable higher-order thought, namely a higher-order thought *about* that state. Thus, consciousness is a kind of higher-order representing of lower-level mental states and processes. The higher-order thought confers intransitive consciousness on the mental state it is about. In fact, a mental state is intransitively conscious exactly insofar as there is a higher-order thought which is transitively conscious *of* it. This model does not lead to an infinite regress, however, since the higher-order thought does not itself have to be conscious. This will only be the case if it is accompanied by a third-order thought (Rosenthal, 1997, p. 743). It is this model which then allows Rosenthal to make his distinction between non-introspective conscious thoughts, and introspective conscious thoughts. A mental state is non-introspectively conscious when accompanied by a second-order thought. Introspection occurs when the second-order thought is accompanied by a third-order thought that makes the second-order thought conscious (Rosenthal, 1997, p. 745).

One question which any higher-order representation theory has to answer is the following: Why is the second-order thought, B, directed at the first-order mental state, A? What is it that makes B conscious of A? Rosenthal writes that a 'higher-order thought, B, is an awareness of the mental-state token, A, simply because A is the intentional object of B' (Rosenthal, 1993, p. 160). At the same time, however, Rosenthal is well aware that the relation between the mental state and the higher-order state that makes it conscious is unlike ordinary intentional relations. On the one hand, we only regard mental states as being conscious if we are conscious of them in some suitably unmediated way, namely directly and non-inferentially.[7] On the other hand, Rosenthal argues that for a mental state to be conscious, is not simply for us to be directly conscious of it; we must be directly conscious of being *ourselves* in that very state: 'Only if one's thought is about oneself as such, and not just about someone that happens to be oneself, will the mental state be a conscious state. Otherwise it might

---

[7] Rosenthal (1997), p. 737. Otherwise, an unconscious mental process would qualify as conscious, simply because we could infer that we would have to have it.

turn out in any particular case that the state was a state of somebody else instead.'
(Rosenthal, 1997, p. 750; cf. 1997, p. 741.)

Why does Rosenthal feel obliged to make this crucial specification, which as we
shall soon see is fatal for his own theory? Why is it necessary that my consciousness
of a mental state includes a consciousness of *myself* being in that very mental state?
Let us employ a distinction between two kinds of self-reference, one external and the
other internal, to clarify the argument. The external kind of self-reference is the one
available from the third-person perspective. I can refer to an object by way of a proper
name, a demonstrative or a definite description, and occasionally this object is myself. When I refer to myself in this way, I am referring to myself in exactly the same
way that I can refer to Others, and Others can refer to me (the only difference being
that I am the one doing it, thus making the reference a self-reference). Apart from
being external and contingent, this kind of self-reference is also non-emphatic, since
it can occur without my knowledge of it, that is, I can refer to myself from the third-
person perspective without realizing that I myself am the referent. In contrast, the
self-reference available from the first-person perspective is of an internal and
emphatic kind. When one is directly and non-inferentially conscious of one's own
occurrent perceptions or pains, they are characterized by a first-personal givenness,
that immediately reveals them as being one's own. When I am aware of an occurrent
pain, perception or thought, the experience in question is given unmediated, non-
inferentially and non-criterially as *mine*, i.e., I do not first scrutinize a specific perception or feeling of pain, and subsequently identify it as being mine. If I am dizzy I
can neither be in doubt nor mistaken about who the subject of that experience is, and it
is nonsensical to ask whether I am sure that I am the one who is dizzy, or to demand a
specification of the criteria being used by me in determining whether or not the felt
dizziness is really mine.

Obviously, any convincing theory of consciousness has to account for the first-
personal or egocentric givenness of our conscious states, and has to respect the difference between our consciousness of a foreign object (that we encounter in any ordinary intentional act) and our self-awareness (that we presumably encounter in the
relation between a second-order thought and a first-order mental state). Any convincing theory of self-awareness has to be able to explain the distinction between *intentionality*, which is characterized by a *difference* between the subject and the object of
experience, and *self-awareness*, which implies some form of *identity*. The decisive
question is whether Rosenthal's (and Armstrong's) model can do that. Rosenthal
argues that a perception is given as a perception that *I* am having as a result of it being
the object of an unconscious second-order mental state. But will this really do the job,
will this really permit us to explain the first-personal givenness of the experience?

Any higher-order representation theory operates with a duality of moments. One
mental state is taking another mental state as its object, and we consequently have to
distinguish the two. Of course, it is essential for the higher-order representation
theory to overcome or negate this division or difference and to posit both moments as
identical (cf. below) — otherwise, we would not be aware that we were *ourselves* in
that very state. But why should an interaction between otherwise unconscious
processes cause one of them to become conscious? Why should the fact of being the
intentional object of an unconscious higher-order act confer first-personal givenness
or 'myness' on an otherwise unconscious first-order mental state?

The higher-order thought theory claims that an act of perception, in order to manifest itself phenomenally (and not merely remain *unconscious*), must await its objectivation by a *subsequent* higher-order thought. But in order for the act of perception to appear as *my* act, as an act or state that *I* am in, it is not sufficient that the act in question is grasped by a higher-order thought. As the previous distinction between emphatic and non-emphatic self-reference illustrated, there is a difference between being aware of some self and being aware of oneself. If I am to realize — as Rosenthal admits — that the first-order experience is *mine*, i.e., that it is an experience that I am in or having, it is not enough that I am *de facto* thinking of it, I also need to know of the identity between myself and the act in question. In other words, the first-order experience must be grasped as being identical with the higher-order thought. Since a *numerical identity* is excluded, the identity in question must be that of belonging to the same subject or being part of the same stream of consciousness. This poses a difficulty, however, for what should enable the unconscious higher-order thought to realize that the act of perception belongs to the same subjectivity as itself? If it is to encounter something as itself — if it is to recognize or identify something as itself — it obviously needs a prior acquaintance with itself (Cramer, 1974, p. 563). In order to identify something as oneself one has to hold something true of it that one already knows to be true of oneself. This self-knowledge might in some cases be grounded on some further identification, but the supposition that *every* item of self-knowledge rests on identification leads to an infinite regress (Shoemaker, 1968, p. 561). As Shoemaker has made clear, this even applies to introspection. Thus, it will not do to claim that introspection is distinguished by the fact that its object has a property which immediately identifies it as being me, since no other self could possible have it, namely the property of being the private and exclusive object of exactly my introspection. This explanation will not do, since I will be unable to identify an introspected self as myself by the fact that it is introspectively observed by me unless I know it is the object of *my* introspection, i.e., unless I know that it is in fact *me* that undertakes this introspection, and this knowledge cannot itself be based on introspection if one is to avoid an infinite regress (Shoemaker, 1968, pp. 562–3).

IV

First-personal givenness cannot come about as the result of the encounter between two unconscious acts. Consequently, the higher-order thought must either await a third-order thought that will confer consciousness on it, in which case we are confronted with a vicious infinite regress, *or* it must be admitted that it is itself already in a state of phenomenal consciousness *prior to its objectivation*, and that would of course involve us in a circular explanation, presupposing that which was meant to be explained, and implicitly rejecting the thesis of the higher-order thought theory of consciousness: that all phenomenal consciousness is brought about by a process of higher-order representation (cf. Henrich, 1970, p. 268; 1982, p. 64; Frank, 1991, pp. 498, 529).

If a higher-order representation theory is to explain phenomenal consciousness, it has to explain the unique first-personal manifestation of our conscious states, but this is exactly what it fails to do.

Thus, it is highly questionable whether one can account for the unique first-personal givenness of consciousness by sticking to a traditional model of object-consciousness and then simply replacing the external object with an internal one. In fact, when one is non-introspectively conscious of one's thoughts, feelings, beliefs and desires, one is not *given* to oneself as an *object* at all. And this is exactly what Rosenthal overlooks.

More generally, there is reason to warn against taking phenomenal consciousness as a relational property, be it a relation between two acts or a relation between the mental state and itself (cf. Henrich, 1966; 1970; Cramer, 1974; Pothast, 1971). Every relation entails a distinction between two (or more) relata, and it is doubtful whether one could account for the immediacy, unity and infallibility of self-awareness (particularly its so-called *immunity to the error of misidentification*), if it were in any way a mediated process. As a result, the first-personal givenness of an experience cannot come about as the result of a self-identification, a reflection, an inner vision or introspection, nor should it be conceived as a type of intentionality or as a conceptually mediated propositional attitude, all of which entails the distinction between two or more relata. The basic self-awareness of an experience is not mediated by any foreign elements such as concepts and classificatory criteria. It is an immediate and intrinsic *self-acquaintance* which is characterized by being completely *irrelational*.[8]

We consequently have to choose the second of the following two theories:

(1) Consciousness is strictly and exclusively conscious of the intentional object. There is no simultaneous self-awareness. Thus the act itself is unconscious, but it can be made conscious through a subsequent, higher-order intentional act, which takes the first act as its object. In this way consciousness can be compared to a knife, which is able to cut other things, but not itself.
(2) Consciousness is self-luminous. It is characterized by intentionality, but being intentionally aware of objects, it is simultaneously self-aware through and in itself. Its self-awareness is not due to a secondary act or reflex but is a constitutive moment of the experience itself, and consciousness can consequently be compared to a flame, which illuminates other things, and itself as well (Kern, 1989, pp. 51–3; Henry, 1963, p. 173).

The criticism directed at the higher-order thought theory has not been meant to imply that reflective self-awareness and objectifying self-thematization is impossible, but merely that it always presupposes a prior unthematic and pre-reflective self-awareness as its condition of possibility. Thus, it is necessary to distinguish *pre-reflective* self-awareness — which is an immediate, implicit and irrelational, non-objectifying, non-conceptual and non-propositional self-acquaintance — from *reflective* self-awareness — which, at least in certain forms, is an explicit, conceptual and objectifying thematization of consciousness. Rosenthal's higher-order thought theory might at most throw light upon *explicit* self-experience, but not upon the origin of self-awareness as such.

Our acts are pre-reflectively self-aware, but they are also accessible for reflection. They can be reflected upon and thereby brought to our attention (Husserl, 1952, p. 248) and, as both Husserl and Sartre have pointed out, an examination of the

[8] Frank (1986), pp. 34, 61. This raises a question however concerning the infrastructure of self-awareness, addressed elsewhere (see Zahavi, 1998b; 1999).

particular intentional structure of reflection can substantiate the thesis concerning the existence of a pre-reflective self-awareness.[9] The reflected act must already be self-aware, since it is the fact of it being already mine, already being given in the first-personal mode of presentation that allows me to reflect upon it. And the act of reflection must also already be pre-reflectively self-aware, since it is this that permits it to recognize the reflected act as belonging to the same subjectivity as it*self* (Henry, 1965, pp. 76, 153).

V

Let us at this point take a brief look at Strawson's analysis of the self in this volume. Although careful reading of his text at the level of an analysis of single sentences may reveal some agreements between his arguments and our own exposition, there are nevertheless outweighing overall differences, linked to a lack of an adequate frame of reference in Strawson's version of phenomenology.

Strawson emphasizes that a phenomenology of the self must precede any metaphysics of the self. He commits himself, however, from the outset, to a materialistic metaphysics, in a way not unlike that of Rosenthal: the self must be, and will ultimately be, captured not only as a thing, but as a thing which is just as physical as a cow.[10] This metaphysical commitment, despite Strawson's programmatic exclamation of the primary task of phenomenology, cannot avoid contaminating and unnecessarily complicating his analysis.

A more strict phenomenological approach would be to start by asking *how the world and my experiences of it are given to me.* As we have insisted above, original self-awareness does not arise from criterial self-identification, reflection or introspection. To be self-aware is not to apprehend a pure self *distinct* from the experience and then to merge these two together. There is only one component in the self-awareness so described, which means that the experience *is* and *is present to itself*, and it is this very self-presence or self-manifestation which constitutes the self in its most original and fundamental form as *ipseity*. The 'I', the subject of *self*-awareness, is simply a feature of the givenness of the experience. More precisely, the self is disclosed as the invariant dimension of first-personal givenness in the multitude of my intentional acts. Radically speaking, specific modalities of intentional experience are mere modifications of this field of self-presence before the world (Klawonn, 1991, p. 72–85; Henry, 1963, p. 173). There is no difference between the *givenness* of self and the *self-in-itself*, or between the phenomenon of self and its metaphysical nature. Reality is here the same as appearance.[11]

The lack of a phenomenology of *ipseity* creates difficulties in Strawson's further elaboration of the experiential characteristics of the self.

Singularity of the self, both in its synchronic and diachronic experiential aspects, poses immense difficulties: what is a sufficient duration of the 'hiatus-free' episodes of self-consciousness to guarantee the diachronic self-identity, how may the self be

---

[9] Husserl (1973c), pp. 492–3, Sartre (1943), p. 20. As Sartre writes about reflection: 'Elle implique une compréhension pré-réflexive de ce qu'elle veut récupérer comme motivation originelle de la récupération' (Sartre, 1943, p.195). Cf. Henrich (1970), p. 265.

[10] Strawson, p. 21. We are not unaware that Strawson elsewhere acknowledges (Strawson, 1994) that the current concept of matter is insufficient for this purpose.

[11] This is not to say that the phenomenal self might not have *causes*, e.g. cortical brain activity, but these causes are certainly not to be identified with the *self-in-itself.*

located within the saccadic flux of 'radically disjunct irruptions' of our conscious life (Strawson, p. 18), what are the roles of memory, narrative and personality character- istics? Since finally no phenomenological grounding of the singular unity of the self can possibly follow from these second order aspects of the life of consciousness, Strawson concludes, by reference to psychological empirical research, that, 'If there is any support for the belief in the long-term continuity of the self in the nature of moment-to-moment consciousness, *it is derived indirectly from other sources* — the massive constancies and developmental coherencies of *content* that often link up ex- periences through time, and by courtesy of short-term memory, across all the jumps and breaks of flow.'[12] We may even be tempted to suspect that the operation involved in providing the self with a sense of permanence must be executed through a subper- sonal, inferential process, electing or computing the degrees of the content resemblances. In this case the self will emerge as a truly constituted, representational mental object.

But contemplating self-identity and wishing for an ice cream may surely either coexist or rapidly follow each other, and such two contents, if occurring only occa- sionally, cannot amount to a status of a sufficient cause of my feeling myself as being a 'permanent mental thing'. On the contrary, we would claim that *ipseity*, as an un- mediated self-awareness, is a precondition of identity to be experienced across time, saccadic jumps and diversity of mental contents (Klawonn, 1991, pp. 230–1; Henry, 1963). If a memory of a past event is to provide me with a sense of personal continu- ity, it must necessarily entail that the event is remembered as an event *which hap- pened in my field of self-presence*, as an event in the field of first-personal givenness (Klawonn, 1991, pp. 196–202). For this reason, any philosophical account of self- identity, which omits the notion of the original self-awareness and ipseity, becomes question-begging.

VI

Phenomenological interest in schizophrenia research belongs to a longstanding and rich tradition in philosophical thought that draws upon examples from pathology, e.g. Bergson's interest in *aphasia research*, Goldstein's work on *Gestalt psychology*, Merleau-Ponty's on *corporeality*, Binswanger's on the structures of the *Lifeworld* and, more recently, by Gallagher on the *body schema* (Gallagher and Meltzoff, 1996).

The relationship between psychopathology and neurology on the one hand, and phenomenology on the other, can be considered as a particular instantiation of what Gallagher (1997) summarizes as possible ways in which cognitive science and phe- nomenology may interact: (1) a relationship of mutual constraint; (2) a relationship of mutual enlightenment.

Gallagher points out that a relationship of strong constraint must pose a relation- ship not merely of analogy but, recalling Gestalt psychology, isomorphism between the phenomenological analysis and the hypothetical underlying (subpersonal) mechanisms. This requirement amounts to a type-to-type identity theory, which has been long ago discredited for several conceptual and empirical reasons (Searle, 1992). In our view, examples from pathology enrich each side of the relation by dis-

---

[12] Strawson, p. 19; our italics. This is a peculiar, question-begging, argument. As far as perceptual content is concerned, its coherence or familiarity is not only a matter of 'objective' sensory data, but is to a large extent linked to its organization which is dependent upon the subject itself.

closing novel solutions to refractory problems or by revealing hitherto unsuspected difficulties.

In the case of schizophrenia, there is a long line of phenomenological research (Minkowski, 1927; Binswanger, 1956; Blankenburg, 1971; Parnas and Bovet, 1991; Sass, 1992) aiming at comprehension of the symptomatology and its evolution. More recently, phenomenology has been viewed as particularly needed to address questions of pathogenetic mechanisms (Mishara *et al.*, 1998). Psychiatric phenomenology in its clinical application is not an application of ready-made concepts to empirical data, although the conceptual framework is anchored in the phenomenological tradition. Rather, in the encounter with his patient, the clinician is attempting to disclose fundamental forms of intentionality (*Being-in-the-world*) by way of their pathological distortions. This task is achieved by focusing on *ways* of experiencing rather than on the *contents* of experience, through an imaginative reduction of multifarious and accidental clinical features, into more essential, organizing patterns (Parnas and Bovet, 1995).

To put it differently, the phenomenological approach to schizophrenia is based on the premise that the schizophrenic abnormalities involve such profound deviations from aspects of normal human experience that they exhibit usually taken-for-granted, unnoticed conditions of normal daily experience. In a certain sense, the lifeworld of the schizophrenic patient reveals itself after a certain suspension of common-sense assumptions about existence and experience. To say that schizophrenia involves disorders of the self is, at one level, the merest commonplace. The most prominent of the so-called psychotic symptoms in the advanced stages of the disease involve a fundamental alteration of the sense of possession and control of one's own thought, action, sensation, or emotion as exemplified by this report from a patient with chronic schizophrenia:

> When I ate this morning, I felt as if somebody else's head would also be there and would eat with me. It feels like other people would stick their head into my head. When I am chewing, it seems that another tongue comes and takes the food (Angyal, 1936, p. 1036).

Such florid psychotic symptoms are frequently associated with a loss of motivation toward action, a fundamental decline in the vitality or dynamism of the self. 'Da ist ein Ich einfach nicht mehr da,' said Kraepelin, the founder of this disease entity.

We particularly wish to draw attention to clinical manifestations of self-disorders that occur in early stages of the development of schizophrenia, manifestations that may be detectable in prodromal or even premorbid phases of the illness, when the patient is not yet psychotic, but experiences a profound and alarming change, which may be almost ineffable (Parnas, forthcoming). These disorders are, in the early phases, less dramatic than those, like the one quoted above, encountered in the later stages, and are often communicated by the patient as non-specific complaints such as fatigue, depression or lack of energy. If not sufficiently explored, they are frequently overlooked by the treating physician. These disorders are in fact the early, etiological foundation of later, more florid or chronic developments; an understanding of their nature is pertinent to neurobiology, cognitive science and phenomenology. In particular, reports of such patients may shed light on the nature of self and self-experience. The example presented below (the patient's anonymity being preserved) is typical of the characteristics of the disturbed self-experience in early schizophrenia:

A young male patient, high-school graduate, employed as an unskilled worker, hospitalized at the age of 22, reported that during several years he was bothered by a strange feeling of not participating fully in the interactions with his surroundings. He was never entirely *present,* in the sense of never being entirely absorbed or engaged in daily interactions. This experience of disengagement from the world was accompanied by an enhanced tendency to reflect and observe himself. He summarized his condition in one sentence: 'My first personal life has been lost and has been replaced by a third person perspective'. He provided an example: listening to music on his hi-fi he would have an impression that he did not really receive the musical tune in its natural fullness, 'as if something was wrong with the sound itself', and he would try to regulate the parameters of his hi-fi equipment, to no avail, only to realize that he was 'internally monitoring' his own receptivity to music, his own being affected by music, as if he was witnessing his sensory processes rather than possessing them: 'I am being heard!!'. He often engaged in reflection on self-evident daily matters and had difficulties 'in letting things and matters pass by'. He complained of 'not having a stable perspective', i.e. he would regard any matter from all possible points of view with a consequent indecisiveness, feeling of floating around, and, in the end, abstention from action and withdrawal. Periodically, he experienced his own movements as reflected upon and de-automatized. Episodically, his inner speech thinking acquired acoustic quality confined to his skull, becoming a sort of loud monologue. He considered all these experiences as morbid, or at least, not usual. (Parnas *et al.*, forthcoming.)

We have chosen this case from a series of patients from an early recognition study (see Parnas, forthcoming). We would like to highlight certain typical aspects, emphasized in psychopathologic phenomenological research (Blankenburg, 1972; Sass, 1992; Parnas and Bovet, 1991) which illustrate a particular transformation in the structure of experiencing. There is a change on the level of intentionality, in the sense that the perceptual world has changed and acquired more distance, and there is an incipient fragmentation of meaning. However, equally striking is the change in self-experience. What happens here is that the *ipseity*, the normally tacit or unnoticed 'myness' of the experience, which is a precondition or a medium of any natural, spontaneous and absorbed intentionality, is deranged, and becomes an object of introspective intentionality. In this way the patient's perception becomes deprived of its normal *ipseity* matrix. His altered self-presence leads to a phenomenological distance in his perceptual experience: perception is not really felt and he is never really present. There is a peculiar splitting in an observing and observed, represented ego, and the patient reports increasing objectivation of introspective experience.[13] Inner speech is transformed from a medium of thinking to an object-like entity with quasi-perceptual characteristics.

In fact, the patient's report is close to the account of the self which we criticized in the previous sections: the self as an object — a representation — and self-consciousness as a consequence of an objectifying intentional act. If we consider the schizophrenic experience along the lines proposed by phenomenology, we may conclude that the presented case illustrates phenomenal priority, in the sense of foundation, of unmediated self-awareness as an intrinsic feature of experience, and a secondary and derived status of self-awareness, linked to acts of reflection and objectivation. The dissociation, which our patient exhibits between his experience and his experiencing,

---

[13] Similar altered states may occur as a result of excessive introspection or meditative practice (cf. Hunt, 1986)

or his experiencing of his own experience, points to the original identity of self-awareness and intentional experience.

VII

Why does the phenomenological approach to consciousness continue to be ignored by analytical philosophy of mind, and what are its major advantages *vis-à-vis* 'folk psychology'? Why have recent analytical philosophy of mind and cognitive science, despite their increased occupation with phenomenal consciousness, made such scant use of continental phenomenology? Why do they, if they at all acknowledge the resources to be found in the philosophical tradition, bypass Husserl, Sartre, Merleau-Ponty and Henry, and return all the way to Kant, James or Brentano?[14] Surely, one reason is the fact that continental phenomenology has evolved as an independent tradition, with its own method, topics, and rather complex terminology. Another reason is an amazing number of misunderstandings concerning its precise nature. If one consults the entry on Husserl in the *Oxford Dictionary of Philosophy*, one will for instance read that Frege took Husserl's initial work to be characterized by an 'impenetrable fog', and learn that Husserl had a penchant for an obscure terminology, but that he is well-known for having advocated a transcendental idealism which bracketed all external questions, and took a solipsistic, disembodied Cartesian ego as its starting point (Blackburn, 1994, p.181). Such a presentation might extinguish any initial interest.[15]

Why should one prefer continental phenomenology to 'folk psychology'? Because the former can provide far richer and far more refined analytical and systematical descriptions than the pre-scientific insights of the latter. To investigate the first-personal dimension thoroughly calls for a number of methodological interventions, a fundamental change of attitude, a process of purification, or as Husserl would put it, a kind of *phenomenological reduction*,[16] and cannot simply be left to folk psychology. As phenomenology has repeatedly pointed out: the so-called natural and pre-scientific attitude is in fact suffused with heavy metaphysical presuppositions and theoretical prejudices, and it is a mistake to assume that we can obtain the raw atheoretical data serving as constraints for our theoretical models on the basis of common-sense assumptions. The primary concern of the phenomenological analyses is to provide an adequate description of the phenomena. It is not to find room for consciousness within an already well established materialistic or objectivistic framework. In fact, the very attempt to do the latter, thereby assuming that consciousness is merely yet another (physical or psychical) object in the world, might very well prevent one from disclosing — let alone clarifying — some of the most interesting aspects of consciousness, including the true epistemical and ontological significance of the first-person perspective.

---

[14] To mention one example, Flanagan makes extensive use of James' analysis of the stream of consciousness, thereby disregarding the fact that Husserl's investigation of inner time-consciousness — albeit considerably more difficult — is generally regarded as being superior (cf. Linschoten, 1961; Brough, 1972; Cobb-Stevens, 1974; 1998).

[15] To mention but a few recent works undermining this interpretation: Hart (1992); Bernet (1994); Depraz (1995); Steinbock (1995) and Zahavi (1996; 1999).

[16] For a more detailed examination of Husserl's different ways to the phenomenological reduction, see Depraz (1999).

Rosenthal's argumentation exemplifies two assumptions that phenomenology has been to wont to criticize. First, it clearly shows the danger of basing one's investigation on a prior commitment to the project of naturalization rather than on phenomenological evidence. Instead of examining the actual givenness of consciousness, certain models are ruled out in advance. Secondly, it is simply a mistake to think that recognizing something as intrinsic will put a stop to further analyses. As numerous phenomenological analyses show there is far more to the question of phenomenal consciousness than a mere recognition of its existence. To elucidate structures and principles of phenomenal consciousness requires investigations into the connection between self, person, subjectivity, first-personal givenness, thematic and marginal consciousness, reflective and pre-reflective self-awareness, time-consciousness, body-awareness etc. That is, it calls for a disciplined approach and cannot simply be left to folk psychology.[17]

The problem of consciousness should not be addressed on the background of an unquestioned objectivism, but in connection with overarching epistemological and transcendental considerations. Frequently, the assumption has been that a better understanding of physical systems will allow us to understand consciousness better, and rarely, that a better understanding of consciousness might allow us to understand the metaphysical nature of physical reality better. But if one simply presupposes the validity of naturalism, and conceives of, say, perceptual consciousness as a causal relation between two different and separate *objects*, a psychical and a physical, one might already have presupposed far too much. This is why the theory of intentionality has often assumed a central position in phenomenological thinking. The primary concern of phenomenology is not to answer how a physical world could give rise to a first-person perspective, but to examine how objectivity and intersubjectivity are established from a first-person perspective.

Through the study of the world-directedness of consciousness, it is possible not only to achieve insights into the structure of subjectivity, but also into the nature of objectivity. That something like a conscious appropriation of the world is possible does not merely tell us something about consciousness, but also about the world. Thus part of the phenomenological work is to examine different types of objects exactly as they are intended and given, that is, as correlates of intentional experiences. But to examine the objects in their manifestation or significance for consciousness is exactly to examine and clarify dimensions of the objects, and not parts or structures of consciousness. For that very reason, it is simply wrong to identify phenomenological descriptions with introspection, as it has occasionally been done. The aim of the phenomenological reduction is not to effect a radical introspection, it is not to look inside, but to gain new insights into that which manifests itself, and into its condition of possibility.

This way of discussing consciousness — as the constitutive dimension that allows for identification and manifestation, as the 'place' 'in' which the world can reveal and articulate itself — is quite different from any attempt to treat it (folk psychologically or neurophysiologically) as merely yet another (psychical or physical) object in the world. It is of course true that phenomenology, apart from its orientation towards the

---

[17] For more detailed phenomenological analyses of these issues, cf. Zahavi (1998a; 1998b; 1998c). For a full scale presentation and discussion of the theories of self-awareness found in some recent analytical philosophy of mind, in the Heidelberg-school and in phenomenology, cf. Zahavi (1999).

givenness of objects, is also concerned — in its so-called *noetic* analyses — with disclosing the intrinsic structures of experience, but even these analyses can hardly be called introspective, since phenomenology does not share the central assumption of introspective psychology: that the object under investigation is an intramundane psychical entity. To use the classical formulation, phenomenology is not concerned with empirical consciousness, but with transcendental subjectivity.

References

Angyal, A (1936), 'The experience of the body-self in schizophrenia', *Archives of Neurology and Psychiatry*, **35**, pp. 1029–53.

Armstrong, D.M. (1993), *A Materialist Theory of the Mind* (London: Routledge).

Bernet, R. (1994), *La vie du sujet* (Paris: PUF).

Binswanger, L. (1956), *Drei Formen missglückten Daseins : Verstiegenheit, Verschrobenheit, Manieriertheit* (Tübingen: Niemeyer).

Blackburn, S. (1994), *The Oxford Dictionary of Philosophy* (Oxford: Oxford University Press).

Blankenburg, W. (1971), *Der Verlust der natürlichen Selbstverständlichkeit. Ein Beitrag zur Psychopathologie symptomarmer Schizophrenien* (Stuttgart: Enke).

Block, N., Flanagan, O. & Güzeldere, G. (ed. 1997), *The Nature of Consciousness* (Cambridge, MA: MIT Press).

Brough, J.B. (1972), 'The Emergence of an Absolute Consciousness in Husserl's Early Writings on Time-Consciousness', *Man and World*, **5**, pp. 298–326.

Cobb-Stevens, R. (1998), 'James and Husserl: Time-consciousness and the intentionality of presence and absence,' in *Self-awareness, Temporality, and Alterity*, ed. D. Zahavi (Dordrecht: Kluwer Academic Publishers).

Cramer, K. (1974), '"Erlebnis". Thesen zu Hegels Theorie des Selbstbewußtseins mit Rücksicht auf die Aporien eines Grundbegriffs nachhegelscher Philosophie', in *Stuttgarter Hegel-Tage 1970*, ed. H.-G. Gadamer (Bonn).

Depraz, N. (1995), *Transcendance et Incarnation* (Paris: Vrin).

Depraz, N. (1999), 'The Phenomenological reduction as praxis,' *Journal of Consciousness Studies*, **6** (2–3), pp. 95–110..

Flanagan, O. (1992), *Consciousness Reconsidered* (Cambridge, MA: MIT Press).

Frank, M. (1986), *Die Unhintergehbarkeit von Individualität* (Frankfurt am Main: Suhrkamp).

Frank, M. (Ed. 1991), *Selbstbewußtseinstheorien von Fichte bis Sartre* (Frankfurt am Main: Suhrkamp).

Gallagher, S. and Meltzoff, A.N. (1996), 'The earliest sense of self and others: Merleau-Ponty and recent developmental studies', *Philosophical Psychology*, **9**, pp. 211–33.

Gallagher, S. (1997), 'Mutual enlightenment: recent phenomenology in cognitive science', *Journal of Consciousness Studies*, **4** (3), pp.195–214.

Goldman, A.I. (1997), 'Consciousness, folk psychology, and cognitive science', in Block *et al.* (1997).

Güzeldere, G. (1997a), 'The many faces of consciousness: A field guide', in Block *et al.* (1997).

Hart, J.G. (1992), *The Person and the Common Life* (Dordrecht: Kluwer Academic Publishers).

Henrich, D. (1966), 'Fichtes ursprüngliche Einsicht', in *Subjektivität und Metaphysik. Festschrift für Wolfgang Cramer*, ed. D. Henrich & H. Wagner (Frankfurt am Main: Klostermann).

Henrich, D. (1970), 'Selbstbewußtsein, kritische Einleitung in eine Theorie', in *Hermeneutik und Dialektik*, ed. R. Bubner, K. Cramer, R. Wiehl (Tübingen).

Henrich, D. (1982), *Selbstverhältnisse* (Stuttgart: Reclam).

Henry, M. (1963), *L'essence de la manifestation* (Paris: PUF).

Henry, M. (1965), *Philosophie et phénoménologie du corps* (Paris: PUF).

Henry, M. (1989), 'Philosophie et subjectivité', in *Encyclopédie Philosophique Universelle, Bd.1.: L'univers philosophique*, ed. A. Jacob (Paris: PUF), pp. 46–56.

Hume, D. (1888), *A Treatise of Human Nature* (Oxford: Clarendon Press).

Husserl, E. (1952), *Ideen zu einer reinen Phänomenologie und phänomenologischen Philosophie II*, Husserliana IV (Den Haag: Martinus Nijhoff).

Husserl, E. (1959), *Erste Philosophie II (1923-24)*, Husserliana VIII (Den Haag: Martinus Nijhoff).

Husserl, E. (1962b) *Phänomenologische Psychologie*, Husserliana IX (Den Haag: Martinus Nijhoff).

Husserl, E. (1973a), *Cartesianische Meditationen und Pariser Vorträge*, Husserliana I (Den Haag: Martinus Nijhoff).

Husserl, E. (1973b), *Zur Phänomenologie der Intersubjektivität I*, Husserliana XIII (Den Haag: Martinus Nijhoff).

Husserl, E. (1973c), *Zur Phänomenologie der Intersubjektivität III*, Husserliana XV (Den Haag: Martinus Nijhoff).

Hunt, H. T. (1986), 'A cognitive reinterpretation of classical introspectionism,' *Annals of Theoretical Psychology*, **4**, pp. 245–90.

Jackson, F. (1982), 'Epiphenomenal qualia', *Philosophical Quarterly*, **32**, pp. 127–36.

James, W. (1890), *The Principles of Psychology*, 2 vols (London: Macmillan and Co.).

Kern, I. (1989), 'Selbstbewußtsein und Ich bei Husserl', in *Husserl-Symposion Mainz 1988* (Stuttgart: Akademie der Wissenschaften und der Literatur), pp.51–63.

Klawonn, E. (1990), 'On personal identity: defence of a form of non-reductionism', *Danish Yearbook of Philosophy*, **25**, pp. 41–59.

Klawonn, E. (1991), *Jeg'ets Ontologi* (Odense: Odense Universitetsforlag).

Linschoten, J. (1961), *Auf dem Wege zu einer phänomenologischen Psychologie* (Berlin: de Gruyter).

Locke, J. (1975), *An Essay concerning Human Understanding* (Oxford: Clarendon Press).

Lycan, W.G. (1997), 'Consciousness as internal monitoring', in Block *et al.* (1997).

McGinn, C. (1997), 'Consciousness and content', in Block *et al.* (1997).

Minkowski, E. (1927) *La schizophrénie. Psychopathologie des schizoïdes et des schizophrènes* (Paris: Payot).

Mishara, A., Parnas, J. & Naudin, J. (1998), 'Forging the links between phenomenology, cognitive neuroscience, and psychopathology: The emergence of a new discipline', *Current Opinion in Psychiatry*, (in press).

Nagel, T. (1974), 'What is it like to be a bat?' *The Philosophical Review*, **83**, pp.435–50. [Reprinted in Block *et al.* (1997)].

Nagel, T. (1986), *The View from Nowhere* (Oxford: Oxford University Press).

Parfit, D. (1987), *Reasons and Persons* (Oxford: Clarendon Press).

Parnas, J. and Bovet, P. (1991), 'Autism in schizophrenia revisited,' *Comprehensive Psychiatry*, **32**, pp. 1–15.

Parnas, J. and Bovet, P. (1995), 'Research in psychopathology: epistemologic issues', *Comprehensive Psychiatry*, **36**, pp.167–81.

Parnas, J. (forthcoming), 'From predisposition to psychosis: Progression of symptoms in schizophrenia,' *Acta Psychiatrica Scandinavica*, (in press).

Parnas, J., Jansson, L., Sass, L. & Handest, P. (forthcoming), 'Self-experience in the prodromal phases of schizophrenia: A pilot study of first-admissions', *Neurology, Psychiatry and Brain Research*, (in press).

Pothast, U. (1971), *Über einige Fragen der Selbstbeziehung* (Frankfurt am Main: Vittorio Klostermann).

Rosenthal, D.M. (1993), 'Higher-order thoughts and the appendage theory of consciousness', *Philosophical Psychology*, **6**, pp. 155–66.

Rosenthal, D.M. (1997), 'A theory of consciousness', in Block *et al.* (1997).

Rudd, A. (1998), 'What it's like and what's really wrong with physicalism: A Wittgensteinian perspective', *Journal of Consciousness Studies*, **5** (4), pp. 454–63.

Sartre, J-P. (1943), *L'Étre et le néant* (Paris: Tel Gallimard).

Sass, L.A. (1992), *Madness and Modernity. Insanity in the Light of Modern Art, Literature, and Thought* (New York: Basic Books).

Searle, J.R. (1992), *The Rediscovery of the Mind* (Cambridge, MA: MIT Press).

Shoemaker, S. (1968), 'Self-reference and self-awareness', *The Journal of Philosophy*, **65**, pp. 556–79.

Smith, D.W. (1989), *The Circle of Acquaintance* (Dordrecht: Kluwer Academic Publishers).

Steinbock, A. (1995), *Home and Beyond* (Evanston, IL: Northwestern University Press).

Strawson, G. (1994), *Mental Reality* (Cambridge, MA: MIT Press).

Strawson, G. (1997), '"The self"', *Journal of Consciousness Studies*, **4** (5–6), pp. 405–28. Reprinted in this volume, pp. 1–24.

Strawson, P.F. (1959), *Individuals* (London: Methuen).

Van Gulick, R. (1997), 'Understanding the phenomenal mind: Are we all just armadillos?', in Block *et al.* (1997).

Zahavi, D. (1996), *Husserl und die transzendentale Intersubjektivität. Eine Antwort auf die sprachpragmatische Kritik* (Dordrecht: Kluwer Academic Publishers).

Zahavi, D. (1998a), 'Self-awareness and Affection', in *Alterity and Facticity. New Perspectives on Husserl*, eds. Depraz & Zahavi (Dordrecht: Kluwer Academic Publishers).

Zahavi, D. (1998b), 'The fracture in self-awareness', in *Self-awareness, Temporality, and Alterity. Central Topics in Phenomenology*, ed. Zahavi (Dordrecht: Kluwer Academic Publishers).

Zahavi, D. (1998c), 'Brentano and Husserl on self-awareness', *Etudés Phénoménologiques*, **27-28**, pp.127–68.

Zahavi, D. (1999), *Self-awareness and Alterity. A phenomenological Investigation* (Evanston, IL: Northwestern University Press).

Part 4

Pathologies of the self

Shaun Gallagher and Anthony J. Marcel

The Self in Contextualized Action

This chapter suggests that certain traditional ways of analysing the self start off in situations that are abstract or detached from normal experience, and that the conclusions reached in such approaches are, as a result, inexact or mistaken. The chapter raises the question of whether there are more contextualized forms of self-consciousness than those usually appealed to in philosophical or psychological analyses, and whether they can be the basis for a more adequate theoretical approach to the self.

First, we develop a distinction between abstract and contextualized actions and intentions by drawing on evidence from studies of rehabilitation after brain damage, and we introduce the notion of intentional attitude. Second, we discuss several interesting conclusions drawn from theoretically and experimentally abstract approaches. These conclusions raise some important issues about both the nature of the self and reflexive consciousness. At the same time they indicate the serious limitations concerning what we can claim about self and self-consciousness within such abstract frameworks.

Such limitations motivate the question of whether it is possible to capture a sense of self that is more embedded in contextualized actions. Specifically, our concern is to focus on first-person approaches. We identify two forms of self-consciousness, ecological self-awareness and embedded reflection, that (1) function within the kinds of contextualized activity we have indicated, and (2) can be the basis for a theoretical account of the self. Both forms of self-consciousness are closely tied to action and promise to provide a less abstract basis for developing a theoretical approach to the self.

To get clear about philosophical problems, it is useful to become conscious of the apparently unimportant details of the particular situation in which we are inclined to make a certain metaphysical assertion.
                                                                    Wittgenstein (1958)

The self that we are does not possess itself; one could say that it 'happens'.
                                                                    Gadamer (1976)

Overt action is indivisible . . . it is the whole individual who acts in the real environment.
                                                                    Neisser (1988)

Surprising and seemingly counter-intuitive results are not uncommon when philosophers, psychologists, and neuroscientists, employing a variety of first- and third-person approaches, search for an adequate model of the self. At least one philosopher equates the self with a momentary existence so that we are said to live through a large number of consecutive momentary selves (Strawson, 1997). Other philosophers, introspectively exploring the stream of consciousness, fail to find anything at all that resembles a self (Hume, 1739). Psychological and neurological observations and experiments (concerning, for example, Dissociative Identity Disorder and split-brain phenomena) suggest the possibility of more than one self to a single human organism. (Radden, 1998; Gazzaniga, 1978; Sperry, 1968a,b). Neuroscientists seem quite intent on demonstrating that what we call the self is either nothing more than a set of neuronal processes (Crick, 1994) or what such a set of processes produces (Ramachandran and Hirstein, 1997). Others think that the various ideas of the self as unitary, unique, familiar, autonomous, and so forth, attributable to common sense or to Enlightenment or Romantic conceptions, amount to naive delusions, convenient defence mechanisms, or, at best, abstract centres of narrative gravity.[1]

When faced with a range of questions about self (questions pertaining to identity, experience of self, nature of self, and so forth) most theorists approach the topic in a manner that is abstract or detached from behaviour and action normally embedded in pragmatically and socially contextualized situations. When, for example, philosophers employ reflective introspection in order to search for the unity of consciousness or 'the self' as an element in consciousness, they choose a framework for their investigation that is not equivalent to the framework within which people normally act. The introspective framework takes consciousness and the self as objects and thereby fails to capture their role in the realm of action, where they are specifically not objects. Similarly, psychological experimentation sometimes places subjects in circumstances where they are called upon to view their own body or their own thinking processes in an abstract and detached way. We argue, in this chapter, that these various approaches to developing a model of the self, either through methods of reflective self-consciousness or by means of scientific experimental investigation, have been conducted from perspectives that remain relatively abstract in a way that disqualifies, or at the very least places qualifications on many of these findings. We want to define what these perspectives have in common, that is, in what sense they are abstract. We also want to suggest that most of the controversies, problems and paradoxes concerning the notion of self are the result of searching for the self within these abstract perspectives. We suggest a different starting point and strategy for developing models of a self which is more contextualized within the realm of action. The idea is that within a more contextualized framework one is able to formulate a theory that is 'closer to the ground' and less abstract.

Insights developed in certain neuropsychological studies suggest a way to define the deficiency of the above-mentioned approaches, and to project a path that would

[1]   Sartre (1957) views the notion of the ego as a defence mechanism that protects us from the anxiety associated with an authentic realization of our absolute freedom. Recently, Varela, Thompson and Rosch (1991), integrating a Buddhist psychology with a cognitive science approach, conclude that 'the ego-self that everyone clings to and holds most dear,' doesn't really exist, and that this fact can be 'profoundly transformative' (pp. 80–1). However, as the authors acknowledge, whether *this* kind of a self exists or not, does not rule out the existence of other kinds of self. For the concept of 'centre of narrative gravity' see Dennett (1992).

lead to a more comprehensive and less abstract model of the self. Moreover, for this more comprehensive model, considerations about agency and ethical action are most pertinent. We are led to a perspective that takes ethics (in the most general sense of 'having to do with how one lives one's life') as a suitable starting point for working out an understanding of the notion of self. In contrast, in most traditional philosophical approaches to the question of personal identity, the starting point is purely epistemological or metaphysical, with the result that only in the end and as a seeming after-thought does one try to sort out the implications for the ethical realm of action.[2]

On this score, Galen Strawson's (1997) model of the self is not unconventional within the discourse of philosophy. He sets out to develop a phenomenologically informed metaphysical (specifically, for Strawson, materialist) conception of the self.[3] This approach leads him to a conception of the self as a relatively short-lived mental thing, a temporary subject of experience. Along the way he mentions, but then excludes from the essential aspects of self, the ideas that the self can ordinarily be thought to have character or personality, and to be conceived as an agent. He offers only a short discussion of personality in which he takes the state of depersonalization to be the essential aspect of a mental self. This he describes as a 'bare locus of consciousness . . . void of personality, stripped of particularity of character, a mere (cognitive) point of view', which one might experience as 'the result of exhaustion or solitude, abstract thought or a hot bath'. Strawson contends that a sense of self such as this survives depersonalization, and since even in normal circumstances personality is something that goes unnoticed and undetected as an object of experience, personality and character are accessories, not essentials to the sense of self. In Strawson, then, no less than in the philosophical tradition that stretches from Locke to Parfit (see, e.g., Parfit, 1984), the ethical dimensions of self are usually explored only in terms of what implications or consequences an already worked-out conception of self may hold in such respects.

We have two final introductory remarks. First, we want to be clear that although this chapter is centrally concerned with the nature of the self, there is a necessarily related issue that we address, namely, the question of access to the self, and whether there can be certain forms of self-consciousness that are not abstractions from contextualized activities. The promise of a sound basis for the development of a theoretical conception of a contextualized self is only good if in fact there are reliable forms of contextualized self-consciousness, since the primary method for getting a grasp on the self is through first-person self-experience. Beyond this, however, the question of access is essentially linked with the question of the nature of the self. Consider an animal that has no experience or awareness of its actions. It has no access to something that we would call self. We are inclined to say that such an animal *has* no self. The question of self or personal identity is an issue only for an animal which has some access to itself within the context of its own behaviour; *access to 'itself'* actually helps to make possible *the existence of 'its self'*. Access (self-consciousness) is constitutive of self.

---

[2] Carol Rovane's recent book, *The Bounds of Agency* (1998) makes a similar point. Her analysis, which ends up defending the notion of psychological continuity, leads in a very different direction from the one taken here however.

[3] As several commentators have already pointed out, Strawson's phenomenology is not the methodological phenomenology developed by Husserl and his followers, but more of an informal introspection. See Sheets-Johnstone (1999), and Zahavi and Parnas (1998).

Second, we wish to be clear that in sketching an approach to a conception of a self in contextualized action, we do not assume that there is only one kind of self or that an explanation of the contextualized self will be an explanation of every sense of self. Other approaches, such as the Meadian analysis of a socially constituted self, or the notion of an autobiographical self, can reveal important and valid conceptions of self.

Intentional Attitudes and Contextualized Action

Central to our proposal are two concepts: the *intentional attitude* of a person and *contextualized action*. The intentional attitude of a person consists of the content of their current purposive intentions which is itself a function of their attentional focus. It is inferred from the performance of perceptual, motor and linguistic activities, from phenomenological report, and also from the task demands and external situation. The total context of an action is made up of the intentional attitude and the external context, which we see as largely but not totally interdependent. Intentional attitude and contextualized action will be more fully specified below. Different kinds of contextualization can be distinguished by considering the variety of ways in which the effects of brain damage are affected by or mitigated by factors most easily described on the personal level, especially in terms of the intentionality of the behaviour involved. However, while we make broad categorizations of intentional attitudes and contextualizations in regard to the data discussed below, we suppose that they vary continuously and are a complex mix.

In certain approaches to rehabilitation of function after brain damage attempts are made to elicit the behaviour that is impaired or inaccessible.[4] Apart from the rehabilitative motives for this, if it is possible to elicit otherwise inaccessible behaviour or function, that which is effective in eliciting it is of great and obvious theoretical relevance. Consider first the implications of Leontiev and Zaporozhets' (1960) research on rehabilitation of impairments in hand use. They showed that in some cases hand movements can be more effectively rehabilitated by having the patient perform the impaired behaviour in the context of meaningful activity than in the exercise of isolated movement. In patients suffering from ideomotor apraxia, who are otherwise unimpaired in perception, comprehension, or motor performance, actions that cannot be produced on request or by imitation, can be produced or improved when they are performed in the course of normal activities that include such actions. Marcel (1992) found this same phenomenon in experiments with motor-impaired neurological patients who showed characteristics of ideomotor apraxia in manual function but were not classified as ideomotor apraxics since their motor impairments were identified as relatively peripheral (rather than of central origin). These patients showed a significant improvement in various aspects of motor control and fluency in impaired behaviours when performed as meaningful actions, over their performance when elicited as decontextualized behaviours. More significantly, in almost all of these cases even further improvement was found when nominally the same movements

---

[4] For example, in the therapeutic procedure called 'deblocking' or 'stimulation' technique (Weigl, 1961; Weigl and Kreindler, 1960). The assumption made in the stimulation approach to therapy is that the impaired function is not completely lost, but rather is inaccessible. The attempt is made to find an appropriate method of elicitation so that the patient might be able to recover, rather than relearn, the function in question.

were performed in a situation, usually a social situation, in which the movements constituted actions with personal and culturally derived signification.

For example, a woman who had difficulty in grasping, in lifting, and in motor fluency when asked to lift a cylinder of the weight and size of a glass of liquid and to move it toward or away from herself, showed clear improvement in her performance when spontaneously drinking during a meal. This same woman was even more proficient, almost normal, in the very same movements when serving mugs of tea to guests in her home, although not when clearing up the mugs. A second patient who had co-ordination, timing and sequencing problems in finger control, found it difficult to copy letter-like figures, but improved when writing words to dictation, and performed best when writing her plans and achievements in her diary.

On the basis of such observations and of follow-up experiments, Marcel (1992) distinguished three levels of performance, the baseline level plus the two levels of improvement. These levels of performance turned out to be associated with two things: the degree of semantic or pragmatic contextualization,[5] and social or self signification. In all but one of the patients examined by Marcel, differences in the nature of intention strongly correlated with performance differences. Marcel labelled the performance levels, simply, Levels 1, 2 and 3. Level 1 (worst) performance was obtained in situations in which the patient was instructed to carry out a disembedded, meaningless or purely procedural action (often the case in psychological or neuro-logical experimentation or examination). Level 2 performance was obtained in con-textualized actions or activities that involved a pragmatic significance or purpose relative to the patient (in the above examples, drinking at a meal, washing dishes, writing to dictation). Level 3 (best) performance was obtained in actions that were personally significant or that derived their signification from the social and cultural system (in the above examples, serving tea to friends, writing in a diary; in other cases, cutting bread or meat for others at a family meal, dealing cards at a real game). Level 3 performance, involving improvement to normal or near-normal performance, appeared to be associated with intentions which implicitly refer to self, in those cases in which cultural practice usually assigns such symbolic signification. For example, grasping mugs of tea and giving them to guests is underlain by the intention to 'offer hospitality', a cultural practice which contributes to the constitution of the social competence and self-esteem of the agent. Following such changes in intention, a specific motor performance can move from impossible, or near impossible (Level 1), to possible or improved (Level 2), to relatively fluent (Level 3). Actions do not need to be performed in the presence of others to have a social signification. However many of them were so performed. One might think that performance of such actions in the presence of others would lead to greater 'self-consciousness' which would *disrupt* the fluency of action. In experiments, Marcel found that this did often occur. What is important is that in real social situations, after initiation of the activity, the opposite (greater fluency) occurred.

In the cases examined by Marcel, different performance levels appeared to correspond to differences between three kinds of intentions.

---

[5] It will be clear from the following analysis that 'semantic or pragmatic' refers to a situation in which there is a meaningful intention on the part of the agent, or in which meaningful action is possible.

- Intentions that are relatively *abstract or decontextualized* (i.e. that have no purpose beyond the task itself or compliance).

- Intentions that are *pragmatically contextualized* (e.g. those involving purposive behaviour, or the exercise of an already known intention).

- Intentions that are *socially contextualized* (e.g. those involving self-reference or other persons — where the self is socially embedded by action and where actions both express and signify competence in a social and emotional role).[6]

We can enlarge on these distinctions by first defining them in terms of the contextualization of actions which correspond to them, and then by characterizing their respective attentional foci.

An abstract *or decontextualized* action is one which is detached from what would ordinarily be considered a significant context or where the person has no normal or good reason for doing what is asked other than voluntary compliance. A good example can be found in an experimental situation in which the experimenter asks the subject to perform a simple movement, e.g., touching one's own nose. A *pragmatically contextualized* action is one that is relatively more informed by a meaningful structure (relative, of course, to the individual subject) and is performed in the course of a natural activity whose purpose arises from personal projects and concerns. These two kinds of action closely align with Kurt Goldstein's (1940) distinction between *abstract* and *concrete* behaviour. Concrete behaviour, corresponding to pragmatically contextualized action, is behaviour that a subject performs and has a reason to perform in a situation that is closer to real-life (e.g. scratching, or swatting a fly from one's own nose, or showing someone else where a mark is, in contrast to the behaviour of touching one's nose on command, as in the clinical test).[7] A *socially contextualized* action is not only one where the agent is embedded in a social context, but where the action has meanings defined by cultural categorizations ('gestures') and represent states of the self in regard to others. It is rare that pragmatically contextualized actions are not also socially contextualized. However, this does not mitigate the distinction.

It is important to note that a specific kind of behaviour or movement cannot be categorized *per se* as having any one kind of intentional or contextualization status exclusively. The distinctions between these actions are relative to the agent's intentions, and to different reasons for action or the relative absence of reason (e.g. for no reason other than compliance in the case of an experiment). To point, or touch, or scratch: these are not *intrinsically* abstract or concrete behaviours; their status in this regard depends on intention. For example, a movement of one's hand to a specific

---

[6] These three kinds of intention can be exactly exemplified by three kinds of utterance, all of which have the 'objectively' identical external phonological form.
    (a) You agree to read aloud a list of pronounceable letter-strings that are orthographically non-words, one of which is PHYRE.
    (b) You answer the question 'what results if you set light to dry wood?' with the word 'fire'.
    (c) You see that an office has caught light and is burning and run out shouting the warning 'fire!'
The manner of the utterance of identical phonology would differ, but crucially it would do so because the content of the intention would differ, and this varies in accord with the situation.

[7] Like the patients discussed above, Goldstein's neuropathological patients often failed on tasks defined on an abstract level. Patients would be unable to perform abstract movement but could perform the mechanically equivalent movement in more concrete situations.

part of one's own body may be (nominally) mechanically identical in all three levels of action described above.[8]

The intentional attitudes of the distinctions sketched above are characterized by differences in their attentional focus. The notion of an abstract or decontextualized action indicates one characterized not only by a lack of contextualization but also by some degree of relatively high-level cognition or conscious attention directed to the particular behaviour itself (e.g. understanding instructions and deliberately translating them into motor actions that one monitors). When, for example, I am told to walk a straight line as part of a neurological examination, I am more conscious of my movement than if I am simply walking to open a door for a friend. The notion of a pragmatically or socially contextualized action indicates one with higher degrees of intentional content (one that is purposive and involves intentions that go beyond that behaviour itself) and a relatively low-level of attention targeted to the particular behaviour in question. So, for example, in walking to open the door for a friend I will not be thinking of (or possibly not even be aware of) how I am moving my legs; one might say that my walking is an unthinking (close-to-automatic) aspect of the larger intentional action. It is also possible that the very same motor functions which formed the conscious theme of the subject's activities in the abstract situation are, in a more contextualized setting, incorporated into and become an intrinsic part of a larger task that bestows meaning on the particular movement. The task itself may not be particularly meaningful (for example, washing dishes within an experimental or therapeutic situation); but relative to the task a particular hand movement takes on meaning and is generated by that meaning.

Of course, in many social situations what matters to the agent is indeed the *manner* of the action, e.g., walking elegantly or nonchalantly. We suggest that disruption of the intended behaviour in such cases is due to the behaviour being the *explicit focus of consciousness* rather than an *implicit aspect of the intention*. For example, it is important for the actor, dancer or athlete, once having worked on such aspects of movement, to demote them from the focus of conscious intention in performance. The main point here is the difference in intentional attitude when the behaviour in question is the explicit focus of conscious attention as opposed to when it is an implicit aspect of the intention.

One can find numerous examples of behaviour on these different levels across many different behavioural domains: perceptual, cognitive, linguistic, motor, and emotional.[9] Marcel and his colleagues presented auditorily, single, three-syllable nonwords (e.g. 'miladu') to a patient with conduction aphasia (a form of aphasia that involves difficulty with repetition, especially of nonsense words). The patient was asked to repeat each of them. She was able, at best, to repeat single syllables, sometimes combining the consonant and vowel of different syllables, sometimes making phonemic paraphasias. When the task was redefined and the requirement of repetition was an *implicit* requirement of a request simply to say which one of three auditorily presented nonsense words she preferred (using the same stimulus set as before), now the patient succeeded in 28 out of 30 trials in properly remembering and pronouncing one of the three-syllable nonwords. This task implicitly required repetition, but that

---

[8] Of course there are what O'Shaughnessy (1980) calls 'sub-intentional actions', such as tongue movements while writing, that are irrelevant to the main activity and are voluntary, but 'unaware'.

[9] Goldstein (1940) presents numerous examples.

aspect was embedded in the intention of telling which word she preferred, a task that included an aspect of personal intentionality. Repetition, in this case, was made possible by making it an implicit rather than explicit part of the agent's intentions.[10] Of course the total situation had now changed, because of what was being asked of the patient; and thus the role of the questioner was different (an enquirer after personal preference rather than a tester of competence in a task known to be frustratingly difficult). This in turn changes the intentional attitude, from attempting to repeat to expression of preference.

That the meaning content of an intention according to which the action is performed has an effect on performance, can be seen in a study by Brouchon *et al.* (1986). In both optic ataxic patients and in normal subjects, perceptual-motor coordination in what is mechanically the same movement is qualitatively influenced by whether the instruction is 'to reach for and touch' or 'to indicate' an object. Movements performed under different descriptions or instructions entail differences in the subject's intention; the second instruction insofar as it requires deixis (pointing) implicates communicative reference to another person.

Another example is both clear and dramatic. It involves congenitally deaf users of American Sign Language (ASL) who suffer from hemispatial neglect following stroke. In cases of left hemispatial neglect (Jeannerod, 1987) subjects entirely ignore their left perceptual and/or motor field, or the left side of their body. Such patients do not refer to things in their left hemispace and have a tendency to fail to perceive or attend to what is to their left. They obviously experience difficulty with spatial tasks that are in or that refer to left hemispace; so, for example, they may be unable to map out a room or properly describe the layout of objects in space. It is important to note that some of the syntactic and discursive aspects of ASL make use of space. For example, when entities are introduced in discourse they are each assigned a spatial location around the signer which is returned to for anaphoric (especially pronominal) reference. The same ASL users with acquired hemispatial neglect who ignore their left and have profound difficulties with tasks in their left perceptual field and left peripersonal space have no problem or pathology in discursive or syntactic use of left hemispace when involved in socially contextualized communicative acts of signing (Poizner *et al.*, 1987). This suggests that it is what the space represents, within an intentional context, that matters. In the conversational situation peripersonal space, rather than representing only itself, represents the reference and pragmatics of discourse for the subject acting in a culturally determined sign system, just as phonology does for the normal speaker.

Changes in the content and organization of the agent's intentions result in changes in the performance level of action. In many of the cases cited, even in normal subjects, behaviour tends to break down and become disintegrated in decontextualized tasks. In such tasks the opportunity has been reduced for the content of the intention to go beyond the immediate task. In pragmatically and socially contextualized tasks

---

[10] See Marcel (1992) for summary of this study. The patient's performance following a redefinition of task provokes the question of whether the patient's short-term auditory-verbal memory was impaired or whether her difficulty involved access to and use of her memory. Goldstein describes a similar case involving memory. 'The patient has the material in his memory, but he is unable to use it freely; he can use it only in connection with a definite concrete situation, to which it must seem to him to belong' (1940, p. 51).

behaviour tends to be more integrated, presumably because the agent's intentions encompass more than the immediate action itself, their attentional focus goes beyond it, and its significance is part of the larger projects and concerns of the person.

These generalizations do not hold in all cases, however. There are many pathologies (for example, some instances of aphasia and associative agnosia) where patients perform worse at the semantic or pragmatic levels and better at the lower or more abstract level — some aphasic patients may be able to apprehend sensory and lexical characteristics of words, but not their meaning; many agnosic patients can perceive sensory aspects of objects but fail to know what the object is or how to use it even when in context (see Marcel, 1983). It is difficult, however, to find corresponding clearcut instances in normal subjects for two reasons. First, normal people have the ability to behave in a decontextualized manner, even if less well; and can bestow meaning on it. Second, conscious attention is normally directed to the highest semantic or functionally useful level of behaviour — in perception, at the level of objects and action, in language, at the level of communicative pragmatics. Difficult, but not impossible. In the midst of a highly contextualized social situation, the normal person may suddenly become overly self-conscious of his/her own movements or speech and suffer a corresponding performance decline. When a poorly skilled reader devotes more attention to coding processes, he/she may lose consciousness of meaning (see Marcel, 1983). These examples, however, also indicate how the availability and execution of behaviour is influenced by the description or the intention under which such behaviour is generated. Personal goals and motives, as well as the social pragmatics of the situation (always defined relative to the subject), can clearly provide the energizing mechanism which transforms intentions into action. For our purposes here, the distinctions between performance levels are useful simply for indicating and providing evidence for the distinctions between intentional attitudes, even if performance levels are not strictly correlated with specific kinds of such attitudes in all cases.[11]

At this point we can fill out our definition of intentional attitude and add some comments. The intentional attitude is characterized not only by its level of contextualization but by its attentional focus (e.g. on the action itself versus its function or signification: lifting a glass, drinking, offering hospitality) and correspondingly the breadth of that focus (whether it is restricted to the action *per se* or goes beyond it temporally or socially). Attentional focus can be more radically divergent: on the self or the world, inner or outer directed. In such cases it is more evident that its breadth is relatively independent of its object or directionality. It is worth emphasizing that the increased breadth of attentional focus, which corresponds to contextualization, does not imply that all such content is explicit in the person's conscious experience. When the act of passing mugs of tea is embedded in the larger project of hospitality to guests, one's intentions extend to that project, but it is rare that one is immediately aware of all of this or of its significations.

The intentional attitude is also characterized by the *mode* of attention. In an *observational mode* one is detached from that which is the focus of attention; in a *non-observational mode* one is immersed in it. This corresponds to being in a state of reflexive or nonreflexive consciousness respectively. Furthermore, while there is a

---

[11] The relation between performance level and intentional attitude as defined above, will vary across individuals and across different pathologies.

correlation between the external situation and the intentional attitude, they are independent. In one and the same situation a person can change their attitude. Indeed this is just what is learnt in certain meditation and therapeutic techniques. For example, in depression the cycle of negative thoughts about the self and the inability to take action which maintain and increase the mood can be broken insofar as the person is able to learn to attend to the world and projects beyond themselves (see Teasdale, in press).

The importance for the concepts of self and self-consciousness of the foregoing discussion will become evident in the context of the following examination of the unity of consciousness.

Unity and Abstractness

The question of the unity of consciousness is one that is often raised in philosophical and psychological investigations into the nature of the self. Our intention is not to address the difficult problem of the unity of consciousness, but to examine the ways in which philosophers and psychologists attempt to address this problem. We want to suggest that various answers to this question are shaped by the kinds of behavioural situations in which philosophers and scientists are inclined to conduct their investigation.

Nagel, for example, takes issue with an assumption which underpins the idea of a mentalistic self, and which thus remains operative in many philosophical analyses of the self. The suspect assumption is what we might call the *assumption of the unity of reflexive consciousness*: that 'a single mind has sufficiently immediate access to its conscious states so that, for elements of experience or other mental events occurring simultaneously or in close temporal proximity, the mind which is their subject can also experience the simpler *relations* between them if it attends to the matter' (Nagel, 1975, p. 239). Through an examination of cases of split-brain patients Nagel is led to a certain scepticism: 'I believe that consideration of these very unusual cases should cause us to be skeptical about the concept of a single subject of consciousness as it applies to ourselves' and, by extension, to others (p. 242). Rather than thinking in categories that involve the unity of consciousness, he suggests, we need to think in terms of behavioural functions that are normally integrated but that can be dissociated in either experimental situations or cases of brain damage.

If one adopts Nagel's perspective, if, for example, one examines dissociative states of consciousness, it seems quite reasonable to question the notion of a unitary self (Marcel, 1993). As Nagel points out, it is not unusual to assume that the unity of self is based on the unity of consciousness. But then, on close inspection, the unity of consciousness does not seem to hold up to philosophical reflection. One need only think of Hume's famous and failed introspective attempt to locate the self in consciousness, and his conclusion that what we call the self is nothing but a bundle of impressions; or of Strawson (1997), who presents a similar although less bundled example. One possible response to such conclusions is to ask about the agent involved in doing the reflecting, so that, even if Hume consistently finds a bundle of different impressions, he does so from a consistently unified perspective (see Gallagher, 1992). This idea, again, involves the assumption of the unity of reflexive consciousness. The argument would be that even if phenomenal consciousness is not unified, at least our (second-order) access to it is, and that unity provides, in part, for the veracity of a more detached reflection.[12]

The same assumption, that the subject's reflexive consciousness is unified, operates in many psychological studies. Psychological experiments are often set up on the assumption that the test subject has a unified consciousness.[13] This assumption is implicit in the fact that the mode of report (the subject's mode of response) is not expected to make any difference in the content of what subjects actually report as their experience. This is clearly a Cartesian assumption: subjects have direct access to their experience (e.g. either they see or they don't see a certain visual stimulus) and the way they report on that experience is immaterial to what that experience is. Consider, however, the following experiments which suggest disunity in reflexive consciousness.

In a set of experiments that began as studies on a subject with blindsight, Marcel (1993) was led to test normally sighted subjects. In one experiment 10 normally sighted subjects were asked to discriminate on each trial between the presence and absence of a luminance increment in a target light, using a threshold increment value which yielded for each subject 50% correct guesses and 25–30% reports of 'definitely seen'. On each trial subjects responded simultaneously in three response modes: by eye-blink, by finger-press on a button, by oral 'yes/no'. In different blocks of trials they were asked either to *report their experience* of a luminance change or to *guess presence/absence* of a change. In both cases they were asked to respond 'as fast as possible but as accurately as possible'. Latencies of the responses indicated that they were not reflexes. The results for guessing showed very little difference between the response modes. However the dramatic finding was that in the condition requiring report of experience, on identical trials the responses dissociated across different modes. For example, people would simultaneously indicate 'yes' with their eye-blink but 'no' with the finger-press, or 'yes' with both eye and finger but 'no' with the oral response, and the reverse also occurred. Overall accuracy of report (correct vs. false positives) differed significantly between the three modes; it was best for eye-blink and worst for oral report. Although subjects correctly remembered the instructions, when reports were made fast they did not realize (even when questioned immediately

---

[12] Even detached reflection has experiential and, in that sense, phenomenal content (and this means that it can become the object of a further reflection). Insofar as reflective consciousness takes conscious experience as its object, as in the kind of reflective introspection often found in philosophical analyses of the self, it is twice removed from the conscious experience that is its object, and depends on the more immediate reflexive access we have to experience. This kind of reflective stance is taken by Edmund Husserl, for example, in his complex phenomenological analysis of the temporal stream of consciousness. Despite his trust in reflection, however, Husserl notes:

> We must therefore distinguish: the pre[reflective] being of experiences, their being before we have turned towards them in reflection, and their being as [reflected] phenomena. When we turn towards the experience attentively and grasp it, it takes on a new mode of being; it becomes 'differentiated', 'singled out'. And this differentiating is precisely nothing other than the grasping [of the experience]; and the differentiatedness is nothing other than the being-grasped, being the object of our turning-towards' (Husserl 1991, p. 132).

Husserl means that the reflective act lifts the reflected part of consciousness out of the stream of consciousness, freezes it when in fact that freezing distorts its nature. So the reflecting is just this differentiating of the reflected part from the stream. For further discussion, see Gallagher (1998).

[13] Even the experimental examination of split-brain patients starts with this assumption since instructions are given to the subject as if he or she were a single individual.

after a trial) that there was a discrepancy between the response modes of their reports. This discrepancy did not occur in the guessing conditions.

In another experiment, again with 10 normally sighted subjects and again with either guessing or report, each response mode was tested separately, i.e. on a block of trials subjects responded with only one kind of response on each trial. Also in separate blocks of trials subjects either had to respond as fast as possible or had to wait for a signal, delayed by 2 or 8 seconds, before responding. It was found that relative accuracy was the same for each response mode as when they had been performed simultaneously. Again it was found that in all response modes guessing was more accurate than report, and that accuracy did not differ between response modes for guessing, but did so for reporting. In neither experiment was the non-difference for guessing due to performance being at ceiling, i.e. as high as logically possible. This second experiment shows that the discrepancy between report modes was not due simply to having to make three responses on each trial, nor to the order of or delay in such reports.

The importance of this is that traditionally, in psychological experiments on nonconscious perception and blindsight, greater accuracy of guessing than reports is interpreted as reflecting the presence of nonconscious perception versus conscious perception. Nonconscious information is taken to guide or have a causal effect on guessing, while having a very much smaller role in affecting the rational descriptions, in report, of the subject's conscious perceptual experience.

How should we interpret these data? First, conscious detectability of experience appears to differ across different modes of report. Subjects on the same trial are reporting with a button press that they see a light and reporting orally that they do not see a light, or vice versa. The second experiment shows that this contradiction does not depend on the requirement of making simultaneous reports; that is, it is not a property of the requirement to make more than one report on a single trial. If reports are indeed reports of experience[14] then it appears that an experience is not independent of report, but depends on the mode of the report. This may mean that the nature of an intended report influences experience,[15] but since in the experiment involving simultaneous reports all three report modes were intended, this cannot be a complete explanation. An alternative and preferred hypothesis is that different ways of reporting have differential access to an experience. This calls into question the existence of a unitary reflexive consciousness, or a unitary subject of experience responsible for report.[16] It suggests not only a distinction between phenomenal experience (the sensed experience of the light) and reflexive consciousness (the awareness that we

[14] There are several good reasons to believe that they are reports of experience. First, spontaneous latencies are too long to be reflexes. Second, subjects, when asked, insist that their responses are 'reports'. If people deny awareness of such stimuli, they are usually unwilling to make voluntary responses (see Marcel, 1988). Finally, there are significant differences in results between responses in the case of reports of experience and guesses in the absence of conscious perception.

[15] Bisiach, Berti and Vallar (1985) suggest that the nature of the response used to report a visual experience can alter the memory of the experience in as little as two seconds.

[16] Similar dissociation in reflective consciousness was found by Cumming (1972). Subjects were shown letters briefly and laterally masked, and were asked to indicate the presence of a specified target letter by pressing a key. Asked to respond quickly, subjects 'tended to respond to the presence of a target letter with a fast press of the "target-present" key, and then, a moment later, to verbally apologize for having made an error, when in fact they had been correct'.

are experiencing something, which becomes the basis for the report), but disunity in the latter. The apparent contradictions revealed in the experiments (e.g. a subject's reports that he is both experiencing the light and not experiencing the light) are resolved on the supposition that the experience is differentially available to divisions of reflexive consciousness.

The supposition of disunity in reflexive consciousness is reinforced in cases of anosognosia (when patients demonstrate a lack of awareness of their deficits or impairments). In some cases, patients seem to demonstrate both awareness and non-awareness of their neurological problems. For example, a patient may verbally admit or complain of his hemiplegia (unilateral paralysis), and at the same time try to act as if he were normal. On the other hand, some hemiplegic patients appear unaware of their deficit, and deny it if questioned, but never attempt to initiate activities requiring coordinated use of limbs on both sides (Bisiach and Geminiani, 1991).

In another set of observations (Marcel, 1993; Marcel *et al.*, under review) sixty-four hemiplegic patients who were anosognosic for their plegia were asked to rate (1) their own ability on activities that involve coordinated activities of limbs on both sides (e.g. tying a knot, clapping) and (2) the questioner's ability to do such tasks *if the questioner were in the same condition as the patient.* Half of the patients were asked to rate (1) first, and (2) later; the other half were asked to rate these in reverse order. In such instances, many patients rate their own ability as perfect but claim that the questioner, if in their own (the patient's) condition, would not be able to perform the task, 'because you would need both hands'. In each case (1 and 2) a reflective stance is taken, but in (1) patients fail to recognize their deficit while in (2) they affirm it. Patients failed to notice the inconsistency between their responses. Some of these self-contradicting patients showed another dissociation of awareness involving self-knowledge. When asked whether each arm was at all weak they casually denied any weakness in their plegic arm. However, when asked immediately after, in a confidential manner, 'Is this arm ever naughty? Does it ever not do what you want?', several patients, although bemused at this question when referred to their nonplegic arm, answered affirmatively when referred to their plegic arm. (One patient said 'Oh yes! In fact if it doesn't do what I want, I'm going to hit it.') It seems that patients' awareness of their state and abilities is split and contradictory, and depends upon the kind of personal stance that they take.

Because reflexive consciousness is thought to have a close connection with self-hood (Kihlstrom, 1993; Marcel, 1993; Nagel, 1975), such considerations lead again to scepticism about the concept of a single subject of consciousness. If reflexive conscious states can be dissociated, then there is little reason to assume a unified self, or even a single self in one body or brain.

Nagel (1986) moves beyond the assumption of the unity of reflexive consciousness and furthers the discussion by considering an alternative hypothesis to mentalism, namely, the equation of self and brain. Not unlike Strawson's stance on materialism, he embraces the 'dual aspect theory' of self, and maintains that brain states are both physical and mental. For him, this means that the referent of the psychological subject is actually the brain, something 'which is the persisting locus of mental states and activities and the vehicle for carrying forward familiar psychological continuities when they occur.' Nagel continues:

I could lose everything but my functioning brain and still be me. . . . If my brain meets these conditions then the core of the self — what is essential to my existence — is my functioning brain. . . . I am not just my brain. . . . But the brain is the only part of me whose destruction I could not possibly survive. The brain, but not the rest of the animal, is essential to the self (1986, p. 40).

One may thus be tempted to push aside the perplexities involved in dissociations of reflexive consciousness and the problems of psychological discontinuity, the subject of seemingly interminable philosophical discussions, by appealing to reductionist neuroscience.[17] Yet, reductionist or functionalist interpretations of neurological evidence do not appear to settle the philosophical problems of the self, since the diversity of such interpretations make it possible to develop various and incommensurable models of the self that simply mirror the philosophical theories.[18] If the framework of inquiry is set by the usual kinds of questions posed in philosophical investigation or at the level of psychological or neurological experimentation, then the answers that seem most natural are those that are framed in terms of consciousness and/or the brain. Here again we find the traditional problems and paradoxes that keep the issue completely unsettled, and that make up the majority of the philosophical and psychological history of these concepts. What we need to be clear about, however, is that in all of these approaches the self is being sought from an *abstract and detached* behavioural perspective.

We have characterized abstract behavioural situations in terms of a decontextualization. It is also possible that a subject may actually be reduced to abstract or detached behaviour by various pathologies or in certain limit situations (involving fatigue, illness, and so on). We want to suggest that philosophical methods which involve introspective self-consciousness or the hyperreflective analysis of behaviour may also place the reflecting agent in an abstract behavioural situation or a detached stance. Reflective self-consciousness (the unity of which is itself in question) involves something like artificially (and sometimes experimentally) pulling back from particular contextualized activities and posing a question from an abstract or detached point of view. Not only questions such as 'What is the I?' or 'What is the self?' or 'How can I account for the unity of consciousness?' but also the practice of reflective introspection itself shift and redefine our intentions away from what may have been an active engagement with the world. As in some experimental situations, such questions involve shifting the focus of attention away from purposive activity involving meaningful objects and other persons, to our own movements and modes of consciousness. Such hyper-reflection is a third-order cognitive activity, once

[17] This temptation is often accompanied by a certain discounting of the difference between the discourse of neuroscience and the personal-level discourse involved in the description of self and self-consciousness. There are many objections to this move. One is Dennett's (1969) — that different entities are involved at different levels of discourse. Another is simply that when someone refers to their self, they are not referring to their brain, with which they have no acquaintance. For our purposes here we forego any objections that are rightly made to this conflation of discourses.

[18] Contrast, for example, the details of Dennett's (1991) abstract centre of narrative gravity, Damasio's concept of a 'neural self' which, not unlike Galen Strawson's model, is, at each moment, 'constructed, from the ground up' (1994, p. 240), and the account provided by Ramachandran and Hirstein (1997) which regards the self as a delusion. Disagreements among these accounts involve both philosophical and neurological details.

removed from reflexive consciousness, and twice removed from phenomenal experience or the behavioural level at which we find contextualized action.

Donaldson (1978) has pointed out that such academic and analytic attitudes are the goal of much of Western schooling and involve the ability to detach one's consciousness from determination by worldly and pragmatic contexts. Such attitudes are often difficult to learn because they involve addressing specific aspects of pre-semantic levels of representation in perception and action, when we are normally inclined to operate at the semantically or pragmatically contextualized level. For example, in order to learn to read (new words) in an alphabetic orthography, one has to attend to auditory words at the level of the sequence of phonemes and to desist from attending to their wholes and their meaning.

It is in this kind of detached, abstract, analytic attitude that, as philosophers or scientists, we start to search for and account for the self. To ask, for example, 'What is the self *per se*, or essentially, or *in itself*?' is to ask 'What is the self, apart from or outside of any particular context?' Philosophical and scientific questioning itself may be quite contextualized in social and professional settings. But the very nature of the questions (for example, 'What makes me or someone else an identical self across any number of particular contexts and behaviours?') and the preferred methods for answering them, lead us to seek answers that are abstracted and that exist in abstract decontextualized behavioural situations. In such an approach, one looks for something relatively general — the subject of experience, independent of any particular experience, and thus independent of any particular context.

Methodological frameworks in philosophy and the sciences lead us to believe that we are working out solutions on a relatively basic level when we do this kind of analysis. It is clearly a mistake, however, to think of the more abstract behavioural level as more basic than contexctualized behavioural levels. The experimental data cited in the first section (i.e., the fact that, at least in some cases, performance of abstract behaviour is frequently impaired first and to a higher degree while performance remains more intact in pragmatically and socially contextualized action) suggests that abstract behaviour may not be more basic than contextualized behaviour. Socially contextualized behaviour is not built out of abstract behavioural components; rather, abstract 'components' are simply abstractions of more contextualized behaviours. We do not intend this as a developmental statement — that is, our claim is not that more complex social behaviour is not built up from more simple behavioural components as the individual matures, etc. What we want to say is that complex social behaviour is more than the sum of its parts (indeed it is not clear that it really has independent parts), and that meaning (or meaningful action) cannot be analysed in purely mechanistic or atomistic terms.

It is important to note that dissociations such as those in reflexive consciousness shown by the experiments cited above, are not usually observed by either the subject (since one can logically never directly experience more than one consciousness or self) or even by others. What we come to consider to be the self from the perspective of abstract behavioural situations like those produced in philosophical reflection or in much scientific experimentation, is no more than a detached snapshot of a self that quite possibly functions in a more integrated manner in socially contextualized situations.

Our claim is not that reflexive awareness and a more detached reflective consciousness[19] are not involved in the workings of the self, but that by focusing on detached or decontextualized states philosophers like Hume, Nagel and Strawson, as well as psychologists and neuroscientists, are searching for the self in the wrong way, or certainly in a way that will give a partial and distorted picture. If the self cannot be accounted for purely in terms of reflexive consciousness or purely in terms of brain functions (both, of course, necessary conditions), neither can it be adequately accounted for by a dual-aspect theory that would locate it in a mix of brain and reflexive consciousness, if that theory is developed in a framework that is built around abstract behavioural situations. The answer, however, is not to abandon the notion of a self, but to start the search at a different level.

The Self in Personal and Social Pragmatics

We have argued that in general, and for the most part, philosophical reflection operates in such a way, and psychological and neurological experiments are designed in such a way, as to limit the subject to abstract intentional attitudes or to a detached stance. And it is within the limits of such situations that philosophers and psychologists pose and answer abstract questions about the self, the unity of consciousness, and so forth. It is to be noticed that this limitation holds for both first- and third-person approaches.

Is it possible to develop an approach to the self that would take its bearing within pragmatically and socially contextualized action, i.e., where the subject is in a non-reflective intentional attitude? What does the self look like in such behavioural situations? What kind of access do we have to the self in such cases? If we take a third-person perspective we easily discover, not a unitary phenomenon, but a self with multiple but relatively integrated aspects. That is, as social psychology often suggests, the subject (i.e. the actor) plays different social roles within different social contexts. As an academic or scientist my socially contextualized behaviour is typically circumscribed so that I represent myself in a certain way. As a family member, citizen, religious practitioner, sports enthusiast, my various activities are characterized in relatively different roles and vocabularies, and so on. So in my various activities, I am many different selves to many different social groups. Following this approach it seems that even in socially contextualized situations, we can discern multiple selves, albeit in a somewhat different way from Nagel or Strawson. It is not uncommon, however, to think of these different roles or aspects as being integrated in some relatively rough way. The concept of 'character' or 'person' is sometimes used to indicate that an agent has or manifests some relatively stable and consistent characteristics across all of these roles. This relatively integrated agent in some way constitutes what is ordinarily called the self.[20]

---

[19] By reflexive consciousness we mean a second-order awareness directed at and capable of reporting phenomenal experience; reflective consciousness is a detached, offline or introspective consciousness.

[20] Kathleen Wilkes (1988) argues in this way. Pragmatic support of this view can be found in legal and political systems that treat one agent as responsible for actions, no matter under what role description the action has been perpetrated (unless the agent is deemed to have been in a fugue state). In short, one can sort this issue out with relative ease on third-person approaches since there are acceptable and practical ways to adjudicate alternative descriptions (multiple selves vs. unitary agent) of socially contextualized behaviour.

The approach we outline below is not inconsistent with such third-person views. Our question, however, concerns the possibility of gaining *first-person* access to the self in socially contextualized behavioural situations. For our purposes here, we leave the third-person framework aside in order to explore two first-person approaches.

Certain forms of reflective self-consciousness, especially a methodological hyper-reflective or introspective consciousness, where attention is focused on one's own consciousness, are characteristic of abstract behaviour in detached states and pathologies, as well as in philosophical reflection and certain limit situations like fatigue and illness. In contrast, in most pragmatically and socially contextualized behaviour, when our attention is directed toward the external environment and we are involved in meaningful activity, both our reflexive and reflective consciousness are in many respects non-operative. Indeed as Csikszentmihalyi (1978) has shown, when people have been totally involved in an activity (e.g. rock climbing, problem solving) they retrospectively report that they were aware of the immediate situation but say that they cannot report the content of their conscious awareness at the time.[21] Our intentionality is directed to things and other people; our consciousness is immersed in our projects. If we attempt to turn our reflective regard from our projects to the structure of consciousness, or the self, we alter our intentional structure, and the self who had been immersed in those projects is now abstracted from them. We end up with something akin to an artificially produced dissociated state: a self which is engaged in a project of reflecting, and a self which has been reflectively abstracted from the situation that had engaged it. Precisely in this disengagement, the reflected self ceases to be itself. Is there a way to capture the pre-reflective self, which, in any particular situation, is caught up in a unity of action?

It might seem that our only access to this pre-reflective self is either just the kind of abstract self-reflection that we have criticized, or the third-person observations that we have just set aside. If this were the case, then our position would not be unlike a Kantian faith in a transcendental entity which is distorted in every attempt to capture it. We admit that even these detached kinds of access, scientific and philosophical reflection and third-person observation, do provide some information about the pre-reflective self, but that the information is both abstract and incomplete, and in that sense distorted. We want to suggest two other kinds of access. The first one involves proprioceptive and ecological self-awareness. The second is a form of first-person contextualized access that we call 'embedded reflection'.

Ecological self-awareness

Within Gibsonian psychology one finds the concept of a non-observational access to what Neisser (1988) has termed an ecological aspect of self (see Butterworth, 1995; 1998; Marcel and Dobel, under review). This involves the idea that the information that I receive about the world includes, implicitly, information about my own self (specifically about egocentric perspective and spatial embodiment). To whatever

---

[21] The notion that we are not conscious of our situation and actions while driving a familiar route in a car is unwarranted. Rather, our reflexive or reflective consciousness is not focused on these things at the time of the activity, and we cannot, therefore, consciously recollect them. While both first-order conscious experience and second-order reflexive consciousness may be necessary for later episodic memory, the lack of formation of episodic memories, or the inability to remember episodically does not imply an absence of consciousness at the time of the original event.

extent this information is part of conscious experience, for example, in the form of proprioceptive awareness and awareness of egocentric self-location, it provides some sense of myself as an experiencing organism. My perception of the world is at the same time shot through with information about my own embodied position in that world. Ecological information (from both exteroceptors and interoceptors) about perceptual perspective, embodiment, and motor activity not only facilitates motor control, it provides a basis for distinguishing between self and non-self.[22] Although much of the detail about bodily position and movement *vis-à-vis* the environment, detail which is absolutely essential for motor control and physical action, is not conscious, whatever *is* conscious does not present itself as detailed information about various parts of my body. Rather, it manifests itself as an integrated or global sense of where I am spatially in relation to the immediate environment and what, in any particular situation, I am capable of doing. In effect, ecological access provides a pre-reflective sense of the self as a spatial presence and a set of capabilities.

When my attention or conscious activity is directed toward the environment or toward some project, the content of proprioceptive awareness, in this Gibsonian sense, tells me, for example, whether I am moving or staying still, whether I am sitting or standing, whether I am reaching or grasping or pointing, whether I am speaking or maintaining silence, whether I am thinking or not.[23] Proprioceptive awareness thus provides an immediate experiential access to my pre-reflective, embodied self, even as I, as an agent, am not reflectively seeking myself, but am engaged in pragmatically and socially contextualized action. This is precisely what cannot be fully grasped in approaches that proceed reflectively within situations where the ecological sense is overtaken or dominated by reflective consciousness. One reason for this inability, so far unmentioned, is that in states of reflexive self-consciousness one's focal attention is by definition focused on oneself. Removing one's attention from the world and from one's goals destroys or makes perceptually recessive the self that is expressed in action. There is nothing mysterious about this. It is simply that an agentive self, as it removes itself from action to reflection, cannot perceive itself (as acting in the original action). David Rosenthal (1993) has noted a related point: pre-reflective phenomenal states can be *expressible* without being *reportable*. Only the content of second-order reflexive states of awareness can be reported (Marcel, 1993). This suggests that insofar as there is a contextualized self (a self contextualized in and by perception and action) it is something which can be expressed in action, emotion,

---

[22] This ecological sense is present from the very beginning of life. See Gallagher and Meltzoff (1996) and Butterworth (1995).

[23] James Gibson defines this ecological perspective in the following terms.

> Awareness of the persisting and changing environment (perception) is concurrent with the persisting and changing self (proprioception in my extended use of the term). This includes the body and its parts and all its activities from locomotion to thought, without any distinction between the activities called 'mental' and those called 'physical' (1987, p. 418).

We also want to include in the concept of an ecological aspect of self what Neisser (1988) terms the interpersonal aspect of self. That is, we live in an environment that is not only physical but also social, and in social contexts we are constantly (but not necessarily consciously) provided with information about ourselves from the way others react to us. This represents a conflation of Neisser's two kinds of self which in other contexts are quite useful to keep apart. The idea that the self is unavoidably interpersonal is nicely captured in Varela's thought that the self 'cannot be separated from the distributed, multiple others which are our inescapable human ecology' (1996, p. 340, note 7).

or in certain attitudes, but not necessarily something which can be reported. To be reported it would need to be encountered in Hume's sense, that is, it would require second-order reflexive awareness. Reflexive awareness, however,   necessarily involves an experiential separation between that of which one is aware (the object of reflexive consciousness) and the subject of awareness. This is the very activity which removes the self from the original action and decontextualizes it. The reflecting agent, which *expresses* itself in the action of reflecting, can only *report* on a self that is no longer in action.

The ecological self discussed above is a self that is perceptually specified. There is, however, another but related kind of embedded self-awareness, where the self is a more positive presence, but where the self is still not experienced as an objective 'Me' as it appears to a subjective 'I' (i.e., a self-awareness which is not a second-order reflexive awareness of a self separate from the perceiver). This is the sense of agency. When one is aware of one's actions at the time of acting, one experiences them as owned, as one's own. One does not experience them as unowned or as another's. In this respect one experiences oneself; and this is the case when we are involved in our actions, as opposed to being reflexively or retrospectively aware of them. The online sense of agency is thus complementary to the ecological sense of self in perception. Marcel (forthcoming) has argued that in one's immediate phenomenology during action, the owner or agent of action is not represented as separate from the action, but is an intrinsic property of action itself, experienced as a perspectival source. Findings in two areas of research concerned with awareness of bodily action and with felt ownership of bodily action point to a common conclusion.

First, experimental research on normal subjects by Marcel (ongoing) and by Jeannerod (Fourneret and Jeannerod, 1998) suggests that awareness of one's action is based not so much on actual feedback from movement itself or from peripheral effort associated with such movement, but more on that which precedes action and translates intention into movement — high-level motor commands, experienced as 'tryings'. Further, research by Haggard (Haggard and Eimer, in press; Haggard and Magno, in press) which correlates initial awareness of action with recordings of the Lateralised Readiness Potential and with Transcranial Magnetic Stimulation, strongly indicates that one's initial awareness of a spontaneous voluntary action is underlain by the motor commands relating to the effectors to be used. That is, although the content of experience is the action, its source is in fact what lies between intention and performance. It is important to note that the cerebral area centrally involved in this is the Supplementary Motor Area.

Second, the prime and most compelling instance of experienced dis-ownership of action is Anarchic Hand Syndrome (della Sala *et al.*, 1994). In this neurological syndrome one hand acts purposefully and wilfully against the person's conscious intentions and their efforts to suppress it. The action, but not the bodypart involved, is experienced as another's. Such patients do not have a delusion that someone else *is actually* doing it, i.e., they do not take the experience for reality, but it is a genuine 'as if' experience. It should be noted that, in contrast with this, in Tourette's Syndrome and Obsessive-Compulsive Disorder, and often in schizophrenia, the action itself is experienced as owned but the source of the action, an intention or command, is what is dis-owned. Indeed stimulation of the Central Thalamic Nucleus produces hand movements, and subjects have no idea why they did them, but the actions are not disowned (Hécaen et al., 1949). Thus awareness and ownership of intention is not crucial to ownership of action *per se*. While lesions to the Basal Ganglia–Cortical loops are often implicated in Anarchic Hand Syndrome, the most frequent and common lesion site is the Supplementary Motor Area — as noted above, the site of activity found to be associated with normal awareness of action.

On the basis of such evidence, Marcel (forthcoming) suggests that immediate awareness and experienced ownership of action go together and lie in the specific 'trying' underlain by pre-action specifications. It is logically necessary that such specifications for bodily action are in an egocentric frame of reference, since they specify movements in space from the body's points of origin. Furthermore, for commensurability with spatial targets, bodily disposition has to be represented in egocentric coordinates. In the phenomenology of the normal person such action specifications yield a perspectival sense of the source of action, in which spatial points of origin and the spatiality and physics of intended action are specified (a counterpart in action to the egocentric perspectivalness of perception). This amounts to ownership of action in spatial terms and an immediate sense of agency. This sense of ownership is different from the sense of ownership for sensations, bodyparts or thoughts. It should also be noted that in this case the owner, the self in action, is not a substantive entity but a source. In Anarchic Hand Syndrome, the patient is (neurologically) deprived of the phenomenology of *this* source of action, and a different route to action is involved. The patient's awareness of the movements may be by means of internal proprioception, but his awareness of the wilfulness of the hand's actions is external, through haptic contact with it via other of his bodyparts and through his inability to suppress it. This proposal also accounts for several aspects of anosognosia for plegia, since patients without any loss of proprioception per se nonetheless experience movement in their paralysed limb as they had intended it (Marcel et al., under review).

This perspectival sense of self as agent is normally set against and supported by a long-term background sense of agency (Marcel, forthcoming). This latter involves not only awareness that one has intentions but crucially the sense that one's actions, or rather one's tryings, are *reliably effective*, i.e., that spontaneous movements do come about in accordance with intentions that conform to the physics of the environment and the body. However, the main point is that the data suggest that self-awareness, experienced as ownership of action, is an intrinsic property of action itself, and is perspectival. It is thus complementary to the ecological sense of self in perception, and likewise involves no reflexive or detached self-consciousness.

Ecological self and temporal extension

Ecological self-awareness is normally considered to be momentary, providing a sense of posture or movement at any particular instant. But proprioceptive and ecological awareness also must include a sense of self over time, a sense of self as temporally extended. Even if our bodily position and embodied activities are constantly changing, and in that sense, impermanent or non-persisting, ecological self-awareness gives us more than just a snap-shot profile of our posture, location and action. Implicit in this kind of self-awareness is a sense of *what I have just been doing*, and, of equal importance, *what I can do*, and *what I am just prepared to do*, a sense of capability which goes beyond the momentary. This sense of capability implicitly involves a continuity from past experience, since my capabilities are to some extent created and constrained by my past experience as well as my present situation. This is not episodic memory, which can provide a sense of personal continuity; the kind of continuity at stake in ecological self-awareness is a continuity that involves past learning and that is implicit in motor capabilities such as riding a bicycle or swimming. This sense of capability also involves a projection of possible movements or actions, which are constrained and enabled by the present position of my body or my present embodied activities. In this sense, ecological self-awareness involves not a temporal knife-edge experience, but a changing 'specious present' that opens in the directions pertinent to the actor's intentional activities. William James' (1890) notion of the specious present has been recast by contemporary psychologists as 'working memory' (e.g. Baddeley, 1990; 1992). We concur insofar as working memory is conceived of as attentional involvement in current projects, but not insofar as it is conceived of as a subpersonal representational mechanism.

Two related questions can be raised here. First, is the self that is expressed and realized in contextualized action temporally extended? Second, is the self in action *experienced* as temporally extended further than the immediate past and future?

To address the first question, the self realized and expressed in action is temporally extended insofar as one's actions are informed not just by one's individual procedural learning, but by one's past experience, by beliefs, lasting attitudes, moral positions, by one's personal knowledge, concerns, and practical interests. One's actions are often so informed by reflection on and recollection of episodic memories and autobiography. More to the point, however, and despite the contribution of reflection and recollection, one's actions do seem to be informed by such things nonreflectively. This is partly what we will refer to as 'character' (see below). It is perfectly true that self-image and the avowals of character witnesses are no guarantee of what one will actually do or be capable of. Nonetheless there is a degree of consistency in an individual that is captured by the notion of disposition. Such a notion does not necessarily require either conceptual representation or reflective consciousness.

Regarding the second question, there are two respects in which temporal extension of self may be experienced in embedded action. The first of these is a primitive sense of time reflected by the 'aspectual' use of verbs, separable from tense *per se*. McCormack and Hoerl (in press) point to the fact that prior to children's appropriate use of verb tense and prior to evidence for episodic memory proper, they are sensitive to temporal aspect, which marks not only completion versus continuation of action but also the difference between actions that are punctate versus extended (e.g. hit vs swim). Consider the differences between: I do it (now), I am doing it, I do it (habitually), I am about to do it, I complete it, I have completed (just done) it, I initiate it. Many of these temporal aspects of action are made available to us and are differentiated by our ecological awareness discussed above. But others, such as the generic 'I do *x*' (i.e. habitually), suggest that the very doing of an action brings into the momentary proprioceptive awareness of the actor the sense that he knows how to do *x* (the sense of capability discussed above) and either generic knowledge that he has done it before or even episodic memories of the action.

Episodic memory involves a second respect in which we may have an awareness of our own temporal extension in action. As opposed to deliberate attempts to recall episodic memories, preparation for and performance of action may bring to mind other instances of performance of that action by oneself. Even if one does not have a sense of specific times or occasions of such episodic memories of doings, they nonetheless give one a sense of other instances of oneself as the identical first-person agent — as the perspectival source of action. Such awareness is not of long-term continuity, but of re-emergence or re-identification. While we do not doubt that people have a detached conception and belief in their long-term continuity, we are doubtful that people have an immediate *sense* or *awareness* of such permanence, other than when engaged in detached consideration of their personal narratives.

A somewhat more reflective awareness of temporal continuity is provided when, within activity or the planning of action, we deliberately recall episodic memories or consider how to behave. In the final section we suggest that this kind of reflection may also be 'embedded'.

The Ethical Self

What we want to call 'embedded reflection' is not the same as the hyperreflective or introspective consciousness we identified in previous sections as a form of abstract, decontextualized behaviour. We may state the difference in this way. Embedded reflection is a first-person reflective consciousness that is embedded in a pragmatically or socially contextualized intentional attitude and the corresponding actions. It involves the type of activity that I engage in when someone asks me what I am doing or what I plan to do. In such reflection I do not take consciousness or 'the self' as a direct or introspective object of my reflection; I do not suddenly take on the role of a phenomenologist or theorist for the sake of answering the question. Rather I start to think matters through in terms of possible actions. I treat myself (I discover myself) as an agent. In such situations, my attention is directed not in a reflective inspection of consciousness as consciousness, but toward my own activities in the world where my intentions are already directed. Often my aim in such reflection is not to represent my 'self' to myself, as if it were a piece of furniture in my mind, but to continue certain actions or to explain myself in terms of my actions.[24]

Korsgaard (1991) distinguishes between *being engaged in a conscious activity* and *being conscious of an activity*. If, for example, I move across the room in order to pick something up and hand it to another person, I am engaged in a conscious activity of voluntary movement and I know what I'm doing. If forced to express it I may say 'I'm getting that book for my friend'. Part of that conscious activity may include an aspect of embedded reflection, and I may be thinking to myself, as I move, that I had better get this book to show my friend what I was talking about. Embedded reflection in this case is part of my engagement in the conscious activity of getting the book. If my actions call for a momentary or ongoing consideration of my intentions, this sort of reflective consciousness does not necessarily involve an interruption of or detachment from action. Certainly I may be engaged in getting the book and I may be simultaneously formulating a commentary ('Listen, I'm just going to get that book in the

[24] Much of what we say in this section resonates well with points made about 'embodied reflection' by Varela *et al.* (1991). Invoking a Buddhist tradition, they suggest 'a change in the nature of reflection from an abstract, disembodied activity to an embodied (mindful), open-ended reflection' (p. 27; also see pp. 27–31). Like their work, our remarks here are also informed by the phenomenological tradition. The notion of embedded reflection echoes Heidegger's and Merleau-Ponty's critiques of the detached attitude.

next room') which may even serve to improve my actions, or clarify my contextual-ized intention. For example, not infrequently we may arrive at a destination, knowing that we came for some specific purpose, but unable to remember precisely what that purpose was. In some such cases, we may forget our intention precisely because we are so immersed in the immediate action. When, however, we do not lose track of our intention, embedded reflection can be reflexively directed to the intention itself. In such cases, embedded reflection can assist in keeping our intentions accessible, not as certain contents for epistemological investigation, but as pragmatic guides to our actions. Within this kind of self-reflection or reflection on my intentions, I would not necessarily be reflecting on the fact of my moving — on how my legs are moving or on how my arm reaches for the book — nor would I be thinking of the fact that my thoughts about the book are indeed conscious and perhaps organized in a successive way, etc. All of these things constitute the possible subject matter for a more abstract, theoretical or phenomenological reflection, but that would be something more than and different from embedded reflection.

We are not claiming that embedded reflection is such that on its own it could pro-vide a theory of the self, as, for example, one might claim for a scientifically or phe-nomenologically trained reflection. Indeed, a theoretical model of the self is always going to be something more abstract than the kind of insight provided by embedded reflection. It is the nature of theory to involve generalization and to move beyond par-ticulars. If reflection is embedded, it is embedded precisely in the particulars of an individual's life. We suggest, however, that theoretical models of the self ought to start closer to the level of the embedded reflective access we have to our own action and experience, rather than with detached introspective reflection on the nature of consciousness or self. Furthermore, an investigation of the self or personal identity that takes its bearing from embedded reflection and action is not necessarily naive, or uninformed by scientific or systematic considerations. One can educate embedded reflection and make it rigorous and systematic, even if it cannot be theoretical in the sense of being generalizable. Indeed, we find indications of this in long-established and sophisticated traditions of ethical thought.

One kind of embedded reflection is moral deliberation, in which I attempt to answer the question (posed by myself or by others): What do I plan to do? This kind of deliberative reflection includes what Charles Taylor (1985) calls 'strong evaluation,' a reflection on one's own desires and beliefs in which we evaluate our desires and not just the objects that we desire. Nonetheless, when we evaluate our desires, beliefs, and intentions in this way, we do not evaluate them as psychological or epistemologi-cal entities, nor do we report them as contents of our consciousness as such. Rather we evaluate them in their transparency, that is, in terms of our commitment to acting on them.[25] Taylor importantly points out that such strong evaluations are 'anchored' in feelings, emotions and aspirations, and can move us to take action about the way that we take action. Such reflective evaluation is embedded in what we inherently take to be meaningful and important, in our purposive designs for life, in what we intend to do. When in such evaluative explication we define or redefine our desires

---

[25] This notion of transparency derives from Wittgenstein and is discussed in Evans (1982) and Moran (1997). The idea is that, when I am asked what I believe about *x*, I respond by talking about *x*, not about the psychological or epistemological status of my belief. That is, we are aware of the content of our beliefs rather than of our beliefs *as beliefs*.

and intentions, we make constant reference to the way we are living or want to live our lives. It is at this level that episodic memory and certain emotions (especially emotions with a self-reflexive and temporal aspect, such as guilt, pride, hope or relief) can inform embedded reflection and provide a sense of continuity over time, and a sense of responsibility for actions.

To the extent that I come to realize that I am responsible for my actions, and feel so, I recognize a self that I have been, and that I continue to be, or that I want to transform by my actions. Insofar as I am willing to accept the consequences of my actions, or even insofar as I attempt to avoid the consequences of my actions, I am not only making reference to a pragmatically embedded self that is relatively integrated, i.e., dispositionally consistent over time, but I am able to provide an account of that self in the form of a reflective justification, a narrative, or an autobiography.[26] To be sure, such an account will be an explanation or interpretation, but it will be one that is tied to the reality of my own actions, and in that sense it will be a model of my own self. The referent of such reflection and expression is precisely a self that is instantiated in actions across a variety of personally and pragmatically contextualized situations. This notion of the self is best thought of as an *ethical or pragmatic identity*, for it is one that develops within a way of life (an *ethos*) and on a personal level.

Korsgaard suggests that ethical identity can be thought of as a unity of consciousness, but not in the sense of a unified collection of experiences. 'The unity of consciousness consists in one's ability to coordinate and integrate conscious activities' (1991, p. 329). Perhaps we should not call this a unity of consciousness so much as a unity of active life. It is a unity in the particular way that we habitually tend to be engaged *in intentional actions*, rather than a unity of our consciousness *of such activities*. The unity here pertains to agency and capability for action, and involves, not a reflective retrospection that bestows identity on past experiences, but a prospective, embedded reflection that accompanies intentional action and helps to constitute capability. To be sure, deliberation among alternatives and the evaluation of their implications, happen, but not on an abstract theoretical level. Rather, deliberation goes on in the light of one's desires, beliefs, ambitions, hopes, and attitudes toward other people.

Ethical terms such as *integrity*, *disposition*, *constitution* and *character* may signify more appropriately than epistemological or ontological concepts, such as the unity of consciousness or permanence over time, the important aspects of personal identity. Indeed, the central issue for us is not the question of unity, or the possibility of one or many selves. There may be no secure unity of self to be found in ethical behaviour, and we can certainly find examples of ethically inconsistent behaviours within the same individual. By character or disposition we do not mean an essence or thing; nor are these concepts captured by nineteenth-century conceptions of motive and cause that are conceived to be bound up in a nexus that lies beneath the subject and that putatively unifies the phenomenal discontinuity of someone's existence, experience and actions. Character is formed by and continues to be formed by experience and by actions. What we are describing as the ethical self (involving character, disposition, and action capabilities) is generated in and through action.

Outside of pragmatically and socially contextualized actions, the self can only be pictured in an abstract snapshot, through a kind of reflection or experiment that robs it

---

[26] Again, we do not claim that there is any immediate sense of unity of self or of long-term temporal continuity. Rather, in feeling responsible for our actions such unity and permanence is *implied*.

of a rich *ethos*. The self, insofar as this signifies who the subject actually is, comes to exist and is articulated in the social and personal pragmatics and in action contexts that are characterized primarily in personal and social terms. Who I am gets expressed (and is constituted) in my actions towards others and my interactions with them. The personal self comes to exist as such only within such pragmatically and socially contextualized behavioural situations, that is, in action contexts that are characterized primarily in personal and social terms. The vocabulary of self is one that applies to my social interactions, my ethical projects, my meaningful intentions, my moral responsibilities, and to my bodily movements and linguistic competencies *insofar as they are taken up in such situations*.

Certainly what we have said about ecological access and embedded reflection is not a complete characterization of the ethical self. Each self has a certain 'depth' that can be traced out across an individual's own history (including upbringing and individual life experiences), dispositional attitudes and concerns, and traced through the effects that culture and particular constraints imposed by various other factors (such as language, class, gender and race) have on the individual's practical interests, projects and goals. To the extent that individual desires, as well as cultural practices and the performance of social roles, are developed and enacted most fully in behaviour that is defined by personal and social dimensions, the fuller picture would still require that the notion of self be described in vocabulary that is intrinsically related to pragmatically and socially contextualized behaviour. Who I am is most often tied to what I do, or what I can do, or how I express myself in such contexts, even if such actions and expressions cannot capture the full depth of the self.

One finds only incomplete or distorted aspects of the self in isolated or decontextualized movements, in physical mechanisms or functions that can be dissociated in an abstract fashion, or in metaphors such as the flow of consciousness or momentary Strawsonian 'pearls'. Theories that start with abstract behavioural levels base their models of the self on partial, and sometimes distorted aspects of the self — aspects of body image, mechanical movements, syntax and grammar, the starts and stops of a conscious stream, but not on moving and speaking persons. In pragmatically and socially contextualized interactions, however, we find persons who are immersed in purposive projects and are conducting meaningful communication.

Our intention here has not been to work out the details concerning the structure of the ethical self, or how ecological aspects relate to the relatively integrated agent referenced in embedded reflection. We have not tried to explicate precisely how abstract reflective consciousness or psychological experimentation may provide positive snapshots of a self that is more, or less, integrated than its representations. Our intention, rather, has been to indicate an appropriate starting point for building a more adequate and less abstract model for explaining selves.

References

Baddeley A.D. (1990), *Human Memory* (Hove, UK: Lawrence Erlbaum).

Baddeley, A.D. (1992), 'Working memory', *Science*, **255**, pp. 556–9.

Bisiach, E., Berti, A. and Vallar, G. (1985), 'Analogical and logical disorders underlying unilateral neglect of space', in *Attention and Performance XI*, ed. M.I. Posner and O.S.M. Marin (Hillsdale, NJ: Lawrence Erlbaum).

Bisiach, E. and Geminiani, G. (1991), 'Anosognosia related to hemiplegia and hemianopia', in *Awareness of Deficit after Brain Injury*, ed. G.P. Prigatano and D.L Schacter (Oxford: Oxford University Press).

Brouchon, M., Joanette, Y. and Samson, M. (1986), 'From movement to gesture: "here" and "there" as determinants of visually guided pointing', in *Biological Foundations of Gesture*, ed. J.L. Nespoulos, A. Perron, and R.A. Recours (Hillsdale, NJ: Erlbaum).

Butterworth, G. (1995), 'An ecological perspective on the origins of self', in *The Body and the Self*, ed. J. Bermúdez, A. Marcel & N. Eilan (Cambridge, MA: Bradford/MIT Press).

Butterworth, G. (1998), 'A developmental-ecological perspective on Strawson's "The Self" ', *Journal of Consciousness Studies*, **5** (2), pp. 132–40.

Crick, F. (1994), *The Astonishing Hypothesis: The scienctific search for the soul* (London: Simon & Schuster).

Csikszentmihalyi, M. (1978), 'Attention and the holistic approach to behaviour', In *The Stream of Consciousness*, ed. K.S. Pope and J.L. Singer (New York: Plenum Press).

Cumming, G.D. (1972), 'Visual perception and metacontrast at rapid input rates', Unpublished DPhil thesis, University of Oxford.

Damasio, A. (1994), *Descartes' Error: Emotion Reason, and the Human Brain* (New York: Grosset/Putnam).

della Sala, S., Marchetti,C. and Spinnler, H. (1994), 'The anarchic hand: a fronto-mesial sign', in *Handbook of Neuropsychology, vol. 9*, ed. F. Boller and J. Grafman (New York: Elsevier).

Dennett, D. (1969), *Content and Consciousness* (London: Routledge and Kegan Paul).

Dennett, D. (1991), *Consciousness Explained* (Boston, MA: Little, Brown and Company).

Dennett, D. (1992), 'The self as a center of narrative gravity,' in *Self and Consciousness: Multiple Perspectives*, ed. F. Kessel, P. Cole and D. Johnson (Hillsdale, NJ: Erlbaum).

Donaldson, M. (1978), *Children's Minds* (Glasgow: Fontana).

Evans, G. (1982), *The Varieties of Reference* (Oxford: Oxford University Press).

Fourneret, P. and Jeannerod, M. (1998), 'Limited conscious monitoring of motor performance in normal subjects', *Neuropsychologia*, **36**, pp. 1133–40.

Gadamer, H-G. (1976), *Philosophical Hermeneutics*, trans. and ed. David E. Linge (Berkeley, CA: University of California Press).

Gallagher, S. (1992), 'The theater of personal identity: From Hume to Derrida', *The Personalist Forum 8 (1992)*, pp. 21–30.

Gallagher, S. (1998), *The Inordinance of Time* (Evanston, IL: Northwestern University Press).

Gallagher, S. and Meltzoff, A. (1996), 'The earliest sense of self and others: Merleau-Ponty and recent developmental studies', *Philosophical Psychology*, **9**, pp. 213–36.

Gazzaniga, M.S. (1978), 'On dividing the self: Speculations from brain research', in *Neurology: Proceedings of the 11th World Congress of Neurology*, ed. W.A. deHartog Jager *et al.* (Amsterdam: Excerpta Medica).

Gibson, J.J. (1987), 'A note on what exists at the ecological level of reality', in *Reasons for Realism: Selected Essays of James J. Gibson*, ed. E. Reed and R. Jones (Hillsdale, NJ: Erlbaum).

Goldstein, K. (1940), *Human Nature in the Light of Psychopathology* (Cambridge, MA: Harvard University Press; reprinted by Shocken Books: 1963).

Haggard, P. and Eimer, M. (in press), 'On the relation between brain potentials and the awareness of voluntary movements', *Experimental Brain Research*.

Haggard, P. and Magno, E. (in press), 'Localising awareness of action with Transcranial Magnetic Stimulation', *Experimental Brain Research.*

Hécaen, H., Talairach, J., David, M. and Dell, M.B. (1949), 'Coagulations limitées du thalamus dans les algies du syndrome thalamique: résultats thérapeutiques et physiologiques', *Revue de Neurologie*, **81**, pp. 917–31.

Hume, D. (1739), *A Treatise of Human Nature*, ed. L.A. Selby-Bigge (Oxford: Clarendon Press, 1888, 1975).

Husserl, E. (1991), *On the Phenomenology of the Consciousness of Internal Time (1893-1917)*, trans. J. Brough. Collected Works IV (Dordrecht: Kluwer Academic).

James, W. (1890), *The Principles of Psychology* (New York: Dover Publications, 1950).

Jeannerod, M. (1987), *Neurophysiological and Neuropsychological Aspects of Spatial Neglect* (Amsterdam: Elsevier).

Kihlstrom, J.F. (1993), 'The psychological unconscious and the self', in *Experimental and Theoretical Studies of Consciousness,* Ciba Foundation Symposium # **174** (Chichester: John Wiley & Sons).

Korsgaard, C.M. (1991), 'Personal identity and the unity of agency: A Kantian response to Parfit', in *Self and Identity: Contempoary Philosophical Issues*, ed. D. Kolak and R. Martin (New York: Macmillan).

Leontiev, A.N. and Zaporozhets, A.V. (1960), *Recovery of Hand Function* (London: Pergamon).

Marcel, A.J. (1983), 'Conscious and unconscious perception: An approach to the relations between phenomenal experience and perceptual processes', *Cognitive Psychology*, **15**, pp. 238–300.

Marcel, A.J. (1988), 'Phenomenal experience and functionalism', in *Consciousness in Contemporary Science,* ed. A.J. Marcel and E. Bisiach (Oxford: Clarendon Press).

Marcel, A.J. (1992), 'The personal level in cognitive rehabilitation', in *Neuropsychological Rehabilitation*, ed. N. Von Steinbüchel, E. Pöppel and D. Cramon (Berlin: Springer).

Marcel, A.J. (1993), 'Slippage in the unity of consciousness', in *Experimental and Theoretical Studies of Consciousness*, Ciba Foundation Symposium # 174 (Chichester: John Wiley & Sons).

Marcel, A.J. (forthcoming), 'The sense of agency: Awareness and ownership of actions and intentions', in *Agency and Self-Awareness*, ed. J. Roessler and N. Eilan (Oxford: Oxford University Press).

Marcel, A.J. and Dobel, C. (under review), 'Confusing frames of reference in real space and in imagination — the stabilizing effect of perceptual input'.

Marcel, A.J., Tegnér, R. and Nimmo-Smith, I. (under review), 'Anosognosia for plegia: Specificity, extension and partiality of bodily unawareness'.

McCormack, T. and Hoerl, C. (in press), 'Memory and temporal perspective: The role of temporal frameworks in memory development', *Developmental Review*.

Merleau-Ponty, M. (1962), *Phenomenology of Perception*, trans. Colin Smith (London: Routledge and Kegan Paul).

Moran, R. (1997), 'Self-knowledge: Discovery, resolution, and undoing', *European Journal of Philosophy*, 5 (2), pp. 141–61.

Nagel, T. (1975), 'Brain bisection and the unity of consciousness', in *Personal Identity*, ed. John Perry (Berkeley, CA: University of California Press).

Nagel, T. (1986), *The View from Nowhere* (Oxford: Oxford University Press).

Neisser, U. (1988), 'Five kinds of self-knowledge', *Philosophical Psychology*, 1, pp. 35–59.

O'Shaughnessy, B. (1980), *The Will*. 2 vols. (Cambridge: Cambridge University Press).

Parfit, D. (1984), *Reasons and Persons* (Oxford: Oxford University Press).

Poizner, H., Klima, E.S. and Bellugi, U. (1987), *What the Hands Reveal about the Brain* (Cambridge, MA: MIT Press).

Quinton, A. (1975), 'The soul', in *Personal Identity*, ed. John Perry (Berkeley, CA: University of California Press).

Radden, J. (1998), 'Pathologically divided minds, synchronic unity and models of the self', *Journal of Consciousness Studies*, 5 (5–6), pp. 658–72.

Ramachandran, V.S. and Hirstein, W. (1997), 'Three laws of qualia: What neurology tells us about the biological functions of consciousness', *Journal of Consciousness Studies*, 4 (5–6), pp. 429–57.

Rosenthal, D.M. (1993), 'Thinking that one thinks', in *Consciousness*, ed. M. Davies and G.W. Humphreys (Oxford: Blackwell).

Rovane, C. (1998), *The Bounds of Agency* (Princeton: Princeton University Press).

Sartre, J-P. (1957), *Transcendence of the Ego: An Existentialist Theory of Consciousness*, trans. Forrest Williams and Robert Kirkpatrick (New York: Farrar, Straus and Giroux).

Sheets-Johnstone, M. (1999), 'Phenomenology and agency: Methodological and theoretical issues in Strawson's "The Self"', *Journal of Consciousness Studies*, 6 (4), pp. 48–69.

Sperry, R.W. (1968a), 'Mental unity following surgical disconnections of the cerebral hemispheres', *The Harvey Lectures*, Series 62 (New York: Academic Press).

Sperry, R.W. (1968b), 'Hemisphere deconnection and unity in conscious awareness', *American Psychologist*, 23, p. 723.

Strawson, G. (1997), '"The Self"', *Journal of Consciousness Studies*, 4 (5–6), pp. 405–28. Reprinted in this volume, pp. 1–24.

Taylor, C. (1985), *Human Agency and Language: Philosophical Papers I* (Cambridge: Cambridge University Press).

Teasdale, J.D. (in press), 'Emotional processing, three modes of mind, and the prevention of relapse in depression', *Behaviour Research and Therapy*.

Varela, F. (1996), 'Neurophenomenology: A methodological remedy for the hard problem', *Journal of Consciousness Studies*, 3 (4), pp. 330–49.

Varela, F., Thompson, E. and Rosch, E. (1991), *The Embodied Mind* (Cambridge, MA: MIT Press).

Weigl, E. (1961), 'The phenomenon of temporary deblocking in aphasia', *Zeitschrift für Phonetik, Sprachwiss und Kommunikationsforschrift*, 14, pp. 337–64.

Weigl, E. and Kreindler, A. (1960), 'Beiträge zur Auffassung gewisser aphasischer Störungen als Blockierungserscheinungen', *Archiv fur Psychiatrie und Zeitschrift für Gesamte Neurologie*, 200, pp. 306–23.

Wilkes, K.V. (1988), *Real People: Personal Identity without Thought Experiments* (Oxford: Clarendon Press).

Wittgenstein, L. (1958), *The Blue and Brown Books* (Oxford: Basil Blackwell).

Zahavi, D. and Parnas, J. (1998), 'Phenomenal consciousness and self-awareness: A phenomenological critique of representational theory', *Journal of Consciousness Studies*, 5 (5–6), pp. 687–705.

Jonathan Cole

On 'Being Faceless'
Selfhood and Facial Embodiment

The horror of being faceless, of forgetting one's own appearance, of having no face. The face is the mirror image of the self. (Hull, 1992.)

He kissed me, or perhaps I should say that he kissed my face, as I wasn't in it at the time. (Williams, 1992.)

I have a notion which has stayed with me over much of my life that it is possible to live in your head, entirely in my head. Whether that came out of my facial problem I don't know . . . ('James' from an interview cited in Cole, 1998.)[1]

Unquestioning Beginnings

Though I have not met him I suspect that Galen Strawson is healthy and passably handsome. He is also an intellectual with a well developed introspective cognitive awareness. I say this not because I think all philosophers are handsome or particularly healthy, I have met enough of them to know this is not true, but simply because his account of the self has no room for embodiment.

For most people a sense of self includes an embodied component: when describing our selves we describe those aspects of our physical bodies which can be easily codified: height, hair colour, sex, eye colour. Even when we consider ourselves we tend not to consider our intellectual cognitive characteristics but our describable anatomy. Wittgenstein's dictum, 'the human body is the best picture of the human soul', is relevant here but I would like to go further: the body-part we feel most embodied in is our face, even though it is difficult to describe and so forms little part of how we describe ourselves to others.

The face is an unique identifier, allowing observable differentiation from others, (identical twins excepted). It also shows our approximate age, our gender and something of our health, and how tired we are. Through it we can reveal, or attempt to conceal, our emotions. It also, perhaps most importantly, allows shared emotions and

[1] The narratives in this chapter [and the theoretical constructs] are taken from some of the longer and more wide-ranging interviews with people with unusual facial problems for my book, *About Face* (unless stated otherwise all quotations are from this source.) I am very grateful to them for allowing me to listen to and then publish their accounts. I am also happy to acknowledge the constructive advice of Shaun Gallagher.

relationships between people to a level and refinement not observed in other species. To understand the important effect of facial experience on our whole experience of, and sense of, self I suggest that we have to do more than construct experiments or introspect; we have to enter the experiences of others for whom there is a facial problem.

In this chapter I present narratives of subjects with facial problems of various sorts, showing the effect of these on their selfhood. This in turn will suggest how important embodiment and our social relations are in the development and maintenance of sense of self, and how in these relations emotional expression has a role to play. The chapter will thus argue against a strictly cognitive view of the self. I have included narratives not only of those with unusual faces, e.g. the disfigured, but also those whose experience of the faces of others is unusual, e.g. the blind and the autistic. Throughout, my approach will be to explore function by looking at the consequences of loss. In this approach the subject's experiences, as reflected in the opening quotations, are central. Lastly I will also argue that by considering the evolution of the face we may catch a glimpse of our own origins as socially intelligent emotional beings.

My interest in the subject of faces was first kindled when, at a clinical neurological meeting, an elderly woman, Mary, was brought in for our examination and opinion. She had lost speech, probably due to a stroke. What was unusual, however, was that she had also lost facial expression. This made the group of clinicians uneasy since they could not 'make her out'. She offered to write out her answers to their questions but time was short and the offer politely refused. When she had left the room the doctors conferred about the nature of her problem, its site and the possibility of treatment. Some doctors suggested she was demented since she had been unable to respond to us, and a large part of that perceived lack of presence was due to her facial lack: without face she had become in some way invalid as a person.

I reconstructed her case by talking with her (via a portable typewriter) and by talking with her daughter. It turned out that her loss of facial expression had been completely unnoticed by her family, and even by her husband, before a doctor had pointed it out. The family had just thought she was depressed by other aspects of her illness. Bell's (1933) suggestion that we are scarcely conscious of the familiar seemed borne out by her family and, I readily admitted, in my own experience. For until I saw Mary I too had given little thought to the relation between the face and the self: the face was always there and so unquestioned.

This unquestioning was also apparent later when I went to a seminar arranged by Bencie Woll. When deaf subjects communicate by sign language, with their arms and hands, they look at each other's faces. Facial action is used to communicate linguistic and affective information. How, I wondered, did the deaf separate this linguistic facial action from the affective expressions they, and we more familiarly, use the face for? Helpful though the deaf volunteers were, the seminar was close to a disaster. The congenitally deaf could see no problem: the two parts of their facial action merged seamlessly and unconsciously together in such a way that, despite my questioning and probing, they were unable to discriminate. For an understanding of the face I had to go to those with something wrong: only then could I reflect from their experience back to our own.

Congenital Blindness: 'Conscious of the Smile'

I began by asking people who were blind from birth about their experiences of face. They, after all, would never have seen another face, but could make facial expressions, and feel those expressions, through internal feedback or proprioception. Darwin (1965) had observed congenitally blind people and shown that their enjoyment smiles and expressions of anger were similar to sighted people's. Indeed he used this as evidence for the innateness of some facial expressions. What was less clear was whether such a group of people used their faces for social purposes, say when greeting a friend. Did the face have any privileged position in their body image in the absence of sight? Lastly, I was most interested to see how congenitally blind people construct others' identities.

For Peter White, a television and radio broadcaster who has been blind since birth, the questions were easy. He had never even considered the construction of self in others, much less considered it a problem: all was in the voice. Character, mood and even person are constructed as fully from voice as in a seeing person from voice and sight. His self, he thought, 'resided in voice', as we reside in the face and voice. That is not to say, however, that there was exact homology. Some emotions and moods he agreed were heard more in the voice, as others were seen better on the face. He also viewed his face from the inside in curiously proprioceptive terms rather than in our external visual manner:

> I have always been fairly conscious of the smile. A smile is a physical entity to a blind person because of the sensation that generates it inside. It's almost in the throat, a bubbly feeling. You're not necessarily going to laugh. You can feel your face twist and certain muscles relax so you know intellectually that this changes the shape of your face. In contrast I don't know how much I give away of myself in sadness. I am aware of non-communication with my face tightening up and closing up. I am not so aware of it as in smiling.

Sadness was often silent in a way happiness was not, as though some emotional states evolved to be communicated more than others. He accepted also that blindness may have imposed an intimacy in his relations with others, in the sense he tended to know a few people well, and know his immediate family through touch as well as sound. He was clear, however, that facial projection to and from others was of importance. Despite its not being seen, face was a method of contacting others.

> The face is not doing something that's very conscious or vital to my existence but it is doing something that I want to communicate. . . . in order to interact and talk with people you present your face to them. It's not just a place where your voice comes out of, it allows contact with others.

Next I went to talk with David Blunkett in the House of Commons. He is Secretary of State for Education in the 1997– Labour government and has also been blind since birth. He too takes all from the voice and yet is aware of the face disclosing feelings and mood. As a corollary of this he is aware also of the need to control it, for he does not have the non-verbal feedback from others to alert him to the effect his facial expression is having on others. In his forties he is beginning to realize that his face may not be reflecting his feelings, and that this may promote misinterpretations of which he is poorly aware.

On television I have to remember that people are more impressed, or depressed, by how you look than by what you say. Politics is now so much image and atmosphere. People have said to me recently that part of the difficulty fellow politicians in the House of Commons have in relating to me is that sometimes my body language is very dismissive. Now there's a thought. Does that mean my face is dismissive? Am I dismissive in my manner, face and other actions?

Blindness is asymmetric — the blind are always on show to the world and yet unable to perceive much of the feedback. David was describing how he felt at times divorced from what his face was telling people and how, as he concentrated on a question, his face gave wrong signals. He told me that, while congenitally blind children have innate use of the face for enjoyment smiles, he never learnt to smile socially when greeting. He thought that such social use of the face might be taught, to avoid blind children being considered austere.

Loss of Sight, Loss of Face, Loss of Self?

The experience of those who go blind as adults was revealed to be an infinitely different experience. John Hull, who went completely blind in his forties, wrote about some of these experiences in his book, *Touching the Rock* (1992). This diary covered the first few years of blindness and the profound mental adjustments he was forced to make. In my later conversation with him I asked him about his experience in the decade or so after blindness, much of which was not described in his earlier account.

Over the first few months of post-blindness he had almost been taken over by faces as they flooded into his imagination. Sitting alone, his thoughts were all but overwhelmed at times by the faces of friends and of people infrequently seen, even school friends from decades previously. Without seen faces, remembered ones, and unbidden ones welled into his consciousness. He described how the faces of those he could hold onto were like portraits in a gallery. In his imagination he would walk around rooms looking at people he knew he could never see again. As the months went by, however, he noticed that some portraits were now missing. Those he met in his daily life vanished first, as their visual representations were slowly replaced by something else, less describable. Another person who went blind as an adult told me how, in the months after blindness, when meeting new people he would give them the imagined face of someone he had known while sighted, as a way of giving them an identity and character. He needed a face to make a person. This helped, until their self-identity turned out to be different to the one he had given them. Hull found it easier to remember what people looked like whom he had not met since he lost sight. In those with whom his relationship was continuous he simply imposed his living relationship with them on his old visual memory.

In the months after going blind he was tortured by a loss of identity resulting from his blindness:

> To what extent is the loss of the image of the face connected with loss of the image of the self? (Diary [in Hull, 1992], 25 June 1983).

He became aware of facial actions in a way we usually are not. Motor programs, which for most of us are non-conscious, became conscious and began to enter his self image.

Nearly every time I smile, I am aware of it . . . aware of the muscular effort: not that my smiles have become more forced . . . but it has become a more or less conscious effort. It must be because there is no reinforcement . . . no returning smile . . . like sending off dead letters. . . . I can feel myself stopping smiling . . . must ask someone if it is true. (17 September 1983).

In those first three years after blindness he began to explore the voice far more and was amazed, and excited, to learn that for him, as for Peter White, all the emotion which is in the face was also in the voice. Intelligence, colour, light and shade, melody, humour, grace, accuracy, laziness, carelessness and monotony — as well as vocabulary and precision of language — all became revealed aurally. Crucially though, he realized that he was far more passive, and depended on people disclosing themselves through speech. There were, for instance, no covert looks at a person when they were off-guard.

Despite all the daily practical problems following blindness it was the lack of contact with people and, particularly, with their faces that led to his becoming depressed and introspective. He had been quite confident initially but slowly he realized that his continuing social existence depended on a continuing visual memory of others, and of their faces. Just as when sighted people who shut their eyes still envisage the world through a visual memory, so John retained a visual memory of others for some time. He became most depressed not when he went blind but as these visual — mainly facial — images faded and he finally left the visual world, nearly two years after the loss of sight itself.

At one level this meant a loss of an already established visual category of identified others and of self, of visually embodied selves. But along with this there was also a most important and poorly-defined loss of relish and enjoyment in others. This reduced relationship with them underpinned his depression. There was a time when he would retreat to his bedroom and lie for hours under a blanket, trying desperately to find a way out into the world of others again.

Slowly, and through prolonged and persistent cognitive effort, he learnt to reconstruct his new world of relationships, and social existence, without vision. On meeting him, I began by asking how he constructed identity and character without a seen face.

I no longer have a visual image. I don't any longer know or care if they're tall, short, fat, thin, bearded or what, don't give a damn. It doesn't occur to me to construct a physique through the voice. It takes time, more time perhaps. Everything is in the voice.

What was second, or rather first, nature for Peter White, John had to learn to do, constructing individuality from hearing over months and years of cognitive effort.

I instantly know what my closest friends are thinking and feeling because it's all in the voice — but they have to speak. There is a big problem with the child and the face. It's hard to tell moods. If my thirteen year old is taciturn a glance at his face would tell me how he was. When one of my children isn't feeling very well I stretch out my hand and say, 'Well, you're hot, you're cold, you're clammy or sweaty.' I could tell those things but all the subtlety, the diagnosis of emotion of that child, experiencing whether the child is wan or pale I can't tell, nor can I with Marilyn (his wife). I only have the voice. I might hold the hand but I wouldn't know what was happening because of an alienation from the face.

At an emotional level, anger, impatience, such emotions are more easily expressed in the voice than thoughtfulness or sadness. It is very difficult to detect sadness. My emotional range is narrowed. This is something I feel most acutely when I'm telling stories to my children, and an even worse time is when I want to listen to music with them.

I suggested that I could tell a joke, or share an experience, several times to different sets of people and find it funny each time because they renewed it through sharing.

I'm not getting the feedback that allows that refreshment and rejuvenation. I would love my son Tom say to come and listen to a Beethoven Violin Concerto but he would be sitting there next to me and I have no way of knowing what it means to him. When it's finished I'd say at the end, 'Well what's it like?' and he'd say, 'Great,' and walk off and I still wouldn't know.

I suggested that he thought that the face expresses emotion in the finest way.

Exactly. And with music it's not what you say afterwards, it's the little glances that you show as it reaches its climax and you know you're in the music together and there's no fellow feeling without contact with the face.

I continued that normally one never consciously constructs character and feelings towards someone — it just happens. I asked if once blind he had to become more intellectual, and if these constructions required effort and thought.

Marilyn and I have sweated blood on this one because it was so difficult for the sighted person to enter into that world. A year or two ago we had a visitor when Joshua was about three; when the friend had gone Marilyn said, apropro of nothing, 'What comes into your mind when I say Joshua?' I said, 'Well, Joshua.' And she said, 'What, what exactly is it?' 'Well, it's the memory running through my hand, the feeling, kicking, laughing body, of throwing him over my shoulder. Joshua's tummy when I put my hand on it in the bath and the things Joshua and I have done together.' 'Yes, but what of Joshua himself?' 'If you mean what does he look like — nothing.' 'I can't bear that, I can't bear to hear you say that, because I feel that I'm closer to our friend who just left because she and I share the same Joshua.' I had to reply that I did not really know what she meant, 'Darling, but if we are going to say do we share the same Joshua we might as well say "Do we share the same world?" and in saying "do we share the same world" there is a deep and important sense in which we do not. We do not share the same world.'

I asked if he knew what he looked like himself.

I don't know what you mean by look like. The category of 'looking like' has disappeared with me. I can remember passport photographs and things like that but they're irrelevant.

Trying to see the interaction between thought and facial action, I asked him: if he thought of something funny, did he think, and then realize that he was smiling?

That's such a good question. I am sometimes fearful that my face is becoming less expressive but Marilyn tells me this is not the case and that I have no need to worry about that, but I feel it. I often feel that I'm thought to be too serious. It's hard for a blind person to have fun in a way because so much of the fun is visual and shared, especially in the family. People making funny faces, teasing each other and I can be out of it. It's so instantaneous, it can't be expressed in speech and I'm sometimes conscious of being heavy. I try to make up for that by hearing. Laughing together is one of the best things.

Normally, enjoyment smiles, social smiles, family smiles are all entwined together, feeding off each other and creating new smiles. Not just smiles and happiness — sadness, say, has a large facial component and a large social, figure of eight, existence. That was something John found difficult with, and through, the voice. I asked if he smiled as much when on his own.

I am not sure. Not knowing about other person's tears is worse than not knowing about smiling. Tears are silent. It's perhaps more important to know about tears than about smiles. Tears take longer, laughter is so ephemeral. I think there's no doubt that the loss of the face is a profound loss. A deeply dehumanising loss. Having said that the experience of living without faces does present another facet of human relationships which has its own adaptations and compensations.

If subjects suffering from congenital blindness had little problem in constructing identity and character from the voice, they were aware of some problems in the way others might perceive them. Peter White remarked that he was aware that people said he had a smile in his voice, and wondered whether he had consciously put it there. David Blunkett was concerned that people might consider him austere because he was not so adept at a social use of his face. The experience of learning to live in a blind world as an adult was very different. For John Hull the lack of sight of others, and the loss of social relationships through shared facial expression, was perhaps the most profound and difficult aspect of blindness. This loss had taken him to despair, and beyond, and had forced him to consider the validity of his own self and own soul. Reconstruction of a new and altered world of social relationships, and of self, had required a huge cognitive effort not just to learn to overcome the inconveniences of practical day to day living, but even more so to regain a full awareness of the presence of others.

Möbius Syndrome: 'Living in my Head'

Acquired blindness allows some reflection on the consequences of losing the sight of oneself and of others. The loss was not exclusively facial, though the subject's experience did reveal the primacy of facial experience in selfhood and affective communication. There is, however, a condition which may be considered exclusively facial. In Möbius syndrome subjects are born without the ability to move any of the muscles of facial expression, or to move their eyes laterally.

The syndrome was first described by Paul Möbius, a nineteenth-century German neurologist. Diane Williams, an American nurse who has the syndrome, wrote of her problems, 'I am unable to raise my eyebrows, close my eyes tightly, move my eyes to the side, smile or move my lips . . . my face has a mask-like appearance' (Goldblatt and Williams, 1986). People with Möbius then have no movement of the facial muscles, they have drooping and wide eyes, and a narrow open mouth. In addition they have an associated problem with sideways movement of the eyes, so that in order to gaze at something, or someone, they have to move the whole head.

Their lack of facial expression and their mask-like faces lead to a stigmatisation which obviously colours their early social development. However the syndrome leads to other less expected consequences. I spoke with several people with Möbius about their experiences. One man, James, was in his fifties. In his family he was not singled out and his facial problem was hardly mentioned. This was a wonderful beginning, though it is less clear if it prepared him for the inevitable problems of school and even university. He described how he was a loner, even at Cambridge, where he studied theology. He divided people into two groups, those that did not want to have anything to do with him and those who did. He described feelings of low self worth, of isolation, even in company, and of loneliness. Worse perhaps, he seemed to have lost sight of the fact that many of these feelings were related to his facial problems, thinking instead that was just the way he was, and that he was a failure. The Möbius appeared so obvious, and yet he had repressed it in considering his feelings and self-esteem.

> I have a notion which has stayed with me over much of my life — that it is possible to live in your head, entirely in my head. Whether that came out of my facial problem I don't know.

This reduced embodiment had isolated him from the world and also led him away from the physical origin of the problem. He also described the problems of never having experienced happiness, or sadness, or anger, through facial expression. This reduced embodiment seemed to have several consequences. There was a dissociation from feelings: 'feelings', he described, had a more thinking aspect which were then turned into feelings almost intellectually. When he met his wife, 'I think initially I was thinking I was in love with her rather than feeling it: it was some time later when I realized that I really felt in love.' This dissociation re-emerged later:

> I do think I get trapped in my mind or my head. I sort of think happy or I think sad, not really saying, or recognizing, actually feeling happy or feeling sad. Perhaps I have had a difficulty in recognizing that which I'm putting a name to is not a thought at all but it is a feeling, maybe I have to intellectualize mood. I have to say this thought is a happy thought and therefore I am happy. Of course since I have never been able to move the face, I've never associated movement of the face with feeling of an emotion. If I have expressed any emotion I must have spoken it, or I might put my arm around someone of course.

This lack of engagement in an emotional existence, which may have arisen from the lack of facial expression of feeling, was experienced both by James and others with Möbius. With this there was also a terror that emotions might run out of control. It seems that we need to express powerful feelings in order to calibrate them. James suggested that,

> I have a fear of being out of control with emotions, feeling something that I can't manage. I have also found it very difficult to communicate feelings throughout my life, though I think I am getting better at it now. I don't really know how I communicate happiness or sadness. That's a very hard question. Some people cry when they're sad. I don't think I cry. I am afraid of such feelings. I try and shut them off.

I asked if since he had never been able to reinforce his feelings by their expression in his face, and possibly in his body, he thought those feelings might be less experienced. He agreed, 'I think you're right. These feelings are there but they are probably reduced. I've often thought of myself as a spectator rather than a participant.'

Another person with Möbius had suffered severe panic attacks with sufficient episodic loss of control that she had been hospitalized and sedated — her feelings of frustration and pain once welled up were uncontrolled. In contrast a young boy with Möbius I met was described by his parents as so placid they hardly ever knew what he was thinking. His never got excited, even at Christmas.

There seems little doubt that the stigmatization secondary to James' unusual face, coupled with a dissociation of emotion from its expression to others and to himself, led to profound effects on his sense of self. His choice of the ministry for a profession may have been, in part, to gain a ready identity as a 'man of the cloth'. Recently he has left work as a parish priest as he began to explore himself as a person and, in particular, as a person with a face. 'People, they are their faces. I think now I would like to be my face'. I asked if he felt he had lost a sense of self, or was trying to recover it, by leaving active ministry.

Had I ever had it? I was losing me as a priest but trying desperately to recover just me, James. Yes, this is a new thought. Perhaps I had spent my life as someone else in order not to be me. Me is something I see in the mirror. I have always had a difficulty with mirrors and photographs. I don't like being confronted by me.

'But the "me" you see is not the "me" that you are.'

No. That's true. But even in a mirror it's an image, a partial image. I don't want to but I have to look in a mirror, and apart from shaving I never do. I may have turned my back on my face. I hadn't thought of it but I certainly may have done, much more than I had ever realized or supposed. This idea I mentioned earlier of attempting to live behind it may well be an escape from something I found intolerable. But I now realize that some things which may have been due to the condition I felt were just down to me. Rather than saying that the condition has made life difficult I have been saying I have made life difficult. It was my fault. I have failed.

I suggested that to become a whole person he had to look in the mirror and say, 'This is my face but I am not this: I exist behind and yet beyond it.'

Yes, I think you're right. One of the things I think that's happening now is that I have a sense of becoming freer. Freer in the sense of becoming more myself, not playing a role. I certainly wanted to try and explore me behind the mask of the priesthood. If you say where does 'me' now reside, I think I am slowly coming out of my head a bit. I am not sure I can locate where I am but I don't think I am entirely in my head or even my mind. I have an expression of living 'a life of the mind', but I do accept that the mind is not easily able to communicate its thoughts or even its feelings. I think I was out of touch with my feelings, or I suppressed a lot of them.

It was clear from talking with a number or people living with Möbius that the loss of facial movement had led them to a range of experience beyond the imagination of most of us. Their loss of facial expression had reduced their emotional experience and control, and distanced themselves not just from others, but also from their own experienced embodiment. Their facial stigma, and their inability to co-ordinate gaze, meant they were further disadvantaged in not observing others frequently. They had been led, or forced, to live in their heads. Yet if this was a purely intellectual existence it was not that of the balanced enquiring philosopher, but a measured attempt at self preservation.

Bell's Palsy: 'Emotional Limbo'

Just as congenital blindness is a very different condition to mature onset of blindness, so too loss of facial expression must be a very different experience to having never had it. Such a fate does fall to some people with Parkinson's disease, when it can, unfortunately, be remorseless though slowly progressive. Fewer people have ever been facially immobile and then recovered. Medically this is a very rare event, found usually in a rare number of cases of bilateral Bell's palsy affecting the facial nerves. One such case was Oliver, an architecture student in his early twenties. He developed an immobile face whilst at university, existed with it for around six months and then recovered slowly, whilst at home.

Whilst facially immobile he had noticed a reduction in his relish and enjoyment of the world. I reminded him that stuck at home instead of university, and with a worrying illness, one would expect to feel low. He agreed, but then carried on,

> I suppose I didn't feel constantly happy, but then I didn't feel sad . . . I felt almost as if in a limbo between feelings — just non-emotional . . . I don't know . . . it was within myself, an emotional limbo. I still felt happy to see or hear something I liked, but I didn't think that I felt it as much because I was not actually smiling. I started to write a diary . . . Writing it out helped a lot. Such and such has happened and I feel this. Writing allowed me to express.

It seemed very likely that losing facial animation meant not only losing expression and communication with others but led to a reduced intensity of, and delineation of, feeling within oneself. That he was able to reflect on this, whilst temporarily without facial expression, throws into relief the difficulties those with Möbius had, who have never known what it is to move their faces. The experience for Oliver however was not altogether negative:

> I felt like someone always wearing a mask, but not as you might expect. The facial problem was a bit like a mask, a mask of anonymity, partly because I was shy and uncertain of myself. But a mask can also act as a protective barrier — my face became such a mask for me and I was hiding behind it and getting more confidence. Then knowing that people would be unsure of me because of my condition it made me, enabled me, to be more forceful and less hesitant. I became more positive. I made more effort to communicate verbally and by gesture. I would wave my arms around like a Frenchman.

That such a huge loss of function had actually been beneficial was extraordinary. I paraphrased Wittgenstein, that the face is transparent and allows you to 'see through it . . . to the person', to the soul.

> My soul, I think, was more in my voice. I noticed that on the telephone I had difficulty in controlling my own emotional state because I could not control my face — my face did tie in with this. You can be in a foul mood normally and speak on the phone as though happy. With the condition I could no longer do that. I could not lie.

His temporary facial paralysis had forced him to consider many matters in his relations with others and in his perception of himself as a person. Extraordinarily he had used this period as one of asylum from the intensity of social play which we, particularly as young adults, experience and he returned to that world wiser — an unexpected consequence of living 'without face'.

Autism: Push Button Expression

Talking with people who existed without seen or moved faces allowed some insight into the centrality of the face, and facial expression, as a representation of self, and of reaching out to others. These narratives told of the face reflecting the importance of embodiment and our social existence. I next went to a group of people who had practically no sociability and little apparent use for facial expression. Their main problem was a much more widespread and pervasive developmental neurological disorder. In his original description of a group of children with the disorder which now, in part, bears his name, Asperger (1944) wrote:

... autistic children have a paucity of facial and gestural expression. In ordinary two-way interaction they are unable to act as a proper counterpart to their opposite number, and hence they have no use for facial expression as a contact-creating device.

The whole of the problem of autism has yet to be encompassed. For some it can be understood in terms of a defect of theory of mind, in that people with autism cannot understand that others have minds and feelings. For others that cognitive theory is secondary to a lack of inter-personal relatedness and a lack of reaching out to others. Some talk of information overload, which makes sounds frighteningly loud and incoherent, the visible world overwhelming, preventing any meaningful interpretable sense of what is external. This overload also, it is apparent, exists in autistic subjects' inner states too, so that any sense of a unified self can be missing.

All these approaches have their merits. Here, however, is not the place for a detailed discussion on the phenomenology of autism. In trying to analyse the condition there has been much work on the use of face by autistic subjects. Some have suggested that they ignore faces, others that they can interpret easy expressions like happiness, but are lost when it comes to facial expressions which require interpretation of motive in a manner which requires understanding of a theory of mind (Baron-Cohen, 1995; Baron-Cohen et al., 1993; Hobson, 1993). One difficulty in defining autism concerns understanding what it is like to be autistic: for this autobiographical accounts are required and yet, historically, these have been scarcely possible given the problems inherent in the condition. Fortunately, recently, some such accounts have been forthcoming and something of the autistic subject's disordered, fractured existence has been made public (Frith, 1991; Grandin and Scariano, 1986). Donna Williams has written two books of autobiography about her autistic spectrum disorder (1992; 1994). She describes her condition as being a neurological problem (rather than a developmental psychiatric one), denying her emotional expression and understanding. It is clear, however, that her problem involves all aspects of her being. At one point in her first book she clearly describes how she has hardly any sense of body image or of embodiment:

> My hand was placed randomly on my leg. Suddenly I became aware of inner feeling in both my hand and my leg at the same time. 'I can feel my leg,' I shouted in fear. 'I can feel my hand and my leg!'... I moved my hand to my arm and fearfully whispered, 'I've got an arm.' I felt it not on my hand from the outside, as usual, but from the inside. 'Arm' was more than a texture; it was an inner sense.
> My hands went up to my face. My face was there from the inside. My body was more than just a series of textures that my hands knew, an image my eyes saw ...

If she had problems with her self image at the most profound level, then her problem with accessing others was not surprising. Despite these difficulties, however, even from early childhood, when her ability to find any sense or reason in her world was severely limited, the face still played some role in defining people and so represented both threat and hope. She wrote that as a child she 'avoided looking into other people's eyes, but could look into those of young baby brother,' who was less threatening. Once, she thought, her father's eyes seemed to be crying out to reach her.

We normally learn to understand more complex facial expressions as the appreciation of more complex emotions develops. Young children, for instance, find happiness and sadness more easily communicated via the face than the more subtle expressions, say of interest or concern, that they do not yet fully understand. Children with autism seem unable to connect scarcely understood facial movements with feelings in order to learn something of themselves and their social existence. Donna learnt to behave in a way which allowed her to function, painting a smile across her face, trying 'to impersonate my version of happy'. Smiling was not a pretence but a necessary way of existing. At home there was one person she could look at, her reflection in a mirror. 'At home I would still spend hours in front of the mirror, staring into my own eyes and whispering my name . . . frightened at losing my ability to feel myself.'

Once, as an adolescent, she met a boy, 'He kissed me — or perhaps I should say that he kissed my face, as I wasn't in it at the time.' To become too close was to be overwhelmed by the 'otherness' of that person, and to risk losing all connection to the fragile sense of 'self'. Time and time again she writes of how she would paint on a smile, learnt from a TV soap, to hide from others her true feelings. Slowly the sharing of attention was not just seen as a threat, though the face and its gaze continued to represent an overwhelming presence of another. Slowly she began to see what faces meant for relatedness. In her early twenties she watched as a small child greeted her mother and father,

> I watched the ease with which she hugged her parents. I watched the expression on her face . . . What she did was not just for image, for acceptance. It was not out of insecurity to make sure they would still like her. There was something happening for her that affected not her expression but the change in her expression. What she did had come from feelings, and the change in her expression seemed like a dialogue between her and her parents.

Fascinated by Donna's first hand accounts of her disorder and how face was represented in it, I corresponded with her, mainly by phone and fax, trying to order her thoughts about her problem with faces, and how it could reflect on the use of faces for us all. She replied that the problem with faces was based on several things.

There was a fear based on learning that looking would cause people to attempt to engage her in interaction. This, in turn, would engulf her fragile sense of selfhood in a flood of 'other'. It would also evoke body-sensation caused by intense emotion that would be beyond her ability to process, and, therefore, be confusing and frightening, as well as being physically intolerable. There was also a concern that what was shown on faces would only be inconsistently comprehensible, and would soon cause information overload.

There was also a problem in not being able to bear looking because what she did see suggested 'that people were not true to their self and that made them scary'. She could see this when the eyes had no correlation to the expression of the rest of the face, and she was struck fiercely by the impact of this asymmetry. Its implications were that these people were somehow dangerous because their real self was not accessible. It is not clear here if she is describing her inability to appreciate the social use of the face which we all employ for much of the time. But it is clear that she was searching for something that connected her self, whatever perception or realization of it that she had, and her facial expression.

> I did not empathize with what the face was expressing but with the system that the facial disconnections spoke of. When I searched in my own eyes, [when looking in a mirror for hours on end] I did not look at my face, I searched for connectedness between soul and expression through body — most of the time I found none, except in my eyes. Sometimes

I saw dead eyes in an animated face, sometimes I saw alive eyes in a disconnected face. I also avoided looking at faces because of the meaningless of their component parts, [which] led to non-interpretable sensory-based behaviours and curiosity which were generally not welcomed.

She was aware of some of the effect her interest was having on others, even though she had no ability to empathize with them.

I also did not like the shock of finding I had touched or stared at a part of someone's face and then realized that these parts belonged to the person. The jolt always disturbed me. I did not learn to stop touching or staring at people though I learned to stop touching hair, comparing noses and staring at blemishes. Another disturbance in looking at people was that being echopraxic [mimicking their movements because they had taken over her actions], taking on their postures and facial expressions unintentionally, disturbed me and sometimes disturbed them.

It disturbed me because I just wanted to keep my own body connectedness intact and not have to have it trail off like that, like a wild horse. Sometimes others had more control over my body than I did and I did not like to experience that, when I realized I had slipped into involuntarily mimicking them.

We all have a body image, which involves, in part, a conscious perception of our own embodied self viewed as a whole, and a body schema, a non-conscious, or pre-conscious system, which co-ordinates sensory feedback and motor control (Gallagher and Cole, 1995). Here, and in a later passage, she suggests that she did not have a body image, did not have a conscious and accessible sense of herself as a whole, as a person. She could walk and eat and so forth, without conscious attention according to stored repertoires, and was not aware of herself doing these things. She existed at the level of the body schema and occasionally had an image imposed on her by the presence of another, or from a mirror image.

Not being able to make consistent sense of facial expression also meant there was no consistent reward in what it was meant to express. This was worse with overload which could mean that 30% comprehension could slip to 10% or nil. I also think that relying upon pattern [rote learning of facial expressions] made reliance upon interpretation a late, acquired second language and so interpretation was generally a redundant system, because I already had one that I trusted far more in terms of my own social/emotional/perceptual/ sensory reality.

She began to achieve some consistent interpretation around 10 years old. Moreover her system seems to make interpretations of others, and of their feelings, from surprising things.

I could tell mood from a foot better than from a face. I could sense the slightest change in regular pace and intensity of movement of foot. I could sense any asymmetry in rhythm that indicated erraticness and unpredictability. I could sense the expressive from the reactive. Facial expression, by comparison, was so overlaid with stored expression, full of so many attempts to cover up or sway impression that the foot was much truer. I used sound in the same way, even breathing. Intonation aside, I could sense change in regular rhythm, pace, intensity and pitch. I think these things may be how animals make sense of people.

Now in her thirties, she has some knowledge of what she is doing with the face.

Yes, I have come to externally monitor my own facial expression. Through this I can often tell when a disconnected expression is on my face, but I can also tell when, much more occasionally, a connected emotion has made the physical connection to facial expression. I do feel that I have connected expression but it gets lost when experiencing other. I feel that in place of this, I learn to stick stored expressions on and over time, these became triggerable responses in response to patterns of behaviour, though still disconnected to emotion — push button expression.

Self and face were not linked. Triggerable, reactive defence, like what comes out in disconnected facial expression is stored repertoire, the result of brain but not of mind. I distinguish between the brain (instinctual involuntary adaptations) and the mind (the self which has volition). The only point at which the mind comes into this is where it chooses to allow the adaptations of the brain to govern without a psychological fight.

But despite these problems she is now aware of faces as ways of joining up with others. In corresponding I had mentioned Merleau-Ponty's saying about existing in another's facial expression.

I liked the Merleau-Ponty thing, that I exist in another's facial expression. . . . Certainly, it was the reaction of others to my 'characters' that encouraged reliance upon mechanical, disconnected expression in place of self expression, and helped develop a sort of defence of those characters as 'selves'. Yet, for me, it was that rare experience of seeing in someone's eyes that they had seen me in there — beyond the suffocation of these distorting facades — that told me that I did exist. This was like oxygen to a flame about to go out and it fired the fight for expression of selfhood, for which I had almost exhausted all hope.

I still do not feel right with the idea that I am my body, I have had the experience of this but it is not consistent. Mostly I think I exist in my sub-conscious or pre-conscious mind — not easily voluntarily accessible except through writing, music and painting. In daily life, my self is often inaccessible on a voluntary and conscious level, though it is certainly triggerable and able to be evoked. Much of my life is spent either writing, composing or in the company of someone with whom I feel safe to mirror or be triggered by. Mostly my direction is dictated by the things around me, rather than by conscious mind. I am stuck with this but if I go to winge all I have to do is to think about all the low functioning autistic people who do not have this adaptation. Then there is no winge or moan.

There are many problems for those with autistic disorders. Yet in their relations with others, in their social existence, the absence of which has fascinated since the disorder was first described, faces and facial expression have been used to try and get inside the condition from the outside. Now through Williams' work, and those of others, biographical and autobiographical accounts are emerging. As Oliver Sacks (1995) has written, each individual is different and ideally requires their own account. Williams is unlikely to be typical, and that she can express herself this well is unusual in itself. But her account of her facial problems does allow some insight into her world and, in turn, some of her insights into how her problems in her relatedness to others have a facial dimension reflects back to our own use of faces.

Facing Emotion, Facing Consciousness, Facing the Self

My approach to exploring the relation between face and self has been unusual. In listening to the narratives of those with facial problems I have attempted, by understanding the effect of their facial experience on their perception of themselves, to reflect on our normal facial functioning. This approach has led me to stress the importance of our emotional lives on selfhood and self-esteem. It has also, inevitably, placed the face in a central role in these matters.

In focusing on the importance of the face in selfhood I might be criticised for ignoring the huge evolutionary developments of language and of intellect. Might we not now live in a more cognitive world, having left purely affective emotional responses behind a little? Though more recent evolutionary cognitive developments have had a huge effect on our perception of self and of others, we still remain driven to surprising degree by an emotional perspective. Antonio Damasio (1995), for instance, has shown how some people with frontal lobe damage to the brain can have retained intellect and memory but can be without emotional responses. They are unable to function in the world because decisions about even simple matters, say like what to eat or where to go, depend on an emotional valence.

Yet I would hesitate to suggest that emotion and the face have no relation to the more phylogenetically recent intellectual functions for which we are renowned. In evolutionary terms the development of mobile expressive faces may be of great importance in the development of our intellectual cognitive identities. If, as has been suggested by Donald (1993), intelligence arose in a social setting to manage the complex social groups that were one reason for the success of early primates, then the evolution of facial expression, which allowed expression of inner affective states, may have been a necessary development for subsequent changes.

The importance of mutual gaze and shared visual attention have been stressed by workers investigating theory of mind mechanisms, as a way children learn that others share mental states. How this knowledge originates has, however, proved more difficult to determine in such a theoretical framework. For Peter Hobson (1993) the way out of this difficulty is to suggest that, 'children's understanding of unobservable mental states is not so mysterious once one sees that they begin by understanding mental states that are observable'. By this he means that inner emotional states are seen and recognized as such, innately and initially, by children on the face. Anger, happiness and a number of other emotions are seen on the face. Later in development cognitive strategies for interpersonal skills may come more to the fore, but at the beginning was not the thought, or the word, but the feeling, seen facially. Meltzoff and Gopnik (1993) go further and suggest that in early experience babies learn something of emotion, and how it is experienced, by taking the facial expressions of others and, by imitation, feeling their own faces to be like others. This is clearly impossible for those with Möbius, and some of their problems in the full embodied experiencing of emotion and in interpersonal relatedness have been discussed. In the case of Donna's autism imitation was possible, but with no connection between face and self, nor face and soul. She was able either to paint a smile on her face to get by with others, or in an echopraxic take-over have a smile put there by others. Neither of these was the imitative and shared expression/emotion of Meltzoff and Gopnik.

For Wittgenstein (1980) the face is the interlocutor between the self and the world, and facial action and feeling are intimately linked. 'We describe a face immediately as sad. . . even when we are unable to give any other description of the features. "We see emotion." — As opposed to what? — We do not see facial contortions and then make the inference that the other person is feeling joy, grief, boredom.' In agreement, and correctly, Hobson (1993) writes, that normally,

> the perception is not a two stage process of which the first stage is the perception of . . . behavioural or bodily form, and the second is an intellectually-based attribution of meaning. Rather the perception is of the meaning itself. . . . To perceive a smile is to be inclined to feel certain things.

We describe a face immediately as sad, radiant, bored, even when we are unable to give any other description of the features. Grief, one would like to say, is personified in the face. This is essential to what we call 'emotion'.

'The content of an emotion — here one imagines something like a picture. The human face might be called such a picture . . .' (Wittgenstein, 1980). Wittgenstein's book, *Remarks on the Philosophy of Psychology*, was about many things, but perhaps most about the relations between what is within us and its expression. For him visual representation, via the face, was a most important aspect of our expression of inner states and of self. The mind, consciousness, is on the face, to be seen. Such themes also occupied Merleau-Ponty, whose discussions considered the relation of emotion and consciousness. 'What is it to be moved, what is the meaning of emotion? Can one conceive of a consciousness which is incapable of emotion?' (1964). One might suggest that some people with autism have a form of consciousness, but it seems fragmented and incapable of having sufficient aspects, on-line together, for either fully formed self awareness, or to enter others' experiences. Neither can autistic subjects apparently recognise their poorly formed emotions, let alone express them either in their own bodies, for themselves, or for others. The frontally damaged subjects described by Damasio may have a full memory and cognitive powers but, without an emotional valence, may be deficient in interpersonal relations. Both groups then have an impoverished and reduced consciousness. Merleau-Ponty went on to suggest that, 'the intellectual elaboration of our experience of the world is constantly supported by the affective elaboration of our inter-human relations'.

It is clear that consciousness without this affective component is very different to that which exists with a fully-formed emotionally aspect. Whilst the detailed relations between the evolution of face and facial expression, social intelligence, and theory of mind remain unclear, it is clear that in evolutionary terms the development of mind and of face have gone together. It is indeed difficult to imagine how the kind of regulation of emotion in complex social groups that is seen in primates and, particularly, in humans could have arisen without the refinement in feeling and in its expression (through face). The *Oxford English Dictionary* gives its first definition of consciousness as, 'knowing something of others, knowing in yourself'. In this sense consciousness may have been first considered as something that happens not only in oneself, but also between people, and one important way to communicate is through facial expression. If, as is thought, our evolution proceeded for sometime before the development of language then 'knowing something of others' may initially have evolved in an affective, emotional milieu rather than through linguistic cognitive channels. If so then this communication of inner states may have depended to some extent on the evolved face.

A picture, or even moving pictures, as suggested by Wittgenstein are understandable yet poor analogies, for the face involves an injunction not only to express, and to observe expressions, but to immerse oneself in what is expressed and to feel something of it oneself. Though complementary to body language, in this it may go beyond what is usually considered to be expressed through posture. Expressions actually help in constituting what is within. A face, therefore, is not only an expression of a self available for others to read, but to some extent the self is constituted in the face and developed, and experienced, in the interaction between faces.

This empathic component probably has no analogies because it is unique in the animal kingdom and indeed helps define us all, bar those with autism. Consciousness, knowing with others, 'knowing something of others, something in yourself': in one of its original senses the definition carries with it some recognition of self and others in relation to one another. Facial expressions are concerned not only with communication outwards, but with relatedness and sharing of feeling.

Self and Social Existence

Merleau-Ponty was in no doubt as to the importance of our social relationships for the expression of, and indeed existence of, a well developed sense of self and of the centrality of the face in this expression: 'I exist in the facial expression of others, as they do in me' (1964). This truth is shown in those with facial problems. Their unusual faces prevented any reflection in the facial expression of others but that which reinforced their separateness and alienation. For example a charity concerned with the social and hence personal rehabilitation of those with facial disfigurement (Changing Faces), seeks for its clients other avenues of expression, and to give them the means to manage social interactions independently of their faces, as individuals with personal gifts to offer, not as people defined by their stigma. Many of their clients' first requirement was to be able to stand gazing at each other, such was their depression with their perceived facial problem and their poor self esteem. Many said that they came to group sessions just to experience friendship once more.

We may now see how the various case histories and narratives are related. The different categories of problems, blindness, Möbius, Bell's palsy and autism — some congenital, some experienced later — blur and overlap at the face. All tell of a disconnection between mind and body in a very specific way, between that part of mind concerned with emotion and its elaboration in the face.

Their narratives tell of difficulties in the calibration and experience of emotion and of the essential, deeply embedded, role of the face in our perception of self. Their profound difficulties in a social existence keep returning us to the crucial part that existence plays in our well being. Those who were hardly aware of the facial origin of their problems show how deep within us are these matters, that they are only brought to light by a shattering disconnection between personality and the face.

Autism of course is not a face problem in the way Möbius syndrome is. Despite these differences, those with Möbius have, at times, been labelled autistic because their facial immobility has prevented normal social interaction and emotional expression. In people with facial problems their low self esteem led to an almost autistic withdrawal from others. If emotions need expression, through feelings in the body, then it follows that a lack of experience of feeling, from the face, may lead to a reduced ability for emotional experience itself. Oliver, with the Bell's palsies, described being in an emotional limbo, not knowing what he felt, and resorted to a diary to write down and try to reach his emotions.

It becomes clear from those who have lost facial animation how crucial is that facial embodiment for our emotional existence. One could even legitimately ask why, when we talk of 'embodiment', is there no term for facial embodiment? Is it because it is so obvious we cannot see it? James, 'the spectator', who has never known such embodiment, described a curious detachment, thinking he was happy rather than feeling it. Without feelings from the face, emotions may be less clearly defined and so less fully experienced, and James was less able to enter the full presence of others. I once suggested to him that seeing someone else, and seeing how they felt, were the beginnings of relating to them. He replied,

> I have not tried to think about how they feel. I have not done this by looking, communication for me began with the words, it was language and by thought that my relationship was formed.

But we have seen how inadequate many of these purely cognitive-based relations are. To live, 'in one's head', or without the emotional interpersonal relatedness which the face allows, leads to an almost unimaginable impoverishment of self. It is through exploring the experiences of such people that we can realize the nature of these selves, and, by reflection, the nature of our own selves and our dependence on face. And finally, only then, with understanding and empathy can we seek to help such people, and ourselves.

References

Asperger, H. (1944), 'Die "autischen Psychopathen" in Kindesalter', *Archiv für Psychiatrie und Nervenkrankenheiten*, **117**, pp. 76–136. For an English translation, see Frith (1991).

Baron-Cohen, S. (1995), *Mindblindness* (Cambridge, MA: MIT Press).

Baron-Cohen, S., Tager-Flusberg, H. and Cohen, D.J. (1993), *Understanding Other Minds, Perspectives from Autism* (Oxford: Oxford University Press).

Bell, Charles (1833), *The Hand: Its Mechanism and Vital Endowments as Evincing Design*. Bridgewater Lecture Series. Reprinted by Pilgrims Press, 1979.

Cole, Jonathan (1998), *About Face* (Cambridge, MA: MIT Press).

Damasio, Antonio (1995), *Descartes' Error: Emotion, Reason and the Human Brain* (New York: Putnam).

Darwin, Charles (1965), *The Expression of the Emotions in Men and Animals* (Chicago: University of Chicago Press).

Donald, Merlin (1993), *Origins of the Modern Mind* (Cambridge, MA: Harvard University Press).

Frith, U. (1991), *Autism and Asperger Syndrome* (Cambridge: Cambridge University Press).

Gallagher, Shaun and Cole, Jonathan (1995), 'Body image and body schema in a deafferented subject', *Journal of Mind and Behaviour*, **16** (4), pp. 369–90.

Goldblatt, D. and Williams, D. (1986), ' "I am Smiling!" Möbius syndrome inside and out', *Journal of Child Psychology and Psychiatry and Applied Disciplines*, **1**, pp. 71–8.

Grandin, Temple and Scariano, M.M. (1986), *Emergence Labelled Autistic* (Novato, CA: Arena Press).

Hobson, R.P. (1993), *Autism and the Development of Mind* (Hillsdale, NJ: Erlbaum).

Hull, John (1992), *Touching the Rock* (New York: Random House).

Meltzoff, A. and Gopnik, A. (1993), 'The role of imitation in understanding persons and developing a theory of mind', in Baron-Cohen *et al.* (1993).

Merleau-Ponty, Maurice (1964), *The Primacy of Perception* (Evanston, IL: Northwestern University Press).

Sacks, Oliver (1995), *An Anthropologist on Mars* (New York: Knopf).

Williams, Donna (1992), *Nobody Nowhere* (London: Corgi Books; New York: Random House).

Williams, Donna (1994), *Somebody Somewhere* (New York: Random House).

Wittgenstein, Ludwig (1980), *Remarks on the Philosophy of Psychology* (Chicago: University of Chicago Press).

Louis A. Sass

Schizophrenia, Self-consciousness, and the Modern Mind

This chapter uses certain of Michel Foucault's ideas concerning modern consciousness (from The Order of Things) *to illuminate a central paradox of the schizophrenic condition: a strange oscillation, or even coexistence, between two opposite experiences of the self: between the loss or fragmentation of self and its apotheosis in moments of solipsistic grandeur.*

Many schizophrenic patients lose their sense of integrated and active intentionality; even their most intimate thoughts and inclinations may be experienced as emanating from, or under the control of, some external being or mysterious foreign soul ('I feel it is not me who is thinking'; 'I have been programmed'). Yet the same patients may also experience the self as pre-eminent, all-powerful or all-knowing ('My thoughts can influence things'; 'This event happens because I think it'). Here one may feel confronted with the very paradigm of irrationality: profound contradictions suggesting regression to primitive 'primary-process' thinking or utter collapse of the higher faculties of mind.

I argue, however, that these dualities so basic to schizophrenia can best be understood very differently: as consequences of a kind of alienation and hyper-self-consciousness ('hyper-reflexivity') that is closely analogous to what occurs in the post-Kantian era of Western intellectual history. The parallel dualities of modern thought have been most extensively discussed by Foucault, who describes paradoxes, tensions and other dilemmas central to what he calls the modern 'episteme'; these result from what Foucault sees as the modern human being's introverted and ultimately self-deceiving preoccupation with, and overvaluing of, the phenomenon of his own consciousness. Parallels between these contradictions and those characteristic of several withdrawn schizophrenic individuals are described and analysed. The chapter concludes with an Afterword in which some possible neurobiological underpinnings of these schizophrenic experiences are discussed.

There is a strange duality lodged at the heart of the schizophrenic condition. On the one hand, such patients tend to lose their sense of active intentionality and integrated selfhood. Instead of serving as a kind of anchoring centre, the self may be dispersed outward, where it fragments into parts that float among the things of the world; even one's most intimate thoughts and inclinations may appear to emanate from some external source or mysterious foreign soul — as if they were 'the workings of another psyche' (Bleuler, 1950, p. 128). (These are the well-known 'first-rank symptoms' of Kurt Schneider [Mellor, 1970].) On the other hand, the patient's own consciousness can come to seem pre-eminent and all-powerful: one's own consciousness may seem poised at the controlling centre of the universe, with everything arrayed about it as around some constituting solipsistic deity. Patients may state: 'My thoughts can influence things.' 'This event happens because I think it.' 'To keep the world going, I must not stop thinking.' But they may also say: 'I feel that it is not me who is thinking.' 'Feelings are not felt by me, things are not seen by me, only by my eyes' (quoted in Spitzer, 1990, pp. 393–4).

This sort of duality may be the most dramatic illustration of the paradoxical or contradictory quality that is so characteristic of schizophrenia, a condition in which, as the Russian psychologist Vygotsky (1987) once noted, every major symptom seems to be matched by a 'countersymptom, its negative double, its opposite'. Although evidence for this peculiar duality is widespread, it has not been accorded as much attention as it deserves. Both Bleuler (1950, p. 54) and Jaspers (1963, p. 413) remarked on the tendency for the megalomania of such individuals to be mixed with feelings of persecution, powerlessness and inferiority. The same patient who declares himself to be omnipotent will also say that he does not exist, or that his body or his thoughts are under alien control; the patient who claims to be all-knowing also complains of being mystified by the workings of either real or delusional phenomena; the patient who claims he can conjure whole worlds in or out of existence nevertheless complains that mysterious machines, lasers, or electrical forces are controlling his thoughts, actions, or field of awareness. As John Haslam wrote in 1810, in what is widely regarded as the first psychiatric description of a schizophrenic patient, this sort of person is 'sometimes an automaton moved by the agencies of persons . . . at others, the Emperor of the whole world' (Carpenter, 1989, p. 332).

But it is not merely that such patients tend to shift readily between what seem to be opposite kinds of claims: they may even maintain both positions at the same moment, often without being troubled by the apparent inconsistency. Thus while the schizophrenic person is as liable to identify himself with god as with a machine, perhaps the most emblematic delusion of this enigmatic illness is of being a sort of God-machine, a kind of all-seeing, all-constituting camera eye. One patient recalled that, during an intense period of his psychosis, tables and chairs had seemed unreal to him — only 'projections in my mind'; yet he had also found himself uncertain of the very existence of his mind, doubting that 'it is me thinking, myself' (Rosser, 1979, p. 182).[1] Another schizophrenic person whom I interviewed wrote that he felt himself to be a sort of brain in a vat, and that it was as if everything he experienced, including all the objects of his gaze, were but a train of illusions produced in him by evil scientists. In his case, the sense of derealization, of perceiving a merely subjective reality, seemed to attest less to an intuition of limitless power or epistemological centrality than to an awareness of the narrowness or blindness of his own restricted perspective. One might suppose that a person who constitutes the universe could never be surprised, and could not, therefore, experience the fear of the unknown, since, of necessity, nothing could lie outside his awareness or his control. Yet many schizophrenics *are* preoccupied with just this kind of pervasive paranoia: though subjectivized, even

---

[1] A similar experience is described in this statement from another schizophrenic person: 'Now the question is, cannot a human brain under certain circumstances become so perverted as to recognize for itself, and *without the volition of its bearer*, the acts of other individuals as belonging to its life, as falling within its own memory?' (Landis, 1964, p. 195, emphasis added). In this bizarre and characteristically schizophrenic experience, external events ('the acts of other individuals') are somehow felt to be incorporated by the ego, owned by the self, yet what might seem the most crucial act of all, this very incorporating or owning, is not *itself* felt to be under the person's own control.

quasi-solipsistic at times, their worlds are shot through with a curious anxiety and suspiciousness, as if they experienced their actual thoughts and perceptions against the backdrop of an unspecifiable and threatening unknown. It seems that, in the autistic and withdrawn stages of schizophrenia, the one who is all-knowing may nevertheless feel ignorant or blind; the all-powerful one may nevertheless feel passive and afraid.

Schizophrenia has often been defined by its bizarre and alienating qualities, by its evocation in other people of the so-called 'praecox-feeling' (from the older term for schizophrenia: dementia praecox) — the sense of encountering someone who, in the words of Manfred Bleuler (1978, p. 15), seems 'totally strange, puzzling, inconceivable, uncanny, and incapable of empathy, even to the point of being sinister and frightening.' According to Karl Jaspers' (1963, p. 577, also pp. 447, 578–83) influential 'doctrine of the abyss', typical schizophrenic symptoms are simply incomprehensible to the normal person; they are 'entirely inaccessible to us', ' "mad" in the literal sense'. The symptoms I have been describing may well seem the very paradigm of madness or irrationality: for they involve not just deviations from normal human life but the most profound forms of self-contradiction — a flouting of what, since the ancients, has been considered the fundamental rule of reason, the identity principle or law of contradiction which states that it is impossible to affirm both p and not-p. Such patients claim to have a nearly divine intelligence yet to be incomparably stupid; to have limitless powers yet to be completely impotent; to be God himself yet to be nothing more than the beeping of a computer that was programmed during their sleep (last example from Glass, 1985, p. 147). To Freudians, this sort of tolerance of contradiction has generally suggested regression to the primitive a-logic of 'primary-process thinking'. Those of a more cognitivist persuasion might see it as a simple collapse of the higher faculties of mind. I will argue, however, that these incongruities can also be viewed in a rather different light: it turns out that these dualities so basic to the schizophrenic condition are, in fact, very close to a set of contradictions and paradoxes that are no less central to modern thought — to the era of western intellectual history when consciousness first comes to know itself as such, to take itself as an object or to appreciate its own subjective being and register its own contribution to the world that it knows. Indeed, if 'rationality' can be defined as 'reflexivity' — as what the scholar A.W. Gouldner (1976, p. 49) calls 'the capacity to make problematic what had hitherto been treated as given; to bring to reflection what had only been used; . . . to think about our thinking' — we might even say that these forms of incongruity can sometimes be products of a kind of hyperrationality. They may, in a sense, be forms of irrationality that are generated by rationality itself.

The various paradoxes, oscillations, and interdependencies which are at issue have received their most extensive discussion in *The Order of Things* (1994; original title, *Les Mots et les Choses*) — Michel Foucault's famous and forbidding study of the taken-for-granted modes or structures of knowing (*epistemes*, he calls them) that have channelled thought in the major epochs of Western history since the Renaissance. Foucault is perhaps the greatest contemporary chronicler and analyst of the nightmare side of modern times, and the prime critic of what he sees as its myths of emancipation and enlightenment through self-knowledge. In the final two chapters of this dense, at times almost cryptic work, Foucault describes the modern mode of thought as riven by deep contradictions, by tensions, paradoxes, and other dilemmas so varied and convoluted as nearly to defy summary. All these dilemmas do, however, have something in common: they all derive from a certain duality in the status of human consciousness — a duality bound up with what might be termed modern man's 'hyper-reflexivity', with what Foucault sees as his ultimately self-deceiving preoccupation with, and overvaluing of, the phenomenon of his own consciousness. In a moment I shall describe some of these dilemmas, but first, several preliminary remarks are in order.

This essay presents the culmination of the argument of my recent book, *Madness and Modernism: Insanity in the Light of Modern Art, Literature, and Thought* (1992; see also Sass, 1994). Like the book, the present essay could best be described as an exercise in comparative phenomenology — hermeneutic phenomenology, to be precise. What I shall be proposing is not a causal explanation focusing on the etiology or pathogenesis of schizophrenia, but a description, or interpretation, that is intended to bring out central features of characteristic forms of schizophrenic experience and expression; I shall use analogy in an attempt to change the way schizophrenic symptoms are seen, so that these symptoms will begin to make sense, or make sense in a new way. The analogies are taken from the art, literature, and thought of the past two centuries, the age that culminates in the modernism and postmodernism of the last one hundred years; it is here that one finds the clearest and most carefully analysed manifestations of the features that I consider to be most central to schizophrenia — namely, phenomena of intense self-consciousness and alienation, the turning inward and away from social life and practical activity and from emotion that I shall call 'hyper-reflexivity'.

To adopt such a view of schizophrenia is to run counter to some of the deepest assumptions about madness in western thought. Going back to Plato, and even to the pre-Socratics, madness has nearly always been associated with a lowering of the level of consciousness, with a dimming of awareness or with some kind of lack of knowledge or insight — in effect, with irrationality. It has been seen either as involving primitive/infantile and Dionysian modes of experience or else as a kind of dementia. Infant, wildman, broken brain: these, for many centuries, have been the dominant models for understanding madness. Perhaps the key recent ancestor in biological psychiatry is the influential nineteenth-century neurologist, J. Hughlings Jackson, who believed that mental disorders always involve a decline of the higher or more rational functions, usually accompanied by disinhibition of what is lower; but one might also mention the views of Emil Kraepelin, Kurt Goldstein, Henry Maudsley, and many others (see Sass, 1992, pp. 1–5, 16–23, 375–84; also Clark, 1981, pp. 275, 284; re. Jackson in particular see Berrios, 1985; 1991; Stengel, 1963). Despite some exceptions, similar conceptions remain dominant in present-day psychiatry and clinical psychology, especially in the United Kingdom and North America. Thus we find schizophrenia prominently described as resulting from a 'broken brain' (Andreason, 1984) or an 'unsupervised brain' (Liddle, 1992), or as manifesting an incapacity for meta-representation (in the characterization recently espoused by C.D. Frith [1994], a view highly reminiscent of Kurt Goldstein's [1940/1963; 1944/1964] notion of loss of the 'abstract attitude'); along with psychoanalytic concepts that emphasize revival of immature forms of ego functioning and self-world fusion or the schizophrenic's refusal of mature capacities for symbolic representation.[2]

_____

[2] This is not the place to discuss the neurobiology of schizophrenia in any detail (for extended discussion, see Sass, 1992, pp. 374–97, 'Appendix: Neurobiological Considerations'). I want to make

Among the exceptions, those whose views do not follow the traditional vision of madness I have just described, are Wolfgang Blankenburg (1991), Bin Kimura (1992), Josef Parnas and Pierre Bovet (1991; also Bovet and Parnas, 1993), John Cutting (1990), and, from earlier in this century, Eugene Minkowski (1927). Also congruent with my own emphasis on schizophrenic hyperreflexivity and alienation is the following statement by Robert Cancro, who manages to avoid the common tendency to understand so-called negative symptoms in purely deficit terms:

> If there are symptoms that are unique to our conceptualization of schizophrenia, they are the negative symptoms. . . . It is the turning inward, the pseudo-introspective quality, the turning away from reality, the preoccupation with inner experience and the inner voice, and the withdrawal from the outer world that define schizophrenia (in Sobel *et al.*, 1996).

In one sense, of course, the common tendency to equate madness with irrationality can hardly be mistaken. Indeed, the claim is virtually a tautology — if by 'rationality' we mean reasonableness, practical efficiency, agreement with others, social appropriateness, openness to dialogue, and the like. But the dominant conceptions have typically gone beyond mere judgments of impracticality, eccentricity, or unreasonableness. It has been assumed that the schizophrenic person's point of view is not merely idiosyncratic, off-putting or socially dysfunctional but actually incorrect, unintelligent, or otherwise inferior according to some essential or universal human standard.

It would also be foolish to deny that schizophrenia can lack orderliness and ready intelligibility, that it can display forms of violent contradiction and nearly impenetrable obscurity. What I shall argue below, however, is that, at least in many cases of schizophrenia, the forms of disorganization and dysfunction at issue may involve something surprisingly intricate and complex. (The heterogeneity of what Bleuler aptly termed the *group* of schizophrenia*s* must be acknowledged; it may well limit the applicability of my interpretation to a subset of patients with this diagnosis.) What occurs in this illness is often a kind of hyperconsciousness combined with alienation from one's own body, emotions, and thoughts as well as from the social and practical world. Often this hyperreflexivity (a condition that often involves, but is not restricted to, hyperrationality) brings on a kind of self-undermining — like something that turns inward on itself until, finally, it collapses of its own accord. I shall argue that many of the seemingly irrational aspects of schizophrenia are, in fact, less a matter of brute and incomprehensible contradiction than of paradox: the paradoxes of the reflexive. The nature of possible neurobiological underpinnings for such a condition is a fascinating question which I shall address only briefly in an Afterword.

Two additional points should be clarified before proceeding. First, as I use it, 'hyper-reflexivity' has a rather broad meaning. The term 'reflexive' denotes any action, entity, or event that is 'directed or turned back on itself,' particularly any action or process that is 'directed back on the agent or the grammatical subject' (Webster's Ninth New Collegiate Dictionary, p. 990). What I call hyperreflexivity is not

---

it clear, however, that I am by no means opposed to neurobiological accounts of this condition. I reject only what might be described as reductionistic accounts — those which treat mind as entirely an epiphenomenon of brain processes or which assume (in the manner of Hughlings Jackson) that lesions or other cerebral abnormalities always result in a decline or lessening of the 'higher' cognitive functions of rationality, self-consciousness and volition. For further discussion, see the afterword at the end of this article.

restricted to intellectualized or potentially verbalizable forms of introspection or reflective psychological insight, but can also include non-intellectual modes of experience, modes that may even be capable of precluding or replacing forms of
consciousness commonly associated with the exercise of practical or analytic intelligence. A good example is the tendency (found in schizophrenics, meditators, as well
as psychological introspectionists such as Titchener [Hunt, 1995, pp. 201, 214;
Sass, 1994, pp. 88–97]) to focus attention on kinesthetic sensations that would not
normally occupy the focus of awareness, so that these bodily sensations come to
monopolize one's awareness and to be experienced as akin to external objects existing in the outer world (Sass, 1992, pp. 213–41; see also Sass, 1994, pp. 88–97).

Also, I am not claiming that characteristics involving hyperreflexivity are found
only in such patients, Like virtually any aspect of mental processes, the forms of reflexivity and alienation that I emphasize are not unique to any diagnostic group or
personality type, but only more prominent or less prominent in them. Neither schizophrenia, nor modernism, nor hyper-reflexivity is a phenomenon with sharp boundaries or a readily definable single essence. Here I shall adopt something like an
ideal-type approach which allows me to generalize readily about the schizophrenic
individual without dwelling too much on exceptions and qualifications. As Max
Weber (1949, p. 90), who first described the notion of the ideal type, acknowledged,
such an approach is unabashedly perspectival and partial in nature, accentuating features that are characteristic of the phenomena at issue but not applying equally well,
or in the same way, to all instances of the type. Also, the patients I use to illustrate my
points are in some respects atypical, given their uncommon articulateness and the
highly creative or coherent nature of their delusions or quasi-delusional preoccupa-
tions. I would argue, however, that although they may not *typify*, they do in some
sense *epitomize* the schizophrenic condition — bringing out, with special clarity, features that are present in a significant number of patients in the schizophrenia spectrum. Among other things, this may help to clarify some of what may underlie the not
infrequently noted tendency for schizophrenic patients to become preoccupied with
'the deepest questions' (Bleuler, 1950, p. 67) and 'profound philosophical queries'
(Snyder, 1974, p. 5), with 'concepts such as timelessness, world, god, and death [that]
become enormous revelations [but] which when the state has subsided cannot be re-
produced or described in any way' (Jaspers, 1963, pp. 115, 284; see also Sass, 1992,
p. 7). In a moment we shall examine some of these features. But first let us leave
schizophrenia to the side, looking instead at Foucault's illuminating discussion of
some related aspects of the modern condition.

The Doublet of Modern Thought

In *The Order of Things*, Foucault identifies the advent of the modern mode of thought
and self-knowledge, what he calls the modern *episteme*, with the innovations of Kantian philosophy. It was Kant who decisively introduced a new kind of self-
consciousness, a dual self-consciousness in which human subjectivity came to be understood — and potentially, experienced — as, at the same time, both a knowing subject and a primary object of knowing. With his notion of the categories or forms of
understanding — temporal, spatial, causal, and so forth — to which all human experience must necessarily conform, Kant emphasized the transcendental role of the mind

in shaping the world we experience. At the same time Kant's self-reflexive focus on these categories or forms also had the effect of turning subjectivity into a prime object of study, a quasi-empirical entity that would itself be investigated by newly developing human sciences that aspired to specify the nature or explain the sources of these very categories or cultural forms. According to Foucault, the duality of this new kind of human self-awareness had some peculiar, even self-contradictory, implications and consequences.[3]

Suppose subjectivity is conceived in transcendental terms, as the medium *by* which everything is known or *in* which it has its being: how then, let us ask, is it possible for subjectivity itself ever to *be* known? Would this not require the impossible: that subjectivity should turn around on itself, becoming an object within its own field, within the medium that it itself is? (How, after all, can that which is the condition of possibility *for* all manifestation, actually come to manifest itself?) Foucault (1994, pp. 341–3, 364) describes the human sciences of the modern *episteme* as suffering from a 'confusion of the empirical and the transcendental'. Because they treat 'as their object what is in fact their condition of possibility', he writes, these sciences are doomed to certain 'warped and twisted forms of reflection' — to futile contortions of thought that will continually evoke, yet continually frustrate, the hope for some profound insight into subjectivity and its relationship to the world.

A second consequence of the Kantian duality — of what Foucault (1994, p. 318) calls the 'empirico-transcendental doublet' of modern thought — is a certain polarization or duality in the status of human consciousness and, potentially, in the individual person's sense of self. If human consciousness is in some way the source or foundation of all reality (or, at least, of all reality that can possibly be of relevance to beings such as ourselves), then consciousness, or the human self, might seem to hold a position of ultimate sovereignty and omniscience. If all knowledge is 'but pictures, representations', as the post-Kantian philosopher Fichte (1910, pp. 91, 83) declared, that is, if there *is* no independent, material world because the world 'arises only through knowledge', then why, Fichte asked, should you 'tremble at a necessity which exists only in thine own thought [or] fear to be crushed by things which are a product of thine own mind'.

Yet, if consciousness has also come to be the object of new disciplines that seek to understand its causes and processes of functioning, it is also being assimilated to the natural order of determined or otherwise limited entities. Far from being sovereign, mind is discovered to be constrained by all the rules of material causality, biological law, and historical process. Another post-Kantian philosopher, Arthur Schopenhauer (1928, p. 27), describes this dual condition when he speaks of the antinomy whereby consciousness, the 'supporter of the world, the universal condition of all that appears', also recognizes itself to be merely a 'modification of matter' thus to be 'just as necessarily wholly dependent upon a long chain of causes and effects, which have

---

[3] The following paragraphs are based, somewhat loosely, on pp. 294–387 of Foucault's *The Order of Things* (1994). It should be emphasized that we will be concerned here with Kant as a cultural figure and general source of intellectual influence — with Kantianism, if you will. This need not always be the most accurate reflection of all the complexities and subtleties of what Kant actually wrote. We can think of Kantianism as 'a tendency, a spirit, a disposition to interpret life and human nature and the world in a certain general way — a tendency . . . capable of . . . expressing itself in numerous mutually hostile teachings' (Royce, 1919, p. 2). For discussion of some of the internal contradictions in Kant, see Strawson (1966, pp. 11–44).

preceded it, and in which it itself appears as a small link'. What results is a curious co-existence of, or oscillation between, feelings of puniness and of ultimate centrality, of being merely a thing among things and of being the source and 'the center of the world'.

A closely related paradox concerns the mind's sense of the status of its own knowledge. The very idea that forms of knowing or categories of understanding actually *constitute* our experience may suggest that understanding our own minds (the locus of these forms and categories) can give us comprehensive and reliable insight into the basic structure of the universe that we encounter (see Royce, 1919, pp. 73–4, on these tendencies in post-Kantian idealism). After all, if all of relevant existence presents itself *to* consciousness, then it might seem that an exhaustive investigation of the form and contents of consciousness might be able to reveal the whole of Being, including the nature of consciousness itself. (For some of the post-Kantians, it was doubly inconceivable that mind — whose defining criterion was the presence of self-consciousness — would not be conscious of its own nature. Thus J.G. Fichte [1910] could argue that an object was 'thoroughly transparent to thy mind's eye, because it is thy mind itself'.) But the notion of constituting categories also has implications that tend to deflate any pretensions to omniscience, for such a notion suggests that consciousness has certain limits: though the domain of consciousness may feel immense, without visible boundary, and self-transparent, it must also seem narrow, for now one is likely to recognize at least the abstract possibility of inconceivable realities — realities potentially accessible to *other* forms of mental life but whose very nature excludes them from comprehension by one's own, all-too-human mind. (There is also the possibility that the nature of one's own mind will seem unknowable: after all, if one can know only that which *conforms* to certain forms and categories of intuition and understanding, how, then, can one know these very forms or categories themselves? Would this not require the ability to get *outside* these categories, which by definition is impossible?)

Here, then, are the dual and rather paradoxical results of Kantian reflection, an introverted process whose effect, in Hegel's words, is 'to withdraw cognition from an interest in its objects and absorption in the study of them, and to direct it back upon itself' (quoted in Griswold 1988, p. 150). To the extent that one focuses on the world, the world feels subjectivized, even subordinate to one's will; but to the extent that one focuses on one's own mind or thinking, consciousness itself begins to seem at a remove — alien, constrained, and inherently obscure. So consciousness in the post-Kantian age comes to seem profoundly ambiguous: all-powerful and all-knowing (a kind of deity who thinks the world) but also objectlike and finite — determined, knowable, as well as limited in its capacity *to* know.

In *The Order of Things* Foucault is concerned with explicitly theoretical modes of thought. His analysis of the modern episteme offers what Hubert Dreyfus and Paul Rabinow (1982, p. 43) have rightly described as 'astonishing synoptic insight into the tortured turnings of two hundred years of complex and tangled thought' in philosophy and the human sciences. Foucault does not, however, provide any real indication of the implications these post-Kantian forms of reflection might have at the lived and more immediate level of individual human experience. Something of the concrete existential consequences is conveyed in an early work by Franz Kafka, 'Description of a Struggle' (1971), a short story that is perhaps the most perfect evocation in western literature of the full range of schizophrenic or schizophrenialike experience — from schizoid self-consciousness, isolation, and hyperscrutiny through self-alienation and solipsism and on to the fragmentation or total dissolution of both self and world.

Kafka's 'Description of a Struggle' is told from the point of view of a man who seems to lack any capacity for direct, unproblematic engagement with the world, and who lives instead within the confines of his own head. The narrating consciousness of this fictional work (and along with this, the reader's experience) wavers between grandiosity and abjection, between the euphoria of solipsism and the nausea or terror of world-dissolution that express the two sides of the empirico-transcendental doublet. Thus one finds oneself, much of the time, occupying a transcendental position, in fact an almost solipsistic one — identifying with a narrator who experiences himself as the centre of the universe. Yet one also experiences the self as alienated and passive: instead of owning his own experience, the narrator is continually discovering his thoughts and feelings outside himself, as the experiences of an other who is, in fact, only a simulacrum of himself (that is, the narrator repeatedly encounters some other person who begins to narrate his own experiences, yet the experiences described turn out to be uncannily similar to those of the original narrator). In this way, we could say that what *was* primarily a godlike entity — the narrator's all-constituting ego — is continually being transformed into an empirical object existing with*in* his own (and one's own, the reader's) field of awareness. Also, the events that occur generally have a quality of unreality, of being mere subjective illusions: 'the stones vanished at my will', writes the narrator, who also describes seeing 'a squirrel of my whim' perched at the end of a trembling branch (pp. 21–3) — yet these events seldom appear to be anticipated or willed: they are like dream images that roll without warning across the horizon of awareness.

Kafka's story perfectly exemplifies the dizzying shifts of modern thought: a characteristic veering between a bracing sense of absolute epistemic omnipotence, omniscience and freedom; and an equally compelling experience of the self as limited, determined and blind. And this parallels quite precisely the above-mentioned duality in schizophrenia — that condition in which patients are liable to experience themselves both as ultimate solipsistic centres and as mechanical and fragmented beings (a kind of transcendental xerox machine, a camera recording the world, or a deified corpse-with-insomnia); and where they often claim to know and control everything, yet nevertheless to fear unknown dangers lurking all about them and to feel confronted by some collosal riddle.

The Consciousness Machine

Both sides of this duality found in schizophrenia — the solipsistic grandiosity as well as the felt impotence and ignorance — are exemplified by a famous example of a delusion which is described in a classic essay by the psychoanalyst Victor Tausk. In his essay, published in 1919, Tausk (1933) describes a patient, Natalija, who claimed that all of her actions as well as experiences were actually under the control of an influencing-machine. This machine, which partially resembled her own body, existed in some distant place where it was being manipulated by mysterious men. If her arm or leg moved, this was not because she, Natalija, had moved it of her own accord, but because the mysterious men had moved the arm or the leg of the distant machine. If

Natalija saw or smelled something, this was not because there was really an object before her or a scent in her immediate vicinity, but because the men had shown a slide before the eyes or placed a scent under the nostrils of the machine.

One implication of this delusion — which is the classic example of the 'influencing-machine delusion' — is that it places the patient, Natalija's, own person or consciousness at the very centre of the universe, in a position of great epistemic importance.[4] Natalija believed, after all, that what she saw were but pseudo-objects, slide-images displayed before the eyes of the Natalija-machine; this suggests that the persons and things of which she was aware must not have seemed truly independent beings, solid objects existing apart from her, but mere images existing for her alone, indeed, actually constituted by the fact of her perceiving them. (Over time, in fact, Natalija began to perceive the world as if it lacked substance in a rather literal way: increasingly the world appeared to her to be only a two-dimensional image, existing in a single plane.) At the same time, the very notion of a mysterious influencing device, a mechanism with invisible parts and obscure functions, controlled by unidentified men who display only certain images before her sense organs, suggests that Natalija did not feel wholly identified with or in control of her experiences, and, in addition, that there were other, unknown realities beyond those that happened to appear before her own, carefully manipulated field of awareness.[5] (Presumably, these unknown realities would include all that the men do *not* place before the machine's sense organs and, in addition, the epistemic mechanism itself and the processes of manipulating this apparatus — which, as Tausk notes in his article, tend to remain obscure, even completely unimaginable, to patients who have such delusions.)

In these paradoxes of Natalija's delusion, there is the suggestion that her experience may suffer from certain forms of 'essential instability' and 'precariousness' which Foucault (and others) have discerned in the human sciences of the modern episteme, sciences that engage in what Foucault (1994, p. 343) describes, somewhat hyperbolically, as 'warped and twisted forms of reflection'. After all, according to the 'logic' of a delusion like that of Natalija, the very things that cause or bring about all the images of her subjectivized world — namely, the mysterious men and the influencing machine itself — would themselves have to be mere images or representations. For, if *everything* she experiences is an illusion, merely a slide-image or the like, should this not apply to the Natalija-machine also — since she is aware of it? (And interestingly enough, the components of Natalija's machine itself did, over the course of time, begin to take on a two-dimensional quality, as if they too were entering the realm of images! [Tausk 1933, p. 533]). But how, then, could a mere vision, an insubstantial figment in her mind, actually have the causal powers of an influencing mechanism, a mechanism that could create these very images?

The situation is no less paradoxical if we begin on the other side of the doublet, with the supposed objectivity and causal power of the mind-machine; for given such an arrangment, we must ask how Natalija could possibly *know* these very facts about the finitude or limitedness of her own consciousness? If she sees only the images, has

[4] Although this implication is not stressed by Tausk, it is suggested by the structure of Natalija's delusion.

[5] Incidentally, there is a close and interesting analogy between the condition implied by Natalija's delusion and the new conception of the nature of vision that developed in the early nineteenth century, at the beginning of the modern *episteme*; see Crary (1990). discussed in Sass (1997, pp. 208–10).

only the thoughts, which the machine and its manipulators allow her to 'see' or to 'think', how, then — short of being shown slide-images of the machine itself, and of the entire system which includes the machine[6] — would it be possible for Natalija to know the conditions, causes, or limits of her own finite and manipulated awareness? Doesn't her knowledge *of* these facts suggest that she must somehow be able to catapult herself out of the condition which these very facts describe?

At least on a logical level, then, the universe of the influencing-machine is fraught with irresolvable contradictions. But, though it may well be logically impossible, it was nonetheless quite actual: it did exist — and not merely as an isolated belief but, it would seem, as a particular mode of existence that was given expression in a delusional claim having implications of a peculiarly metaphysical or ontological kind. If we consider Natalija's delusion and the sort of experiential world it seems to imply, we realize, in fact, that the condition in which she lived must have involved a kind of perpetual oscillation: in one moment, the feeling that the entire universe, influencing-machine and all, was but a figment of her own, all-constituting ego, but in the next, the sense that her own consciousness, represented by the mysterious machine, is a mere thing among things, an objectified, partially unknown thing that is subject to the effects of external causes. Her fate, then, is very like that of the modern episteme that Foucault describes: it seems that Natalija existed in a kind of fitful equivocation between objectification of the self and subjectification of the world, between self-abnegation and self-deification, between a sense of finitude and of the infinite.

'A Metaphysical Illness'

To some readers, my interpretation of Natalija may seem over-elaborate, perhaps even fanciful, especially given the lack of direct quotations from the patient in Tausk's article. But many of these themes do preoccupy other schizophrenics as well, and it will be useful to consider a patient who is more explicit in describing the nature of his problems. One exceptionally articulate and self-aware schizophrenic man in his early thirties, whom I shall call Lawrence, gave a particularly clear account of some of the symptoms and the paradoxes we have been examining, capturing the two sides of the doublet in a distinction he made between two types of thinkers or ways of thinking.

Lawrence had been hospitalized many times; all of the statements quoted below come from his twelfth period of hospitalization. On this, his twelfth admission, he offered the following as his chief complaint: 'I have a metaphysical illness; my mind is rapidly deteriorating.'[7] Somewhat later in this period of hospitalization, Lawrence complained of being misunderstood by the staff on the ward: 'Just because they don't understand me they think [I'm speaking] word salad.' 'I'm not crazy: mad, perhaps, but not crazy,' he said, explaining that to be 'mad' was to be driven 'to the extremes of experience, to experience ideas at the extreme; but [the ideas I had were] all true so I wasn't crazy'.

---

[6] This is something Tausk would surely have mentioned if it were part of her delusion. If, however, this *were* the case — had Natalija felt that she knew the machine through being shown slide images of it — then she still could not have been sure that the slide images were veridical or that the machine itself was anything more than another illusion.

[7] All quotations from Lawrence were reported to me by a colleague who served as his therapist. Some of their sessions were tape recorded; in others the therapist took verbatim notes, or recorded the conversation from memory immediately after the session.

The notions that preoccupied Lawrence — constituting what the treatment staff thought of as his 'delusional system' — centred on his distinction between what he referred to as 'intuitive' and merely 'mechanical' or 'empirical' types of thinkers. Lawrence considered the vast majority of human beings to be of the latter sort — not truly living minds but only 'organic machines' or 'mental vegetables' who lacked a real soul; what appeared to be thinking on their part was, in fact, not really thinking at all, but only the mechanical retrieval and processing of facts and memories from a memory bank. (Incidentally, Lawrence considered psychiatry to be a particularly egregious example of merely empirical thinking. As he once put it to his therapist: 'I feel psychiatry is a lot of empirical nonsense, no offense. I object to empiricism — it's all based in facts — the logos is absent.')

In the past, Lawrence had generally counted himself among the other group, the 'intuitive thinkers', those capable of 'conceiving abstractions' and of having truly original thoughts. To be an intuitive thinker was clearly bound up with experiencing the ascendancy and self-sufficiency of one's mental essence; for, as Lawrence explained in one therapy session, 'the intuitive thinker knows his mind because he *is* his mind. You are it and it's you. It's not an asset; it's total identification there.' He described any kind of compromise as 'a sin for the intuitive thinker; I just never compromised; I was in search of mental purity.'

The condition of Lawrence's 'intuitive thinker' seems to display all the characteristics of one side of the empirico-transcendental doublet of modern thought. In this mode of self-consciousness — which Foucault (1972, p. 203) would later term 'transcendental narcissism' — consciousness declares its unlimited freedom, its utterly self-creating nature, and its indubitable lucidity as an ultimate source of truth. The sense of solipsistic power, along with its attendant anxieties, is clear enough in the following statements which Lawrence made to his therapist:

> You can't imagine how terrifying it is to realize that you're in a world of organic machines with the intuitions that enable you to create truths. . . . Where ideas and thoughts permeate all that you are — where all you need to do is to be able to conceive of something for it to come true. I could create the events of my universe by just thinking them, believing them to be true. . . . What really terrified me was when I realized that I could conceive of wrenching the world from its axis. Do you know how it would feel to have that kind of power? You see, you're protected from that kind of power . . . that is, not being a true intuitive thinker you're incapable of creating truths. For you, death could only come through interventions in your physiology. For me, all I would have to do would have been to think in certain ways in order to achieve physical death. It would not have had to involve physiological damage. One time I was sitting in a chair and I felt myself capable of thinking myself to death — I felt an incredible sense of calm come over me . . .

Lawrence's sense of having special knowledge, a kind of all-encompassing divine insight, pertained especially to what he called the realm of 'abstraction', and, in particular, to the workings of the mind and its fundamental relationship to the world. Lawrence spoke, for example, of having discovered the science of 'psychomathematics,' which concerned the abstract principles of mental functioning and constituted what he called 'a discrete mathematical theory of the intuitive and non-intuitive mind' (mathematics being, in his view, 'the logos of the mind'); and he claimed to have 'come to understand the mind more completely than, and please pardon what may seem to you my grandiosity, more completely than anyone possibly in the history of mankind'. 'I never did figure out the soul,' Lawrence acknowledged, 'but in coming to understand the mind in its relationship to the physical, I came to resolve the mind-body problem'. Since abstractions were, as Lawrence put it, 'the only reality', and 'the most concrete thing there is', psychomathematics 'had substance, it was real.' But psychomathematics, it seems, was an essentially reflexive, hence a peculiarly intransitive science — a matter, as it were, of the mind watching itself as it idled in neutral. Thus Lawrence explained that this intuitive science of the mind 'required no research whatsoever' and had no purpose beyond its own, self-generated coming into being: 'I applied it as soon as I discovered it; the discovery was the application'.

This essential intransitivity, this quality of self-referentiality and self-enclosure, is related to the combination of grandiosity along with limitation that was characteristic of his solipsistic claims — claims that generally applied only within a self-referential or subjectivized domain. It was clear, for example, that Lawrence did not experience his own godlike control as affecting events that were intersubjectively recognizable or objectively real. Thus he explained to his therapist that she need have no fear; his wrenching of the world's axis would have no effect on her. Also, the self-engendered death to which he referred lacked the finality of a *real* death (Lawrence claimed to believe he'd already been dead once, and that his redemption actually lay in this kind of death, which would eventually lead to enlightenment — in his opinion, 'heaven is eternal enlightenment'). The same holds for his claims of special insight — which, in reality, pertained only to a restricted range of phenomena: to the realm of what he called 'truth' as opposed to mere 'facts'. 'Facts are nothing; it's truth that's important,' he explained. 'I've never been wrong though I may have been mistaken', he would say, thereby acknowledging that he made no claim to special expertise or knowledge regarding the concrete, arbitrary, purely objective — and for him, ultimately trivial — real-world phenomena that are the standard preoccupation of merely 'empirical' minds. In true Kantian fashion, Lawrence was concerned with features of experience that have a more general, formal, or seemingly necessary status — that is, with truths about the nature of mind and world that could presumably be uncovered by a kind of transcendental reflection or introspection.

In the past, Lawrence would say, he had experienced himself mostly as what he called an intuitive thinker, though the sense of quasi-solipsistic power and insight had never been the sole theme of his experience. But now, with the passage of time, he seemed to be veering more and more often into an antithetical mood; as he rather eerily expressed it, there had been 'a change in the configuration of the void'. For the intuitive thinker, the immanent objects and the structures of one's own experience will seem to be of paramount importance; whatever eludes this constituting consciousness will seem somehow trivial — mere empirical facts ('I used to live my ideas; they surrounded me; I lived in the plasma of my ideas'). But now Lawrence was beginning to feel just the opposite — as if the realm of truth had been closed off to him and he were being presented only with illusions. 'My intelligence is my portal to reality and the glass is clouding over,' he said. And on another occasion: 'I am like the person in Plato's cave. All I see is the images reflected from reality; all I see is the verisimilitude of reality, not reality itself. I've lost access to reality, it's really horrendous.' There were moments, in fact, when Lawrence felt that he was becoming even more mechanical and ignorant than the organic machines he so despised, moments when it seemed to him that he had lost all his intelligence: 'My truths were reduced to facts, and now I'm starting to forget the facts.' 'Sometimes I can become deluded into thinking I still do have intelligence, although the reality is that I've lost my mind completely.' 'I am devolving into a mental vegetable.'

It may be tempting to think that Lawrence's sense of mental degeneration might reflect some actual decline of cognitive capacity, perhaps secondary to actual neurophysiological deterioration (e.g. cell loss in his brain). Although such a possibility certainly cannot be ruled out, upon reflection it hardly seems, by itself, to provide an adequate account. For one thing, the deterioration Lawrence experienced was by no means gradual or continuous: there were many shifts back and forth between what he called the 'intuitive' and the 'mechanical' condition, sometimes from day to day but also from hour to hour.[8] Even more telling is the lack of any real evidence of lowered cognitive capacity during many of those periods when he bitterly complained of mental debility. We must remember, after all, that at the very moments of claiming to *be* in some kind of severely deteriorated state, Lawrence was simultaneously *describing* this condition in a most articulate, even eloquent fashion (speaking, e.g., of portals 'clouding over', or 'Plato's cave') — which is hardly consistent with his claim of being a kind of mental vegetable. Sometimes he would say he had lost all ability to understand written and spoken language, to grasp 'the formal aspects of the language, the grammatical structures of the sentences' ('This morning I couldn't even understand *Life Magazine*, and that's written for morons,' he once said), but if asked to explain what he had just read or heard, he was perfectly capable of doing so — though all the while he would insist that he was simply carrying out some merely 'syntactic' or purely 'mechanical' processing rather than displaying the true understanding of a 'living mind'.

But if Lawrence's mind was not actually deteriorating, at least according to conventional standards, how, then, is it possible to account for the *sense* of mental decline that he felt at certain moments? What was it that caused this individual to lose a feeling of understanding things, or of owning or identifying with his own conscious processes?

Actually, various factors seemed able to undermine Lawrence's sense of mental vitality. It was vulnerable, for instance, to mood shifts and also to changes in his psychiatric medications (he spoke, e.g., of having once 'lost his soul' when he was given psychotropic medications that, as he put it, were 'spiritually contra-indicated'). At times, the sense of decline seems to have reflected his own disdain for what were in fact perfectly normal processes of everyday practical thinking — processes that struck him as lifeless and banal in comparison with the more abstract, transcendental reflections of his 'intuitive' periods. (And, interestingly enough, what Lawrence experienced as deterioration seems to have impressed others as an improvement — presumably because, by their standards, his thinking — now focused on mere empirical

---

[8]   In the following account of a late-night conversation with a mental-health worker, Lawrence describes his oscillating sense of losing and regaining his intelligence. 'We really were having a stimulating discussion,' he reported. 'I felt as if I were truly gaining back some of my intelligence.' At that point, another staff member appeared, interrupting the ongoing conversation by using what Lawrence described as 'that horrible word they use so often around here — "inappropriate".' As Lawrence explained: 'He [the second staff member] said it was inappropriate to be having a one-on-one at that hour . . . what I seemed to be wanting to talk about was not important enough. . . . And what, I ask you, could be more important than the recovery of one's mind? I tried to reason with him; and remember, I had a good deal of my intelligence back, the very intelligence that I then lost this morning.'

facts — had become more relevant and clear: 'People kept thinking I was regaining my brilliance, but what I was really doing was retreating to simpler and simpler levels of thought. But to the empiricists I was recovering.')

When Lawrence himself attempted to explain his supposed mental decline, he put the primary emphasis on his own, at least quasi-wilful mental activity. In this reflexive or intransitive realm, to believe something was tantamount to making it true, especially if the mind's object was itself; and so, as Lawrence explained, 'I believed that I could destroy my mind; I could conceive of [this destruction], and I made it into my own truth . . . in my own global system, and so it became true.'[9] Particularly destructive, in his view, was the process of introspection itself. 'My downfall was insight,' he explained, '. . . too much insight can be very dangerous, because you can tear your mind apart.' 'Well, look at the word "analysis",' he said on another occasion. 'That means to break apart. When it turns in upon itself the mind would rip itself apart.' He spoke of 'doing six self-analyses simultaneously'; and of how he needed to change his living environment often, because he knew that, once everything around him had been scrutinized, his mind would then turn inward and begin undoing itself, leading him eventually to the feeling of having no real mind at all: 'Once I started destroying [my mind], I couldn't stop.'

In the following statement, offered in response to a question from his therapist, we can see how Lawrence's relentless self-scrutiny could fix upon certain routine mental operations, thereby seeming to confirm his sense of being nothing more than some kind of data-processing machine:

> . . . because there's nothing there, no cognition at all. I'm actually deluding myself into thinking I could think. I was trying to think of an answer to that question, but I'm incapable of thinking. Because I was actually searching my memory-bank and generalizing slightly from the dialectical juxtaposition of a couple of memories. . . . non-mechanical thinking? — I can't conceive of that any more. I can give you labels that have lost their meaning to me.

Here Lawrence seems to have been experiencing the second kind of reflective self-awareness inherent in the doublet — not the subjectivizing kind which experiences the world as if it were pulsating with the mind's constituting power (as in 'intuitive thinking'), but the objectifying sort where the mind turns more directly upon itself, coming to experience itself as just another empirical, even mechanical object, constrained by all the determinisms of the natural order.

Foucault's discussion of the modern episteme helps us see that these two ways of experiencing one's mind can have a profound interdependence — like the systole and diastole of the same reflexive process. It seems that the reflexive move, the turning-inward, has the potential of bringing on the condition and contradictions of the doublet: for insofar as one focuses on the world, it is liable to seem like *my* world; but insofar as one focuses more directly on thoughts or feelings, these will seem to exist out-there and apart.[10] And so, in the realms both of madness and of modernism, we

---

[9] Lawrence also spoke of an occasion when he was able to arrest the deterioration of his mind simply by believing that he had reached bottom.

[10] If we think of experience as having two aspects, mental acts and their objects, then (borrowing the vocabulary of the philosopher Samuel Alexander), we could describe the reflexivity of the modern doublet as a situation in which that which is normally 'enjoyed' (the mental act) comes to be 'contemplated', and in which that which is normally 'contemplated' (the object of awareness) comes to be subjectivized (see Passmore, 1968, p. 268).

find, tightly intertwined, a solipsism that would elevate the mind and derealize the world along with a self-objectification that would rob the subject of its transcendental role as a centre of power and knowledge. This parallelism of paradoxes is no mere co-incidence: what we are discovering in both domains are characteristic paradoxes of the reflexive, contradictions generated by the alienation and hyper-self-consciousness that are central to both schizophrenia and the modern mind.

Concluding Remarks

Psychosis has nearly always been seen as antithetical to higher forms of thought or consciousness — as a condition involving decline or even disappearance of rational factors in the organization of human conduct and experience. Madness as irrational-ity: this is the key idea that, in various forms but with few true exceptions, has echoed down through the ages. But as we have seen, many of the core features of the quintes-sential form of madness — schizophrenia — can be understood in a very different way. Indeed, they sometimes appear to involve an almost opposite condition: not a dimming but a heightening of conscious awareness, especially of self-consciousness of various kinds, and an estrangement not from reason but from the emotions, in-stincts, and the body—the condition I have termed hyperreflexivity.

It would obviously be wrong to view these forms of hyperreflexivity as being es-sentially volitional in nature, as if the fragmentation and dislocation in question were purely the result of some perverse strategy engaged in willfully. The processes that can dissolve the sense of being an integrated or coherent self in active engagement with the world can, in fact, be experienced by the schizophrenic individual as some-thing imposed upon him, or that happens to him even against his will. This was clearly the case with one schizophrenic woman who described what she called 'the splitting "dialectic" and the splitting "egos which inspect each other".' She was de-scribing processes of self-monitoring that tended to occur when she was participating in a conversation, and that seemed to have an almost mechanical inertia of their own and to lead to unwanted and painful consequences: 'then I, through this combination of myself projecting into the other person, and the other person in itself, am moni-tored to react as expected,' she said, 'and that happens so rapidly that I, even if I had wanted to, am unable to stop myself. And after that, I am left by myself and very lonely' (quoted in Stromgren, 1987, p. 49). It seems very likely that various neuro-cognitive abnormalities could be involved in conditions of this kind — whether by providing the immediate substrate of these hyperreflexive processes or by creating conditions that might elicit forms of self-distancing and analytic scrutiny in some more indirect, perhaps defensive, manner. (This will be discussed in more detail in the Afterword below.)

Some of the aspects or features of experience that we have been considering — such as the self-conscious awareness of one's own subjectivity, or a sense of detach-ment from the surrounding sensory and social world — have often been thought to be intimately associated with the capacity for volitional self-control, indeed, to be neces-sary components of volition in its highest or purest form (e.g. Goldstein & Scheerer, 1941, pp. 22–9). But as we have seen, these features themselves can seem to impose themselves on the schizophrenic individual — and in doing so they often serve to undermine the normal sense of the self as an active centre or source that possesses its own experiences or controls its own action and thoughts.

A proper understanding of these kinds of disorder demands an appreciation of the rather paradoxical nature of the phenomena at issue. It seems clear, in any case, that we need to go beyond the standard polarities of defence/deficit or act/affliction that have channelled and continue to channel so much of our thinking about madness. We need to recognize, for instance, that it is both true and not true that such patients lack awareness of and control over themselves. What patients like those we have been considering often seem unable to control is self-control itself; what they cannot get distance from is their own endless propensity for detachment; what they cannot be conscious of is their own hypertrophied self-consciousness and its effect on their world. What prevents them from returning to a more normal existence is no simple failure of consciousness or of will but, we might say, an inability to *desist* from knowing and from willing — an inability to let oneself be caught up in and carried along by the ongoing flow of practical and social life. A schizophrenic man named Thomas Hennell (1967, p. 210) seems to have grasped something of the paradoxes that are involved: 'The introverted mind believes itself busy, yet produces nothing,' he wrote in his autobiographical book, *The Witnesses*. 'Its self-torture is partly involuntary, but partly willful: for that which ambitiously directs it increases its painful labor.'

Finally we might note that such a reading of schizophrenic experience casts a different light on the famous 'praecox-feeling', the sense of essential strangeness and incomprehensibility emphasized by various European psychiatrists (Rumke, 1941/1990), and which Jaspers associated with the fundamental mutations of self-hood and volition that are characteristic of schizophrenia. What is strange or alienating to the observer about such patients as Natalija or Lawrence may not be *just* the patient's sheer different-ness from oneself, but something more closely bound up with what the patient is actually experiencing. Indeed, rather than indicating a total failure of empathic comprehension, the praecox-feeling which is evoked in the interviewer may in fact indicate a *shared* sense of alienation; it may involve some accurate intuition of the profound *self*-estrangement which the patient him or herself is really going through.

An Afterword: Some Reflections on Neurobiology

In the preceding pages and elsewhere (Sass, 1992; 1994), I have portrayed schizophrenia as a hyper-self-conscious, often hyper-cerebral condition, an illness in which the capacity for spontaneous activity and ready engagement with the world are diminished, and where there may be an exaggerated (and usually dysfunctional) reliance on coping via deliberation, abstraction, contemplation and withdrawal. It is important to address the question of possible neurobiological bases for such a condition. Given the continuing influence of certain traditional assumptions about mind/brain relationships in mental disorder, it is possible that some readers may assume — quite mistakenly in my opinion — that the account offered here is somehow in conflict with an acknowledgement of the role of neurobiological abnormalities in schizophrenia. Some brief discussion of these issues therefore seems appropriate (for lengthier discussion, see Sass 1992, pp. 374–97).

As is well known, one of the most influential formulations of the traditional assumptions was put forward by the British neurologist J. Hughlings Jackson at the end of the nineteenth century. Inspired in part by the evolutionism of his time, Jackson postulated levels in the nervous system that differed according to their degree of organization and of volitional control. In Jackson's view, the *sine qua non* of all mental disorders, neurological as well as psychiatric, was a decline or disintegration of the higher or more quintessentially human mental capacities — including the capacities for volition, logical reasoning, abstraction, and self-conscious awareness. As Jackson (1873, p. 84, quoted in Harrington, 1987, p. 211) wrote in a typical passage: 'That parts suffer more as they serve in voluntary, and less as they serve in automatic operations is, I believe, the law of destroying lesions of the cerebral nervous centers.' Going along with this, as a secondary consequence, there was often an increase of lower or more primitive mental processes, which were supposedly released due to the failure of the higher levels to exert their normal inhibitory control. Charles Mercier, Jackson's disciple and close friend, could not have been more explicit: 'In every case of insanity, the essential feature is defect,' he wrote. 'In no case does disease make a real, fruitful addition to function. The affection of function is always in the direction of loss, of deficit, or diminution . . . in all cases of insanity, the real and important aberration is not necessarily the most conspicuous feature — the over-action — ... but the degradation of action to a lower plane' (quoted in Clark 1981, p. 284). (On Jackson and his influence, see Sass, 1992, pp. 377–8; Clark, 1981; Stengel, 1963.)

The continuing emphasis on lowered mental level or loss of rationality in schizophrenia is exemplified by many subsequent authors, including Kurt Goldstein (1944/1964), who was himself influenced by Hughlings Jackson and whose notion of abstract-versus-concrete modes of functioning has exerted a powerful influence in psychology, psychiatry and neurology since the 1920s. In Goldstein's view, the schizophrenic is characterized by an impairment of the 'abstract attitude' that has various manifestations — including a tendency to respond in quasi-automatic fashion to sensory stimuli, to be 'given over and bound to the immediate experience of a given thing or situation in its particular uniqueness', to prefer 'situations of activity [in which] objects are experienced as things for definite use', to have difficulty adopting a hypothetical or fictitious attitude, and to lack 'generic words which signify categories or classes' (1944/1964, pp. 18, 23–5), Notions akin to those of Jackson and Goldstein are prominent in contemporary psychiatry (Sass, 1992, pp. 375–84). Obviously, these ideas are in fundamental contradiction with my own portrayal of schizophrenia as a hyperreflexive condition characterized by alienation from (or suppression of) the more spontaneous forms of bodily activity and response and the more primitive realms of affect and instinct, and by an exaggerated reliance on abstraction, self-consciousness, and dysfunctional forms of deliberation.

This is not the place for a general survey of the contemporary neurobiology of schizophrenia. But in order to explore this conflict of views, and to indicate how neurobiological abnormalities might contribute to the symptoms I emphasize, it is useful to focus on some specific neurobiological hypotheses prominent in the past decade. I will concentrate on the work of Daniel Weinberger and others concerning 'hypofrontality' — that is, the pattern of decreased activity in the dorsolateral portion of the prefrontal cortex, usually occurring in conjunction with heightened activity in subcortical limbic areas, particularly the hippocampus. (I hold no special brief for the hypofrontality hypothesis, by the way. But owing to its prominence, and to the fact that it seems at first so *in*consistent with my own portrayal of schizophrenia, it will serve very well as an example.)

Given the traditional tendency to view the prefrontal cortex as the seat of all higher cognitive capacities, the finding of hypofrontality in the schizophrenic brain certainly appears, at first blush, to be consistent with the traditional models of Jackson, Goldstein, and others. It is hardly surprising, therefore, that the original portrayals of hypofrontality were thoroughly Jacksonian or Goldsteinian in spirit, with hypofrontality being interpreted as an index of a general decline of higher and more quintessentially human psychological functions. In formulations reminiscent of Goldstein's 'loss of the abstract attitude', Weinberger and his co-authors speak, for instance, of a supposed incapacity to form abstract concepts, shift mental sets, reason deductively, or exercise independent judgment. This decline was assumed to be accompanied by release or disinhibition of affect, instinct, automatic and primitive action patterns, or archaic memories housed in the more 'primitive' temporal lobe (which contains the hippocampus, among other structures) (Goldberg *et al.*, 1987; Weinberger *et al.*, 1986; see also Andreasen, 1986). In one article, Weinberger (1987) even went so far as to speculate that this neurobiological model might provide a physiological explanation for the classic psychodynamic model of schizophrenia, with 'inadequate ego defenses' reflecting hypofunction in the prefrontal cortex and 'overwhelming instinctual forces' reflecting subcortical dopamine disinhibition'. As often occurs with scientific findings, these early interpretations now appear somewhat oversimplified. More recent interpretations of the significance of hypofrontality have had a rather different cast.

Hypofrontality is now more likely to be described not as an index of the loss of higher capacities such as reason and abstraction, but as a more specific as well as complicated disturbance pertaining to action: namely, as a decline in the capacity (or, possibly, the propensity) to engage in controlled, sustained, and self-monitored forms of practical activity coordinated with external cues, probably in association with disturbances of immediate or working memory. Thus Weinberger and Lipska (1995, p. 90) describe poor performance and hypofrontal patterns of brain activation in schizophrenia as specific to tasks that involve 'calling up information from memory, holding it in mind for short periods, updating it frequently, and coordinating it with other mental activities in the services of a response'; they acknowledge that schizophrenics do not manifest this abnormal pattern on certain other tasks, including tasks calling for effortful exercise of abstract reasoning (pp. 90–1). Subcortical functions have also come to be viewed rather differently, with certain 'lower' areas, particularly the hippocampus and related temperolimbic areas, now seen as serving sophisticated *cognitive* functions — for example, the so-called 'comparator function', which involves a complex interplay of action plans, perception, and decision-making processes that allows for the registering of novel or unexpected stimuli as well as for the inhibiting of attention or orienting responses to very common and familiar stimuli (see Gray *et al.* ,1991).[11]

---

[11] I cannot resist noting that the interpretations of the significance of hypofrontality offered by Weinberger and associates have come to be very congruent with the interpretation I suggested in 1992 (see Sass 1992, pp. 388-92).

One current way of understanding the pattern of hypofrontality along with sub-cortical hyperactivation that schizophrenics demonstrate on certain tasks, is to inter-pret this pattern as a consequence of frontal-temperolimbic disconnection in which working memory — a frontal function — fails to inhibit startle or orienting responses that are mediated by limbic areas (Weinberger and Lipska, 1995). These latter responses must be suppressed in order to allow the shift from explicit or focal to tacit or subsidiary awareness that is required for the development of spontaneous skilful action (see Polanyi, 1964). One might argue that this shift from focal to tacit aware-ness is also necessary for one to have a coherent sense of self or the experience of a direct relationship to a coherent outer world.

The most fundamental sense of selfhood involves the experience of self not as an *object* of awareness but, in some crucial respects, as an unseen point of origin for action, experience, and thought. What William James (1981, p. 286) called (perhaps somewhat misleadingly) the 'central nucleus of the Self' is not, in fact, experienced as an entity in the focus of our awareness, but, rather, as a kind of medium of aware-ness, source of activity, or general directedness toward the world. A coherent sense of self would seem to require, therefore, that certain phenomena — including the kines-thetic and proprioceptive sensations that provide us with information about our body's stance and movement, and inner speech, which often serves as the medium of our thinking — be experienced in an implicit or subsidiary manner; that is, that we be able to dwell with*in* these elements of experience, to know them in a subsidiary fash-ion while we direct our focal attention toward the world or the objects of our thought. The disturbances of working memory or comparator function supposedly present in schizophrenia would prevent this from occurring. And when focal or explicit atten-tion *is* directed at phenomena that would normally be experienced in a tacit manner, these normally 'inner' phenomena are liable to take on some of the quality of external objects: phenomena that would normally be 'inhabited' as part of the self thereby come to seem extruded, resulting in a fragmenting or centrifuging of the experiential sense of self (see Sass, 1992, pp. 213–41, 473–5; also Frith, 1979; Hemsley, 1998). Inappropriate direction of focal attention is also liable to disrupt the figure/ground or object/horizon structure of our experience of the outer world. Normally, focal atten-tion is not directed toward familiar stimuli; these are instead allowed to merge into an only implicitly noticed, taken-for-granted background or horizon of awareness which frames the more novel or otherwise significant stimuli and allows these latter to stand forth in the focus of our awareness (see Heidegger, 1962; also Hemsley, 1992; Sass, 1992, pp. 43–74).

It should be clear, then, that hypofrontality along with temperolimbic hyperactivity need not be conceived in neo-Jacksonian or Goldsteinian terms. Indeed, one could argue that these patterns might well constitute the neurobiological underpinnings of some aspects of the schizophrenic hyperreflexivity I describe. Instead of being asso-ciated with a general decline of rational or higher capacities, hypofrontality may instead indicate incapacity for, and/or withdrawal from, world-oriented practical activity — a withdrawal that may in turn encourage self-consciousness and that could therefore be a prerequisite for a sense of alienation from the self as well as for solipsistic-like experiences (re. the latter point, see Wittgenstein's association of pas-sivity and staring with solipsism, discussed in Sass, 1994). According to this hypothe-sis, temperolimbic hyperactivation may not be associated with influx of the passions or other primitive aspects of the psyche but, rather, with a kind of undirected hyper-consciousness that contributes to a subtle sense of alienation from the world, as well as to the fragmentation and sense of extrusion of the self — for instance, of kines-thetic sensations and inner speech. (It may also contribute to solipsistic experiences, since these developments could make one more aware of normally unnoticed psycho-logical processes that mediate our experience of the world, and could also make one more aware of the field of awareness as such.)

It is also worth noting the fact that hypofrontality often occurs in conjunction with heightened activity of *posterior* parts of the brain. The frontal cortex has often been believed to be the locus of all higher intellectual functions; in the nineteenth century, in fact, the anterior–posterior axis of the brain was often thought to correspond, on the psychological plane, to a dimension of abstract-versus-concrete forms of conscious-ness, or else to a distinction of intellectual-versus-instinctual-and-appetitive func-tions (Harrington, 1985, p. 622; 1987, p. 225). If this were true, the pattern of hypofrontality along with posterior hyperactivity would clearly fit the general models of Goldstein and Jackson.[12] Contemporary neuroscience recognizes, however, that certain forms of abstract reasoning and logical thinking tend to activate not frontal - areas but parts of the posterior lobes (see e.g. Berman *et al.*, 1988, re. activation patterns with the Ravens Progressive Matrices test; see also Harrington 1987, p. 225 fn, on some precursors of this view). A more accurate characterization of the anterior-posterior axis might therefore emphasize the role of the frontal lobes in the control of goal-directed action and that of the posterior lobes in subserving sensory reception and knowing. Thus it has been suggested that the pattern of relative increase of poste-rior and decrease of anterior activation sometimes found in schizophrenia, could be a sign of *hypo*intentionality combined with *hyper*gnosia (Ingvar and Franzen, 1974). The British psychiatrist Hayes Newtington, writing in 1909, gave a related but more colourful description when he spoke of 'the contemporaneous existence in one brain of morbid apathy and active, though misguided cerebration' (quoted in Barham, 1984, p. 38). Such a formulation is consistent with my own discussion of how passivi-zation combined with hyperconsciousness may underlie some of the transformations in the experience of self and world that occur in this illness.

A schizophrenic patient named Jonathan Lang (1940) captures exactly this condi-tion in describing his own abnormal experiences. He describes what he calls 'schiz-ophrenes' such as himself as tending to withdraw from 'sensorimotor activity' and to be dominated, during all their waking hours, by what he terms 'central-symbolic, par-ticularly verbal activity', often involving the use of abstractions. Though acknowl-edging his own difficulties with 'sensory discrimination' and 'neuro-muscular coordination', Jonathan Lang goes on to criticize studies of concept-formation that attempt to describe 'the *general* mental level of the schizophrene' on the basis of sensorimotor tests alone (it is worth recalling that the Wisconsin Card Sorting Test, which is used in the study of hypofrontality, has a significant sensorimotor compo-nent). Lang argues that one must also consider what he calls the 'ideological level' (i.e. the level of inner symbolic thought), for this, he says, 'is the most highly devel-

---

[12] It is worth noting, however, that Jackson and some other British neurologists were exceptions on this issue, tending to oppose what Harrington (1987, p. 225n) calls 'the old prejudice that everything that counted in a person was to be found up front.'

oped level' in 'ideocentric schizophrenes' such as himself — persons for whom the 'search for abstractions' is actually their most central quest.

References

Andreasen, N. (1984), *The Broken Brain: The Biological Revolution in Psychiatry* (New York: Harper and Row).
Andreasen, N. (1986), 'Is schizophrenia a temperolimbic disease?', in *Can Schizophrenia Be Localized in the Brain?*, ed. Andreasen (Washington DC: American Psychiatric Press).
Barham, P. (1984), *Schizophrenia and Human Value* (Oxford: Blackwell).
Berman, K.F., Illowsky, B.P. and Weinberger, D.R. (1988), 'Physiological dysfunction of dorsolateral prefrontal cortex in schizophrenia: IV, Further evidence for regional and behavioral specificity', *Archives of General Psychiatry*, **45**, pp. 616–22.
Berrios, G. (1985), 'Positive and negative symptoms and Jackson', *Archives of General Psychiatry*, **42**, pp. 95–7.
Berrios, G. (1991), 'French views on positive and negative symptoms: A conceptual history', *Comprehensive Psychiatry*, **32**, pp. 395–403.
Blankenburg, W. (1991), *La Perte de L'Evidence Naturelle*, translated from the German by J-M. Azorin and Y. Totoyan, (Paris: PUF).
Bleuler, E. (1950), *Dementia Praecox or the Group of Schizophrenias*, translated from the German by J. Zinkin (New York: International Universities Press).
Bleuler, M. (1978), *The Schizophrenic Disorders*, translated from the German by S.M. Clemens, (New Haven, CN and London: Yale University Press).
Bovet, P. and Parnas, J. (1993), 'Schizophrenic delusions: A phenomenological approach', *Schizophrenia Bulletin*, **19**, pp. 579–97.
Carpenter, P.K. (1989), 'Descriptions of schizophrenia in the psychiatry of Georgian Britain: John Haslam and James Tilly Matthews', *Comprehensive Psychiatry*, **30**, pp. 332–8.
Clark, M.J. (1981), 'The rejection of psychological approaches to mental disorder in late nineteenth-century British psychiatry', in *Madhouses, Mad-Doctors, and Madmen: The Social History of Psychiatry in the Victorian Era*, ed. A. Scull (Philadelphia: University of Pennsylvania Press).
Crary, J. (1990), *Techniques of the Observer* (Cambridge, MA: MIT Press).
Cutting, J. (1990), *The Right Cerebral Hemisphere and Psychiatric Disorders* (Oxford, New York and Tokyo: Oxford University Press).
Dreyfus, H. And Rabinow, P. (1982), *Michel Foucault* (Chicago: University of Chicago Press).
Fichte, Johann Gottlieb (1910), *The Vocation of Man*, translated from the German by W. Smith (Chicago: Open Court Press).
Foucault, M. (1972), *The Archaeology of Knowledge*, translated from the French by A. Sheridan Smith (New York: Harper Colophon).
Foucault, M. (1994), *The Order of Things* (New York: Vintage Books).
Frith, C.D. (1979), 'Consciousness, information processing, and schizophrenia', *British Journal of Psychiatry*, **134**, pp. 225–35.
Frith, C.D. (1994), 'Theory of mind in schizophrenia', in *The Neuropsychology of Schizophrenia*, ed. A.S. David and J.C. Cutting (Hove, UK and Hillsdale, NJ: Lawrence Erlbaum).
Glass, J.M. (1985), *Delusion* (Chicago and London: University of Chicago Press).
Goldberg, T.E., Weinberger, D.R., Berman, K.F. *et al.* (1987), 'Further evidence for dementia of the prefrontal type in schizophrenia', *Archives of General Psychiatry*, **44**, pp. 1008–14.
Goldstein, K. (1940/1963), *Human Nature in the Light of Psychopathology* (New York: Schocken Books).
Goldstein, K. (1944/1964), 'Methodological approach to the study of schizophrenic thought disorder', in *Language and Thought in Schizophrenia*, ed. J.S. Kasanin (New York: W.W. Norton).
Goldstein K. and Scheerer, M. (1941), 'Abstract and concrete behavior: An experimental study with special tests', *Psychological Monographs*, **53** (2), pp. 1–151.
Gouldner, A. W. (1976), *The Dialectic of Ideology and Technology* (New York: Seabury).
Gray, J.A., Feldon, J., Rawlins, J.N.P., *et al.* (1991), 'The neuropsychology of schizophrenia' (with peer commentary), *Behavioral and Brain Sciences*, **14**, pp. 1–84.
Griswold, C.L. (1988), *Platonic Readings* (New York: Routledge and Kegan Paul).
Harrington, A. (1985), 'Nineteenth-century ideas on hemisphere differences and "duality of Mind"', *Behavioral and Brain Sciences*, **8**, pp. 617–34.
Harrington, A. (1987), *Medicine, Mind, and the Double Brain* (Princeton NJ: Princeton University Press).
Heidegger, M. (1962), *Being and Time*, trans. J. Macquarrie and E. Robinson (New York: Harper and Row).
Hemsley, D.R. (1992), 'Cognitive abnormalities and the symptoms of schizophrenia', in *Phenomenology, Language, and Schizophrenia*, ed. M. Spitzer, F. Uehlein, M.A. Schwartz and C. Mundt (New York: Springer Verlag).

Hemsley, D.R. (1998), 'The disruption of the "sense of self" in schizophrenia: Potential links with disturbances of information processing', *British Journal of Medical Psychology*, 71, pp. 115–24.

Hennell, T. (1967), *The Witnesses* (New Hyde Park, NY: University Books).

Hunt, H.T. (1995), *On the Nature of Consciousness* (New Haven, CN and London: Yale University
Press).

Ingvar, D.H. and Franzen, G. (1974), 'Distribution of cerebral activity in chronic schizophrenia', *Lancet*,
December 21, 1974: pp. 1484–6.

Jackson, J.H. (1873), 'On the anatomical and physiological localisation of movements in the brain', *The
Lancet*, 1, pp. 84–5, 162–4.

James, W. (1981), *The Principles of Psychology* (Cambridge, MA: Harvard University Press).

Jaspers, K. (1963), *General Psychopathology*, trans. J. Hoenig and M.W. Hamilton (Chicago: University
of Chicago Press).

Kafka, F. (1971), 'Description of a struggle', in *The Complete Stories*, translated from the German by
T. Stern and J. Stern (New York: Schocken Books).

Kimura, B. (1992), *Ecrits de Psychopathologie Phenomenologique*, translated from the Japanese by Joel
Bouderlique (Paris: PUF).

Landis, C. (Ed. 1964), *Varieties of Psychopathological Experience* (New York: Holt, Rinehart and
Winston).

Lang, J. (1940), 'The other side of the ideological aspects of schizophrenia', *Psychiatry*, 3, pp. 389–93.

Liddle, P. (1992), 'The unsupervised brain: Persistent features of schizophrenia', *British Journal of Psychiatry Review of Books* (January 1992), pp. 1–3.

Mellor, C.S. (1970), 'First rank symptoms of schizophrenia', *British Journal of Psychiatry*, 117,
pp. 15–23.

Minkowski, E. (1927), *La Schizophrenie* (Paris: Payot).

Parnas, J. and Bovet, J. (1991), 'Autism in schizophrenia revisited', *Comprehensive Psychiatry*, 32,
pp. 7–21.

Passmore, J. (1968), *A Hundred Years of Philosophy* (Harmondsworth, UK: Penguin Books).

Polanyi, M. (1964), *Personal Knowledge: Towards a Post-Critical Philosophy* (New York and Evanston:
Harper and Row).

Rosser, R. (1979), 'The psychopathology of feeling and thinking in a schizophrenic,' *International Journal of Psychoanalysis*, 60, pp. 177–88.

Royce, J. (1919), *Lectures on Modern Idealism* (New Haven, CN: Yale University Press).

Rumke, H.C. (1941/1990), 'The nuclear symptom of schizophrenia and the praecox feeling', *History of
Psychiatry*, 1, pp. 331–41.

Sass, L. (1992), *Madness and Modernism: Insanity in the Light of Modern Art, Literature, and Thought*
(New York: Basic Books; Harvard University Press paperback edition, published in New York and
London, 1994).

Sass, L. (1994), *The Paradoxes of Delusion: Wittgenstein, Schreber, and the Schizophrenic Mind* (Ithaca,
NY and London: Cornell University Press).

Sass, L. (1997), 'The consciousness machine: Self and subjectivity in schizophrenia and modern culture',
in *The Conceptual Self in Context*, ed. U. Neisser and D. Jopling (New York: Cambridge University
Press).

Schopenhauer, A. (1928), *World as Will and Idea* (book 1, section 7), in *The Philosophy of Schopenhauer*
(New York: Modern Library).

Snyder, S. (1974), *Madness and the Brain* (New York: McGraw-Hill).

Sobel, W., Wolski, R., Cancro, R. and Makari, G.J. (1996), 'Interpersonal relatedness and paranoid
schizophrenia', *American Journal of Psychiatry*, 153, pp. 1084–7.

Spitzer, M. (1990), 'On defining delusions', *Comprehensive Psychiatry*, 31, pp. 377–97.

Stengel, E. (1963), 'Hughlings Jackson's influence in psychiatry', *British Journal of Psychiatry*, 109,
pp. 348–55.

Strawson, P. (1966), *The Bounds of Sense: An Essay on Kant's Critique of Pure Reason* (London:
Methuen).

Strömgren, E. (1987), 'Autism', *European Journal of Psychiatry*, 1.

Tausk, V. (1933), 'On the origin of the "influencing machine" in schizophrenia' (first published in
German in 1919), *Psychoanalytic Quarterly*, 2, pp. 519–56.

Vygotsky, L.S. (1987), 'The psychology of schizophrenia', *Soviet Psychology*, 26, pp. 72–7.

Weber, M. (1949), *The Methodology of the Social Sciences* (New York: Free Press).

Weinberger, D.R. (1987), 'Implications of normal brain development for the pathogenesis of schizophrenia', *Archives of General Psychiatry*, 44, pp. 660–9.

Weinberger, D.R., Berman, K.J. and Zec, R.F. (1986), 'Physiological dysfunction of dorsolateral prefrontal cortex in schizophrenia: I. Regional cerebral blood flow evidence', *Archives of General Psychiatry*,
43: pp. 114–24.

Weinberger, D.R. and Lipska, B.K. (1995), 'Cortical maldevelopment, anti-psychotic drugs, and schizophrenia: A search for common ground', *Schizophrenia Research*, 16, pp. 87–110.

Jennifer Radden

Pathologically Divided Minds Synchronic Unity and Models of Self

Introduction[1]

In this chapter, I explore the implications of adopting one model of self rather than another in respect to one particular feature of our mental life. The need to explain synchronic unity in normal subjectivity, and also to explain the apparent and puzzling absence of synchronic unity in certain symptoms of severe mental disorder, I show, becomes more pressing with one particular model. But in the process of developing that explanation we learn something about subjectivity and perhaps also something about brain functioning.

How many models of self are there? It depends in part on what ranks as a model of the self. Does an explicitly 'no self' or 'no subject' theory such as we associate with postmodernist deconstruction qualify as a model of self? Does a relational self theory, which posits that selves are to be understood not as entities but as relations? Maybe, maybe not. At any rate, I am going to exclude both of these together with (some versions at least of) the Buddhist, certainly with the Goffmanesque and other variants on them, narrowing my focus to models which regard the self as something more than a mere set of relations, and more than a completely misleading description (or what Ryle would have called a category mistake), as postmodern deconstructions appear to do.

It seems true of the more robust models of self that they come in at least two forms. There is the self of Cartesian and Kantian tradition which offers us an unchanging and transcendental subject of experiences; on the other hand, there is the empirical self embraced by social science constructivists (or constructionists), and found in the work of contemporary 'reductionist' philosophers like Parfit (also Mead, Cooley, James and most of social science in the twentieth century). For brevity I shall refer to these as the *transcendental subject* model, and the *reductionist* model, respectively.

The details of the first of these, the transcendental subject model, require little introduction, but let me briefly summarize aspects of the second model. The reduc-

[1] This paper was presented at the Brain and Self Workshop at Copenhagen and Helsinor, Denmark, in August 1997, and I am grateful to many people who commented on it at that meeting. I also wish to acknowledge several astute and helpful readers for *JCS* for their comments and suggestions.

tionist model emerges out of a famous moment in the history of philosophy: Hume's fruitless search for the Cartesian subject and his conclusion that strict identity was not a characteristic of the self. A reductionist account of the self, such as we find in the neo-Humean theories of Parfit, is non-essentialist and relativistic. The concept is (1) derived from a form of empirical observation, i.e., phenomenologically, (2) content and purpose dependent, (3) compatible with a 'scalar' notion of the sameness or identity through time whereby a later self may be the same or 'identical' with an earlier one to a greater or lesser degree, and as a consequence (4) not bound by the customary presumption whereby persons or selves come one to a bodily lifetime.

My interest here is in one feature that distinguishes these two models. The transcendental subject model occludes a distinction which the reductionist model permits us to see: the distinction between the self's unity viewed in *diachronic* terms (i.e., through stretches of time) and viewed in *synchronic* terms (at a particular time). Questions about the self's diachronic unity concern its identity or sameness through stretches of time, such as 'Is she the same person now as she was ten years ago?' or 'Am I the same person as I was ten years ago?' Questions about the self's synchronic unity concern its unity at a given time, such as 'Are all these simultaneous experiences experiences of mine?' The normal self's synchronic and diachronic unity are, as Galen Strawson[2] has emphasized, grounding aspects of phenomenologically confirmed subjectivity.

This distinction between the self's diachronic and synchronic unity is occluded in the transcendental subject model. The Cartesian subject, or self, was thought to encompass a unifying principle. This principle linked items in the mind or consciousness both at a given time, and through time, ensuring perfect identity throughout the individual's lifetime. Since *the same principle* served to unify the self at a given time and through stretches of time, little emphasis was placed on these distinguishable kinds of unity or oneness involved, diachronic and synchronic. If, as Hume suggests, there is no introspectively identified unchanging subject of experiences, then the unifying function allegedly ensured by that subject is lost. On Hume's positive account of self-identity, that function devolved onto the imagination. Although he did not seem to recognize the matter of synchronic unity, still Hume's account apparently provided for it. If I could not mistake my bundle of experiences for yours, or question whether some experiences were mine, then it must be because the imagination ensured unity. Thus, on a Humean account, also, these two separable unifying functions must depend on a single source or principle.

Interestingly and confusingly, although Hume was critical of the transcendental subject model and is the founder of this second, reductionist alternative, *he* did not fully acknowledge the distinction between the unity of the self at a given time, and the continuity of experiences and traits scattered across stretches of time, thus failing to raise, or answer, the distinctly synchronic question, 'what makes all these present experiences mine?'

This omission confirms one interpretation of some puzzling passages in Hume, suggesting that for him the distinction between the two kinds of unity was illusory. On this interpretation he made what, at least from a phenomenological standpoint, must be seen as a mistake, by treating each separate perception we apparently experi-

---

[2] All references to 'Strawson' in the current chapter are to Galen Strawson's opening chpater in this volume (pp. 1–24).

ence *simultaneously* as actually *sequential*. The sounds, thoughts, sights and sensations experienced at a given moment each actually succeed each other, in his view, albeit with 'inconceivable rapidity', which will make imperceptible their being a sequence rather than simultaneous. (Hume 1965, p. 252) All separable perceptions shared the same feature: not only those which appeared to do so, but also those which did not, occurred sequentially.

Another passage from Hume's discussion may be read to refute this interpretation. On the following page, he states of the mind that 'There is properly no simplicity in it at one time . . .' allowing us to recognize that the many discrete impressions occurring in the mind *at a given time* may be what in parallel, simultaneous sequences succeed each other with 'inconceivable rapidity', i.e. , that the mind at any given time comprises a multitude of ever-changing elements. The first reading, while apparently more compatible with Hume's failure to explicitly address the question of synchronic unity, perhaps nonetheless misinterprets the referent of his claim about an inconceivably rapid succession.[3]

Were we to adopt the first interpretation of Hume's discussion, we should accuse him of an error in phenomenological terms. (The analysis attributed to Hume on this interpretation may not be correct in brain science terms, either. See Galen Strawson's discussion of empirical work on the three-second dimension of the 'Now' [Strawson, pp. 9–10].) Philosophers refer to a '*specious present*', (This is Strawson's 'hiatusfree periods of thought or experience.') Following Grice's early work (Grice 1941) the specious present is usually defined (phenomenologically) in the following way:

> Experiences E1 and E2 are united at a time or in a specious present, just when they are believed, on the basis of memory or introspection, to be simultaneous. And within the specious present, separable 'impressions' such as the sounds, thoughts, sights and sensations experienced at a given moment, occur not sequentially but simultaneously.

I assume we can and should reject Hume's oddly counter-empirical (and counter-phenomenological) presumption — if he *is* guilty of such a presumption — that all perceptions must be sequential. And if so, we can say that by embracing the reductionist model, we are required to distinguish these two separate aspects of the self's alleged unity, and to consider separately each of these kinds of questions, the diachronic 'What makes me the same person now as I was ten years ago?' and the synchronic 'How do I know all these simultaneous experiences are experiences of mine?' Moreover, having adopted a reductionist model of self, we may say, *we are required to account for synchronic unity*, the oneness or 'mineness' seeming to bind together all the parts of my experience within any given specious present.

Here I focus my attention on the second sort of question, about synchronic unity (How do I know all these experiences are experiences of mine?), laying aside considerations about diachronic unity, and also laying aside the reasoning by which the

---

[3] I am grateful to Jonathan Shear for help in recognizing this second, alternative reading of the crucial sentences in Hume. Because on the most natural reading of the 'which' in the first passage quoted ('that they are nothing but a bundle or collection of different perceptions, which succeed each other with an inconceivable rapidity, and are in perpetual flux and movement.' [page 252]), its referent is the perceptions, and because of Hume's failure to address the synchronic question, I am still inclined to accept the first interpretation. The apparently contradictory claim on the following page that. 'There is properly no simplicity at one time' must be read, along with the rest of the sentence and the remarks that follow, as a reiteration of Hume's general resistance to the idea of a simple, identical subject of experiences 'housing' the sequence of perceptions.)

reductionist model might be seen as preferable to the traditional Cartesian-Kantian model positing a transcendental subject. Certain aspects of the self's synchronic unity have particular bearing for a discussion of self and brain. I want to explore what sort of claims are claims about the self's (alleged) synchronic unity, grammatical, or psychological? And to direct that exploration, I want to look at abnormal psychology, particularly some cases of mental or psychological disorder which seem to challenge the synchronic unity which presents itself as a given in normal subjectivity. Once we have embraced a reductionist model of self, again, we are required to find some account which accommodates not only the synchronic unity we associate with the normal experience of self, but also the odd descriptions of fractured subjectivity we find in psychopathology.

In what follows I use the term 'divided mind' in a slightly technical way to describe degrees of synchronic disunity found in these states of pathology. 'Mind' here alludes to the set of a person's psychological states. (For a fuller development of the concept of divided minds, see Radden 1996.) Two things must be clear about these pathologically divided minds. (1) Normal minds are not *strict* synchronic unities — there are heterogeneities in ordinary synchronic experience, for instance when we are of two minds or ambivalent over something: what I am calling a divided mind is more divided than that. And (2) certain conditions of disease and injury to the brain (and mind) result in such radical synchronic fracture that the term 'divided mind' is also inapplicable because the term ' mind' is inapplicable. There is *no longer* a mind in the massive amnesias resulting from dementias like Alzheimer's Disease and from head injury. (We shall return to these conditions later in this chapter.) So 'divided minds' cases fall between (1) and (2).

More fractured than (1), but less fractured than (2), lie a diverse cluster of disorders and symptoms. These include the disunity evidenced in descriptions of Multiple Personality Disorder (otherwise known as Dissociative Identity Disorder and henceforth referred to as MPD/DID in this discussion), and the felt division and disownership experienced subjectively in ego-alien, 'made' experiences, such as thought insertion, which are associated with schizophrenia. These disorders and symptoms each invite interpretation as pathologically divided minds, as do certain other conditions including states of possession, hypnoid states and other dissociative conditions effected in the laboratory, as well as more commonplace experiences of depersonalization and derealization. My discussion will be limited to the first two, however: the so-called 'co-consciousness ' of MPD/DID, and ego-alien experiences such as thought disorder. They are in my assessment the most vivid, and the best-understood states and thus the most plausible candidates for this description of divided minds.

There seem to be several inquiries here. First, what *is* the evidence for the degree of synchronic disunity here termed divided minds? And second, what are we to make of such evidence, i.e., how should these experiences be described? Third, do they tell us something interesting about the brain? In looking at this last question, I want to examine a methodology associated with what is known as top-down explanation; more particularly, I want to see if we can learn about the brain from pathological states by a 'deficit' model. Central cases of the deficit model of top-down explanation demonstrate something about the functioning of the normal brain by discovering the area or state of the brain whose damage has resulted in this defect.

What is the Evidence for Divided Minds?

Evidence of divided minds comes from several sources, the above collection of symptoms and disorders shows. Notable among these is evidence of *shared knowledge* and *waverings* indicative of the 'coconsciousness' attributed in cases of MPD/DID.

Very briefly, since its notoriety precedes it, this odd disorder (MPD/DID) involves the apparent presence of several fairly well developed personalities alternating control of the same body, at least one of which is ignorant of at least some of the states and activities of another through a process of psychogenic amnesia, or dissociation. (These separate selves are sometimes known as alters, and I will refer to each alter's alternating states of control as its reign.) I have argued elsewhere that in particular case descriptions rigorous criteria for the notion of a separate self will frequently prevent us from acknowledging these MPD/DID alters as selves, strictly understood (Radden 1996). Nonetheless, for our purposes here, the symptoms of MPD/DID look to be evidence of divided minds and the term 'selves' will be used loosely to describe the alters attached to a multiple person or 'multiple.'

Shared knowledge, apparently acquired firsthand by non-reigning selves through forms of eavesdropping, or listening in on the experience of the reigning self, constitutes one form of evidence for divided minds. Seemingly less common is the alleged interference from other selves reflected in the occasional waverings of the reigning self — interruptions and anomalies in the smooth flow of control linking the reigning self's cognitive states and desires to their execution. Such evidence and its interpretation will be my initial focus here. Evidence of divided minds from each source is equivocal, in my assessment. Neither publicly observable non-verbal evidence of disunity nor verbal reports of felt division or possession will eventually prove sufficient to refute certain philosophical claims, and common-sense presumptions, about the self's unity. These empirical findings deserve close examination, nonetheless, for they are opaque — open to, and even inviting of, conflicting interpretation.

In order to narrow our discussion, we must formulate the particular claim in support of which these several forms of evidence will be reviewed.

The dispositional understanding of selves makes relatively uncontroversial any answer to the question of whether selves are to be regarded as simultaneous rather than sequential. Granted the satisfaction of certain criteria built into the notion of self (a self must have some duration, for instance: however distinctive, the fleeting occurrence of a set of traits is something less than a self) several selves sharing the same body may be said either (a) to coexist, or (b) to succeed one another, and the considerations affecting our decision to put it one way, rather than another, are not philosophically weighty. In contrast, the decision to speak of simultaneous, rather than successive, centres of awareness will be more problematic. Awareness is not usually treated as a dispositional concept. Thus the claim that more than one separate centre of awareness inhabits the same body at the same time is a philosophically significant one with serious conceptual implications. It will affect how we must understand selves and minds; it has bearing on the notions of awareness and of subjectivity.

The more significant philosophical claim, that there are *separate simultaneous centres of awareness,* is the one toward which our evaluation of the evidence from abnormal psychology will be directed.

Does the evidence suggest that the divided states of awareness in MPD/DID are (a) simultaneous or (b) successive? These alternative interpretations ((a) and (b)), may be illustrated through the case of a multiple known as John Woods. (Armstrong, 1997) John Woods, a college student who killed two women, was examined by Judith Armstrong after the crime. Woods proved to comprise two additional selves or alters. Armstrong's clinical account includes exchanges between herself and these separate selves, and one of these, named Donnie, is portrayed as possessing the epistemic advantage of knowing about the crime perpetuated by John.

Divided minds in MPD/DID

It will be useful to distinguish two kinds of evidence available to observers here, that known to us through non-verbal behaviour of the multiple, and that known to us from the subject's verbal report.

Evidence of simultaneous divided awareness or what is sometimes known as co-consciousness that may be identified through non-verbal behaviour is of two kinds. First there is shared knowledge, i.e. the indication at t2 that the non-reigning self (here, Donnie) is in possession of information acquired by the reigning self (here, John) at t1; the fact that if put to the test Donnie could identify the murder weapon, for example. Second, there are observable waverings in the reigning self's progress, which seem to indicate interference from a cognizant but non-reigning self.

Shared knowledge: If a non-reigning self (Donnie) exhibited non-verbal evidence that he knew P at t1, must we conclude that the awareness was simultaneous? Several possible interpretations avoid such an inference. The simplest of these is that while Donnie acquires sensory information at t1, that information was acquired without his having been aware (or been able to become aware) at t1, of this acquisition. Another interpretation is that at t2 John informed Donnie that P. Relying on a non-verbal evidence, there seems to be no better grounds for ascribing awareness at t1 to the non-reigning self (Donnie), than for attributing sense-produced knowledge that P after t1. Not all sensory information we acquire is or could be acknowledged in subjective awareness. Certainly we sometimes extend the word 'awareness' just as we extend 'perception', so that it encompasses sensory input of this subliminal kind. It may even be that this looseness in the notion of awareness explains the commonly found attribution of two separate awarenesses to the putatively divided mind of MPD/DID. But rather than attributing simultaneous separated awarenesses to the multiples' two selves, it seems simpler, and at least equally plausible, to suppose that the distinctive cognitive states were derived in the way normal persons acquire beliefs based on unnoticed sensory input.

We could of course attempt to elicit Donnie's knowledge that P by asking him what he knew after t1, and perhaps Donnie will offer a verbal report, as he apparently did in his interview with Anderson. But obvious difficulties stand in the way of eliciting verbal report with multiples. First, it is not always possible to 'call up' the relevant alter for an introspective report; and second, an alter in a 'bystander' position is no more able to exert verbal control than any other kind of control. So asking Donnie may be the most obvious, but not the easiest approach.

Waverings: A brief example of wavering from real life will illustrate (this case was described to me by Stephen Braude): a multiple is grocery shopping, filling her cart with the staples of an adult diet. What occurs next appears to be inconsistency.

Although she lives alone and has no apparent need for them, she reaches for several brightly-colored packets of animal-shaped children's cereal. The hypothesis proposed to account for this wavering is that the impulse was not hers, but rather a challenge to her reign interjected by another self, a child alter. To the observer of her non-verbal behaviour then, this apparently aberrant and alien impulsive intervention reflected a wavering in the steady course of the adult reigning self's agency.

Viewed at any given time, at least from what we can infer through observation of the subject's non-verbal behaviour, the short-term waverings of multiples do not constitute very strong evidence in support of the presence of simultaneous divided centres of awareness. First, the rarity of these waverings is itself puzzling. If the multiple comprises all these contenders for control, why is there not more of a visible struggle for ascendancy, we want to ask? Why do other selves meekly accede to the power of the reigning self so often? Second, when such a struggle is alleged to take place, what do we observe publicly? An eccentric taste in cereal, or a self-indulgent impulse. Nothing more. Moreover, resort to verbal report will likely only yield an account from the reigning alter: perhaps a report of an alien impulse, or usurped control. By their nature, waverings are short-lived and incomplete challenges to the reigning alter's control.

Although I shall not deal with these other cases here, I would add that analogous reasoning is invited when we reflect on non-verbal behavioural evidence for two other phenomena suggestive of divided minds: the postoperative behaviour of commissurotomy patients, and the hidden observer phenomenon associated with the experimental study of hypnoid states. (See Radden, 1996)

Let us return to Armstrong's clinical description.

> Donnie... described himself to me as someone who likes to watch people, be nice to people and go to school...Donnie told me that he was watching throughout most of the attack [by Woods on one of the women]. . . . Although he was watching, Donnie said that he was unable to describe much of what had happened because he was too scared to think. He felt as if he were back in his childhood, where everything was 'wild and confused' and he had 'wanted to leave but I was trapped.' (Armstrong, page 15)

Donnie knew about John's crime because as he said, he watched — and 'watched' here implies some form of direct personal awareness. If, after the crime, Donnie had merely known it had occurred, then this is not obviously so, as we have seen. But if Donnie watched while John committed the crime, then Donnie's presence looks to have been simultaneous with John's.

This description introduces the phenomenon described as *co-presence* which we associate not only with descriptions of MPD/DID but also with states of so-called possession. There are several kinds of direct verbal report which provide the evidence for co-presence. One is Donnie's claim to have watched John's deed. Another derives from first person reports of the reigning self in MPD/DID. Just as the multiple whose selves have been effectively integrated through therapeutic intervention complains of a feeling of loneliness, so clinical descriptions sometimes attribute an accompanied feeling on the part of a reigning self when another self is present (Putnam, 1989). Thus John might have admitted to a sense of Donnie's presence (he did not, in this particular case).

The evidence of co-presence in MPD/DID apparently offers some support for the thesis that there are divided minds, although as I shall show presently, it still fails to unseat certain philosophical and commonsense convictions about synchronic unity.

Parallels between co-presence and ego-alien experience

The puzzling and even paradoxical nature of the verbal evidence for divided minds such as this is diminished by the use of proper names in case descriptions of MPD/DID. Donnie's claim to have watched while John acted has a comprehensible quality in part because we inevitably assimilate it to the normal model where Donnie and John are two spatio-temporally distinct persons. But this is misleading. For Donnie to claim to have watched John is for Donnie to have asserted that he experienced doing something which was not, in some sense, *his doing*, and thus, at least in some sense, not his experience. (This is not to say that Donnie did not experience his body being directed by John's will. But it is to emphasize the difficulty we have describing this state of affairs in ordinary English, and I will return to this point later in the chapter.) Put this way, verbal report as evidence for divided minds parallels other reports of subjectively experienced disunity, such as that reported in ego-alien experiences like thought insertion (and also, perhaps, possession, depersonalization and derealization).

I do not mean to equate these experiences. They differ not only etiologically and clinically but phenomenologically. Nonetheless, as instances of synchronic disunity, they share much in common and may be subject to the same analysis. And in fact once we have temporarily set aside nosological, syndromal and other categories in order to compare these experiences of disunity, we find in descriptions of ego-alien experiences such as thought insertion more vivid and richly developed descriptions than are yielded through accounts of MPD/DID such as Armstrong's report.

Divided minds in thought insertion and other made or ego alien states

Seeming failures and errors of self attribution and cases of the 'disowning' of experience have long been described in accounts of mental disorder. The group of symptoms discussed here are characteristically cognitive and affective. They involve the subjective belief that they originate outside the person's own mind or will. They are also accompanied by feelings of alienation. These experiences, sometimes known as ego-alien, may best be summed up in the term 'disownership'.

Associated with schizophrenia is thought insertion, the occurrence of thoughts judged by the patient to be another's. The experience is as of their having been placed in the patient's mind from some outside source. Not only thoughts but feelings, impulses and actions are described in this language of alienation or disownership. States and actions not acknowledged to be the patient's own, are known as 'made' responses. Thus 'made' feelings were reported by one patient in the following way:

> I cry, tears roll down my cheeks and I look unhappy, but inside I have a cold anger because they are using me in this way, and it is not me who is unhappy, but they are projecting unhappiness on my brain. They project upon me laughter, for no reason, and you have no idea how terrible it is to laugh and look happy and know it is not you, but their emotions. (Davidson and Neale 1986, p. 340)

'Made' volitional acts, or 'dissociated will' are described similarly. The patient feels that her actions result from a consciousness and will other than her own. Not merely does she experience an irresistible and unwanted impulse whose origin feels to be external, however. In addition, the impulses in and movements carried out by her body feel to be another's. Rather than being active in bringing them about, she experiences her body as the other's passive instrument.

These kinds of 'disownership' experience challenge a very fundamental aspect of normal subjectivity, the assumption, conviction, and sense that all and only my experiences — my thoughts, feelings, impulses to act and seemingly voluntary actions — are *mine*.

Stephen Braude's taxonomy of self ascription is initially helpful in distinguishing the several different epistemic attitudes adopted in these curious cases toward what are seemingly one's own experiences (Braude, 1991). A state is indexical when a person *believes it to be his or her own*, autobiographical when a person *experiences it as his or her own*. The ambiguities involved in some disownership experiences seem to go beyond these categories, however. The patients described do not experience their made responses as theirs. Rather they experience them as alien. Nor, in one way, do they believe them to be theirs. Yet in another respect these descriptions reveal that the subject both knows the experience to be hers (and 'owns' it) and experiences it as hers. The patient quoted speaks of unhappiness, a felt state, in her brain. So although they are both non-indexical and non-autobiographical, disowned experiences are not *simply* non-indexical and non-autobiographical.

If divided minds means simultaneous separated centres of awareness, then the evidence seems to direct us toward contradictory conclusions. On the one hand, we want to insist, the mere fact that these are subjective experiences ensures their unity. When they are a reflection of a subjective report, and not merely deductions from non-verbal behaviour, they are a report, finally, from one, albeit fractured, centre of awareness. Spoken in the language of the first person singular, they could only be so, it would seem — unless we accommodate the bizarre possibility that two distinct centres of awareness or 'minds' might each, independently, entertain identical thoughts and issue an identical set of words *at the same time*. (If such a state of affairs were countenanced, though, by the identity of indiscernibles we would surely judge ourselves dealing with one rather than two centres of awareness.) And this seems to preclude their constituting evidence in support of separate centres of awareness. On the other hand, these odd disownings and detachments between 'this experience' and the quality of 'mineness' seem to impel us to look more closely at what we may take for granted about self-ascription in the normal case. Perhaps these abnormal cases reveal that the process by which the self-attribution of our experiences is effected must be recognized to be a process, requiring in every case something like an inferential step from 'this experience' to 'my experience'.

With apparently contradictory conclusions indicated by the evidence, we need the help of philosophy; let us look at philosophical theories of self-ascription or 'ownership.'

Philosophers have customarily approached the question of ownership or 'self-ascription' with reference to (i) the normal case, in which ownership is assumed, and to (ii) the subjective or phenomenological perspective. In a common formulation, the philosophical question has been, 'How do I know that my experiences are mine?' It is understood here, that I do know. The question is not about identification or re-identification — whether my experiences might be mine — but about epistemological features of my conviction over an incontrovertible fact.

Philosophical accounts of ownership show what is to be said about disowned experiences even before real case material need be introduced. Until recent interest in abnormal psychology, disowned experiences have been treated as hypothetical cases, or logical possibilities, at best.

The Meaning of the Evidence for Divided Minds

(i) Logico-grammatical theories

Different philosophical accounts share the tenet that ownership it is grammatically guaranteed. Our usual understandings of concepts like 'experience', and 'self', it seems widely agreed, prevent my speaking of having experiences which are not mine. Making the point that all my experiences are mine, Sydney Shoemaker asserts that an experiencing is something whose existence is 'adjectival upon' a subject: the states of a self are as attached to that self as are its attributes to a material thing — its shape to a book, for example. And we can no more speak of the experience without its subject, than of the shape without the book whose shape it is (upon which it is adjectival). (Shoemaker, 1986) So convinced were many philosophers that all and only my experiences are mine, that the so-called philosophical problem of ownership was dismissed by some as a non-problem.

Philosophical explanations of why our experiences come owned, and whether it is significant, differ, however. In traditional Kantianism, for example, a transcendental unifying principle — unavailable to subjective experience — had ensured ownership. A nonempirical posit explains, and necessitates, the grammatical fact. In the pared-down Humean and neo-Humean tradition that eschews transcendental entities, the inviolable unity ensured by ownership grammar is still maintained. But within this tradition also are to be found divergent accounts of the meaning and significance of that grammar. Some theorists emphasize the psychological necessity of ownership. It is a feature of humans, shaped, perhaps, by evolutionary imperatives, as Flanagan, Dennett and others have suggested, that we own all and only our experiences (Flanagan, 1992; Dennett, 1991). It may be a contingent fact that we have evolved this way: nonetheless, the form of our proprietary grammar could not now be otherwise.

Despite such differences, each of these analyses, from Kant to Dennett, rejects the possibility of radical disownership, and it is their points of agreement that require our attention initially. If ownership is ensured, as each of these otherwise disparate theories suggests, instances of disowned experience, hypothetical or real, must each submit to the same analysis. The mental patient's complaint that she is experiencing another person's thoughts and feelings would have to be dismissed as misleading or mistaken description. The putatively disowned experiences of multiplicity, possession or thought insertion encountered in abnormal psychology must be understood to reduce to some form of unfounded false belief or to an infelicity of expression. 'This experience is not mine' cannot express a warranted belief. And nor can it be an expression of a pathologically-wrought delusion, since that would suggest that a contingent, not a grammatical fact guarantees our normal proprietary grammar.

The ownership grammar view — and approach — appears to find some correspondence and, thus, corroboration, in the way paranormal phenomena are portrayed. (I have reservations about ESP. But we do not need to accept the evidence for telepathy to acknowledge how it *ought to be described,* were compelling instances found.) The hypothetical telepathic awareness by which person X was said to enjoy access to the contents of the mind of another person (person Y), could only be understood as the recurrence (in X's mind) of an exactly similar token of Y's thought. X experiences Y's thoughts, only in the sense that Y experiences thoughts qualitatively the same as Y's. (Braude, 1986) They are X's own thoughts, not Y's, and in that sense X is entitled to use the possessive grammar of ownership with regard to them: 'They are mine'

Related to these observations is a feature noted by philosophers emphasizing the privileged access or privacy we enjoy in relation to our mental states. In the phenomenal or mental realm, distinctions like that between *seems* and *is,* which undergird the activity of doubt, have no purchase. To doubt is also to think, as Descartes pointed out. (Descartes, 1647) But without the possibility of doubt, we have no way to question whether an apparently owned experience might be disowned. If they are experiences, then they must be owned. Despite the alien and detached quality of this phenomenal feel, these states are objects of awareness. As such, however alien they may be described as feeling or seeming, however removed, remote and separated, they are the subject's *own* experiences, and none other's.

Are these patients suffering from symptoms of disownership just guilty of confusing expression? The ownership grammar analysis encourages us to examine the language in which any clinical experiences of disownership are reported. 'Some of *my* mental contents feel not to be mine' (my emphasis), '*My* actions do not emanate from my will (but from an alien possessor's).' Those possessives seem an admission that while something is wrong, unusual or alien about these experiences and actions, they are nevertheless the person's own, and self-ascription is not, in one respect, in question. Perhaps a less confusing account introducing *as if* language would entirely capture all that such avowals can coherently mean. Thus: 'It feels as if this feeling (I experience) were not mine', or 'It feels if my actions do not emanate from my will.'

An explanation for some of these strange locutions is not hard to find either. Our speech is filled with ambiguities of identity language, ambiguities only resolved by attention to semantic context. Such ambiguity seems sufficient to have distorted the meaning, or intent, of these introspective reports and descriptions of unusually divided experience. By insisting that she is thinking another's thoughts, a patient may mean merely that the content of her thought echoes the other's, i.e. her thought, is qualitatively similar to — though not numerically identical with — his. Since context alone allows us to distinguish when a phrase like 'the same thought' is used in each way, the confusion comes by default : there exists no unambiguous linguistic form for the patient to employ.

Thus far we have considered the grammatical answer to the question of how disownership experiences are to be understood. Let us look now at the psychological answer.

(ii) Psychological-brain deficiency theories

Although in normal psyches 'this experience' is inextricably linked to 'my experience', perhaps under conditions of stress or mental illness these ties give way. Perhaps, that is, disownership experience finds a mirror in some deviation from the normally functioning brain. If there are psychological reasons for ownership grammar as some theorists have proposed, rather than logical ones, then abnormal cases such as disownership experience may indicate a breakdown of the usual *psychological* connections. If this were true, notice, then the puzzling disownership claim that 'Not all my experiences are mine' would have to be regarded not as a grammatical infelicity, nor as an unfounded false belief, but as a pathologically wrought *delusion*.

Before we rush to pin the phenomenological tail on the neurobiological donkey, let us note something else, however. Fractured and divided as they are, disownership experiences do not simply constitute a challenge to the self's capacity to distinguish self from non-self, to separate my experiences from those which are not mine. The patients described earlier do not have any doubt that it is their *own* mind on which are imposed others' thoughts, feelings and impulses, their own body made the instrument of others' actions. Nor, in the case of co-presence or possession, does the reigning subject doubt the boundary between herself and the other self 'accompanying' or 'invading' her. To the contrary, it is the sharpness of the boundary between the reigning self and her ghostly accomplice that constitutes this symptom and accounts, indeed, for the qualitative distinctness of this experience. These symptoms do not provide evidence that the *boundary* between self and non-self is eroded or absent.

Something more can be learned from this last-mentioned feature of disownership experiences, and it is of some methodological significance. The experiences that are our particular concern do not reveal a breakdown or incapacity of self-attribution as such. But nor will any symptoms which, *as observers*, we might begin to understand. Disorders more extreme than those we have been considering may truly rob the person of the ability of self-ascription — along with robbing them of a self at all. Attempts to understand autism have postulated something to this effect, as have descriptions of those suffering the extreme disintegration or fragmentation associated with brain damage, degenerative diseases such as Alzheimer's, and even forms of schizophrenia. But significant in these suggestions is that they are mere *postulation* — tentative *interpretations of non-verbal behaviour.*

Such interpretations may even be based on verbal behaviour of a kind: after all, words issue from the lips of these severely disordered and disintegrated patients. But they do not come from *subjective or introspective report*, conveyed in the proprietary grammar of the first person. This is because for intelligibility such report requires a unified subjectivity. Such discourse presupposes the capacity to recognize that however alienated and detached from them I may feel, I know that my experiences are mine.

Philosophical claims about ownership are not, or not exactly, refuted by the particular states of disownership isolated here, then. While they remain intelligible, first person accounts of disownership experience continue to uphold the presumption that all and only my experiences are mine.

Yet in revealing where the usual cohesion of experience is fractured, these reports can also reveal something about self-ascription, something which the oneness of normal, non-pathological experience conceals. This is illustrated in recent writing by George Graham and Lynn Stephens. (Graham and Stephens, 1994a, 1994b, 1994c) These authors assert that normal self-ascription — applying 'my experience' to 'this experience' — is analyzable into two elements. One may be said to concern ownership (Experience M occurred to me), but the other more precisely concerns *agency* (Experience M is my mental action). The disownership experiences of mental disturbance reflect a separation of these two elements observed by normal grammatical possessive forms.

These authors consider cases of disownership experience such as that of the patient who claims that she has the thoughts of another and their term to describe such experience is introspective alienation. A person suffering from introspective alienation with respect to a mental episode M, Graham and Stephens explain, acknowledges that he is the subject in whom M occurs but feels that somebody else is the agent of M. (Graham and Stephens, 1994b) Graham and Stephens derive this distinction from another philosopher, Frankfurt. Frankfurt has tried to distinguish and define a sort of mental state associated with normal experience which goes undistinguished in the usual grammar and language of ownership — unbidden thoughts. Of such thoughts, which seem to occur to us without our will or wish, Frankfurt has postulated that they are not rightly deemed thoughts that we *think* at all, but rather thoughts which we find occurring in us. (Frankfurt, 1976)

If we accept the Graham-Stephens-Frankfurt use of the distinction between thoughts we think, and thoughts which merely occur in us, then self-ascription, and the grammar of ownership, are ambiguous. 'This is my experience' accommodates 'This is not my experience.' Thus, while expressing confusing beliefs, the subject of disownership experience does not utter claims that are incoherent or unintelligible.

> The sense in which she attributes the thought to herself is not the same as the sense in which she attributes it to the other and denies that it is hers. So her attributions may be taken literally and they are mutually consistent. One answers the question 'Who is the subject in whom M occurs?' The other answers the question 'Who is the agent who produces M (wherever M occurs)?' (Graham and Stephens, 1994b)

The force of this analysis, as these authors recognize, depends on two additional elements. It requires a useful explanation of when and why the subject disowns some experiences in this way. And it calls for an account of why the common and normal experience of unbidden thoughts, which seem to invite the same analysis, has failed — until Frankfurt's analysis — to receive it.

These authors offer both. A self-referential, narrative explanation of my mental states and behaviour is sometimes available through my understanding or 'theory' of my self. (This 'theory' is understood as a set of enduring intentional states sufficient to yield such explanation.) If my theory of myself ascribes to me the relevant intentional states, or if it appears to be random, *and not the apparent product of some other intentional source*, I unquestioningly and fully regard this episode as mine. In this case, agency and ownership elements are both present. If my mental states or behaviour are inexplicable in terms of these intentional states, then they are judged as something which happens to me, but which is not mine. Unbidden thoughts, although they happen to me, are not the seeming product of another source of agency for they lack the coherence, intelligence and direction that invites us to postulate a separate agentic source.

Until philosophers directed their attention away from normal psychology and toward abnormal states and experiences, they failed to recognize the complexities in the seemingly simple judgements of ownership, and in the proprietary grammar associated with self-ascription.

Reconciling (i) and (ii)

With this account of the complexities underlying self-ascription we seem also provided with a means of reconciling the apparently conflicting explanations of the inviolable unity of self-consciousness put forward by different theorists. Those whose explanation is logical and those whose explanation is psychological may each be right. My ownership of those of my states of which I am subjectively aware at a given time is ensured by the grammar of 'experience'. But 'my experience' contains two parts. My experience is mine in emanating from a unified subjectivity, this is logically guaranteed. It is not mine when disownership renders it not my mental action. This is a psychological matter. The judgement that this experience is mine involves the logically ensured element, but also a psychological element which relates to agency. To the question of whether the grammatical necessity of ownership is logical or psychological, the answer may well be that it is both.

So these patients' inviolable ownership of their experiences is compatible with their believing those experiences — falsely, but not incoherently — to be other selves' experience. It is also compatible with their believing them to be, and or experiencing them as alien, and or believing them to emanate from an alien source. But whatever extremes of inner heterogeneity the divided minds of disownership experience reveal, and whatever disunities of self they suggest, they are none sufficient to elude the conclusion that the self of a given moment *known to us from the intelligible self narrative of subjective report* (not merely inferred through an observation of behaviour) remains one while it is many. (Galen Strawson's recent work conforms with this conclusion. Any candidate for being an experience of the mental self as synchronically single, he asserts, '*will have to be an episode of explicitly self-conscious thought*, and there is a crucial (trivial) respect in which no such episode could be experience of the mental self as synchronically multiple' [p. 12, my emphasis].)

Pathological Disownership, Deficit Studies and the Brain

Pathological cases of synchronic disunity reveal a distinction obscured by the apparently indissoluble unity of normal experience. And this distinction invites analysis on the so-called deficit study methodology associated with the work of thinkers like Nelkin, Van Gulick and Metzinger (Nelkin 1994, 1996; Van Gulick 1994; Metzinger 1995). This methodology utilizes the evidence of cases in which one function or ability is lost or impaired in order to show the existence of independent modules or functional units in the underlying organization of cognition.

The neurologist Ronald Melzack postulates that the brain contains a 'neuromatrix', or network of neurons which, in addition to responding to sensory stimulation, continuously generates 'a characteristic pattern of impulses indicating the body' (Melzack, 1989, page 123). This pattern is a brain's 'neurosignature'. Melzack uses the neurosignature to explain phantom limb phenomena, but it may also be implicated in the normal sense of ownership we have in relation to our mental states. Damage to or interference with a brain's neurosignature may account for these pathological experiences of disownership.

Alternatively, Vogeley invites us to implicate the pre-frontal cortex as the source of this proprietary sense (Vogeley, 1997). The work of Vogeley and others suggests a number of functions for this area of the brain. The prefrontal cortex serves as a kind of clearing-house for all sensory modalities. It is closely related to the affectively important limbic system. And it distinguishes 'self' from 'other' — at least in a sense consistent with Frith and Concoran's (1996) notion of providing an 'other minds paradigm'.

Thus, whether as the result of a breakdown in the brain's neurosignature function, of damage to the prefrontal cortex, or some other neurobiological deficiency, the patient experiencing disownership pathology is subject to a functional agency deficit: she can recognize her experience *as* hers, but not recognize its agency, on the Graham-Stephens-Frankfurt analysis of this psychopathology. What appeared in normal experience as one function, has revealed itself to be two, suggesting the presence of two independent modules or functional units in the brain.

Conclusion

Having adopted a reductionist model of self we are required to account for synchronic unity, the oneness or 'mineness' binding all parts of my experience at a given time. Two kinds of theories are distinguishable, those which propose a logical or grammatical necessity to explain our experience of synchronic unity in normal subjectivity, and those which explain it as an important but psychological fact about human experience. Each account must not only tell us what to say about the unity we associate with normal subjectivity, however; it must also permit us to explain and account for the descriptions of seemingly divided minds we find in psychopathology.

These two theories treat the divided minds of disownership experience differently. On the first, disownership experience reflects either an ungrounded false belief or a linguistic infelicity. On the second, however, disownership experience may reflect a confusing truth: the sufferer correctly recognizes that his experience is not his own in one very important sense — it is not a mental action, that is, to all appearances, not a product of his own volition. This distinction between ownership and agency aspects of subjectivity, which is obscured in the indissoluble unity of normal experience, seems to point to a research agenda for future deficit studies using a form of top-down explanation to illuminate the structure and function of the brain.

References

Armstrong, J. (1997), 'The case of Mr Woods', Unpublished paper.
Braude, S.E. (1986), *The Limits of Influence: Psychokinesis and the Philosophy of Science* (London: Routledge and Kegan Paul).
Braude, S.E. (1991), *First Person Plural: Multiple Personality and the Philosophy of Mind* (London: Routledge).
Davidson, G. and Neale, J. (1986), *Abnormal Psychology: An Experimental Clinical Approach*, 4th edition (New York: John Wiley and Sons).
Dennett, D. (1991), *Consciousness Explained* (Boston, MA: Little Brown & Co.)
Flanagan, O. (1992), *Consciousness Reconsidered* (Cambridge, MA:MIT Press)
Frankfurt, H. (1976), 'Identification and externality', in *The Identities of Persons*, ed. A. Rorty (Berkeley, CA: University of California Press).
Frith and Concoran (1966) *Theory of Other Minds Paradigm*
Graham, G. and Stephens, G.L. (1994a), 'Mind and mine', in Graham and Stephens (1994b).

358 J. RADDEN

Graham, G. and Stephens, G.L. (ed. 1994b), *Philosophical Psychopathology* (Cambridge, MA: MIT Press).

Grice, H.P. (1941), 'Personal identity', *Mind*, **50**, reprinted in *Personal Identity* , ed. J. Perry (Berkeley, CA: University of California Press, 1975).

Hume, D. (1967), *Treatise on Human Nature*, reprint of 1888 edition, ed. L.A. Selby-Bigge (Oxford: Clarendon Press).

Melzack, R. (1989), 'Phantom limbs, the self and the brain', The D.O. Hebb Memorial Lecture, *Canadian Psychology*, **30**, pp. 1–16.

Metzinger, T. (ed. 1995), *Conscious Experience* (Paderborn: Schöningh / Thorverton, UK: Imprint Academic).

Nelkin, N. (1994), 'What is consciousness?', *Philosophy of Science*, **60**, pp. 419–34.

Nelkin, N. (1996), *Consciousness and the Origins of Thought* (Cambridge: Cambridge U.P.).

Putnam, F. (1989), *Diagnosis and Treatment of Multiple Personality Disorder* (New York: Guilford Press).

Radden, J. (1996), *Divided Minds and Successive Selves: Ethical Issues in Disorders of Identity and Personality* (Cambridge, MA: MIT Press).

Shoemaker, S. (1986), 'Introspection and the self', in *Studies in the Philosophy of Mind*, ed. P.A. French, T.E. Uehling and H.K. Wettstein, Midwest Studies in Philosophy, No. 10 (Minneapolis: University of Minnesota Press).

Strawson, G. (1997), '"The self"', *Journal of Consciousness Studies*, **4** (5–6), pp. 405–28. Reprinted in this volume, pp. 1–24.

Van Gulick, R (1994), 'Deficit studies and the function of phenomenal conscious', in Graham and Stephens (1994b).

Vogeley, (1997), 'The prefrontal cortex as basic constituent of the self', Paper given at the Brain and Self Workshop, August 21–24, 1997, Elsinore, Denmark.

Part 5

Meditation-based approaches

Robert K.C. Forman

What Does Mysticism Have To Teach Us About Consciousness?

Introduction: Why Mysticism?[1]

One of the most exciting aspects of consciousness studies is the way that it has become a forum in which so many distinct fields can interact on a single question, that of consciousness. I know of no other subject which has brought together so many voices, from so many fields, to swirl around a single topic. It is exciting to be a part of this debate.

In this chapter I would like to bring the findings of my somewhat unusual but increasingly accepted field — mysticism — to the discussion, for I think they may offer some helpful insights about consciousness. Why? When a biologist seeks to understand a complex phenomenon, one key strategy is to look to at it in its simplest form. Probably the most famous is the humble bacterium *E. coli*. Its simple gene structure has allowed us to understand much of the gene functioning of complex species. Similarly many biologists have turned to the 'memory' of the simple sea slug to understand our own more kaleidoscopic memory. Freud and Durkheim both used totemism, which they construed as the simplest form of religion, to understand the complexities of religious life.[2] The methodological principle is: to understand something complex turn to its simple forms.

Mystical experiences may represent just such a simple form of human consciousness. Usually our minds are an enormously complex stew of thoughts, feelings, sensations, wants, snatches of song, pains, drives, daydreams and, of course, consciousness itself more or less aware of it all. To understand consciousness *in itself*, the obvious thing would be to clear away as much of this internal detritus and noise as possible. It turns out that mystics seem to be doing precisely that. The technique that most mystics use is some form of meditation or contemplation. These are procedures that, often by recycling a mental subroutine,[3] systematically reduce mental activity. During meditation, one begins to slow down the thinking process, and have fewer or

---

[1] An earlier version was given at the conference, *Toward a Science of Consciousness*, Tucson, Arizona, April 1996.

[2] I am indebted to the psychologist of religion William Parsons, in a private communication, for this observation.

[3] See here Ornstein (1976).

less intense thoughts. One's thoughts become as if more distant, vague, or less preoc-
cupying; one stops paying as much attention to bodily sensations; one has fewer or
less intense fantasies and daydreams. Thus by reducing the intensity or compelling
quality of outward perception and inward thoughts, one may come to a time of greater
stillness. Ultimately one may become utterly silent inside, as though in a gap between
thoughts, where one becomes completely perception- and thought-free. One neither
thinks nor perceives any mental or sensory content. Yet, despite this suspension of
content, one emerges from such events confident that one had remained awake inside,
fully conscious. This experience, which has been called the pure consciousness event,
or PCE, has been identified in virtually every tradition. Though PCEs typically happen to any single individual only occasionally, they are quite regular for some practitioners.[4] The pure consciousness event may be defined as a wakeful but contentless
(non-intentional) consciousness.

These PCEs, encounters with consciousness devoid of intentional content, may be
just the least complex encounter with awareness *per se* that we students of consciousness seek. The PCE may serve, in short, as the *E. coli* of consciousness studies.[5]

But the story does not stop here. Regular and long-term meditation, according to
many traditions, leads to advanced experiences, known in general as 'enlightenment'.
Their discriminating feature is a deep shift in epistemological structure: the experienced relationship between the self and one's perceptual objects changes profoundly.
In many people this new structure becomes permanent.[6]

These long-term shifts in epistemological structure often take the form of two
quantum leaps in experience; typically they develop sequentially.[7] The first is an
experience of a permanent interior stillness, even while engaged in thought and activity — one remains aware of one's own awareness while simultaneously remaining
conscious of thoughts, sensations and actions. Because of its phenomenological dualism — a heightened cognizance of awareness itself plus a consciousness of thoughts
and objects — I call it the dualistic mystical state (DMS). The second shift is
described as a perceived unity of one's own awareness *per se* with the objects around
one, an immediate sense of a quasi-physical unity between self, objects and other
people. States akin to this have been called 'extrovertive-' or sometimes 'nature-'
mysticism; but I prefer to call it the unitive mystical state, UMS.[8]

---

[4]   See the articles in Forman (1990) and Section I of Forman (1998).

[5]   Bruce Mangan (1994) suggests this when he says that 'mystic[al] encounters . . . would seem to
      manifest an extreme state of consciousness' (p. 251).

[6]   James' famous characterization of mysticism in *The Varieties of Religious Experience* states that a
      defining feature of mysticism is 'transiency' (James, 1902/1983, p. 381). My evidence says this is
      simply wrong.

[7]   I say typically because sometimes one may skip or not attain a particular stage. Ken Wilber (1980)
      claims sequence. William Barnard (1995), however, disputes this claim of sequence.

[8]   One key element of the UMS is that it is a *permanent* shift in the structure of awareness. 'Extrovertive'
      mysticism, a term coined by W.T. Stace, implies that one has mystical experiences out in the world,
      while we are 'extrovertively' aware. Zaehner coined the term 'nature mysticism' to describe such
      paths as Zen or Taoism, which describe mystical experiences in nature. This he distinguishes from the
      theistic traditions, among others. But in the UMS, as I understand this form of life, the sense of being in
      contact with the expansive emptiness that extends beyond the self, *never* fades away, whether one is in
      nature or in the city, whether the eyes are open or closed, and whether one is a Zen Buddhist, a Jew or a
      Christian. Thus each of these accepted terms define this experience too narrowly, and thus I coin my
      own broader term.

Like the PCE, these latter two may serve as fertile fields for students of consciousness to plough. To understand them, I want to introduce the idea of the *relative intensity* of a thought or desire. Some desires have a high relative intensity. Let's say I am walking across the street when I see a huge truck hurtling at me. Virtually 100% of my attention is taken up with the truck, the fear, and getting out of the way. It is virtually impossible for me to think about anything else at that time. I don't even consider keeping my suit clean, how my hair might look, the discomfort in my tummy, or the classes I will teach tomorrow. The fear and running are *utterly* intense, we might say, consuming nearly 100% of my attention.

That evening, I come home starved, and rush to the fridge. I may be civil to my kids and wife, but I have very little patience. My desire for food is very intense, for it preoccupies most of my consciousness, but it consumes less of my attention than did jumping away from the truck.

Some thoughts consume very little of my attention. Driving to work the next day, for example, I might ruminate about my classes, remember the near miss with the truck, half hear the news on the radio, and think about getting that noise in the car fixed — nearly all at once. None of these thoughts or desires is very intense, for none has a strong emotional cathexis that draws me fully into it. My attention can flow in and out of any of them, or the traffic ahead, effortlessly. In short the intensity of a thought or desire tends to increase with the amount of my consciousness that is taken up with that thought or feeling. Conversely, the thought's intensity tends to lessen when I am able to retain more attention for other issues, and for my wider perspective.

Now, as I understand them, advanced mystical experiences result from the combination of regular PCEs plus a minimization of the relative intensity of emotions and thoughts. That is, over time one decreases the compulsive or intense cathexis value of *all* of one's desires. The de-intensifying of emotional attachments means that, over the years, one's attention is progressively available to sense its own quiet interior character more and more fully, until eventually one is able to effortlessly maintain a subtle cognizance of one's own awareness simultaneously with thinking about and responding to the world: a reduction in the relative intensity of *all* of one's thoughts and desires.

This state of being cognizant of one's own inner awareness while simultaneously maintaining the ability to think and talk about that consciousness offers students of consciousness a unique situation. For these subjects may be both unusually cognizant of features or patterns of their own awareness and also able to describe them to us: a kind of ongoing microscope on human consciousness. In short, while not as phenomenologically simple as PCEs, these experiences may provide us with highly useful reports about the character of human awareness.

Several additional preliminary matters: First, perforce we will be drawing conclusions based on the experiences of a very few people. Most of us haven't had any experiences like the ones I will describe, and some may sound pretty strange. Yet we often do generalize from the unusual to the general. Just think how much we have concluded about consciousness from a very few: epileptics, people with unusual skull accidents or brain injuries, the man who mistook his wife for a hat, etc. From the *pathology* of a very few we have learned a great deal about the relationship of one side of the brain to the other, of two kinds of knowing, of information storage and retrieval, of impulse control, etc. Indeed it is common practice to take data about a few unusual individuals and generalize it to the many. Here again we are studying the data of a few. But rather than the pathological, we will be studying people — Teresa of Avila, Vasubandu, Ramana Maharshi, etc. — who are not 'pathological' but unusually self-actualized.

Should we not be as willing to learn from the experiences of the unusually healthy as we are to learn from the unusually diseased?

The second matter is definitional: What do we mean by mysticism? What is generally known as mysticism is often said to have two strands, which are traditionally distinguished as *apophatic* and *kataphatic* mysticism, oriented respectively towards emptying or imagistically filling. These two are generally described in terms that are *without* or *with* sensory language. The psychologist Roland Fischer has distinguished a similar pairing as *trophotropic* and *ergotropic*, experiences that phenomenologically involve inactivity or activity. *Kataphatic* or imagistic mysticism involves hallucinations, visions, auditions or even a sensory-like smell or taste; it thus involves activity and is *ergotropic*. *Apophatic* mystical experiences are devoid of such sensory-like content, and are thus *trophotropic*. When they use non-sensory, non-imagistic language (cf. Smart, 1982), authors like Eckhart, Dogen, al-Hallaj, Bernadette Roberts and Shankara are all thus *apophatic* mystics. Because visions and other ergotropic experiences are not the simple experiences of consciousness that we require, I will focus my attentions exclusively on the quieter *apophatic* forms.

Finally, I want to emphasize that phenomenology is not science. When we describe these experiences, we do not gain hard scientific proof thereby. There can be many ways to explain an unusual experience: one might say it was the result of what one ate for dinner, a faulty memory, psycho-somatic processes, a quantum microtubule collapse, or an encounter with Ultimate Truth.[9] Without further argumentation, phenomenology cannot serve as the sole basis for any theory of reality. It may be taken only as a finger, *pointing* in some direction, rather than *conclusive evidence* for or against a particular thesis. This is how I see my role in this chapter. I will simply describe mystical experiences as accurately as I can, and say where I see their fingers pointing. That is, I will attempt to coax metaphysical hypotheses out of these phenomenological descriptions.

First-person reports, especially those that are about unusual experiences are, of course, notoriously unreliable. When an epileptic says that 'the table seemed wavy', or when a man asserts that his wife is a 'hat', these reports are not taken as data about the world, but about their condition.[10] One may want to assert that a mystic's report should be regarded similarly.

But we must be careful here, for first-person reports can also be veridical or even sources of wisdom. For example, in the kingdom of the blind, the 'first-person' report of a sighted fellow that 'the mountain peak near the village is in the shape of five fingers' may be regarded as the rantings of a lunatic or as information about the mountains. Similarly, when Woodward and Bernstein spoke with the Watergate informant 'Deep Throat', they could have taken his utterances as paranoid ramblings, data about his developing psychosis, or as information about the Nixon administration.

---

[9] These may not be mutually exclusive. See, for example, neurologist Oliver Sacks' comments on migraines and mysticism in the case of Hildegard of Bingen (Sacks, 1994, pp. 238–9).

[10] I am grateful for Joseph Goguen, private communication, for articulating this question so clearly.

How can we determine which way to regard the unusual first-person reports of the mystics? If we were Woodward and Bernstein, how would we decide? Common sense seems a good place to begin. We might ask, does Deep Throat, or the mystics in our case, *seem* unconnected or delusional? I believe most of us would say no. In fact many regard Meister Eckhart, Teresa of Avila, the authors of the Upanishads, and others who tell us of such experiences as unusually wise. Certainly they do not seem utterly unhinged, physically ill, etc. Secondly, we might ask, do others in a situation similar to Deep Throat's describe things similarly? In our case, assuming reasonable cultural differences in language and detail, do mystics from around the world describe things largely similarly? Here again the answer is yes. We shall find a reasonable amount of similarity among their descriptions, a family resemblance, They tend to confirm each others reports. Finally, is there other confirming evidence for our Deep Throats' claims? Here the information is not in: just how consciousness works, relates to the world or the brain, is anything but established.

In sum, it makes sense to regard the mystics' unusual reports about the world as more like those of a Deep Throat than those of an epileptic. But also, again as with Deep Throat, the information we can glean from them is not, by itself, reliable enough to base a theory of consciousness solely on it. It will take the hard-working Woodwards and Bernsteins in the scientific and philosophical trenches to verify or deny the suggestions of our Deep Throats.

Three Mystical Phenomena and their Implications

Pure consciousness events

Let me begin by offering several reports of the first of the mystical phenomena I mentioned above, the pure consciousness event (PCE). First, from Christian mystical literature,[11] St. Teresa of Avila writes of what she calls the 'orison of union':

> During the short time the union lasts, she is deprived of every feeling, and even if she would, she could not think of any single thing. . . . She is utterly dead to the things of the world . . . I do not even know whether in this state she has enough life left to breathe. It seems to me she has not; or at least that if she does breathe, she is unaware of it. . . . The natural action of all her faculties [are suspended]. She neither sees, hears, nor understands (James, 1902/1983, p. 409).[12]

Several key features of this experience jump out. First, Teresa tells us that one reaches this 'orison of unity' by gradually reducing thought and understanding, eventually becoming 'utterly dead' to things, encountering neither sensation, thought nor perceptions. One becomes as simple as possible. Eventually one stops thinking altogether, not able to 'think of any single thing . . . arresting the use of her understanding . . . utterly dead to the things of the world'. And yet, she clearly implies, one remains awake.[13]

---

[11] Forman (1990) offers a rich compendium of reports of the PCE. I have intentionally offered here several reports of this experience that are not included there.

[12] James is quoting from St. Teresa of Avila, *Interior Castle*, in *Oeuvres,* trans. Bouix, vol. 3, pp. 421–4.

[13] The mystic apparently remains conscious throughout. Although Teresa does not explicitly say the mystic is not asleep, I cannot imagine anyone spilling so much ink on merely sleeping or blacking out, or on something like a coma. See below for more explicit statements to this effect.

Meister Eckhart describes something similar as the *gezucken,* rapture, of St. Paul, his archetype of a transient mystical experience:

> ... the more completely you are able to draw in your powers to a unity and forget all those things and their images which you have absorbed, and the further you can get from creatures and their images, the nearer you are to this and the readier to receive it. If only you could suddenly be unaware of all things, then you could pass into an oblivion of your own body as St Paul did, ... In this case ... memory no longer functioned, nor understanding, nor the senses, nor the powers that should function so as to govern and grace the body ... In this way a man should flee his senses, turn his powers inward and sink into an oblivion of all things and himself (Walshe, 1982, p. 7).

Like St. Teresa, Eckhart specifically asserts the absence of sensory content ('nor the senses'), as well as mental objects ('devoid of' memory, understanding, senses, etc.). One becomes oblivious of one's 'own body' and 'all things'. In short one becomes unaware of all things', i.e. devoid of all mental and sensory content.

The absence of thought and sensation is repeated in the following passage from the Upanishads when describing the state these early Hindu texts call *turiya,* the 'fourth'.

> Verily when a knower has restrained his mind from the external, and the breathing spirit (*prana*) has put to rest objects of sense, thereupon let him continue void of conceptions. Since the living individual (*jiva*) who is named 'breathing spirit' has arisen here from what is not breathing spirit, therefore, verily, let the breathing spirit restrain his breathing spirit in what is called the fourth condition (*turiya*) — Maitri Upanishad 6:19 (Hume, 1931, p. 436).

Here again one has 'put to rest objects of sense', i.e. gradually laid aside all sensations, and continued 'void of conceptions', i.e. not thinking. And yet the Upanishads are insistent that one remains conscious, indeed becomes nothing but consciousness itself. The consciousness that one reaches in *turiya* comes to be known in Samkhya philosophy as *'purusha'*, often translated as awareness or consciousness itself, that which 'illuminates' or 'witnesses' thoughts, feelings, and actions.[14] The *purusha* or awareness that one reaches during this experience is described as 'sheer contentless presence (*sasksitva*) . . . that is nonintentional' (Larson, 1979, p. 77).

Here is a report from the present author's own twenty-eight year practice of neo-Advaitan (Hindu-derived) Transcendental Meditation, which suggests the persistence of consciousness throughout such events.

> Sometimes during meditation my thoughts drift away entirely, and I gain a state I would describe as simply being awake. I'm not thinking about anything. I'm not particularly aware of any sensations, I'm not aware of being absorbed in anything in particular, and yet I am quite certain (after the fact) that I haven't been asleep. During it I am simply awake or simply present.
>
> It is odd to describe such an event as being awake or being present, for those terms generally connote an awareness of something or other. But in this experience there is no particular or identifiable object of which I am aware. Yet I am driven to say I am awake for two reasons. First, I emerge with a quiet, intuited certainty that I was continually present, that there was an unbroken continuity of experience or of consciousness throughout the

---

[14] These two are not quite equivalent. *Atman,* when seen in its fullest, according to the Upanishads and to Advaita Vedanta, merges with *Brahman,* and thus is experienced as including the object or content of perception. *Purusha,* according to Samkhya, is more an independent monad. It thus remains forever separate from its content. But the two both represent the human awareness, however differently understood.

meditation period, even if there seemed to have been periods from which I had no particular memories. I just know that there was some sort of continuity of myself (however we can define that) throughout.[15]

In Buddhism such pure consciousness events are called by several names: *nirodha-samapatti*, or cessation meditation; *samjnavedayitanirodha*, the cessation of sensation and conceptualization; *sunyata*, emptiness; or most famously, *samadhi*, meditation without content (cf. Griffiths, 1990). What is most fascinating about traditional Buddhist explorations of this state is that despite the fact that one is said to be utterly devoid of content, according to Yogacara Buddhist theorists one's consciousness is said to *persist* as 'some form of contentless and attributeless consciousness' (Griffiths, 1990, p. 83). That is, despite the fact that one is not aware *of* any specific content or thought, 'something persists' in this contentlessness, and that is consciousness itself: 'I, though abiding in emptiness, am now abiding *in the fullness thereof*' (Nagao, 1978, p. 67). When discussing this possibility that one may abide in the 'fulness' of 'emptiness', Vasubandu states:

> It is perceived as it really is that, when anything does not exist in something, the latter is empty with regard to the former; and further it is understood as it really is that, when, in this place *something remains, it exists here as a real existent*[16]

In sum, the PCE may be defined as a wakeful but contentless (non-intentional) experience. Though one remains awake and alert, emerging with the clear sense of having had 'an unbroken continuity of experience', one neither thinks, nor perceives nor acts. W.T. Stace (1960):

> Suppose then that we obliterate from consciousness all objects physical or mental. When the self is not engaged in apprehending objects it becomes aware of itself. The self itself emerges. The self, however, when stripped of all psychological contents or objects, is not another thing, or substance, distinct from its contents. It is the bare unity of the manifold of consciousness from which the manifold itself has been obliterated (p. 86).

Now what implications can we draw from the pure consciousness event about the nature of human consciousness?

1. We have a pattern here that is seen across cultures and eras. This, in combination with the reports offered in *The Problem of Pure Consciousness,* suggests that the phenomenon is not an artifact of any one culture but is something closer to an experience that is reasonably common and available in a variety of cultural contexts.[17]

2. Thomas Clark and other defenders of functionalism have suggested that consciousness is *identical to* certain of our information-bearing and behaviour-controlling functions, even going so far as to define it thus (Clark, 1995, p. 241).

---

[15] This account is taken from Forman (1998).

[16] Vasubandu commentary on Vs. 1.1 of the Madhyanta Vibhaga, quoted in Nagao (1978). Vasubandu is here wrestling with just the focus that made Yogacara so distinctive and clear. In its focus on the *alayavijnana*, it deals directly with the question of what remains in 'cessation meditation'. Steven Collins (1982) believes this is a mistaken view of the nature of *samadhi*, though unfortunately he never directly confronts such Yogacara texts. For comparable analyses from a Zen perspective, with explicit comparisons with Yogacara, see e.g. Chang Chen Chi (1970), pp. 167–71.

[17] See especially Forman (1990), Part I.

Others have suggested that consciousness is an artifact or an epiphenomenon of perception, action and thought, and that it arises *only* as a concomitant of these phenomena. Our accounts tend to *dis*confirm this view, which is generally argued on *a priori* grounds. Rather they suggest that consciousness *does* persist even when one has *no* perception, thought or evaluation. This suggests that consciousness should not be defined as merely an epiphenomenon of perception, an evaluative mechanism, or an arbiter of perceptual functions, but rather as something that exists *independently* of them.

3. Some have suggested that if we can understand how we can tie together perceptions and thoughts — the so called binding problem — we will *ipso facto* understand consciousness.[18] Now, how we bind together perceptions *is* a very interesting question for cognitive psychology, neurobiology and philosophy of mind. But even if we understand how we do tie together perceptions, we will not *necessarily* understand the phenomenon of consciousness *per se* thereby, for according to these mystical accounts, it is more fundamental than a mere binding function.[19] These reports suggest that binding is something done *by* or *for* consciousness, not something that creates consciousness.[20]

4. Our evidence suggests that we should conceptually and linguistically differentiate *merely* being aware or awake from its functional activities. Accordingly, I propose to use the terms as follows: (i) 'awareness' and 'consciousness' for that facet of consciousness which is aware within itself and which may persist even without intentional content; (ii) 'awareness of' and 1consciousness of' to refer to that feature of experience which is cognizant when we are *intentionally* aware of something; and (iii) 'pure awareness' and 'pure consciousness' to refer to awareness without intentional content.[21]

5. Reports of pure consciousness suggest that, despite the absence of mental content, the subjects were somehow aware *that* they remained aware throughout the period of the PCE . Apparently they sensed a continuity of awareness through past and present. If they did, even though there was no content, then they must have somehow *directly* recalled that they had been aware despite the absence of

---

[18] This debate goes back at least to Kant's criticism of Hume's 'associationism' in the eighteenth century. For a discussion of contemporary parallels, see Hardcastle (1994).

[19] If we think in a socio-cultural way here, we might note that our long western worldview, with its roots in the Judaeo-Christian past, in the protestant capitalistic history, and in the history of science, would tend to favour a definition of consciousness in active, masculine, intentional, and 'doing' terminology. Thus consciousness is, in this view, always vectorial, intentionally pointing towards this or that. Such a definition fits how people are expected to act in such a culture. Contemplative traditions and the east, on the other hand, tend to be more open to defining consciousness as *awareness per se*, or just being. In the west we may take these to be too passive, feminine, but they 'fit' the more station-oriented caste and natal-status behavioural patterns. My thanks to Bill Parsons for this observation.

[20] Logically: awareness is a necessary but not sufficient condition for binding; binding is neither a necessary nor sufficient condition for awareness.

[21] This usage preserves Deikman's (1996) separation of awareness from the other senses of 'I', and Chalmers' (1995) similar distinction. My thanks to Jonathan Shear for pointing out that I have reversed Chalmers' terms (he calls awareness in itself 'consciousness' and connects its various functional phenomena with the term 'awareness'). I believe that my usage is in better accord both with ordinary speech and the traditional scholarly use of 'pure consciousness' and 'pure consciousness event'.

remembered content.[22] This implies human awareness *has* the ability to tie itself together and to know intuitively that it has persisted.[23]

We may want to say that being conscious seems to entail this sort of direct self-recollection, a presence to oneself that is distinct from the kind of presence we have to perceptions and other intentional content. In this sense, the pure consciousness event tends to affirm Bernard Lonergan's distinction between our conscious presence to intentional objects and our consciousness of consciousness itself:

> There is the presence of the object to the subject, of the spectacle to the spectator; there is also the presence of the subject to himself, and this is not the presence of another object dividing his attention, of another spectacle distracting the spectator; it is presence in, as it were, another dimension, presence concomitant and correlative and opposite to the presence of the object. Objects are present by being attended to but subjects are present as subjects, not by being attended to, but by attending. As the parade of objects marches by, spectators do not have to slip into the parade to be present to themselves; they have to be present to themselves for anything to be present to them (Lonergan, 1967, p. 226, quoted in McCarthy, 1990, p. 234).

In sum, the PCE militates towards a distinction between consciousness or awareness *per se* and its usual binding, relational and culturally-trained processes. It suggests that consciousness is more than its embodied activities.

The dualistic mystical state, the peculiar 'oceanic feeling'

The second mystical phenomenon bears a dualistic pattern. Let us look at a few reports. The first comes from the autobiography of a living American mystic, Bernadette Roberts, middle-aged ex-nun, mother, housewife, and author of *The Experience of No-Self*. She had been in the practice of meditating in a nearby monastery, she tells us, and had often had the experience of complete silence we described above. Previously such experiences had sparked fear in her, perhaps a fear of never returning. But on this particular afternoon, as her meditation was ending,

> once again there was a pervasive silence and once again I waited for the onset of fear to break it up. But this time the fear never came. . . . Within, all was still, silent and motionless. In the stillness, I was not aware of the moment when the fear and tension of waiting had left. Still I continued to wait for a movement not of myself and when no movement came, I simply remained in a great stillness (Roberts, 1984, p. 20).

She became silent inside but, to her surprise, did not emerge from that silence. She stood up and walked out of her chapel, 'like a feather floats in the wind', while her silence continued unabated. No temporary meditative experience, this was a permanent development of that quiet empty interior silence.[24]

> . . . Once outside, I fully expected to return to my ordinary energies and thinking mind, but this day I had a difficult time because I was continually falling back into the great silence (*ibid.*).

---

[22] See the extended discussion of this possibility in Forman (1998).

[23] Here language fails us. The awareness is not in any sense conscious *of* the passage of time; rather I am suggesting that awareness ties itself together through what an external observer would note as the passage of time.

[24] William James' thought that mysticism is 'transient', i.e. short lived, clearly does not capture Bernadette Roberts' experience, nor many of the experiences documented in this section.

She 'remained in a great stillness', driving down the road, talking on the phone, and cutting the carrots for dinner. In fact that inner stillness was never again to leave her.

She experienced her interior silence as her original 'consciousness', by which I understand that she experienced it as devoid of the intellectual self-reflection that generally accompanies experiences. She describes this new state as a continuation of what she had encountered when she was in her meditative silence (PCE); only here she remains fully cognizant of her own silent awareness even while active.

My own previously published autobiographical report of such a state also associates a permanent interior silence with consciousness:

> This began in 1972. I had been practicing meditation for about three years, and had been on a meditation retreat for three and a half months. Over several days something like a series of tubes (neuronal bundles?) running down the back of my neck became, one by one, utterly quiet. This transformation started on the left side and moved to the right. As each one became silent, all the noise and activity inside these little tubes just ceased. There was a kind of a click or a sort of 'zipping' sensation, as the nerve cells or whatever it was became quiet.[25] It was as if there had always been these very faint and unnoticed activity, a background of static, so constant that I had never before noticed it. When each of these tubes became silent, all that noise just ceased entirely. I only recognized the interior noise or activity in these tubes in comparison to the silence that now descended. One by one these tubes became quiet, from left to right. It took a couple of weeks and finally the last one on the right went *zip,* and that was it. It was over.
>
> After the last tube had shifted to this new state, I discovered that a major though subtle shift had occurred. From that moment forward, *I was silent inside.* I don't mean I didn't think, but rather that the feeling inside of me was as if I was entirely empty, a perfect vacuum.[26] Since that time all of my thinking, my sensations, my emotions, etc., have seemed not quite connected to me inside. It was and is as if what was *me,* my consciousness itself, was (and is) now this emptiness. The *silence* was now me, and the thoughts that have gone on inside have not felt quite in contact with what is really 'me,' this empty awareness. 'I' was now silent inside. My thinking has been as if on the outside of this silence without quite contacting it: When I saw, felt or heard something, that perception or thought has been seen by this silent consciousness, but it has not been quite connected to this interior silence.

In this experience the silence is explicitly associated with awareness. It is experienced as 'the I', 'what was really me', 'my consciousness itself'. Somehow this area in the back of the head seems to be associated with being aware; as it became silent, a sense of the self or consciousness itself within became more articulated, and was now experienced as silent.

Like Roberts', this shift to an interior silence was permanent.[27] Thus we should call it a state, not a transient experience. I call it the dualistic mystical state (DMS).

Descriptions of a DMS are surprisingly common in the mystical literature. Teresa of Avila writes of such a dualistic state. Speaking of herself in the third person, I believe, she writes:

[25] Here I am struck by the parallel with the rapid shifting of a physical system as it becomes coherent. Disorganized light just 'shifts' or 'zips' into laser light nearly instantaneously.

[26] Writing this, I think of the parallel between this sense and Bernadette Robert's sense of having lost the usual 'unlocalized sense of herself'.

[27] It is my impression that the awareness of the specific locations within the body is not essential to this transformation.

However numerous were her trials and business worries, the essential part of her soul seemed never to move from [its] dwelling place. So in a sense she felt that her soul was divided . . . Sometimes she would say that it was doing nothing but enjoy[ing] itself in that quietness, while she herself was left with all her trials and occupations so that she could not keep it company (Peers, 1961, p. 211).

She too describes an experience in which, even while working and living, one also maintains a clear sense of the interior awareness, a persisting sense of an unmoving silence at one's core.

Meister Eckhart describes something similar, calling it the Birth of the Word In the Soul. One of Eckhart's clearest descriptions is from the treatise 'On Detachment'. It analogizes the two aspects of man with a door and its hinge pin. Like the outward boards of a door, the outward man moves, changes, and acts. The inward man, like the hinge pin, does not move. He — or it — remains uninvolved with activity and does not change at all. This, Eckhart concludes, is the way one should really conduct a life: one should act yet remain inwardly uninvolved. Here is the passage:

And however much our Lady lamented and whatever other things she said, she was *always in her inmost heart in immovable detachment*. Let us take an analogy of this. A door opens and shuts on a hinge. Now if I compare the outer boards of the door with the outward man, I can compare the hinge with the inward man. When the door opens or closes the outer boards move to and fro, but the hinge *remains immovable* in one place and it is not changed at all as a result. So it is also here . . . (Clark and Skinner, 1958, p. 167; emphasis mine.)

A hinge pin moves on the outside and remains unmoving at its centre. To act and yet remain 'in her inmost heart in immovable detachment' depicts precisely this dualistic life. One acts, yet at an unchanging level within retains a sense of something unmoving. One lives a dichotomous existence. Inside, she experiences an interior silence, outside she acts. Elsewhere Eckhart describes what this is like:

When the detached heart has the highest aim, it must be towards the Nothing, because in this there is the greatest receptivity. Take a parable from nature: if I want to write on a wax tablet, then no matter how noble the thing is that is [already] written on the tablet, I am none the less vexed because I cannot write on it. If I really want to write I must delete everything that is written on the tablet, and the tablet is never so suitable for writing as when absolutely nothing is written on it. (*ibid.*, p. 168.)

The emphasis in this passage is on the achievement of emptiness within. One has 'deleted' everything inside; one comes to a 'Nothing' inside; the tablet is 'blank'. When one is truly empty within, comes to 'the Nothing,' what goes on 'outside' is of lesser significance, for it is unconnected to the inner 'nothing'. Only once this interior 'Nothing' is established does one truly begin 'acting rightly'. This is highly reminiscent of the empty interior silence achieved by our other reporters.

In sum, in this DMS the subject has a sense, on a permanent or semi-permanent basis, of being in touch with his or her own deepest awareness, experienced as a silence at one's core, even while remaining conscious of the external sensate world. Awareness itself is experienced as silent and as separate from its intentional content.

This dualistic mystical state seems to evolve gradually into another state. First this author's own experience:

Over the years, this interior silence has slowly changed. Gradually, imperceptibly, this sense of who I am, this silence inside, has grown as if quasi-physically larger. In the beginning it just seemed like I was silent inside. Then this sense of quietness has, as it were *expanded* to permeate my whole body. Some years later, it came to seem no longer even limited to my own body, but even wider, larger than my body. It's such a peculiar thing to describe! It's as if who I am, my very consciousness itself, has become bigger, wider, less localized. By now it's as if I extend some distance beyond my body, as if I'm many feet wide. What is *me* is now this expanse, this silence, that spreads out.

While retaining something of the dualistic character, the sense of the self or awareness itself here seems to have become as if quasi-physically expanded, extending beyond the felt borders of the usual physical frame. It is important to note that exterior perception has not changed here, only the sense of what consciousness itself is. That will change in the next state.

Freud called this a 'peculiar oceanic feeling', which seems to communicate both the ineffability and the expanded quality of such a sense of consciousness.[28] Yet at this point this sense of an inner expanse does not yet seem to 'touch' or affect the perception of objects.

Being in the middle of an expanse is reminiscent of the well known passage from Walt Whitman. As if having a conversation with his soul, he recalls,

I mind how once we lay, such a transparent summer morning,
Swiftly arose and *spread around me* the peace and knowledge that pass all the argument of the earth.[29]

Here the sense of inner silence, the peace, is experienced as part of the world. But note again that Whitman does not suggest that the peace is *within* the world.

The sense seems to be that what one is, one's awareness itself, is experienced as oceanic, unbounded, expanded beyond the limits of the body. Here, I believe, a theist might plausibly associate this silence, that seems to be both inside and yet quasi-physically expansive, with God. If this is true, then St. Teresa's 'Spiritual Marriage' is very much like this one. In it, one is permanently 'married' to the Lord,

. . . the Lord appears in the centre of the soul . . . He has been pleased to unite Himself with His creature in such a way that they have become like two who cannot be separated from one another: even so He will not separate Himself from her. [In other words, this sense of union is permanent.] The soul remains all the time in [its] centre with its God. . . . When we empty ourselves of all that is creature and rid ourselves of it for the love of God, that same Lord will fill our souls with Himself (Peers, 1961, pp. 213–16).

To be permanently filled within the soul with the Lord may be phenomenologically described as experiencing a sense of some silent but omnipresent, i.e. expansive, 'something' at one's core. If so, this becomes remarkably like the other experiences of expansiveness at one's core that we have seen before. (Once again, the expanse is not described as permeating the world, as it might in the next 'state'.)

This sense of an interiority that is also an expanse is reconfirmed by her disciple St. John of the Cross, who says, 'the soul then feels as if placed in a *vast* and profound solitude, to which no created thing has access, in an *immense* and *boundless* desert'.

In sum, the interior silence at one's core sometimes comes to be experienced as expanded, as if being quasi-physically larger or more spacious than one's body. Now, what might this DMS suggest? It offers several tantalizing hints about consciousness.

---

[28] Freud was employing a phrase from his correspondence with Ramakrishna's disciple Romain Rolland. See Parsons (forthcoming).

[29] Walt Whitman, quoted in James (1902/1983) p. 396, no reference.

1. Human capacity includes more epistemological modalities than is generally imagined. It is clear from these reports that one can be self-reflexively cognizant of one's own awareness more immediately than usual. The contemplative life can lead one to the ability to be aware of one's own awareness *per se* on a permanent or semi-permanent basis. This is not like taking on a *new awareness*. None of our sources describe this as a sense of becoming a different person, or as a *discontinuity* with what they had been. Rather the descriptions are that of becoming more *immediately* cognizant of the awareness they had always enjoyed.

2. We suggested above that consciousness should not be defined in terms of perceptions, content, or its other functions, for in the DMS awareness continues even when perceptions do not. Here awareness is not only not implicated with thoughts and perceptions, but is *experienced* as entirely different in quality or character — unchanging, without intrinsic form — than its content. It is also experienced as unconnected with its intentional content. Even thoughts do 'not quite contact it'. Awareness itself is experienced as still or silent, perceptions as active and changing. Therefore instead of defining awareness in terms of its content, we should think about awareness and its mental and sensory *functions* as two independent phenomena or processes that somehow interact.

3. The sense of being expanded beyond the borders of one's own body, what Freud called the 'peculiar oceanic feeling', is a very peculiar sense indeed. Yet if we take these wide-spread reports seriously, as I think every open-minded thinker should, what do they suggest?

    The phenomenology, simply put, suggests that consciousness is not limited to the body. Consciousness is encountered as something more like a field than a localized point, a field that transcends the body and yet somehow interacts with it.[30]   This mystical phenomenon tends to confirm William James' hypothesis in his monumental *Principles of Psychology* that awareness is field-like. This thought was picked up by Peter Fenwick and Chris Clarke in the Mind and Brain Symposium in 1994, that the mind may be non-localized, like a field, and that experience arises from some sort of interplay between non-localized awareness and the localized brain.[31] It is as if these mystical reporters had an *experience* of just the sort of field-like non-locality of awareness these theories hypothesize.

    The heretical suggestion here is not that there is a ghost in the machine, but rather that there is a ghost in and *beyond* the machine! And it is not a ghost that thinks, but a ghost *for which* there is thinking and perception.

4. The experience of awareness as some sort of field points towards the theory that consciousness is more than just the product of the materialistic interactions of brain cells, since it can be understood in two ways. First it may mean that like a magnet, the brain 'produces' a field which extends well beyond its own physical borders. The slow growth of the sense of an experience suggests this.

    Or, conversely, the field-like experience may suggest that awareness somehow

[30] Of course, that implies that one has some sort of non-sensory sense, the ability to sense one's own expansive presence even though there are no visible mechanisms of sensation. But is that so strange after all? If we can sense our own awareness directly in the pure consciousness event, why shouldn't we be able to sense something of its non-limited character on a more permanent basis?
[31] See Freeman (1994) for a brief report and Clarke (1995) for the full text of Chris Clarke's talk.

transcends individual brain cells and perhaps the entire brain. This suggests a new way to think about the role of the physical body. Brain cells may receive, guide, arbitrate, or canalize an awareness which is somehow transcendental to them. The brain may be more like a receiver or transformer for the field of awareness than its generator: less like a magnet than like a TV receiver.

The unitive mystical state

Our last commonly reported mystical experience is a sense of becoming unified with external objects. It is nicely described by the German idealist Malwida von Meysenburg:

> I was alone upon the seashore ... I felt that I ... return[ed] from the solitude of individuation into the consciousness of *unity with all that is*, [that I knelt] down as one that passes away, and [rose] up as one imperishable. Earth, heaven, and sea *resounded as in one vast world encircling* harmony. . . . I *felt myself one* with them ... (von Meysenburg, 1900; emphasis mine).

The keynote of Malwida's experience is that in some sort of immediate or intuitive manner she sensed that she was connected with the things of the world, as if she was a part of them and they part of her. It is as if the membranes of her experienced self became semi-permeable, and she flowed in, with or perhaps through her environment.

A similar experience is described in Starbuck's 19th century collection of experience reports. Here again we see a sense of unity with the things of the world.

> ... something in myself made me feel *myself a part of something bigger* than I ... I *felt myself one with* the grass, the trees, birds, insects, everything in nature. I exulted in the mere fact of existence, of being apart of it all, the drizzling rain, the shadows of the clouds, the tree-trunks and so on.

The author goes on to say that after this experience he constantly sought these experiences of the unity between self and object again, but they only came periodically. This implies that for him they were temporary phenomena, lasting only a few minutes or hours.

This sense of the unity between self and object, the absence of the usual lines between things, is clearly reminiscent of Plotinus's *First Ennead* (8:1).

> He who has allowed the beauty of that world to penetrate his soul goes away no longer a mere observer. For the object perceived and the perceiving soul are *no longer two* things separated from one another, but the perceiving soul has [now] within itself the perceived object (quoted in Otto, 1930, p. 67).

Again we have a lack of boundaries between consciousness and object. It is not clear from this passage if Plotinus is describing a transient or a permanent experience. Yet some reporters clearly tell us that such an experience can be constant. Though it is often hard to distinguish biography from mythology, Buddhist descriptions of Sakyamuni Buddha's life clearly imply that his Nirvana was a *permanent* change in epistemological structure. Similarly the Hindu term for an enlightened one, *jivanmukti* (enlightened in active life), clearly suggests that this experience can be permanent.

Notice how different these reports are from our DMS descriptions of an inner expanse. There we saw no change in the relationship between the subject and the perceived world. Here 'the object perceived and the perceiving soul' are now united. 'I felt myself one with the grass, the trees, birds, insects, everything in nature.'

One of the clearer descriptions of this state comes from Krishnamurti, who wrote of his his first experience of this sort, in August, 1922:

On the first day while I was in that state and more conscious of the things around me, I had the first most extraordinary experience. There was a man mending the road; that man was myself; the pickax he held was myself; the very stone which he was breaking up was a part of me; the tender blade of grass was my very being, and the tree beside the man was myself. I also could feel and think like the roadmender and I could feel the wind passing through the tree, and the little ant on the blade of grass I could feel. The birds, the dust and the very noise were a part of me. Just then there was a car passing by at some distance; I was the driver, the engine, and the tires; as the car went further away from me, I was going away from myself. I was in everything, or rather everything was in me, inanimate and animate, the mountain, the worm and all breathing things. All day long I remained in this happy condition.

Perhaps the most unmistakable assertion that these shifts can be permanent comes from Bernadette Roberts. Sometime after her initial transformation, she had what is clearly a development *on* her earlier dualistic sense of an expanded consciousness. She writes:

I was standing on [a] windy hillside looking down over the ocean when a seagull came into view, gliding, dipping, playing with the wind. I watched it as I'd never watched anything before in my life. I almost seemed to be mesmerized; it was as if I was watching myself flying, for there was not the usual division between us. Yet, something more was there than just a lack of separateness, 'something' truly beautiful and unknowable. Finally I turned my eyes to the pine-covered hills behind the monastery and still, there was no division, only something 'there' that was flowing with and through every vista and particular object of vision. . . . What I had [originally] taken as a trick of the mind *was to become a permanent way of seeing and knowing* (Roberts, 1984, p. 30; italics mine).

She describes this 'something there' that flowed with and through everything, including her own self, as 'that into which all separateness dissolves.' She concludes with an emphatic assertion: 'I was never to revert back to the usual relative way of seeing separateness or individuality.' Again we have a state, not a transient episode.

We could multiply these examples endlessly. This unitive mystical state (UMS), either temporary or permanent, is a very common mystical phenomenon. It is clearly an evolution of the previous sense. First one continues to sense that one's awareness is expansive, field-like, and that the self is experienced as larger, expanded beyond the usual boundaries. One feels oneself to be 'a part of something bigger', which is to say, senses a lack of borders or a commonality between oneself and this expanse. Indeed, in Bernadette Roberts' case, her sense of 'something there' *followed* and was an evolution of her initial dualistic mystical state. But now this perceived expansion of the self is experienced as none other than, permeating with and through, the things of the world. One's boundaries become as if permeable, connected with the objects of the world. The expanded self seems to be experienced as of the same metaphysical level, or of the same 'stuff', as the world. Despite the grammatical peculiarities, 'what I am *is* the seagull, and what the seagull is, *I* am'.

From this fascinating phenomenon we may note several implications for our understanding of consciousness.

1. The perceived 'spaciousness' of awareness suggests, I said above, that consciousness is like a field. These unitive experiences reaffirm this implication and suggest that such a field may not only transcend our own bodily limits, but somehow may interpenetrate or connect both self and external objects. This is of course strikingly parallel to the physical energy fields and/or the quantum vac-

uum field said to reside at the basis of matter, for these too are both immanent within and also transcendent to any particular expression, a parallel that Fritjof Capra, Lawrence Domash and others have been quick to point out.

2.   The perception of unity holds out the possibility that the field of awareness is common to all objects, and however implausibly, among all human beings as well. It indicates that my own consciousness may be somehow connected to a tree, the stars, a drizzle or a blade of grass and, paradoxically, to yours. Thus these unitive experiences point towards something like a primitive animism, Leibnitz's panspsychism and Griffin's suggestion of a pan-experientialism, that experience or some sort of consciousness may be 'an ingredient throughout the universe, permeating all levels of being'. All this, however, opens up another Pandora's box of peculiar questions: most obviously what might the conscious-ness be of a dog, flower, or even a stone? Does the claim of a perceived unity merely point to some ground of being, and not a consciousness that is in any sense self-reflective like our own consciousness? Or if you and I share conscious-ness, can I experience what you do? If not, why not?

3.   Not everyone who meditates encounters these sorts of unitive experiences. This suggests that some may be genetically or temperamentally predisposed to mysti-cal ability; borrowing from Weber, the 'mystically musical'.

     One might suggest that the mystic's awareness is categorically different than other peoples', i.e. that it is connected to the world in an ontologically deep way that the rest of ours is not. I find this unconvincing, since every mystic I have read says he or she began as an 'ordinary', i.e. non-mystical, person and only came to realize something of what he or she 'had always been'. Whichever explanation we opt for, however, it is clear that there is some ability the mystics have been able to develop — through meditation or whatever — that most of us have not.

Conclusions

Our three modalities of mystical experiences point clearly towards a distinction between awareness *per se* and the ordinary functional processes of sensation, percep-tion and thought. They suggest that awareness is not *constructed* out of the material processes of perception or perhaps the brain, but rather they suggest a distinction and / or interaction between consciousness and the brain. Furthermore, they suggest that awareness may have a non-localized, quasi-spatial character, much like a field. Finally they tend to suggest that this field may be transcendental to any one person or entity.

I want to end by restating my earlier caveat. Phenomenology is not science. There can be many ways to explain any experience, mystical or otherwise, and we should explore all of them. But in the absence of compelling reasons to deny the suggestions of their reports, we would be wise to seriously examine the direction towards which the finger of mysticism points. If the validity of knowledge in the universities is indeed governed, as we like to claim, by the tests of evidence, openness and clarity, then we should not be too quick to throw out the baby swimming in the bathwater of mysticism.

References

Barnard, William (1995), 'Response to Wilber', unpublished paper delivered to the Mysticism Group of the American Academy of Religion.

Chalmers, David J. (1995), 'Facing up to the problem of consciousness', *Journal of Consciousness Studies, 2* (3), 1995, pp. 200–19.

Chang Chen Chi (1970), *The Practice of Zen* (New York: Perennial Library / Harper Row).

Clark, Thomas W. (1995), 'Function and phenomenology: closing the explanatory gap,' *Journal of Consciousness Studies, 2* (3), pp. 241–54.

Clark, James M. and Skinner John V. (1958), *Meister Eckhart: Selected Treatises and Sermons* (London: Faber and Faber).

Clarke, C.J.S. (1995), 'The non-locality of mind', *Journal of Consciousness Studies, 2* (3), pp. 231–40.

Collins, Steven (1982), *Selfless Persons* (Cambridge: Cambridge University Press).

Deikman, Arthur (1996), ' "I" = Awareness', *Journal of Consciousness Studies, 3* (4), pp. 350–6.

Forman, Robert K.C. (ed. 1990), *The Problem of Pure Consciousness* (New York: Oxford University Press).

Forman, Robert K.C. (1998) *Mysticism, Mind, Consciousness* (Albany, NY: SUNY Press).

Freeman, Anthony (1994), 'The science of consciousness: non-locality of mind' [Conference Report], *The Journal of Consciousness Studies, 1* (2), pp. 283–4.

Griffiths, Paul (1990), 'Pure Consciousness and Indian Buddhism,' in *The Problem of Pure Consciousness*.

Hardcastle, Valerie (1994), 'Psychology's "binding problem" and possible neurobiological solutions', *Journal of Consciousness Studies, 1* (1), pp. 66–90.

Hume, Robert (trans. 1931), *The Thirteen Principle Upanishads* (London: Oxford University Press).

James, William (1902/1983), *The Varieties of Religious Experience* (New York: Longmans, Green and Co.; reprinted in Penguin).

Larson, J.G. (1979), *Classical Samkhya: An Interpretation of its History and Meaning* (Santa Barbara: Ross / Erikson).

Lonergan, B. (1967), *Collection*, ed. Frederick Crowe (New York: Herder and Herder).

McCarthy, Michael H. (1990), *The Crisis in Philosophy* (Albany: SUNY Press).

Mangan, Bruce (1994), 'Language and experience in the cognitive study of mysticism — commentary on Forman', *Journal of Consciousness Studies, 1* (2), pp. 250–2.

Nagao, Gadjin M. (trans. 1978), 'The Culasunnata-Sutta (Lesser discourse on emptiness)' translated as, '"What Remains" in Sunyata: A Yogacara interpretation of emptiness', in *Mahayana Buddhist Meditation*, ed. Minoru Kiyota (Honolulu: University Press of Hawaii).

Ornstein, Robert (1976), 'The techniques of meditation and their implications for modern psychology', in *On The Psychology of Meditation*, Claudio Naranjo and Robert Ornstein (New York: Penguin).

Otto, Rudolf (1930), *Mysticism East and West*, trans. Bertha Bracey and Richard Payne (New York: Macamillan).

Parsons, William (forthcoming), *The Enigma of the Oceanic Feeling* (Oxford University Press).

Peers, E. Allison (trans. 1961), *The Interior Castle* [Teresa of Avila] (New York: Doubleday).

Roberts, Bernadette (1984), *The Experience of No-Self* (Boulder: Shambala).

Sacks, Oliver (1994), 'An anthropologist on Mars' [interview with Anthony Freeman], *Journal of Consciousness Studies, 1* (2), pp. 234–40.

Smart, Ninian (1982), 'Interpretation and mystical experience', *Sophia, 1* (1), p. 75.

Stace, W.T. (1960), *Mysticism and Philosophy* (London: Macmillan Press).

von Meysenberg, Malwida (1900), *Memoiren einer Idealistin*, 5th Auflage, iii. 166. Quoted in James (1902/1983), p. 395.

Walshe, M.O'C. (1982), *Meister Eckhart, Sermons and Tractates*, Vol. 1 (London: Watkins).

Wilber, Ken (1980), *The Atman Project* (Wheaton, IL: The Theosophical Publishing House).

Jeremy Hayward

A rDzogs-chen Buddhist Interpretation of The Sense of Self

A rDzogs-chen (Tibetan Buddhist) interpretation of the sense of self is presented that is grounded in the disciplined method of shamatha-vipashyana meditation. This model of self/non-self agrees with Strawson's analysis as far as the discontinuity of self, but elaborates the momentary self not as any kind of 'thing', but as an energy process having both particle-like and field-like aspects. The moment-by-moment appearance of a sense of self is described as arising in stages over a finite duration from a background of non-dual intelligence and energy. There are implications for further scientific research into the structure of self-consciousness as well as for the cultivation of individual wisdom and compassion.

Introduction

Galen Strawson[1] claims that the self should be considered to be a single thing, onto-logically distinct from other things, yet discontinuous as a function of time. He suggests the image of a string of pearl-like things, as an image of a self. This image of individual short moments of experience, captures one aspect of the Buddhist notion of 'egolessness', namely, the discontinuity of the self. However, the Buddhist analysis of experience questions the notion of 'thingness', or distinct ontological existence, altogether and raises some further questions: do the discontinuous moments of experience themselves have structure; how are they held together so that we have the sense that they all belong to the same string (my particular self); is there any experience (clearly not that of a 'self') in the gaps between the moments of experience of a self.

Presumably Strawson bases his analysis on some kind of first-person observation. However, he does not describe any specific method of observation and so one supposes that his method is informal introspection, which is notoriously problematic (Lyons, 1986; Varela *et al.*, 1991). In this chapter I will discuss the structure of the self from the point of view of the Buddhist analysis of experience which is based on the disciplined examination of first-person experience through the well-tested method of shamatha-vipashyana meditation (SVM), which I will describe in detail

---

[1] All references to 'Strawson' in the current chapter are to Galen Strawson's opening chapter in this volume (pp. 1–24).

later (Thrangu, 1993; Varela *et al.*, 1991). This analysis agrees that the self is discontinuous, but goes further than that. Experience does appear to have particle-like aspects, whose discontinuity we gloss over to create our usual sense of a permanent, continuous self. However, the very notion of the self as some kind of 'thing', continuous or discontinuous, is itself superficial. At a deeper level of analysis, the momentary experience of a self is itself a dynamic process dependent on interconnected causes but having no substantial reality. A particle–field analogy for experience would be more apt than the string-of-pearls analogy. Experience is particle-like in that our sense of self *appears* to be ontologically distinct, relatively permanent and localized, more or less in our head or heart, depending on our cultural conditioning. But, according to the Buddhist analysis, experience also has a field-like, that is a non-local, aspect. In other words, some aspect of experience is not localized and may not even be confined by the conventional experiential categories of space and time.

The Method of Shamatha-Vipashyana Meditation

In practising the method of shamatha-vipashyana meditation (SVM) I sit with my legs crossed, my palms resting on my thighs, back straight, eyes open with gaze down. The practice is just to pay attention to whatever thoughts, feelings and bodily sensations arise to awareness, as they arise, and let them go when they want to go. The effort is to be direct and clear, not rejecting thoughts, feelings or sensations that feel bad (immoral, stupid, etc.), not trying to hold onto positive feelings or thoughts, nor to think any particular thoughts or follow a special train of thought. Being gentle with my thoughts and feelings, I try to be open to them, but not to encourage them unnecessarily, just to let them be there as they are.

As I sit there I pay attention to my body resting on the cushion; experience the solidity and earthiness of my body; feel the heart beating in my chest and the blood pulsing through my body. In particular, I pay attention to the breath as it goes out of my body. When my attention wanders off, and I forget that I made the decision to pay attention to my thoughts and emotions, getting *lost* in thinking something, then I bring my attention gently back to my breath. This gives my attention a kind of anchor that holds it here and now, as all kinds of different thoughts and emotions arise.

The practice can be compared to a naturalist looking for hours at a time, for days on end, at ground hogs in a field, popping in and out of their holes, until he becomes so familiar with their movements that he loses his feeling of being separate from them. He begins to develop a sense of the overall patterns of behaviour of the ground-hogs as well as an intimate feeling for each of the members of the tribe he's watching. At this point the naturalist may have direct insight into the behaviour of ground hogs.

The practice of SVM has two components. The first is *shamatha*, most frequently translated as *tranquillity* (Thrangu, 1993) or, more literally, *development of peace,* but also called *mindfulness* (Trungpa, 1995). The second, *vipashyana,* is more frequently translated as *insight* (Thrangu, 1993) or *awareness* (used in a technical sense, not in the general sense commonly interchangeable with consciousness, Trungpa, 1995). These correspond to the two aspects of the way mind functions: focusing on one activity or thought, and having a broad, panoramic sense of our experience. Mindfulness and awareness are simple processes that occur naturally in every moment of our experience to a lesser or greater extent, but they are usually scattered and hidden from us and are usually unavailable to us as tools we can use. Yet people do use them instinctively. Mindfulness is just paying attention. We all pay attention when something invites us to, for example when we hear a strange sound or see an interesting person. We try to pay attention when listening to a boring lecture, but no doubt find our mind constantly wandering off. Even when we really want to learn a task, we often have a great deal of difficulty attending. Awareness is opening our minds at each moment and taking in a broad spectrum of perception and feeling. Again, this can occur quite naturally. If you play a musical instrument in an orchestra, for example, you have to pay attention to the details of your own part while at the same time having a panoramic awareness of what the rest of the orchestra and the conductor are doing.

William James (1961) wrote,

> The faculty of voluntarily bringing back a wandering attention, over and over again, is the very root of judgment, character and will. No one is *compos sui* if he have it not. An education which should improve this faculty would be education *par excellence*. But it is easier to define this ideal than to give practical direction for bringing it about.

Mindfulness-awareness is precisely such 'practical direction for bringing it about.' I was once describing mindfulness-awareness meditation to someone who had responsibility for training the Air Traffic Controllers in Canada. He exclaimed, 'But this is just what Air Traffic Controllers need!' He explained that these are precisely the two aspects they urgently need in their job. They need to be able to pay very pr incrementallyecise attention to their own screen and the planes that they are directly responsible for — mindfulness. But as well they need to have a constant sense of the broad picture of the airspace altogether — awareness.

The *mindfulness* aspect of the formal practice is paying close and direct attention to one's thoughts, emotions, bodily sensations. It is identifying fully with one's bodily sensations, thoughts, and emotions, so that there is nothing left over, no self-consciousness, no watcher, no split mind. It is not *watching* what we are doing but simply *being* what we are doing, thinking, and feeling in its smallest detail. There are various specific techniques for resting the mind in the present in this way, focusing on the breath being the most common. This practice of taming the wildness of the mind brings about a sense of rest and tranquillity which enables one to be not caught up on one's thoughts and emotions and therefore to see their nature clearly and directly.

The practice of *awareness* depends on the settling of mind in the practice of mindfulness. When we *are* fully present, we can begin to take an inquisitive interest in the environment within which our actions and thoughts take place. With awareness, we realize that our thoughts, emotions, and perceptions are not solid 'things', but are simply patterns of energy. Awareness is said to cognize the associations and causal connections to each smallest thought or sense perception, unraveling and revealing the details and causal processes of thought and perception itself. This cognizing is not at the level of self-consciousness, but more at the level of direct intuition, much as we intuit the inner presence of our own bodies, or know the presence of the environment around us without deliberately paying attention to it, yet can become immediately attentive to any sudden change in that presence. It is similar to Whitehead's sense of 'causal efficacy' (Whitehead, 1959) which constituted a challenge to Hume's analysis of causality as mere regularity of association.

This unravelling of the causal process is described as six particular 'discoveries' (Thrangu, 1993; Trungpa, 1974): first comes discovery of 'meaning', which means being able to distinguish the meaning of a perception from its name. We are said to become free from the ensnarement of words and language, and are therefore able to have an exact and precise relationship to words, to use them powerfully to cut through mental gossip and ignorance. The second discovery is of 'object'. Here it is said that we begin to see the actual patterning that we are projecting onto our perceptions, and to be able to distinguish a perception that genuinely corresponds to something in the environment from one that is at the level of fantasy or mental creation. The third is the discovery of 'nature', or 'mark': how the first bare perception expands into our projected world, by categorizing and proliferation of concepts.

Fourth is the discovery of 'direction' or 'sides', which means knowing when these proliferations lead towards or away from further awareness. Therefore it means knowing what to do and what not to do from the point of view of awareness. Fifth is the discovery of 'time', which means realizing how concepts, as memory of the past and anticipation of the future, are entering into each moment of perception; knowing what you are experiencing now and seeing clearly how past and future are entering into this. Sixth is discovery of 'insight', which is realizing the deep conceptual frame of reference involved in each moment of perception, our personal 'belief system', and therefore not necessarily being trapped in it. One begins to see how each moment of experience is grounded in some relative frame of reference that, until one saw it, one took for granted. It is claimed that one can become aware even beyond the reference of self and other to the entire process of the arising of perception; how each moment leads to the next and gives rise, causally, to the next. It is described as seeing cause and effect directly, seeing how present action leads to future result. These six discoveries are said to arise after one has become quite proficient at attending to the smallest fluctuations or flickerings of thoughts with their surrounding atmosphere of meanings.

In some early Buddhist schools, the development of shamatha is carried to its farthest extent before the insight of awareness is cultivated, and joined with mindfulness. In most modern schools, the two are cultivated simultaneously from the beginning. The joining of mindfulness and awareness is regarded as the most important point. It is said that this will bring the discovery of beauty, harmony and clarity of perceptions, which exist beyond ego. This transformation of perception *is* sacredness in the Buddhist tradition. There is no other world than this one, but this one is said to be immeasurably more vast than our *ideas* of it. And through the practice of SVM one can, it is claimed, experience that vastness, sacredness, and inherent meaningfulness in each detail. This transformation of our ordinary perceptual world comes from ceasing to ignore what is so close to each one of us that we cannot see it without it being pointed out.

The process of SVM is not the same as the conventional idea of introspection. It differs from introspection in that the meditator is not looking 'inwards' at something that is imagined to be 'my mind', and is not specifically interested in 'consciousness'. SVM, mindfulness-awareness meditation, is not merely subjective, although it clearly does not make the artificial distinction between subject and object that science is conventionally believed to make. It is not 'objective' but it *is* inter-subjectively testable. It is a method that has been applied over and over again, with repeatable results.

However, because our experimental material is in this case our own minds, and because we may well not like what we find (especially as we come closer and closer to discovering the fluctuating, impermanent nature of the self), there is a very strong possibility of self-deception. Therefore SVM practice depends on there being a community of practitioners and a guide who has already, at least partially, accomplished the training. Without such a community and guide, just because of this potentiality for self-deception, SVM practice is very much a hit and miss affair, in which one might easily get lost. These checks and balances by which the practice of SVM is kept from becoming mere introspection or dangerous fantasy, are akin in some ways (though not identical) to those used by the ordinary scientific community.

Studies to Verify the Meditative Insights

Various studies have been done to try to develop some understanding of the practice of meditation within the context of third-person discourse, the only sphere of discourse available to conventional science with its deceptive emphasis on 'objectivity'. For example, clinical psychologist Daniel Brown (Brown, 1986) compared the meditation practices of three different traditions: the Theravadin Buddhist traditions, the Tibetan Buddhist Mahamudra tradition, and the Hindu yoga tradition of Patanjali. Brown suggests that the path of meditation of each of these traditions can be broken down into eighteen stages and that there are very significant parallels in the changes of the perceptual process accompanying each stage. He also shows how the very early stages of all three traditions can be interpreted in terms of the stages of perception outlined by cognitive psychology.

The cognitive stages Brown identifies are: first, discriminatory thinking about the object ceases, the meditation disrupts the categorizing mind and returns to the actual physical features of perceptual objects. For example, a stick is seen as colour and form but remains without the attached meaning 'stick'. The second stage is one in which the object appears to change dramatically in size; there is a destabilizing of the perceptual phenomenon of 'size constancy': for example as you move an outstretched thumb towards you, it appears to move closer without changing in size. This is an important element in the primitive recognition of patterns as definite objects. Next the meditator observes the reversal of the primary pattern formation. According to cognitive psychologists and on neurological grounds, it appears that, in ordinary perception, a synthesis of the senses occurs first, followed by primary pattern recognition. At this stage of meditation this is reversed so that the primary pattern of an object is lost, followed by the loss of the sensory synthesis. At this point the meditator has deconstucted the gross perceptual world altogether.

The next, more advanced, stages of mindfulness-awareness meditation bring the letting go of subtle attachments to the 'I' construction, as well as to the time–space matrix. At this point the meditative experience is one of non-dual perception of flashes of brilliance, energy and clarity, free from concepts of self, of space, or of time. At the end of the session, the meditator, arising out of this non-dual state, is able to see the perceptual world of space, time and the duality of subject and object return, and the reconstruction of the gross perception of an 'outside' world with recognizable 'objects'. Between meditation sessions, the advanced meditator is able to see the ordinary world as a perceptual construction just as he did as he went into and out of the non-dual state of being.

Brown, together with his colleagues, have corroborated some of these traditional descriptions of meditative experience in clinical tests. In one extensive series of tests, meditation subjects at various levels of practice, as designated by meditation masters, were submitted to Rorschach tests. Brown also travelled to Asia to give similar tests to several meditation masters. The results could quite clearly be correlated with some of the stages described above.

In another series of tests Brown used a tachioscope, a machine that is able to present images to a subject at durations of thousandths of a second, much shorter than a normal subject can detect. Brown reports studies of visual sensitivity done on people who had undergone an intensive three-month training in insight meditation. The training seems to have made the meditators more sensitive to perceptual events. For example, in one test a series of lights were flashed for periods lasting just a fraction of a second, some too short to be seen normally. The meditators tested were able to detect much shorter flashes than was possible before they began the training. Their visual detection abilities were also much sharper than were those of people given the same test who had not been in the training course.

In other research, Brown found that some students, classified as 'adept meditators' were able to describe subtle events in perception that are ordinarily unnoticed. For example, in a test where two lights are flashed in a sequence so quickly that they blend into a single flash on an untrained person's perception, these subjects reported distinctly perceiving as separate moments the beginning of the flash, the flash itself, the ending of the flash and the gap before the next flash, perceptual events that usually go by in a blur.

Extensive studies have been done on the EEG patterns of meditators in comparison with those of non-meditators (Pelletier, 1978). The number and complexity of variables involved in most of these studies, including the type of meditation practised, the degree of genuine accomplishment of the practitioner, the philosophical viewpoint of the experimenter, and the physiological variables, make it difficult to come to any general conclusions. It is quite clear, however, that there is a correlation between physiological state as measured by EEG and the meditative state of the subject. Beyond simply showing a correlation between brain activity and meditation, these investigations tend to confirm two of the claims of the meditators. First, alpha activity was not different with eyes open or closed. In fact Buddhist mindfulness-awareness meditation is usually practised with the eyes open since the intention is not to enter a trance state in which one is cut off from the world but rather to sharpen and clarify ones senses. This is further corroborated by the lack of habituation to sensory stimuli, in this case a series of clicks. The normal untrained subject does show habituation — if a tap is dripping it disturbs us at first but then gradually we cease to notice it, city dwellers barely notice the sound of traffic which to a visitor is highly disturbing. The lack of habituation of Zen practitioners during and after a meditation session is a simple confirmation of their claim that their practice makes them more rather than less sensitive to their sensory surroundings.

The Analysis of Experience in Shamatha-Vipashyana Meditation

Since Buddhism does not start from the point of view of an observing self, experience is not analysed from the 'objective' point of view, as if one's own experience were an object outside of oneself, or were the experience of a stranger. Nor is experience analysed purely subjectively, as if it were the make-believe of each individual and had no common elements from person to person. It is the claim of Buddhism that the felt, direct qualities of one's experience are common to all and can be seen and analysed impartially, without prejudice or prejudgment, if there is the intention and the method to do this. At the same time 'impartiality' and 'non-judgment' should not be confused with 'objectivity'.

From the point of view of Buddhist meditation, what is real, all that actually exists, are *dharmas* (Conze, 1970; Late and Napper, 1980; Guenther and Kawamura, 1975). Dharmas are momentary elements of experience, flashing in and out of existence and directly knowable to the cognizing mind, *which is itself one of these momentary dharmas*. Each dharma is not further subdividable; they are the elementary components of experience. Each dharma 'carries its own mark', i.e. it has a defining characteristic which distinguishes it from other dharmas. In fact a dharma should be regarded as *none other* than its defining characteristic. A dharma is not some kind of substance that supports qualities, it simply *is* that quality. Through a variety of interconnected causes and conditions, particular dharmas arise at any moment and are the experienced characteristics at that moment. And a particular moment of experience is, in turn, *nothing other* than this particular conglomeration of dharmas, including the momentary cognizing dharma. All persons, objects and facts can be understood as combinations of elemental dharmas. The analysis of experience into dharmas is known as abhidharma, which literally translates as 'the nature of now'.

There are a number of ways by which the dharmas may be categorized, but one of the most common and fundamental is the division into five groups known as the *skandhas*, or 'heaps': *form, feeling, recognition, formation* and *consciousness*. Each skandha is simply a bundle or a heap of dharmas, and the human personality, as well as the world of objects constructed by perceptual experience, is found to consist simply of a conglomeration of these five heaps, ceaselessly changing from moment to moment. Joining in a natural, automatic, causal process, abiding momentarily and then separating again, the constant turmoil of dharmas gives the appearance of the world as we know it. The skandhas, or heaps of dharmas, are themselves in constant flux as different dharmas enter and leave. In the early schools of Buddhism, the skandhas are regarded as components of the personality of an individual that are continuously present as threads running through every moment of experience (Conze, 1970; Norlha, 1986).

The dharma analysis of the early schools of Buddhism gave rise to a profound understanding of the nature of human perception, and this understanding of perception was the underpinning of all later Buddhist discovery. The analysis of experience into dharmas is considered a necessary first step in discovering the nature of experience and perception. The transition from earlier to later schools of Buddhism should be regarded like the transition from arithmetic to calculus, the later schools building on the insights of the earlier, rather than rejecting them (Guenther, 1972; Klein, 1986).

Analysis of experience into its elementary components, or dharmas, espouses neither the idealistic nor the materialistic view. Dharmas are neither merely ideas of an isolated self nor are they lumps of material stuff existing independently of mind. The view of experience we are presenting here probably comes closer to the 'panexperientialist physicalism' of David Griffin and Alfred North Whitehead (Griffin, 1997a; Whitehead, 1929; 1967) than to either materialism or idealism. Both materialism and idealism assume the mind/matter, subject/object split as givens, whereas these dualities might better be considered historical/cultural artifacts. Dharmas arise and depart from presence prior to the conceptual designations of self and other, inner and outer, mind and matter. And in this view, the dichotomies of self and other, inner and outer, mind and matter are not fundamental realities, exisiting in some 'objective' real world. Rather the dichotomies themselves are artifacts of the process of experience. And, ultimately, even the belief that the dharmas *exist* as real independent entitites leads to serious problems which can only be resolved by the realization that the dharmas, too, are subtly conceptual and ultimately empty of self-existence or substantiality. To go further into this ultimate Buddhist analysis would take us too far afield for the present purposes.

The Five Skandha Description of Momentary Experience

Dharma analysis of experience breaks down each moment of experience into its component dharmas. Having done this, it is, of course, desirable to understand how these dharmas combine into the apparent unity of experience. The contemplative vajrayana tradition of Tibetan Buddhism, specifically the rDzogs-chen[2] teachings, uses the skandha categories in an analysis of how each moment of experience arises within a background of non-dual space–awareness–energy (Kongtrül, 1982; Trungpa, 1978; Hayward, 1987).

The development of a moment of experience is not instantaneous, it develops over a very brief period of time. The duration of an experiential moment has been variously estimated by Buddhists, from approximately 1/500 second (Trungpa, 1978) to 1/75 second (Conze, 1970). This sequential process can be described in five stages corresponding to the five skandhas, culminating in a conscious experience. In this context, rather than static heaps of dharmas, the skandhas could more usefully be regarded as stages in the heaping process by which a moment of dualistic experience — experience *of* an object *by* a separate subject — arises from that non-dual background.

I will now describe the five skandhas as they enter into a moment of experience. First it is important to understand that in this view the skandhas arise as momentary flashes within the non-dual background which has qualities of insight, awareness, and energy, but is *not localized* in space. The sense of being localized in this particular body comes in only during the rapid process of building a moment of perception.

---

[2] rDzogs-chen, Complete Perfection, is taught principally by the Nyingma, or Ancient, school of Tibetan Buddhism, founded by Padmasambhava in the eighth century C.E. These teachings are said to come from the highest level of meditative realization. In the vast compendium of Buddhist philosophy, psychology, and meditative disciplines of the four main schools of Tibetan Buddhism, compiled in the nineteenth century by the great Jamgön Kongtrül, the rDzogs-chen teachings constitute the final stage of nine stages, or 'yanas', of meditative development.

Form (rupaskandha) consists of eleven dharmas. The first ten are the five senses, sight, hearing etc. and the five sense objects, colour, sound etc. The eleventh is form without sensory manifestation, which includes imaginary forms, hallucinations and visions. *Form* is the only skandha which corresponds to the external physical-material world. The other four skandhas correspond to the mental side of the mind/body system. The physical-material world is known as data presented to the senses. However in this case, not only the sense objects themselves such as colour and sound are included, but also the *senses* of seeing, hearing and so on. This reflects the fact that, if we do not forget the role of our own psychophysical organism in the act of perception, then we find that what appears to mind at a moment of perception of an object of sight is that object *together with* the sense of seeing, and so on for the other senses. We never *merely* see a flower, we always experience *seeing* the flower at the same time.

Form is the first activation of the five senses. This is a primitive stage, not by any means *'self*-conscious'. It is a preconscious recognition, or apperception, of patterning. It is without interpretation other than the distinction between 'outside' and 'inside', between 'that' and 'this'. The sixth sense, cognitiveness, is felt as 'this', or 'inside'. The patternings in the five senses, arising from the first contact between the sense organs and sense objects, are felt as 'outside'. This includes the proprioceptive sense of neurology, which is the inner sensation of owning a body: for the primitive sense of 'mind', or cognitiveness, the body perceived through this inner sense, is 'other' or 'outside'.

The second stage of perception is the skandha of *feeling (vedanaskandha)*. Having made the first basic split between 'inside' and 'outside' and having acknowledged, apperceptively, the sensory patternings in the 'outside', there is a reaction of *feeling* towards these patternings. *Feelings* are relative to the survival of the primitive sense of self that has already appeared at the level of *form*, determining what sensory dharmas are attended to. Thus feelings are positive, negative, or neutral, depending on whether the 'outside' patternings are apprehended as supportive, threatening, or neither supportive nor threatening to self.

Feeling is the automatic affective response to form, before any higher conceptual processes enter in. It is a bare reaction of 'pleasant' (what one would like to grasp onto and seems to confirm the nascent sense of 'self', felt at this stage simply as 'this', 'here'), 'unpleasant' (what one would like to reject and threatens to harm 'this'), or 'neutral' (what has no bearing on the continuation of the nascent self). This does not refer to a distinct emotional response, but to a simple positive, negative or neutral evaluation which accompanies cognition of any primary form. While *form* corresponds to the 'physical-material' pole of dualistic experience, and the last three skandhas, three through five, correspond to the 'mental pole', the second skandha, *feeling* connects 'mind' and 'body'. In 'body' it manifests as the inner feeling of the body as pleasurable, painful or neutral, the proprioceptive sense. Feeling manifests in 'mind' as affective arousal, the instinctual response to the basic thingness of the 'outside' and the basic response of 'like' or 'dislike' towards our bodily sensations.

In the third stage, the skandha of *recognition (samjnaskandha)*, feelings refer back to the inside which then reaffirms itself and tries to take charge as a kind of switchboard or central processor, to use the analogy of computers. *Recognition*, also sometimes translated as *discernment*, is the first recognition or discernment of a specific object. It is the beginning of concept formation. It forms the concept of one's 'self' as that 'self' relates to the particular form occupying ones attention. It abstracts the characteristics of any object which has been determined by *feeling* to be of interest to oneself, either positively or negatively, thus enabling one to grasp onto it and hold it in one's field of attention, that is, to draw it into one's world.

This is the first actual cognition of a separate sense of self, together with the first cognition that a perception of a specific object with specific characteristics is taking place, and a grasping onto that object as meaningful. There are primitive judgments involved at this level, judgments of 'near' or 'far', 'large' or 'small', 'strange' or 'familiar', 'looming' or 'receding', 'frightening' or 'relieving'. All of these judgments are in reference to the 'inside', now apprehended as a distinct self, and the 'outside' grasped onto as distinct 'objects' or 'things', but, as yet, without specific characteristics.

The fourth skandha, *formations* or *mental elements (samskaraskandha)* comprises all mental contents other than *feeling* and *recognition*. It comprises the conceptual contents of experience: a variety of positive, negative and indifferent emotions; simple and complex thought patterns as well as systems of thought such as various philosophical, religious, psychological belief systems; and various mental functions and attitudes are all included in this category.

Formation is the stage at which intellect, as naming and meaning interpretation, comes in. It is the level at which complexes or formations of concepts with affects are projected onto the 'outside' together with names. There is recognition of actual objects. A chair is recognized as a chair, with all the connotations of chairness. A chair is a thing to sit on, it is also the thing we first stood on to wash dishes as a proud little boy, it is also an example of a seat, something we offer to our guests, and so on. That voice is the voice of my friend, Nicholas, whom I knew at college, and who first taught me the meaning of emptiness, and so on. All the belief systems we have, philosophical, religious, economic, political, personal and so on, are stored and ready to be applied to a developing perception at the level of *formation*. *Formation* therefore takes its name because it is at this level that the perception is unified into a coherent recognizable thing, a form with a name.

The skandha of *formation* includes positive and negative emotions that are also sometimes referred to as 'wholesome', or 'healthy', and 'unwholesome', or 'unhealthy', factors. The distinction between 'healthy' and 'unhealthy', is not made from the point of view of an externally imposed moralism, but refers to the immediately felt quality of mind, and the direction towards which that felt quality tends. The dharma of 'cheerfulness' brings with it a positive attitude and a tendency to openness. The dharma of 'meanness' brings with it an attitude of depression and a tendency to restriction. The factors taken to be wholesome are simply those which tend towards the realization of egolessness, and the unwholesome factors are those which tend to strengthen the tendency towards ego-fixation. The point is not to make judgments about this, but to see it impartially.

The fourth skandha occurs still below the threshold of what we normally take to be consciousness, that is the dualistic consciousness of the normal waking or dreaming state. The fifth skandha is known as *consciousness (vijnanaskandha)*. In the early schools, this was equated with mind or heart (citta) and referred to that which knows or cognizes the other dharmas. Vijnana was sometimes divided into six consciousnesses depending on which other dharmas arose with it. In that scheme there were five vijnanas corresponding to each of the five senses and a sixth vijnana which cognized the mental dharmas. This sixth vijnana is a rather condensed category, containing the qualities of illumination and clarity of self-cognition as well as the discrimination and 'taking account of' involved in cognition of other. It is also sometimes termed 'heart' to indicate the sense of immediate presence felt as each conglomeration of dharmas arises, abides momentarily, and decays. Later schools separated out these functions to give a much clearer sense of that notoriously tricky notion, consciousness (Guenther, 1989).

At the stage of the skandha of *consciousness* we are, finally, conscious of a thought or a perception. *Consciousness* is a narrative which gives the *formations* a context. It is like a radar beacon which constantly circulates checking out the coherence and meaningfulness of the entire scene. It fills in any gaps it finds with its projections or reasonable hypotheses as to what is there, so that there are no uncertainties. We know we are here in this familiar and recognizable world. Anything which does not fit in is finally excluded at the level of *consciousness*. *Consciousness* keeps up a storyline as to what is going on to provide continuity from moment to moment. Our conscious life follows this story line as far as it is able and so long as no incoherence is able to break through it.

What we normally think of as 'waking consciousness' or 'self-consciousness' is a combination of the fourth and fifth skandhas, but all five skandhas are occurring in every moment of experience. Our attention is normally of such a course grade that we experience the skandhas lumped together in a continuous 'stream of consciousness'.

This then is the process of perception divided into five stages as discovered in the practice of mindfulness-awareness meditation. Notice that affective reaction enters at a very early stage into the formation of the momentary self. Thus, from the point of view of this analysis the attempt of Strawson and other cognitive philosophers to define a self in purely 'cognitive rather than affective' terms is clearly inadequate. Concept is present in the sense of the involvement of images projected by the developing sense of self all the way from the stage of *form* to the stage of *consciousness*. So long as the five skandhas are all stuck together as I have presented them, and experienced as one stream of consciousness, then that stream of consciousness is the end of a long train of inferential perceptions. 'Inferential' perception refers to perception which is mediated by concept, image or word. It is perception of an image of the situation rather than the situation itself. In other words so long as our awareness dwells in the fifth skandha of *consciousness*, then that consciousness itself is the object of each successive moment of perception. We perceive only our narrative of the world and never perceive the world as it is. Under these circumstances, even *form* is experienced inferentially, mediated by concept.

Continuity *versus* Discontinuity

Normally, owing to the coarse degree of perceptual processing of which we are conscious, we experience continuity. But the awareness of finer levels of perceptual processing seen in meditative training shows discontinuity of experience. The apparent continuity of a world of relatively permanent but changing things is put together by consciousness, rather as a movie is seen as continuously changing scenes even though it is in fact a series of still shots.

Between moments of experience of self are gaps in which there is no sense of self or of separateness from what is being experienced. The early Buddhist schools referred to the momentary gaps in the flow of moments mechanically succeeding each other as the appearance of an unconditioned dharma. By this they meant a dharma which is not conditioned at all by previous patterns. It enters in freely and brings with it a sense of freedom from habitual thought. It is not a part of the skandha system. This unconditioned dharma is called 'nirvana', literally 'extinction'. This does not mean the extinction of all experience, but only of the grasping onto the belief that one is a permanent self.

The discovery of discontinuity is capable of resolving some questions in the understanding of the mechanics of perception as well as in the understanding of the spiritual path. As far as spirituality is concerned, it suggests that the wisdom of egolessness is not some state of mind or of being that has to be 'attained' as something foreign to one's present state, nor is it a 'higher' state of being, nor does it belong to another realm outside of this universe. It is a fundamental, ever-present, aspect of one's ordinary being, which is normally covered up due to ignorance and bewilderment, believing in ego's continuity, and which can therefore be uncovered by knowledge and insight.

However discontinuity raises a new question: how is there apparent continuity? If there is no ego, or self, what is it that experiences continuity? How is it that I experience this particular stream of thoughts and emotions as a continuous stream and that I remember previous moments as belonging to me? Beyond this, what is it that aspires to and realizes egolessness? In some sense the tension which arises in one's mind as one contemplates this question is the essence of the spiritual path: if there is no ego, who or what am I, or am I not? For this reason some traditions remained altogether silent on this issue, feeling that to give any answer would simply further the practitioners' clinging to ego. The Buddha remained silent when the philosopher asked such questions, and the Zen Buddhist tradition of Japan, too, remains silent.

However other schools *do* try to answer this question, and one could almost regard the question as the key problem which gave rise to so many different schools in the history of Buddhism. Some early schools, basing their interpretation of experience on dharmas, tried in one way or another to introduce some special dharma which acted as a kind of glue which held together each individual, personal stream of dharmas. But all of these attempts were, in the end, unsatisfactory. Either the special dharma was too vague to have any power to really maintain the sense of continuity, or it was too definite and gave rise in the end to heresies which were accused of reintroducing the idea of a self.

The apparent continuity of experience could perhaps be likened to the apparent continuity of a tornado. The tornado appears to move across the countryside as a unity but is nothing other than the moving pattern of an unceasing flux of air molecules and of whatever debris is drawn up into it. The appearance of a unity comes from the pattern of motion. Likewise, the personality and the apparent continuity of a self may be nothing other than the ceaseless activity of a stream of dharmas held together as a temporary unity by the force of habitual patterns.

The rDzogs-chen teachings, as we have seen, point out that the momentary self, built from the skandha process, arises within unbounded, non-localized openness. This completely open, unbound, and undivided presence is, of course, inaccessible to the methods of dualistic science, to dualistic observation. But, it *is* said to be directly accessible (not as dualistic experience, however), within the gap between two moments of dualistic experience, as spacious and vast, with a quality of peacefulness and brilliance. Within that openness there is primordial non-dual intelligent insight, known as *rigpa* in Tibetan (Reynolds, 1989). The way the arising of perceptions in the skandha process appears to *rigpa* is said to be like reflections, *as* in a mirror, though there *is* no mirror, just the reflections (Laycock, 1998).

Buddhists claim, not that the space of awareness, insight, rigpa, *exists*, in contrast to *not* existing, but rather that the dichotomy of existence or non-existence does not apply here. This vast expanse of openness is full of potentiality, yet contains no forms, dichotomies, or boundaries, therefore it is called 'emptiness' or 'nothingness' in the Buddhist tradition, which should not be confused with nihilistic voidness. It is no *thing*, yet it is, as Zen master, Shunryu Suzuki, wrote,

> . . . something which has no form and no colour — something which exists before all forms and colours appear. This is a very important point. . . . It is absolutely necessary to believe in nothing. But I do not mean voidness. There is something, but that something is something which is always prepared for taking some particular form, and it has some rules, or theory, or truth in its activity (Suzuki,1973).

Within that openness — Suzuki's 'nothing, which is something' — sparks, or flashes, of primordial intelligence continually arise from moment to moment. Such a flash may recognize the non-dual openness within which it arose, and rest back into that. Alternatively there may be an ignoring (*marigpa, ma-* meaning 'not') of the primordial background intelligence, and thus a clinging to the feeling of separate existence, which leads to panic. With the panic, the energy becomes frozen into a first, primitive distinction between self and other. This is the beginning of the first skandha, the skandha of *form*.

It may be worth pointing out at this stage that merely reading a description of the skandhas without direct experience of the process of perception through the practice of SVM can take one only so (not very) far toward understanding that process. It is rather like a colour-blind person trying to understand the difference between red and blue by reading about it, or like a person with no education in tensor calculus trying to decide whether he or she believes in black holes.

Correlation Between the Analysis of Perception in Buddhism and the Sciences

There are correlations between the view of momentary experience presented here and some work in the sciences of mind that does suggest that perception is an active process in which the 'outside world' and the 'self', are to some extent a mutual co-fabrication (Varela *et al.*, 1991); that perception spans a finite duration (Varela *et al.*, 1981; Popper & Eccles, 1981); that our conscious perception and action is affected by emotional bias beyond our conscious control (Dixon, 1981; Merikle and Daneman, 1998); and that it occurs in stages involving an initial perception with some conceptual content, an emotional response, a verbal meaning analysis, and finally consciousness (Rock, 1983; Wilding, 1982). These potential areas of cross-over between Buddhist meditative insight and experimental psychology are related to specific details of a directly observable process and provide suggestions for further research.

We will not, however, find any reference to the non-dual background of primordial insight-energy-awareness in the scientific account of perception/cognition. The sciences have not yet realized the need to take account of first person experience and to train attention to fine time intervals, thus revealing the discontinuity of the perceptual/cognitive process. Furthermore, *rigpa* can only be pointed to, but not literally described, by symbolic means, such as language. Objective science deals essentially in the symbolic representation of experience but does not speak of direct experience itself — which is the only experience we actually know. We might expect that the sciences of mind will be able to clearly delimit the boundaries of the discontinuity of perception, perhaps to the point of the origin of the split between self and world. But we would not expect that the cognitive sciences, with their present dualistic methods and attitudes, will be able to penetrate beyond those boundaries to the unconditioned basis of experience.

However, there may be some scientific evidence suggesting a non-local aspect to awareness, for example in the work on psychokinesis and remote viewing conducted in a number of laboratories (Jahn and Dunne, 1987; Radin, 1997). Although this work is controversial amongst committed materialists, it seems very important to make a truly impartial assessment of it. Proponents of this work claim that the results are robust and repeatable. If this is so, then it creates very serious difficulties for the standard reductionist materialist worldview. And, indeed, these difficulties seem to be a major reason — more, I think, than inadequacy of the experimental method or the strength of the results — for discounting the work (Radin, 1997; Griffin, 1997b). I mention this work not because I believe that the Buddhist analysis needs 'scientific' support. On the contrary, I suggest that the Buddhist view provides a cogent, rational, non-theistic perspective within which the data of so-called 'extra-sensory' perception can be understood and which can at the same time accomodate much of conventionally accepted science. The non-dual perspective presented here, like the pan-experientialist physicalism of Griffin and Whitehead, is capable of accomodating observations like those of Jahn and Dunne and several other laboratories, while not in contradiction with the data of normal science. Such perspectives can provide intelligent alternatives to the spiritually impoverished world-view of reductionist materialism.

Conclusion

In conclusion, the Buddhist theory of mind is based on a disciplined, well-tested and inter-subjectively verifiable method of first-person investigation of experience, and goes far beyond Strawson's string-of-pearls theory. This method indicates that the self is not any kind of solid 'thing', neither a relatively permanent thing, nor a string of momentary things. Rather experience is a discontinuous dynamic process of momentary events in which concatenations of dharmas arise, stay together for a fraction of a second, and then dissipate. The sense of a continuous self arises out of the habitual, mechanical repetition of certain patterns of dharmas, including the patterns that provide the sense of having a physical body. The background intelligence-energy, *rigpa*, within which this process occurs is beyond the boundaries of conventional, conceptual space and time. It is neither mind-stuff, nor matter-stuff, but is primordial to both, having the qualities of openness, energy, awareness and insight. This process can be described in five sequential stages, though one must be careful not to think of these stages as taking place in objective 'time' since the experience of time, like that of space, arises as a high level abstraction out of ordinary dualistic experience. One analogy for the way the space- and time-bound self manifests out of the space- and time-symmetrical background of rigpa is the appearance of a space-binding crystallization pattern out of a space-symmetrical super-cooled fluid (Guenther, 1989).

It is possible, through the practice of shamatha-vipashyana meditation, to join one's awareness with the background, rigpa, while not losing the awareness of a self in its world. This identification with rigpa is known as egolessness. Thus, egolessness is not a state in which there is no sense of self at all. Rather it is a state in which the self is perceived not as a solid permanent thing relative to which one's life should be directed, and which needs to be constantly defended, but as a constant momentary flashing into existence out of a boundless background. Gradual identification with the background, rather than with the illusion of a permanent self, brings a sense of harmony, clarity, wisdom and energy to one's life. Furthermore, the realization of egolessness does not consist of 'getting rid of' the self, but of seeing it as a merely useful practical tool. Therefore movement toward egolessness does not imply withdrawal from the mundane world in the world-denying attitude that has been mistakenly imputed to Buddhism by theistic religious scholars. Rather, because it involves the removal of the delusion of a self separate from the world, it brings one into a more direct and real appreciation of life as it is. Thus, the Buddhist insight into the process of perception is not a mere 'objective' conceptual exercise, but understands and takes responsibility for the implications for living a human life implied by its researches.

References

Brown, D. (1986), in *Transformations of Consciousness*, K. Wilber, J. Engler and D. Brown (Boston, MA: Shambhala Publications).

Conze, E. (1970), *Buddhist Thought in India* (Ann Arbor, MI: University of Michigan Press).

Dixon, N. (1981), *Preconscious Processing* (New York: Wiley & Sons).

Griffin, D. (1997a), 'Panexperientialist physicalism and the mind–body problem', *Journal of Consciousness Studies*, 4, (3), pp. 248–68.

Griffin, D. (1997b), *Parapsychology, Philosophy, and Spirituality: A Postmodern Exploration* (New York: SUNY Press).

Guenther, H. (1972), *Buddhist Philosophy in Theory and Practice* (New York: Penguin).

Guenther, H. (1989), *From Reductionism to Creativity: rDzogs-chen and the New Sciences of Mind* (Boston, MA: Shambhala Publications).

Guenther, H. and Kawamura, L. (1975), *Mind in Buddhist Psychology* (Emeryville, CA: Dharma Publishing).

Hayward, J. (1987), *Shifting Worlds, Changing Minds: Where the Sciences and Buddhism Meet* (Boston, MA: Shambhala Publications).

Jahn, R.G. and Dunne, B.J. (1989), *Margins of Reality: The Role of Consciousness in the Physical World* (New York: Harcourt, Brace, Jovanovich).

James, W. (1961), *Psychology: A Brief Course* (New York: Dover).

Klein, A. (1986), *Knowledge and Liberation* (New York: Snow Lion Publications).

Kongtrül, Jamgön, Lodrö Thaye [Jam mgon Kong sprul blo 'gros mtha' yas] (1982), *The Treasury of Knowledge* [*Shes bya kun khyab mdzod*], 3 vols. (Peking)

Late, R. and Napper, E. (1980), *Mind in Tibetan Buddhism* (Valois, NY: Gabriel).

Laycock, S.W. (1998), 'Consciousness it/self', *Journal of Consciousness Studies*, 5, (2), pp. 141–52.

Lyons, W. (1986), *The Disappearance of Introspection* (Cambridge, MA: MIT Press).

Merikle, P.M. And Daneman, M. (1998), 'Psychological investigations of unconscious perception', *Journal of Consciousness Studies*, 5 (1), pp. 5–18.

Norhla, Lama (1986), in *The Dharma*, Kalu Rinpoche (New York: SUNY Press).

Pelletier, K. (1978), *Toward a Science of Consciousness* (New York: Delta).

Popper, K.R. and Eccles, J.C. (1981), *The Self and Its Brain* (New York: Springer International).

Radin, D. (1997), *The Conscious Universe: The Scientific Truth of Psychic Phenomena* (New York: HarperEdge)

Reynolds, J.M (trans. 1989), *Self-Liberation Through Seeing with Naked Awareness* (Barrytown, NY: Station Hill Press).

Rock, I. (1983), *The Logic of Perception* (Cambridge, MA: MIT Press).

Strawson, G. (1997), '"The self"', *Journal of Consciousness Studies*, **4** (5–6), pp. 405–28. Reprinted in this volume, pp. 1–24.

Suzuki, S. (1973) *Zen Mind, Beginner's Mind* (New York: Weatherhill)

Thrangu, K. (1993), *The Practice of Tranquility and Insight: A Guide to Tibetan Buddhist Meditation* (Boston, MA: Shambhala).

Trungpa, C. (1974), *Vajradhatu Seminary Transcripts, Hinayana-Mahayana, 1973* (Halifax: Vajradhatu Publications).

Trungpa, C. (1978), *Glimpses of Abhidharma* (Boulder, CO: Prajna Press).

Trungpa, C. (1995), *The Path is the Goal, A Basic Handbook of Buddhist Meditation* (Boston, MA: Shambhala Publications).

Varela, F.J., Thompson, E. and Rosch, E. (1991), *The Embodied Mind: Cognitive Science and Human Experience* (Boston, MA: MIT Press).

Varela, F., Toro, A., Roy, John E. and Schwartz, E. (1981), 'Perceptual framing and cortical alpha rhythm', *Neurophysochologia*, **19** (5), pp. 675–86.

Whitehead, A.N. (1929), *Process and Reality* (New York: Free Press).

Whitehead, A.N. (1959), *Symbolism: Its Meaning and Effect* (New York: Putnam).

Whitehead, A.N. (1967), *Science and the Modern World* (New York: Free Press).

Wilding, J. M. (1982), *Perception: from Sense to Object* (London: Hutchinson).

Steven W. Laycock

Consciousness It/Self

There is no place to seek the mind;
It is like the footprints of the birds in the sky.
(Robert Sohl, in Sohl & Carter, 1970, p. 27)

For better or for worse, I find myself in the company of the 'misers' of Galen Strawson's[1] portrayal who, in response to the question, 'Is there such a thing as the self?'
rejoin: 'Well, there is *something* of which the sense of the self is an accurate representation, but it does not follow that there is any such thing as the self' (Strawson, p. 6;
italics original). Far from representing a form of 'metaphysical excess' (p. 5), the
rejoinder seems faithfully and reliably phenomenological. We need not assume that
reflection ('self'-reflection) is mere fabrication, or that it *crucially* distorts the thematic posit that funds our sense of self. The focus, recognition and contextual sensitivity that condition perception may, and admittedly do, limit and modify the activity
of reflection as well. Observation disturbs the observed. And likewise, reflection may
well compromise its object. But the product of this 'compromise', the object *as disturbed*, the reflective posit *as distorted*, is nonetheless 'there', for reflection. If the
way a given object appears to us is a function of our perspectival insertion into the
visible world, we need not deny that the world still appears to us in just this way. And
analogously, our 'sense of self' may represent — in fact, *faithfully* represent — the
resultant 'distortion', but it would be a breach of logic to infer from this that our
'sense of self' therefore represents a *self* untouched by distortion, an independent,
'undistorted' self. Indeed, if reflection distorts, we would have no reflective access to
an undistorted self, and would thus have no phenomenological warrant for assuming
its existence. *Pace* Strawson, however, the 'something' represented by our 'sense of
self' is not some *thing*. It is not 'as much a *thing* or *object* as any . . . grain of salt'
(p. 21), but rather, as we shall see, an atmospheric haze, or at best, an adventitious
'sheen'.

Be this as it may, however, the reflective representation, faithful or disloyal, could
be a disclosure *of the self* only if it were possible to speak of consciousness it/self;
only, that is, if it rendered the 'self' of consciousness it/self. And this, I propose, it
patently cannot do. Merleau-Ponty affirms that 'consciousness has a "*punctum cae-
cum*" . . .' (1962, p. 247), a blind spot. The transparentism which I adopt here is rooted

---

[1] All references to 'Strawson' in the current article are to Galen Strawson's keynote paper in this volume (pp. 1–24).

in Buddhist insights according to which consciousness does not 'have', but rather *is*, a 'blind spot' in the sense that it in no way appears to 'itself'. And this, of course, engenders a cascade of implications with regard to the nature of consciousness and its alliance with 'things' — the 'things' of neurophysiology (neural events and processes) and the mental 'things' of Strawson's ontology (i.e. selves). Strawson's extraordinarily sensitive description of the 'fundamental experience of consciousness' as 'one of *repeated returns into consciousness from a state of complete, if momentary, unconsciousness*' (p. 18; italics original) is, as he recognizes, remarkably consonant with the Buddhist theory of *bhavanga* (cf. his footnote 27), the continuous discontinuity (or discontinuous continuity) of experience that constitutes the transtemporal unity of our conscious lives. If it is true, as Strawson claims, that 'conscious thought has the character of a (nearly continuous) series of radically disjunct irruptions into consciousness from a basic substrate of non-consciousness', if '[i]t keeps banging out of nothingness', if 'it is a series of comings to' (p. 18), we should expect, not that each such 'bang' would be a pearl-like self (cf. p. 20), but that, in principle, no 'pearl' can represent consciousness it/self. No 'pearl' in the diachronic string is, then, self-conscious. No 'pearl' is, or has, a self.

While the eye is, of course, a vital condition of visibility, perennial Buddhist wisdom conveys that the eye cannot see itself. Indeed, '[e]ven the sharpest sword cannot cut itself; the finger-tips cannot be touched by the same finger-tips. *Citta* [mind] does not know itself' (Murti, 1987, pp. 317–18). Thus, as Dōgen affirms, '[s]ince there is no mind in me, when I hear the sound of raindrops from the eave, the raindrop is myself'.[2] This is not, of course, a postulation of identity. As Wittgenstein discerned, 'to say of two things that they are identical is nonsense, and to say of one thing that it is identical with itself is to say nothing at all' (1974, 5.5303, p. 52). Dōgen is not putting forward the implicitly dualistic claim that the raindrop (one thing) is identical with the self (another), but is rather giving voice to the abrogation of dualism. For the eye, there is no eye. For the mind, there is no mind. And for the subject there is no *subject*, and consequently no counterposed *object*. For enlightened perception, the raindrop is not, then, an object *identical* with the self. It is rather *non-different*. For there is, and in principle can be, nothing, no thematizable mark or feature, in virtue of which subjectivity can be distinguished from objectivity.

Dōgen is not, then, positing the Self as a Great Object, a great *One* that absorbs or sublates the multiplicity of narrowly circumscribed selves. To count, even to *one*, assumes a duplicity of counter and counted. Thus, Dōgen's radical non-dualism is incompatible with the postulation of reality as unitary or single, as a 'uni/verse', a bounded *whole* delivered to our apprehension in a single (*uni-*) turn (*versus*), and is incompatible, *a fortiori*, with the perception of this purported unity as identical with the self. Berg expresses a dimension of Dōgen's insight in his assertion that 'I'm not here so I see everything . . .' (Berg, 1991, p. 31). But this 'everything' is neither a uni/verse nor *a* (one) universal Self. The eighth-century Ch'an teacher, Chih of Yun-chu, proclaimed: 'There is seeing, but nothing is seen'. A monk queried: 'If there is nothing seen, how can we say there is any seeing at all?' Said Chih: 'In fact there is no trace of seeing'. The monk inquired: 'In such a seeing, whose seeing is it?' In Chih's response: 'There is no seer, either' (Suzuki, 1956, p. 207). Egolessness (Pāli: *anatta*;

---

[2] Quoted in Kotoh, 1987, p. 206.

Sanskrit: *anatman*) prompts the question, 'Where is this "I"? What does it look like?' (Suzuki, 1981, p. 115). And an expectable Buddhist response is that it 'looks like' nothing at all.

The 'I', understood — not *à la* Sartre — as a transcendent *Gestalt* of states, actions and qualities, the objectified 'outside' of consciousness, but as the 'seer', the agency (if not the agent) whereby being is disclosed, is in no way present to our intuition. In response to Shen-hsiu's postulation of the mirror-likeness of the mind (*hsin ju ming ching t'ai*), Hui-neng (CE 638–713), the sixth ancestral teacher of the *Ch'an* tradition, countered that there never was a mind-mirror (*hsin ching i fei t'ai*). The reciprocal repulsion of these diptych deposits is, however, impelled by a merely superficial contradiction. Probing beneath the surface, we find not only compatibility, but co-entailment. For if mind (*hsin*) is, indeed, like a mirror (*ching*), or like a mirror-stand (*ching t'ai*), if consciousness is, indeed, like the eye, then nothing reflected, nothing perceived, is 'itself'. *For* the mirror, there *is* no mirror.[3] The point remains the same if, contrary to the prevailing tradition of interpretation, the 'stand' (*t'ai*) of 'mirror--stand' is given the accent. On this reading, Shen-hsiu claims that the *stand*, or stance, the modality of perspectival insertion, and not the mirror, is the analogue of mind. On the concomitant reading, Hui-neng would contribute the insight that views, perspectives, modes of givenness, can be recognized *as such* only by effecting a reflective withdrawal of engagement. *For* the stand, there is no stand. From 'within' a given modality of perspectival engagement, there is neither *within* nor *without*. A per/spective is *seen-through*, not *seen*. A 'perspective' is not a *perspective* for itself, but only for the 'other', the reflecting consciousness. And in this way, 'the concept of a non-unified or decentered (the usual terms are *egoless* or *selfless*) cognitive being is the cornerstone of the entire Buddhist tradition' (Varela *et al.*, 1992, p. xviii). Consciousness is 'decentered' in its being perpetually displaced beyond direct figural objectification. And the typical, and unenlightened, reaction to decentering, 'self'-effacement, impelled by the presumption that there *must* be a consciousness 'itself', is narcissistic. In Dillon's words, 'we find the familiar figure of philosophical Narcissus still absorbed in his own reflection . . . Narcissus has always sought his reflection outside himself. He has always sought what he lacks to be himself in the Other that is beyond himself: Narcissus has always been decentered' (1991, p. x). Merleau-Ponty writes, 'I am a self-presence that is an absence from self' (1962, p. 250). Thus, '[v]ision . . . is the means given me for being absent from myself, for being present at the fission of Being from the inside . . .' (1964, p. 186). The 'depersonalization' of which Strawson speaks (1997, p. 418) is thus a fundamental and ineluctable status, not a contingent and optional modality. Consciousness is hopelessly anonymous.

The mirror, understood not as a quasi-opaque visibility, another object in the room made present and visible by its frame (or perhaps its stand), the glare and discoloration of its glass, the irregularities of its tain, but as the pure functioning of mirror[*ing*], is constituted precisely by its having no 'self'. It 'itself' cannot be seen. And for it, from its 'own' perspective, there is neither ownness nor perspecting. Or as Levin puts it, 'to be "possessed by" the visible is to be a *cogito* dispossessed: an ego not in total possession of itself; an ego not totally present to (for) itself' (1991, p. 69). The mind-

[3] For a fuller exposition of the narrative implications of the gāthās of She-hsiu and Hui-neng, see Laycock, 1994a.

mirror of the Buddhist tradition is not merely lacking a few degrees in 'total possession of itself', it is totally lacking in self-possession. Yet this momentous absence is constitutive for the mirror. For the mirror, *to be* is exactly *not* to 'own' a self. As Dews explains, '[t]his is because, however many times it is reduplicated, the image of the observer seeing him- or herself, which appears in the mirror, must always remain the object of an uncaptured *pre-existing gaze*' (1988, pp. 87–8). It is not that the mirror is 'devoid' of self, that a void remains where the self *could*, perhaps *should*, be. It is not that the mirror has been dispossessed of that which is most intimately its 'own'. Rather, it is essentially, necessarily, originally selfless. Thus, Buddhist transparentism cannot be assimilated to a subject/object dualism, the subject, or 'self', being an unspeakable residue after all objectivity has been excluded. To be sure, as Merleau-Ponty tells us, '[a] Cartesian does not see *himself* in the mirror; he sees a dummy, an "outside" . . .' (1964, p. 170). But this is not to say that the mirror 'itself' is the self posed against the objective other. *For* the mirror, there *is* no mirror 'itself'.

There is in Sartre's early thinking a similar 'transparentist' strain — though it sits uneasily beside a disrupting conception of conscious 'ectoplasm', the conception of a subtle, ghostly presence that imbues consciousness and conditions its visibility to reflection. Consciousness is 'all lightness, all translucence' (1972, p. 42). But at the same time, it offers to 'impure and conniving' reflection — a modality of reflection 'which effects . . . a passage to the infinite' (p. 64) and thus 'affirms *more* than it knows' (p. 65) — an 'outside', a certain indistinctness, a spectral haze, 'as if interiority closed upon itself and proffered us only its outside; as if one had to 'circle about' it in order to understand it. . . .' (p. 84). Phyllis Morris helpfully discriminates transparency from translucency (cf. 1992, p. 105), citing the *Larousse* definition of the latter term as 'that which allows light to pass without at the same time permitting one to see objects clearly through its thickness: frosted glass is translucid'.[4] A later version offers a somewhat more abstract, less nuanced, definition: 'Said of a substance which allows light to pass, but through which one does not neatly distinguish objects'.[5] The translucent is, to some degree, in some respect, opaque. It is 'impure', muddied, only partially capable of transmitting illumination, as if an otherwise crystalline consciousness were pervaded by a tincture of color or discernible quality that offered to reflecting consciousness 'something', however subtle, to *see*. 'Indistinctness', this qualitative pervasion, 'is interiority seen from the outside; or, if one prefers, indistinctness is the degraded projection of interiority' (1972, p. 85).

Sartre was not himself perfectly lucid about the distinction, and seems to have modulated unconsciously from a transparentist to an ectoplasmic (translucentist) conception of consciousness. Yet, *pace* Sartre, while consciousness may be 'pure translucidity', it is, nonetheless 'pure' — and a merely translucid consciousness is 'impure', clouded and diffused in some degree by a permeating positivity of phenomenal quality. Moreover, the admitted shift in his thinking from an anonymous consciousness to a conception of [*con*]sciousness — a knowing (*scientia*) ineluctably accompanied by (with: *con*-) a non-positional awareness of the event of knowing

[4] Translucidité: qui laisse passer la lumière, sans permettre toutefois de voir clairment, les objets à travers son épaisseur: les verres dépolis sont translucides (quoted from *Larousse Classique*,1957, in Morris,1992, p. 116, n. 8).

[5] Se dit d'une substance qui laisse passer la lumière, mais au travers de laquelle on ne distingue pas nettement les objets (*Larousse,*1979, p. 1923).

'itself' — is at least a movement *from* a certain transparentism. Sartre insists that the least hint of content, a wisp of discoloration 'in' consciousness, 'would divide consciousness'. It 'would slide into every consciousness like an opaque blade'. It would 'tear consciousness from itself', and would be 'the death of consciousness' (p. 40). And if '[a]ll is clear and lucid in consciousness . . .' (p. 40), then, in particular, there should be no ectoplasmic haze, no indeterminate qualitative pervasion, no 'matter', no *hylè*, no matter how subtle. And even supposing the ectoplasmic conception were primary, Sartre is not spared inconsistency. For the translucid is transparent in one respect and opaque in another. If consciousness is translucid, it admits of 'respects', thus becoming multiperspectival, and thus exceeding in its *being* any particular *appearing*. If transcendence is invariance (thus in/difference) across the varying and different modes of appearance (respects), then consciousness would be transcendent. Yet if consciousness, voracious for presence, is like '[t]he spider which draws things into its web, coats them with its own drivel, and slowly swallows, reducing them to its own nature' (cf. Cumming, 1965, p. 19), it preys upon the different and can hardly be 'indifferent' to differing manifestations of presence.

If, then, consciousness is present to itself, it is self-predatory. Yet this macabre feast is necessarily partial. We may not yet have rid ourselves of 'that primitive illusion . . . according to which to know is to eat — that is, to ingest the known object, to fill oneself with it (*Erfüllung*), and to digest it ("assimilation")' (Sartre, 1971, pp. 258–9), but to the extent that consciousness is 'itself' transcendent, to the extent then, that it *has* an 'itself', consciousness as reflectively known 'remains in the same place, indefinitely absorbed, devoured, and yet indefinitely intact, wholly digested and yet wholly outside, as indigestible as stone . . . the "digested indigestible ". . .' (p. 739). But a consciousness which submits to 'the absolute law of consciousness for which no distinction is possible between appearance and being' (1972, p. 63) cannot, in principle, display itself in a manifold (or even a duality) of 'respects'. Consciousness is the 'identity of appearance and existence' (Sartre, 1971, p. 17). It is 'pure "appearance" in the sense that it exists only to the degree to which it appears' (p. 17). To whatever extent it appears, it appears exactly *as it is*. It cannot appear in alternative 'ways'. And if it be suggested that transparency and opacity are second-order traits, and do not, then characterize the 'itself' of consciousness, we would have, not a phenomenology, but a metaphysics of consciousness. I suggest, then, that we take the early transparentism seriously. It is admittedly a recessive trait in Sartre's thinking (and a dominant trait in Buddhist thought). But it is undeniably *there* — and, I believe, arguably preferable. Invoking Emerson, we are not content with a 'smallminded' accusation of inconsistency. Sartre's recessive transparentism is rather to be honoured for its revolutionary disruption of phenomenological method.

In the *Transcendence*, Sartre attempts to reconcile the utter transparency of consciousness with its presence to reflection by positioning the two, respectively, in the arms of an ostensible distinction between the 'inside' and the 'outside' of consciousness. Granted that 'an absolute interiority never has an outside' (1972, p. 84), yet the psychic, 'the transcendent object of reflective consciousness' (p. 71), *is* its outside. If this doublet of depositions is not to lapse into logical chaos, the 'outside', the indeterminate shimmer, of consciousness, must be comparable to the glare which renders an otherwise transparent pane of glass visible. What is observed in reflection is not a ghostly mist which suffuses consciousness, but a merely superficial glint. To the extent that the psychic (the 'glint') is an appearance *of consciousness*, consciousness could not be intrinsically 'empty' and transparent. Outside has invaded inside. And to the extent that the psychic is adventitious, reflection, though it retrieves the surface glare, would nonetheless be incapable of apprehending consciousness 'itself'.

The ego, for Sartre, is a *Gestalt* comprised of such external 'glints', a configuration of states, actions and qualities (we might prefer 'dispositions') that display their superficiality to an 'impure' reflecting consciousness incapable of confining itself to the immediate given. The excess of posit over intuition that characterizes 'impurity' entails more than a certain temporal dilation that delivers the objects of reflection to consciousness as perduring despite their punctal immediacy, their momentariness. It represents a confusion of 'glint' and transparency, a willingness to attribute *to pre-reflective consciousness* what belongs properly only to reflection. We need not assume that reflection fabricates its subject-matter. Reflection need not be a species of hallucination. But as refraction is distinct from the pure transparency of glass, so the psychic is distinct from consciousness. It is an adventitious dance of presence available only to reflection. Sartre tells us that the 'self' of reflective self-consciousness is ejected from consciousness 'like some noisy visitor' (1984, p. 324). I would rather say that prereflective consciousness has no self to 'eject'. Reflection thematizes exactly what is *not* consciousness, and cannot bring to presence that which *is*. And since reflection disrupts the immediate life of prereflective consciousness, and recaptures it only subsequent to this disruption, we must credit Derrida's remark that '[a] more or less argot translation of the *cogito*' would be: 'I am therefore dead'. And '[t]his can only be written' (1986, p. 92). Reflection feeds only upon the past, upon the husks of experience that have elapsed, lapsed, rendered up their vitality and become hollow form. The 'self' thematized in reflection, the agency thus recaptured, is lifeless. It has no voice. And reflection can only inscribe the site of a once-living experience. Thus, in Blanchot's consonant affirmation, '[w]hen the Cartesian "I think, therefore I am" is written it is, in effect, rewritten as "I think, therefore I am not".' (1973, p. 99.) Or Trinh thi Minh-hà remarks, '[t]o see one's double is to see oneself dead' (1989, p. 22). Reflection kills. Or it trades in corpses. The living heart of consciousness is empty. It embraces no self, and thus has no self-presence to offer. It follows, then, that the ego, as the overall configuration of the psychic, as the seeming, but impossible, 'outside' of consciousness, is not the self *of consciousness*. The shimmer of the psychic is like the lines of a sketch. But this sketch is not a sketch *of consciousness*. For consciousness is strictly invisible to reflection. The glare serves to locate the glass. But it is an *index*, not a *part*, of the glass. Otherwise, if it were, in some sense, an aspect *of the glass* (as distinct from its transparency), then consciousness (the 'glass') would be possessed of a perspectival depth, a density incompatible with the identity of being and appearing.

The Sartrean ego 'is a virtual locus of unity' (1972, p. 80). It *is* a unity, rather than *posessing* unity. Strawson's self, 'thought of as single in the way in which a single marble . . . is single . . .' (Strawson, p. 8), seems, conversely, to *possess* unity, without *being* a unity. The Sartrean ego is complex (or *is*, rather, a complexity). But it is doubtful, in this case, that 'the experience of radical complexity . . . clearly depends on a prior sense of the mental self as synchronically single', that ' "multiple" is a characterization that is applied to something that must have already presented as single in order for the characterization to be applied at all', as Strawson (p. 13) asserts. The ego is rather like a melody. 'The unity here comes from the absolute indissolubility of the elements which cannot be conceived as separated, save by abstraction' (Sartre, 1972, p. 73). And 'it is useless to presuppose an X which would serve as a support for the different notes' (p. 73). 'Such an X would, by definition, be indifferent to the psychic qualities it would support. But the ego . . . is never indifferent to its states; it is "compromised" by them' (p. 74). The ego is 'compromised' by its elements in the same way that a configuration of pebbles is fundamentally modified by addition and deletion. Four stones 'form' a rectangle. Add one, and the emergent *Gestalt* is a pentagon. Remove one, and we see a triangle. *What* is seen is not indifferent to its elements. And beyond the elements, there is not, in addition, some mysterious 'extra' thing, an 'X' reposing in absolute singularity beyond the multiplicity of its elements. And likewise, the Sartrean ego is simply the inextricable being-together of the states, actions and qualities that constitute it. It *is* a unity, without being a 'thing' that *has* unity.

Sartre, of course, is not an unqualified Cartesian. His antisubstantialism dispatches this possibility. The for-itself is a 'non-substantial absolute' (1971, p. 17). And his characterization of the in-itself as being '*what* it is', being, that is, identical with its attributes both collectively and severally — 'the yellow of the lemon . . . *is* the lemon' (p. 257) — completes his repudiation of substance. The in-itself and the for-itself are not separate Cartesian substances. Nor is consciousness in any sense some[*thing*] that stands in a relation of duality to the in-itself. It is rather the absence (or better: the evacuation) of being. And being-in-itself, finally, is not wholly devoid of self. Rather, '[i]t is this self. It is itself so completely that the perpetual reflection which constitutes the self is dissolved in an identity. . . . In fact being is opaque to itself precisely because it is filled with itself. This can be better expressed by saying that *being is what it is*' (p. 28). The in-itself is 'glued to itself'. It inheres 'in itself without the least distance', and is thus 'an immanence which can not realize itself' (p. 27). Transparency implies the transitive deferral of selfhood. To *see* consciousness ('itself') is to see *through* it. Its 'self' *is* this deferral. Reflective consciousness effaces 'itself' in the face of prereflective consciousness of the world; and prereflective consciousness effaces 'itself', in turn, in the face of the world. Only one 'face', one manifestation, remains for both. The (ostensibly) 'two' cannot be distinguished. The transparent is not an intuitive presence, but rather the condition for the phenomenal opacity of being-in-itself. But it is not clear how being can be characterized as 'opaque', if not by contrast to an equally phenomenal transparency which Sartre's postulation of 'the noema in the noesis; . . . the inherence in itself without the least distance' (p. 27) rules out. Without reflective distantiation, reflection resolves into opacity. And from the standpoint of reflection, 'distance' vanishes. In Sartre's quasi-mythical formula, '[e]verything happens as if, in order to free the affirmation *of* self from the heart of being, there is necessary a decompression of being' (pp. 27–8). Self-presence, the 'affirmation *of* self', 'supposes that an impalpable fissure has slipped into being . . .' (p. 124). Levinas forwards the same point: 'In the identity of self-presence — in the silent tautology of the prereflexive — lies an avowal of difference between the same and the same, a disphasure, a difference at the heart of intimacy' (1991, pp. 212–3). But if 'presence is an immediate deterioration of coincidence . . .' (Sartre, 1971, p. 124), it would be utterly undetectable, since absorption into the opaque is indiscriminable from the interposition of a wholly transparent distance, the fissuring of being. If being 'fissures', we could not notice it. Or at least we could not discriminate the opening of a fault in being from the pervasion of consciousness by an ectoplasmic haze.

In Corless' quip, 'Descartes said, "I think therefore I am", but Buddhism replies, "Think again".' (1989, p. 125.) Sartre did, in fact, 'think again', and discerns that 'the consciousness which says *I Think* is precisely not the consciousness which thinks' (1972, p. 45). This reflective 'synthesis of two consciousnesses, one of which is consciousness *of* the other' (p. 44) is 'detotalized', ruptured. Sartre, no less than Buddhism, would reject Valéry's assumption that '[b]etween what I say and what I hear myself say, no exteriority, no alterity, not even that of a mirror seems to interpose itself . . . The [interior] voice . . . can accomplish the circular return of the origin to itself'.[6] For Valéry, interior speech is '[l]ike a closed circuit' and is 'similar to the snake biting its tail'.[7] But in a rumination more consonant with Sartre's persuasion, 'Who speaks, who listens? It is not exactly the same . . . The existence of the speech from self to self is the sign of a *cut*.'[8] In reflection, consciousness is severed, breached. And to this extent, the ventriloquism of Sartre's reflective syn-thesis is Derridean. 'Do not forget,' admonishes Derrida, 'that you are the nucleus [*le noyau*] of a rupture.' (1978, p. 67.) In Dews' explication, '[t]here is no domain of 'phenomenological silence', of intuitive self-presence prior to the representational, and therefore divisive, function of language' (1988, p. 19).[9] While I agree with Strawson that the self is more than a 'grammatical error', and thus with his rejection of Kenny's (1988) proposal that ' "the self" is a piece of philosopher's nonsense consisting in a misunderstanding of the reflexive pronoun' (p. 4; quoted by Strawson, p. 1), the ostensible representation of consciousness to 'itself' in reflection, or rather its dis/placement, is effected, as Sartre sees, by a certain 'saying'.

The projected affirmation, 'I Think', on the part of the reflecting consciousness which merely *says* 'I Think', but does not think — or which, rather, is represented as saying so, since, unthinking, it is also mute — is an echo, the reflection (or re/flexion) of a primal institution of voice. Ventriloquism is the comportment of 'a consciousness which imprisons itself in the world in order to flee from itself' (1972, p. 80), thus projecting upon the *I Think* 'a degraded and bastard spontaneity, which magically preserves its creative power even while becoming passive' (p. 81). The *cogito* is thus 'an ontological puppet, whose inventor [i.e., Descartes] at the same time sketched a new figure of the philosopher as transcendental-talking ventriloquist . . .' (Granel, 1991, p. 148). Thus, '[c]ogito means everything, except *I think*' (Henry, 1991, p. 116). Sartre assumes, by contrast, that prereflective consciousness imbibes an exalted and legitimate spontaneity, an authentic originality of which the reflective representation

---

[6] Quoted in Derrida, 1982, p. 127.

[7] Valéry, *Cahiers* 24, 1940, quoted in Derrida, 1982, p. 287.

[8] Valéry, *Cahiers* 7, 1920, p. 615, quoted in Derrida, 1982, p. 189.

[9] The self-referential pronouns of Vietnamese, for example, are inextricably bound up with the social relationship in which one stands with respect to others. There is no transcontextually invariant 'I'. Rather, Vietnamese offers a suite of self-referential pronouns which, at best, we could translate: *I-as-your-brother, I-as-your-uncle, I-as-your-father*, etc. There is no self-reference independent of other-reference, and, I maintain, the very conception of 'self' that subordinates this curious linguistic phenomenon is reticular and relational, not monadic and unitary, certainly not marble- or pearl-like. The Vietnamese self is breached — one might say fragmented — in virtue of the manifold ways in which it is referred to. Cf. Laycock (1994b).

is but a faded copy. But originality is lost in the reflective synthesis. Not only does the presumptive 'original' impress its outlines upon the reflective representation, but representation, in turn, determines and informs its object, the 'original', at least to the extent that reflection can only recapture an elapsed event of thinking, a discarded husk, and not the live upsurge of present and engaged consciousness.

Reflection can never be strictly simultaneous with its posit. And as co-determinants, reflection and 'original' mirror each other without primacy.[10] As Trinh thi Minh-hà confirms, '[n]o primary core of irradiation can be caught hold of . . .' Indeed, '[i]n this encounter of I with I, the power of identification is often such that reality and appearance merge while the tool itself becomes invisible' (1989, p. 22). In reflection, as in prereflective consciousness, the mind-mirror 'becomes invisible'. There is neither primary reality nor a merely apparent representation, but the endless free fall of reflection within reflection swallowed up in the 'abyss' of the *mise-en-abîme*. 'There are,' as Magliola tells us, 'things like reflecting pools, and images, an infinite reference from one to the other, but no longer a source, a spring. There is no longer a simple origin. For what is reflected is split *in itself* and not only as an addition to itself of its image. The reflection, the image, the double, splits what it doubles.' (1986, p. 9.) We cannot, then, accept Nozick's view that '[t]he self which is reflexively referred to is synthesized in the very act of reflexive self-reference' (1981, p. 91), since what is 'synthesized' in reflection is not the self, nor even a consciousness *of* the self, but the consciousness of an intimate, but still alterior, 'other'. There is no genuine 'self'-reference.

In *Being and Nothingness*, Sartre proposes an extraordinary analysis of consciousness — a proposal made all the more remarkable by the devilish difficulty of 'defining' this elusive term. As consciousness of the very terms in which a purported definition would be couched, consciousness drops back, eludes capture. 'What is consciousness?' can only be answered by 'Consciousness is not a "what".' It cannot itself be subsumed under a kind of thing. It is rather the condition of there being, for us, any kind of thing at all. And besides, consciousness has no 'itself'. There *is* no 'consciousness *itself*' to be defined. Sartre's analysis ingeniously takes advantage of precisely this perplexity. Consciousness is analysed as an event of differing, repulsion, dis-identification: nihilation, the 'making-nothing' of plenary being-in-itself, its 'decompression', that amounts to its internal disintegration, 'an expanding destructuring of the in-itself . . .' (1971, p. 133). Nihilation is thus the institutive event of '[s]ubjectivity, as the absolute other of everything that is other than it, subjectivity in the modern sense, as a realm of pure, uncontaminated, transparent interiority . . .' (Madison, 1990, p. 30). Consciousness is not the subject term of a relation of differing, something different, a substance that differs. It is rather the very event of differing. And its relationship to 'what' it *is* — its essence, or in the idiom of the *Transcendence*, the ego — is that of transcendence, surpassing, not that of subsumption. Its elusiveness, its perpetual slipping out from under any categorial imposition, is not a hindrance to definition. It is rather definitive of consciousness. Consciousness is defined as indefinable. Its essence follows it like the wake of a ship. It cannot simply *be* what it is. The 'glint' is no longer simultaneous with consciousness. And in becoming past, the self has sacrificed its life. Death has interposed itself between con-

---

[10] A more nuanced critique of Sartre's presumption of primacy or originality on the part of pre-reflective consciousness is presented in Laycock (1989).

sciousness and its wake. Consciousness, as perpetual transcendence, is a continual process of dying to 'itself'. The ego or essence, the 'what', of consciousness is like the lifeless, calcified deposit of the living coral, or like the dead skin sloughed off by a live snake. The self is not what consciousness *is*, but what it *was*. Every attempt to surmount consciousness, to fix it, through reflection, in its essence, succeeds only in clutching at ashes. Live consciousness is never what its 'self' is.

Sartre assumes that we can never be in a position reflectively to *say* 'I am consciousness, but I am unconscious of being conscious'. The 'position' we assume in order to *say* 'I am conscious' is *already* reflective. We *already* know that we know or we would be unable authentically to *say* that we know. And to this extent, Sartre acknowledges this postulate of Cartesian self-lucidity: to know is to know that one knows. He insists that 'if my consciousness were not consciousness of being consciousness of the table, it would then be consciousness of the table without consciousness of being so. In other words, it would be a consciousness ignorant of itself, an unconscious — which is absurd' (1971, p. 11). Sartre has, however, given away too much to Descartes. For to be in a position to *say* that I know is precisely *no longer* to know. We can never be in a (reflective) position to say that we *are* conscious — only that we *have been* conscious. Sartre insists that it is entirely possible — indeed, predominantly actual — to know without being in a position to *say* that we know, but he does not abandon, but rather modalizes the simultaneous knowing of knowing co-occurrent with positional knowing. If it were exceptionlessly true that consciousness entails consciousness *of* consciousness, each act of consciousness would then set off an infinite iteration: consciousness of . . . of . . . of . . .   But Sartre's discrimination of positional from non-positional consciousness will not permit this regress to begin. Roquentin, the diarist of Sartre's *Nausea*, writes: 'I *was* the root of the chestnut tree'. And to this extent Sartre seems to express a certain transparentism. But this is immediately qualified: 'Or rather I was entirely conscious of its existence. Still detached from it — since I was conscious of it — yet lost in it, nothing but it' (1964, p. 131).

For Sartre, to be *positionally* consciousness is to be *non-positionally* conscious of being *positionally* conscious. Formally considered, any modalization of consciousness would serve the same end. The specific conception of *non-positional* consciousness is not indispensable. But what makes it *true* that to be positionally conscious is to be —-ly conscious of being positionally conscious? Sartre clearly assumes that something of this form *is* true. He assumes, more specifically, that consciousness appears *to itself* in the very act of being conscious of the world — not, of course, as a figural objectivity, but as a background presence that 'haunts' the act. 'Subjectivity', in Henry's depiction, 'is the pathetic immediation of appearing as auto-appearing, such that, without this pathetic grasp of appearing in its original appearing to itself, no appearing . . . would ever appear' (1991, p. 116). Non-positional self-awareness, Sartre's 'prereflective *cogito*', assumes that, in 'auto--appearing', something appears. This non-positional consciousness (of) consciousness (to display Sartre's suggestive iconography) is a consciousness, not of the direct 'posit' installed by a 'positing' of consciousness, but of the background (ontological) 'presupposition' of consciousness. In the non-positional mode, consciousness relegates 'itself' to the background. Its self-presence, thus 'itself', is disclosed as an ectoplasmic haze at the margin of the field. But the untenability of this view is patent. First, we must wonder why the 'self' of consciousness disclosed in the non-positional self-awareness of the act is confined to the peripheral region of the field. Is consciousness *itself* no more than a marginal awareness? Or more poignantly, is the direct presentation of a figural object not equally an enactment of consciousness *itself*? If the 'itself' of consciousness is not displayed in positional consciousness, and if the background presentation of positional consciousness is, indeed, a presentation of consciousness *itself*, then non-positional consciousness cannot be a display of consciousness *itself*. Self-presence is not, then, intrinsic to consciousness. But if self-presence suffuses consciousness like milk that modifies the presentation of coffee, but remains, nonetheless, distinct no matter how well mixed, or rather, like a haze that modulates our perception of the environment without in any way being identical with the space that it inhabits, then a non-positional consciousness (of) the 'self--presence' of consciousness is in no way a consciousness of consciousness *itself*. Moreover, the qualitative modification of a transparent medium merely renders this medium translucent. The spiritual quasi-opacity accorded to non-positional consciousness cannot be intrinsic *to consciousness*. Otherwise, it would be equally present to positional consciousness. And if it is thus adventitious, it is not the *self*-presence of consciousness at all.

We are driven, then, to repudiate, not consciousness, but consciousness *itself*. What reflection reveals of consciousness is an adventitious 'glint', an ossified deposit, but not consciousness *itself*. And what a prereflective consciousness (of) consciousness reveals is at best an ectoplasmic haze — but again, not consciousness *itself*. But to say that consciousness is devoid of 'itself' is to assume what the recessive strand of Sartre's early thinking requires: utter transparency. To 'see' consciousness at all is precisely to see *through* it, to see what it sees. It is the absolute and remainderless effacing of 'itself' in the face of its object. But if so, then reflection simply collapses into prereflective consciousness. Or rather, the difference is purely and simply a difference of object — in the one case, a glint, a mist, the corpse of a once-living act; in the other, a table or a coffee cup.

'Transparency' can be understood functionally or substantially. It can, that is, refer to the pure event of luminal permissiveness, the non-hindrance, non-impedance, that conditions the passage of light; and it can also refer to the quality of a transparent substance, a pane of glass, for example. Indeed, for Sartre, '[c]onsciousness has nothing substantial' (1971, p. 17). And 'it is precisely because consciousness is pure appearance, because it is total emptiness (since the entire world is outside it) — it is because of this identity of appearance and existence within it that it can be considered absolute' (p. 17). As a 'non-substantial absolute' (p. 17), consciousness cannot be transparent in the substantival sense. But it is this sense that best accords with a conception of consciousness *itself*. The transparent glass offers 'itself' to vision through its glare. The event of openness does not. And it is to the precise extent of its freedom from refraction, colouration and distortion that the glass illustrates the function of transparency. There would be no transparent glass — with its glint and partial opacity — without transparency. And we can thus say that consciousness conditions, makes possible, what Sartre calls the psychic without being the psychic. Consciousness is related to the presentation of 'itself' as a necessary condition. But as a 'miser', rooted in Buddhist transparentism, and tendentiously engaged with the translucentist strain of Sartre's thought, I urge that this presentation, though, perhaps, a faithful disclosure of the 'glint', is in no way the presentation *of the self*.

References

Berg, Stephen Berg (1991), 'To the Being we ere', in Johnson *et al.* (1991).

Blanchot, Maurice (1973), *Thomas the Obscure*, R. Lamberton, trans. (New York: David Lewis).

Cadava, Eduardo, Connor, Peter and Nancy, Jean-Luc (ed. 1991), *Who Comes After the Subject?* (New York: Routledge).

Corless, Roger J. (1989), *The Vision of Buddhism: The space under the tree* (New York: Paragon House).

Cumming, Robert Denoon (ed. 1965), *The Philosophy of Jean-Paul Sartre* (New York: Vantage).

Derrida, Jacques (1978), *Writing and Difference*, trans. Alan Bass (Chicago: University of Chicago Press).

Derrida, Jacques (1982), *Margins of Philosophy* (Chicago: University of Chicago Press).

Derrida, Jacques (1986), *Glas*, trans. J. P. Leavey and R.A. Rand (Lincoln, NE: University of Nebraska).

Dews, Peter (1988), *Logics of Disintegration: Post-structuralist thought and the claims of critical theory* (London: Verso).

Dillon, M.C. (1991), 'Preface: Merleau-Ponty and Postmodernity', in *Merleau-Ponty Vivant* (Albany: SUNY Press).

Granel, Gérard (1991), 'Who comes after the subject?', in Cadava *et al.* (1991).

Henry, Michel (1991), 'The critique of the subject', in Cadava *et al.* (1991).

Johnson, Galen A. and Smith, Michael B. (ed. 1990), *Ontology and Alterity in Merleau-Ponty* (Evanston, IL: Northwestern University Press).

Johnson, Kent & Paulenich, Craig, (ed. 1991), *Beneath a Single Moon: Buddhism in contemporary American poetry* (Boston, MA: Shambhala).

Kenny, A. (1988), *The Self* (Marquette: Marquette University Press).

Kotoh Tetsuaki (1987), 'Language and silence: self-inquiry in Heidegger and Zen', in Parks (1987).

Larousse de la Langue Française (1979, Paris: Librairie Larousse).

Laycock, Steven W. (1989), 'Sartre and the Chinese Buddhist theory of noself: The mirroring of mind', *Buddhist–Christian Studies*, **9**, pp. 25–42.

Laycock, Steven W. (1994a), *Mind as Mirror and the Mirroring of Mind: Buddhist reflections on western phenomenology* (Albany: SUNY Press).

Laycock, Steven W. (1994b), 'The Vietnamese mode of self-reference: A model for Buddhist egology', *Asian Philosophy*, **4**, pp. 53–69.

Levin, David Michael, (1991) 'Visions of narcissism: Intersubjectivity and the reversals of reflection', in Dillon (1991).

Levinas, Emmanuel (1991), 'Philosophy and awakening', in Cadava *et al.* (1991).

Madison, Gary Brent (1990), 'Flesh as otherness', in Johnson and Smith (1970).

Magliola, Robert (1986), *Derrida on the Mend* (West Lafayette, IN: Purdue University Press).

Merleau-Ponty, Maurice (1962), *The Visible and the Invisible,* trans. Colin Smith (New York: Humanities Press).

Merleau-Ponty, Maurice (1964), *The Primacy of Perception And Other Essays on Phenomenological Psychology, and the Philosophy of Art, History and Politics*, ed. James M. Edie (Evanston, IL: Northwestern University Press).

Morris, Phyllis Sutton (1992), 'Sartre on the self-deceiver's translucent consciousness', *Journal of the British Society for Phenomenology*, **23**.

Murti, T.R.V. (1987), *The Central Philosophy of Buddhism: A study of the Madhyamika system* (London: Allen & Unwin).

Nozick, R. (1981), *Philosophical Explanations* (Oxford: Clarendon Press).

Parks, Graham Parkes (ed. 1987), *Heidegger and Asian Thought* (Honolulu: University of Hawaii).

Sartre, Jean-Paul (1964), *Nausea*, trans. Lloyd Alexander (New York: New Directions).

Sartre, JeanPaul (1971), *Being and Nothingness: An essay on phenomenological ontology*, trans. Hazel E. Barnes (New York: Washington Square Press).

Sartre, Jean-Paul (1972), *The Transcendence of the Ego: An existentialist theory of consciousness,* trans. Forrest Williams & Robert Kirkpatrick (New York: The Noonday Press).

Sartre, Jean-Paul (1984), *The War Diaries of Jean-Paul Sartre: November 1939/March 1940,* trans. Quintin Hoare (New York: Pantheon).

Sohl, Robert & Carr, Audrey (ed. 1970), *The Gospel According to Zen: Beyond the death of God* (New York: Mentor).

Strawson, Galen (1997), '"The Self"', *JCS*, **4** (5–6), pp. 405–28. Reprinted in this volume, pp. 1–24.

Suzuki, Daisetz Teitaro (1956), *Zen Buddhism* (New York: Doubleday Anchor).

Suzuki, Daisetz Teitaro (1981), *The Zen Doctrine of No-Mind: The significance of the Sutra of Hui-Neng (Wei-Lang)*, ed. Christmas Humphreys (New Beach: Samuel Wiser).

Trinh thi. Minh-hà (1989), *Woman, Native, Other: Writing Postcoloniality and Feminism* (Bloomington: Indiana University Press).

Varela, Francisco J., Thompson, Evan and Rosch, Eleanor (1992), *The Embodied Mind: Cognitive science and human experience* (Cambridge, MA: The MIT Press).

Wittgenstein, Ludwig (1974), *Tractatus Logico-Philosophicus*, tr. D.F. Pears and B.F. McGuinness, (Atlantic Highlands, NJ: Humanities Press).

Jonathan Shear

Experiential Clarification of the Problem of Self

I

The topic of self-knowledge has been central to Western philosophy since its inception in ancient Greece. In the modern era the three great philosophers, Descartes, Hume and Kant accordingly held that self-knowledge should be expected to provide the 'Archimedean point' for all knowledge, the 'capitol or centre' of all human understanding, and the 'supreme principle for all employment of the understanding', respectively. Despite its continuing importance, the topic has proved problematic, as Descartes, Hume and Kant's own analyses clearly illustrate. Descartes held with common sense that we have clear intuitive knowledge of the self as *single, simple* and *continuing*. Hume, responding to Descartes, looked within and argued that he could find nothing at all corresponding to the notion, and that it was thus *empty of all significance*. In return Kant argued, paradoxically, that *both* Descartes and Hume were correct: Descartes in that we *have to have* such a self, and Hume in that there is *no possibility whatsoever* of experiencing it, or indeed of knowing it as anything but an *abstract vacuous cipher*. Since subsequent philosophical discussions of the self have largely been reaction to these analyses and conclusions, it will be worth reviewing them briefly here.

Descartes sought an indubitable ground for all knowledge, and concluded that he located it in awareness of his own self-existence. *Cogito ergo sum*, or, in modern English, 'I am conscious, therefore I exist'.[1] For, Descartes argued, one cannot coherently doubt one's own conscious existence, since the very act of doubting implies it. Or, put linguistically, one can never truly say 'I do not exist'. But if one necessarily exists, *what is it* that exists? Descartes concluded that the self that we know indubitably exists is a *consciousness*, the *selfsame* consciousness, *single, simple* and *continuing* throughout one's awareness (Descartes, 1971, pp. 66 ff., p. 121, etc.). This view of course resonates deeply with our common sense. And we should note that it is not only our modern Western 'common sense' that this view accords with, but also that of

---

[1] Traditionally, Descartes' *cogito* used to be translated as 'I think'. Yet Descartes, in both the Latin and French editions, makes it clear that what he intends is what we would now call 'being conscious' rather than merely 'thinking', including, for example, willing, sensing and imagining, as well as such things as asserting, understanding, and doubting. Compare, for example, Anscombe and Geach's now widely used translation of the *Meditations* in their *Descartes: Philosophical Writings* (1971).

very different cultures, as, for example, the many references in Asian Buddhist and Vedantan texts to this view of self as the common one clearly show.[2]

Hume's critique of Descartes, however, proved devastating to Descartes' position. For when he looked within, Hume reported that he could not find anything in his experience corresponding to Descartes' single, simple, continuing self:

> When I enter most intimately into what I call *myself*, I always stumble on some particular perception or other, of heat or cold, light or shade, love or hatred, pain or pleasure. I never can catch *myself* at any time without a perception, and never can observe anything but the perception (Hume, 1978, p. 252).

These results, of course, have accorded with those of almost every commentator since. Thus, while self is supposed to be 'something simple and continu'd' and 'that to which our several impressions are suppos'd to have a reference', it is introspectively clear that we have 'not the least idea' of what such a thing could be. In short, our ordinary notion of self must be some kind of commonsensical 'fiction' (Hume, 1978, pp. 251 ff.).

What then, on Hume's account *is* the self? Hume offered the first of what later came to be called 'logical construction theories' (LCTs) which attempt to account for our concept of self entirely in terms of a 'collection' or 'bundle' of experiences connected by some 'logical' relationship. This approach became the dominant one among English-speaking philosophers in our century. In Hume's original theory the relationships were contiguity and resemblances of our perceptions; later theorists often used complex sorts of memory relationships.

There are, however, real problems with this approach. Indeed, Hume himself rejected it in the famous 'Appendix' to his *Treatise* (Hume, 1978, pp. 633–6) where his critique and 'collection' theory first appeared. The critical passages of this Appendix are very compact, and their argument is not transparent. But the basic idea is clear: the fact, as Hume argues, that each of our perceptions is 'a distinct existence', separable (in principle, if not in fact) from all the others, implies that no perception can contain any content implying any real connection with the others. This, however, in turn implies that there is no possibility of properly deriving from the actual content of our perceptions any principle capable of unifying them into a 'whole mind' or self. We will return to this line of argument in the next section. First let us now see how Kant's critique strengthened major aspects of *both* Hume's sceptical difficulty *and* Descartes' positive claim.

Kant argued, with Hume, that no overall principle of unity can be derived from the content of any of our experiences. Nevertheless, he also argued that such an overall unity, which he called 'the transcendental unity of apperception' must be *presupposed* as 'the supreme principle of all employment of the understanding'. All of our experience, inner and outer, Kant argued, is extended in time, and all outer experience extended in space as well. Thus, for example, if an experience, whether inner or outer, had no temporal extension, it would be too short to be perceived, and if an outer experience had no spatial extension, it would be too small to be seen. Consequently, Kant argued, every experience, whether inner or outer, must have separate *parts*. Thus a

---

[2] Thus the fashionable view, often expressed by philosophers from Ryle onward, that we modern Westerners find Descartes' view 'commonsensical' only because of the influence of his views today, is clearly incorrect. For a discussion of the cross-cultural commonality of core components of our notions of self, see Shear (1996).

visual experience, for example, must have a left and a right, and a top and a bottom, etc. (Kant, 1965, pp. 129 ff.).[3]

But for any experience to exist as a single experience, all of its parts must be given to a single experiencer. If you look at your hand and see it, you will necessarily see a left and a right aspect. These will be parts of *your* experience. If, for example, one person saw only the left aspect (say, the little finger) and another only the right (say, the thumb), then these would be *different* experiences (above and beyond being had by different people) from your original one. And even for each of these different experiences, a single person would have to see both the left and the right aspects, too, or that experience would not have existed either. Similarly, Kant argues, if each of a number of people (heard or) thought only a single word of an extended sentence, no one would experience the entire sentence or thought (Kant, 1965, p. 335). In ways such as these Kant argued that self as single, simple and abiding, is the absolutely necessary precondition for the existence of any experience or thought whatsoever.

So far, then, Kant would support Descartes. But he also argued, strengthening Hume, that there is absolutely no possibility of having any experience, or even any definite concept, of this necessarily inferred unitary self. Kant's arguments here are complex, and not always clear. But his conclusions are. And one of his major conclusions about the self is that *it cannot have any experiential quality* of its own at all. That is, it has to be a 'pure, original unchanging consciousness', a 'bare consciousness' with 'no distinguishing features' of its own. We will return to this conclusion in the next section below. The next step of Kant's argument is easy to follow, however. For if all of our experience is of qualities extended in time and/or space (as argued above) and the self is necessarily qualityless with no distinguishing feature of its own, there is no possibility either of experiencing it, or even generating any graspable concept of it. Therefore the self, however necessary it might be, is knowable only as a blank abstraction, 'a something = X', as he puts it, completely ungraspable, as well as unexperienceable, in itself (Kant, 1965, pp. 329 ff.).

Thus the paradox: self as single, simple and continuing is at once both *absolutely necessary* and *absolutely unexperienceable and unknowable*. In other words, Descartes and Hume are *both* importantly correct — and this amounts to a paradox which, as Kant put it, 'mocks and torments' even the wisest of men. In short, the concept of self is at once both (i) absolutely necessary and (ii) entirely vacuous and ungraspable.

II

These arguments are all well-known to students of philosophy. But since they underlie so much of our contemporary discussion of self, it will be worthwhile to unpack their logic a little more. Hume's rejection of the existence of any internal perception adequate to our ordinary notion of self is of course well-known and well-accepted. But his rejection of his own — and all other — LCT's is neither so well understood, nor so influential. It is not, however, hard to see how, as Hume suggested, all LCT's must be inadequate to capture our ordinary notion of self. First, let us put the argu-

---

[3] Interestingly, this holds for inner visual experiences as well as outer ones. While for Kant such experiences are not 'spatial' in the sense of having parts that are spread out over (and synthesized in) the one 'real' external space, they are nevertheless *phenomenologically* 'spatial', having a phenomenal 'left' and 'right', etc. requiring a Kantian synthesis in order to be experienced at all.

ment formally: suppose, for example, the self to be some collection of perceptions de-fined by an empirical relation R. That is, suppose that there is some such R capable of defining one's self. Then R must be able to distinguish between (i) perceptions that it includes in the collection identified as one's self and (ii) those that it excludes. Next consider any one, say P, of the possible perceptions outside the collection R specifies as (supposedly) constituting one's self. Since P is a possible perception, one can (without contradiction) imagine having it. That is, it is logically possible, if not possi-ble in empirical fact, that one could find oneself having just this particular perception. But then one would be having a perception outside the bundle specified by R and supposedly constituting one's self, contrary to the definition of R. The conclusion, of course, is that no such relation R could serve to define our ordinary, commonsense notion of self.

Since the above argument is a bit abstract, let me give a concrete example. Sup-pose, in accord with Hume's original proposal, that every member of the collection of perceptions (supposedly) constituting one's self has to be related to the others by the relation R, 'recognized spatial contiguity', that is, that all of one's perceptions must be connected by the recognized spatial contiguity of their content. This would make it impossible for one to become unconscious and wake up in an environment having no recognized spatial relationship to the environment where one went to sleep. For one would then be having perceptions P outside the collection, defined by the contiguity-relation R, supposedly constituting the self. Yet we can easily imagine people having such spatial discontinuities in their experiences without having to be different selves. Indeed, people obviously sometimes *do* have such spatial discontinuities in their experience, as, for example, happens when people become unconscious and wake up in environments perceptually non-contiguous to those where they went to sleep. And surely no-one would want to say they had to become *different individuals* for having done so. Alternatively, consider a relation R_1 defined in terms of 'perceived contigu-ity to one's (physical) body'. This relation would imply that it couldn't be the case that one's body could be destroyed, and one find oneself in heaven, or reincarnated, or simply disembodied in some realm or other. Now it may be the case that one will *in fact* cease to exist if one's body is destroyed. But it is surely not impossible to *imagine* otherwise. Indeed, most of the people of the world indeed *believe* otherwise (i.e. that they will somehow survive bodily death). Thus it is clear that this R_1, too, is incapable of capturing our ordinary notion of self as something that can (at least logically, if not factually) undergo such a sequence of experiences.

Such examples can be multiplied without end. They illustrate that there is an im-portant sense in which we conceive of ourselves purely as experiencers, capable in our conception, if not in objective fact, of being independent of any particular context and/or set of experiences. And this implies, as the above argument in terms of Ps and Rs showed in abstract general form, that our selves, as ordinarily conceived, cannot be captured by any set of experiences. For it shows that *whatever* relation is chosen, there will be examples that show its inadequacy. In short, Hume's sceptical despair of ever coming to an adequate account of self by virtue of any LCT whatsoever appears very well taken.

Let us now turn to Kant's conclusion that the self must be a 'qualityless pure con-sciousness', a 'bare consciousness' with 'no distinguishing quality of its own'. Kant's arguments are embedded in the details of his epistemological and psychological theories, and are, as noted, often difficult to follow. But the gist of his reasoning is easy to understand. Roughly put, he argues that the self has to be an aspect of (or at least connected to) all of one's possible experiences. Otherwise these experiences would not be *one's own*, and one would not be able to say of them 'I have them', 'I recognize them', 'They are *mine*', etc. So far, this seems sensible enough. But, strikingly, in itself it seems to imply that the self must be *qualityless*. For suppose the self *did* have some distinguishing empirical quality Q. Then Q would have to be an ubiquitous quality, since self has to be an aspect of (or connected to) every part of every one of one's experiences,[4] and as the distinguishing characteristic of self, Q would have to be there, too. That is, it would be impossible for one to have any experience where Q was absent, and Q could never be identified as an empirical quality or distinguishing characteristic in the first place. Thus, by analogy, suppose the self to be the glass of one's glasses. If the glass had any colour, say green, this colour would colour *all* experiences equally, and this would imply that the colour would not be knowable as an empirical quality or distinguishable characteristic at all.

In short, Hume and Kant's analyses appear to lead to the striking conclusion that self cannot be experienced, or even defined, in terms of any empirical quality, or even any empirically significant set of empirical qualities, at all.

III

Indeed, it is easy to see from the perspective of common sense, that is, quite aside from formal philosophical analyses, how problematic the notion of self really is. Each of us naturally feels we are a person, a single continuing something. As James put it, each of us feels that we are an 'Arch-ego, at the center of our own experiences', which, as Locke put it 'owns and imputes its experiences to itself', one and the same throughout one's life. At least this is what common sense would hold, unless we become confused by reading too much philosophy. But what *is* this sameness? It seems to be extremely difficult to identify. Consider, for example, *the body*. One's body changes throughout one's life. One can remember events that one experienced as a small child, and one remembers them as *one's own*, despite the fact that one's body was very different. One's personality changes, too, yet one remembers events from the time one was a young child or a teenager as *one's own*, even if one had a very different personality then. These observations clearly suggest that there must be an aspect of one's ordinary concept of self that one takes to be different from either one's body or one's personality, all matters of abstract philosophical analysis aside.

This is even easier to see if we turn our consideration from waking consciousness to that of dreams. One common type of dream involves experiencing oneself as having a different body from the one one has in reality. This dream-experienced 'body' can even be a non-human type of body, such as that of an animal. Yet when one wakes and remembers the dream, one is sure that it was *one's own* dream, that *one* had the dream one is remembering. This makes it clear, again, that there is an important aspect of our commonsense notion of self that is independent of identification with one's body (various philosophical arguments for the necessity of body-grounded self-identification notwithstanding). Of course, the point here is not that one is, or even could in fact *be*, independent of one's body; it is just that people sometimes do

---

[4]   Indeed, as Kant put it, all of one's experiences are *in* one's self. Thus self has to be *there* wherever any part of any one of one's experiences exists.

experience themselves (as well as naturally conceive themselves) *as* being independent of it. This independence is made even clearer by the common sort of dream where one appears to be a *disembodied* spectator, watching the dream action from some vantage-point or other, like a video-camera.

The case of *personality* is similar. People often do things in dreams that they 'wouldn't dream of' doing (in the waking state). In other words, we often do things in dreams that lie entirely outside our consciously conceived personality. Even more, it is also a common experience to observe the dream-action in a completely impersonal, emotionally neutral way when one finds oneself a disembodied dream-spectator. Nevertheless, even if there is neither body nor personality there (in the dream), one is sure that *one* was there, oneself, watching the action. But *what* was watching? It seems ungraspable.

These experiences, of course, are not universal. But they are very common. Each time, for example, I poll groups of philosophically innocent students, easily one-quarter or more say they have had the above experiences. At the very least these experiences show something of how discoordinated a basic aspect of our deeply held, naive commonsensical notions of self are from anything graspable in terms of body, personality or, indeed, any identifiable empirical qualities at all.

Such simple reflections on common sense in short make it clear that the puzzles about self generated by Descartes', Hume's and Kant's philosophical analyses are not off the mark. For a deep aspect of self as we ordinarily conceive it does seem to be both continuing ubiquitously throughout our experience and completely ungraspable in terms of empirical qualities whatsoever. It is thus not hard to see why Hume ended his analysis with sceptical despair and Kant with mocking and tormenting paradox.

IV

The above analyses reflect the problematic sorts of discussions of self in Western philosophy over the past few centuries. Interestingly, if we turn from Western analyses to those of Asian civilizations, however, we find their philosophical discussions in general, and discussions of self in particular, often embedded in what amounts to an expanded experiential context that includes experiences generally not even referred to, much less emphasized, in Western discussions of self. These experiences have been taken seriously enough by a variety of Eastern traditions that they have developed a variety of meditation procedures designed specifically to produce them. One of the experiences, often called the 'pure consciousness' experience, will prove to be highly relevant to our own discussion. Different traditions use different terminology to refer to the experience, and they interpret it from different metaphysical perspectives. But its identifying characteristic, namely, that it is *devoid of all empirical content whatsoever*, is found in common in tradition after tradition. This identifying characteristic, to be sure, is at first likely to appear a bit odd to us, if not simply unintelligible. It will therefore be useful to take a brief look at standard accounts of the experience, taking them at face value, and suspending for the moment all questions about their reliability and intelligibility.

We should first note that nothing much can be said about the experience itself. For its identifying characteristic is that it is devoid of all empirical content. That is, as texts from many traditions emphasize, the experience has absolutely no discernible sensations, perceptions, images, thoughts, etc., in it. Indeed, by all reports, it does not even have a spatio–temporal manifold for such phenomenological objects to be located in. What then is the experience *like*? It is not *like* anything. What is it remembered *as*? Not *as* anything. Nevertheless it *is* remembered. One remembers having the experience, but there is nothing 'to' it. No content, shape, structure, or anything else. Thus, not surprisingly, it is often referred to as 'pure consciousness' (since there had to be consciousness for there to be a rememberable experience), 'pure being' (since nothing positive can be said about it except that it *was*), and 'pure void' (since it is utterly devoid of content).

More, of course, can be said about the procedures developed in different cultures and traditions to produce the experience. Many such procedures exist, with those of Zen and Transcendental Meditation (TM) being the most widely known throughout the world. Some of these procedures are easy and widely applicable, others are very difficult and masterable only by a few people after years of dedicated work. The methods range, for example, from Zen's *koan* practices (concentration on intellectually unsolvable connundra to 'freeze' the mind) and 'doubt sensation' (to loosen one's attachment to everything) to TM's use of *mantras* (mental repetition of specific sounds to let one relax utterly, while remaining awake). Although less widely known, Western practices, such as medieval Christianity's focusing on 'unknowing' (to cause all ordinary mental processes to stop), exist as well. The proponents of such procedures appear to be unanimous in their claims that the procedures actually have to be practiced to really be understood. Nevertheless something of their overall logic is easy to comprehend. For they are all designed to allow one's attention to withdraw from all ordinary contents of awareness, including finally even the procedure itself, the idea being that once all phenomenal objects (including the components of the procedure itself) are gone from one's awareness — while one nevertheless stays awake — what remains can only be awareness or consciousness itself.[5]

Thus, particularities of methods aside, what remains, according to a wide spectrum of traditional accounts, is what can be called pure qualityless conscious itself. Consider, for example, the following accounts from several different traditions. First, from Chinese Ch'an (Zen):

> When the mind is reduced to impotency, it is compared in the Ch'an [Chinese Zen] texts to that of a withered log, an unconscious skull, a wooden horse, a stone girl and an incense burner in a deserted temple. . . . The mind, thus stripped of all its activities [thought, feeling, experiencing, etc.], will be reduced to impotency and will vanish sooner or later. . . . This death of the mind leads to the resurrection of the self nature (Luk, 1961, pp. 20–1).

Japanese Zen:

> The time comes when no reflection appears at all. One comes to notice nothing, feel nothing, hear nothing, see nothing. . . . But it is not vacant emptiness. Rather it is the purest condition of our existence (Katsuki Sekida, in Austin, 1998, p. 473).

The ancient Indian *Mandukya Upanishad*:

> Turia [the 'fourth' state of consciousness, after deep sleep, dreaming, and ordinary waking] is not that which cognizes the internal (objects), not that which cognizes the external (objects), not what cognizes both of them, not a mass of cognition, not cognitive, not non-cognitive. (It is) unseen, incapable of being spoken of, ungraspable, without any distinctive marks, unthinkable, unnamable . . . .The fourth [state, turia] is that which has no

elements, which cannot be spoken of . . . non-dual . . . . He who knows it thus enters the self with his self (Radhakrishnan, 1981, pp. 698 & 701).

And modern Vedantan TM:

> When the subject is left without an object of experience, having transcended the subtlest state of the object, he steps out of the process of experiencing and arrives as the state of Being . . . beyond all seeing, hearing, touching, smelling and tasting — beyond all thinking and beyond all feeling. This state of . . . unmanifested, absolute, pure consciousness . . .' (Maharishi, 1967/1981, p. 52).

From the above examples we can immediately see two things, first that texts from different traditions, in different cultures with different metaphysics, take great pains to emphasize that the experiences they are describing are to be understood as absolutely devoid of phenomenal content. Secondly, they also associate the experience with what they take to be the true, underlying nature of self. Similar descriptions, and similar claims of relation to the self, are also found (although, to be sure, less frequently) in Western texts as well, as in the following example from a medieval version of Christianity's *Pseudo-Dionysious*:

> Through . . . passing beyond yourself and every other thing (and thereby cleansing yourself from all worldly, physical, and natural love, and from everything that can be known by the normal processes of mind) . . . . Enter into this darkness with love . . . this supreme and dazzling darkness . . . [and experience] the self in its naked, unmade, unbegun state (*Pseudo-Dionysius*, 1978, pp. 209–13).

Such texts and claims raise many questions of course. These include hermeneutical questions about the appropriateness of taking descriptions from different cultures as being of the same (type of) experience, and methodological questions about how seriously to take subjective reports of unusual experiences in the first place. We will return to these questions later. For now, however, let us turn to the question of the significance of the experience for our examination of the nature of self.

V

As we have seen, identification of the experience in question with a fundamental underlying stratum of self is quite common. However, our concern here is not so much with how ancient traditions have interpreted the significance of the experience *vis-à-vis* the self, but only with how *we* should interpret it.[6] Nevertheless, the basic intuition underlying the common identification of the experience of pure qualityless awareness with the self is not difficult to understand. For, as noted above, from the perspective of common sense it seems apparent that if one takes everything away while remaining conscious, what remains has to be one's self.

It is also easy to see that the analyses of Descartes, Hume and Kant outlined above serve to *identify* the experience in question *as* experience of self. For it is obvious (i) that this experience, and only this experience, can fulfill Kant's otherwise paradoxical 'pure consciousness', 'bare consciousness', 'devoid of all distinguishing marks'. It is also (ii) the only experience that could give experiential significance to the notion of the commonsensical simple consciousness, underlying but distinct from all our changing perceptions, proposed by Descartes and Locke but rejected despair-

---

[6] This identification, to be sure, is not universal, and there are Buddhist traditions which, while clearly identifying the experience in question, also hold, in opposition to the Zen, that there is no true 'self' to be discovered in the first place.

ingly (as unexperienced) by Hume. And (iii) it is the only experience that could give experiential significance to the notion of self as independent of all collections of experiences, as implied by our analysis of common sense. In short, this and only this experience can allow us to resolve the relevant (phenomenological) tensions within and between Descartes, Hume and Kant, not to mention the tensions between these philosophical analyses and common sense, in an experientially significant way.[7]

Thus, in sum, we can see both (1) how the expansion of the domain of experience provided by Eastern meditation techniques helps us resolve major Western philosophical problems about the self, and (2) how the same Western philosophical analyses in turn help identify the experience as being of self.[8] This analysis also (3) allows us to 'save' common sense, at least to the extent indicated above. But common sense would naturally also ask: If this qualityless pure consciousness is the self, and it is ubiquitous, why is it so obscure? The answer, I think, is straightforward: it is ordinarily obscure precisely *because* it is (a) qualityless and (b) ubiquitous. It is a psychological commonplace that that which is constant in experience becomes 'filtered out', with attention going to what is changing (compare information theory's definition of information as 'news of a difference'). Thus *if* pure consciousness is constant, it is easy to see why it is not attended to until attention is drawn to it — much, for example, as one is unlikely to notice the background temperature of a comfortable room. For since infancy our attention, in the name of functional efficiency, has been drawn to the ever-changing qualities of our environment in order to learn to deal with them properly. Moreover, because pure consciousness has no distinguishing characteristics at all, the only way to actually draw attention to it is to allow all the other objects of attention to be withdrawn from our awareness while we remain awake. (By analogy, one ordinarily may be unlikely to notice anything but the images projected on the screen while a movie is playing, but one can easily be led to become aware of the flat imageless screen itself if the moving images are brought to a halt with the light still on.)

On this account, then, it should not be surprising that after one's attention has been drawn frequently to pure consciousness in meditation (with all other objects of awareness absent), it should become possible to recognize it at will afterward, even when the other ordinary components of experience have returned to one's awareness (much, perhaps, as one may notice the flatness of the screen even after the movie has started up again), as meditation traditions often report.

In short, these experiential reports suggest (1) that pure consciousness may well be a ubiquitous component of our experience, (2) that our ordinary (and ordinarily paradoxical) sense of self reflects a subliminal awareness of this ubiquitous pure consciousness, and (3) that after we become clearly aware of it as it is in and by itself in meditation, we can then come also to recognize it *as* ubiquitous — as self is supposed to be.

----

[7] It should be emphasized that the conclusion drawn here is entirely phenomenological and epistemological, resolving problems arising from the seeming impossibility of locating anything in experience corresponding to the relevant notions of self, and not ontological at all.

[8] Thus this analysis also supports, with uniquely Western lines of reasoning, the identification of the experience with the self, common to many but not all Eastern traditions. That is, it gives independent Western support for Yoga, Vedanta and Zen's identification of the experience and the fundamental nature of the self as opposed to Therevada Buddhism's emphasis on the (apparently opposing) doctrine of 'non-self'.

VI

The above analyses have proceded by taking the widespread, cross-cultural accounts of pure consciousness experiences at face value, and assumed the appropriateness of talking about a single identifiable pure consciousness experience. But serious questions about this approach can be raised here, and the most important critiques and questions should at least be mentioned, namely, the (i) hermeneutical — questioning whether there can be *one* experience, the same across different cultures, (ii) phenomenological — asking if the experience can really be *qualityless*, and (iii) methodological — asking *how can we determine* if these odd experiential reports have any objective significance at all? These critiques all involve complicated issues. Nevertheless a few brief remarks may be useful.

(i) *The hermeneutical critique* is based on the following line of reasoning: All experience, as a matter of empirical fact, is shaped and constructed out of culture-dependent components (symbols, images, expectations, etc.). This obviously implies that it is impossible to have the same experience across different cultures. This critique had been influential for a decade or more. Yet it is quite easy to respond to: The defining characteristic of the pure consciousness experience is the *complete absence* of all empirical content. Thus any experience properly identified as a pure consciousness experience is outside the range of all the components (symbols, images, expectations, etc.) hermeneutical thinkers are concerned with. Furthermore, it is easy to see that the pure consciousness experience is logically unique. For if two experiences are phenomenologically different, at least one of them must have some content and cannot be an instance of a pure consciousness experience. In short, any two experiences that fit the defining characteristic of pure consciousness experiences have to be the same, whatever the surrounding cultural context might be.[9]

(ii) *The phenomenological critique* has more substance. For it is not implausible to suspect that putative examples of pure consciousness experiences might have *some* content, though too abstract to be noticed and identified by the ordinary observer. That is, there might be some content in the experience that would be apparent to one who had undergone sufficient phenomenological training to uncover typically unnoticed subtleties of one's experience. Here one can readily allow this logical possibility. Nevertheless, there would still be a *family* of closely related experiences well-defined here, and the members of this family would, at least to a first approximation, still serve (with slight modification) to fulfill the arguments about self outlined above.[10]

(iii) *The methodological question* is, I think, the most important one, namely, how to tell if reports of pure consciousness experiences are anything more than mere reports. Here some kind of objective corroboration is needed. But how could this be possible for such contentless subjective experiences? The response is in terms of actual research on meditation subjects. Quite a bit has been done here, much of it on subjects practising the TM technique (presumably, according to the research literature, because of the ease of the practice, consistency of results, and ready availability of experienced subjects). Here we have the ordinary methodological constraints on subjects' reports, typical of those in psychological research in general. More to the

---

[9] For extended discussions of the hermeneutical critique, see Shear (1990) and Forman (1990).

[10] For further discussion of these phenomenological questions see Shear (1999a).

point, a variety of physiological correlates of the experiential reports has been observed, including unusual EEG coherence, marked reduction of metabolic activity, and, most strikingly, periods of *complete cessation of respiration* (measured, for example, by essentially flat pneumotachygraphic tracings) highly correlated ($p < 10^{10}$) in experimental settings with reports of the experience (Farrow and Hebert, 1982). Furthermore, this same correlate (cessation of respiration) of the experience is reported and emphasized in meditation texts from ancient and contemporary China and India, in the contexts of Zen, Yoga and Tibetan Buddhism.

Thus, when the same unusual experiential accounts, found in very different belief-contexts, are correlated with the same unusual (often unconscious) physiological parameters, it would strain credulity to think that these correlations occur just by chance. The reasonable inference is that the experiential accounts reflect the natural subjective response to the unusual correlated physiological state, rather than to the radically different, often opposing cultural, belief, and expectation-contexts in which the reports happen to be embedded. In short, the reasonable conclusion is that the reports do indeed reflect an objective phenomenon, namely, the culture-independent psychophysical state in question. Finally, we can also note that this common psycho-physiological conjunction across very different cultures and belief-contexts re-inforces the lack of relevance of the hermeneutical culture-embeddness objection, and the phenomenological objection as well.[11]

It is important to note here, however, some things that the above account does *not* do. In the first place, the account is purely phenomenological (a matter of experience and its relation to our concepts), and not at all ontological. Indeed, this is part of its strength. No particular ontological position is presumed, and the analysis is compatible with substance and non-substance theories of self, and non-dualisms (whether idealist, materialist, or neutral-monist) and dualisms, indifferently. For it is derived from examination of our experience and ordinary concepts, quite apart from any determination of these ontological questions.[12] And however these questions may be resolved, our experiences, our commonsense concepts, and their relations remain what and as they are. But while the above account of self has no ontological significance, it does appear to enable us both to clarify the significance of our commonsense intuitions and to resolve long-standing conceptual problems about the self in a way compatible with common sense.

VII

Let us now see what this analysis might imply for Galen Strawson's discussion of self.[13] Strawson begins his chapter by claiming that each of us has a 'sense of mental self' [or 'SMS'], an 'ordinary human sense of self' as

> being . . . a mental presence . . . a single mental thing that is a conscious subject of experi-
> ence, that has a certain character or personality, and that is in some sense distinct from all
> its particular experiences, thoughts and so on.

Further, he asserts, this

---

[11] For further discussion of these methodological questions see Shear (1999a).

[12] In particular we can note that nothing at all is implied here about ontological questions of agency, mind-body relations, or ultimate identity (as in Vedanta) or plurality (as in Yoga and common sense) of selves.

[13] All references to 'Strawson' here are to Galen Stawson's opening chapter in this volume (pp. 1–24).

sense of mental self . . . comes to every normal human being, in some form, in childhood. The early realization of the fact that one's thoughts are unobservable by others, the experience of the profound sense in which one is alone in one's head — these are some of the very deepest facts about the character of human life, and found the sense of mental self (Strawson, p. 3).

These claims seem to me on the whole[14] to be reasonable beginning points for Strawson's analysis. The claim that some such sense of mental self comes to any normal person in childhood is be well-supported by extensive studies of cognitive development in early childhood (Wellman, 1990). The cross-cultural nature of this notion of self is, for example, clearly indicated by the many references to it as the ordinary (if 'unenlightened') notion of self in texts of Buddhism, Yoga and Vedanta. It is just this commonsensical notion of self which has proved so philosophically difficult, in the absence of knowledge of the experience of pure consciousness. And it is this same commonsensical sense of self that the analysis above intends to clarify, using expanded phenomenological knowledge of mind made available by traditional Eastern meditation techniques.

Strawson, of course, also uses a phenomenological approach to re-examine this ordinary sense of mental self,[15] in this case the results of his own simple introspection:

> (1) Human thought has very little natural phenomenal continuity or experiential flow — if mine is anything to go by. . . (2) It keeps slipping from mere consciousness into self-consciousness and out again . . . (3) When I am alone and thinking I find that my fundamental experience of consciousness is one of *repeated returns into consciousness from a state of complete, if momentary, unconsciousness* . . . (4) [C]onscious thought has the character of a (nearly continuous) series of radically disjunct irruptions into consciousness from a basic substrate of non-consciousness. (5) It keeps banging out of nothingness; it is a series of comings to (Strawson, pp. 17–18) [numbers added].

This phenomenological account, however, raises a number of problems. For it is hard to understand just what kinds of breaks of consciousness Strawson intends to describe. Sentence (1) is about discontinuity of *thought*. Sentence (2) is about contrasts between 'mere consciousness' and 'self-consciousness'. If Strawson is referring here to contrasts between episodes where discursive thought (a) is and (b) is not noticeably present, this amounts to discontinuity of thought and is consistent with (1). But then he (3) refers to breaks in *consciousness*, contrasting 'consciousness' and 'complete unconsciousness'. This, of course, is consistent with the 'non-consciousness' of (4), but not, seemingly, with the notion of breaks in (2). It is then also unclear why such unexperienced, completely unconscious episodes should be regarded (4) as a '*substrate*' (emphasis added) for one's conscious experiences. And this question of 'substrate' becomes even more acute when Strawson (5) refers to the emergence of consciousness from the breaks as coming 'out of *nothingness*' (emphasis added).

I am not suggesting that Strawson does not have the kinds of experience he is attempting to describe, but only that his description as it stands is not entirely clear. Are the described breaks (or 'gaps', as he elsewhere calls them) in ordinary con-

---

[14] The one exception is Strawson's locating the sense of self as 'in the head' rather than 'in the mind;' for different individuals may of course also locate this sense in different parts of the body, as, for example, in the chest or heart.

[15] Strawson notes we do of course also have other senses of self, as when we conceive of ourselves as mental-and-non-mental things, human beings considered-as-wholes. These other senses of self, however, lie outside the scope of his (and our own) phenomenological analysis.

sciousness (i) conscious without discursive awareness, or (ii) non-conscious? If they are non-conscious (or unconscious), why should they be regarded as being a substrate from which conscious states emerge rather than merely some distinct state of unconsciousness that they alternate with? If they are truly *nothingness*, how are we to understand them as being some sort of *substrate*? Moreover, if they are 'unconscious nothingness', it would appear that their existence, as well as their role as substrate for emergence — could not be known by any direct phenomenological acquaintance, but only by inference from the experience of discontinuities within Strawson's consciousness. And it would then be unclear why recognition of mere discontinuities within consciousness should imply anything more about an underlying substrate than the discontinuities of sleep or anaesthesia would.

These ambiguities make it difficult to know just what sort of phenomena it is that Strawson has in mind, much less analyse their implications. Our discussion of pure consciousness, however, may prove helpful here. For it allows us to distinguish two possible interpretations of Strawson's account. In the first, the gaps Strawson refers to are not *given* in awareness but really are 'unconscious nothingness', known only by inference from the recognition of discontinuities. In the second, they are known through direct phenomenological acquaintance, and are 'mere [or pure] consciousness' (described as 'unconscious' only in the sense of being 'unconscious of' any particular content).

Let us now see what the implications of Strawson's account for the pure consciousness theory of self under these two interpretations would be. If, as in the first interpretation, the gaps (i) are known only discursively, then their supposed existence would pose no more problem for the pure consciousness theory of self than the existence of any other, more ordinary unexperienced gaps, such as those of sleep and anaesthesia. For this theory was articulated in terms of the nature of periods when we are, rather than when we are not, conscious, and nothing has changed at all about the logical relationship of pure consciousness to *these* periods. Thus none of the arguments offered above for identifying experience of pure consciousness as experience of the self would be changed. On the other hand, if, as in the second interpretation, the gaps (ii) *are* known by direct experience, then their complete absence of empirical content would identify them as episodes of pure contentless consciousness, and the presence of additional instances of pure consciousness episodes would of course present no obstacle to the pure consciousness theory of self. Thus in neither case would Strawson's phenomenological account — even if, as not established, both introspectively correct and properly generalizable to other people[16] — pose any problem for the theory of self we have been articulating.

[16] Most of us, of course, do not experience our awareness as filled with the gaps Strawson describes, so Strawson would have to argue that our awareness really is filled with such gaps, although we don't notice them. To make this more than an odd postulate, he would need to suggest that we can come to discover this putative fact, and offer some means for doing this. Interestingly, in a footnote (p. 422) Strawson does refers us to a discussion of 'gaps' as displayed through advanced Therevada Buddhist meditation practice. But here we find more than one sort of gap discussed, and also contrasting uses of the 'string of pearls' metaphor (for normal mental contents, and for underlying substrate). Also, since the 'gaps' discussed in both Buddhist and Vedantan texts are typically said to be orders of magnitude more closely packed than those of Strawson's account (cp. Hayward, 1998, p. 618), Strawson's momentary unitary 'selves' would have to be *merely* apparent, and composed of huge numbers of other, very short-lived selves rather than 'real' unities. In short, these meditation-related accounts rather than supporting Strawson's phenomenology, raise more as yet unanalysed problems.

The pure consciousness theory of self outlined above, based on expanded phenomenological knowledge derived from traditional meditative procedures and contemporary research, attempts to clarify both our ordinary intuitive and our traditional philosophical views of self. Strawson, on the other hand, offers a 'string of pearls' theory in which what we intuitively take to be a single, continuing self is actually nothing but a sequence of short-lived (usually one or two second) selves strung together. He supports this view with his 'gap' phenomenology, based on his own introspection. However once we have a pure consciousness theory of self, it is easy to accommodate Strawson's phenomenology (or phenomenologies, under the two interpretations above) without needing to resort to such a counter-intuitive view.

VIII

There are, of course, many aspects of our notion of self that the pure consciousness theory of self outlined here has not attempted to address. For the theory is, as noted, ontologically neutral, and compatible with the widest variety of different ontologies. On the other hand the theory does, I think, have significant implications for questions of personal identity, emotional maturity and moral values; but exploring these topics here would take us too far afield (but see Shear, 1990; Shear & Jevning, 1999). Enough, however, has hopefully been said to show something of the potential value for our traditional philosophical discussions of self of taking into account the pure consciousness experience, widely discussed in Eastern, but not Western, philosophical traditions. For if the phenomenological analyses above are even roughly correct, it would appear that the experience 1) is capable of resolving some major Western issues about self, 2) clarifies our commonsense intuition, and 3) is properly identified by philosophical analysis as being experience of self itself.

References

Austin, James H. (1998), *Zen and the Brain* (Cambridge: MIT Press).
Descartes, René (1971), *Meditations*, in *Descartes: Philosophical Writings*, translated by Elizabeth Anscombe and Peter T. Geach (Indianapolis: Bobbs-Merrill).
Farrow, J.T. and Hebert, R. (1982), 'Breath suspension during the transcendental meditation technique', *Psychosomatic Medicine*, **44** (2), pp. 133–53.
Forman, Robert (1990), *The Problem of Pure Consciousness* (Oxford: Oxford University Press).
Hayward, J. (1998), 'A rDzogs-chen Buddhist interpretation of the sense of self', *Journal of Consciousness Studies*, **5** (5–6), pp. 611–26.
Hume, David (1978), *A Treatise of Human Nature* (Oxford: Oxford University Press).
Kant, Immanuel (1965), *Critique of Pure Reason*, trans. Norman Kemp Smith (NY: St. Martin's Press).
Luk, Charles (ed/trans. 1961), *Ch'an and Zen Teaching, Vol. 2* (London: Rider and Co.).
Maharishi, Mahesh Yogi (1967/1984), *Bhagavad Gita: A New Translation and Commentary* (Washington DC: Age of Enlightenment Press).
Pseudo-Dionysius (1978), 'Pseudo-Dionysius' Mystical Theology', in *The Cloud of Unknowing and Other Works*, trans. Clifton Wolters (Harmondsworth: Penguin Books).
Radhakrisnhan, S. (trans. 1981), *The Principal Upanisads* (London: G. Allen & Unwin Ltd.).
Shear, Jonathan (1990), 'Mystical experience, hermeneutics, and rationality', *International Philosophical Quarterly*, **30** (4), pp. 391–401
Shear, Jonathan (1996), 'On a culture-independent core component of self', in *East-West Encounters in Philosophy and Religion*, ed. Ninian Smart and B. Srinivasa Murthy (Long Beach: Long Beach Publ.).
Shear, Jonathan (1999), 'Ethics and the experience of happiness', in *Crossing Boundaries: Ethics, Antinomianism, and the History of Mysticism*, ed. G. W. Barnard and J.J. Kirpal (New York: SUNY Press).
Shear, Jonathan and Jevning, Ron (1999), 'Pure consciousness: Scientific exploration of meditation techniques', *Journal of Consciousness Studies*, **6** (2–3), pp. 189–210.
Strawson, Galen (1997), 'The self', *JCS*, **4** (5–6), pp. 405–28. Reprinted in this volume, pp. 1–24.
Wellman, H.M. (1990), *The Child's Theory of Mind* (Cambridge, MA: The MIT Press).

Arthur J. Deikman

'I' = Awareness

Introspection reveals that the core of subjectivity — the 'I' — is identical to awareness. This 'I' should be differentiated from the various aspects of the physical person and its mental contents which form the 'self'. Most discussions of consciousness confuse the 'I' and the 'self'. In fact, our experience is fundamentally dualistic — not the dualism of mind and matter — but that of the 'I' and that which is observed. The identity of awareness and the 'I' means that we know awareness by being it, thus solving the problem of the infinite regress of observers. It follows that whatever our ontology of awareness may be, it must also be the same for 'I'.

'I'

We seem to have numerous 'I's.[1] There is the I of 'I want', the I of 'I wrote a letter', the I of 'I am a psychiatrist' or 'I am thinking'. But there is another I that is basic, that underlies desires, activities and physical characteristics. This I is the subjective sense of our existence. It is different from self-image, the body, passions, fears, social category — these are aspects of our person that we usually refer to when we speak of the self, but they do not refer to the core of our conscious being, they are not the origin of our sense of personal existence.

> *Experiment 1:* Stop for a moment and look inside. Try and sense the very origin of your most basic, most personal 'I', your core subjective experience. What is that root of the 'I' feeling? Try to find it.

When you introspect you will find that no matter what the contents of your mind, the most basic 'I' is something different. Every time you try to observe the 'I' it takes a jump back with you, remaining out of sight. At first you may say, 'When I look inside as you suggest, all I find is content of one sort or the other.' I reply, 'Who is looking? Is it not you? If that "I" is a content can you describe it? Can you observe it?' The core 'I' of subjectivity is different from any content because it turns out to be that which witnesses — not that which is observed. The 'I' can be experienced, but it cannot be 'seen'. 'I' is the observer, the experiencer, prior to all conscious content.

In contemporary psychology and philosophy, the 'I' usually is not differentiated from the physical person and its mental contents. The self is seen as a construct and the crucial duality is overlooked. As Susan Blackmore puts it,

---

[1]   I am indebted to David Galin and Eleanor Rosch for their helpful comments during the development and writing of this manuscript.

> Our sense of self came about through the body image we must construct in order to control behaviour, the vantage point given by our senses and our knowledge of our own abilities — that is the abilities of the body–brain–mind. Then along came language. Language turns the self into a thing and gives it attributes and powers. (Blackmore, 1994)

Dennett comments similarly that what he calls the 'Center of Narrative Gravity' gives us a spurious sense of a unitary self:

> A self, according to my theory, is not any old mathematical point, but an abstraction defined by the myriads of attributions and interpretations (including self-attributions and self-interpretations) that have composed the biography of the living body whose Center of Narrative Gravity it is (Dennett, 1991).

However, when we use introspection to search for the origin of our subjectivity, we find that the search for 'I' leaves the customary aspects of personhood behind and takes us closer and closer to awareness, *per se*. If this process of introspective observation is carried to its conclusion, even the background sense of core subjective self disappears into awareness. Thus, if we proceed phenomenologically, we find that the 'I' is identical to awareness: 'I' = awareness.

Awareness

Awareness is something apart from, and different from, all that of which we are aware: thoughts, emotions, images, sensations, desires and memory. Awareness is the ground in which the mind's contents manifest themselves; they appear in it and disappear once again.

I use the word 'awareness' to mean this ground of all experience. Any attempt to describe it ends in a description of what we are aware *of*. On this basis some argue that awareness *per se* doesn't exist. But careful introspection reveals that the objects of awareness — sensations, thoughts, memories, images and emotions — are constantly changing and superseding each other. In contrast, awareness continues independent of any specific mental contents.

> *Experiment 2:* Look straight ahead. Now shut your eyes. The rich visual world has disappeared to be replaced by an amorphous field of blackness, perhaps with red and yellow tinges. But awareness hasn't changed. You will notice that awareness continues as your thoughts come and go, as memories arise and replace each other, as desires emerge and fantasies develop, change and vanish. Now try and observe awareness. You cannot. Awareness cannot be made an object of observation because it is the very means whereby you can observe.

Awareness may vary in intensity as our total state changes, but it is usually a constant. Awareness cannot itself be observed, it is not an object, not a thing. Indeed, it is featureless, lacking form, texture, colour, spatial dimensions. These characteristics indicate that awareness is of a different nature than the contents of the mind; it goes beyond sensation, emotions, ideation, memory. Awareness is at a different level, it is prior to contents, more fundamental. Awareness has no intrinsic content, no form, no surface characteristics — it is unlike everything else we experience, unlike objects, sensations, emotions, thoughts, or memories.

Thus, experience is dualistic, not the dualism of mind and matter but the dualism of awareness and the contents of awareness. To put it another way, experience consists of the observer and the observed. Our sensations, our images, our thoughts — the mental activity by which we engage and define the physical world — are all part of the observed. In contrast, the observer — the 'I' — is prior to everything else; without it there is no experience of existence. If awareness did not exist in its own right there would be no 'I'. There would be 'me', my personhood, my social and emotional identity — but no 'I', no transparent centre of being.

Confusion of Awareness and Contents

In the very centre of the finite world is the 'I'. It doesn't belong in that world, it is radically different. In saying this, I am not suggesting a solipsistic ontology. The physical world exists for someone else even when I am sleeping. But any ontology that relegates awareness to a secondary or even an emergent status ignores the basic duality of experience. Currently, there are many voices denying the dualistic ontology of awareness and contents. For example, Searle attacks mind–body dualism, regarding consciousness (awareness) as an emergent property of material reality. He likens it to liquidity, a property that emerges from the behaviour of water molecules composed of hydrogen and oxygen — atoms that do not themselves exhibit liquidity. 'Consciousness is not a "stuff", it is a *feature* or *property* of the brain in the sense, for example, that liquidity is a feature of water' (Searle, 1992).[2] But liquidity, understandable as it may be from considerations of molecular attraction, is part of the observed world, similar to it from that ontological perspective. To state that the subjective 'emerges' from the objective is quite a different proposition, about which the physical sciences have nothing to say.

Colin McGinn also insists that there is no duality of mind and matter — all can ultimately be explained in physical terms — but he asserts that the critical process by which a transition occurs from one to the other will never be understood because of our limited intellectual capacity (McGinn, 1991). McGinn believes that the observer/observed duality is apparent rather than real; there is a physical transition from the observed to the observer. But the ontological gap between a thought and a neuron is less than that between the observer and the observed; there is nothing to be compared to the 'I', while thoughts and neurons are linked by their being objects of observation, contents of 'I', sharing some characteristics such as time and locality.[3] Granted that a blow on my head may banish 'I', its relationship to the observed is fundamentally different from anything else we can consider. The best that can be said for the materialist interpretation is that the brain is a necessary condition for 'I'.

Confusion about 'I'

One can read numerous psychology texts and not find any that treat awareness as a phenomenon in its own right, something distinct from the contents of consciousness. Nor do their authors recognize the identity of 'I' and awareness. To the contrary, the phenomenon of awareness is usually confused with one type of content or another. William James made this mistake in his classic, *Principles of Psychology*. When he

---

[2] Liquidity may not be the best example of emergence; both hydrogen and oxygen exhibit liquidity at very low temperatures.

[3] For an interesting discussion of this point, see William James' essay, 'Does consciousness exist?' (James, 1922).

introspects on the core 'self of all other selves' he ends up equating the core self with 'a feeling of bodily activities . . .' concluding that our experience of the 'I', the subjective self, is really our experience of the body:

> . . . *the body, and the central adjustments* which accompany the act of thinking in the head. *These are the real nucleus of our personal identity*, and it is their actual existence, realized as a solid, present fact, which makes us say 'as sure as I exist' (James, 1950).

To the contrary, I would say that I am sure I exist because my core 'I' is awareness itself, my ground of being. It is that awareness that is the 'self of all other selves'. Bodily feelings are *observed*: 'I' is the observer, not the observed.

Beginning with behavioural psychology and continuing through our preoccupation with artificial intelligence, parallel distributed processing, and neural networks, the topic of awareness *per se* has received relatively little attention. When the topic does come up, consciousness in the sense of pure awareness is invariably confused with one type of content or the other.

A few contemporary psychiatrists such as Gordon Globus (1980) have been more ready to recognize the special character of the self of awareness, the observing self, but almost all end up mixing awareness with contents. For example, Heinz Kohut developed his Self Psychology based on considering the self to be a superordinate concept, not just a function of the ego. Yet he does not notice that awareness is the primary source of self experience and concludes: 'The self then, quite analogous to the representations of objects, is a content of the mental apparatus' (Kohut, 1971).

We see the same problem arising in philosophy. After Husserl, nearly all modern Western philosophical approaches to the nature of mind and its relation to the body fail to recognize that introspection reveals 'I' to be identical to awareness.[4] Furthermore, most philosophers do not recognize awareness as existing in its own right, different from contents. Owen Flanagan, a philosopher who has written extensively on consciousness, sides with James and speaks of 'the illusion of the mind's "I"' (Flanagan, 1992). C.O. Evans starts out recognizing the impor tance of the distinction between the observer and the observed, 'the subjective self', but then retreats to the position that awareness is 'unprojected consciousness', the amorphous experience of background content (Evans, 1970). However, the background is composed of elements to which we can shift attention. It is what Freud called the preconscious. 'I'/awareness has no elements, no features. It is not a matter of a searchlight illuminating one element while the rest is dark — it has to do with the nature of light itself.

In contrast, certain Eastern philosophies based on introspective meditation emphasize the distinction between awareness and contents.[5] Thus, Hindu Samkhya philosophy differentiates *purusa*, the witness self, from everything else, from all the experience constituting the world, whether they be thoughts, images, sensations, emotions or dreams. A classic expression of this view is given by Pantanjali:

> Of the one who has the pure discernment between *sattva*
> (the most subtle aspect of the world of emergence)
> and *purusa* (the nonemergent pure seer)
> there is sovereignty over all and
> knowledge of all.   (Chapple, 1990.)

---

[4]   Robert Forman is an exception. See Forman (1993).

[5]   For discussions of this point and its relationship to philosophical problems see Forman (1990b) and Shear (1990).

Awareness is considered to exist independent of contents and this 'pure consciousness' is accessible — potentially — to every one. A more contemporary statement of this position is given by Sri Krishna Menon, a twentieth century Yogi:

> He who says that consciousness is never experienced without its object speaks from a superficial level. If he is asked the question 'Are you a conscious being?', he will spontaneously give the answer 'Yes'. This answer springs from the deepmost level. Here he doesn't even silently refer to anything as the object of that consciousness (Menon, 1952).

In the classical Buddhist literature we find:

> When all lesser things and ideas are transcended and forgotten, and there remains only a perfect state of imagelessness where Tathagata and Tathata are merged into perfect Oneness . . . (Goddard, 1966).[6]

Western mystics also speak of experiencing consciousness without objects. Meister Eckhart declares:

> There is the silent 'middle', for no creature ever entered there and no image, nor has the soul there either activity or understanding, therefore she is not aware there of any image, whether of herself or of any other creature' (Forman, 1990).

Similarly, Saint John of the Cross:

> That inward wisdom is so simple, so general and so spiritual that it has not entered into the understanding enwrapped or clad in any form or image subject to sense' (1953).

The failure of Western psychology to discriminate awareness from contents, and the resulting confusion of 'I' with mental contents, may be due to a cultural limitation: the lack of experience of most Western scientists with Eastern meditation disciplines.[7]

Eastern mystical traditions use meditation practice to experience the difference between mental activities and the self that observes. For example, the celebrated Yogi, Ramana Maharshi, prescribed the exercise of 'Who am I?' to demonstrate that the self that observes is not an object; it does not belong to the domains of thinking, feeling, or action (Osborne, 1954). 'If I lost my arm, I would still exist. Therefore, I am not my arm. If I could not hear, I would still exist. Therefore, I am not my hearing.' And so on, discarding all other aspects of the person until finally, 'I am not this thought,' which could lead to a radically different experience of the 'I'. Similarly, in Buddhist *vipassana* meditation the meditator is instructed to simply note whatever arises, letting it come and go. This heightens the distinction between the flow of thoughts and feelings and that which observes.[8]

Attempts to integrate Eastern and Western psychologies can fall prey to the same confusion of 'I' and contents, even by those who have practised Eastern meditation disciplines. Consider the following passage from *The Embodied Mind*, a text based on

[6] For a detailed account see Daniel Goleman, 'The Buddha on meditation and states of consciousness', in Shapiro and Walsh (1984).

[7] The key activity of modern Western psychotherapy is to enhance the experience of the observing self, discriminating it from the contents of the mind. Indeed, Freud's basic instructions on free association bear a striking resemblance to the instructions for *vipassana* meditation (Deikman, 1982).

[8] In Buddhism, the meditation experience may be given different interpretations. Walpole Rahula is emphatic in saying that Buddha denied that consciousness exists apart from matter and therefore rejected the idea of a permanent or enduring Self or Atman (Rahula, 1959). In contrast, D. T. Suzuki identifies the Self with absolute subjectivity (Suzuki *et al.*, 1960). However, both Vedantic and Buddhist commentators agree on the illusory nature of the self-as-thing.

experience with mindfulness meditation and correlating Western psychological science with Buddhist psychology.

> ... in our search for a self ... we found all the various forms in which we can be aware — awareness of seeing and hearing, smelling, tasting, touching, even awareness of our own thought processes. So the only thing we didn't find was a truly existing self or ego. But notice that we did find experience. Indeed, we entered the very eye of the storm of experience, we just simply could discern there no self, no 'I' (Varela *et al.*, 1991).

But when they say, '... *we* just simply could discern there no self, no "I"', to what does 'we' refer? Who is looking? Who is discerning? Is it not the 'I' of the authors? A classic story adapted from the Vedantic tradition is relevant here:

> A group of travellers forded a river. Afterwards, to make sure everyone had crossed safely, the leader counted the group but omitted himself from the count. Each member did the same and they arrived at the conclusion that one of them was missing. The group then spent many unhappy hours searching the river until, finally, a passerby suggested that each person count their own self, as well. The travellers were overjoyed to find that no one was missing and all proceeded on their way.

Like the travellers, Western psychology often neglects to notice the one that counts. Until it does, its progress will be delayed.

Similarly, discussions of consciousness (awareness) as 'point of view' (Nagel, 1986) or 'perspective' do not go far enough in exploring what the 'first person perspective' really is. In my own case, it is not myself as Arthur Deikman, psychiatrist, six feet tall, brown hair. That particular person has specific opinions, beliefs, and skills all of which are part of his nominal identity, but all of which are observed by his 'I', which stands apart from them. If awareness is a fundamental in the universe — as proposed most recently by Herbert (1994), Goswami (1993) and Chalmers (1995) — then it is 'I' that is fundamental, as well, with all its ontological implications. Arthur Deikman is localized and mortal. But what about his 'I', that light illuminating his world, that essence of his existence? Those studying consciousness, who can see the necessity for according consciousness a different ontological status than the physical, tend not to extend their conclusions to 'I'. Yet, it is the identity 'I' = awareness that makes the study of consciousness so difficult. Güven Güzeldere (1995) asks:

> Why are there such glaring polarities? Why is consciousness characterized as a phenomenon too familiar to require further explanation, *as well as* one that remains typically recalcitrant to systematic investigation, by investigators who work largely within the same paradigm? (Güzeldere, 1995.)

The difficulty to which Güzeldere refers is epitomized by the problem: Who observes the observer? Every time we step back to observe who or what is there doing the observing, we find that the 'I' has jumped back with us. This is the infinite regress of the observer, noted by Gilbert Ryle, often presented as an argument against the observing self being real, an existent. But identifying 'I' with awareness solves the problem of the infinite regress: we know the internal observer not by observing it but *by being it*. At the core, we *are* awareness and therefore do not need to imagine, observe, or perceive it.

Knowing by being that which is known is ontologically different from perceptual knowledge. That is why someone might introspect and not *see* awareness or the 'I', concluding — like the travellers — that it doesn't exist. But thought experiments and introspective meditation techniques are able to extract the one who is looking from what is seen, restoring the missing centre.

Once we grant the identity of 'I' and awareness we are compelled to extend to the core subjective self whatever ontological propositions seem appropriate for awareness. If awareness is non-local, so is the essential self. If awareness transcends material reality so does the 'I'. If awareness is declared to be non-existent then that same conclusion must apply to the 'I'. No matter what one's ontological bias, recognition that 'I' = awareness has profound implications for our theoretical and personal perspective.

References

Blackmore, Susan (1994), 'Demolishing the self', *Journal of Consciousness Studies*, **1** (2), pp. 280–2.

Chalmers, David J. (1995), 'The puzzle of conscious experience', *Scientific American*, December, pp. 80–6.

Chapple, Christopher (1990), 'The unseen seer and the field: consciousness in Samkhya and Yoga', in Forman (1990a).

Deikman, Arthur (1982), *The Observing Self: Mysticism and Psychotherapy* (Boston, MA: Beacon Press).

Dennett, Daniel (1991), *Consciousness Explained* (Boston, MA: Little, Brown & Co.).

Evans, C.O. (1970), *The Subject of Consciousness* (London: George Allen & Unwin Ltd.).

Flanagan, Owen (1992), *Consciousness Reconsidered* (Cambridge, MA and London: MIT Press).

Forman, Robert K.C. (ed. 1990a), *The Problem of Pure Consciousness — Mysticsim and Philosophy* (New York: Oxford University Press).

Forman, Robert (1990b), 'Eckhart, Gezuken, and the ground of the soul', in Forman (1990a).

Forman, Robert (1993), 'Mystical knowledge: knowledge by identity', *Journal of the American Academy of Religion*, **61** (4), pp. 705–38.

Globus, Gordon (1980), 'On "I": the conceptual foundations of responsibility', *American Journal of Psychiatry*, **137**, pp. 417–22.

Goddard, Dwight (ed. 1966), *A Buddhist Bible* (Boston, MA: Beacon Press).

Goswami, Amit (1993), *The Self-Aware Universe: How Consciousness Creates the Material World* (New York: Putnam).

Güzeldere, Güven (1995), 'Problems of consciousness: a perspective on contemporary issues, current debates', *Journal of Consciousness Studies*, **2** (2), pp. 112–43.

Herbert, Nick (1994), *Elemental Mind: Human Consciousness and the New Physics* (New York: Plume Penguin).

James, William (1922), *Essays in Radical Empiricism* (New York: Longmans, Green and Co.).

James, William (1950), *The Principles of Psychology: Volume One* (New York: Dover).

John of the Cross, St. (1953), *The Complete Works of St. John of the Cross, Vol. 1* (Westminister: Newman Press).

Kohut, Heinz (1971), *The Analysis of the Self* (New York: International Universities Press).

McGinn, Colin (1991), *The Problem of Consciousness: Essays Towards a Resolution* (Oxford: Blackwell).

Menon, Sri Krishna (1952), *Atma-Nirvriti* (Trivandrum, S. India: Vedanta Publishers).

Nagel, Thomas (1986), *The View from Nowhere* (Oxford: Oxford University Press).

Osborne, Arthur (1954), *Ramana Maharshi and the Path of Self-Knowledge* (London: Rider).

Rahula, Walpola (1959), *What the Buddha Taught* (New York: Grove Press).

Searle, John (1992), *The Rediscovery of the Mind* (Cambridge, MA: MIT Press).

Shapiro, Deane H. and Walsh, Roger N. (ed. 1984), *Meditation: Classical and Contemporary Perspectives* (New York: Aldine).

Shear, Jonathan (1990), *The Inner Dimension: Philosophy and the Experience of Consciousness* (New York: Peter Lang).

Suzuki, D.T., Fromm, Erich and De Martino, Richard (1960), *Zen Buddhism and Psychoanalysis* (New York: Grove Press).

Varela, Francisco J., Thompson, Evan and Rosch, Eleanor (1991), *The Embodied Mind: Cognitive Science and Human Experience* (Cambridge, MA: MIT Press).

Part 6

Further methodological questions

José Luis Bermúdez

Reduction and the Self

Galen Strawson's opening chapter[1] offers us one way of modelling the self, one that starts from the phenomenology of the sense of self and derives from that metaphysical conclusions about the nature of the self. Strawson is surely correct to hold that phenomenological considerations cannot be ignored in thinking about the metaphysics of the self. I am not as convinced as he is, however, that phenomenology is the royal road to metaphysics. What I want to sketch out in this short chapter is another approach to the metaphysics of the self, one that is driven by reductivist concerns. As far as I can see it is an open question whether there are any global points of disagreement between us (although there are certainly some local ones).

Intertheoretic reduction is a well established scientific phenomenon. Apparently autonomous bodies of scientific theory have at regular intervals in the history of science been shown to be either derivable from or explicable in terms of other, more fundamental, parts of scientific theory. Prime examples include the reduction of classical thermodynamics to statistical molecular mechanics and the explication of classical genetic theory in terms of molecular biology. It is not surprising that scientific reduction is a tantalising ideal for ontologically-minded philosophers. Ontology is the business of explaining what types of entity the world contains, and most ontologists are understandably concerned to minimise the number of distinct types of entity that exist. But if a theory containing one, perhaps problematic, type of entity can be reduced to a theory in which that first type of entity does not feature but which instead appeals to a second, perhaps less problematic, type of entity, then it might be thought that one need only have the second type of entity in one's ontology. The work done by the initial theory can be done without positing the existence of the problematic type of entity at all. Philosophers who believe that this can be done are said to be reductionists with respect to the type of entity that is eliminated.

But there is another side to scientific reductions. Showing that one area of science is reducible to another more fundamental part of science does not show that the reduced theory is in any sense false. Quite the contrary. There is a sense in which the theory that is reduced acquires the legitimacy of the theory to which it is reduced. When the reducing theory is a well-established and powerful scientific theory, then the reduced theory becomes continuous with it and therefore to a certain extent validated by it — although the existence of the reduction shows that it might in principle be dispensed with. This second aspect of scientific reductions is no less philosophi-

---

[1] References to 'Strawson' are to this volume, pp. 1–24, unless otherwise stated.

cally appealing than the first. Although the view is slightly out of favour now, there are philosophers who hold that without a reduction of mental states (like beliefs and desires) to physical states the reality of mental states is in doubt (Churchland, 1981).

Of course, it is a pressing question whether these motivations for reductionism are compatible. There is a *prima facie* tension between ontological reduction and reductive legitimation (Wright, 1986, 1.4). I do not want to go into this general issue here, however. This is partly because positions on this issue will depend upon views about the nature of causality. But it is also because the balance between the two will be different for different cases of reduction. The classic philosophical reductions tend to be more reductively legitimating than ontologically reductive. By philosophical reductions I means those reductions in which what is being reduced is not a part of science. A reduction of folk psychology to neurophysiology would be a paradigm of such a philosophical reduction, as would a reduction of the so-called secondary qualities to the so-called primary qualities. Such philosophical reductions are, it seems to me, more likely to be reductively legitimating than ontologically reductive because they work to defuse *prima facie* conflicts between different and seemingly incompatible modes of explanation. They bring the apparently anomalous within the orbit of the comprehensible. Philosophical reductions, I should add, are unlikely to be carried out by philosophers.

The type of philosophical reduction most frequently discussed in the literature is that of folk psychology to neurophysiology. This reductive project is motivated by the thought that the apparently problematic and anomalous domain of the psychological can be brought within the ambit of the natural sciences by mapping mental states onto more basic physical/biological processes whose interactions will eventually be explicable in neurophysiological terms. Sensory neurophysiology is at the moment in too undeveloped a state for the prospects of the reductive project to be properly evaluated in purely scientific terms. Nonetheless, the general flavour of the philosophical discussion of the reductive project has been highly critical. There is a range of reasons for this, some more respectable than others, but one good way to understand what is at stake in the resistance to reduction is through the idea that the concept of a self or person has a central and irreducible role to play in our understanding of mental states.[2] Let me explain.

Suppose one thinks that selves or persons form a distinct natural kind, with criteria of identity and individuation fundamentally different from those of any other type of entity in the world. That is, to use an Aristotelian vocabulary, suppose that persons are members of a distinctive natural class of substances — that they form a distinctive category with its own principles of classification. This would entail two consequences, both of which are highly inimical to reductionism (Lowe, 1995). The first consequence concerns the relation between the particular mental states and the persons who 'own' them. It is that we have to view mental states as modes of the substance that is the person to whom those mental states are ascribed. If this is right, then mental states (or, more cautiously, *some* mental states) are essentially individuated with reference to persons.[3] There is no way of identifying a mental state without iden-

---

[2] I shall use 'self' and 'person' interchangeably.

[3] The global thesis is defended by P.F. Strawson (1959, chapter 3), while Cassam (1992) defends the more local thesis.

tifying it as the mental state of some person. This would be fatal to the project of psycho-physical reductionism, because the base for any such reduction would consist of physical states which are not essentially individuated with reference to persons.

There is a second consequence. Assume that persons are members of a substantial kind. Part of what we mean by saying that something is a member of a substantial kind is that it is subject to the laws which are distinctive of that kind. When that substantial kind is a natural kind, those laws will be natural laws. So, it follows that persons will be the subject of distinctive natural laws. Now, this in itself is not directly inimical to reductionism, but it is when we combine it with a popular view of what characterizes those distinctive natural laws which apply to the putative substantial kind of persons — namely, that they are governed by normative ideals of rationality in a way that other natural laws, such as those governing the behaviour of neurophysiological states, are not.

Neither of these consequences of viewing selves or persons as a substantial kind seems to me to be at all attractive. On the other hand, it is not clear to me that we *do* have to view persons or selves as a substantial kind. There is room, I think, for a form of reductionism about the self. On this sort of view the world can be described in impersonal terms, and the concept of a self or person is, although undoubtedly useful, theoretically dispensable. We do not need to ascribe mental states to persons, and it is a mistake to think that there are any distinctive natural laws peculiar to those things to which we do ascribe mental states, even the most complex ones.

The key motivation for reductionism about the self, to my mind, derives from the more general attractiveness of the overarching project of psychophysical reductionism. Putting this to one side for the moment, however, there are two further motivating arguments that might be adduced in support of reductionism about the self. The first line of argument has been developed at considerable length by Derek Parfit (1984). It starts with a version of the general ontological principle that there is no entity without identity, interprets this so that it is satisfied only if there is always a determinate answer to the question of whether the putative entity has continued or ceased to exist, and then deploys thought experiments and Sorites-style reasoning to show that cases can be imagined where there is no such determinate answer.

To appreciate a second motivating argument for reductionism one can do no better than cast one's mind back to the eighteenth century and in particular to David Hume. Hume envisioned and tried to carry out a naturalization of the mind. He called for a science of man that would do for the study of human nature what Newtonian physics had done for the study of the natural world. A Humean science of man is one that explains human psychology, both cognitive and moral, in terms of natural causal laws that show how individual mental states give rise to each other and to actions. Hume's psychological laws are, of course, associationist, but there is no need to follow him in this. The crucial point is that the laws that govern the behaviour of mental states are laws that hold over individual mental states, like thoughts, volitions and emotions. It is not surprising that Hume should have been the first reductionist about the self, for on his view of psychology the only interesting psychological facts there are are facts about the relations between mental states. Hume's reductionist theory of the self, the so-called bundle theory, is a natural corollary of his science of the mind. There is no room in the science of man for any person or self to 'own' mental states, and so it is natural to see the mind as just a collection of mental states.

The Humean point, it seems to me, is this. The only items that we need in our psychology are those which feature in the law-governed explanations provided by the science of man, which we might perhaps prefer to call cognitive science. There is no place in our ontology for anything that does not feature in such explanations. But psychological explanation is concerned purely and simply with mental states and how they are related to each other and to physical states. The only place there might be for the self or the person in one's ontology would be if selves and persons could be *reduced* to relations between mental states and/or physical states. Selves are not causally efficacious — so why say that they exist if they cannot be reduced to collections of interrelated things that are causally efficacious?

My discussion of reductionism in this short chapter will be limited. I will only discuss one narrow class of mental states, namely, those bound up with the capacity for first-person thought. By this I mean the capacity to think thoughts whose natural linguistic expression is the first-person pronoun — thoughts it would be natural to express with sentences of the form 'I am F'. Autobiographical memories of particular episodes in one's life are an obvious example, as are self-ascriptions of sensations and reports of one's intentions. First-person thoughts have been held by many philosophers to pose an insuperable problem for reductionism about the self, and hence by extension for the more general project of psychophysical reductionism.

Why might one think that first-person thoughts are problematic for reductionism? Let us start with the proposition that a thinker's first-person thoughts are inferentially integrated, where this means that from any two premises, both stated using the first-person, it is legitimate for the thinker to draw inferences which presuppose the identity of the thing referred to in the two premises — namely, himself. This applies both to straightforward self-predications, such as 'I am happy' and to more complicated first-person mental states like autobiographical memories. Let me call these *first-person inferences*. Objections to reductionism often start from the question: what explains the legitimacy of first-person inferences? The anti-reductionist has a simple answer. The truth conditions for the first-person pronoun are, according to the anti-reductionist, that any token of 'I' refers to the person who produces it. The legitimacy of first-person inferences is simply that the same person produced all the relevant tokens of 'I'.[4] But this account obviously makes constitutive reference to persons. How can the reductionist deal with first-person inferences?

Obviously, reductionism cannot accept the account of the truth conditions of the first-person pronoun just given. The reductionist has to say something like: any token of 'I' refers to the suitably interconnected series of mental and physical states of which it forms a part. Of course, reference to an interconnected series of mental and physical states is not what we intend to achieve when we use the first-person, but it is not generally true that we can refer only to what we intend to refer to. It is true when reference is fixed by definite descriptions, but the reference of the first-person pronoun is not fixed by definite descriptions. So, how does the reductionist move from this to an account of first-person inference? The move is straightforward. first-person inferences are legitimately made when the relevant tokens of 'I' all occur within the same series of mental and physical states.

---

[4] This line of argument is pressed in chapter five of Campbell (1994). For further discussion see Bermúdez (1995b).

Of course, though, the crucial difficulty which reductionism faces has been glossed over. What is it for a series of mental and physical states to be suitably interconnected in a way that will make it a suitable referent for a token of the first-person pronoun? A reductionist with functionalist sympathies will obviously want to appeal to causal links as the factors which sort out mental states into what one might describe neutrally as separate *psychological spaces*. The first-person pronoun refers to a series of mental and physical states that are causally connected to form a distinct psychological space. What sort of causal connections are these? In the case of first-person thoughts a functionally minded reductionist will stress the immediate implications that first-person thoughts have for action, or the causal connections between today's self-ascriptive thought 'I am tired now' and tomorrow's autobiographical memory 'I was tired yesterday'.

How might this causal account help us with the problem of first-person inference? The functionally minded reductionist could well say the following. What is going on in first-person inferences is explicable in terms of a disposition to draw first-person conclusions from a set of first-person premises. What makes those first-person premises the thoughts that they are is precisely that they have a propensity to interact causally in such a way as to bring about the thought that is the conclusion of the inference. On this view there is no mystery about first-person inference. The existence of first-person inferences is just a function of the causal roles of first-person thoughts.

Many opponents of reductionism will think that this account is based upon the very basic mistake of failing to distinguish between causal and normative relations. What is significant about first-person inferences, critics would say, is precisely that they are inferences — that the truth of the premises entails the truth of the conclusion. This normative relation of entailment is fundamentally different from the factual relation of causation — or so it is often said (McDowell, 1985; Campbell, 1992).

It is most plausible, I think, to take it as a claim about explanation. The suggestion is that simply saying that the existence of certain first-person thoughts produces a disposition to generate first-person inferences leaves it unexplained *why* this should be the case.[5] There is an obligation to explain what is going on here — an obligation that can be discharged only by recognizing that the same person is the subject of all the first-person thoughts in the inference. It is because the same person is the subject of all the thoughts that the entailment holds, and the fact that the entailment holds is what legitimates the first-person inference.

But how exactly is this supposed to work? There is one way of taking it which is clearly false. Suppose 'A' and 'B' are two first-person thoughts, appropriately related. Conjoining 'A' and 'B' obviously entails the conjunctive thought 'A & B', but it is not the case that if I think 'A' and I think 'B' I must think 'A & B'. The conjunctive thought is distinct from the conjunction of the two individual thoughts. This is just an application of the familiar principle that we can think thoughts without thinking everything that they entail — or even the most obvious things that they entail. So, first-person inferences are not *dictated* by logical relations of entailment. What work, then, is the appeal to normative relations actually doing? The idea is presumably that they are in some sense *warranted* by such normative connections in a way that they cannot be when the connections are construed causally or functionally.

---

[5] See Cassam (1992), p. 378.

But here too it is hard to extract a clear thesis. It is far from obvious that first-person inferences are the sorts of things that need justification or warrant in any epistemologically interesting sense. To get any sort of purchase on this idea we would need to show the possibility of a situation in which a first-person inference causally or reductively specified was not justified. That is, we would need to make it credible that, for any functional or causal characterization of first-person inferences, a first-person conclusion, say 'I am F and G', might be derived in the appropriate causal or functional way from the first-person thoughts 'I am F' and 'I am G' in a way that would count as an unjustified first-person inference. I can think of no such cases. But without such an example to hand it is unclear what content there is in the charge of conflating the causal with the normative, and hence how we are to evaluate the more general anti-reductionist argument.

Scepticism about the explanatory power of appealing to normative relations between states of a single person is reinforced when we consider a case where the conjuncts 'A' and 'B' and the conjunction 'A & B' are actually explicitly thought. *Ex hypothesi* we have a normative entailment. But in what sense is this normative entailment underwritten by appeal to persons? Again, it is not very clear. We want to know why *these* two first-person thoughts lead to *this* first-person conclusion — as opposed, of course, to these other first-person thoughts (over there, as it were) which are completely uninvolved. The anti-reductionist answer is that the first lot of thoughts belong to person A while the second lot belong to person B. But why is this informative? How is person A distinguished from person B? There is a very basic problem here. If A and B are persons who are the subjects of mental and physical states then either these persons are something over and above the sum of the relevant mental and physical states, suitably organized, or they are not. If they are indeed something over and above those states, then it is not clear how they are to be distinguished since *ex hypothesi* it cannot be in either physical or mental terms. But if on the other hand it is accepted that persons are no more than sum of the relevant mental and physical states, then in ascribing a mental state to a particular person we seem to be doing no more than specifying the connections that it holds to certain other mental and physical states. It would seem then that we are right back where we started. We still don't have an explanation of the connections between *these* first-person thoughts and *those* first-person thoughts, because the relativization to persons that was supposed to explain it presupposes those very connections.

One might wonder at this point whether we need an explanation at all. Why not just take the connections between first-person thoughts to be basic? It might be thought, for example, that it is just a brute fact that *these* first-person thoughts are causally connected with *those* first-person thoughts. These given causal connections are all that we need to define a distinct psychological space. Distinct psychological spaces are defined as those collections of mental states across which the appropriate causal connections hold.

It is obvious why an anti-reductionist would be unhappy with this sort of deflationary theory. But it seems to me that it should be no more appealing to a reductionist. It is foreign to the reductionist spirit to allow brute psychological facts about the relations between mental states. But this leaves us in an unappealing position. On the one hand, we need to find some explanation of the connections that weld mental states into distinct psychological spaces. But on the other hand, relativization to persons is clearly not going to achieve this. What if anything is?

There are, it seems to me, two elements in a satisfactory explanation of the unity of a psychological space. The first element derives from the physical realization of the relevant mental states.[6] The second derives from the content of those states. Let me take these in order. The reductionist needs to explain what grounds the causal connections between mental states in a single psychological space. The simple solution is to say that these causal connections hold in virtue of the existence of suitable neural pathways between the states in the central nervous system that realize the mental states in question. The propensity of today's self-ascription 'I am in pain' to generate tomorrow's autobiographical memory 'I was in pain yesterday' is due to the fact that the two thoughts are realized in a brain so constituted that thoughts of the first type tend to give rise to thoughts of the second type. Of course, it is not sufficient to say that it is simply a function of their both being realized in the same brain, for it is well known that the appropriate neural pathways can fail to hold within a single brain. It is the existence of the pathways not the singleness of the brain that is important.

But there is more to the existence of a single psychological space than the existence of appropriate causal connections between mental states. Defining the unity of a psychological space is equally a matter of capturing what it is that makes the states within that space internally coherent. What confuses matters here is the thought that capturing the internal coherence of a psychological space requires showing how all the states in that psychological space cohere with each other. This is what leads the anti-reductionist astray, because the anti-reductionist tries to find global internal coherence in the supposed fact that they all belong to the same person. But the internal coherence of a psychological space can be captured without a common owner for all the mental states in that psychological space. It is a function of the coherence of content across all the perceptually-based states within that psychological space. By a perceptually-based state I mean one whose content is partly perceptual, and this will obviously include certain types of memory and certain types of intention. Perceptually based states are important here because of their foundational role in the acquisition of knowledge and beliefs. To the extent that there is one thing in common to all mental states in a given psychological space, apart from membership of that psychological space, it is that they are all ultimately grounded in an internally coherent series of perceptually-based states.

Of course, explaining how this grounding works is a matter for the combined efforts of epistemology and psychology, and all I want to do now is make some rather programmatic comments about the more basic notion of an internally coherent set of perceptually-based states. The internal coherence of perceptually-based states is, it seems to me, based upon the spatio-temporal continuity of the body which is their point of origin. The bodily point of origin is part of the content of perception. It is part of what it is that is actually perceived. Correspondingly, the fact that a body takes a single trajectory through the world is reflected in the content of the perceptually-based states associated with that body. Those perceptually-based states reflect a point of view, a perspective on the world (to use two rather overworked terms). It is a fact

---

[6] This is not presupposing the truth of the thesis of psychophysical reductionism. Almost all anti-reductionists would accept that mental states are realized in physical ones. What they deny, of course, is that this is a reductive relation achieved through psychophysical laws.

about the content of the perceptually-based states within a psychological life that they reflect a point of view upon the world (Bermúdez, 1995a; 1998). Here, it seems to me, is where we will find the beginnings of an explanation at the level of content of the unity of a psychological life. Extending the explanation will involve specifying more closely what it is for a series of perceptually-based states to reflect a point of view upon the world, and then specifying how other non-perceptually-based states are epistemically grounded in perceptually-based states.

The need for unity in the content of perceptually-based states associated with a body is sufficient, I think, to raise serious doubts about the possibility which Galen Strawson canvasses in the opening chapter of a three-bodied creature nonetheless thinking of itself as 'I'. The continuity of a single path through space–time is part of what grounds and makes possible the ways of thinking of oneself that ground first-person thought and linguistic self-reference (Bermúdez, 1998). It would take a lot to persuade me that one could have the latter without the former. In this respect the three-bodied example which Strawson puts forward is significantly different from the three-brains example which he also offers in support of his thesis of the irrevisable sense of the synchronic singleness of the mental self. Strawson seems absolutely right that the discovery that one's psychophysical life is in fact underwritten by three brains would not compromise one's sense of psychophysical unity. But this is in large part because the existence of the three brains would not compromise the continuity and singleness of one's path through space-time. The same can be said for Strawson's use of Kant's hypothesis in the Paralogisms of the sequence of selves.[7] Discovering that this was true would leave untouched the point of view upon which the sense of a single self largely depends.

Many anti-reductionists, however, would feel that this account of unity of content has effectively abandoned reductionism, because of the central role played by the body. My account of the unity of content has whatever plausibility it does have, they might argue, only to the extent that the person can be identified with the body. But this is not reductionist at all, because the concept of a person is still in play. In fact it is a perfectly respectable position in the philosophy of personal identity — one that is often termed animalism, because it identifies persons with human animals (Snowdon, 1995).

It is widely held that animalism represents a coherent anti-reductionist position. As far as I can see, though, this is false. Let us go back to the original characterization of the position to which reductionism is opposed. The question at issue is whether persons form a distinct natural kind — whether persons are natural substances. This is equivalent to the question whether persons have criteria of identity and individuation distinct from those of any other kind of thing. But from this perspective animalism is a reductionist thesis. If, as animalism suggests, persons just are living organisms of a particular species, then persons don't have distinctive criteria of identity — they have pretty much the same criteria of identity as any other type of organism. Of course, there are the differences between organisms that are a function of the differences between species. But these are surely trivial. If anti-reductionism about persons is to be interesting it must be saying more than this. The existence of a class of persons is philosophically challenging only in so far as it does not map onto the class of human beings. For example, the view that persons are a substantial kind seems *prima facie* to

---

[7] For further discussion of Kant's argument in the Paralogisms and how it bears upon contemporary discussions of personal identity see Bermúdez (1994).

stand in the way of general psychophysical reductionism, because it would entail that psychological states and bodily states are essentially individuated as modes of fundamentally different substances. But, on an animalist view of the matter, this is not the case. Both mental states and, say, neurophysiological states are modes of precisely the same thing — the living human organism. This is hardly an obstacle to psychophysical reduction.

The moral to draw, then, is that the only form of anti-reductionism about the self which is remotely defensible really collapses into reductionism. All other forms of anti-reductionism seem to fail because it is not at all obvious that we *have* to individuate mental states by ascribing them to persons. Although we *can* do so, the proper names denoting persons seem really to pick out interconnected series of mental and physical states. Each such series seems to be unified psychologically in two ways. First, in virtue of the existence of appropriate neural pathways connecting the physical states that realize those mental states. Second, as a function of the internal coherence of the contents of the perceptually-based states within that life, and of the foundational role that those states have for other states within that life. Describing a series of mental states as forming a unified psychological life in virtue of these two features provides the impersonal description that reductionism about the self requires.

This is a sketch of a research programme. The real work will come in spelling out just how these two features act together to create a unified psychological life. Without such a detailed account reductionism about the self will not have been placed on a solid footing. What should be clear, however, is that anti-reductionism about the self is far from being the insuperable obstacle to general psychophysical reduction that it is often taken to be.

References

Bermúdez, J L. (1994), 'The unity of apperception in Kant's *Critique of Pure Reason*', *European Journal of Philosophy*, **2**, pp. 213–40.

Bermúdez, J.L. (1995a), 'Ecological perception and the notion of a nonconceptual point of view' in Bermúdez *et al.* (1995).

Bermúdez, J.L. (1995b), 'Aspects of the self', *Inquiry*, **38**, pp. 489–501.

Bermúdez, J.L. (1998), *The Paradox of Self-Consciousness* (Cambridge, MA: MIT Press).

Bermúdez, J.L., Marcel, A. J. and Eilan N. (1995), *The Body and the Self* (Cambridge, MA: MIT Press).

Campbell, J. (1992), 'The first person: The reductionist view of the self', in Charles & Lennon (1992).

Campbell, J. (1994), *Past, Space and Self* (Cambridge, MA: MIT Press).

Cassam, Q. (1992), 'Reductionism and first person thinking', in Charles and Lennon (1992).

Charles, D. and Lennon, K. (1992), *Reduction, Explanation and Realism* (Oxford: Oxford University Press).

Churchland, P.M. (1981), 'Eliminative materialism and the propositional attitudes', *Journal of Philosophy*, **78**, pp. 67–90.

Lowe, E.J. (1995), *Subjects of Experience* (Cambridge: Cambridge University Press).

McDowell, J. (1985), 'Functionalism and anomalous monism', in *Actions and Events: Perspectives on the Philosophy of Donald Davidson*, ed. E. Lepone & B. McLaughlin (Oxford: Basil Blackwell).

Parfit, D. (1984), *Reasons and Persons* (Oxford: Oxford University Press).

Snowdon, P. (1995), 'Persons, animals and bodies' in Bermúdez *et al.* (1995).

Strawson, G. (1997), '"The Self"', *Journal of Consciousness Studies*, **4** (5–6), pp. 429–57. Reprinted in this volume, pp. 1–24.

Strawson, P.F. (1959), *Individuals* (London: Methuen).

Wright, C. (1983), *Frege's Conception of Numbers as Objects* (Aberdeen: Aberdeen University Press).

Mait Edey

Subject and Object

Dividing the Universe

A concept of self is commonly thought to have meaning only by virtue of a distinction between self and not-self. A conceptual boundary is drawn, and (in a common assumption) the universe of everything that exists is divided into two parts. One part is myself, and the other is everything which is not myself.

The referent of the pronoun 'I', when I use it, is myself. But the referent of 'self' varies with context, and not merely because we each may seem to draw a different boundary when we say 'I'. Radically different concepts and theories of self, some of them mutually incompatible, are found in psychology, sociology, philosophy, religion, artificial intelligence, and ordinary talk and opinion. These different concepts and theories draw the self/not-self boundary in radically various places. Different theorists tell me that I am, for example:

- a body consisting of matter; • a mind; • a body/mind;
- a living organism; • an organism's behaviour and/or functions;
- a person, as defined in part by social roles and relationships;
- an artifact of my culture; • an information processing program or programs;
- an immortal soul; • a kind of narrative, or a centre of narrative gravity.

Though they divide the universe differently, and draw different boundaries, these concepts or theories have in common that they do all divide the universe somehow and do all draw a boundary somewhere.

Questions about the nature of the self are often linked to questions about the nature of consciousness. The assumption that the self is something in the universe, or one part of the universe distinguishable from the rest, is linked to the assumption that consciousness is a state or property of some part of the universe, whether of an organism, a person, a brain, part of a brain, or perhaps even a machine.

To focus on the relationship between self and consciousness, it may help to prune away some distracting connotations. The various items on the list above, in their various contexts, recall controversial issues in philosophy, religion, and several sciences. These may distract us from an inquiry on what seems to me a more fundamental level. So let us focus the meaning of 'self' here in terms of such familiar distinctions as between, for instance, observer and observed, seer and seen, hearer and heard, or thinker and thought, where the role of consciousness is explicit. Such pairs generalize to the distinction between subject and object.

The two related assumptions just mentioned — (1) that I am a discrete part of the universe with some sort of boundary (physical, functional or conceptual) marking the division between me and the rest, and (2) that consciousness is a property of some part of the universe — are so deeply ingrained in much contemporary thought that to question them may seem ridiculous. But in my opinion it is exactly here that progress toward clear thinking about consciousness is blocked. A genuine breakthrough requires abandonment of these two assumptions. To that end let us examine the neglected distinction between subject and object, not in terms of some presupposed theory or other, but as we actually make it prior to any theory or opinion whatsoever. The distinction we actually make is not a matter of dividing the universe.

Making the Distinction Between Subject and Object

Here I use the term 'object' broadly. Let it refer to anything anyone might be aware of or pay attention to. It refers, then, not only to 'physical' objects, but also to such 'mental' entities or processes as pains, sensations, memories, images, dreams and daydreams, emotions, thoughts, concepts, desires, and so on. That is, any of these may be objects of attention or pass in and out of awareness.

Let the term 'subject' refer to I-who-am-aware, whatever opinion we may hold of what that 'I' may be. To be a subject, in this sense, is to be aware or conscious. I, subject, can be aware of some object; I can focus awareness in attention paid to that object; and I can distinguish myself from the object I attend to.

Now, you may believe that you are one of the items mentioned on the list above. At some earlier time in your life you may have believed you were a different item, and have since changed your mind. Or you may identify with some other item not on the list, or you may have no opinion or be suspending judgment.

But the crucial point to emphasize is this: the distinction between subject and object, and our capacity to make it, are prior to self-identification with any such item whatsoever. The distinction is prior to any particular opinion or theory about what the subject may be. By 'prior' I mean that I must already have realized THAT I am before I can even begin to wonder WHAT I am, much less decide that I am such-and-such.

At any time that you are aware of some object, or attend to some object, you won't normally have any trouble distinguishing it from yourself as subject, regardless of what you may believe about the nature of the self or of consciousness and their relation to the world. That is, you're likely to know, immediately, without having to stop and think it over, or having to collect any evidence, which is you and which is the object. You can distinguish yourself as subject from any object whatsoever ('physical' or 'mental') any time you direct your attention to that object and realize that it is not that object which is aware and paying attention, but you. The real nature of the object and the real nature of the subject may be baffling mysteries, but these mysteries are no barrier whatever to knowing which is obviously which.

Of course, if we define 'subject' as some part of the universe, with a boundary, we may well be confused about which is which. Confusion about the boundaries of the self can even become a psychiatric problem. Such a definition commits the fallacy of objectification, which occurs any time we attempt to define 'subject' in terms of objects. There will be deep philosophical questions no matter how we ground our definition, but confusion and anomalies are guaranteed if we do not ground it in the distinction we actually make.

For example, you may hold the opinion that you, the subject, are a biological organism. But this is merely a theoretical conception. The distinction itself is prior to this or any other theory. If you think you are a biological organism, you classify your hand as part of you, since it is part of the organism. But if you look at your hand, or become aware of it in any way, you experience it as an object of attention, and in this respect can distinguish it from yourself as subject. (In a statement of the form 'I am aware of X', 'hand' is among the possible variables.) It is worth emphasizing again that you don't make this distinction as an implication of whatever theory you might have about the self. Indeed, the conspicuous lack of fit between the distinctions you actually make and any theory based on objectification is the cause of all the familiar anomalies and puzzles of consciousness studies.

If we rigorously and systematically discriminate subject and object often enough, long enough, and on sufficiently various occasions, it is likely to dawn on us sooner or later that the subject is not an object. The subject is not any particular object or any combination of objects. The chief barrier to drawing this conclusion is conceptual. Prevailing conceptions of mind or consciousness, based on the unquestioned assumption of objectification, impose constraints on what we allow ourselves to realize. And once we have adopted a conception we become attached to it.

Consciousness Is Not a Property

Some of the most difficult and contentious issues in the philosophy of mind arise from the assumption that consciousness or subjectivity is to be understood as a state or property of something, or defined in terms of some state or property. Nowadays the most popular properties are physical, behavioural, or functional. Such familiar problems as the other-minds problem, the zombie problem, and the Turing test problem tempt us to seek such a definition. With a definition in hand we can hope to construct theories about consciousness and even claim we have explained it. But then somebody always objects that our definition has missed the essential meaning.

As Stevan Harnad has asked: how can we know that the identifying properties we choose are actually the right ones, in the absence of any understanding of how they relate to consciousness itself? As for 'consciousness itself', he wondered: 'What is it that something would lack if it lacked consciousness yet had the property you picked out?' (Harnad, 1994).

The other-minds problem and its variations are generated by a question: how do I justify my belief that you (or somebody else, or an animal, or perhaps a machine) are conscious?

Obviously, as a practical matter I use behavioural clues as evidence to answer the question: are you conscious? But those clues do not define the meaning of my question or of my conclusion. What then is that meaning? I can wonder if you are conscious, in the first place, only if I have already realized that I am conscious. And it is only my realization that I am conscious which defines what I mean by 'conscious' or 'consciousness'. What I have realized must be the actual referent of the word 'consciousness'.

I do not wonder whether I am conscious. I already realize I am conscious. My realization is peculiar in two respects whose significance is crucial. First, it is peculiarly obvious. Second, I don't attribute consciousness to myself on any grounds whatever. I haven't reasoned it out. I haven't looked for clues. I haven't decided what empirical evidence is relevant, and collected that evidence. No evidence is relevant. My realization that I'm conscious is neither verifiable nor falsifiable. It is not testable at all.

These peculiarities are the case because my realization is not the attribution of some property to some system. It has nothing to do with properties or their attribution. I may have a theory that I am this or that kind of a system, and I may have been led to assume that consciousness is a property of the system, but that is not what I actually realize. I don't conclude that I have passed an operational test. I don't actually check myself out to see if I exhibit any particular behavioural or functional properties. So such criteria do not define what I mean when I say that I am conscious. Therefore they cannot define what I mean when I conclude that you are conscious, unless we are willing to say that the term 'conscious' is used here in two entirely different senses, which of course gets us nowhere.

The Conflation of Two Distinctions

No end of confusion is generated by the conflation of two different distinctions: the distinction between subject and object and the distinction between mind and matter. The conflation generates an ambiguity in the meanings of the very terms 'mind' and 'consciousness' before analysis even begins. The ambiguity leads to equivocation — the shift of a term's meaning during the process of reasoning. In this case the shift is that 'mind' and 'consciousness' are used to refer sometimes to objects and sometimes to the subject, often in the same context or argument, without the shift being noticed. We inherit this conflation from Descartes, but have neglected to eliminate it along with his substance dualism.

Descartes' mind/body distinction remains fundamental to the contemporary discussion even though few contemporary philosophers and scientists are substance dualists. Fundamental issues are still conceived in terms of, on the one hand, mind (sometimes called — in the interests of analytic tractability — mental events, mental states, or mental properties), and, on the other, body or matter (events in, states of, or properties of, the brain). The mind–body problem is taken to be the problem of how to conceptualize, describe, and account for the evident relationships between these two categories of phenomena.

In this traditional conception the subject is thought to be an aspect of mind, even while mind is thought to consist of such things as thoughts, feelings, sensations, pains, and emotions. But simply by being aware of such mental phenomena I can distinguish them, as objects of awareness, from myself as subject. They are not the subject aware of them.

Much recent attention has been given to such problems as the relationship between mental objects and their neural correlates. The discussion often appears to assume that this is the fundamental philosophical problem of mind or consciousness. It is an interesting problem, to be sure, but it is not fundamental in the sense assumed, because it fails even to inquire how to conceptualize the subject, or consciousness, as distinct from all objects, whether mental or physical.

We can discard Descartes' dualism and still retain two important insights he chose to emphasize. First, he recognized that there is something peculiarly obvious about the realization of consciousness. And second, he grasped a relationship between consciousness and being: 'I think, therefore I am'. His expression of what he realized may be thought problematic, but I am nevertheless capable of realizing for myself that I am conscious, or that I am, and that there is some intimate connection between these two propositions. The obviousness of what I realize is not compromised in the slightest by my difficulties in conceptualizing or expressing it.

Unfortunately, having realized the subject, or consciousness-being, Descartes then went on to conceive the subject in objective terms, as 'mind', an immaterial substance in the world. 'I' became 'it'; subject was mistaken for a kind of non-spatial object existing as part of the universe, and all the familiar difficulties of the mind–body problem arose.

Subject and Being

Descartes failed to conceptualize coherently the implications of his basic insight, but its expression was correct in that he said 'sum' (I am) rather than 'existo' (I exist). 'Being' and 'existence' sometimes seem to be taken as synonyms. So it might be supposed that 'I exist' and 'I am' can be used to make the same statement. Indeed, there is plenty of blur in ordinary usage. But I suggest that there is a fundamental distinction to be made (whether or not we are accustomed to using the terms 'being' and 'existence' to make it), and that it is illuminating to see how this distinction relates to that between subject and object, and to what may seem to be the paradoxical nature of the subject.

The apparent paradox is this. On the one hand, my realization of consciousness/being/subject is utterly obvious and beyond doubt. But this obviousness may seem to collide with the realization that the subject is no kind of object, and is nowhere to be found, and therefore should not be supposed to exist.

Lest the distinction between being and existence be mistaken as a relic of scholastic hairsplitting, a quick etymological digression is in order. Partridge's 'Origins' says that 'exist' is from the Latin, formed by adding the prepositional prefix 'ex' to the root 'sist'. 'Sist' is from 'sistere', meaning to stay, in the sense of staying a mast: to cause to stand. 'Ex' means 'out' or 'outward'. So 'exsistere' means to stand forth, to emerge outward. (Partridge, 1983, p. 625.)

This etymology suggests that to say that something exists means that it stands forth or emerges as one object distinguishable from others; that is, it becomes figure as opposed to ground.

Runes' *Dictionary of Philosophy* (1955) gives for 'existence': 'The mode of being which consists in interaction with other things.' Interaction, of course, implies distinction and multiplicity. Many things exist, and they exist by virtue of being distinguishable from one another. The dictionary adds: 'The state of being actual, the condition of objectivity . . . Opposite of essence' (p. 102).

'Essence', said to be the opposite of 'existence', is from the Latin 'esse', to be. 'Essens' is a participle form, meaning 'being'. It may seem odd to say that existence and being are to be contrasted, but the intended sense is clear if we relate them to figure and ground. The objects of my awareness exist, but my being is the ground of their existence in awareness. The ground is not itself a figure, or object.

Implications

The related propositions that the subject is not an object, and that consciousness is not a property, have radical implications for the philosophy of mind or consciousness studies. They imply that consciousness, or the subject, or the self as most narrowly defined, is not to be identified with any entities or processes to be found as objects of attention in the world. Such an implication is likely to be resisted, because its acknowledgment means abandonment of much current theory, indeed of an entire dominant paradigm.

Nevertheless, it now seems academically respectable to say that consciousness must be conceived as something deeper than a mere physical or functional property which some things have and some things do not. It has become almost respectable to argue that consciousness must be somehow a more fundamental feature of reality. How can we make sense of such a claim? Panpsychism is mistaken, if it merely enlarges the number of objects thought to display consciousness as a property. I suggest another course: that we consider the terms 'consciousness' and 'being' as alternative attempts to conceptualize the same realization.

Something is realized, something important enough to constitute an evolutionary threshold between humans and (probably) all other terrestrial species. It is not simply conceptual and is certainly not perceptual. My dog doesn't seem to realize it, and I didn't realize it at the age of three or four. How to express it? I can say I realize that I am, or that I'm conscious, and that these seem equivalent. If they don't seem equivalent at first glance, I presume to suggest that this is because the common conceptualization of consciousness is still so defective, and because the common assumption is still that 'I am' refers to the existence of a person, or an organism, or whatever one's preferred set of objects may be.

When I realize that I am, or am conscious, I'm not realizing anything about any objects or contents of mind or awareness. I realize consciousness (or awareness, or subjectivity) itself. My realization that I am conscious is not tied to awareness of any particular objects. Indeed, it has more to do with realizing the potential absence of any particular object or objects. In realizing the potential absence of any particular objects, I realize myself or my being ('I am') as distinct from all objects. As Descartes saw, correctly in my opinion, to realize consciousness or self is to realize being.

To say that the concepts of consciousness and self are linked with the concept of being does imply a radical expansion of the discussion. If the concept of consciousness is hard, the concept of being is no easier. There is as yet no conceivable scientific approach to the problem of being, sometimes expressed (e.g. in Heidegger, 1959) as the question: Why is there anything at all, rather than nothing? Actually, this question, as phrased, seems rather to pose the problem of existence: why are there objects, rather than nothing? Similarly, the basic problem of consciousness, as often conceived, can be expressed in the question: Why does anything appear at all, rather than nothing? This question too appears to inquire about objects. Yet both questions imply something further. The existence of objects presupposes their distinction from a ground; the appearance of objects presupposes their distinction from a subject to which they appear. But further discussion of the implied relationship between subject and ground is far beyond the scope of this short chapter.

References

Harnad, S. (1994), 'Why and how we are not zombies', *JCS*, **1** (2), pp. 164–5.
Heidegger, M. (1959), *An Introduction to Metaphysics*, tr. R. Manheim (Newhaven, CT: Yale Univ. Pr.)
Partridge, E. (1983), *A Short Etymological Dictionary of Modern English* (New York: Greenwich House).
Runes, D. (ed. 1955), *Dictionary of Philosophy* (Ames, IA: Littlefield, Adams).

Tamar Szabó Gendler

Exceptional Persons

On the Limits of Imaginary Cases

It is of great use to the sailor to know the length of his line, though he cannot with it
fathom all the depths of the ocean. It is well he knows that it is long enough to reach the
bottom at such places as are necessary to direct his voyage, and caution him against running upon shoals that may ruin him.

John Locke, *Essay Concerning Human Understanding*, I:I:6

I: Introduction

The problem of personal identity

The question of personal identity (at least as it concerns contemporary Anglo-
American materialist philosophers) is the question of what the necessary and sufficient conditions are for a person at some later time to be identical with a person at
some earlier time.[1] Phrased in the language of standard discussions of the issue, the
question is: under what conditions are we correct in saying that P_2 (a person who exists at t_2) is the same person as P_1 (a person who exists at t_1)?[2] The question is a special
case of the more general question of the identity conditions for entities over time: under what conditions are we correct in saying that E_2 (an entity of sort E which exists at
t_2) is the same E as E_1 (an entity of sort E which exists at t_1)?

Responses to this question of personal identity by those who think it has a determinate categorical answer tend to be of two sorts: either it is suggested that some sort of
physical characteristic — such as having the same body — serves as the basis for
identity over time, or it is suggested that some sort of *psychological* or *mental* charac-

---

[1] For a non-materialist discussion in the same tradition, see the contribution by Swinburne in Shoemaker
and Swinburne (1984). The topic of personal identity has produced an enormous literature;
comprehensive on-line bibliographies of recent books and articles on the subject are available at
http://gort.canisius.edu/~gallaghr/pi.html and http://ling.ucsc.edu/~chalmers/biblio5.html. Two of
the best introductory discussions of the issues involved are Shoemaker's contribution to Shoemaker
and Swinburne (1984), and Noonan's survey of early modern and recent discussions in Noonan
(1989). The most useful collections of classic papers on the topic remain Perry (1975a) and Rorty
(1976); a particularly sophisticated collection of recent papers can be found in Dancy (1997).

[2] Strictly speaking, this is the question of *diachronic* identity for persons. The expression might also be
used to refer to the question of *synchronic* identity for persons. For a clear introduction to the relation
between the two questions, see Perry (1975b).

teristic — such as having the same memories — serves that role.[3] That these are the two sorts of answers that have been offered should not be surprising. We are, after all, physical beings whose most notable feature is our psychological characteristics; what is essential to who we are is presumably either the distinctive set of beliefs, desires, memories, etc. which together constitute our character, or the distinctive configuration of molecules which together constitute our body, or, perhaps, some combination of the two.

What may be surprising is how investigations of this question tend to proceed.[4] Ever since Locke (and particularly in the last 50 years or so) the philosophical literature on personal identity has centred on arguments of a certain type. These arguments use an assumed convergence of response to purely imaginary cases to defend revisionary conclusions about common-sense beliefs concerning the nature or importance of personal identity. So, for instance, one is asked to contemplate a case in which A's brain is transplanted into B's body, or a case in which some of C's memories are implanted in D's brain, or a case in which information about the arrangement of the molecules which compose E is used to create an exact replica of E at another point in space–time.[5]

Thinking about these cases is supposed to help us tease apart the relative roles played by features that coincide in all (or almost all) actual cases, but which seem to be conceptually distinguishable. So, for instance, even though we can ordinarily assume that the beliefs, desires, memories, etc. which are associated with a given body will not come to be associated with another body, it does not seem to be in principle impossible that such a state of affairs should come about. Indeed, it seems that we can describe a mechanism by which such a situation might come about: for instance, A's brain (and with it A's beliefs, desires and memories) might be transplanted into B's body. And since the scenario described strikes us as something of which we can make sense, it seems we can make judgments of fact or value about which of the two factors really matters in making A who she is. We might ask, for instance, whether it would be true to say that A had survived in a body that used to belong to B, or whether it would be right to punish the B-bodied human being for A's actions, or whether if we were A before the intended operation, we ought to worry about what would be happening to the B-bodied person afterwards. And on the basis of these judgments about what we would say in the imaginary case, we can return to the actual case having learned something about which features are essential and which accidental to our judgments concerning the nature or value of personal identity. My goal in this chapter is to suggest reasons for thinking that this methodology may be less reliable than its proponents take it to be, for interesting and systematic reasons.

---

[3] In addition, there are those who suggest that both factors are necessary, for instance, that what is required for P_1 and P_2 to be the same person is that P_2 have more than 50% of P_1's brain, along with P_1's core psychology (Unger, 1990).

[4] Consider, for instance, the following quote, taken from a book intended for a lay audience entitled *Persons: What Philosophers Say About You*:

  Philosophers frequently dream up weird examples to test their understanding of concepts. With respect to persons, they talk about machines that can duplicate human behavior and appearance, brain transplants, mind interchanges, teletransportation . . . This tends to alienate people in other fields who wonder what philosophers have been smoking (Bourgeois, 1995, p. 19).

[5] In speaking of 'A's brain' or 'B's body', I am speaking loosely, since precisely what is at issue is what sort of thing 'A' or 'B' might be. I trust that this loose talk will not be misleading.

Questioning the methodology

In general, two sorts of objections are offered when appeals to such scenarios are made.[6] The first type involve substantive disputes about particular cases: whether, for instance, divided consciousness can be imagined 'from the inside', or whether brain transplants are biologically possible. The second type concern a far more general issue: whether our concepts should (or could) support all of the implications of our beliefs concerning what is practically, physically, or conceptually possible. Those who make such objections have been partially heeded; appeals to thought experiments in discussions of personal identity are now often prefaced by a discussion of the feasibility of the scenario described, and sometimes by a discussion of the legitimacy of the methodology as such.[7] But with a few exceptions,[8] I think both critics and defenders have located the problem in the wrong place.

Certainly, *pace* extreme critics, there is nothing wrong with the methodology of thought experiment *as such*. After all, a thought experiment is just a process of reasoning carried out within the context of a well-articulated imaginary scenario in order to answer a specific question about a non-imaginary situation. Such hypothetical test cases play perfectly unobjectionable roles in legal reasoning, linguistic theorizing, scientific inquiry and ordinary conversation. And there is nothing categorically wrong with thought experiments that concern technologically or biologically or even physically impossible situations. Again, such purely counterfactual test cases play unobjectionable roles in each of the areas listed above. Rather, I will argue, the legitimacy or illegitimacy of thought experimental reasoning in a particular case depends upon the structure of the concept which the thought experiment is intended to illuminate. If the concept is structured around a set of necessary and sufficient conditions, *and* if these conditions play a role in how it is that we identify candidates as falling under that concept,[9] then imaginary cases may help us to separate essential features of the concept from accidental ones. But if the concept is not structured in that way, or if the features in question do not govern our application of the concept, then imaginary cases are likely to be misleading.[10, 11]

---

[6] See especially Wilkes (1988). Cf. also: Johnston (1987; 1989; 1992); Quine (1972); Robinson (1988); Snowdon (1991). For more general discussions of the methodology, see Sorensen (1992) and the papers collected in Horowitz and Massey (1991). See also the somewhat spotty listing at http://astro.ocis.temple.edu/~souder/thought/index.html.

[7] For a sophisticated example, see Unger (1990), pp. 7–13; for critique, see Rovane (1994).

[8] In particular, the argument I present below owes a tremendous amount to the work of Mark Johnston.

[9] In the psychological literature on concepts, this is generally referred to as the 'classical view', and is widely regarded by psychologists as inadequate in accounting for all but a few of our concepts. (For surveys of this literature, see Smith and Medin, 1981; Medin and Smith, 1984; Komatsu, 1992; for a very brief overview, see Medin and Goldstone, 1994.) I think this dismissal is overhasty, in part for the reasons discussed in Rey (1983; 1985). But since I agree in the case on which I am focusing that the view cannot account for the concept in question, I will not pursue these general issues further.

[10] For incisive discussion of these issues, see Johnston (1987). For reasons similar to my own, Johnston contends that these conditions are not met when we think about imaginary cases involving the concept 'person'.

[11] I suspect it is this distinction that explains the widespread sense that thought experiments are less problematic in science than in philosophy. It is certainly true that scientific concepts are, in general, more likely than non-scientific concepts to be structured around necessary and sufficient conditions that play a role in how we identify instances that fall under that concept.

My main contention in this chapter is that the concept of personal identity belongs to the second of these classes. Although philosophers from Locke on are correct in recognizing that a conceptual distinction can be drawn between what Locke (1710/1975) called the 'man' (or human animal) and what he called the 'person' (or set of distinct psychological characteristics), it does not follow that we are able to make informative judgments about many of the combinatoric arrangements in which these features might appear. For the fact that two features can be conceptually separated in the sense that we can imagine the one obtaining without the other in some particular case does not mean that those two features are conceptually distinct in the sense that we can make reliable judgments about them, considered in isolation. Conceptual separability guarantees conceptual distinctness only if our knowledge of the necessary and sufficient conditions of a concept is what governs our application of that concept; in other cases, we have no such guarantee.

So even if we are aware that the two features need not coincide in all possible cases, the fact that they coincide in all (or even in nearly all) actual cases may mean that there is no ascertainable fact of the matter about how we would or should respond to either in isolation. For while we may be able to make sense of exceptional situations where they come apart, we do so only by relating them back to ordinary cases where they coincide. But this means that our evaluation of the exceptional case will depend upon which mapping we use in making this assimilation. And this means that our ability to make sense of such cases outruns our ability to make reliable judgments about them.

I think this is what explains both the appeal and the inconclusiveness of thought experiments about personal identity.[12] As a matter of evolutionary fact, human persons are entities which are both biological organisms and self-conscious loci of psychological characteristics. And while these features are clearly conceptually separable — we can easily make sense of cases in which the purely biological kind 'human animal' and that kind's most striking characteristic: 'self-conscious locus of psychological characteristics' come apart — it is not clear that we can make informative *judgments* about them. For although the world forces us to think about certain exceptional cases in which a single body may be able to support more than one collection of psychological attributes (cases, for instance, of multiple personality, or of other sorts of dissociation and compartmentalization, or of memory loss and subsequent relearning), it does not present us (at least according to those whose views are the targets of my discussion) with cases in which a single set of psychological characteristics may be present in more than one body, either diachronically or synchronically.[13] And this contingent fact — that is, the fact that in almost all cases, a single mind is associated with a single body — plays a central role in how it is that we make judgments about the nature and

---

[12] For a related but somewhat different take on this question, see Rovane (1994, as well as 1998, especially chapter 2).

[13] In saying this, I do not mean to deny that there are purported cases of reincarnation, memories of past lives, soul-transfer, etc., and that commitment to the existence of such phenomena may play a central role in the conceptual schemes of millions, even billions, of people. But as far as I can tell, these purported facts play no part whatsoever in the conceptual schemes of those who make use of the sorts of imaginary cases that I will discuss below. (I thank an anonymous reviewer for *Journal of Consciousness Studies* for reminding me of the provincialism of ignoring such views.)

importance of personal identity.[14] For it is the lens through which we view the cases where the one–one coincidence does not hold.

Below, I will describe a widely-discussed imaginary case to which our responses seem to be frame-dependent; how the story is told affects how the story is evaluated. This phenomenon is easily explained if we assume that the way we make sense of such cases is by assimilating them to a class of cases with which we are familiar. Whichever of the story's features are made salient by the particular presentation will thus serve as the basis for assimilation to the ordinary cases in which the contingently associated features that together comprise ordinary cases of personhood coincide. On a biological or psychological view of personal identity, however, one or another of the responses could legitimately be criticized as mistaken. For reasons that I will discuss after I present the case, I think both responses are at least rationally permissable.

Plan for the rest of the chapter

In the remainder of the chapter, I will proceed as follows. In section II, I will briefly summarize Locke's views on the identity conditions governing objects, organisms, and persons, and describe the famous thought experiment from which modern discussions of personal identity take their inspiration. The purpose of this section is two-fold: first, to provide an example of the sort of analysis that is offered in discussions of the identity conditions for entities over time; and second, to do so in the context of the Lockean framework, which has served as a jumping off point for subsequent discussions.[15] Readers familiar with Locke's writings might skip this section without losing the thread of the argument. In section III, I will identify what I take to be the crucial aspects of Locke's thought experiment, and explain how contemporary cases can be seen as continuous with it. The purpose of this section is to identify some central assumptions which underlie contemporary discussions of the nature and importance of personal identity, and to amass intuitive support for my claim that we can make sense of cases about which we cannot make judgments. Again, the details of this section are not essential to my main argument, so readers familiar with contemporary Anglo-American literature on the nature and importance of personal identity may wish to read these pages rather quickly. The principal argument is picked up again on page 602, where I consider a particular case in some detail (that described by Bernard Williams in 'The self and the future'[1970]), and suggest a way of understanding the case in light of a more general strategy for understanding how we make sense of exceptions.

---

[14] To repeat: this is so even if there are a small number of actual exceptions.

[15] Cf. Harold Noonan's remark that just as '[i]t has been said that all subsequent philosophy consists merely of footnotes to Plato', of personal identity 'it can truly be said that all subsequent writing has consisted merely of footnotes to Locke*' (Noonan, 1989, p. 30). Whether this is an accurate description depends, of course, upon exactly how much new material can be included in (metaphoric) footnotes. But it certainly provides a rough indication of Locke's centrality, and some justification for my beginning my discussion only with Locke (as opposed to with Plato or Aristotle), and for my beginning my discussion already with Locke (as opposed to with Bernard Williams or Derek Parfit).
　　* Which would make them, I suppose, sub-footnotes to Plato.

II: The Lockean Background[16]

Locke on the identity of men and of persons[17]

Modern discussions of the metaphysics of personal identity can be traced to Locke's chapter 'Of identity and diversity' in his *Essay Concerning Human Understanding* (Locke 1710/1975, Book II, chapter XXVII). There Locke defends a view that identity is 'suited to the Idea' (§7); that is, that criteria for identity (over time) are criteria for identity as an X (over time), and that these criteria, in turn, can be categorized into several clusters, each involving different *kinds* of identity criteria. With this in mind, then, Locke sets out to provide a general taxonomy of types of identity over time for various sorts of bodily substances: first non-living, then living.[18]

The primitive bearers of bodily identity on the Lockean picture are atoms, which are the basic units of matter. So long as an atom exists, there can be no question about its identity; being fundamentally simple, the atom exists unchanged as long as it exists at all (§2). At the next level of complexity come simple clumps of matter, where 'two or more Atoms [are] joined together into the same Mass'; here continued existence requires the continued contiguity of the body's subparts, whatever the arrangement (§3).

A very different sort of criterion governs Locke's remaining categories — plants, animals, and human beings; for entities of these sorts, identity is a function not of sameness of matter, but of sameness of life. A plant, such as an oak tree, is the same plant so long as it follows a natural course of events determined by its organic unity as a living entity of a particular sort, regardless of radical changes in its form (say, from acorn to sapling) or the particular matter that makes it up (§4). Similar criteria govern animals, whose identity comes from the internally-driven unified participation of the various parts in a continuing life (§5). Finally, Locke turns to the criterion of identity for man, which is nothing more than a special case of animal identity (§6).

Thus far, Locke has introduced two sorts of identity criteria: non-living (non-artifactual) bodily substances retain their identity through identity of matter, and living bodily substances retain their identity through identity of life. This latter criterion is intended to satisfy two constraints simultaneously: first, to permit continued attribution of identity in the face of change (§6), and second, to do so without eliminating the ground for drawing distinctions between separate individuals (§7). That is, in providing a theory of identity for human beings over time, a distinction must be drawn between the sorts of changes which are entity-preserving (such as growth, or getting drunk, or the loss of a limb), and the sorts of changes which are entity-destroying

---

[16] My discussion in this section is not intended to do justice either to the details of Locke's view, or to the many issues of identity over time which thorough discussion of the view would require. For discussion of the former, the reader might fruitfully consult Mackie (1976, especially chapters 3, 5 and 6), Alston and Bennett (1988) or, for a general overview, Noonan (1989, chapter 2); a bibliographic exploration of the extensive literature on the latter question might reasonably begin with the sources listed in Noonan (1989, pp. 255–9).

[17] Throughout this section, for convenience of exposition, I follow Locke's terminology in using 'man' as a general (gender-neutral) term for human animals, and 'person' as a general term for human beings considered as psychological entities. In later sections, I make use of the terms 'Lockean men' and 'Lockean persons' respectively.

[18] I here neglect Locke's discussion of other sorts of substances — God and finite intelligences — about which identity judgments might be made. For reasons that Locke explains clearly in §2, these do not raise the sorts of puzzles that are raised when we make identity judgements about complex bodies.

(such as transformation into a beast, or death). The criterion of 'participation in a single continued Life', which is nothing more or less than the criterion for animal identity, is meant to capture precisely this distinction.[19]

The main negative conclusion of the first part of Locke's discussion is that none of the criteria of identity for bodily substances over time can do justice to what Locke will call *personal identity*. So the discussion thus far can be seen as prefatory to Locke's famous distinction between 'man' and 'person', and the corresponding distinction between the identity suited to the idea of the one, and the identity suited to the idea of the other (§7). Whereas *man* is an animal, that is, a 'living organized Body' of 'a certain Form' (§8), a *person* is 'a thinking intelligent Being, that has reason and reflection, and can consider itself as a self, the same thinking thing in different times and places' (§9). That is, a person is a self-conscious reflective being whose awareness of itself as a thinking thing over time is what serves to make it the same self.[20] The criterion of identity for personhood is 'sameness of . . . rational Being', and the personal analogue to 'participation in a single continued Life' is participation in a single consciousness: life unifies men, consciousness unifies persons.

The prince and the cobbler

With this distinction in place, Locke goes on to discuss a number of imaginary cases designed to buttress his analysis of personal identity, the most famous of which is the story of the prince and the cobbler.[21] He writes: 'Should the soul of a prince, carrying with it the consciousness of the prince's past life, enter and inform the body of a cobbler, as soon deserted by his own soul, everyone sees that he would be the same person with the prince, accountable only for the prince's actions: but who would say it was the same man?' (§15).

Locke's story is motivated by a desire to avoid putting excessive weight on a certain uniformity in the world — that persons and men coincide with sufficient regularity that the distinction between them seems to have gone unnoticed. In order to establish that the two are conceptually separable, he employs a technique well-known from scientific methodology: that two features can be shown to be discrete if it is possible for each to obtain without the other. If the story Locke has described makes sense to us, then the conceptual distinction he wishes to draw must also make sense. But this alone does not show that we can make reliable judgments about Lockean persons as self-standing entities. So let us look a bit more closely at why Locke's story seems to make sense, and why that does not show what Locke and his followers have taken it to show.

Crucial elements of the Lockean story

Locke's scenario has the following crucial elements:

(1) The set of psychological characteristics ('personality') previously associated with one body comes to be associated with another body, in such a way that it

---

[19] 'The Identity of the same *Man* consists . . . in nothing but a participation in the same continued Life, by constantly fleeting Particles of Matter, in succession vitally united to the same organized Body' (§6).

[20] 'For since consciousness always accompanies thinking . . . in this alone consists *personal Identity, i.e.* the sameness of a rational Being: and as far as this consciousness can be extended backwards to any past Action or Thought, so far reaches the Identity of that *Person*' (§9).

[21] Locke's less-famous cases — including those of the Christian Platonist, the Mayor of Queensborough, the Day-man and the Night-man, and so on — are described in the surrounding sections.

seems to the rest of the world that the Y-body manifests the personality previously associated with (the) X-(body); and it feels to the to the Y-body person [that is: the X-soul person] as if she has obtained a new body.

(2) The story describes a mechanism — the movement of the consciousness-carrying soul from one body to the other — by which the changes described in (1) come about.

(3) The mechanism is such that the X-personality is manifest in the Y-body because some substance that was present in the X-body is now present in the Y-body.

That is, the Lockean story depends upon the following three things: (1) that we can make sense of a story in which two personalities 'switch bodies'; (2) that we can describe a mechanism by which such a switch might take place; (3) that that mechanism involves some transfer of substance. What (2) and (3) help us to see is how we are able to think of the scenario described in (1) as coherent; by providing us with a narrative about how the surprising state of affairs described in (1) might come about, they help make the situation seem less mysterious. But from the fact that we can tell a story about how the world might come to be configured in some way other than the way it actually is, it does not follow that we will be able to make judgments about the various combinations of the features Locke has isolated. As the combinations grow more complex, we see that the initial illusion of certainty about the simple case was only that: an illusion.

So in the next section, I will trace the ways in which a number of widely discussed contemporary thought experiments can be seen as arising out of Locke's original case. My purpose in doing so is twofold: to demonstrate the continuity of contemporary cases with their early modern predecessors;[22] and to show how the increasing complexity which these cases introduce in no way disrupts our ability to make sense of them, but wreaks havoc with our ability to make reliable judgments.

III: Variations on the Lockean Story

Transferring matter

In direct descendents of Locke's story, only (2) is altered. Instead of the 'soul . . . carrying with it the consciousness of the prince's past life', it is the brain of the first character (carrying with it the consciousness of the character's past life) which is imagined to have been transplanted into the body of the second character. As with Locke's story, the intuition this is standardly taken to evoke is that the person has moved from one body to another. A typical presentation of this sort of story is the following:

> Imagine . . . that in the twenty-first century is it possible to transplant brains, as it is now possible to transplant hearts, and let us suppose that the brain of a Mr Brown is transplanted into the skull of a Mr Robinson. . . . The result of the operation, call him Brown-

---

[22] In the anti-thought experiment literature, one occasionally encounters remarks which suggest that the methodology is unique to contemporary Anglo-American philosophy (and hence can be dismissed out of hand as contrary to 'real' philosophy). The lie is given to this claim quite early in one's search for a counter-example: at least by the time that one opens Plato's *Republic* to the story of the Ring of Gyges. (Indeed, if Nicholas Rescher is to be believed, thought experiments were present at Western philosophy's birth; see Rescher, 1991.)

son, will then be a completely healthy person . . . with Robinson's body, but in character, memories and personality quite indistinguishable from Brown. . . . Most modern philosophers who have reflected on this case . . . have found that they could not honestly deny that Brownson, in the case imagined, was Brown (Noonan, 1989, pp. 4–5).[23]

Let us call this the 'brain transplant case'. A minor variation on this story is one in which the brains of the two characters are switched, so that, for instance, just as Brown's brain is transplanted into Robinson's skull, Robinson's is transplanted into Brown's (see, for instance, Perry, 1975b, pp. 3–6). On the standard interpretation, just as we would be inclined to say that Brownson is Brown, so too would we be inclined to say that Robin is Robinson. Let us call this the 'brain switch case'.

But the brain has a certain complexity which has led philosophers to consider a variation on the brain transplant case which is referred to as 'fission'. Following the appearance in the philosophical literature of an article entitled 'Brain bisection and the unity of consciousness' (Nagel, 1971), in which the results of Sperry's split-brain research were presented, philosophers began to consider the possibility that a single brain might in principle be able to support two loci of consciousness.[24] And if this is so, then it seems to be a shallow rather than a deep truth that various processes are localized in one or another brain hemisphere, rather than being spread throughout the brain as a whole. But from here it seems only a minor idealization to imagine a case in which all of the features of Brown's personality are realized in his brain twice-over, such that the transplant of either half to Robinson's body would be sufficient to give us a human being with all of Brown's memories, beliefs, desires, etc. But if either half would be sufficient, then we might also coherently imagine a third case, in which after being removed from Brown's body and divided in two, one half of Brown's brain is transplanted into Robinson's body, and the other half is transplanted into a third body, that of Robinson II. But then, is Brown Brownson, or Brownson II, or both, or neither? It seems clear that he cannot be both, for surely Brownson and Brownson II are distinct individuals, and if Brown were identical with both, then they would have to be identical with each other. But it seems equally problematic to say that he is one as opposed to the other; for what could make it the case that he is Brownson instead of Brownson II? And it seems no more plausible to say that he is neither one; after all, were it not for the existence of Brownson II, he would surely be identical to Brownson, and it seems odd to say that twice-over survival is tantamount to death.

Reconfiguring form

The case of fission is indeed deeply perplexing, and to say more about it here would distract us from my main line of argumentation even more than we have been already.[25] Instead, I turn to cases in which (3) is denied, that is, cases in which it is

---

[23] This version of the story derives from Shoemaker (1963).

[24] Discussions of similar cases, in which persons were simply hypothesized to 'split like amoebas', were present in the literature before mid-century. But it was only when philosophers were able to identify a mechanism by which such a process might 'actually' occur that discussion began to take on the proportions it currently has. (To be fair, there are additional factors, both micro- and macro-sociological, which may also explain the swelling literature.)

[25] Three of the most subtle and influential discussions of this case are Wiggins (1980), Parfit (1984/1987) and Johnston (1989). For a more comprehensive survey of responses, see Noonan (1989). See also the essays collected in Dancy (1997).

imagined that it is not the transfer of some substance, but rather the transfer of some information by which the circumstance described in (1) comes about. We can call these cases the 'brain state transfer case', the 'brain state exchange case' and the 'brain state duplication case'. We might, for instance, imagine a machine which scans all of the information about the configuration of the pre-switch X's brain, and then uses this information to reconfigure the brain of pre-switch Y so that the brain in Y's body comes to support all of the memories, beliefs and desires of the pre-switch X.[26] The outcome of such a process is functionally identical to the outcome of the brain transfer described above; the Y body manifests the memories, beliefs and desires of the pre-switch X, and does so because pre-switch X did. And, of course, as with the brain transfer case, we might imagine slight variations: a more complicated version of this story wherein the brain-structures of the two characters are switched, or a case in which the duplication (or multiplication) occurs without disrupting the original.

But if the correct set of instructions is enough to allow us to reconfigure one brain in such a way that it supports the psychological characteristics previously associated with another brain, then with a slightly more complicated set, we ought to be able, at least in principle, to assemble a brain, or indeed a whole human being, out of simple bits of matter of the same sort of which the original was composed. So we might imagine a case of 'teletransportation', where one or more exact duplicates of a human being would be brought into existence at a spatially remote location as a result of information garnered about the structure of the original being.

And if this is in principle possible, then it also seems possible, in principle at least, that matter might come to be configured in that way without this configuration being the result of information-transfer as described above. That is, it seems that what might be called 'independent replication' is at least in principle possible, wherein one or more exact duplicates of a human being would be brought into existence at a spatially remote location not as a result of information garnered about the structure of the original being, but as a result of some causally independent process.

Let me summarize the variations I have described on the basis of the assumptions that underlie them:

(4) assuming that the source of psychological content is localized, this could be removed and transplanted to another body (brain transfer, brain exchange);

(5) assuming that the source of psychological content is localized, redundantly realized and divisible such that either half might adequately serve as the basis for full psychology, it could be divided and doubly transplanted (fission);

(6) assuming that the source of psychological content might be realized in another physical entity of similar basic structure, the matter of that entity might be reconfigured in a way that would render it structurally identical to the original (brain state transfer, brain state exchange, brain state duplication);

(7) assuming that the same arrangement of the same kind of matter would produce the same macrostructural properties, one or more exact duplicates could, in principle, be generated at a spatially remote location (teletransportation);

[26] For early discussions of this case, see Shoemaker (1963) and Williams (1970).

(8) assuming that the same arrangement of the same kind of matter would produce the same macrostructural properties, one or more exact duplicates could, in principle, be spontaneously generated at a spatially remote location (independent replication).

It seems to me undeniable that we can make sense of such scenarios. Each represents a state of affairs that seems metaphysically, perhaps even physically possible. But this does not mean that we can make reliable judgments about how we would or should respond to such scenarios, were we to encounter them. In the next section, I will say more about this contention in the context of one particular case.

The self and the future

I now want to consider one particular case in some detail. In 'The self and the future', Bernard Williams describes an imaginary case in which one is asked to contemplate a machine of a sort rendered practicable by (6) above: when two individuals, A and B, are hooked up to the machine, it reconfigures the A-brain in such a way that it comes to be associated with all of the psychological states previously associated with the B-brain/B-body person, and reconfigures the B-brain in such a way that it comes to be associated with all of the psychological states previously associated with the A-brain/A-body person.[27] With this in place, Williams asks the reader to consider the following two stories.

In the first, one imagines A, faced with the prospect of being connected up to the machine in question. From the machine will emerge two persons: the first, the A-body person, will have the body previously associated with A, but all of the psychological states previously associated with B; the second, the B-body person, will have the body previously associated with B, but all of the psychological states previously associated with A. Before the operation, A is told that one of the two resultant persons will be given a large financial reward whereas the other will be tortured. A is asked to decide, on purely self-interested grounds, whether the reward should go to the A-body person or the B-body person.

As the case is presented, it seems sensible for A to direct the reward towards the B-body person. Among the other evidence that seems to support this decision as being correct is the fact that, when the operation is over and the goods are distributed, the B-body person — whose memories and desires correspond to those of the pre-operational A — will say rightly: 'This is just the outcome I selected! And how glad I am that I so chose.' Whereas, presumably, if the reward went to the A-body person, the B-body person would remark with outrage: 'Why am *I* sitting here in great physical discomfort, when what I requested was the reward?' (cf. Williams, 1970, pp. 48–50). The intuition evoked by this first version is that we seem to be able to make sense of there being some sort of procedure whereby two persons could, so to

[27] As one of the central cases in the personal identity literature, Williams' story has received wide discussion. A nice overview of the various responses, along with defence of Noonan's own take on these questions, can be found in Noonan (1989), chapter 10. In light of this extensive literature, my rather flat-footed presentation of the story may strike readers familiar with these discussions as rather naïve. But my purpose in presenting this case is to talk about what role imaginary cases *in themselves* can play in deciding the sorts of questions they are credited with deciding. I have no doubt that imaginary cases considered in conjunction with well-worked-out philosophical theories can do many many things.

speak, 'swap bodies'. To the extent that I bear to my future self a relation of rational prudential concern, I might properly bear that relation to someone with whom I shared no physical matter at all.[28]

The second scenario is the following. One imagines A to be in the hands of a particularly dastardly surgeon, who tells A: 'Tomorrow, you will be subjected to great physical discomfort. But before this happens, you will be operated upon with the following effect. "[Y]ou will not remember being told that this is going to happen to you, since shortly before the torture something else will be done to [you] which will make [you] forget the announcement." Indeed, you will "not remember any of the things [you are] now in a position to remember." In fact, at the moment of torment you will "not only not remember the things [you are] now in a position to remember, but will have a different set of impressions of [your] past, quite different from the memories [you] now have" — a set of memories and impressions that exactly fit the past of some other person.' Of this situation, Williams writes: 'Fear, surely, would still be the proper reaction: and not because one did not know what was going to happen, but because in one vital respect at least one did know what was going to happen — torture, which one can indeed expect to happen to oneself, and to be preceded by certain mental derangements as well.'[29]

The intuition evoked by this second version — which is, of course, just a one-sided presentation of the original scenario — is that we seem to be able to make sense of there being some sort of procedure whereby two persons could, so to speak, 'swap minds'. To the extent that I bear to my future self a relation of rational prudential concern, I might properly bear that relation to someone with whom I shared no psychological connections at all. My biological animal seems also to be *me*.[30]

Having presented these two versions of the story, Williams goes on to introduce a series of cases leading up to the story with which we were just presented:[31]

(9) First case: 'A is subjected to an operation which produces total amnesia'.

(10) Second case: 'amnesia is produced in A, and other interference leads to certain changes in his character'.

(11) Third case: 'changes in his character are produced, and at the same time certain illusory "memory" beliefs are induced in him' which do not correspond to the memories of any actual person.

---

[28] If, however, as Derek Parfit has argued, 'identity is not what matters' for rational prudential concern, then the case does not allow us to conclude anything about the identity of the person towards whom the prudential concern is directed (see Parfit, 1971; 1984/1987). I think Parfit is wrong about this, but presenting my reasons here would take us too far afield.

[29] Williams (1970), p. 52. The reader who finds such a response completely alien — as one of the anonymous referees for the *Journal of Consciousness Studies* apparently did — might think about the following structurally similar scenario. Suppose that in old age you suffer from a debilitating brain disease which leaves you unable to remember any of your earlier experiences, and which produces in (what was) your brain all sorts of apparent memories unrelated to your own past. Would you not be self-interestedly concerned if you heard that 'your' body was then scheduled to undergo some sort of physical torture? Would you think that you yourself had already died, at the moment when you lost your memories?

[30] For an extended defence of the view that we are essentially human animals, see Olson (1997). For a discussion of some of Olson's claims, see Gendler (1998).

[31] All quotations in this paragraph from Williams (1970), pp. 55–6.

(12) Fourth case: 'the same as [(11)], except that both the character traits and "memory" impressions are designed to be appropriate to another actual person, B'.

(13) Fifth case: 'the same as [(12)], except that the result is produced by putting the information into A from the brain of B, by a method which leaves B the same as he was before'.

(14) Sixth case: 'the same happens to A as in [(13)], but . . . a similar operation is [also] conducted in the reverse direction', resulting in corresponding changes in B.

In general, consideration of this series of stories has evoked three different sorts of responses. Williams himself contends that our inclination to say that A would be right to be prudentially concerned about what would happen to the A-body person in the first (amnesia) case carries through all the way to the fifth (brain state transfer) case; and since the difference between the fifth and the sixth case does not involve any difference in what happens to *A*, then it carries through to the sixth case as well. So the correct criterion of identity, Williams thinks, is a bodily criterion. By contrast, advocates of the psychological criterion of personal identity conclude just the opposite. Already in the first case, they contend, what matters for prudential concern has been lost; the Lockean person associated with the A-body has already been eliminated by the process which produces amnesia. So from the very beginning, the A-body person does not have warranted prudential concern for any of the characters described in the six cases.[32] Finally, some have taken the scenario to show that both lay legitimate claim on our intuitions,[33] and that what the case shows is that our concept of person is not definitively committed to the primacy of one or the other.[34]

In short, the Williams story perfectly illustrates the claim I have been making: that our ability to make *sense* of imaginary scenarios in which features that coincide in nearly all actual cases are recombined in novel ways far outruns our ability to make *judgments* about them. We may well feel that a scenario is perfectly coherent, without knowing what we would do or say were we to encounter it. In such circumstances, our evaluation of the case is likely to depend upon how the case is presented.

---

[32] More complicated versions of this view draw the line somewhat later along the spectrum. See, for instance, Noonan (1989).

[33] See, for instance, Carol Rovane's extremely interesting discussion of this case and its implications in Rovane (1998), chapter 2. Unfortunately, I encountered Rovane's view after I had already completed all but final revisions on this chapter.

[34] One might say, for instance, that the story provides evidence in favour of a 'closest continuer' theory: that 'to be something later is to be its closest continuer' (Nozick, 1981, p. 33). According to such a theory, to be X later is to be whatever entity it is that most closely matches the profile of characteristics associated with being X (provided that the entity matches this profile sufficiently closely to be a candidate). The closest continuer view raises certain perplexing metaphysical puzzles about the extrinsic determination of identity. (See, for instance, Johnston, 1987, and Noonan, 1989, for objections.) But I am not convinced that the question of personal identity is straightforwardly metaphysical in the way critics of the closest continuer theory assume it must be. (For further brief remarks on this suggestion, see Gendler, 1998.)

IV: The Moral of the Stories

Decision-making and assimilation to a class of familiar cases

Consider the following situation, which is standard fare in discussions of rationality.[35] Suppose that on your way to see a play, you lose a ten-dollar bill from your wallet. Upon arriving at the theatre, you discover this loss. However, you still have money in your wallet, and tickets to the play are $10 each. Do you still buy a ticket? A vast majority of people answer 'yes'.[36] By contrast, consider the following case. You have already purchased a $10 ticket for the play, but upon arriving at the theatre, you discover that you have lost the ticket. Would you buy another ticket? Most people answer 'no'.[37]

Clearly, however, at some level these cases are the same. They differ only in the form of the $10-item lost: in the first case, the $10 lost is in the form of cash, which is the paradigmatically interchangeable commodity; in the second case, the $10 lost is in the form of a ticket which is directly related to the expected gain (seeing the play).[38] But as far as their implications for action in this particular case are concerned, this difference is trivial: the purchase of the ticket is imagined to have been basically effortless; to acquire a second would be equally trifling. Indeed, the similarity between them can be seen from the fact that one can easily talk oneself out of either reaction by assimilating the first case to the second, or the second case to the first. So it seems *prima facie* irrational to treat the cases differently. If we can see that, deep down, all we have are two alternate descriptions of the same state of affairs, how can we justify our inclination to deal with them asymmetrically? To do so seems to be to give justificatory import to factors which ought not to matter: how could the mere fact that we describe something in one way rather than another justify such a striking difference in the attitudes we bear towards it?

Although I agree that it is not rationally *mandatory* that the attitudes we take towards the two situations should differ, I also do not think that it is rationally *prohib-*

---

[35] This case, along with a number of others, is first discussed in Tversky and Kahneman (1981). Again, to those familiar with the enormous literature on these subjects, my discussions here may seem superficial. As before, since the point I am trying to establish is a simple one, the many nuances of recent discussions are not relevant to my purposes. The reader interested in following up on these issues might fruitfully begin with the papers collected in Kahneman *et al.* (1982). For a collection focusing on the philosophical implications of this research, see Moser (1990). For a collection of recent papers with extensive bibliography, see Goldstein and Hogart (1997).

[36] The question was phrased as follows: 'Imagine that you have decided to see a play where admission is $10 per ticket. As you enter the theater, you discover that you have lost a $10 bill. Would you still pay $10 for a ticket to the play?' Out of nearly 200 subjects, 88% answered 'yes'; 12% answered 'no'. (Tversky and Kahneman, 1981, p. 457.)

[37] 'Imagine that you have decided to see a play and paid the admission price of $10 per ticket. As you enter the theater you discover that you have lost your ticket. The seat was not marked and the ticket cannot be recovered. Would you pay $10 for another ticket?' Out of 200 subjects asked, 46% said 'yes'; 54% said 'no'. (Tversky and Kahneman, 1981, p. 457.)

[38] Tversky and Kahneman diagnose the outcome as follows: 'The marked difference between [the two cases] is an effect of psychological accounting. We propose that the purchase of a new ticket in [the second case] is entered in the account that was set up by the purchase of the original ticket. In terms of this account, the expense required to see the show is $20, a cost which many of our respondents apparently found excessive. In [the first case], on the other hand, the loss of $10 is not linked specifically to the ticket purchase and its effect on the decision is accordingly slight.' (Tversky and Kahneman, 1981, p. 457.)

ited. That is, I think that it is rationally *permitted* that we should take these different perspectives, and I want to say a few words about why. In general, when we make decisions, we make sense of the particular scenario with which we are confronted by assimilating it to a class of familiar cases.[39] Since in general it is economically unwise to indulge ourselves by automatically replacing any item that breaks or is lost, and since we treat the lost ticket case under that rubric, we are hesitant to buy another. And since in general it would make us unhappy to deny ourselves enjoyment in one sphere whenever something has gone wrong in another, and since we treat the lost $10-bill case under that rubric, we are prepared to spend the money. Even when the baseline similarity between the two cases is brought out to us, we may maintain that it makes good sense to treat them differently, since each is best understood as belonging to one of two classes of cases between which we make a justifiable distinction.

With this idea in place, let us return to the Williams case. The perplexity there, you will recall, is that our response to the case seems to be frame-dependent. On one way of telling the story, we are inclined to take it as evidence in favour of the hypothesis that personal identity over time is a matter of physical continuity; on another, we are inclined to see it as supporting the view that personal identity over time is a matter of continuity of psychology. The discussion above suggests a diagnosis of the difference in response. In the first presentation, when we try to make sense of the story in light of our general assumptions about ordinary cases of personal identity, we focus on issues involving the body. And in ordinary cases, continuity of body assures continuity of personhood. So when the Williams story is framed in a way that foregrounds the bodily perspective, we take this feature to be sufficient for continuity of personhood. Likewise with the second presentation. Framed in a way that highlights the psychological continuity involved, the case is assimilated to ordinary cases under the following line of reasoning. We notice that there is a feature possessed by the B-body person — psychological continuity — which suffices for continuity of personhood in ordinary cases. And so we are inclined to take that feature as decisive in this case as well.

We have, then, a story about *how* we come to treat the two presentations so differently; we make use of a process of reasoning of which we make use in other cases as well. We assimilate a situation under one description to one class of cases, and we assimilate that same situation under another description to a different class of cases. But it could be that in so doing we are making a mistake. Just as one might defend a substantive global theory of rationality according to which one or the other of the attitudes towards the missing $10/ticket is seen as categorically correct, so too might one defend a theory of personal identity according to which one or the other of the views we have been considering actually captures the truth about the nature and importance of personal identity. Indeed, this is precisely what the sorts of thought experiments described in the previous section seek to establish; they offer carefully described scenarios in which relevant and irrelevant features can be separated out so that we can determine which are essential and which accidental. If I am right in my claim that such cases do not, in general, show what their advocates purport that they show, I need to offer further reasons.

---

[39] I take this analysis from Nozick (1993), chapters 1 and 2. Among other things, Nozick there suggests that the bringing about/allowing distinction in ethics might be viewed as an example of the sort of baseline effect which Kahneman and Tversky have discussed (see Nozick, 1993, p. 60, fn). For two independently-arrived-at workings-out of this idea, see Horowitz (1998) and Kamm (1998).

Exceptions and norms

I have suggested above that the structure of the concept 'person' is such that it applies
in central cases as the result of the correlative appearance of a set of frequently-
associated characteristics, and to other cases as the result of our assimilation of them
to these central cases. In defending this view, I now describe two strategies which
might be employed when confronted with exceptional cases.

The *exception-as-scalpel* strategy uses exceptional cases as a way of progressively
narrowing the range of characteristics required for the application of a concept by
allowing us to isolate the essential features for concept-application from those which
are merely ordinarily correlative. So, for instance, suppose that entities which fall
under a certain concept generally have characteristics a, b, c, d and e. Suppose further
that we come upon some entity which falls under the concept, but which has only
b and d. We are then entitled to conclude that of the five characteristics typically associated with entities of the type under discussion, at most only b and d are required
characteristics of any entity which falls within the purview of the theory. By contrast,
the *exception-as-cantilever* strategy views the category-membership of exceptional
cases as essentially reliant on the ordinary instances against which they can be seen as
exceptions. So, for instance, suppose again that entities which fall under the concept
in question generally have characteristics a, b, c, d and e, and suppose further that
some entity is found which has only b and d, but which nonetheless falls under the
concept. According to the second strategy, the proper thing to say about the entity in
question is that it falls under the concept only because it is similar in certain crucial
ways to more typical instances of entities which the theory describes.

Applying the exception-as-scalpel strategy to the Williams case, we discover the
following. The first presentation reveals that physical continuity is not necessary for
diachronic personal identity; since it seems that there are cases where a person's
future self might share none of her original physical matter. The second presentation
reveals that psychological continuity is not necessary for diachronic personal identity, since it seems that there are cases where a person's self might share none of her
original psychological characteristics.[40] Moreover, neither feature could be sufficient, unless the pre-operation individual is supposed to be identical to both her con-
tinuers in the second scenario. So neither physical nor psychological continuity is
either necessary or sufficient for diachronic personal identity.[41] This suggests that our
concept of 'person' is not organized around a set of necessary and sufficient condi-

---

[40] Alternatively, one might follow Parfit in saying that prudential concern need not track identity, in
which case thinking about these scenarios tells us nothing decisive about personal identity (since the
evidence they used in favour of the attribution of identity was: projected prudential concern).
Depending on whether one thinks that prudential concern generally tracks identity, and depending on
which sorts of cases 'generally' is supposed to cover — all normal cases? all actual cases? all
(technologically, biologically, physically, metaphysically, logically) possible cases? — our projected
judgments about a particular scenario will turn out to be very, somewhat, or not at all relevant to
determining the identity conditions for personhood over time. But this only helps to make my point. If
judgments about prudential concern are relevant to making such determinations, then I refer the reader
to my argument in the paragraph to which this footnote is attached. If judgments about prudential
concern are not relevant to making such determinations, then it is unclear how contemplation of the
sorts of imaginary scenarios described in the literature is supposed to give us the right sort of
information (since it seems that our primary basis for judgments about identity is projection of
prudential concern).

[41] Cf. Johnston (1987) for related discussion of these points.

tions that play a role in how we identify candidates as falling under that concept.[42] The exception-as-scalpel strategy cuts away too much. By contrast, consider the exception-as-cantilever strategy. On this strategy, the Williams case is to be understood as follows. The first presentation reveals that there are imaginable cases in which we would be inclined to attribute diachronic identity in the absence of any sort of psychological continuity; the second presentation reveals the same about physical continuity. But rather than concluding something about the (lack of) necessary and sufficient conditions for the application of the concept 'person', the exception-as-cantilever strategy tells us to conclude this about our classification of these exceptional cases as cases where diachronic personal identity obtains: our decisions about these cases are justified by the rational permissibility of assimilating them to ordinary cases. In the first scenario, we focus on the similarity that concerns physical continuity; in the second, we focus on psychology. But in both cases, we are cantilevering out from the set of generally-obtaining correlations which characterize ordinary cases.[43] The persons in these far-fetched stories are persons by courtesy only.

Conclusion

Thinking about actual and imaginary exceptional cases is indispensable if we wish to avoid mistaking accidental regularities for regularities which reflect a deeper truth about the world. And because the world does not provide us with easily accessible instances of all the combinations there might be, thought experiment — the contemplation of a well-described imaginary scenario in order to answer a specific question about some non-imaginary situation — is an indispensable technique: in philosophy, in science, and in ordinary reasoning. At the same time, critics of this methodology have correctly pointed out that it can be misused. Most have suggested that constraints be imposed on the sort of possibility involved in the imaginary scenario; that the more far-fetched the case, the less likely it is to be informative.

I have tried to show that this analysis locates the problem in the wrong place: the risk of misusing thought experiment arises not from the outlandishness of the scenarios, but from the structure of the concept which the thought experiment is intended to explore. Concepts structured in certain ways (those which are organized around a set of necessary and sufficient conditions which play a role in our identification of instances of that concept) can be clarified by means of the *exception-as-scalpel* strategy described in the last section; those which are structured in other ways may require us to treat *exceptions as cantilevers*. I have argued that the concept of person, and with it, the concept of personal identity, is a concept of the latter sort. Diachronic personal identity is a matter of the continued coincidence of enough of the factors that ordinarily allow us to persist over time: psychological, physical, and perhaps even social factors play a role.[44] We can make sense of cases where one or another of these features is absent. But this does not mean that our evaluations of them will be reliable guides to what matters in ordinary cases. For, as I have argued throughout this piece,

---

[42] Cf. Wittgenstein's discussion of 'games' in Wittgenstein (1953).

[43] To use a slightly different metaphor: the 'persons' in these stories come in through the back gate — but the only reason there is a back gate for them to come in through is that ordinary cases form the fence.

[44] See, for instance, Whiting (1986), Schechtman (1996) and Velleman (1996) for discussion of the role played by self-consciousness in 'making' future selves.

our ability to make sense of exceptional situations far outruns our ability to make reliable judgments about them.

Acknowledgements

For comments on earlier material from which this chapter is descended, I am grateful to Robert Nozick, Derek Parfit and Hilary Putnam; for more recent discussion, I thank Shaun Gallagher, John Hawthorne, Zoltán Gendler Szabó and two anonymous referees for the *Journal of Consciousness Studies*.

References

Alston, William and Bennett, Jonathan (1988), 'Locke on people and substances', *Philosophical Review*, **97**, pp. 25–46.
Bourgeois, Warren (1995), *Persons: What Philosophers Say about You* (Waterloo, ON: Wilfrid Laurier University Press).
Cockburn, David (ed. 1991), *Human Beings* (Cambridge: Cambridge University Press).
Dancy, Jonathan (ed. 1997), *Reading Parfit* (Oxford: Blackwell).
Gendler, Tamar Szabó (1998), 'Review of Eric Olson's *The Human Animal*', *Philosophical Review*, **107**.
Goldstein, William M. and Hogart, Robin M. (ed. 1997), *Research on Judgment and Decision-Making* (Cambridge: Cambridge University Press).
Horowitz, Tamara (1998), 'Philosophical intuitions and psychological theory', *Ethics*, **108** (2), pp. 367–85.
Horowitz, Tamara and Massey, Gerald (ed. 1991), *Thought Experiments in Science and Philosophy* (Savage, MD: Rowman and Littlefield).
Johnston, Mark (1987), 'Human beings', *Journal of Philosophy*, **84** (2), pp. 59–83.
Johnston, Mark (1989), 'Fission and the facts', in *Philosophical Perspectives, 3*, ed. James E. Tomberlin (Atascadero, CA: Ridgeview Publishing Co.).
Johnston, Mark (1992), 'Reasons and Reductionism', *Philosophical Review*, **101** (3), pp. 589–618.
Kahneman, Daniel, Slovic, P. and Tversky, A. (1982), *Judgement Under Uncertainty: Heuristics and Biases* (Cambridge: Cambridge University Press).
Kamm, Frances Myra (1998), 'Moral intuitions, cognitive psychology, and the harming-versus-not-aiding distinction', *Ethics*, **108** (3), pp. 463–88.
Komatsu, Lloyd K. (1992), 'Recent views of conceptual structure', *Psychological Bulletin*, **112** (3), pp. 500–26.
Locke, John (1710/1975), *An Essay Concerning Human Understanding*, edited with a forward by Peter H. Nidditch (Oxford: Clarendon Press).
Mackie, J. L. (1976), *Problems from Locke* (Oxford: Clarendon Press).
Medin, Douglas L. and Goldstone, Robert L. (1994), 'Concepts', in *The Blackwell Dictionary of Cognitive Psychology*, ed. Michael W. Eysenck (Cambridge, MA: Blackwell).
Medin, Douglas L and Smith, Edward E. (1984), 'Concepts and concept formation', *Annual Review of Psychology*, **35**, pp. 113–38.
Moser, Paul (ed. 1990), *Rationality in Action: Contemporary Approaches* (Cambridge: Cambridge UP).
Nagel, Thomas (1971), 'Brain bisection and the unity of consciousness', *Synthèse*, **22**. Reprinted with new pagination in Perry (1975a).
Noonan, Harold (1989), *Personal Identity* (London and New York: Routledge).
Nozick, Robert (1981), *Philosophical Explanations* (Cambridge, MA: Belknap/Harvard Univ. Press).
Nozick, Robert (1993), *The Nature of Rationality* (Princeton: Princeton University Press).
Olson, Eric (1997), *The Human Animal: Personal Identity Without Psychology* (Oxford: Oxford UP).
Parfit, Derek (1971), 'Personal identity', *Philosophical Review*, **80** (1). Reprinted with new pagination in Perry (1975a).
Parfit, Derek (1984/1987), *Reasons and Persons* (Oxford: Clarendon Press).
Perry, John (ed. 1975a), *Personal Identity* (Berkeley and Los Angeles: University of California Press.
Perry, John (1975b), 'The problem of personal identity', in Perry (1975a).

Quine, W.V. (1972), 'Review of *Identity and Individuation*', *Journal of Philosophy*, **69** (16), pp. 488–97.

Rescher, Nicholas (1991), 'Thought experimentation in presocratic philosophy', in Horowitz and Massey (1991).

Rey, Georges (1983), 'Concepts and stereotypes', *Cognition*, **15**, pp. 237–62.

Rey, Georges (1985), 'Concepts and conceptions: A reply to Smith, Medin and Rips', *Cognition*, **19**, pp. 297–303.

Robinson, John (1988), 'Personal identity and survival', *Journal of Philosophy*, **85** (6), pp. 319–28.

Rorty, Amelie (ed. 1976), *The Identities of Persons* (Berkeley, CA: University of California Press).

Rovane, Carol (1994), 'Critical notice: Peter Unger's *Identity, Consciousness and Value*', *Canadian Journal of Philosophy*, **24**, pp. 119–33.

Rovane, Carol (1998), *The Bounds of Agency* (Princeton: Princeton University Press).

Schechtman, Marya (1996), *The Constituion of Selves* (Ithaca, NY: Cornell University Press).

Shoemaker, Sydney (1963), *Self-Knowledge and Self-Identity* (Ithaca: Cornell University Press).

Shoemaker, Sydney and Swinburne, Richard (1984), *Personal Identity: Great Debates in Philosophy* (Oxford: Basil Blackwell).

Smith, Edward E. and Medin, Douglas L. (1981), *Categories and Concepts* (Cambridge: Harvard U.P.).

Snowdon, P.F. (1991), 'Personal identity and brain transplants', in Cockburn (1991).

Sorensen, Roy (1992), *Thought Experiments* (Oxford: Oxford University Press).

Tversky, Amos and Kahneman, Daniel (1981), 'The framing of decisions and the rationality of choice', *Science*, **211**, pp. 453–8.

Unger, Peter (1990), *Identity, Consciousness and Value* (New York and Oxford: Oxford U.P.).

Velleman, J. David (1996), 'Self to self', *Philosophical Review*, **105** (1), pp. 39–76.

Whiting, Jennifer (1986), 'Friends and future selves', *Philosophical Review*, **95** (4), pp. 547–80.

Wiggins, David (1980), *Sameness and Substance* (Cambridge, MA: Harvard University Press).

Wilkes, Kathleen V. (1988), *Real People: Personal Identity without Thought Experiments* (Oxford: Clarendon Press).

Williams, Bernard (1956/1973), 'Personal identity and individuation', reprinted with new pagination in Williams (1973).

Williams, Bernard (1970/1973), 'The self and the future', reprinted with new pagination in Williams (1973).

Williams, Bernard (1973), *Problems of the Self* (Cambridge: Cambridge University Press).

Wittgenstein, L. (1953), *Philosophical Investigations* (Oxford: Blackwell).

Mary Midgley

Being Scientific About Our Selves

The current narrowing of the notion of 'science' to exclude reference to anything subjective is perfectly acceptable in the physical sciences but it cannot accommodate psychology. This has become clear from the dismal failure of behaviourism. The enormous opportunity we now have for better thinking will be wasted if we merely go on devising thought-systems which look vaguely scientific (as behaviourism did) instead of ones that actually help us to understand human life. A striking example of such an etherial, quasi-scientific system is 'memetics'.

'Science', Old and New

Philosophers are well known to like talking about ambiguous words. But I shall not apologize for drawing attention here to two words, two ideas which are causing so much trouble at present that they are surely worrying most of us already. The first one is *scientific*, the second is *self-knowledge*.

To start with *scientific* — This word now has two distinct meanings contrasting it with two distinct sets of opposites. On the one hand it can be a quite general word of praise, meaning simply *thorough* and *methodical* as opposed to casual, vague or amateurish. In that sense historians or linguists or logicians can be called scientific — or unscientific — just as properly as astronomers. On the other hand, the word can also be a strictly factual one meaning 'concerned with the *natural* sciences' as opposed to other studies. In this sense (but not in the other) we can talk about *bad science*. In this sense, even a bad and casual book about astronomy counts as a scientific book, but a good and thorough book about history is *not scientific*. This, of course, is the familiar principle on which bookshops and libraries organize their shelving.

This is not a trivial ambiguity. It is part of a general confusion about the kind of praise that is conveyed by the notion of science, a confusion which is causing a lot of trouble. When the two meanings get mixed, it becomes obvious by definition that the methods of the natural sciences are not just the best methods but the only ones that are intellectually respectable. They are therefore all that we need and can rightly be described as *omnicompetent*. Thus Peter Atkins (1995):

> Although poets may aspire to understanding, their talents are more akin to entertaining self-deception. They may be able to emphasise delights in the world, but they are deluded if they and their admirers believe that their identification of the delights and their use of poignant language are enough for comprehension. Philosophers too, I am afraid, have contributed to the understanding of the universe little more than poets. . . . They have not contributed much that is novel until after novelty has been discovered by scientists. . . . While poetry titillates and theology obfuscates, science liberates (pp.123–4 and 129).

This idea that 'scientific' methods are quite simply the only good methods and should therefore be extended to cover every subject-matter, including our understanding of ourselves, was put forward early in the nineteenth century by Auguste Comte and others. It is still a powerful faith, devoutly preached by many people today. So far as it is true at all, it depends entirely on what you mean by 'scientific'. Before considering this, however, I want to say a word first about the target area, the site to which it is now proposed to extend this empire — about my other troublesome concept, *self-knowledge*.

Knowing Ourselves

Self-knowledge is a notion that is not always fully examined when academics talk about 'the self' because that academic self is often taken to be pretty abstract, and so far as it is specified the discussion can often be treated as being about other people's selves rather than one's own. But in everyday life self-knowledge is rather an important topic, one that crops up often in our personal affairs and has a strong moral bearing. Like other reflexive words such as *self-deception* and *self-control,* self-knowledge raises puzzles (which do interest academics) about how subjects can somehow become their own objects — who is doing the knowing or controlling and who is being known or controlled? Such words make it clear how terribly complex the human subject is, how many questions are involved in trying to understand it.

This complexity is something that we all know by hard experience because, of course, we often find it very hard to understand both other people's behaviour and our own. But in everyday life we usually accept that we still have to attempt this difficult kind of understanding. Self-knowledge isn't an optional subject like Russian or trigonometry which we can drop if we find it hard. Failure to know ourselves can be a serious moral fault. And one reason why it is a fault is that it blocks our understanding of other people. The sort of basic sympathy and empathy that we need in order to understand others does not work unless we are attentive to our own motives and reactions too. Without that self-critical attitude about how we are behaving to them, we can't hope to understand how they are behaving to us. So, surprisingly enough, in the enterprise of understanding other people, *cognitive success depends on moral attitude*. To get far in this study, you need fairness, honesty, maturity and indeed generosity. This means that there are facts which we cannot reach unless we first get the values right. From the view of facts and values that has been widely accepted for much of this century, that is rather surprising

This surprising fact also applies to more general views about ourselves, views about the kind of entity that we and all other human beings are. What methods do we need for this study? I'd like to quote here a poem by the seventeenth-century poet Sir John Davies because I find the way he uses the word 'know' in it particularly interesting:

> I know my soul hath power to know all things,
> Yet she is blind and ignorant in all.
> I know I'm one of nature's little kings,
> Yet to the least and vilest things am thrall.
> I know my life's a pain and but a span,
> I know my sense is mocked in everything,
> And, to conclude, I know myself a man,
> Which is a proud and yet a wretched thing.

('Man', from the *Oxford Book of English Verse*)

The Importance of Importance

Should we be sceptical about Davies' claim to knowledge? Should we doubt whether he really does know these things and ask for further research? Ought we to say 'but this is only folk-psychology; it remains provisional till more work has been done about the cell-biology and the neurones?' This would surely not be very sensible. The facts that Davies mentions are indeed well enough attested to count as 'known'. They are tacit knowledge. Further detailed evidence for them would not enrich what he is saying and the issue he raises does not concern the details of the facts but how we should respond to them. He is puzzled about the appropriate attitude to this curious self, an attitude which of course is not just a state of emotion but a considered, thoughtful response. He points out that there is good ground, not just for believing that human life is mixed and confusing in this way, but for taking a realistic, non-evasive attitude to its mixedness as a step to dealing with it better.

This involves a moral judgement about how we should proceed, a judgement about what is important, what we should attend to. That kind of judgement is always to be found at the root of metaphysics, including the apparently sceptical kinds of meta-physics (like materialism and determinism) which are sometimes inclined to deny that they are metaphysical at all. It is a judgement about what matters and what does not. Value-judgements of that kind are needed for selection. Without them, we could not form any general view about the human condition, because we could not decide which of a thousand patterns to pick out and study from the welter of experience.

These value-judgements about importance determine, among other things, what limits we set to the self itself, how far we think it extends and how sharply we separate it from what is around it. A self is not a given distinct object like an egg. For instance, the extreme individualistic model of selfhood — the social atomism which underlies Social Contract thinking — treats each self as independent, radically split off from its fellows. But it does not do this on factual grounds. It is not a scientific discovery that selves are in fact separate and egg-shaped. It arises chiefly out of moral indignation at the oppression which has often resulted from a more organic, hierarchical view of people's relations. Social atomism flows from deciding that the bad consequences of hierarchical systems are so important that the conceptual scheme underlying them must be ditched and replaced by a more separatist one.

At the other extreme, the Buddhist view that all separateness is an illusion — that individual selves are more or less arbitrary divisions across the continuum of life — also arises, not out of factual observation, but out of a sense of the harm we do by our tendency to split ourselves off from one another. The different value-judgements that underlie these metaphysical systems are essential to each of them, and besides decid-ing what counts as part of ourselves, these judgements also decide how we conceive the rest of the surrounding world. The independent self of the social contract lives in a world modelled on that of seventeenth-century cosmology. It is a solitary atom gyrating in a social void, a radically solitary rational entity moving among a crowd of others with whom it has no real connection. This is a world, incidentally, which does not easily find room for non-rational humans such as babies and one which can scarcely accommodate non-human nature at all. The Buddhist self, by contrast, lives in a world without frontiers and must recognize a great range of others, human and otherwise, as literally continuous with itself.

These general ways of conceiving the world obviously make an enormous difference, not just to our notions about how we ought to act but also to our views about
which facts we ought to attend to and what methods we should use in thinking about
them. By affecting our selection of topics they alter our factual view of the world as
well as our moral view about how we must deal with it. But neither of them is more
scientific than the other, in the sense in which scientific is a term of praise. In that
sense, either of them can be scientifically or unscientifically developed. We cannot
use the idea of science as a criterion for judging between them.

What Kind of Objectivity?

I have spent some time on this entanglement of fact with value because I want to make
clear at once how impossible it is to apply to these topics the kind of objectivity which
we associate with physical science. That objectivity requires that all observers should
stand at the same point of view and abstract from their individual differences. But this
kind of abstraction simply cannot be used when we are talking about human affairs.
There is no way in which we can collect facts about any significant aspect of human
life without looking at them from some particular angle. We have to guide our selection by means of some value-judgement about what matters in it and what does not.
And these judgements inevitably arise out of each enquirer's moral position. When
they raise difficulties, they need to be justified by explaining that position, not by
ignoring it.

Social and psychological theorists who claim to be operating in a value-free vacuum
outside morality are notoriously deceiving themselves. They simply haven't noticed
their own biases. I think it has now become clear that this was the situation of the
behaviourist psychologists who were so influential during much of the last century.
Watson and Skinner claimed that, in order to be scientific, psychologists should study
people *objectively* in the sense of viewing them solely as physical objects, that is, by
simply ignoring their subjective point of view.

This was not just a proposal for a new scientific method. It was a demand for a new
and very peculiar moral attitude to human life. In his last book, *Beyond Freedom and
Dignity*, B.F. Skinner eventually made that moral attitude explicit, disclaiming all
esteem for the active, creative aspect of human nature and openly asserting the right
of psychological experts to engineer it as they thought best. The exposure of these
views probably played a large part in the subsequent discrediting of his methods.
Until then, however, the idea that a 'scientific' approach demanded this quite impossible abstraction from all views on what mattered in human life was widely accepted.
It did not only allow psychologists to consider themselves scientists. It had the further
and deeper advantage for them of exempting them, as professionals, from the painful
efforts at sympathy and self-knowledge which — as I'm suggesting — normally form
a crucial part of our attempts to understand other people. It allowed them a kind of
detachment in which they could make a positive merit of not knowing how the people
whom they studied felt.

This strange affectation of detachment and ignorance about human experience was
a good deal more extreme than what Comte and the other pioneers had in mind when
they called for the founding of 'social sciences' in the nineteenth century. They simply
wanted to use experimental and statistical methods drawn from physical science in

the study of social affairs so as to make it more systematic. But they took it for granted that these methods could be added to existing ways of thought which were already useful there. For them, the term *scientific* mainly had the general meaning that it had held throughout the Enlightenment. Primarily it meant thinking out problems afresh for oneself rather than relying on authority or tradition. They never envisaged throwing out all existing historical and philosophical methods and replacing them by ones drawn from physical science. Notoriously, Comte himself, when he talked of throwing out religion and metaphysics, only meant throwing out other people's religion and metaphysics and replacing them by better ones of his own invention.

In general, then, these pioneers wanted to combine all useful methods. Thus the new social sciences started life as *sciences* in the old general sense — methodical forms of thought, parallel to history or logic, which would use whatever kinds of reasoning seemed helpful in handling their subject-matter. For instance, social scientists who discuss the scope of their own study, or its history, obviously cannot carry on that discussion by using the methods of physical science. What they are then doing is history or philosophy, whether they notice it or not. Thus Comte himself was not (in the modern sense) a scientist but a philosopher, though not a very good one. Similarly, people today who still echo Comte's philosophical manifestos, as Peter Atkins does, are not doing physical science but are themselves philosophizing, even if not very well.

Popper's Guillotine and the Destiny of Ideologies

What, then, finally broke up this hospitable, inclusive idea of 'science'? The fatal factor seems to have been the steadily growing prestige of the physical sciences themselves. That growth resulted in these sciences acquiring the name of 'science' (par excellence) instead of the former awkward name 'natural philosophy'. And since this prestige accrued chiefly to physics itself — to the enormously popular Newtonian, mechanistic model which dominated the eighteenth-century imagination — physics in turn was seen as the standard model of a science. This notion seemed sensible enough before the great variety of methods that were needed for other studies were noticed. It has persisted, however, without much examination, long after that variety became known and ought to have put it out of business. Thus Rutherford confidently dismissed all studies other than physics as 'stamp-collecting' and Crick (with still less excuse because much later) dismissed them as 'social work'.

What is this really supposed to mean? Physics is a highly abstract and specialized study. It owes its whole success to having deliberately withdrawn from general discourse in the time of Galileo. Obviously, most of the questions that we have to deal with arise outside its province. They cannot be stated in physical terms. For instance, if they are biological questions they need concepts like organism, organ and function, plant and animal, flower and fruit. So how could physics be expected to answer them? Biology is not just a station on a railway-line leading to physics; it is a country on its own on the wider map of explanation. Lewis Wolpert lights up this impasse strikingly in a recent book:

> How can we distinguish between science and non-science? . . . There is a question as to whether the social sciences are really science. . . . The peculiarity of the social sciences is the complexity of the subject-matter. . . . There is little possibility, for instance, of doing

experiments equivalent to those of physics, say, in which it is characteristic to try to vary just one variable at a time, keeping others constant. . . . [Yet] in a sense, all science aspires to be like physics *and physics aspires to be like mathematics* (Wolpert, 1992, pp.124–5 and 121; emphasis mine).

Evidently, the aim of that last aspiration is to have no subject-matter at all. In that kind of purity, mathematics is certainly king. But how could purity of this sort really be the aim of science as a whole? If it were, the claim of science to be explaining the real world would have to be abandoned, and it would certainly be in no position to criticize other methods which did provide such explanations.

Actually, however, this talk of aspiration seems to have a rather interesting aesthetic origin. The familiar claim that 'all the sciences aspire to the condition of physics' is modelled on Walter Pater's remark that 'all the arts aspire to the condition of music'. In both cases, the point seems to rest on abstractness, freedom from the limitations imposed by a particular subject-matter. Whether or no this puts music above the other arts, it is totally mysterious how it should be supposed to put physics above other enquiries. However, the popularity of the Newtonian model did invest physics with a kind of glamour which, during the nineteenth century, led a growing number of prophets to jump onto its bandwagon by claiming that their ideologies were *scientific* — not just in the old sense of being methodical but in the new one of being founded in some way on the physical sciences. Comte himself did this and he had many influential followers, notably Herbert Spencer, who claimed scientific backing for Social Darwinism. Marx also notoriously thought of his world-view as science-based and Engels strongly developed this claim, making the connection with physical science a central plank of later Marxist thought. Freud too relied heavily on claiming scientific status. All these prophets conceived 'science' primarily in general terms as Enlightenment thinking, the opposite of blind tradition and superstition. But they also believed, more specifically, that modern biology and physics directly underpinned their own social and psychological theories.

This proliferation of rival 'scientific' world-views was bound to bring its nemesis. Readers could not go on for ever adjusting themselves, like chameleons, to match all the different colours on this intellectual Turkey carpet and still call the result 'science'. Indeed it is rather surprising now to see how long the plurality was tolerated. Throughout the first half of the twentieth century intelligent people worked amazingly hard to combine obviously incompatible ideas together provided that they were all labelled 'scientific'.

After the second world war, however the guillotine finally came down. Karl Popper then pointed out that the Marxist and Freudian ideologies were not actually constructed by the methods of the physical sciences and could not therefore be described in modern terms as *scientific*. What was unfortunate was that, at this point, there did not follow any proper investigation of what world-views of this kind were if they were not branches of science and what other standards they ought to be judged by. People seem to have been extraordinarily blind to the fact that Marxism and Freudianism were not primarily scientific theories but ideologies, comprehensive attitudes to life, with a strong moral component as well as their factual claims — and that there were many other such attitudes available between which we needed to choose. Discussion of such rival attitudes to life is not a vice nor a waste of time. It is an intellectual necessity, particularly in times of violent change. Popper's work, however, seemed to outlaw all such argument from the province of thought, ruling that, since it was not science, it was *metaphysics* — a word which he used vaguely and which many of his audience took to mean simply nonsense.

There followed a jubilant spasm of unrepentant scientism, not just in the sense that people put too high a value on science in comparison with other branches of learning or culture, but in the wider sense they often forgot that those other branches existed at all. This narrow vision now became explicit. Its prophets tend still to assume, as Atkins does in the recent article I have quoted, that the only available forms of thought other than 'science' are religion and parapsychology. They make no mention of history, law, language or logic and if they mention the social sciences at all they speak of them as dubious entities on the borders of science proper, becoming respectable only when they manage to imitate real science closely. Thus the strange composite intellectual entity called Science now turns out to be not just omnicompetent but unrivalled, the sole representative of rational thinking.

Now of course this crude view is not universally held nor even often defended explicitly today. Many scientists hate it. Atkins' open triumphalism is somewhat unusual. Yet I think he does us a service in making this idea explicit because as a myth, an imaginative pattern underlying more moderate thought, it still is very influential. Irrelevant notions about how to make thought 'hard' and scientific by imitating physical science have repeatedly distorted the social sciences and many other areas of our thought, notably psychiatry. Behaviourist psychology itself was clearly one such imitative project. It has now been discredited because of its inefficiency, and so have many of its fellows. In fact, the enterprise of making all our thought on human affairs conform to physical patterns has proved dauntingly hard. Yet the idea that we must somehow do this difficult thing still haunts us. Many people find the prospect of abandoning that attempt unbearable.

Memes and other Unusual Life-Forms

For breaking this dilemma, two methods are currently being favoured. The first is to do research on some actual, existing, certified branch of physical science such as neurobiology or genetics, and to declare that, in the end, if it is pursued long enough, its results will somehow throw a useful light on human affairs. This path is, of course, only open to trained physical scientists. The second path — which is also open to people in the humanities — is to devise a scheme which *looks* rather like physical science and to claim that it is going to provide, at last, a truly scientific explanation of human life. This is the path that has been followed by a great deal of research on Artificial Intelligence and it is also the one taken by Richard Dawkins in his doctrine of Memes. I think this is an instructive example of the kind of wish-fulfilment that flows from current confusions about what it means to be scientific, so I shall say a bit more about it now.

In the last chapter of *The Selfish Gene*, Dawkins (1976) introduced the notion of memes as 'units of cultural transmission' which were comparable to genes and this idea has been taken up by a number of other sages, most recently by Edward O. Wilson in his book *Consilience*. Wilson hopes that, by dividing culture into these units, he can provide a means of reconciling the humanities and social sciences with physical science. Memes, he says, will form 'the conceptual keystone of the bridge between science and the humanities' (Wilson, 1998, p.136).

But is culture the sort of thing that can be understood by dividing it up into ultimate units? It must be, says Wilson, because atomizing is the way in which we naturally think. 'The descent to *minutissima*, the search for ultimate smallness in entities such as electrons, is a driving impulse of Western natural science. It is a kind of instinct' (p. 50). We need, says Wilson,

> to search for the basic unit of culture. . . . Such a focus may seem at first contrived and artificial, but it has many worthy precedents. The great success of the natural sciences has been achieved substantially by the reduction of each physical phenomenon to its constituents, followed by the use of the elements to reconstitute the holistic properties of the phenomenon (p.134).

In fact (he says) it has succeeded in science so it is bound to succeed in the humanities. How does this actually does work out in practice? The various memeticists use it in rather different ways. Wilson himself at first keeps quite close to the pattern set by the discovery of atoms and electrons. He wants *minutissima* — ultimate units of thought comparable to fundamental particles in physics — and he claims that these units can eventually be linked to particular brain states in a way that will provide a kind of alphabet for a universal brain-language underlying all thought. This is a startlingly ambitious project. But most of the time Wilson seems to forget it completely and describes his particles as units of *culture* — plainly a quite different concept.

The examples which other memeticists give are closer to this model of culture-units. Dawkins himself calls them 'units of cultural transmission', giving as examples 'tunes, ideas, catch-phrases, clothes-fashions, ways of making pots or building arches' to which he later adds popular songs, stiletto heels, Darwinism and the idea of God (Dawkins, 1976, pp. 206–7). None of these very varied things looks much like a Wilsonian ultimate unit of thought. Dawkins, however, is insistent that his items are not mere conventional divisions either. Like electrons they are natural units, fixed, distinct and lasting. On this point Daniel Dennett is still more emphatic. Dennett's long list — even more ostentatiously mixed than the one Dawkins gives — includes *deconstructionism*, *the Odyssey* and *wearing clothes*. He too insists that these are not just arbitrary divisions:

> Intuitively we see these as more or less identifiable cultural units, but we can say something more precise about how we draw the boundaries . . . the units are *the smallest elements that replicate themselves with reliability and fecundity*. We can compare them, in this regard, to genes and their components (Dennett, 1995, p. 344; emphasis mine).

It seems strange, then, that the Odyssey (for instance) contains within it several stories which are well-known in their own right, such as the stories of Scylla and Charybdis and of the Cyclops. *Wearing clothes* is a general term covering a vast range of customs. *Deconstructionism* is a loose name used to describe an indefinite jumble of theories, and *the idea of God* is also a very wide and ambiguous one. None of these items looks in the least like a fixed 'smallest element' that could function as a replicator. But besides this, as Dennett himself points out, none of them is static and immutable, as genes are supposed to be. Customs and traditions of this kind change and develop constantly unless we deliberately fix them, as we do the *Odyssey*, by devices such as printing. The way in which cultural items behave is quite like that of whole organisms but completely unlike the behaviour of genes.

Sometimes, indeed, it does seem that memeticists are comparing their cultural items to whole organisms — to phenotypes — and are positing the memes as hidden entities, unseen 'replicators', occult causes that send these phenotypes leaping from mind to mind. Memetics is then supposed to be parallel to genetics, instructing us in the way that these hidden entities conduct their reproductive business. But it can't do so because there are no such entities. Dennett says that 'These new replicators are, roughly, ideas' (p. 344). But many of the things supposedly replicated, such as Darwinism, are themselves ideas. They cannot need a meta-idea to cause them. The case is not like that of genes which are physical items, sections of DNA observable in the laboratory. In order for human beings to think, feel and communicate, no entities have to be present in them except those human beings themselves. If we want to understand their thoughts and feelings it is the people themselves that we need to understand — a process, as I have been suggesting, which is direct, painful and difficult because it is inseparable from understanding ourselves, but which is thoroughly familiar. Pseudo-genetic occult causes will not help with this nor act as substitutes for it. Memes serve no function and should be cut off with Occam's Razor.

The cultural items which Dennett and Dawkins list are not, then, ultimate, immutable fundamental particles. Nor are they objects made up of such particles, nor phenotypes transmitted by mysterious genes. What they are is aspects of culture, patterns in people's thought and behaviour. Understanding them is not a matter of splitting culture into its ultimate particles because culture is not a substance, a solid stuff of the kind that might be expected to consist of particles. Instead it is a complex of patterns. And *patterns are not the sort of thing that breaks down into ultimate units*.

When we actually want to understand some aspect of culture, such as deconstructionism or the idea of God, we do indeed often analyse it into distinct elements, distinguishing sub-patterns within it. But we do this in accordance with our particular interests at the time, not in the mistaken search for a single basic structure. And before we can make this kind of analysis at all we usually need to look outward for the conceptual background, the wider context of ideas out of which these sub-patterns arise. In the end, *explaining* such things means grasping the motives of the people involved. But this usually cannot be done without a prior outward movement of placing them on a wider map of other ideas and habits, so as to relate the patterns within them to the larger patterns outside. That is what we do in ordinary life when we want to understand such things. And dedicated people who want to understand them more precisely — people such as historians, anthropologists, philosophers, social psychologists, novelists, poets and literary critics — have developed, over time, many subtle ways in which to carry this process further.

That kind of cultural mapping is, in fact, the main business of the humanities, which has been carried on for many centuries and in many cultures. The idea of introducing memetics as the proper way to understand culture is not — as Wilson wants it to be — a useful bridge between this wide range of methods and the physical sciences because it takes no account of these existing methods at all. It simply ignores them and offers a meaningless story about atomic entities as a substitute.

Memetics, in fact, is phlogiston and, what's more, it isn't even useful phlogiston. The idea of phlogiston did have a use, because it marked a blank place on the map, a spot which needed to be filled by a proper theory of combustion. But there is no such blank place on the humanistic map waiting to be filled by this new, quite general proposal about how to start understanding culture. Of course the methods that we now use are grossly imperfect, often terribly faulty. Of course we need constantly to work on them. But they are faulty because of particular faults which require further work to correct them, not because nobody has yet discovered how to start work on this topic at all.

Atomism and Self-Knowledge

These, of course, are alarming words. Can it (you may ask) really be true that very intelligent, high-minded and highly-qualified people are trying to sell us phlogiston? Can it be true that they themselves have bought it? I must certainly explain why I think that so strange a thing is possible. The explanation lies, as I have been trying to suggest throughout this chapter, first in the deep unwillingness of psychologists to understand people by means of the painful, difficult, direct sympathy which is the only effective means of doing so, and second in the huge imaginative force of a certain narrow vision of what it is to be *scientific*, which has been embraced as a substitute for that kind of insight. As Wilson says, this vision centres on the fascination of division into *minutissima*, the ruling obsession with the microscope, an obsession which excludes the use of wider maps and fixes our attention firmly on abstract entities outside the world of our own experience — even when that experience itself is what we are supposed to be studying. At the dawn of modern science in the seventeenth century, this atomistic approach did of course pay tremendous dividends and it has repeatedly proved of huge value since, for instance in the discovery of cells. But never, in any branch of science, has it been the only approach that was needed.

Atomism itself — which of course came originally from Greek philosophers — has an enormous appeal because of its seductive finality. Descartes, describing his search for certainty, laid great stress on the need 'to divide each problem into as many parts as was feasible', aiming to imitate 'those long chains of perfectly simple and easy reasonings by means of which geometers are accustomed to carry out their most difficult demonstrations . . . I knew already that I must start with the simplest objects, those most apt to be known' (*Discourse on Method*, Part Two). He therefore modelled his metaphysical thinking as closely as possible on mathematics, expecting to arrive at a final set of concepts as clear, distinct and separate from each other as those employed in mathematics. Of course this approach made modern physics possible. But it also landed it, for a couple of centuries, with a belief in ultimate, hard, impenetrable and all-explaining atoms, which were viewed as necessary to produce the reductive clarity that scientists aimed at. This hygienic atomism charmed the Enlightenment because it seemed to provide ultimate simplicity and completeness and even a kind of stability, since the atoms last for ever even if we don't. And that charm remains potent today, even though the physical theories that expressed it are now abandoned. The idea of simplifying the shifting chaos of human affairs in this way is hugely attractive, especially to people who have grown up thinking of the atomic pattern as the archetype of all scientific method.

From the seventeenth to the nineteenth century most scientists did think in this way. Since then the original owners of atomism — the physicists — have dropped that seductive vision, recognizing that the world is actually much more complex and much more interconnected. Of course microscopes are still an essential tool for physics, but their usefulness lies just as much in revealing the connections between things as in dividing them into parts. Physicists today, like Buddhists, think in terms of interdependent origination. Many biologists and social scientists, however, still cling to the atomic model and hope to extend its civilizing empire over the tangled rain-forest of human society. But that hope really is mistaken. The atomic vision is just one possible interpretative pattern among many. There are many problems on which it is no help to us, and the understanding of human culture is one of them.

Putting Memes to Work: The Witch-Craze

To show that I am not being arbitrary about this, I will end by looking briefly at how the memetic model would work if we actually did try to use it on a real problem. Dennett, who considers its function more fully than Dawkins, firmly enforces the parallel with 'selfish' genes. It is quite wrong, he says, to try to explain cultural traits by asking what they do for the people who adopt them. Instead, we should recognize that 'a cultural trait may have evolved in the way it has simply because it is advantageous to itself' (Dennett, 1995, p. 362). A human mind is then 'an artefact created when memes restructure a human brain so as to make it a better habitat for memes. . . . Like a mindless virus, a meme's prospects depend on its design — not its internal design, whatever that may be, but the design it shows the world, its phenotype, the way in which it affects things in its environment [namely] minds and other memes' (p. 349). We therefore need memetics to help us grasp the strategies by which memes contrive to infest us even when they are not useful to us, for example: 'the meme for faith, which discourages the exercise of the sort of critical judgement that might decide that the idea of faith was, all things considered, a dangerous idea' (p. 349).

Accordingly, if we want to understand why certain people have faith in something or somebody — for example, why Western people today tend to believe the declarations of scientists — we should not waste our time asking what reasons they might have for putting their trust in that particular thing or person. Instead, we should simply note that an entity called *faith* tends to be successful at parasitizing human brains. The next question, however, is surely: how would this approach give us anything that could be called an explanation of people's actions? Of course it is true that it is often hard to find the kind of explanation that we normally look for — namely, one in terms of reasons and motives. We often cannot find the reasons why people do what they do, and when we do find them they are often bad ones. But if we cannot find those reasons at all there is no way in which we can make sense of their actions.

To enforce his point, Dennett uses examples where the reasons are indeed mysterious, such as having a popular song on the brain when one doesn't even like it. Now these examples are obviously rather rare, which is why we notice them. Most of the time we do have some idea both about why we ourselves do what we do and about why other people do what *they* do. Fashion and custom are, after all, themselves genuine intelligible reasons, even if not specially good ones. They are reasons which relate to peer pressure and to simplifying life by not having to think it out again constantly from scratch. And when we are surprised at being obsessed by some topic which seems unimportant, it is usually worth our while to look for some reason for

this in our own feelings rather than just swatting at it like a wasp and saying 'bother —
another meme'.

However, it is certainly true that there are plenty of cases where we are ignorant or
mistaken both about both our own motives and other people's. This ignorance is
probably what gives the meme idea its only faint plausibility. So I shall end by pointing out how very badly that idea works even in these cases where human motivation
really is mysterious.

The example I shall mention is the witch-craze which prevailed in Europe from the
fifteenth to the seventeenth centuries. That craze was not, as is often supposed,
simply a survival of ancient superstition caused by ignorance, something finally
cured by the rise of science. To the contrary, in the Middle Ages prosecutions for
witchcraft were rare. The church authorities did not think witchcraft was common
and they discouraged witch-hunting because they saw the danger of false accusation.
There was therefore a church canon that set strict limits to it. It was in the Renaissance
that things changed. At that time, as a recent historian puts it:

> The Europeans did three things which set them apart from most other peoples at most
> times and places. Between 1500 and 1700 they set sail in tall ships and colonised most
> quarters of the globe. They made stunning strides forward in the sciences. And they exe-
> cuted tens of thousands of people, mainly women, as witches (Green & Bigelow, 1998).

This attack of frenzy coincided, then, with the increase of knowledge rather than
being cured by it. And, as these authors show, when it finally subsided it did not do so
because science had shown that witchcraft was impossible but because people gradually began to find it psychologically incredible that there was such an organized host
of demon-worshippers. Writers of various kinds greatly helped to nourish this incredu-
lity, but scientific arguments do not seem to have contributed anything particular to it.

Here, surely, is something which needs explaining. And I cite this case because it is
one where explanation by memes would look so easy. We need only posit a new
meme which successfully invades a population that has no immunity to it, a meme
which then declines later as that immunity develops. The meme's success is due to its
own strategy — presumably produced by a mutation — not to any fact about the people it infects. We don't need to look at these people, except perhaps to consider the
general strength of their immune systems. We don't need to relate this meme to any
other cultural viruses or parasites currently infesting the population nor to that population's earlier or later history. We certainly don't need to think about human psychology generally or to look into our own hearts to see what we might learn there
about such conduct. We simply place the whole causation outside human choice.

But, placed there, the meme story simply gives us no explanation at all. What we
actually need, when we are trying to understand such a case, is to grasp how people
could begin to think and act in this way in spite of the beliefs, customs, laws and
ideals which had stopped them doing so earlier. We need, in fact, to understand the
psychology of persecution and to understand it (so to speak) from inside. We need to
penetrate paranoia. And we need this, not just in relation to witch-hunting, but for understanding human conduct in other times and places too, not least in our own lives.

·*Understanding* here does not mean discovering, by research, new facts about its
causation by an imaginary alien life-form. When human beings act, no entities need
be involved in their action except those human beings themselves. Understanding
means essentially self-knowledge, an exploration of what de Tocqueville called 'the

habits of the heart'. Examining the evolutionary strategies of mythical culture-units could not possibly save us the trouble of this painful form of enquiry. What in fact goes on in such investigations — and what has actually gone on over this topic of the witch-craze — is that historians look sympathetically for people's reasons, exploring the expression of those reasons in the documents left by the age. They notice things like the various fears raised by an epoch of violent change, especially fear of the rising status of women at the time — the disintegration of earlier belief-systems — the distraction caused by civil wars — the rising interest in the idea of a devil, and (of course) the particular political interests that could be served by scapegoating a group without power.

All these explanations have some force, all of them do something to make this story more intelligible. None of them explains it completely. This, however, does not mean that historians have failed. These partial explanations can and do still throw light on parallel cases, phenomena such as anti-Semitism and xenophobia. When they are well and seriously worked out, they shed light on the general habits of the human heart. Whether we call that light-shedding scientific is not, perhaps, particularly important.

Conclusion

The reason why I have spent some time putting weed-killer on memetics really is not just wanton destructiveness. I have done so because I believe it is distracting us at a moment when psychology stands a chance of growing in much more useful and real-istic directions. The lifting of the behaviourist tabu on serious discussion of our inner life has released a remarkable flood of interest, a fertile crop of new suggestions which surely needs to be cherished and developed as widely as possible. (This journal is, of course, the scene where much of this new life appears).

What now seems possible is that we can reverse the irrational change which took place a century back, when behaviourism was allowed to drive out a wide range of psychological enquiries of the kind pursued by Dewey and William James, on the quite mistaken ground that it was more 'scientific' than they were. As we now know, it wasn't. It had only managed to master the art of pretending to be scientific by imposing a bogus simplicity, by imitating the externals of physical science. It offered a short cut past the really difficult issue of combining enquiries about the inner and outer aspects of our lives by ruling the inner one out of consideration entirely.

This is no way to run an enquiry. We do not need to make that mistake again. But if we continue to be hypnotized by an uncritical use of the term 'scientific' we shall be in danger of doing so. The dead hand of behaviourism will still control us, leading us always to prefer tidy thought-systems that have a vaguely 'scientific' appearance to ones that don't, regardless of whether they are actually capable of telling us anything of the slightest interest about human life. Our natural resistance to self-knowledge — our chronic unwillingness to look into our own lives in the way that is necessary for real understanding of other people — always inclines us to accept schemes of this sort because they offer to distract us from these disturbing considerations. They make possible the neatly divided academic life whereby 'science' alone is pursued in the university, while all topics of real interest are left at home. This arrangement is, of course, always an option, even indeed a grant-attracting one. But do we really want to be stuck with it? If not, I think there is no substitute for self-knowledge.

References

Atkins, Peter (1995), 'The limitless power of science', in *Nature's Imagination*, ed. J. Cornwell (Oxford University Press).

Dawkins, Richard (1976), *The Selfish Gene* (Oxford: Oxford University Press).

Dennett, Daniel C. (1995), *Darwin's Dangerous Idea* (Harmondsworth: Penguin).

Green, Karen and Bigelow, John (1998), 'Does science persecute women? The case of the 16th–17th century witch hunts', *Philosophy*, **73** (284), April 1998.

Oxford Book of English Verse, ed. Sir Arthur Quiller-Couch, first published 1900 (Oxford: OUP)

Wilson, Edward O. (1998), *Consilience* (New York: Alfred A. Knopf).

Wolpert, Lewis (1992), *The Unnatural Nature of Science* (London: Faber and Faber).

Part 7

Response from keynote author

Galen Strawson

The Self and the SESMET

I: Introduction

I am most grateful to all those who commented on '"The Self"'. The result was a festival of misunderstanding, but misunderstanding is one of the great engines of progress. Few of the contributors to the symposium on 'Models of the Self' were interested in my project: some (like **Olson** and **Wilkes**) were already highly sceptical about the value of talk about the self, others were committed to other projects centred on the word 'self' that made mine seem irrelevant at best and many worse things besides. Large differences in methodological and terminological habits gave rise to many occasions on which commentators thought they disagreed with me although they had in fact changed the subject. So I am not sure anyone found my paper useful. But I found some of the responses extremely useful, especially those that adverted to Eastern and phenomenological traditions of thought.[1]

I decided to take on the self — the self understood as an internal mental presence, a mental entity in the old, strong, classical-philosophical sense — as a lawyer takes on a client. I took my sadly maligned client's innocence and good standing on trust. I took it that there really are such things as mental selves in every sense in which there are dogs or chairs. I then committed myself to making the best case I could for them from a realistic materialist standpoint.[2] My starting assumption was that whatever a self is, it is certainly (a) a *subject of experience*, although it is certainly (b) *not* a person, where a person is understood to be something like a human being (or other animal) considered as a living physical whole.[3]

---

[1] Such as **Forman, Hayward, Laycock, Parnas & Zahavi** and **Shear**.
N.B. In general, when I cite a work I give the date of composition or first publication, while the page reference is to the edition listed in the bibliography. In the case of papers that form part of this symposium, a citation with the author's name in **bold type** without a date indicates that the page numbers refer to the version of their paper reprinted in this volume. In these cases, the bibliography has an asterisk against the author's name and gives details of the original publication in the *Journal of Consciousness Studies*.

[2] A realistic materialist standpoint does not much resemble some of the positions that claim to be materialist — see section **XIII** below.

[3] This immediately separates me from **Bermúdez**, who, like many philosophers, chooses to use '"self" and "person" interchangeably' (p. 432), and peels off into a different debate — along with **Gendler** in her well-balanced piece on thought-experiments. It also separates me from all those in the analytic tradition who think that facts about language suffice to show that 'the self' is either a human being considered as a whole or nothing but a 'mythical entity' (e.g. Kenny, 1988; 1989, ch. 6).

It seems to me that if one is going to take this brief seriously, as a materialist, and try to show that such selves exist, then one must aim to show that they are objects of some sort — concrete objects, not abstract objects — and hence, given materialism, physical objects.[4] This view strikes nearly everyone as obviously — even hilariously — false, and a central aim of this paper is to argue that this reaction stems from a failure to think through what it is to be physical, on a genuine or realistic materialist view, and, equally, from a failure to think through what it is to be an object.[5] I think that one has to solve for three inadequately conceived quantities — *self*, *object*, *physical* — simultaneously, using each to get leverage on the others.

I confess that I was attracted by the counterintuitive sound of the claim that selves are physical objects, and was duly rewarded by the quantity and quality of the protests. But I would have made the claim anyway, because I think it is correct. It is unwise to be gratuitously provocative. In areas like this it is not enough to write so as to be understood; one must write so as not to be misunderstood. Problems of communication that afflict metaphysics in general proliferate like rabbits when the topic is the self.

I will, then, try to clarify what I understand by the words 'object' and 'physical', in the hope that to understand everything will be to forgive everything,[6] and that we can — together with the cognitive self, the conceptual self, the contextualized self, the core self, the dialogic self, the ecological self, the embodied self, the emergent self, the empirical self, the existential self, the extended self, the fictional self, the full-grown self, the interpersonal self, the material self, the narrative self, the philosophical self, the physical self, the private self, the representational self, the rock bottom essential self, the semiotic self, the social self, the transparent self, and the verbal self (cf. e.g. James, 1890; Stern, 1985; Dennett, 1991; Gibson, 1993; Neisser, 1995; **Butterworth**; **Cole**; Gazzaniga, 1998; **Legerstee**; **Gallagher and Marcel**; **Pickering**; **Sheets-Johnstone**), *none* of whom I object to, although I have not chosen to write about them — fall into each others' arms in a passion of mutual understanding and, like Bunyan's pilgrim, go on our way rejoicing.

This paper is only a report on work in progress, however. Much argument is omitted, and I have not thought enough about some of the proposals it contains. Nor have I had space to comment as fully as I would have liked on many of the contributions to the symposium (e.g. **Blachowicz**; **Edey**; **Perlis**; **Ramachandran and Hirstein**; **Radden** and **Tani**).

My brief for the self also led me to conclude that there are many short-lived and successive selves (if there are selves at all), in the case of ordinary individual human beings. Some find this conclusion disappointing — they think it amounts to saying that there is no such thing as the self, or at least no such thing as 'a self worth wanting'

---

[4] Dennett's proposal that the self is a 'center of narrative gravity' (1991, pp. 426–7) does not take the brief seriously in this sense: it denies that there really are such things as selves (and is I believe correct, in so far as selves are taken to be things that persist over long periods of time). **Brook**'s (p. 46) reason for accepting the claim that the self is an object — i.e. that human beings are objects — is ruled out by my starting point as just described.

[5] For one thing, all physical objects are literally processes. If this is a 'category mistake', don't blame me, blame nature — or ordinary language.

[6] In spite of J.L. Austin's remark that to understand everything might only increase one's contempt.

(**Wilkes**, pp. 26, 28, 29, 31, 33). But if 'self' is so defined that its existence necessarily involves some sort of substantial long-term continuity, my aim is to disappoint.

William James also holds that there are many short-lived selves (1890, pp. 360–3, 371, 400–1). I did not know this when writing '"The Self"' because I had never read to the end of his great chapter on 'The Consciousness of Self' and had participated in the common error of thinking that he held the self to *consist mainly of* [*muscular*] *motions in the head or between the head and throat*'(1890, p. 301).[7] Now I know better, and am happy to be on the same side as James. I am also still hopeful of receiving the blessing of certain Buddhists, in spite of widespread scepticism about the validity of my claim to their support,[8] and I hope eventually to show that there is something right about the view of the self famously expounded by Hume in his *Treatise,* and equally famously rejected by him.[9]

The claim that there are many short-lived selves and that they are physical objects may not only look disappointing. It may also look like one of those philosophical views that can perhaps be defended and made consistent and even shown to have certain theoretical advantages, but that remains ultimately boring because it is too far removed from what we feel and what we want.[10] My hope and belief is that it can be made compelling and shown to be natural and true to life, although I suspect that deep differences of temperament will make this hard for some to see. My overall aim is not to produce a piece of irreducibly 'revisionary' metaphysics — one that shows that we are all wrong in our ordinary views.[11] It is to set out some rather ordinary and widely agreed facts in a certain way that I believe to be illuminating and true, although initially rebarbative.

II: The Problem

The notion of the self as we have it is much too baggy and unclear for us to answer questions like 'Do selves exist?', and **Olson** thinks we should stop speaking of selves altogether (p. 49). But psychologists and philosophers and a host of others will never

[7]   This ostensibly ontological remark, which is often lifted out of context and mis-understood, is not a claim about what selves are. It is a claim about what gives rise to our sense or feeling of the self. The question James has asked himself, and is answering (1890, pp. 299, 301–2, James's italics, my underlining), is '*Can we tell more precisely in what the feeling of this central active self consists,* — not necessarily as yet what the active self is, as a being or principle, but what we *feel* when we become aware of its existence?' His final, somewhat tentative reply is that it may be that '*our entire feeling of spiritual activity, or what commonly passes by that name, is really a feeling of bodily activities whose exact nature is by most men overlooked*' — the stress falling heavily on the words 'feeling' and 'activity'. (No trace of this claim remains in the shorter version of the chapter on the self in *Psychology: A Briefer Course* that James published in 1892.)

[8]   **Sheets-Johnstone** quotes Epstein — 'the distinguishing characteristic of Buddhist meditation is that it seeks to eradicate, once and for all, the conception of self as an entity' (pp. 250–1, quoting Epstein, 1995, p. 138–9) — as evidence of the vanity of my aspiration, although I tried to make it clear (cf. e.g. **Strawson**, p. 23 above, and section **XVII** below) that there is no tension between this view and my claim that selves are physical objects.

[9]   Hume (1739), pp. 251–63, 633–6. I think there is something right about it although Hume formulates it badly, gives very bad reasons in its support (as he doubtless knows), and rejects it for reasons that are confused.

[10] **Olson** (p. 59) finds it 'absurd'.

[11] For the distinction between 'descriptive' and 'revisionary' metaphysics, see P.F. Strawson (1959), pp. 9–10.

do as he says, and an alternative approach is to try to clarify and define the notion of the self in such a way that it is possible to answer such questions. Olson doubts that this can be done. He doubts, in fact, that there is any such thing as 'the problem of the self'. But there is a clear sense in which there is a problem of the self simply because there is thought to be a problem of the self; and the main reason why there is thought to be a problem of the self is that there is thought to be such a thing as the self; and the main reason why there is thought to be such a thing as the self — an inner, mental self, 'a secret self . . . enclosed within', a 'living, central, . . . inmost I'[12] — is simply that we have experience that has the *character* of there being such a thing. And this is not, as some have suggested, because we have been misled by words or beguiled by bad religious, psychotherapeutic, or philosophical traditions (Kenny, 1988; 1989). Such experience — I called it 'the sense of the self' in '"The Self"' and will call it 'Self-experience' in what follows — is fundamental to human life. I am puzzled by Steven Pinker when he talks (albeit sceptically) of 'the autonomous "I" that we all feel hovering above our bodies',[13] for if I had to say where I thought ordinary experience imagines the I or self to be, I'd say 'Two or three inches behind the eyes, and maybe up a bit'. But Self-experience doesn't have to involve any particular sense of location in order to be vivid, and to give rise to a genuine problem of the self.

III: Phenomenology and Metaphysics

What is the central question to which we would like an answer — granted that there is a problem of the self? It is, I take it, the straightforward question of fact

(I)   Do selves exist, and if so, what are they like?

But we need to know what sort of things we are asking about before we can begin trying to find out whether they exist.

How should we proceed? Well, it is Self-*experience* that gives rise to the problem — the vivid sense, delusory or not, that there is such a thing as the self. I think, in fact, that it is the whole source of the problem, in such a way that when we ask whether selves exist, what we are actually asking is: Does anything like the sort of thing that is figured in Self-experience exist?[14]

I suggest that there is nothing more at issue than this. And this, just this, is my fundamental move in trying to bring order and a chance of progress into the discussion — in particular, the philosophical discussion — of the self.

Does anything like the sort of thing that is figured in Self-experience exist? The first thing to do is to see what sort of thing is figured in Self-experience. Before we ask the factual or *metaphysical* question

(I)   Do selves exist?

we must ask and answer the *phenomenological* question

(II)   What sort of thing is figured in Self-experience?

---

[12] Traherne (1637–74, first published 1903) and Clough (1862), quoted by Kenny (1989, p. 86).

[13] Pinker (1997), p. 20. Note that this remark is phenomenological; Pinker's (rather unclear) metaphysical proposal is that 'the "I" is . . . a unity of selfness over time, a locus that is nowhere in particular' (p. 564).

[14] I use 'figured' in a highly general sense, one that carries no implication of picturing.

I think this is at first best taken as a question about human beings, as the *local* phenomenological question

(II.1)   What sort of thing is figured in ordinary human Self-experience?

But once we have an answer to the *local* phenomenological question, we have to go on to the more fundamental question, the *general* phenomenological question

(II.2)   Are there other possibilities, so far as Self-experience is concerned? (What sort of thing is figured in the minimal form of genuine Self-experience?)

Once we have an answer to this second question we can go back to the metaphysical question 'Do selves exist?', which we can now address in two versions: 'Do selves exist as figured in ordinary human Self-experience?' and 'Do selves exist as figured in the minimal form of Self-experience?' But we have to begin with phenomenology.[15]

Some cultural relativists doubt that we can generalize about human experience, but it should become clear that the aspects of Self-experience that concern me are situated below any level of plausible cultural variation. Even if there is some sense in which it is true that

> the Western conception of the person as a bounded, unique, more or less integrated motivational universe, a dynamic centre of awareness, emotion, judgement, and action organised into a distinctive whole and set contrastively against other such wholes and against its social and natural background, is . . . a rather peculiar idea within the context of the world's cultures (Geertz, 1983, p. 59, quoted in Watson, 1998),

it doesn't constitute grounds for doubt about the present project.

I should stress that the expression 'Self-experience' is just a phenomenological term: it is a name for a certain form of *experience* that does *not* imply that there actually are such things as selves. My use of the word 'self' is like William James's when he says that we must first try 'to settle . . . how this central nucleus of the Self may *feel*, no matter whether it be a spiritual substance or only a delusive word'. He uses the word 'self' freely as if it refers, while allowing that it may turn out to be 'only a delusive word', and I do the same (James, 1890, p. 298). Every time I use the phrase 'experience of the self' it can, if desired, be read as 'experience (as) of the self'.[16]

Some object that what I call 'phenomenology' is no such thing.[17] It is, however, a matter of the study of certain structures of experience considered just as such, and so fully qualifies for the name 'phenomenology'. I use the term in the standard non-

[15] **Brook** (p. 39) agrees that we must begin with phenomenology, but his reason differs from mine. His basic idea — which deserves serious consideration — is that the self considered as a metaphysical entity is a kind of phenomenologically constituted entity: 'the self is simply what one is aware of when one is aware of oneself [and specifically of one's mental features] from the inside' (p. 41). **Zahavi and Parnas** make a related move when they say that 'there is no difference between the . . . phenomenon of self and its metaphysical nature. Reality here is the same as appearance' (p. 263). I think, in fact, that we have to suppose that there is more to a self than is phenomenally given in this sense (compare the claim that a subject of experience cannot itself be an entirely experiential phenomenon), and this seems to put me at odds with Zahavi and Parnas; but not necessarily with Brook.

[16] Cf. **Strawson**, p. 2 above. **Wilkes** (p. 26) misses this point, taking it that I must suppose there to be a self in talking of a sense of the self.

[17] Cf. e.g. **Sheets-Johnstone**, who criticizes my 'so-called "phenomenological" approach' (p. 231), and **Zahavi and Parnas** (p. 254).

aligned sense, which is widespread in analytic philosophy and has nothing to do with the special use that derives from Husserl.

IV: Phenomenology: Self-experience

But what do I mean by 'Self-experience'? (What, in '"The Self"', did I mean by 'the sense of the self'?) I don't (didn't) mean the 'sense of self' that is discussed in books about 'personal growth' and that is meant to be a good thing. Nor do I mean something that involves one's sense of oneself considered quite generally as a human being. I intentionally avoided the common phrase 'sense of self', using 'sense of *the* self' instead, and giving it an explicit definition: 'the sense that people have of themselves as being, specifically, a mental presence; a mental someone; a single mental thing that is a conscious subject of experience' (p. 3, above). This definition was widely ignored, however, and the move from 'sense of the self' to 'sense of self' caused much misunderstanding.

Jonathan Cole, for example, shifted to 'sense of self' on his first page and contributed an excellent paper, on neurophysiological problems that affect the face, with which I have no disagreement. **Pickering** also dropped the 'the' and changed the subject, choosing to define the self as 'a semiotic process that emerges in a web of relationships'.[18] **Maxine Sheets-Johnstone** also changed the subject in her agreeably hostile paper. Oscillating freely between 'the sense of the self' and 'sense of self', she detailed a number of important facts about normal human experience and mental development. She was wrong, however, to think that these facts conflict with my views either about Self-experience (especially the minimal, non-human case of Self-experience) or about the nature of selves.[19]

By 'Self-experience', then, I mean the experience that people have of themselves as being, specifically, a mental presence; a mental someone; a single mental something or other. Such Self-experience comes to every normal human being, in some form, in early childhood. The realization of the fact that one's thoughts are unobservable by others, the experience of the sense in which one is alone in one's head or mind, the mere awareness of oneself as thinking: these are among the very deepest facts about the character of human life.[20] They are vivid forms of Self-experience that are perhaps most often salient when one is alone and thinking, although they can be equally strong in a room full of people. Many psychologists and anthropologists are quite rightly concerned to stress the embedded, embodied, ecological or 'EEE' aspects of our experiential predicament as social and organic beings located in a

---

[18] This is another interesting paper. Once again my only major disagreement is that there is something he and I disagree about.

[19] Thus I am not 'denying . . . a *developing* sense of the self', or that 'the conceptual sense of self has any foundation in affectivity'. I am not committed to 'an instant self fabricated on the spot' and don't contradict myself when I say (1) that a self is as much a physical object as a cow, and (2) that it is not thought of as being a thing in the way that a stone or a cat is: (1) is a metaphysical claim, (2) is phenomenological (cf. **Sheets-Johnstone**, pp. 248–9). Similarly, my only disagreement with **Legerstee**'s paper on infant self-awareness is on the question whether we disagree. Nor do I disagree with **Butterworth**'s views about 'ecological' aspects of self, given the way he chooses to use the word 'self', although I am sorry to see that psychology has not yet abandoned the false view that children can't attribute false beliefs to others, and don't acquire a 'theory of mind', until they are four (they can be adept at the age of two).

[20] I do not identify them with 'the origin of the sense of mental self' (**Pickering**, p. 73), and can accept the various claims about the development of Self-experience made in this symposium.

physical environment; but they risk losing sight of the respect in which Self-experience — the experience of oneself as a specifically mental something — is, none the less, the central or fundamental way (although it is obviously not the only way) in which human beings experience themselves.

I hear the objection that this is a Western, academic, deskbound, perspective, but I have in mind something that becomes clear after one has got past such objections, something that has now become relatively hard to see. It is, in large part, a simple consequence of the way in which our mental properties occupy — and tend to dominate — the foreground, when it comes to our apprehension of ourselves. It is not only that we are often preoccupied with our own thoughts and experiences, living with ourselves principally in our inward mental scene, incessantly presented to ourselves as things engaged in mental business.[21] It is also that mental goings on are always and necessarily present, even when we are thoroughly preoccupied with our bodies, or, generally, with things in the world other than our own mental goings on. Obviously we can be the subjects of mental goings on without being explicitly aware of them as such. Our attention can be intensely focused outward. But even then we tend to have a constant background awareness of our own mental goings on — it is usually inadequate to say that it is merely background awareness — and a constant tendency to flip back to some explicit sense of ourselves as minded or conscious.

Many lay very heavy stress on our constant background awareness of our bodies, but this awareness is fully compatible with our thinking of ourselves primarily or centrally as mental things, and those who stress somatic awareness may forget that it is just as true to say that there is constant background (as well as foreground) awareness of our minds. Kinaesthetic experience and other forms of proprioceptive experience of body are just that — experience — and in so far as they contribute constantly to our overall sense of ourselves, they not only contribute awareness of the body, they also contribute themselves, together with background awareness of themselves. The notion of background awareness is imprecise, but it seems plausible to say that there is certainly never *less* background awareness of awareness (i.e. of mind) than there is background awareness of body; and unprejudiced reflection reveals that awareness of mind, background or foreground, vastly predominates over awareness of body. Nothing hangs on this quantitative claim, however. For whether or not it is true, the constantly impinging phenomena of one's mental life are far more salient in the constitution of one's sense that there is such a thing as the self than are the phenomena of bodily experience.

Shear, in his contribution to the symposium, points out that it is common to have no particular sense of oneself as embodied when dreaming, although one's sense of one's presence in or at the dream-scene is extremely vivid. Such dream-experience is probably part of our experience from infancy, and doubtless contributes profoundly to our overall sense of the self as a mental something. To consider its experiential character is, as he says, to get an idea of 'how discoordinated a basic aspect of our

[21] Russell Hurlburt made random samplings of the character of people's experience as they went about their daily life by activating beepers that they carried with them: 'it was striking that the great majority of subjects at the time of the beep were focused on some inner event or events, with no direct awareness of outside events at that moment' (Hurlburt *et al.*, 1994, p. 387). Obviously such disengaged thoughts may themselves be focused on outside events — e.g. past events or possible future events. The fact is none the less of considerable interest (it is instructive to watch people as you pass them in the street).

deeply held, naive commonsensical notions of self [is] from anything graspable in terms of body, personality, or, indeed, any identifiable empirical qualities at all' (**Shear**, p. 412).[22]

Independently of this point there is, as **Shear** says, 'an important sense in which we conceive of ourselves purely as experiencers' (p. 410), in a way which is certainly not just a recent and local product of modern (Western) man's 'hyperreflexivity' (**Sass**, p. 322).[23] We may allow **Gallagher's and Marcel**'s phrase 'hyperreflective consciousness' as a description of such Self-experience, but only if we explicitly cancel any suggestion that it is recent and Western and in some way marginal, rather than something that has always been an essential part of the human experiential repertoire — and not restricted to solitary shepherds, spinners, trappers, messengers, farmers or fishermen, or times of 'philosophical reflection and certain limit situations like fatigue and illness' (**Gallagher and Marcel**, p. 289). Many of those who are anxious to dissociate themselves from any 'taint' of 'Cartesianism' and to emphasize their EEE 'enthusiasm for the body' (Shoemaker, 1999)[24] have overcompensated. They have become unable to give a proper place to — clearly see — some of the plainest, most quiet, and most fundamental facts of ordinary human experience.

I am not saying that we don't also naturally experience ourselves as embodied human beings considered as a whole. Obviously we do.[25] Nor am I claiming that Self-experience involves any belief in a non-physical soul. It doesn't. It is as natural and inevitable for atheists and materialists as for anyone else.

V: Phenomenology: The Local Question

Let me now add some detail to this general description of Self-experience. In ordinary human Self-experience, I propose, the self tends to be figured as

[1] a *subject of experience*, a conscious feeler and thinker
[2] a *thing*, in some interestingly robust sense
[3] a *mental* thing, in some sense
[4] a thing that is *single* at any given time, and during any unified or hiatus-free period of experience
[5] a *persisting* thing, a thing that continues to exist across hiatuses in experience
[6] an *agent*
[7] as something that has a certain character or *personality*.[26]

---

[22] To say this is not to say that one could dream in this way if one didn't have (or hadn't once had) normal experience of embodiment. Nor is it to say that there is any sense in which one is or even could be independent of one's body — as **Shear** stresses (p. 411).

[23] **Sass** claims that we must look to 'the [modern] era of western intellectual history' to find the time 'when consciousness first comes to know itself as such', but — waiving objections based on many ancient western and non-western traditions of thought — I would say that this happens, in a deep, plain, unqualified sense, in the case of every normal human being.

[24] Shoemaker is himself a 'friend of the body', as I am, but he senses that we live in a period of excessive reaction to the 'spectre' of 'Cartesianism'.

[25] **Gallagher and Marcel** give some outstanding descriptions of this phenomenon.

[26] I have dropped one of the eight conditions (the ontic distinctness condition) given in **Strawson** (p. 3 above) on the grounds that it is redundant, and have renumbered the others, giving first place, as seems appropriate, to the subject-of-experience condition.

I offer this as a piece of 'cognitive phenomenology': it aims to give the basic *conceptual structure* of our sense of the self, in so far as the self is experienced specifically as an inner mental presence. It does not advert to *affective* elements in our Self-experience, which require separate discussion, but it does not thereby cast any doubt on their profound importance to the overall character of Self-experience, or on the (phylogenetic and ontogenetic) importance of affect in the development of consciousness and self-consciousness, or on the view that 'affects constitute the core of being for many of our higher faculties' (**Panskepp**, p. 127). It just focuses for purposes of discussion on one aspect of the phenomenon that is in question.[27]

All of [1]–[7] need explanation or argument, but here I will add only two brief illustrative comments to what I said in '"The Self"'. First, as far as [4] is concerned, I take the idea of a strongly experientially unified or hiatus-free period of thought or experience as primitive. The conscious entertaining of a thought like 'the cat is on the mat', in which the elements *cat*, *on* and *mat* are bound together into a single thought, is a paradigm example of such a period of experience. So is looking up and seeing books and chairs and seeing them as such. Like Dennett, I take it that such periods are almost always short in the human case, and I believe that there is strong experimental support for this view.

Condition [2], the proposal that a self is experienced as a thing in some sense, is generally doubted, and I defend it in section **VII** below. The general idea is that Self-experience does not present the self as (merely) a state or property of something else, or as an event, or some sort of process. To that extent, *there is nothing else for a self to seem to be*, other than a thing of some sort. Obviously it is not thought of as being a thing in the way that a stone or a chair is. But it is none the less figured as a thing of some kind — something that can *undergo* things and *do* things and, most simply, *be in some state or othe*r. None of these things can be true of processes as ordinarily conceived of.

VI: Phenomenology: The General Question

Conditions [1]–[7] constitute the answer to the *local phenomenological* question, and deliver the following version of the *metaphysical* question: 'Do selves exist as figured in ordinary human Self-experience?' I think the answer is No, and on this I agree with James, Dennett, many if not all Buddhists, and probably with Hume, and even with Fichte. The related question 'What is the very best one can come up with, if one's brief is to argue that selves do exist as figured in ordinary human Self-experience?' is well worth pursuing, but I am going to bypass it and go on to the *general phenomenological* question: 'What is the minimal form of Self-experience?'

---

[27] The term 'cognitive phenomenology' confused many: it is in no sense true that I have a 'determinedly cognitivist' conception of the self (**Butterworth**, p. 203), or attempt to 'define a self in purely "cognitive rather than affective terms"' (**Hayward**, p. 389), or think that 'the self is made up of cognitive phenomena' (**Legerstee**, p. 227), or have 'a strictly cognitive view of the self' (**Cole**, p. 302). More generally, it is in no sense true that I am not interested in, or discount, the affective aspects of Self-experience. (I first used the term 'cognitive phenomenology' in 1980 in discussion of the experience of freedom, which is clearly not just a matter of sensory experience: see Strawson [1986], pp. 30, 55, 70, 96, 107–9. I later took it to cover aspects of the experience of understanding language: see Strawson [1994], pp. 4–13, 182–3; see also Ayers [1991], pp. 277–88, and Pitt [forthcoming]. I have grown accustomed to it, and should have realized that it invited misunderstanding.)

I think that [5], [6] and [7] — long-term continuity, agenthood and personality —
can be dispensed with (remember that we are no longer restricted to the human case),
and that the minimal form of Self-experience is a sense of the self as

[1] a *subject of experience*
[2] a *thing*, in some interestingly robust sense
[3] a *mental* thing, in some sense
[4] *single* at any given time, and during any hiatus-free or strongly experientially
    unified period of experience

Many doubt whether any of [5], [6] and [7] can be dropped, and their dispensability
needs to be argued for at length. But I think that they can be seen to be absent even in
certain human cases.

Some hold that [7], the personality condition, is clearly ineliminable, because to
think in terms of self just is to think in terms of individual personality. But Self-
experience is just: the specific experience of being a mental subject or inner mental
presence; and even if this can involve a sense of oneself as having personality, it
need not.

One way to make this vivid is to appeal to the fact that nearly everyone has at some
time experienced themselves as a kind of bare locus of consciousness, void of personality, but still for all that a mental subject. Equally important, however, is the respect
in which lack of any sense of the self as having personality is normal, in the human
case. One tends to see personality clearly when one considers other people, but not
when one considers oneself. One's personality is usually built so deeply into the way
one apprehends things that it does not present itself to awareness in such a way as to
enter significantly into one's Self-experience. Obviously one may experience oneself
as being in certain moods, but it certainly does not follow that one experiences oneself as having a certain personality. One's own personality is usually something that
is unnoticed in the present moment. It's what one looks through, or where one looks
from; not something one looks at.

What about [6], the agency condition? One of the great dividing facts about
humanity is that some people experience their mental lives in a Rimbaud- or
Meursault-like or fashion, i.e. almost entirely as something that just happens to them,
while others naturally think of themselves as controllers and intentional producers of
their thoughts.[28] The latter group are particularly likely to doubt whether [6] can be
dispensed with, even in non-human cases, and I will not try to convince them here.
What does need to be said, in the context of the symposium, is that there is no tension
at all between the claim that [6] can be dispensed with and facts about the crucial role
of the experience of agency in human mental development, the importance of kinaes-
thesia to human self-awareness, and so on.[29]

---

[28] Rimbaud (1871), pp. 249, 250: 'It's false to say: I think. One ought to say 'it thinks [in] me ... for *I* is an
other ... It's obvious to me that I am a spectator at the unfolding of my thought: I watch it, I listen to it'.
Cf. also Camus (1942; 1960) and the description of the 'Spectator subject' and the 'natural Epictetans'
in Strawson (1986), chs. 12 and 13. Bruner, referring to Happé (1991), notes that 'autists give typically
nonagentive accounts of themselves and their lives' (1994, p. 48), and autism is clearly of great interest
when considering whether [5], [6], and [7] are necessary parts of human Self-experience.

[29] So I have no disagreement with **Legerstee**. The appearance of disagreement arises from three things:
her reading of phenomenological claims as metaphysical claims, her focus on the human case, and her
assumption that I *argue* 'that the "self" is a purely mental entity' (p. 214), whereas in fact I *define* the

VII: Phenomenology: Diachronics and Episodics

Condition [5], the long-term persistence condition, engages with another of the great dividing facts about humanity. Some people have a strongly narrative or (more neutrally) *Diachronic* way of thinking about themselves, a strong sense that *the I that is a mental presence now* was there in the past and will be there in the future. Others have a very different, *Episodic* way of being in time. Episodics, looking out from the present, have very little sense that the I that is a mental presence now was there in the past and will be there in the further future. They are, perhaps, like John Updike when he writes that he has 'the persistent sensation, in my life . . . that I am just beginning' (Updike 1979, p. 239). They relate differently to their autobiographical memories. In my own case, the interest (emotional or otherwise) of my — rather sparse — autobiographical memories lies in their experiential content considered quite independently of the fact that what is remembered happened *to me*. In fact I am strongly inclined to say that the events in question didn't happen to me — to *Me**, to that which I feel myself to be, in having Self-experience — at all.[30] These memories are of course distinctive in their 'from-the-inside' character, and they certainly happened to the human being that I (also) am; but it simply does not follow that they present, or are experienced, as things that happened to Me* as just characterized.

Many are surprised by this last claim. They take it that having a 'from-the-inside' character immediately entails being experienced as something that happened to Me*. But this is not so. The 'from-the-inside' character of a memory can detach completely from any lived identification with the subject of the remembered experience. My memory of falling out of a punt has, intrinsically, a from-the-inside character, visual (the water rushing up to meet me), kinaesthetic, proprioceptive, and so on, but it does not follow that it carries any sense or belief that what is remembered happened to Me*.[31]

It does not follow even when the remembered event is experienced from the inside in emotional respects. I can have a memory that incorporates emotional concern felt from the inside without in any way feeling that what I remember happened to Me*. So the inference from (a) 'The memory has a from-the-inside character emotionally considered' to (b) 'The memory is experienced as something that happened to Me*' is not valid, although (a) and (b) may very often be true together (especially in the case of certain kinds of memory). I find this to be a plain fact of experience. Those who do not may gain a sense of it if they know what it is to be emotionally involved, by sympathy or empathy, in the life or outlook of another person or a fictional character without having any sense that one is that other person or character.[32]

---

notion of self in this way in order to see what can then be made of it (see section **I** above). Nor do I disagree with **Sheets-Johnstone** here. She finds my 'treatment of agency — or rather non-treatment of agency — . . . near astounding' (p. 239), but the principal explanation, apart, perhaps, from differences in the way we experience things, is simple: I am not particularly concerned with the ordinary human case, or indeed with any human case, and certainly not with human developmental necessities.

[30] I introduced 'Me*' in **Strawson**, p. 16 above. It is an essentially phenomenological notion.

[31] For the visual aspect, imagine two video recordings, one from the river bank, one from a camera placed between my eyes.

[32] The common phrase 'empathetic *identification*' can be misleading.

This is obviously not enough to show that Self-experience need not involve [5], experience of the self as having long-term diachronic continuity. Large issues are involved.[33] One concerns another great dividing fact about humanity which can be briefly described as follows. Many think it beyond question that we can and inevitably do (and in any case should) 'create and construct our "selves"' (**Wilkes**, p. 36).[34] Others find such a claim bewildering, in so far as it implies that one's development as a person involves (or should involve) any significant amount of conscious planning, any need for studied reflection on where one has come from or where one is going, any pre-occupation with one's life considered specifically *as one's own life*, rather than as a source of understanding and possible deepening whose instructiveness does not depend internally and constitutively — even if it depends causally — on the fact that it is one's own life.[35] For members of the second group the process is effectively automatic and unpondered; and they may observe that a person could develop just as valuably by empathetic participation — involuntary, unplanned, never consciously mulled over, not a matter of identification in any strong sense — in the experiences of the protagonists of great novels. In general, we can all learn deeply from experience, and from vicarious experience, and develop in various ways, without any particular autobiographical concern with ourselves, and indeed with little reflection on ourselves. The less conscious reflection the better, in many cases. The 'examined life' is greatly overrated.

Diachronics may feel there is something chilling and empty in the Episodic life, but the principal thing about it is simply that it is more directed on the present. The past is not alive in memory, as Diachronics may find, but it is alive — Episodics might say more truly alive — in the form of the present: in so far as it has shaped the way one is in the present. There is no reason to think that the present is less informed by or responsible to the past in the Episodic life than in the Diachronic life. It is rather that the informing and the responsiveness have different mechanisms and different experiential consequences.

VIII: Phenomenology: Me* and Morality

There is one other issue relating to [5] that is worth a comment. I claim in a footnote that the Episodic life may be 'no less intense or full, emotional or moral' than the Narrative or Diachronic life, and Wilkes argues forcefully that this cannot be so:

> Morality is a matter of planning future actions, calculating consequences, experiencing remorse and contrition, accepting responsibility, accepting praise and blame; such mental phenomena are both forward- and backward-looking. Essentially. . . . Emotions such

---

[33] There is more in **Strawson**, pp. 14–19 above, but it is only a summary of a longer work.

[34] For a powerful statement of this position, see Schechtman (1997), ch. 5, 'The Narrative Self-Constitution View': 'baldly . . . stated', her view is that 'a person creates his identity by forming an autobiographical narrative — a story of his life' (p. 93).

[35] Hirst (1994) has an interesting discussion of personal development in people who have severe anterograde or retrograde amnesia, or both, and are to that extent incapable of 'narrative self-construction' of the sort that some believe to be necessary to such development, although they clearly continue to have Self-experience, as does patient 'W.R.', who is 'locked . . . into the immediate space and time' by damage to his dorsolateral prefrontal cortex, in Knight's and Grabowecky's paper 'Escape from Linear Time' (1995).

as love or hate, envy or resentment, would not deserve the name — except in some occasional rare cases — if they lasted for but three seconds, and were thereafter claimed, not by any Me*, but by some former self . . . . The Episodic life could not be richly moral and emotional; we must have a life, or self, with duration. We are, and must consider ourselves as, relatively stable intentional systems. Essentially. (**Wilkes**, p. 27.)

Well, the moral life of Episodics is not the same as that of Diachronics, but that is not to say that it is less moral or less emotional. There are spectacularly different 'varieties of moral personality' in the human species,[36] and members of one variety tend to have an incorrectly dim view of the moral nature of members of another. The question is very complicated, and here the following brief points will have to suffice.

The main problem is that **Wilkes** exaggerates my position. In '"The Self"' I note that I make plans for the future, although I am somewhere down the Episodic end of the human spectrum, and in that sense 'think of myself perfectly adequately as something that has long-term continuity'. I add that 'I'm perfectly well aware that [my past] is mine, in so far as I am a human being considered as a whole', observe that there are certain things in the future — such as my death — and equally certain things in the past — such as embarrassment — that I can experience as involving Me*, and stress the point that 'one's sense of one's temporal nature may vary considerably depending on what one is thinking about' (**Strawson**, pp. 15–17 above).[37] There is, then, no reason why some Episodics may not sometimes apprehend some of their past dubious actions as involving their Me*, and accordingly feel remorse or contrition.

This is not to concede that remorse and contrition are essential to the moral life.[38] There is a great deal more to say, and Wilkes confuses an ontological proposal about the normal duration of human selves (up to three seconds) with a phenomenological description of Episodic experience that does not suggest that the present Me* is experienced as lasting only three seconds.[39] The Episodic life is not absolute in the way she supposes. Human beings fall on a continuous spectrum from radically Episodic to radically Narrative, and may move along the spectrum in one direction or another as they age.

It is true that Episodics are less likely to suffer in Yeats' way —

> Things said or done long years ago,
> Or things I did not do or say
> But thought that I might say or do,
> Weigh me down, and not a day
> But something is recalled,
> My conscience or my vanity appalled.
>   (Yeats, 1933, p. 284)

---

[36] Cf. Flanagan (1991). One particularly striking difference is between those for whom the moral-emotional categories of resentment and humiliation are central, and those for whom they are hardly visible.

[37] One may link up to various discrete, non-narratively apprehended sections of one's past in exactly the way that Locke envisages in his massively misunderstood theory of personal identity (for the correct understanding, see Schechtman, 1997, pp. 105–9).

[38] Note, for example, that matter-of-fact self-criticism — or indeed self-anger — that lacks the characteristic phenomenology of remorse or contrition (or self-reproach, or self-disgust) need not be a morally inferior way of experiencing one's own wrongdoing.

[39] Half an hour is offered as a possible candidate — subject to the point, mentioned above, that 'one's sense of one temporal nature may vary considerably depending on what one is thinking about'.

— even if their lives have been as imperfect as everyone else's. But if they are faced with criticisms from Diachronics who see their lightness as a moral failing, they may observe, correctly, that there is a point (perilously close in some cases) where vanity and conscience — what appears to be conscience — turn out to be a single phenomenon. And this line of thought has striking continuations. It is, for example, arguable that *guilt*[40] is a fundamentally self-indulgent — selfish — moral emotion, as well as a superficial one; although *sorrow* about what one has done is neither selfish nor superficial. Some may suggest that this view of guilt is itself evidence of moral failing, and that someone who holds it cannot fully participate in the moral form of life (although one can hold it while continuing to feel guilt), but they are surely wrong.

This last suggestion shows a serious lack of feeling for human difference, but it isn't as bad as an objection that some (not **Wilkes**) have made, according to which Episodics cannot be properly moral because, in feeling unconcerned in their past, they lack a vital moral constraint on action. This is clearly false. One doesn't have to care about one's past (considered as such) in order to want to act rightly, and in order to do so. One doesn't have to be governed by prudential concern about one's *future past* — the past one will have to live with in the future; one's present commitments — outlook — feelings — awareness of the situation — can be wholly sufficient. Many find concern about the future past completely absent from the phenomenology of moral engagement. Their concern is to do what should be done simply because it is what should be done, or (without the Kantian loop) simply to do what should be done. To be guided by concern about one's future past when making decisions is not to have a distinctively moral motive at all, nor indeed a particularly admirable motive.

I want to finish with phenomenology and get on to metaphysics, but I still haven't discussed the widely rejected[41] phenomenological claim that Self-experience (necessarily) involves [2] experience of the self as a thing in some sense. My optimistic view is that no one will disagree once I have adequately explained what I mean.[42]

IX: Phenomenology: The Experience of the Self as a Thing

The objection to [2] is clear. Why couldn't a self-conscious creature's Self-experience involve experiencing the self as just a property or set of properties of something else (perhaps a human being), or just as a process of some sort?

It depends, of course, on what you mean by 'thing', 'property' and 'process', and by 'experience something as a thing . . . or property . . . or set of properties . . . or process'. I take the words 'thing', 'property' and 'process' to have their ordinary, imprecise pre-theoretical force when they are used phenomenologically to characterize forms of experience. (The issue of how they are best used in metaphysics remains to be considered.)

The question recurs. Must genuine Self-experience really involve [2], experience of the self as a thing of some kind?

[40] Also mentioned by **Wilkes** as important (p. 25).

[41] See for example **Forman**, p. 367; **Hayward**, pp. 380, 392; **Laycock**, p. 396; **Pickering**, p. 65; **Sheets-Johnstone**, p. 249.

[42] I give a further independent argument in 'The Grounds of Self-Consciousness'.

It may seem very hard to be sure, given the vagueness of the word 'thing', and after the discussion of the question 'What is a thing?' in sections **XIV–XVIII** below some may feel that little hangs on the answer. What I have in mind is simply this: Kant is right that 'everyone must necessarily regard himself', the conscious subject, 'as [a] substance', and must regard all episodes of thought or conscious episodes 'as being only accidents of his existence, determinations of his state' (1781–7, A349). As he says, 'the "I" who thinks or is conscious must always be considered in such thought or consciousness as a *subject* and as something that does not merely attach to thought or consciousness like a predicate' (B407).[43]

Kant's main aim in the Paralogisms is to show that one cannot argue from this phenomenological fact to any corresponding metaphysical fact. He points out that it does not follow, from the fact that we must *experience* or regard the 'I' or self as a substance or thing, that it actually *is* a substance or thing, or that we can know that this is so. We cannot, he says, rule out the possibility that the 'I' of thought or consciousness may in the final analysis be just a property of something else, 'a predicate of another being'. It is, he says, 'quite impossible' for me, given my experience of myself as a mental phenomenon, 'to determine the manner in which I exist, whether it be as substance [or object] or as accident [or property]' (B419–20). As a theorist one may believe (as I do) that there is a sense in which the phenomena that constitute selves (if they exist) are 'just' processes in the brain;[44] and one may also think (as I do not) that this view of selves is incompatible with the view that they are things in any worthwhile sense; and so conclude that they are definitely not things (in so far as they exist at all). So be it, Kant will reply. None of this constitutes an objection to the fundamental phenomenological claim that if one has Self-experience at all, one must experience the self as a 'substance' or thing of some kind.

I agree. I have little to add to Kant's arguments and the last paragraph of section **V** above, where it was suggested that the fundamental respect in which the self is apprehended under the category of thing is already manifest in the way in which it is experienced as something that can *have* or *undergo* things like sensations and emotions, something that can *be in some state or other*. No experience that presents something as something that *has experience* or even just as something that can *be in some state or other* can figure it merely as a property of something else, or as a mere process, or event.[45] This is the primary intuition.

It is worth thinking an explicit I-thought like 'I am reading an article' or 'I am present, here, now, thinking that I am present here now'; not simply apprehending the content of some such thought by reading, but stopping to think one through. If, overcoming one's natural contrasuggestibility, one accepts to do this, one encounters, in a vivid way, the inescapable respect in which Self-experience — experience of oneself as a mental subject of experience — must involve figuring the self as a thing in a sense sufficient for the truth of [2].

---

[43] I read 'must' with Pluhar rather than 'can' with Kemp Smith.

[44] For the trouble with 'just' see section **XVII** below.

[45] Here 'property', 'process' and 'event' have their ordinary pretheoretical sense, and 'mere' and 'merely' are added to match.

'But how can you rule out *a priori* the idea that an alien might have Self-experience that figured the self as just a process?'

Well, if it really does have Self-experience, and really does experience itself, when it apprehends itself as a mental self, as a subject of experience that has thoughts and experiences and is in certain mental states, then it experiences the self as a thing in a sense sufficient for my purposes. Kant got it right. If someone says that I have not really given an argument for this, and have merely presented an intuition in a certain way, I will not take it as a criticism. If someone says that I have taken a long time to say something obvious that Kant said long ago, I will accept it as a criticism but I will not mind. If someone says the whole section is a laborious statement of the obvious, I will be rather pleased. If, finally, someone says that any sense of the self as a thing may dissolve in the self-awareness of meditation, I will agree, and reply that in that case Self-experience of the kind that is at present of concern will also have dissolved (this being, perhaps, and after all, the aim of the meditation).

X: Phenomenology: Eyes and *I*s

The preceding sentence raises an important issue. Self-experience is defined as experience that has the character of being of a — the — mental self. But it is not clear that any genuine experience of *what one is considered as a whole and specifically as a mental phenomenon* — call this 'M-experience' — must *ipso facto* be a form of *Self*-experience. It is not clear that all genuine M-experience must have the full structure of Self-experience. By the same token, it is not clear that the minimal case of Self-experience is *ipso facto* the minimal case of M-experience. I suspect that the minimal case of M-experience may be some kind of 'pure consciousness' experience, of the kind discussed by Buddhists and others, that no longer involves anything that can usefully be called 'Self-experience' at all.[46]

I will take this suggestion a little way, in combination with a point about the notion of an object of thought, for some contributors to the symposium focused on such matters, and may feel that their central doubts have not yet been addressed, let alone answered.

When I claim that Self-experience must involve [2] experience of being a (mental) thing of some sort, the sort of self-apprehension that I have in mind need not and typically does not involve targeting oneself as an *object of thought* in a way that opens a path to the well known view that the I or self or subject is 'systematically elusive' to itself and cannot ever truly take itself — i.e. itself as it is in the present moment — as the object of its thought (cf. Ryle 1949, p. 186). I think this view is false, in fact, but the first point to make is that it would not matter to [2] if it were true, for the root thought behind [2] is simply this: if you have Self-experience, you can't *live* yourself, experienced as mental *subject*, as somehow merely a process or property or event. (This thought is, I suppose, very close to triviality, which is a sometimes very good place to be.)[47] In this regard I agree with **Sass** when he says that 'the most fundamental sense of selfhood involves the experience of self not as an *object* of awareness but, in some crucial respects, as an unseen point of origin for action, experience, and

---

[46] In this symposium, see e.g. **Forman**, pp. 362–4; **Hayward**; **Shear**. See also Parfit (1998).

[47] Once, after having given a paper, Brian McGuinness was faced with the objection that one of his claims was trivial. He looked worried for a moment, and then replied 'I *hope* it's trivial'.

thought', and again when he says that 'what William James called . . . the "central nucleus of the Self" is not, in fact, experienced as an entity *in the focus of our awareness*, but, rather, as a kind of medium of awareness, source of activity, or general directedness towards the world' (**Sass**, p. 338, my italics). This is well expressed, and I take it to be fully compatible with the lived sense in which the self is [2] experienced as a thing of some sort. [2] does not require experience of self that is experience (as) of 'an entity in the focus of awareness'.

Is the I or subject none the less systematically elusive? Is there some sense in which genuine self-presence of mind is essentially impossible? The matter requires reflection, but it seems to me that Lonergan, for one, is right when he says that 'objects are present by being attended to, but subjects are present [to themselves] as subjects, not by being attended to, but by attending. As the parade of objects marches by, spectators do not have to slip into the parade to be present to themselves' (Lonergan, 1967, p. 226, quoted by **Forman**, p. 369).[48] **Deikman** makes the same point: 'we know the internal observer not by observing it but by *being* it . . . . knowing by being that which is known is . . . different from perceptual knowledge' (p. 426), as do **Zahavi and Parnas**, introducing the notion of 'the basic self-awareness of an experience', which they describe as 'an immediate and intrinsic self-acquaintance which is characterized by being completely irrelational' (p. 262).[49]

Certainly the eye cannot see itself (unless there is a mirror), and the knife cannot cut itself (unless it is very flexible), and the fingertip cannot touch itself, and one cannot jump on to the shadow of one's own head.[50] It is a very ancient claim, with many metaphorical expressions, that the I cannot take itself as it is in the present moment as the object of its thought, that 'my . . . present . . . self perpetually slips out of any hold of it that I try to take' (Ryle, 1949, p. 187), and several contributors to this symposium concur. **Laycock** expresses the claim in dozens of different ways in his extremely rich Husserlian-phenomenological paper 'Consciousness It/Self', and observes that it is part of 'perennial Buddhist wisdom' (p. 396).[51]

And so it is, considered as a truth about the limitations of a certain form of self-apprehension. But it is as such fully compatible with a claim to which it appears to be opposed, according to which there is another form of self-apprehension in which the I or subject — or just consciousness, if you wish — *can* be directly or immediately explicitly aware of itself in the present moment. I think this is true, and will try to say why. First, though, note that it doesn't matter whether it is true or not when it comes to [2], the claim that Self-experience involves experience of the self as a thing of some sort; for even if the I or subject cannot be explicitly aware of itself as it is in the pres-

---

[48] It is interesting to note how this parallels some of **Gallagher and Marcel**'s remarks about the experience of agency, notwithstanding the strong EEE emphasis of their discussion.

[49] Note that we certainly do not have to suppose that (1), 'knowing by being that which is known', or rather, perhaps, knowing (oneself) by being that which is knowing, entails (2), knowing everything there is to know about that which is known. On a materialist view, one may grant that that which is known, in the case of self-presence of mind of the sort envisaged in (1), has non-experiential being that is not known.

[50] Ryle (1949), p. 187. But perhaps it is high noon. One leans one's head forward and makes a small jump while slightly drawing back one's head.

[51] Cf. also **Deikman** (p. 421): distinguishing between experiencing and 'seeing', which presumably stands for any sort of experientially mediated operation, he says that the 'I' can be experienced, but cannot be 'seen'.

ent moment, [2] remains unaffected as a claim about how one must *live* oneself in having Self-experience.[52]

The view that the mental subject can be aware of itself as it is in the present moment may be challenged as vague and mystical. The systematic elusiveness objection — according to which one cannot after all directly apprehend oneself as mental self or subject or thinker in the present moment — may be redeployed. 'You may think *I am now thinking a puzzling thought*, or *I'm looking down on India*, or just *Here I am*, in an attempt to so apprehend yourself, but in entertaining these contents you necessarily fail to apprehend the thing that is doing the apprehending — the entertainer of the content, the thinker of the thought, i.e. yourself considered as the mental self at that moment. Any performance, as Ryle says, 'can be the concern of a higher-order performance' — one can think about any thought that one has — but it 'cannot be the concern of itself'. When one thinks an I-thought

> this performance is not dealt with in the operation which it itself is. Even if the person is, for special speculative purposes, momentarily concentrating on the Problem of the Self, he has failed and knows that he has failed to catch more than the flying coat-tails of that which he was pursuing. His quarry was the hunter (Ryle, 1949, pp. 188–9).

It is arguable, however, that to think *This very thought is puzzling* — or *I am now thinking a puzzling thought,* or *The having of this thought is strange* — is precisely to engage in a performance that is concerned with itself; so that a certain kind of immediate self-presence of mind is possible even in an intentional, designedly self-reflexive, and wholly cognitive act, quite independently of the truth of the considerations adduced by Lonergan, Deikman, Forman, Shear, and others. It is only when one tries to apprehend that one has succeeded that one triggers the regressive step. It may be added that there does not seem to be any obvious reason why a hunter cannot catch the quarry when the quarry is himself. A detective with amnesia, sitting in her chair and reasoning hard, may identify herself as the person who committed the crime she is investigating. Wandering in the dark, I may get increasingly precise readings regarding the location of my quarry from a Global Positioning System, activate my grabber arms to move to the correct spot and grab, press the grab-function button, and get grabbed.[53]

Actually one can allow, if only for the sake of argument, that concentration on cognitively articulated thoughts like *I am now thinking a puzzling thought* or *Here I am* cannot deliver what is required, or provide a successful practical route to appreciation of the point that it is possible to have genuinely present self-awareness of oneself as the mental subject of experience. For the best route is more direct, and does not involve any such cognitively articulated representations. It is simply a matter of coming to awareness of oneself as a mental presence — as mental presence — in a certain sort of concentrated but global — unpointed — way. It can be done; the object of one's awareness doesn't have to be a content in such a way that it cannot be the thing that is entertaining the content. On this point Ryle and others are simply wrong. There is no insuperable difficulty in the matter of present or immediate self-awareness. I can engage in it with no flying coat-tails time-lag. The case is just not like the case of the

---

[52] So I need not disagree with **Edey** when he claims (p. 443) that 'the subject is not an object'.

[53] There is also the case of Winnie the Pooh and Piglet and the Heffalump (Milne, 1928).

eye that cannot see itself, or a fingertip that cannot touch itself. A mind is, rather dramatically, more than an eye. If Ryle had spent more time on disciplined, unpreju-diced introspection, or had tried meditation, even if only briefly, and in an entirely amateur and unsupervised way, like myself — he would have found that it is really not very difficult — although it is quite difficult — for the subject of experience to be aware in the present moment of itself-in-the-present-moment. As far as the level of difficulty is concerned, it seems to me that is like maintaining one's balance on a bar in a way that is quite hard but not extremely hard. One can easily lose one's balance — one can fall out of the state in question — but one can also keep it. No doubt it is something one gets better at if one practises certain kinds of meditation, in which such self-awareness has the status of a rather banal first step (about which there is extremely wide consensus) towards something more remarkable.

The direct evidence for this, and for 'pure consciousness' experience, is and can only be introspection in the widest sense of the term. Each must acquire it for himself or herself. This does not mean it is not empirical; clearly it is. It does mean that it is not publicly checkable, and it will always be possible for someone to object that the experience of truly present self-awareness is an illusion — produced, say, by Rylean flashes of 'swift retrospective heed' (Ryle, 1949, p. 153).

Whatever one thinks of this, there is another mistake, which may tempt those who carry EEE thinking (see p. 488 above) too far, that can be decisively blocked. There is no good argument from the true EEE fact that naturally evolved forms of conscious-ness are profoundly, and seemingly constitutively, and, in the natural course of things, almost incessantly, in the service of the interoceptive and exteroceptive per-ceptual and agentive survival needs of organisms[54] to the conclusion that Forman (for instance) must be wrong to claim that 'consciousness should not be defined in terms of perceptions, content, or its other functions' (**Forman**, p. 373). Forman holds that in certain meditative states 'awareness itself is experienced as still or silent, perceptions as active or changing. Therefore instead of defining awareness in terms of its content, we should think about awareness and its mental and sensory *functions* as two inde-pendent phenomena or processes that somehow interact.' I think that this notion of interacting processes may be too separatist, and that the contentual features of states of awareness — more precisely, the contentual features of states of awareness that involve content other than whatever content is involved in simple awareness of awareness — should rather be seen as modifications of awareness. But the basic idea of pure awareness or consciousness is not in tension with anything in the theory of evolution by natural selection.

This is a topic that needs a lot more discussion. Here let me say that even if consciousness is not a primordial property of the universe, and came on the scene relatively late, there is no good reason — in fact it doesn't even make sense — to think that it first came on the scene because it had survival value. Natural selection needs something to work on and can only work on what it finds. Consciousness had to exist before it could be exploited, just as non-conscious matter did. I take it that natu-ral selection moulded the consciousness it found in nature into adaptive forms just as it moulded the non-conscious phenomena it found. From this perspective, the task of

[54] Damasio (1994, ch. 10) gives a powerful description of the profundity of the connection between the mind and the rest of the body. Cf. also **Panskepp** on what he calls 'equalia . . . the most ancient evolutionary qualia', **Ramachandran and Hirstein** and Balleine and Dickinson (1998).

giving an evolutionary explanation of the *existence* of consciousness is just like the task of giving an evolutionary explanation of the existence of non-conscious matter (there is no such task). And the evolution by natural selection of various finely developed types of consciousness (visual, olfactory, cognitive, etc.) is no more surprising than the evolution by natural selection of various finely developed types of body. Finally, even if evolved forms of consciousness came to be what they were because they had certain kinds of content that gave them survival value and that were (therefore) essentially other than whatever content is involved in simple awareness of awareness, it doesn't follow that pure consciousness experience is some sort of illusion or mere surface effect: even if pure consciousness experience as we can know it becomes possible only after millions of years of EEE-practical forms of consciousness, it does not follow that it is not uniquely revelatory of the fundamental nature of consciousness.

XI: Transition: Phenomenology to Metaphysics

I have made a negative claim about Self-experience and a positive claim with a rider. The negative claim is that Self-experience does not necessarily involve [5]–[7]: it need not involve any experience of the self as an agent that has long-term diachronic continuity and personality, even if it can do so. The positive claim is that any genuine form of Self-experience must involve [1]–[4]: it must present the self as a subject of experience that is a mental thing that is single at any given time and during any unified or hiatus-free period of experience. The meditative rider to the positive claim is that genuine 'M-experience' (see p. 113 above) — genuine experience of what one is considered as a whole and specifically as a mental phenomenon — need not involve Self-experience.

I turn now from phenomenology to metaphysics, for the phenomenological investigation of Self-experience has duly delivered two versions of the metaphysical question. (1) 'Do selves exist as figured in ordinary human Self-experience?', (2) 'Do selves exist as figured in the minimal form of Self-experience?' I am inclined to answer No to (1) and Yes to (2), but here I will consider only (2).

XII: Metaphysics: SESMETS

Do selves exist as figured in the minimal form of Self-experience? Are there [1] subjects of experience that are [4] single [3] mental [2] things? I think there are, and for the moment I will call them SESMETS (Subjects of Experience that are Single MEntal Things), for this will allow me to put the case for their existence while leaving the question of whether it would be right or best to call them 'selves' entirely open.

In essentials I agree with William James, who holds that 'the same brain may subserve many conscious selves' that are entirely numerically distinct substances. Using the word 'thought' in the wide Cartesian sense to cover all types of conscious episodes, he claims that each '"perishing" pulse of thought' is a self, and in a famous phrase, says that 'the thoughts themselves are the thinkers' (1890, p. 401, p. 371; 1892, p. 191). I think it is clearer to say that the existence of each thought involves a self, or consists in the existence of a self or SESMET or subject of experience entertaining a certain mental content, but the basic idea is the same. The apparent continuity of experience, such as it is,[55] and the consistency of perspective across selves, derives from the fact that SESMETS 'appropriate' — in James's word — the experiential content of the experiences of their predecessors in a way that is entirely unsurprising in so far as they arise successively, like gouts of water from a rapidly sporadic fountain, from brain conditions that have considerable similarity from moment to moment even as they change. Given short-term or 'working' memory, the immediately preceding contents form part of the context in which new contents arise in every sense in which features of the external environment do.

'The I', James says,

> is a *thought*, at each moment different from that of the last moment, but *appropriative* of the latter, together with all[56] that the latter called its own. All the experiential facts find their place in this description, unencumbered with any hypothesis save that of the existence of passing thoughts or states of mind (1892, p. 191; 1890, pp. 400–1).

I take it, then, that there are many SESMETS, in the case of a human being, and that for the most part they exist successively, although I agree with James that there is no theoretical difficulty in the idea that they may also exist concurrently.[57] Each one is an 'indecomposable unity' and 'the same brain may subserve many conscious selves' that 'have no *substantial* identity' (1890, p. 371, p. 401; 1892, p. 181). James expresses himself loosely when he says that the self consists in 'a remembering and appropriating Thought incessantly renewed', for this phrase suggests that selves are things that have some sort of long-term continuity, but his more careful statement of his view explicitly cancels any such suggestion. He knows it is intensely natural for us to think of the self as something that has long-term continuity, and is accordingly prepared to speak loosely in sympathy with that tendency, while holding that it is in fact quite incorrect:

> My present Thought stands . . . in the plenitude of ownership of the train of my past selves, is owner not only *de facto*, but *de jure*, the most real owner there can be . . . Successive thinkers, *numerically distinct*, but all aware of the past in the same way, form an adequate vehicle for all the *experience* of personal unity and sameness which we actually have (1890, pp. 362–3, 360; 1892, p. 181; my emphasis).[58]

A SESMET, then, is a subject of experience as it is present and alive in the occurrence of an experience. It is as EEE — as embodied, embedded and ecological — as anyone could wish. There cannot be a SESMET without an experience, and it is arguable that

---

[55] For doubts see **Strawson**, pp. 17–19 above.

[56] This is surely too strong.

[57] See James (1890), p. 401. Note that there is no more metaphysical difficulty in the idea that a thing that lasts for two seconds can know Latin, be exhausted, kind, and in love, than there is in the idea that an ordinary human being considered during a two-second period of time can be said to have these properties during that time.

[58] Compare Damasio (1994), pp. 236–43: 'at each moment the state of self is constructed, from the ground up. It is an evanescent reference state, so continuously and consistently *re*constructed that the owner never knows that it is being *re*made unless something goes wrong with the remaking' (p. 240). Damasio goes on to say the same about what he calls the 'metaself' (p. 243), which is more closely related to the phenomenon currently under discussion.

there cannot be an experience without a SESMET.[59] I take it that SESMETs exist and are part of (concrete) reality. I think, in fact, that they are physical objects, as real as rabbits and atoms. It is true that this unpopular view depends on taking the words 'object' and 'physical' in an unfamiliar way, but I think that we have to take them in this way when we do serious metaphysics from a materialist standpoint. I will say something about this now, beginning with a brief account of how realistic materialists must understand the physical.

XIII: Metaphysics: Realistic Materialists and the Physical

Step one. Materialism is the view that every thing and event in the universe is physical in every respect. It is the view that 'physical phenomenon' is coextensive with 'real phenomenon',[60] or at least with 'real, concrete phenomenon'.[61] Step two. If one thing is certain, it is that there is conscious experience: it is that *experiential phenomena* — by which I will mean the phenomena of conscious experience considered just in respect of the qualitative character that they have for those who have them as they have them — exist. Step three. It follows that genuine or *realistic* materialists (realistic anybodies) must fully acknowledge the reality of experiential phenomena. Step four. It follows in turn that they must hold that these experiential phenomena are wholly physical phenomena, and are wholly physical considered specifically in respect of their qualitative-experiential character.

Many find it odd to use the word 'physical' to characterize experiential phenomena. Many self-declared materialists talk about mental and physical as if they were opposed categories. But this, on their own view, is exactly like talking about cows and animals as if they were opposed categories. For every thing in the universe is physical, according to materialists. So all mental phenomena, including experiential phenomena, are physical, according to materialists; just as all cows are animals.

So why do materialists talk as if mental and physical were different? What they presumably mean to do is to distinguish, within the realm of the physical, *which is the only realm there is,* according to them, between the mental and the non-mental, or between the experiential and the non-experiential. But their terminology is flatly inconsistent with their own view, and they are in danger of forgetting the first lesson of realistic materialism — which is that if materialism is true, then qualitative-experiential phenomena must be wholly physical, strictly on a par with the phenomena of extension and electricity as characterized by physics. I use the words 'mental' and 'non-mental' where many use 'mental' and 'physical' simply because I assume, as a (wholly conventional) materialist, that every thing and event in the universe is physical, and find myself obliged to put things in this way.

So when I say that the mental and (in particular) the experiential are physical I mean something completely different from what some materialists have apparently

---

[59] If this is so then SESMETs (and hence possibly selves) exist even in the case of unself-conscious beings (cf. Damasio, 1994, pp. 238 and 243). Many, however, will prefer to say that SESMETs exist only in self-conscious beings, or (even more restrictedly) only in the case of explicitly self-conscious experiences. I note this issue in order to put it aside for another time.

[60] I use 'phenomenon' as a completely general word for any sort of existent, abstracting from its meaning of *appearance*, and without any implication as to ontological category.

[61] Some say numbers are real things, but it is agreed that they are abstract objects, not concrete objects in space–time, if they exist.

meant by saying things like 'experience is really just neurons firing'. For I don't mean that all features of what is going on, in the case of conscious experience, can be described by physics (or some non-revolutionary extension of physics). Such a view amounts to radical 'eliminativism' with respect to consciousness, and is mad. My claim is quite different. It is that the experiential (considered just as such) 'just is' physical. No one who disagrees with this claim is a *realistic* materialist.[62]

The next step in realistic materialism is to undercut the common view that the mind–body problem is a problem about how mental phenomena can possibly be physical phenomena *given what we already know about the nature of the physical*. If one thinks this one is already lost. The fact is that we have no good reason to think that we know *anything* about the nature of the physical world (as revealed by physics, say) that gives us any reason to find any problem in the idea that mental or experiential phenomena are physical phenomena, strictly on a par with the phenomena of extension and electricity as characterized by physics. Why do so many think otherwise? Because they are, as Russell says, 'guilty, unconsciously and in spite of explicit disavowals, of a confusion in [their] imaginative picture of matter' (1927a, p. 382). They think they know more than they do. They think, quite wrongly, that they have a pretty good fix on the nature of matter, and are naturally led thereby, as **Zahavi and Parnas** remark, to suppose that 'a better understanding of physical [i.e. non-mental] systems will allow us to understand consciousness better'; thereby ignoring the more plausible view 'that a better understanding of consciousness might allow us to understand the metaphysical nature of physical reality better' (p. 268).

I think that these points about realistic materialism (or whatever you want to call it) are extremely important. Once understood, they suffice to dissolve many people's intuitive doubts about materialism. But I will say no more about them here.[63]

XIV: Metaphysics: Particles, Simples, U-fields

I have claimed that SESMETs have as good a claim to be thought of as physical objects as stars, cats and bosons, and I have tried to check some of the doubts that this claim arouses by giving a brief sketch of what it is to be a realistic materialist. But it also raises a very general metaphysical question about which phenomena are properly said to be things or objects, and it is to this that I now turn.[64] As in '"The Self"' I will appoint Louis as a representative human being, and call the portion of reality that consists of Louis the 'L-reality'. The notion of the L-reality is rough — as a concrete physical being Louis is enmeshed in wide-reaching physical interactions and is not neatly separable out as a single portion of reality — but it is serviceable and useful none the less.

---

[62] In the longer run, I think that the mental/non-mental distinction may need to give way to the — clearer — experiential/non-experiential distinction, but I will continue to operate with the former for the moment.

[63] I discuss the question in Strawson (1994), chs. 3–4, and (forthcoming), following Locke (1690, pp. 311–14, 539–43), Hume (1739, pp. 246–8), Priestley (1777, pp. 103–32), Kant (1781–7, A358–60, A380, B427–8), Russell (1927a, ch. 37, and 1927b, chs. 12–16), Foster (1982, ch. 4), Lockwood (1989, ch. 10), and Chomsky (1995, pp. 1–10), among others.

[64] I often use 'thing' rather than 'object', but I make no distinction between these terms. I am not trying to make things easier for myself by using the former rather than the latter.

I will assume that every candidate for being a concrete thing or object is either a fundamental 'particle' or a 'simple' or 'field' or as I will say *U-field* ('U' for *Ur* or ultimate) or is made up of some number of U-fields in a certain relation. Accordingly I will take it that SESMETS are either single U-fields or made up of U-fields.[65] I agree with van Inwagen (1990, p. 72) that the Leibnizian term 'simple' is preferable to 'fundamental particle' as a term for the ultimate constituents of reality, first because the term 'fundamental particle' has potentially misleading descriptive meaning, provoking a picture of tiny grains of solid stuff that has no scientific warrant, second because many of the things currently called 'fundamental particles' may not be genuinely ultimate constituents of reality.[66] I prefer to use 'U-field' because 'simple', too, carries implications — of radical separateness, non-overlappingness and indivisibility — that are best avoided.[67]

XV: Metaphysics: Subjectivism, Objectivism, Universalism

What, then, is a physical object? It is, no doubt, *some kind of physical unity*. But this is vague, and some philosophers — the *subjectivists* — think that judgements about which phenomena count as objects are never objectively true or false. On this view, there are *no metaphysical facts of the matter*, and whenever we judge something to be an object we (explicitly or implicitly) endorse an ultimately *subjective* principle of counting or individuation relative to which the phenomenon *counts* as a (single) object: we are endorsing an ultimately subjective *principle of objectual unity*.

It is true that many judgements of objecthood — many principles of objectual unity — are so natural for us that the idea they are in any sense subjective seems preposterous. (Nearly all of us think that cups, saucers, meerkats, jellyfish, fingers, houses, planets and molecules are individual objects, and there are clear pragmatic and evolutionary reasons why this is so.) But the subjectivists are unimpressed by this. They deny that the fact that some judgements of objecthood are very natural for human beings entails that those judgements are objectively correct, or record metaphysical facts. If we were electron-sized, they say, our natural judgement about a stone might be that it was a collection of things, a loose and friable confederacy, and not itself a single object. And although it seems uncomfortable at first to think that merely subjective principles of objectual unity underlie our judgements that chairs and stones are objects, the idea becomes increasingly natural as we move away from such central cases. Thus although nearly everyone thinks a chair is a single object, not everyone

---

[65] I will also take it that 'virtual' particles (or U-fields) and 'antimatter' particles (or U-fields) are objects; and that space–time itself may be best thought of as an object (one view worth serious consideration is that it is the only object there is).

[66] One view is that the fundamental particles currently recognized — leptons and quarks — are not strictly speaking elementary and are to be 'explained as various modes of vibration of tiny one-dimensional rips in spacetime known as strings' (Weinberg, 1997, p. 20). Whether this leaves strings in place as ultimates, or only space–time, I do not know.

[67] For purposes of discussion I am taking it that it makes sense to speak of individual U-fields, perhaps by reference to certain particle-like observational effects, and in spite of the phenomenon of quantum entanglement. But nothing much hangs on this. There aren't any U-fields if there is 'structure all the way down' (a view that seems profoundly counterintuitive, but that may have to be taken seriously), and Post (1963) famously suggested that even if there are U-fields, they may have to be seen as 'non-individuals' in some way. Cf. also Lockwood (1989), p. 253; French (1998).

does.[68] And although many think cities, newspapers, galaxies and flutes (assembled from parts) can correctly be said to be single things, quite a few do not. Some think a body of gas is an object, but many do not.

Very few (to move to a distinctively philosophical example) think that three spoons, one in Hong Kong, one in Athens, and one in Birmingham, constitute a single thing, but some do sincerely believe that the three spoons' claim to be considered an individual object is as good as any other. According to one form of *universalism*, an extreme version of this view, any collection of U-fields in the universe, however scattered, counts as a single object in every sense in which a table does. A lepton in your amygdala, a quark in my left hand, and the U-fields that make up the rings of Saturn jointly constitute a single object just as surely as your pen does. No collection of U-fields has a better claim to be an object than any other.

Whatever you think of this form of universalism, it has the merit of being a wholly objectivist theory of objects. It endorses a principle of objectual unity that delivers a clear principle of counting. It tells you that if there are n U-fields in the universe then there are exactly $[2^n - 1]$ objects in the universe. But it also has, in a way, a highly subjectivist or 'post-modern' aura, for it tells you that anything goes and everybody wins, that there is no real issue about whether any particular collection of U-fields is an object or not. It is, accordingly, arguable that genuinely objectivist positions emerge clearly only when more specific and limited principles of objectual unity are endorsed, e.g. by dogmatic common sense, which rules in favour of tables and chairs and against the three spoons; or by Spinoza, who holds that there is, as a matter of fact, only one thing or substance (God or nature, or space–time, as we might now say); or by van Inwagen, who argues very forcefully that only individual U-fields and living beings — and not, say, tables and chairs — are material objects.

Actually, it doesn't matter which side you take in this debate. For if you think that there are indeed objective principles of objectual unity, and therefore that there are indeed metaphysical facts about which phenomena are genuine objects and which are not, then you can take me to be arguing that SESMETs (and thus perhaps selves) are among the genuine objects. If, alternatively, you think that the subjectivist view is best, and that there are no ultimate metaphysical facts about which phenomena are genuine objects, then you may take me to be trying to convince people who are disposed to think of certain but not all collections of U-fields as objects (jellyfish and chairs, but not arbitrarily selected cubic feet of the Pacific Ocean or the three newspapers) that it is at least equally reasonable to think of the collections of U-fields that I choose to refer to by the expression 'SESMETS' (or indeed by the expression 'selves') as objects. Practically speaking, my task is the same.

XVI: Metaphysics: The Nature of Objects

A concrete object, then, is a certain kind of physical unity. More specifically, it is either an individual U-field (subject to the doubt expressed in note 67, p. 122 above) or a number of U-fields in a certain relation. I take it, anti-universalistically, that there are various grades and types of physical unity, and that some candidates for objecthood have a (much) better claim than others; that a human being, say, has a

---

[68] Van Inwagen (1990) does not.

(much) better claim than your lepton + my quark + the rings of Saturn, or the three spoons, or a pile of bricks.

With this in place, consider the following suggestion. As one advances in materialism, deepening one's intuitive grasp of the idea that mental phenomena and non-mental phenomena are equally physical phenomena, one of the things that becomes apparent is that when it comes to deciding which things count as objects and which do not *there are no good grounds for thinking that non-mental criteria or principles of unity* — of the sort that we use to pick out a dog or a chair — *are more valid than mental criteria or principles of unity.*

It is arguable, in fact, that there is no more indisputable unity in nature, and therefore no more indisputable physical unity, than the unity of a SESMET — the unity of a subject of experience that is the subject of, say, a single, unified experience of looking up and seeing books and chairs and seeing them as such, or the subject of the binding or seizing together in thought of the concepts *grass* and *green* in the conscious thought 'Grass is green'.[69] The only comparable candidates that I can think of are space–time, and individual U-fields — if indeed there are any. I agree with the physicist Richard Feynman and the philosopher Peter van Inwagen that things like chairs are distinctly inferior candidates for being objects, when one gets metaphysically serious, and it is arguable that SESMETs are about the best candidates there are for the status of physical objects.

'Hold on. I am prepared to grant, for the sake of argument, that there is a real phenomenon picked out by your use of the word "SESMET". And I am prepared to accept that SESMETs are short-lived. A SESMET, let us say, is: the whole (and wholly material) phenomenon of the live-aware presence of the subject of experience in the present moment of consciousness or in the present hiatus-free period of experience. But why on earth should I also accept that the right thing to say about a SESMET is (A) that it is a *thing* or *object* like a rock, or a mayfly? Why isn't the correct thing to say simply (B) that an enduring object of a familiar sort — viz. Louis, a human being — has a certain *property* at a certain time, in having a certain unified, one-or-two-second-long, subject-of-experience-involving episode of experience? Why, alternatively, can't we say (C) that the occurrence of such an episode is just a matter of a certain *process* occurring in an object at a certain time, and does not involve any further distinct *object*?'

Well, here the canyons of metaphysics open before us. The object/process/property conceptual cluster — the whole object/process/property/state/event cluster — is structured by strongly demarcatory, ontologically separatist habits of thought that are highly natural and useful and effectively inevitable in everyday life, but deeply misleading when taken to have a claim to basic metaphysical truth. I think a little thought strips (B) and (C) of any appearance of superiority to (A), whether or not one is a materialist. I will start with (C), but I can give only brief reasons where others have written books.

---

[69] This is a materialist version of an old thought. I am not suggesting that the subject of experience is the *agent* that *brings about* the binding or seizing, and in fact I do not think that this is so.

XVII: Metaphysics: Object and Process

Any claim to the effect that a SESMET is best thought of as a process rather than an object can be countered by saying that there is, in the light of physics, no good sense in which a SESMET is a process in which a rock is not also and equally a process. So if a rock is a paradigm case of an object in spite of being a process, we have no good reason not to say that a SESMET is an object even if we are inclined to think of it as a process.[70]

In saying this, I don't mean to show any special partiality to the *four-dimensionalist* or *4D* conception of objects as opposed to the *three-dimensionalist* or *3D* conception. I think I can overfly this dispute, noting in passing that there are contexts in which the 4D conception of objects is more appropriate than the 3D conception, and contexts in which the 3D conception of objects is more appropriate than the 4D conception. This debate has its own elegant internal dynamic, and creates contexts in which its disagreements have importance, but it does not really matter to the present question about the existence of mental selves.[71]

'But if there is a process, there must be something — an object or substance — in which it goes on. If something happens, there must be something to which it happens, something which is not just the happening itself. So it can't be true that everything is a matter of process.'

This expresses our pre-theoretical conception of things, but we already know that things are unimaginably strange, relative to our ordinary understanding of them. The general lesson of physics (not to mention *a priori* reflection) is that our pre-theoretical conceptions of *space*, *time* and *matter* are in many respects hugely and provably wrong. So we already have a general reason to be cautious about the claim — which is, after all, a very general claim about the nature of *matter* in *space–time* — that it is a hard metaphysical fact that the existence of a process entails the existence of an object or substance that is distinct from it.

Physics also provides a more specific reason for doubt. For it is of course one acceptable way to talk — to say that if there is a process then there must be something in which it goes on. But physicists seem increasingly content with the view that physical reality is itself a kind of pure process — even if it remains hard to know exactly what this idea amounts to. The view that there is some ultimate stuff to which things happen has increasingly ceded ground to the idea that the existence of anything worthy of the name 'ultimate stuff' consists in the existence of fields of energy — consists, one might well say, in the existence of a kind of pure process which is not usefully or even coherently thought of as something which is happening to a thing distinct from it.[72]

---

[70] The claim is not that everything that is naturally thought of a process is legitimately thought of as an object. (There is no good reason to think of the yellowing of a leaf as an object.) It is only that everything that is naturally thought of an object is legitimately thought of as a process.

[71] For an outstanding piece of arbitration, see Jackson (1994).

[72] Unless, perhaps, that something is space–time itself. But in this case the point remains: for now it looks as if all the more limited phenomena that we think of as paradigmatic objects — stars, tigers, and so on — are to be thought of as local *processes* occurring in the only genuine substance there is: space–time.

Physics aside, the object/process distinction lives — covertly — off a profoundly static intuitive picture of objects and matter: an unexamined, massively influential and massively misleading picture of objects and matter as things whose essential nature can be fully given at an instant. This is one of the main confusions in our 'imaginative picture of matter'. For matter is essentially dynamic, essentially in time. All reality is process, as Whitehead was moved to observe by his study of twentieth-century physics, and as Herakleitos and others had already remarked long ago. We might be well advised to call matter 'time-matter' in contexts like the present one, so that we never for a moment forgot its temporality. We think of it as essentially extended, but we tend to think only of extension in space. But space and time are interdependent. All extension is necessarily extension in space–time.

It follows from this alone, I think, that there is no ontologically weighty distinction between an object and a process. There is no need to invoke relativity theory. For even if relativity theory is false there is no metaphysically defensible concept of an object — a 'spatiotemporal continuant', as philosophers say — that allows one to distinguish validly between objects and processes by saying that one is an essentially dynamic or changeful phenomenon in some way in which the other is not. Nor is there anything in the 3D conception of objects that supports such a view.[73] The source of the idea that there might be some such valid distinction lies in habits of ordinary thought, usually harmless, that are highly misleading in certain crucial theoretical contexts. I believe that we continue to be severely hampered by this; even when we have, in the frame of theoretical discussion, fully agreed and, as we think, deeply appreciated, that objects are entirely creatures of time, process-entities.

XVIII: Metaphysics: Object and Property

It seems to me that these (partly *a posteriori*, partly *a priori*) points about the superficiality of the object/process distinction find a different, irresistible and wholly *a priori* expression when one considers the object/property distinction.[74] Our habit of thinking in terms of this second distinction is ineluctable, and there is a clear respect in which it is even more deeply entrenched than the object/process distinction. And it is perfectly correct, in its everyday way. But ordinary thought is no guide to strict metaphysical truth or plausibility, and one has already gone badly wrong, when discussing what exists in the world, if one draws any sort of ontologically weighty distinction between objects and properties according to which there are objects on the one hand and properties on the other hand.

Clearly there can no more be objects without properties than there can be closed plane rectilinear figures that have three angles without having three sides (the strength of the comparison is intentional). Objects without properties — *bare particulars*, as they have been called — things that are thought of as having properties but as being in themselves entirely independent of properties — are incoherent. For to

---

[73] Nor anything in the 4D view that challenges it — for the fourth dimension is, precisely, that of time, describe it how you will.

[74] Also known as the distinction between particulars and universals, between the particular and the general, between individuals and universals, and so on.

be is necessarily to be somehow or other, i.e. to have some nature or other, i.e. to have properties.[75]

Some, rebounding from the obvious incoherence of bare particulars, suggest that the only other option is to conceive of objects as nothing but collections or 'bundles' of properties. But this option seems no better. Mere bundles seem as bad as bare particulars. Why should we accept properties without objects after having rejected objects without properties?

But this is not what we have done. The claim is not that there can be properties without objects; it is that objects (just) are collections of properties. This debate is as troublesome as it is ancient, conducted as it is against the insistent background rhythm of everyday thought and talk, but the idea is that adequate sense can be given to the admittedly odd-sounding claim that objects are nothing but collections of instantiated properties.

It sounds hugely peculiar, however, to say of a child or a refrigerator that it is strictly speaking nothing but a collection of instantiated properties. In fact it sounds little better than the claim that there are bare propertyless objects. So it is fortunate that there is no need to put things in such troublesome terms. Philosophers have managed to find other ways of describing the object/property topos correctly. When Kant says that 'in their relation to substance, [accidents or properties] are not in fact subordinated to it, but are the way of existing of the substance itself', he gets the matter exactly right, and nothing more needs to be said (Kant, 1781–7, A414/B441).

Armstrong puts the point as follows. We can, he says, '*distinguish* the particularity of a particular from its properties', but

> the two 'factors' are too intimately together to speak of a *relation* between them. The thisness [*haeccitas*] and the nature are incapable of existing apart from each other. Bare particulars are vicious abstractions . . . from what may be called states of affairs: this-of-a-certain-nature (Armstrong, 1997, pp. 109–10).[76]

And states of affairs, one might add, are already static abstractions, vicious or not, from the world-in-time, the essentially dynamic or processual nature of reality.

So the distinction between an object or 'substance' or particular, considered at any given time, and its properties at that time, is, in Descartes' terms, a merely 'conceptual' rather than a 'real' distinction (hence the strong comparison with triangularity and trilaterality). Obviously we want to be able to say, in everyday life, that an object can stay the same while its properties change. Nothing here forbids that way of talking; and there are also theoretical contexts in which one can put things in this way without going wrong. In some theoretical contexts, however, it is essential to maintain a tight grip on the metaphysics of the object/property topos, and to keep Kant's phrase constantly in mind: 'in their relation to the object, the properties are not in fact subordinated to it, but are the way of existing of the object itself'.[77] This, I think, is another point at which philosophy requires a form of meditation, something consid-

[75] I take it that this point is not touched by the claim that one can distinguish between the essential and the contingent properties of individuals, and I am restricting attention, in this discussion, to 'intrinsic', 'non-relational' properties of objects.

[76] Compare P.F. Strawson's philosophical-logical use (1959, pp. 167–78) of the metaphysically suggestive phrase 'non-relational tie' in his discussion of the way in which subject terms and predicate terms are combined in the description of reality.

[77] I have substituted 'object' and 'property' for 'substance' and 'accident' respectively.

erably more than disengaged theoretical assent: cultivation of a shift in intuitions, a learned ability to enable, at least for certain periods of time, a different stress-dynamic in the background of thought.

'All this is very fine. But when one considers a human experience, and hence, on the present terms, an instance of a SESMET, it still seems intensely natural to say (B) that there is just one object in question — namely, a human being like Louis who is a subject of experience and who has the *property* of having an experience of a certain kind — rather than saying that there are really two objects in question, a human being, on the one hand, and a SESMET, on the other.'

True. And yet I think that the two objects claim is correct, although I haven't yet given much of an argument for it, because the objection to the everyday object/property distinction doesn't bear directly against (B) in the way that the objection to the object/process distinction bears against (C).

The direct argument against (B) goes as follows. Consider a human being — Louis — in the light of materialism. Louis is identical with (or is constituted at any time by) a set of U-fields in a certain relation.[78] The same is true of an undetached human hand or pimple. The same is true of a SESMET — the phenomenon of the live-aware presence of the mental subject of experience in the present moment of consciousness or present hiatus-free period of experience. Thus far, then, they are all the same. Now one may grant this similarity, while still wishing to say that a SESMET is a process occurring in a human being, or an aspect of a property — the property of having a certain experience — of a human being. But as one advances in materialism, in one's conception of the nature of a physical object, and in one's intuitive grasp on the point that mental phenomena and non-mental phenomena are equally physical phenomena, one of the things one comes to see, I believe, is that there are in fact no better candidates in the universe for the title 'physical object' or 'substance' than SESMETS.[79] Certainly it seems that there is, in nature, as far as we know it, no higher grade of physical unity than the unity of the mental subject present and alive in what James calls the 'indecomposable' unity of a conscious thought.

Unity, you say, proves nothing about ontological category. Let me re-express the claim. Negatively put, it is that if we consider the phenomenon of the living presence of the subject of experience during an episode of experience, and agree to speak of this phenomenon by saying that a SESMET exists, and make it explicit that we are adopting this (admittedly substantival) form of words without prejudice to any metaphysical conclusions that we may draw regarding its ontological category, then we have no *more* reason to say that it is really just a property (or state) of some other object, or just a process (or event) occurring in some object, than to say that it is itself an object — an instantiated-property-constituted process-object like any other physical object.

Positively put, it is that it is simply correct to say that the SESMET-phenomenon is an object, a physical object. Not only do we have reason to say this given its intrinsic character as a mental unity, and hence a physical unity, in space–time. It is also hard to see that there are any better candidates for the status of physical objects than SESMETS

---

[78] I am using the word 'set' without any theoretical load.

[79] The stress is on 'better'; I'm not saying one can't abandon the category *object*.

or selves — no better candidates, at least so far as this universe is concerned, and as far as our knowledge extends, for the title 'substance'.

'This is charming, but it amounts to very little. You have taken the word "object" and stripped away the features ordinarily thought to distinguish objects from properties and processes in such a way that it is then very easy — not to say empty — for you to call whatever phenomenon you finally identify as the self an object.'

The only thing wrong with this objection is that it misdescribes my route and motivation. True, I think that the phenomenon I am proposing to call a SESMET, and am putting forward as a candidate for the title 'self', is an object. I also think that there is, in nature, no better example of an object.[80] But I do not start from that point and then adjust the metaphysics until it allows me to say this. The metaphysical moves that dismantle the standard frontiers in the object/process/property conceptual cluster seem irresistible in any case.

XIX: Metaphysics: the Transience View

According to the *Transience* view,[81] many SESMETS exist in the case of something like a human being like Louis. Each one is an individual physical thing or object, and a SESMET exists in the L-reality (cf. p. 121 above) whenever there is an episode of conscious experience in the L-reality. How long does a given SESMET last? As long as the experientially unitary period of experience of which it is the subject. How many are there? There are exactly as many SESMETS in the L-reality as there are experientially unitary periods of experience. For each experientially unitary period of experience must have a subject *for whom* it is a unitary, bound experience, a subject that holds it together in such a way that it constitutes an experientially unitary experience — the grasping of a thought-content, the seeing of a bird and the seeing of it as a bird, and so on. If distinguishing and counting such experientially unitary periods of experience is an irreducibly uncertain business, epistemologically speaking, the same goes for the counting of SESMETS. It certainly does not follow that there is any metaphysical indeterminacy when it comes to the question of how many there are (though it may well be rather unimportant how many there are). Either way the facts remain what they are: there are many of these SESMET-involving bindings, in the case of a human being, and the conscious experience — the mental life — of a human being is just the living — the internal inhabitings — of these bindings.[82] When we consider a human being as a persisting psychophysical whole, we can perfectly well speak in terms of there being just one subject of experience. It is only when we decide to think about the Problem of the Self — to press the theoretical, metaphysical question of the existence of the self — that we do better to say that there are many subjects of experience — or selves.

---

[80] It is also, perhaps, the deep original of our active grasp of the notion of unity and objecthood (such a view is entirely compatible with experimental evidence for the innateness of our ordinary concept of a physical object). .

[81] Formerly known as the Pearl View (**Strawson**, p. 20 above).

[82] **Hayward** is wrong to think that I offer 'the image of a string of pearl-like things as an image of the self', or claim that a self is 'a string of momentary things' (pp. 379, 392). **Sheets-Johnstone** makes the same mistake, for I do not claim that we experience the self 'gappily', or that 'the self is something that comes and goes' (p. 251).

The Transience view is so called because of its application to the human case. It does not say that SESMETS are necessarily of relatively short duration. It is only relative to everyday human standards of temporal duration that they appear short-lived, in any case,[83] and it is not a necessary feature of their nature. There may be beings whose periods of hiatus-free experience extend for hours, or for the whole of their existence. This is how I'd expect the divine SESMET to be, if I believed in God.[84] We, however, are not like this. The basic form of our consciousness is that of a gappy series of eruptions of consciousness out of non-consciousness, although the gaps are usually not apparent to casual inspection.[85]

There is no SESMET in the L-reality when there is no conscious experience in the L-reality. A SESMET is present only when there is actual experience or consciousness, and is I believe always short-lived in the human case. So it cannot be identified with a human being considered as a whole, or with a brain, or with a relatively enduring brain structure: it has quite different identity conditions. Most philosophers use the term 'subject of experience', which forms part of the term 'SESMET', in such a way that a subject of experience can be said to exist in the absence of any experience, and many have grown so accustomed to this use, and to identifying subjects of experience with human beings (or other creatures) considered as a whole, that they can no longer hear the extreme naturalness of the other use, according to which there is no *subject of experience* if there is no *experience*; according to which a subject of experience cannot exist at time *t* unless experience exists at *t* for it to be a subject of. I hope that those who find this natural use of 'subject of experience' strained can accustom themselves to it. It is only a matter of terminology, after all, and it is only this indubitably real phenomenon — the subject of experience considered as something that is alive and present in consciousness at any given moment of consciousness and that cannot be said to exist at all when there is no experience or consciousness — that concerns me here.

I take it, then, that there are many SESMETS in the L-reality, and that for the most part they exist successively, and in a non-overlapping fashion, although I agree with William James that there is no theoretical difficulty in the idea that they may sometimes exist concurrently in the L-reality.[86] A SESMET may be short-lived, but it is none the less real, and it is as much a physical object as any piano. Modern physics says nothing about it, or rather, says nothing about its mental being considered specifically as such; but the fact that modern physics says nothing about something is a very poor reason for thinking that the something in question is not physical, or does not exist.

---

[83] Although 10^{-34} sec. is a short time by human standards, it 'seems by the standards of early-universe physics as interminable as an indifferent production of *Lohengrin*' (Ferris, 1997, p. 237).

[84] Perhaps meditation can engender longer periods of hiatus-free thought in human beings (cf. **Pickering**, p. 64).

[85] Cf. **Strawson**, pp. 17–19 above. It doesn't take much to become able to detect them. My talk of an 'irruption into consciousness from a basic *substrate* of non-consciousness' was misleading in this connection (**Strawson**, p. 18 above; see **Shear**, p. 418 for some effective criticism), for I had no metaphysical-substance-like entity in mind.

[86] James (1890), p. 401; cf. **Gallagher and Marcel**, p. 282. **Wilkes'** cases of 'synchronous [multiple] selves' (pp. 33–4) seem to me to support, rather than undercut, my claims about the necessary singleness of a self at a time (**Strawson**, pp. 7–13 above).

XX: Metaphysics: 'I' and 'I'

But what then am I? — to repeat Descartes's question. What am I if the mental subject of experience is not the same thing as the human being? What is the relation between Louis and a SESMET (or self) that exists in the L-reality?

Am I a SESMET, or short-lived self? In one sense No. I am a human being. In another sense Yes, that is precisely what I am, as I speak and think now.

But what then am *I*? Am I two different things, $I_{H(uman\ being)}$ and $I_{S(ESMET)}$, at a given time? Surely that is an intolerable conclusion?[87]

Not at all. It is simply a reflection of how 'I' works. 'I' is not univocal, and can refer to two different things. Or rather, its referential reach can expand outwards in a certain way, so that it can refer to more or less. The same is true of 'here' and 'now', but the phrase 'the castle' provides a better analogy for 'I', given the present concern with objects. Sometimes 'the castle' is used to refer to the castle proper, sometimes it used to refer to the ensemble of the castle and the ground and buildings located within its outer walls. Similarly, when I think and talk about myself, my reference sometimes extends only to the SESMET that I then am, and sometimes it extends further out, to the human being that I am. The castle proper is not the same thing as the castle in the broad sense, but it is a (proper) part of the castle in the broad sense.[88]

The same is true in the case of a SESMET and a human being. Louis is identical with (or is constituted at any time by) a set of U-fields in a certain relation, and a SESMET S existing in the L-reality for a period of time *t* (a two-second interval, say) is identical with (or is constituted at any time by) a set of U-fields in the L-reality in a certain relation.[89] S is a peculiarly shaped thing (it is peculiarly shaped when considered spatially or non-mentally, but not when considered mentally), that has mental being and (I am presuming) non-mental being, and the relation between S and Louis the human being (an object with, say, a seventy-year existence) is a straightforward part-whole relation, like the relation between Louis and one of his toes — or the relation between a morning glory plant and one of its flowers, or between Louis and one of his pimples. That, I believe, is how things are, physically and metaphysically.[90]

---

[87] **Olson** (p. 58–9) asks why we should 'suppose that you and I are [SESMETs]? Why couldn't we be human beings?' Without expecting to satisfy him, I reply that we are both.

[88] Some philosophers refuse to accept that 'I' is not univocal, and appeal to the court of 'ordinary language'. Others have different reasons for insisting on univocality. I will not pursue this here — no contributor to the symposium pursued such objections — except to note that the non-univocality of 'I' is plainly marked in the ordinary use of language (see Strawson, 1999, §2).

[89] The phrase 'a set of U-fields in a certain relation' does not, when used by realistic materialists, refer only or even especially to non-mental, non-experiential phenomena that can be described by current physics or something like it. It refers just as it says: to a set of U-fields in a certain relation, U-fields whose existence in relation is, in the case of a SESMET, as all realistic materialists must agree, as much revealed and constituted by experiential phenomena as by any non-experiential phenomena characterizable by physics. (I am not optimistic about our chances of pinning the U-fields down one by one, for reasons given in Hornsby, 1981, and for reasons deriving from physics; but the claim remains.)

[90] The organization of the set that constitutes S will change during *t*, i.e. during S's existence, not only because each atom will change internally, but also because there will be vast numbers of macroscopic changes, as electrochemical, metabolic and other processes continue. The set's membership may well also change during *t*, and in this respect SESMETs will be like objects of more widely recognized sorts — dogs, human beings, trees, socks — in as much as they are naturally (this is the 'three-dimensionalist' way of describing them) said to be made up of different U-fields at different times.

Some may feel that it is unhelpful to claim that S is a part of Louis, because 'part of' so strongly suggests a persistent spatial part like a finger, but there is no good reason why 'part of' should be restricted to such cases, and no clear lower bound on the period of time required to earn the title 'persistent'. A pimple that lasts for a day is a part of Louis, a flower that lasts an hour is part of a plant, and a carbon atom that takes the following path through Alice is part of Alice:

> Alice drinks a cup of tea in which a lump of sugar has been dissolved. A certain carbon atom that is part of that lump of sugar is carried along with the rest of the sugar by Alice's digestive system to her intestine. It passes through the intestinal wall and into the blood-stream, whence it is carried to the biceps muscle of Alice's left arm. There it is oxidized in several indirect stages (yielding in the process energy, which goes into the production of adenosine triphosphate, a substance that, when it breaks down, provides energy for mus-cular contraction) and is finally carried by Alice's circulatory system to her lungs and there breathed out as a part of a carbon dioxide molecule. The entire process — Alice began to do push-ups immediately after she had drunk her tea — occupied . . . only a few minutes (Van Inwagen, 1990, pp. 94–5).

The thought or experience of which S (and thus Louis) is the subject is like a highly transient flower growing rapidly from nothing into full maturity and fading as rapidly to nothing, or like one sudden arcing jet of water — one of an indefatigable but essen-tially distinct series of such jets — from a powerful fountain with air bubbles in the system. This is the Transience view.

If necessary, I can do without the word 'self' and its plural. Others can use these words for whatever they like. They can say, if they like, that selves do not exist at all. I will be happy to make do with SESMETS — objects whose existence is as certain as the existence of experience, which is certain; things whose existence can and must be as fully acknowledged by Buddhists as by anyone else.

That said, I remain strongly inclined to call SESMETS 'selves', because I believe that SESMETS are located at the centre of what we must mean to be talking about when we talk about the self, or selves, in a way that trumps all other claims to the word 'self'. Talk of SESMETS leaves out a great deal of what some have in mind when they talk of selves, but the central component of the idea of the self is the idea of an inner subject of experience, and in the human case, or so I believe, the existence of inner subjects of experience is, as a matter of empirical fact, just the existence of SESMETS. I think it is a deep and difficult truth, fundamental to the Buddhist tradition and prepared for, in the Western tradition, by Hume, that these short-term selves are what most people are really talking about when they talk about *the* self.

Many agree that the central component of the idea of the self is the idea of an inner subject of experience, but insist that this inner subject is or can be something that has long-term diachronic continuity. On my view, though, this amounts to claiming that a many-membered set or series of SESMETS in a certain relation can be a single subject of experience. But a many-membered set of SESMETS in a certain relation is simply not the kind of thing that can itself be a subject of experience.[91] So there is no place for the persisting self, on the present view. So there is no place for the self at all, as many conceive it.

---

[91] This is not a philosophico-grammatical point about the word 'set', which I am using without any theoretical load, for a set of U-fields in a certain relation can indeed be said to be or constitute a subject of experience, on my view.

XXI: Conclusion

Olson is right that 'self' is used in many different ways (**Olson**, p. 49), but wrong to claim that we should give it up for this reason. Interdisciplinary discussion throws up a chaos of uses, but this turns out to be part of its value.[92] To read all the contributions to this symposium is to see that it is possible to navigate coherently among the many uses and to pursue one's own use fruitfully in the light of one's knowledge of the others. It can be painful at first — one brings cherished habits and sensitivities to the task — but the fall-out from the misprision is, as it accumulates, enlightening. And if one looks down on the debate from high enough, and in a sufficiently pan-dialectical spirit, I think one can see that there is, in spite of everything, a deep consensus about what is being talked about when the self is talked about, shapeshifting though it may be, and structured about various poles (e.g. the high-metaphysical pole and the Ecologically-Embedded-and-Embodied *Lebenswelt* pole) that unite it only by virtue of their dynamic opposition.[93]

References

Balleine, B. and Dickinson, A. (1998), 'Consciousness — the interface between affect and cognition', in *Consciousness and Human Identity*, ed. John Cornwell (Oxford: Oxford University Press).
*Blachowicz, J. (1997), 'The dialogue of the soul with itself', *JCS*, **4** (5–6), pp. 485–508.
*Brook, A. (1998), 'Unified consciousness and the self', *JCS*, **5** (5–6), pp. 583–91.
Bruner, J. (1994), 'The "remembered" self', in *The Remembering Self: Construction and accuracy in the self-narrative*, ed. U. Neisser and R. Fivush (Cambridge: Cambridge University Press).
*Butterworth, G. (1998), 'A developmental-ecological perspective on Strawson's "The self"', *Journal of Consciousness Studies*, **5** (2), pp. 132–40.
Camus, A. (1942/1946), *The Outsider*, trans. Joseph Laredo (London: Hamish Hamilton).
Camus, A. (1960/1995), *The First Man*, trans. David Hapgood (London: Hamish Hamilton).
Chomsky, N. (1995), 'Language and nature', *Mind*, **104**, pp. 1–61.
Clough, A.H. (1862/1974), 'The mystery of the fall', in *Poems* (Oxford: Oxford University Press).
*Cole, J. (1997), 'On "being faceless": Selfhood and facial embodiment', *JCS*, **4** (5–6), pp. 467–84.
Collins, S. (1982), *Selfless Persons* (Cambridge: Cambridge University Press).
*Deikman, A. J (1996), ' "I" = Awareness', *Journal of Consciousness Studies*, **3** (4), pp. 350–6.
Dennett, D. (1991), *Consciousness Explained* (Boston: Little, Brown).
Descartes, R. (1985), *The Philosophical Writings of Descartes*, tr. J. Cottingham *et al.* (Cambridge: CUP).
*Edey, M. (1997), 'Subject and object', *Journal of Consciousness Studies*, **4** (5–6), pp. 526–31.
Ferris, T. (1997), *The Whole Shebang* (London: Weidenfeld and Nicolson).
Flanagan, O. (1992), *Varieties of Moral Personality* (Cambridge, MA: Harvard University Press).
*Forman, R. (1998), 'What does mysticism have to teach us about consciousness?', *Journal of Consciousness Studies*, **5** (2), pp. 185–201.
Foster, J. (1982), *The Case for Idealism* (London: Routledge).
French, S. (1998), 'Withering away physical objects', in *Interpreting Bodies: Classical and Quantum Objects in Modern Physics*, ed. E. Castellani (Princeton: Princeton University Press).
*Gallagher S. and Marcel A. (1999), 'The self in contextualized action', *JCS*, **6** (4), pp. 4–30.
Geertz, C. (1983), 'From the native's point of view: on the nature of anthropological understanding', in *Local Knowledge* (New York: Basic Books).
*Gendler, T. (1998), 'Exceptional persons: On the limits of imaginary cases', *JCS*, **5** (5–6), pp. 592–610.
Gibson, E. (1993), 'Ontogenesis of the perceived self', in *The Perceived Self*, ed. U. Neisser (Cambridge: Cambridge University Press).
Happé, F. (1991), 'The autobiographical writings of three Asperger syndrome adults: problems of interpretation and implications for theory', in *Autism and Asperger Syndrome*, ed. U. Frith (Cambridge: CUP).
*Hayward, (1998), 'A rDzogs-chen Buddhist interpretation of the sense of self', *JCS*, **5** (5–6), pp. 611–26.
Hirst, W. (1994), 'The remembered self in amnesics', in *The Remembering Self: Construction and accuracy in the self-narrative*, ed. U. Neisser and R. Fivush (Cambridge: Cambridge University Press).

[92] In the course of our disagreements we learn as much about striking differences in human Self-experience as about striking differences in theoretical orientation.

[93] I am grateful to Derek Parfit, Edward St. Aubyn, and the editors of the *Journal of Consciousness Studies* for their comments.

Hornsby, J. (1981/1997), 'Which mental events are physical events?', in *Simplemindedness* (Cambridge, MA: Harvard University Press).

Hume, D., (1978), *A Treatise of Human Nature*, ed. L.A. Selby-Bigge and P.H. Nidditch (Oxford: OUP).

Hurlburt, R., Happé, F. and Frith, U. (1994), 'Sampling the form of inner experience in three adults with Asperger syndrome', in *Psychological Medicine*, **24**, pp. 385–95.

Jackson, F. (1994), 'Metaphysics by possible cases', in *Monist*, 77, pp. 93–110.

James, W. (1890/1950), *The Principles of Psychology*, volume 1 (New York: Dover).

James, W. (1892/1984), *Psychology: Briefer Course* (Cambridge, MA: Harvard University Press).

Kant, I., (1781–7/1996), *Critique of Pure Reason*, trans. W.S. Pluhar (Indianopolis: Hackett).

Kenny, A. (1988), *The Self* (Marquette: Marquette University Press).

Kenny, A. (1989), *The Metaphysics of Mind* (Oxford: Oxford University Press).

Knight, R.T. and Grabowecky, M. (1995), 'Escape from linear time: Prefrontal cortex and conscious experience', in *The Cognitive Neuroscieences*, ed. M. Gazzaniga (Cambridge, MA: MIT Press).

*Laycock, S. (1998), 'Consciousness it/self', *Journal of Consciousness Studies*, 5 (2), pp. 141–52.

*Legerstee, M. (1998), 'Mental and bodily awareness in infancy: Consciousness of self-existence', *Journal of Consciousness Studies*, **5** (5–6), pp. 627–44.

Locke, J. (1690/1975), *An Essay Concerning Human Understanding*, ed. P. Nidditch (Oxford: Clarendon).

Lockwood, M. (1989), *Mind, Brain, and the Quantum* (Oxford: Blackwell).

Lonergan, B. (1967), *Collection*, ed. F. Crowe (New York: Herder and Herder).

Milne, A.A. (1928), *The House at Pooh Corner* (London: Methuen).

Neisser, U. (1994), 'Self-narratives: True and false', in *The Remembering Self: Construction and accuracy in the self-narrative*, ed. U. Neisser and R. Fivush (Cambridge: Cambridge University Press).

*Olson, E. (1998), 'There is no problem of the self', *JCS*, 5 (5–6), pp. 645–57.

*Panskepp, J. (1998), 'The periconscious substrates of consciousness: Affective states and the evolutionary origins of the self', *Journal of Consciousness Studies*, 5 (5–6), pp. 566–82.

Parfit, D. (1995), 'The unimportance of identity', in *Identity*, ed. H. Harris (Oxford: Clarendon Press).

Parfit, D. (1998), 'Experiences, subjects, and conceptual schemes', *Philosophical Topics*, 26.

*Perlis, D. (1997), 'Consciousness as self-function', *JCS*, 4 (5–6), pp. 509–25.

*Pickering, (1999), 'The self is a semiotic process', *Journal of Consciousness Studies*, 6 (4), pp. 31–47.

Pinker, sincerely. (1997), *How the Mind Works* (London: Allen Lane).

Post, H. (1963), 'Individuality and physics', *Listener*, **70**, pp 534–7.

Priestley, J. (1777/1965), *Priestley's Writings on Philosophy, Science and Politics*, ed. J.A. Passmore (New York:: Collier).

*Radden, J. (1998), 'Pathologically divided minds, synchronic unity and models of the self', *Journal of Consciousness Studies*, 5 (5–6), pp. 658–72.

*Ramachandran, V. and Hirstein, W. (1997), 'Three laws of qualia: What neurology tells us about the biological functions of consciousness', *Journal of Consciousness Studies*, 4 (5–6), pp. 429–57.

Rimbaud, A. (1871/1972), *Oeuvres complètes* (Paris: Gallimard).

Russell, B. (1927a/1995a), *The Analysis of Matter* (London: Allen and Unwin).

Russell, B. (1927b/1995b), *An Outline of Philosophy* (London: Allen and Unwin).

*Sass, L. (1998), 'Schizophrenia, self-consciousness and the modern mind', *JCS*, 5 (5–6) pp. 543–65.

Schechtman, M. (1997), *The Constitution of Selves* (Ithaca: Cornell University Press).

*Shear, J. (1998), 'Experiential clarification of the problem of self', *JCS*, 5 (5–6), pp. 673–86.

*Sheets-Johnstone (1999), 'Phenomenology and agency', *JCS*, 6 (4), pp. 48–69.

Shoemaker, S. (1999), 'Self, body, and coincidence', *Proceedings of the Aristotelian Society, Supp. Vol.* **73.**

Spinoza, B. de (1677/1985), *Ethics*, in *The Collected Works of Spinoza*, ed. and tr. E. Curley (Princeton UP).

Stern, D. (1985), *The Interpersonal World of the Infant* (New York: Basic Books).

*Strawson, (1997), ' "The Self"', *Journal of Consciousness Studies*, 4 (5–6), pp. 405–28.

Strawson, G. (1999), 'The Sense of the Self', in *From Soul to Self*, ed. J. Crabbe (London: Routledge).

Strawson, G. (unpublished typescript), 'The grounds of self-consciousness'.

Strawson, G. (forthcoming), 'Realistic materialism', in *Chomsky and his Critics*, ed. L. Antony and N. Hornstein (Oxford: Blackwell).

Strawson, P.F. (1959), *Individuals* (London: Methuen).

*Tani, J. (1998), 'An interpretation of the "self" from the dynamical systems perspective: A constructivist approach', *Journal of Consciousness Studies*, 5 (5–6), pp. 516–42.

Traherne, T. (1903), *Poetical Works* (London).

Updike, J. (1989), *Self-Consciousness* (London: Deutsch).

Van Inwagen, P. (1990), *Material Beings* (Ithaca, NY: Cornell University Press).

Watson, D.R. (1998), 'Ethnomethodology, consciousness and self', *JCS*, 5 (2), pp. 202–23.

Weinberg, S. (1997), *New York Review of Books*, June 12 (New York).

*Wilkes, K. (1998), 'ΓΝΩΘΙ ΣΕΑΥΤΟΝ (Know Thyself)', *JCS*, 5 (2), pp. 153–65.

Yeats, W.B. (1933/1967), 'Vacillation', in *The Collected Poems of W.B. Yeats* (London: Macmillan).

*Zahavi, D. and Parnas, J. (1998), 'Phenomenal consciousness and self awareness: A phenomenological critique of representational theory', *Journal of Consciousness Studies*, 5 (5–6), pp. 687–705.

* Indicates a paper reprinted in this volume (see table of contents)

Index